Criminal
— Investigation

Criminal
— Investigation
second edition

John J. Horgan
Resource Assistant, Administration of Justice
Alfred North Whitehead College
University of Redlands
Redlands, Ca.

GLENCOE/McGRAW-HILL
A Macmillan/McGraw-Hill Company

Westerville, Ohio   Mission Hills, California

Peoria, Illinois

Library of Congress Cataloging in Publication Data

Horgan, John J
  Criminal investigation.

  Includes index.
  1 Criminal investigation.   I. Title.
HV8073.H73 1978   364.12   78-13186
ISBN 0-07-030334-7

Criminal Investigation, Second Edition
Imprint 1990

7 8 9 10 11 12 13 14 15 — 00 99 98 97 96 95 94 93 92 91 90

The editor for this book was Susan H. Munger, the art supervisor was George
T. Resch, the cover designer was Edward Smith/Design, and the production
supervisor was May Konopka. It was set in Century Schoolbook by Trufont
Typographers Incorporated.
Printed and bound by R. R. Donnelley & Sons Company.

Contents

Photo Credits

Figure 2-1. Pasadena, California, Police Department. Figure 2-2. Los Angeles Police Department.

Figure 3-1. Los Angeles County Sheriff's Office. Figure 3-7. Los Angeles County Sheriff's Office.

Figure 5-2. Santa Barbara, California, Police Department. Figure 5-3. Bruce Roberts, Photo Researchers, Inc.

Figure 6-1. Betty Lane, Photo Researchers, Inc. Figure 6-3b. Sybil Shelton, Monkmeyer Press Photo Service. Figure 6-5. Syd Greenberg, Photo Researchers, Inc. Figure 6-15. Federal Bureau of Investigation.

Figure 8-3. California Department of Justice. Figure 8-4. U.S. Government Manual, 1977–1978. Figure 8-5. Los Angeles County Sheriff's Office.

Figure 9-1. Libby Wolfe, Police Science Services.

Figure 11-2. Los Angeles County Sheriff's Office.

Figure 15-1. Pasadena, California, Police Department.

Figure 16-2. San Bernardino, California, Police Department.

Figure 18-1. Bureau of Narcotics and Dangerous Drugs, U.S. Department of Justice. Figure 18-5. Santa Barbara, California, Police Department. Figure 18-9 through Figure 18-14. Drug Enforcement Administration.

Figure 19-5. San Bernardino, California, Police Department. Figure 19-7. Sporting Arms and Ammunition Manufacturers' Institute (SAAMI), New York, N.Y. Figure 19-8 through Figure 19-11. San Bernardino, California, Police Department. Figure 19-14 through Figure 19-16. Field Emission Corporation, McMinnville, Oregon. Figure 19-18. Santa Barbara, California, News-Press. Figure 19-19. Los Angeles County Sheriff's Office. Figure 19-20. Photo Researchers, Inc.

Figure 20-2. Los Angeles Police Department.

Preface

This second edition was prepared with the purpose of updating, expanding, and improving the original format. Each chapter has been expanded in order to encompass the widest possible range of useful and authoritative investigating material. A new chapter, "Kidnaping and Extortion," was added in the process.

This book is primarily a text for a course in criminal investigation. The organization of material contributes to good teaching practices and student learning. The techniques of investigation set forth will apply in all areas of the country. The author has a background of twenty-five years in law enforcement. Twenty-two of those years were spent handling criminal investigations, including major case assignments. He is a graduate of the FBI National Academy; has been an associate professor and department head; and is a member of the California Peace Officers Association and the California Association of Administration of Justice Educators.

In the first nine chapters, *Criminal Investigation* discusses those important facets of criminal investigation upon which the ulti-mate success of each case depends. The latter eleven chapters deal with specific crimes and investigative procedures. Police science students and also officers and investigators seeking to increase their knowledge and efficiency in criminal investigation will find this book an informative, educational, and practical text. It is a valuable reference for any officer's police science library and for preparing for promotion examinations.

Grateful appreciation is expressed to Stanley A. Anderson, Department Chairman, Santa Rosa Junior College, and Director, Santa Rosa Center, Northern California Criminal Justice Training and Education System; to Attorney Samuel G. McEldowney, FBI (ret.), Associate Professor, Administration of Justice, Alfred North Whitehead College, University of Redlands; and to Lt. Robert M. Sluder, Los Angeles Police Department (ret.), Assistant Professor, Public Safety Department, San Bernardino Valley College, San Bernardino, Ca., for their valuable assistance in many aspects of this book.

Thanks and appreciation are also extended to the following departments, agencies, and veteran officers whose cooperation was of considerable assistance in the preparation of this text:

California Department of Justice, Special Services Branch

California Highway Patrol

B. Warren Cocke, Assistant Chief, San Bernardino Police Department

District Attorney's Office, Los Angeles County

Drug Enforcement Agency, U.S. Department of Justice

Jack A. Flemming, Coordinator, Police Science, Ventura College, Ventura, Ca.

George Hernandez, Department Chairman, Police Science Department, Grossmont College, El Cajon, Ca.

Vincent Hughes, Coordinator, Police Science, Pasadena City College, Pasadena, Ca.

Robert A. Johnson, Assistant Professor, Administration of Justice and Security Education, Golden West College, Huntington Beach, Ca.

John R. Jones, FBI (ret.)

Inspector Anthony Longhetti, Criminalist, San Bernardino County Sheriff's Office

Los Angeles County Sheriff's Office

Los Angeles Police Department

James Mills, Coordinator, Police Science, College of the Desert, Palm Desert, Ca.

Gerald E. Moore, Coordinator, Police Science, Gavilan College, Gilroy, Ca.

John J. Quinn, FBI (ret.), Legal Instructor, Iowa Law Enforcement Academy, Johnston, Iowa

San Bernardino County District Attorney's Office

San Bernardino County Sheriff's Office

San Bernardino Fire Department

James C. Zurcher, Chief, Palo Alto Police Department, Palo Alto, Ca.

Lastly, I would be remiss if I did not express my gratitude to my former boss, the renowned J. Edgar Hoover, Director, Federal Bureau of Investigation, U.S. Department of Justice, for providing me with the investigative opportunities and assignments that have made this book possible. To the innumerable officers of the city, county, state, and federal agencies with whom I have been privileged to work, I express my thanks.

John J. Horgan, Ph.B., LL.B.

To my wife Margaret
for her invaluable assistance

Guidelines and Requisites for Investigators

CHAPTER 1—

Investigation

An investigation is an observation or inquiry into allegations, circumstances, or relationships in order to obtain factual information. To become a competent investigator one must employ sound, fundamental practices. The first chapter presents many aspects of investigative practice and the requisites that an investigator must have to be successful. Knowledge of the guidelines below will greatly increase the proficiency of an officer, especially when applied to actual work experience. These basic principles may be called the "ABC's" of criminal investigation. The student of police science, the apprentice investigator, or the aspiring officer should study the guidelines carefully. They are the passport to success in the most interesting phase of police work—criminal investigation. Study these guidelines, apply them, and follow them.

Guidelines

1. Make certain as soon as possible whether or not a violation has been committed. First evaluation should always be made to determine the truth or falsity of reported crimes.

2. Respond promptly to a crime. Personnel and equipment can mean the difference between a solved case and an unsolved one.

3. There is no substitute for a thorough investigation. Successful results are proportionate to efforts expended.

4. Ask a lot of questions when seeking information. Responses often furnish valuable information.

5. Recognize the fact that criminals come from all walks of life. They may be butchers, bakers, shoe clerks, musicians, salespeople, socialities, bankers, or anyone from any other station in life; appearances are deceiving.

6. Do not commit yourself as to the guilt or innocence of anyone at a crime scene. Investigators are gatherers of facts. Take whatever action is necessary.

7. Bear in mind that your conduct in investigations may be challenged in court. What you do or fail to do is always subject to scrutiny.

8. Never underestimate your adversary. Expect the unexpected. The "cooperative" suspect may kill the arresting officer in a moment of relaxed vigilance. A "stupid" person may not be as ignorant as he or she pretends. The seemingly "meek" individual may be a knife wielder, burglar, or rapist. Just around the corner "all hell may break loose."

9. Do not be overconfident. Overconfidence may result in conducting incomplete investigations. Thoroughness in obtaining all the available facts is the key to successful prosecutions.

10. Interview, do not be interviewed. Being too accommodating during an interview can result in losing control of the interview or divulging too much information. The result could be a one-sided conversation in favor of the accused in which the interviewee knows as much about the case as the interviewer.

11. Do not jump to conclusions. Good decisions are based on accurate facts. A few seconds of deliberation can help to evaluate the situation, prevent a needless loss of life, and result in better decisions.

12. Act fast, and put first things first. The sequence of action in an investigation is governed by the initial evaluation of the facts.

13. Operate on the premise that a criminal brings something into a crime scene, leaves something behind, or takes something out. A fingerprint, footprint, heelprint, or tireprint may have been left behind. Discarded items, property taken, signs of struggle, or evidence of someone lying in wait could show the presence of the criminals at the scene.

14. Look for "disturbed areas." Watch for the means of entry and exit, places touched, tool marks, and articles moved from their normal position. Missing items, areas trampled, and other disturbances at the scene can also furnish valuable leads to the possible identity of the person involved.

15. Seek the answer to the question, "Why was this particular person or property victimized?" The answer may suggest persons living in the area, a visitor, evidence of previous "casing," the possibility of inside information, or victim involvement.

16. Pay particular attention to the *modus operandi* (method of operation, or M.O.) in every crime situation. Identification of a suspect may result from remembered speech, voice, silence, walk, dress, weapon, or mannerism. The property attacked, object of attack, tools used, or type of transportation involved can also identify a subject.

17. Never take things for granted. Be conscious of identification. Is the person identified correctly? Do not assume that certain investigations were done or completed. False assumptions result in valuable information being overlooked.

18. Work with the evidence at hand. Carefully explore all investigative aspects of evidence obtained at a crime scene. Conduct an immediate investigation to resolve the more critical leads and speed a solution to the case.

19. Make the goal of the investigation of a crime the conviction of the perpetrators. Use acceptable methods and procedures that meet with court standards.

20. Appreciate the importance of accurate observation, recording, collection, and preservation. Handling, identification, and transportation of physical evidence are also significant.

21. Recognize the value of criminalistics. Scientific examinations of evidence can eliminate unnecessary investigation and furnish valuable leads.

22. Know the value of teamwork. The cooperation of many is necessary in crime solving. Hans Gross, an Austrian criminologist and one of the founders of police science, once remarked, "Only the sham knows everything; the trained man understands how little the mind of any individual may grasp, and how many must cooperate in order to explain the very simplest things."

23. Develop informants and sources of information. They are invaluable to an investigator and are a shortcut to crime solutions.

24. Competence as an investigator is achieved by hard work, attention to detail, sacrifice, devotion to duty, study, and continuing education.

25. No investigation is too small or too great to justify the falsification or fabrication of the facts. Such action reflects upon the integrity of the reporting officer, the department, law enforcement, and justice itself. This can only result in general suspicion and distrust.

Requisites for a Successful Investigator

In addition to the guidelines mentioned above, there are many desired attributes which an investigator must have to carry out the job's duties and responsibilities. Some of the special qualities than an officer should have to perform efficiently in an investigation are listed below.

1. Suspicion: Take nothing for granted. Be cautious of obvious things and wary of persons quick to produce identification or alibis. An officer should demand verification wherever possible in order to resolve all doubts.

2. Curiosity: Many cases are solved by officers wondering about things like a statement, unusual dress, a suspicious car, or a person's actions. Habitual inquisitiveness and a desire to learn the truth often reveal important facts that would go unnoticed otherwise.

3. Observation: The use of the five senses plays an important part in the prevention and detection of crime. An officer must remember unusual things about an individual's posture, gait, expression, dress, mannerisms, and other traits. A double-parked automobile or a car left with the motor running should suggest the possibility of a robbery. A loiterer might indicate a lookout and the suggestion of a possible burglary in progress.

4. Memory: The ability to recall facts and past occurrences will assist an investigator in solving crimes. Solutions to difficult cases have often been resolved by a detective's ability to recall minute details of a former criminal's method of operation, physical characteristics, dress, mannerisms, and idiosyncrasies.

5. Ordinary intelligence and common sense: There are very few "instant" solutions to crimes. Cases are solved largely by using good judgment, common sense, and discretion. These are helped by perseverance and the ability to apply proven investigative techniques.

6. Unbiased mind: A biased mind implies prejudgment and results in poor investigations, incorrect conclusions, and unfairness toward complainants, witnesses, and suspects.

7. Avoidance of inaccurate conclusions: Officers should not form conclusions based on past experience with similar cases. A "Peeping Tom" today may be a rapist or robber tomorrow.

8. Patience, understanding, courtesy: Never become irritated with people because they are unable to remember names, dates, places, or other data.

9. Ability to play a role: This attribute is valuable in surveillances, undercover activities, and protecting the investigator's identity. Although the use of disguises is very limited in investigative work, role playing is a useful medium in day-to-day operations.

10. Ability to gain and hold confidence: This requisite is based upon such factors as personality, sincerity, and integrity.

11. Persistence and a tireless capacity for work: Many times information obtained in a case demands immediate investigative action irrespective of time, if successful solutions are to be had.

12. Knowledge of the corpus delicti of crimes: Facts should be developed during investigation to prove each element of the specific crime.

13. Interest in sociology and psychology: An understanding of basic sociological concepts and the problems of dealing with people more effectively is necessary.

14. Ability to recognize persons who are likely to be the subject of police investigations: A knowledge of the activities and methods of operation employed by various types of criminals can prove helpful in crime prevention.

15. Resourcefulness: An investigator must develop the capacity to adapt to all types of situations. Ingenuity suitable to the occasion is necessary.

16. Knowledge of investigative techniques: Such learning will provide the officer with a good foundation with which to conduct better investigations.

17. Ability to make friends and secure the cooperation of others: Contacts and cooperation of many are needed for success in any case.

18. Tact, self-control, and dignity: These are qualities of a professional officer.

19. Interest in job and pride of accomplishment: True success is based on genuine interest. The protection of the citizenry and the successful prosecution of criminals are rewarding goals.

20. Loyalty: Practice loyalty to your profession, your department, your chief, and your co-workers.

Observation, suspicion, curiosity, and knowledge of investigative techniques can all be seen in a case involving a routine stop made by a California Highway Patrol officer. In this instance, the officer learned that his beat partner was chasing a white and blue late model Cadillac on an interstate highway. The information the officer received indicated that the speeding car had run off the road and into the center divider. The driver was apparently drunk. The alerted patrol officer soon observed that the Cadillac was moving erratically on the freeway. The officer followed the suspect Cadillac. He clocked it at speeds well above the legal limit as it crossed over several lane lines during the pursuit. The Cadillac was forced to pull over. The officer noted that the car had Illinois license plates that were old and bent. A check of the license plates revealed that there was no stop against them. They were apparently clear. However, because the driver, a male, exhibited symptoms of intoxication, a series of simple sobriety tests was given to him. The suspect performed poorly on these tests. As a result, the driver was arrested for driving under the influence of alcoholic beverages.

Despite arrest of the driver for intoxication, the officer was still not satisfied with the license plate check. He checked the vehicle identification number. The officer noted that it was not securely attached as it should have been—a violation of the vehicle code.

The curious patrol officer opened the hood of the Cadillac and copied down the identification numbers on the rear of the engine. (These are cross-referenced with the sequential numbers at the end of the vehicle identification number.) The persistent officer then checked the National Automobile Theft Bureau handbook. He ran the vehicle identification number through with the FBI's National Crime Information Center in Washington, D.C. The FBI's reply indicated that the Cadillac was stolen in Chicago. There was a female passenger in the car. She refused to furnish any identification and was placed under arrest for possession of a stolen vehicle. This charge was also filed against the driver.

Then the driver informed the Highway Patrol officer that he had some gold bullion and rare and valuable coins in an overnight case in the back seat. He said that he did not wish to leave this case in the car. With the permission of the suspect, the officer opened the case and found the gold bullion. However, the officer also found 8 ounces of cocaine, a number of blank Illinois drivers' licenses and blank social security cards, and other sets of identification in the suitcase. Bank books, safe deposit keys, and registrations for additional automobiles were also present. While taking inventory of the driver's property, the officer also found a drawing of a doctor's office in a large California city and the names of some law-enforcement officers in Mexican and U.S. border towns. He also found some pay stubs from the Teamsters Union in Chicago.

An FBI fingerprint record check disclosed that the driver was not the person he claimed to be. He was, in fact, a felon with a record dating back to age sixteen. He was now forty-two years old. His record showed the following arrests: murder of a police officer; assault on a police officer; grand theft; grand theft, auto; smuggling; and possession of narcotics. As a result of this routine drunk driver arrest and the astute thinking of the Highway Patrol officer, a major auto theft ring in Los Angeles and Chicago was discovered. The passenger was identified as a prostitute whom the driver had met in Las Vegas, Nevada. Following the conclusion of this case, the patrol officer (a former student of the author's) remarked, "When you get to use your training and see results, it's great to be able to put it all together."

SUMMARY

The twenty-five guidelines set forth in this chapter represent the composite thinking of countless experienced investigators. Their varied experiences as law-enforcement officers are evident in these admonitions and constructive pointers. These principles are by no means the only guidelines that should be taken into account. However, they represent a cross section of important tips which veteran investigators offer to those seeking careers in criminal investigation. Many of the requisites for a successful investigator are gained from patrol service and experience in conducting preliminary investigations.

Resourcefulness Test

Here is a set of hypothetical facts to test your resourcefulness as an investigator. Assume that the case below is assigned to you. After carefully reading the facts of the case, do the following:

1. Indicate what investigation you would conduct to locate this fugitive.
2. Indicate the preparation and approach you would use in an interview with the fugitive's uncle at his office. Use any manner and any pretext you deem suitable in order to learn where the fugitive is.

Facts

You, as a detective, are seeking information leading to the apprehension of JOHN PORTER, a fugitive. He is wanted for the $20,000 robbery of the Acme Finance Company in Los Angeles. The robbery occurred shortly before closing time on January 20, 1979, 0900 hours. This fugitive has been missing since the latter part of February, 1979. Nothing definite has been learned of his whereabouts since that time, but he is thought to be somewhere on the West Coast or possibly in Mexico.

You have information that the fugitive's uncle, FRANK W. PORTER, an attorney in Long Beach, California, knows where the fugitive is and is in communication with him.

FRANK W. PORTER has been practicing law in Long Beach for about a year, and has only mediocre ability. His practice consists mainly of divorce cases. He formerly practiced law in San Jose, California, and was a member of the California State Assembly for two terms. He is extremely vain about his record in the assembly, and his pet subject of conversation is the PORTER thirty-hour work week law, which was overwhelmingly defeated during his second term of office.

FRANK W. PORTER is also known to pride himself upon his various affairs with women. His fondness for JOHN PORTER (fugitive) is based to a great extent upon his nephew's attempt to follow in his uncle's footsteps in this regard. The attorney/uncle has upon several occasions made good on some "hot checks" passed by his nephew to prevent him from going to jail. The attorney does not know that JOHN PORTER is wanted by the Los Angeles Police on a robbery charge. But he is aware that his nephew is wanted by several West Coast police departments on various charges.

The fugitive is the only child of Mr. and Mrs. A. B. PORTER who live at 1200 Maple Street, Long Beach. The parents do not know of the criminal activities of their son. You know the descriptions of the parents and that the father is in the real estate business.

JOHN PORTER is twenty-six years old, 5'10", and 160 pounds. He has dark brown wavy hair, regular features, and extremely white teeth. His Social Security number is 555-41-6234. He is divorced and has one child, six years old. The child lives with his ex-wife, Dorothy, somewhere in San Francisco. The fugitive plays the saxophone and was formerly a member of

Musician's Union 409, AFL-CIO, Los Angeles. His hobbies are hunting, fishing, horse racing, and gambling. He is a medium-to-heavy drinker.

The fugitive attended the University of California at Los Angeles for two years (1974–1976) and excelled in dramatics there. He played with an orchestra at the Beach Combers Club, Palm Springs, California, during the summer of 1978. During the fall of 1978, the fugitive toured the West Coast periodically with the Mad Bombers, a professional dance band, and played occasional dates in Tijuana and Juarez, Mexico.

The fugitive has no known criminal record other than an arrest for disorderly conduct in Los Angeles in March, 1975 or 1976. He is also alleged to be wanted for investigation by the police departments of San Francisco and Seattle. The charges are unknown.

CHAPTER 2—Preliminary Investigation

An investigation should be designed to accomplish justice by determining the accurate detection of the offender and by making it possible in the trial of that defendant to sustain the state's burden of criminal proof beyond a reasonable doubt. The investigation of any crime generally starts with an observation, radio call, or verbal notification. It ends with the arrest and conviction of the suspect. The term "preliminary investigation" in police application has several interpretations depending upon the problem involved. For example, it can be used to determine the urgency of the matter under consideration; for instance, assaults, prowler calls, robberies, silent alarms, injuries, and riots necessitate *immediate action* in order to save a life or apprehend an offender. Other types of offenses (such as vice activities, i.e., narcotics, prostitution, gambling, liquor violations, offenses involving auto theft rings, and thefts perpetrated by fraud) may require evaluation, planning, and a case buildup approach for successful prosecution. Other considerations in a preliminary investigation may be the policy of the specific department or restrictions such as jurisdiction, utilization of discreet approaches, or the use of criminal specialists. It is difficult to describe the limits of preliminary investigation because of the wide variety of incidents that confront the police.

In conducting a preliminary investigation, the investigative inquiry should be directed toward establishing whether a criminal act has been committed and, if so, the type of crime. Should the initial facts prove unfounded or of a noncriminal nature, the matter would be closed with the first report, since the police would have no jurisdiction. If the officer's findings indicate that a criminal violation has been committed, then proof of the corpus delicti of the particular offense must be established. *Corpus delicti* represents the basic elements of an offense specifically set forth in the statute which must be established before there can be a conviction. The identity of the perpetrator is not usually a necessary element of the corpus delicti. Any or all of the elements of a crime can be proven by circumstantial evidence. Thereafter, the facts of the matter are presented to the prosecutor's office, a complaint filed if authorized, a warrant obtained, and an arrest of the suspect made. If the matter requires expeditious attention, then an arrest might be in order as the initial step. Other responsibilities of the first officer at the scene include the securing of all available information, making searches, and preserving evidence.

In types of offenses sometimes referred to as "hot crimes" (assaults, robberies, silent alarms, etc.), the greatest opportunity for apprehension of the suspect is in the first few minutes after the commission of the act. During this time, a criminal is most vulnerable, is apt to make mistakes, is more readily identified, and may still have left evidence of the crime nearby.

A preliminary investigation may be the prelude to an in-depth investigation. The latter is generally made by the detectives who conduct the follow-up investigation, apprehend the offender, and prepare the case for court. These detectives work with the information the police officer accumulates. The first approach to a criminal problem, therefore, is the basic foundation of an investigation. If all available information is not collected, accurately recorded, and intel-ligently processed, much of the follow-up investigation will proceed without the benefit of all the existing facts. This may necessitate repeating much of the preliminary investigation. Teamwork between the patrol and detective division might be compared to a baseball game. If the players do not support their pitcher in the field and at bat, the ball game cannot be won. Likewise, if errors of omission or commission are made in the handling of investigative details of a case, that case would undoubtedly be lost in a court of law.

Principal Objectives of Police Investigation

The objectives of investigation should be thoroughly understood by all investigators. In the previous chapter, guidelines, requisites, and qualifications for the successful investigator were presented. Set forth below are the objectives of police investigation together with the ways in which they are accomplished.

Determine if a crime has in fact been committed — if so, what crime?

This objective is usually accomplished by visual inspection of the crime scene area and interviews with the victim and witnesses. This provides criteria as to whether the reported incident is of a civil or criminal nature.

Identify the offender

In reaching this second objective, investigative activity should include the following: interviews with the victim and witnesses, study and examination of physical evidence, a review of the modus operandi (method of operation), record bureau checks of similar crimes and suspects, utilization of informants and sources of information, and the witness's perusal of available photographic albums of criminal suspects. Other means used to accomplish this goal involve a consideration of the type of property taken or left behind, the vehicle used, and the suspect's peculiarities, conduct, scars and marks, physical defects, and mannerisms. The use of broadcasts, teletypes, artist's sketches or Ident-a-kit photographs, and the aid of other law-enforcement agencies can also be of assistance in the identification of possible suspects.

Apprehend the offender

This third objective is brought about by *immediate action* —the arrest of the suspect at the scene if he is present and there is reasonable cause to believe a felony has been committed. Where the suspect has fled the area and the prospect of his arrest appears likely, hot pursuit would be part of the initial immediate action. If neither of these two conditions exists, the expeditious relaying of descriptive identifying data is made to *other police units* to effect the arrest of the suspect. Additional broadcasts of information are disseminated wherever pertinent.

Where the suspect has been identified, a warrant should be obtained and stops placed with local, state, and FBI identification bureaus to assist in accomplishing this goal. The use of *wanted bulletins* and the services of *informants* may likewise prove to be a useful means of effecting the suspect's apprehension.

Gather and preserve evidence

It is in this area that technical assistance and the facilities of the crime laboratory are of greatest benefit. The obtaining, protecting, collecting, identifying, preserving, and transporting of all physical evidence to the crime laboratory for examination assist in the attainment of this objective. The crime scene must be cleared of all unauthorized persons and protected until it is examined for items of evidence. The protection of evidence is accomplished by covering the sus-

pect area with such protective materials as paper, boxes, and barricades. Rope and guards can also be used until processing is completed. In each instance, the item or section involved will dictate the type of protection to be used.

Prior to the gathering of physical evidence, the crime scene should be photographed and sketched. A fingerprint search should be conducted. Casts should be made of the tracks, footprints, and tool impressions if these are found. Evidence such as fibers, particles of clothing, threads, hair, bloodstains, cigarette butts, footprints, tools, markings, shells, bullets, writings, are of particular significance in criminal cases. Generally speaking, an item is considered to be evidence if (1) it tends to show the identity of the suspect (fingerprints, footprints, palm prints, etc.); or (2) it tends to show the manner or method in which the crime was committed (weapons, forged checks, or other instruments).

Aid in the prosecution and conviction of the perpetrator

In carrying out this fifth objective, all reports needed for presentation in court are prepared. Those of other crimes in which the suspect is believed implicated are also made ready. Reports submitted to the prosecutor should be so comprehensive that a person without previous knowledge of the case would completely understand them. It is to be emphasized that a good investigation will be reflected in a report that contains (1) victim's statement; (2) witnesses' statements; (3) location, disposition, and finder of the evidence; and (4) officer's summary including the criminal history of the defendant. The report establishes the crime, states all the facts, and identifies the suspect.

Recover stolen property

This sixth goal is attained through such means as interviews with suspects, relatives, associates; legal searches of residence and effects of suspects; checking pawn shops, secondhand stores, junk yards, known "fences," and receivers of stolen property. It is also reached by placing stops with local, state, and federal agencies; putting through all-points or regional broadcasts, bulletins; and exchanging stolen property information with other policing agencies on a mutual basis.

Procedure in Preliminary Investigation

Whenever a crime has been committed, the criminal has disturbed the surroundings in one way or another. It is the investigating officer's task to find the manner in which the crime scene has been altered. From these clues, the officer seeks to identify and apprehend the criminal. Disturbances to a crime scene can be caused by curious onlookers, "helpful citizens," the victim, persons attempting to conceal the crime, newspaper reporters, and others.

Certain procedural steps must be taken by the officers at the scene to create a strong foundation from which to work. The nature and circumstances of the case will determine the order of investigative steps. It is not possible to list all procedural steps, but the following rules have general application to most types of criminal investigations:

1. Waste no time in beginning the investigation. Upon arrival at the scene, be ready to act or react to unexpected happenings that might jeopardize your life. Have a cover plan to prevent the exit of possible suspects before their identification. The specific deployment used will depend on the nature of the complaint and available manpower and equipment.

2. Record the date, time of arrival, visibility, weather, lighting, identity of associate if present, and other conditions that may have a bearing on the crime.

Figure 2-1. Dispatchers play an important role in the preliminary phases of criminal investigation. They are the informational link between headquarters and field operations.

3. Determine whether or not a crime has in fact been committed and, if so, what type of crime it is. Make a rapid visual inspection. The original information many times is misleading, distorted, or too brief to make the necessary evaluation.

4. Advise the radio dispatcher (Figure 2-1) of any needed assistance—medical, ambulance, coroner, photographer, equipment, criminal specialist, or other agencies.

5. Instruct occupants of premises to refrain from touching or disturbing areas that will need to be processed for latent fingerprints, heelprints, footprints, tool marks, or other physical evidence.

6. Isolate and preserve the crime scene. Rope off the area, post guards, and barricade the location if necessary. Exclude unauthorized persons from the scene. Limit authorized personnel to those necessary to carry out the required duties. Make certain the critical area remains under constant protection until processing is completed.

7. Avoid preconceived theories; approach the problem with an open mind. Remember, good decisions are based on accurate facts.

8. Assist the injured when necessary. Recognize the fact that the saving of life comes before the protection of property. Record in detail any statement made by the victim. Take a *dying declaration* (statement given by victim in expectation of death) if the victim appears to be seriously wounded. Outline the body position with chalk or other marking material prior to its removal. Record its exact position in relation to other objects and evidence in your notes. Arrange for an officer to accompany the victim to a hospital in the event hospitalization is required and interview possible.

9. Locate and interrogate suspects, arresting them when there is evidence of guilt (felony cases). Inform any suspects taken into custody that (a) they have a right to remain silent and need not answer any questions; (b) if they do answer questions, answers can be used as evidence against them; (c) they have a right to consult with a lawyer before or during the questioning; and (d) if they cannot afford to hire a lawyer, one will be provided without cost.[1] Make certain the suspect fully understands the above rights and signs a waiver.

10. Arrange for an immediate broadcast if the suspect has already fled from the scene. Furnish the radio dispatcher with any needed information — type of crime, location of occurrence, number of suspects, type of weapons used, direction suspects left scene, description of vehicle if observed, and nature of property taken. Include suspect's age, height, weight, build, color of hair and eyes, complexion, racial descent, scars and marks, oddities in appearance, and clothing worn. Listen to the broadcast to check its accuracy. Dispatch supplemental broadcasts as additional descriptive information is obtained.

11. Identify persons having any knowledge of the crime; separate them in order to obtain their individual accounts of the incident. Include not only eyewitnesses but every witness (before and after the act) who has even the slightest bit of information. Canvass the neighborhood for other possible witnesses. Try to locate people who may have been in the area about the same time of day as the crime occurred — mail carrier, route sales representative, people on way to work, neighborhood children, etc.

12. Take photographs of the crime scene as is. (This is a desirable procedure in many types of felonious cases.) In homicide cases, for example, the use of the camera is a must. Courts are interested in knowing the condition of the scene at the time of the arrival of the investigating officer. Supplement the photographs with a sketch or diagram to show the position of items of evidence. Sketches will reflect measurements and relationships to other objects. Methods of locating objects at a crime scene can be found in Chapter 3.

13. Plan the area to be searched in order to preclude the possibility of any section being overlooked. Use methods similar to those employed in covering a patrol beat (line, circular or clockwise, square, or quadrant). Record the assignments given at a crime scene and detail the work.

14. Place one person in charge of the search. Generally the first detective on the scene is in charge; all others report to that detective for assignments. Appoint one officer to handle all evidence. Maintain an irrefutable chain of custody of all evidence found from the time it was discovered until it is produced in court. The number of officers necessary to conduct the search will depend on the area to be searched and the specific problems involved.

15. Search the scene thoroughly indoors and outdoors. Check first for fingerprints, footprints, tire tracks, weapons, discarded items, or any other materials believed connected with the case. Thereafter, examine the scene for minute bits of evidence. Hairs, textile fibers, rope and string, adhesive tape,

---

[1] *Miranda v. Arizona,* 384 U.S. 436, 444 (1966).

parts of plants, dirt, dust, stains, carpet lint, etc., all have probative value.

16. Place an identification mark on all physical evidence found at the crime scene where it will not interfere with any laboratory examination desired. If the item (liquid, soil, BB shot, etc.), cannot be marked, place the material into an appropriate clean container, seal the container, and mark the seal as well as the receptacle with identifying data.

17. Obtain a detailed description and list of all things taken from the victim or premises no matter how trivial these things seem to be. Include amount or quantity, make, size, model, type, serial number, color, and other identifiable characteristics.

18. Endeavor to locate a weapon if one was used. Find witnesses who can associate the weapon with the suspect or crime scene.

19. Inquire whether the victim can identify the perpetrator. Ask if the victim suspects anyone and the reason for suspicion. List all possible suspects, their addresses, occupations, identification records, and histories.

20. Ascertain in detail how the crime was committed; that is, find out the M.O. (method of operation) and the evidence available to support the M.O., and reconstruct the sequence of events.

21. Determine the possible motive for the crime: love, hate, jealousy, revenge, monetary gain. Consider other possible motives such as alibi for gambling losses, collection of insurance, publicity, cover-up for some other crime, etc.

22. Review the clues found at the crime scene and arrange for coverage of leads which need immediate attention. Initiate teletype messages on wanted persons when there is justification for expeditious attention.

23. Compile a complete, accurate report of the investigation. List only those facts in a report that you can substantiate through your knowledge, physical evidence, or statements made by victim and witnesses.

24. Make sure that all persons, departments, and divisions concerned with the case receive copies of the report.

25. Consider all possible defenses which a suspect might use at a subsequent trial and resolve these during the course of the investigation. Defenses to criminal actions may include alibi, self-defense, intoxication, insanity, duress, character of defendant, entrapment, or necessity.

Investigative procedures pertaining to specific crimes will be found under separate chapter headings in this text.

Following Apprehension of a Suspect

After a suspect is taken into custody and advised of legal rights, the officer has additional investigative responsibilities to fulfill. These include but are not limited to such things as

Searching suspect's person and effects within legal limitations

Making an inventory of all property (clothing, room, car)

Determining involvement or complicity in other crimes

Recovering property

Interviewing relatives and associates

Corroborating information furnished

Cancelling or removal of all stops

Dispatching apprehension teletype

Following through on all leads obtained

Checking reports, teletypes, etc., for possible "connect-ups"

Taking of fingerprints, palmprints, photographs

Obtaining handwriting and voice recording specimens

Disseminating information to other interested agencies

Preparing all reports and materials necessary for trial

Disposing of property in accordance with the policy of the department, district attorney, or court

Field Note-Taking

The subject of field note-taking is germane to criminal investigation whether it concerns itself with preliminary or follow-up procedure. Only information pertaining to police business should be kept in an officer's notebook. Notes should be made on every call or contact made by an officer in the conduct of police business and should be followed by an appropriate report. This procedure is necessary in order that the department head can render a statistical accounting of time to the mayor, city manager, city council, or board of supervisors.

Field notes are necessary because of the inability of people to remember such details as dates, serial numbers, exact words spoken by a victim, suspect, or witness, measurements, etc. Learn to be specific in note-taking. Do not accept general statements such as young, old, short, tall, light, dark, or blue color. Clarify these statements: How long? How old? How short? How tall? How light? How dark? What shade of blue? Make notes as complete as needed for accurate reporting. Record each interview on a separate page. When conducting interviews, it is generally better to permit persons being interviewed to tell the story in their own ways. Ask questions only to keep the interviewee from straying from the facts of the case. Do not start writing immediately. After the person completes a statement, go back over it for details and then take notes. Erasures should not be made on notes taken. Rather, draw a line through any inaccuracies or changes and initial the correction. Be friendly, courteous, and businesslike in all interview procedures. A sketch or diagram often can clear up a point and be helpful to the notetaker when writing a report.

Notes are generally made chronologically in the course of the investigation. They are the frame of reference and the raw sources from which operational reports are prepared. Experience will determine how lengthy the notes should be. In some cases, key words will suffice. In view of the fact that many notes are taken down out of order due to the exigencies of the case, unavoidable interruptions, and other factors, a loose-leaf notebook has the advantage of enabling the investigator to keep pertinent notes together. This will permit organization and reorganization of the notes. Completed notes should be detached and placed in the file of the case to which they relate. Notes made at the time of the investigation can be used later to refresh the officer's memory in court as long as the notes were made when the matter was fresh in mind. However, the defense counsel has the right to cross-examine the officer witness. Therefore, make certain that notes are neat, legible, and accurate.

Occasionally, a person is reluctant to furnish information to an investigating officer when statements are being reduced to writing. In these instances, the investigator should either ask permission to make a few notes or not take any during the interview. However, as soon as possible, while the facts are still fresh in mind, the officer should reproduce all information in writing (out of the presence of the person questioned). The use of portable tape recording machines by some departments enables the officer to concentrate all effort on the interview and assures accuracy in reporting.

The answers to the questions *who, what, when, where, how,* and *why,* along with the certainty of identifying data are key points in the accumulation of information for reports. Never leave the scene of a crime or terminate an interview, if possible, until all available information has been obtained. The above six questions should be kept constantly in mind during all interviews. Before any interview is concluded, the officer should review the notes to be certain that answers to these questions have been obtained. For example,

Who were the persons concerned (names, ages, residences, businesses, telephone numbers, descriptions)? Who did what? Who saw or heard anything of importance? Who handled the evidence? Who discovered the crime? Who had custody of the property last?

What happened? What crime was committed? What time did it occur? What weapon was used? What is the suspect's M.O.? What was the reason for the crime? What was taken? What vehicle, if any, was involved?

When did it occur (time of day)? When was the crime discovered? When were the police notified? When was the victim last seen? When was the property last seen?

Where did it occur? Where was the victim at the time? Where were the witnesses? Where was the suspect first seen? Where was the suspect last seen? From where was the property taken?

How was the crime committed? How did the suspect get to the scene? How did the suspect leave or make a getaway? How many people were involved? How much money or property was taken?

Why was the crime committed (events preceding the offense)? Why did so much time elapse before the police were notified? Why was this particular victim attacked? Why did the suspect commit the criminal act in this particular way?

When property has been taken, descriptive data should include the quantity and kind of article, trade name, physical descrip-

tion, serial numbers, personal identifying marks, damage, age, condition, and current market values.

Obtaining the description of a suspect

This is probably one of the most important steps in the investigation of a crime. Descriptions are intended to set one person apart from others. Every item added to a description reduces the field in which the search is to be made and helps to eliminate possible suspects. Descriptions are often exaggerated by witnesses. In order to overcome this problem, the accepted method used in obtaining a description is *comparison*. Comparison means that the witness will look at one person whose height is known, and will note the differences between that person and the suspect observed. A comparison can also be obtained by having a witness equate the suspect's height with the height of the doorway or with some other object in the room.

In most cases the witness has only looked briefly at the suspect and then under distressing circumstances. The witness will not be able to recall all the elements of a minimum description, but with proper interrogation and the use of comparisons, the interviewer may bring out the descriptive details. Where there are many witnesses, a *composite description* should be compiled from the interviews. For example, if eight witnesses describe the height of a suspect by such observations as 5′8″, 5′8″, 5′9″, 5′9″, 5′9-10″, 5′9-10″, 5′10″, and 5′11″, the composite for the suspect's height would be listed as 5′8–10″.

An officer should endeavor to seek out peculiarities associated with the suspect that become noticeable under varied circumstances. Any one unusual feature may eliminate hundreds of suspects who do not have that particular characteristic. A minimum description of an unknown suspect should include the following: race, nationality, approximate age, height, weight, build, complexion, color of hair, hairline and hairstyle, ears, eyes, eyelids, eyebrows, nose, lips, mouth, teeth, chin, shape of head, beard or mustache, scars, marks, tattoos, voice. Clothing should include hat, jacket, sweater, shirt, tie, trousers, shoes. Noticeable items of jewelry such as watch, watchband, pins, tieclasp, bracelets, and rings should be included.

The investigating officer, in obtaining a complete description of a criminal suspect should always bear in mind that the person who makes an indecent exposure today may be a rapist tomorrow; and the petty thief may be the robber of another day.

Other data that may be considered for inclusion in the investigator's notebook are condition of the premises, evidence of a struggle, remnants of meals, empty glasses, disorder of furnishings, location of physical evidence, and other indications of crime. In addition, the notebook might contain the geography of the scene, such as position of furniture in the room and location of various rooms in relation to the crime scene, with sketches to support this. Descriptions of items of evidence together with the way in which marked, place found, person from whom evidence was received, and disposition should also be noted. Brief notes on statements made by witnesses and suspects should be made. These notes, however, will not replace the detailed statements taken from witnesses and suspects during the investigation.

Results derived from note-taking

Lead to accurate, factual, and complete reporting.

Prevent inaccurate reporting or errors.

Expose discrepancies in statements taken from suspects and witnesses.

Amplify and clarify questionable statements.

Assist in corroborating statements of witnesses, suspects, and victim.

Help to detect fabricated stories when comparison of testimony is made.

Expose untruths and false statements when reviewed.

Assist in prosecution for perjury by detecting falsehoods.

Assist in interrogation of suspects by furnishing an index to the case.

Refute alibis by recording minute details.

Protect the innocent by making a record of facts gathered.

Provide leads to locate suspects, witnesses, evidence, verification, etc.

Protect the officer from false, unfounded charges.

Reflect good police practice.

SUMMARY

Successful results in a case are in direct proportion to efforts expended by officers during the preliminary phase of a criminal investigation. If every bit of evidence is obtained at the crime scene; thorough interviews conducted with the victim and witnesses; appropriate broadcasts made; leads covered in the order of priority; specialists called in where warranted; available sources checked; and accurate reports prepared, then the chances of solving the case are greatly enhanced.

The follow-up or continuing phase of an investigation is generally handled by detective specialists assigned to the division involved. For example, the auto theft, burglary, robbery, homicide, or forgery division.

These officers usually take the case early in the investigation. They have the responsibility for its clearance. The follow-up phase of an investigation may include such activities as reevaluating the initial information, reinterviewing the victim and witnesses, and visiting the crime scene area for any additional evidence that may have been overlooked. In addition, follow-up can involve consulting with fingerprint and laboratory specialists on the evidence collected and covering leads in their order of importance. Other activities include checking *modus operandi* of similar cases for possible connections; arranging for the preparation of a sketch or mechanical photo; searching specialized files on data like scars, marks, tattoos, nicknames, and pawned items. The continuing investigation can entail exhibiting criminal photo albums; conducting liaison with surrounding agencies; checking out possible suspects; preparing reports; consulting with the prosecutor's office; and conducting any other investigation deemed necessary. The type of crime, seriousness of the offense, and information sought are factors determining the kinds of investigation needed.

The taking of complete, legible, and accurate notes during all phases of an investigation is absolutely essential to the preparation of a good report. Notes are the frame of reference and the source from which operational reports are prepared. A good rule to follow is that notes should be retained on any information which might be considered testimony. In judging the efficiency of an investigator, one of the standards used is the quality of the reports submitted. The results derived from note-taking, set forth earlier in this chapter, show why investigators should strive to increase their proficiency in note-taking.

REVIEW QUESTIONS

1. Why is a preliminary investigation important to the investigation of a case?
2. What types of crimes are referred to as "hot crimes"?
3. Why do such criminal offenses as auto theft rings, frauds, and some vice offenses require a case buildup approach?
4. Explain the meaning and importance of the term "corpus delicti."
5. An objective of police investigation is to identify the offender. By what investigative steps or procedures is this accomplished?
6. What are the objectives of a police investigation?
7. What are some of the methods used to recover stolen property?
8. Name six types of crimes which call for immediate action.
9. List ten results that are derived from note-taking.
10. After a suspect has been taken into custody on a felony charge, what other investigative procedures would you undertake before completing your investigation?
11. Write out a list of those items which would be of assistance in describing a person wanted for a criminal offense.

12. In some criminal cases it may be necessary to take a dying declaration from a victim. What must be shown before such a statement is admissible as evidence?

13. When the initial investigation determines that the facts are of a civil nature, how much more investigation should be undertaken?

14. In recording information on stolen property, what descriptive data should be included?

━━━━━━━━━━━━━━━━━━━━ **WORK EXERCISE** ━━━━━━━━━━━━━━━━━━━━

Facts

You (in Car A-57) are dispatched by radio to assist Car A-61 as a backup to check out a suspicious car parked in a supermarket parking lot prior to opening time. Each police car has one officer in it. As you approach the market lot, you observe Car A-61 just ahead of you pulling into the lot and approaching the suspect car. At that time you hear shots fired and see the other officer fall to the ground. You also see the suspect car speed away south from the market on Main Street. What action would you take? Explain.

CHAPTER 3

Collection, Identification, and Preservation of Evidence

A balanced approach to criminal investigation must be concerned with both people and things. Together they constitute the field of physical evidence found in an investigation that will assist in the solution of the crime and the prosecution of the criminal. From the laboratory examiner's viewpoint there are eight important steps.

1. Recognizing or discovering evidence. This is considered the most important step inasmuch as the laboratory can be of assistance *only* when the investigator finds the physical evidence and requests laboratory examination and comparisons.

2. Collecting evidence. This must be done carefully and properly.

3. Packaging evidence to avoid breakage, loss, and contamination.

4. Transporting evidence to the laboratory.

5. Examining evidence in the laboratory.

6. Custody or safekeeping evidence.

7. Transporting evidence to court.

8. Exhibiting evidence in court for the enlightenment of the jury.

The investigator must know what physical evidence is and what types of evidence to expect in a particular crime; how to properly collect, preserve, and transport it; and what the laboratory can do with it. The laboratory is only as good as the investigator. Accordingly, it is the purpose of this chapter to aid the investigator to realize the advantages that can accrue from the careful collection and examination of physical evidence.

Sources of Physical Evidence

In general, physical evidence will be obtained from three main sources: (1) the scene of the crime, (2) the victim, if any, and (3) the suspect and his or her environment.

Crime scene

This will usually be indoors, outdoors, or in an automobile. The procedure will vary somewhat, depending on the locale, but the basic principles will remain the same. The success or failure of a criminal investigation depends upon the thoroughness exercised at the crime scene in recording *all* available information. If every iota of available information is not collected and recorded, the investigation conducted thereafter suffers. The protection and preservation of the crime scene should be maintained while the investigators and technicians proceed to make notes, sketch, photograph, prepare casts, and search the area. Very often the position of articles in a room, in a lot, or throughout a building will relay to the trained eye the events preceding the crime. Never touch, change, or alter anything until identified, photographed, measured, and recorded. Before the actual collection of evidence is started, it is necessary that

All unauthorized persons should be prevented from entering the scene.

Precaution should be taken to prevent contamination and possible loss of microscopic evidence such as hair, fiber, glass fragments, etc.

Photographs of the scene should be obtained from a number of angles. Many times a reevaluation of the overall appearance of the scene is required, and without photographs this study is practically impossible. Pictures should be obtained of the scene only, without spectators or other individuals in the area depicted. It is always desirable to take closeups of the crime scene from all angles. In addition, detailed shots showing the position of special items—body, gun, empty cartridge cases, etc.—should be taken. Notes should be made of all photos.

Photographs taken should be identified by number and described: for example, number 1, photo showing condition of victim's bedroom, upper floor, northwest corner of residence, 2345 Elm Street, Center City, Illinois, 2 P. M. (date), photographer's name, type of camera used, lens opening, shutter speed, film used, position of camera, distance, and lighting.

A general survey of the premises should be made with care to guard against contamination or disturbance of important items.

A sketch should be prepared to show scene conditions, items of importance, and measurements.

In the actual collection of evidence, care should be taken to avoid destroying or adding fingerprints to areas or objects of possible evidential value. After first recording the details, the larger objects at the scene should be placed in a suitable container or wrapped in clean wrapping paper. Identifying data should be placed on a tag tied securely to the article itself and on the wrapper, so that the contents are clearly indicated. Items of clothing or bedding that have not been in contact with each other must be kept separate at all times; thus each article should be wrapped individually. The words "fragile," "corrosive," "flammable," "perishable," or similar notations, should be stamped or printed on the outer wrapper where applicable.

Nonportable items should be dusted for fingerprints if the likelihood of finding fingerprints exists. Thereafter, a search should be made for microscopic evidence and latent fingerprints. Such evidence may include hairs, fibers, minute paint fragments, or dust invisible to the naked eye. The types of evidence and standards to be collected will depend on the nature of the crime and the scene. "Standards" refers to *known specimens* of blood, hairs, fibers, soil, bullets, paper, cloth, paint, etc., which are obtained by the investigator and furnished to the crime laboratory for comparison with *questionable items* of evidence found in an investigation to determine the degree of similarity. A cardinal rule to follow in all cases is to submit sufficient known samples (standards) of materials to the laboratory for the examiner to use in making comparisons with questioned evidence specimens.

Fingerprints are a positive method of identification. Objects that bear fingerprints of the criminal are practically worthless when they bear numerous impressions of others who have handled them. Fingerprints are likely to be found on any varnished or hard, smooth surface. They may also be found on the points of entrance and exit. In addition, fingerprints can be located upon objects that are most commonly touched: glassware, doorknobs, dresser drawers, and content of cabinets. Objects found to have been moved from their usual place are other possible sources. In automobiles, fingerprints are likely to be found on the steering wheel, rearview mirror, instrument panel, registration card holder, doors and windows (particularly on the driver's side), and on items in the glove compartment.

The victim

Apart from the necessary photographs, sketches and examination, which require services of medical and other specialists, particular consideration should be given to the following items:

Clothing   Collect the clothing from the victim of hit-and-run, homicide, kidnapping, sex, or other cases where there has been contact between suspect and victim. Each item should be wrapped separately and transported to the laboratory with a minimum of handling.

Blood   In crimes of violence, the taking of a blood sample from the victim is often essential. Not only is this required for classification of blood type where blood has been shed, but often it is necessary to determine if a victim has been drinking. The blood sample should be taken by a medical doctor or another authorized hospital employee.

Hair   The collection of head hair samples from a body living or dead should be a part of the routine procedure in felonious assault cases. At least twenty hairs collected from several areas of the head are required. A sample of pubic hair should always be obtained from rape victims.

Suspects and their environment

The moment that a suspect is in custody and there is good reason to believe that this person is the criminal, the care previously expended on the collection and preservation of physical evidence begins to pay dividends. The following items of evidence deserve particular consideration:

Clothing   The most important evidence obtainable from a suspect will normally come from the clothing worn at the time of the crime. Apparel may be important in burglary, homicide, kidnapping, aggravated assault, rape, and other cases where there has been contact between suspect and victim. The retention of clothing in other instances should be considered where apparel worn by the suspect is an issue. Careful handling and packaging of this clothing will often result in the finding of almost every category of physical evidence possible.

Hair, Blood, Fingernail Scrapings, and Ear Wax   These may, at one time or another, have to be taken from suspects in order to compare with similar items that may place them at the scene or in contact with the victim.

Searching the Crime Scene

The search is conducted in the area of a crime scene to uncover any physical evidence that could (1) determine the facts of the crime; (2) identify the criminal; and (3) aid in the arrest and conviction of the suspect. The search, although called a crime scene search, is not confined to the specific area of the crime itself. It may extend along the path of the approach and follow the line of flight of the perpetrator. In the mechanics of searching, the investigator might

  Move in straight lines from north to south or east to west.
  Search specific assigned sections or quadrants. This type of search may be used in small or large areas.
  Assign foot or cruising searchers in accordance with such factors as urgency, availability of personnel, mobile equipment, area to be searched, type of search involved. As each assigned area is covered, the searchers are given new sections to cover. All assignments are recorded in order to fix responsibility. This procedure is continued until the area is completely covered.
  Communicate with the person in charge of the search and the participants. When evidence is located, vital information is obtained, or suspects are apprehended, it should be communicated

immediately to the director of the search. This procedure ensures proper correlation of search activities and decisions and is a most important step. (See Figure 3-1.)

Quite frequently, the critical work in a case involving physical evidence is performed at the scene of the crime. The analysis at the laboratory is sometimes a relatively routine procedure. Therefore, in a major case such as a homicide, it may be imperative that a laboratory specialist be called to the scene. Collection of physical evidence by the criminalist will serve two purposes:

1. It will shorten the chain of evidence since the specialist would collect, identify, preserve, and transport the evidence from the crime scene to the laboratory and subsequently into court. This procedure maintains the chain of custody and prevents loss, mishandling, and contamination of the evidence.

2. It will place the collection and preservation of the physical evidence in the hands of the trained specialist who can evelute

Figure 3-1. Uniformed officer pointing out bullet holes in a wall to a homicide detective during a crime scene investigation.

what evidential traces are required and how they can best be obtained.

The methods of searching vary with the crime, type of evidence sought, and the purpose of the search. Guards should be posted at doors, gates, and other entry ways or critical areas as the exigencies demand.

Investigators searching assigned sections should be alert particularly to disturbed areas or indications of tampering such as loose molding, light fixtures, heater ducts, floorboards, new nails or screws, and patches in plaster or cement. They should be attentive to repainting, stains, soil disturbances, new grass, broken twigs, and fresh scratch marks on window areas or walls. Unusual arrangements, dust disturbances, missing objects, and tool marks should be examined carefully. Look for special places of concealment like hidden compartments, false bottoms, hollowed items, and stuffed toys. The extent of the search is dependent upon the facts of the case under investigation. Thoroughness should be the guide in searching. Obvious places such as furniture, beds, vacuum cleaners, and containers should not be overlooked. In the conduct of any search, whether inside or outside, the results are proportionate to the patience, ingenuity, curiosity, and imagination of the searcher.

In the collection of evidence, the courts want to know the following: *Who* found it? *What* did it look like? *When* was it found? *Where* was it found and what was its relation to other objects? The court is interested in knowing where the evidence was held from the time of collection to its presentation at the trial. In order to satisfy these requirements, adequate and complete notes of all evidence found must be recorded accurately. The investigator who finds the evidence should place his personal identifying mark on it. It is preferable to have another investigator present at the time the evidence is located. Such action might preclude the pos-

sibility of exclusion of the evidence in the event the only individual competent to produce it in court is unavailable because of ill health, death, or absence at the time of the trial. The identifying mark should be placed on the object in a permanent manner and in such a way that it can be positively identified. This mark should not be placed on the item where it might destroy any potential area of examination by the laboratory. A knife may be used to mark hard objects; while a pen and ink may be used on absorbent materials.

Evidence, such as bird shot or liquids, that cannot be marked should be placed in an appropriate container. This receptacle should then be sealed and identified on the label. The label or property tag should include title of the case, officer's name or initials, date, time, specific location where found, and case number if available.

Equipment

In preparing for a crime scene search, the facts of the case will govern the type of equipment needed. Evidence tags, containers, assorted envelopes, pillboxes, polyurethane bags, plastic bottles, and cellophane tape may be useful. Equipment such as a compass, axe, pinch bar, chalk, knife, steel tape or ruler, flashlight, latent fingerprint equipment, shovel, probing rod, first aid kit, and metal detectors can also be helpful. Many departments have a prepared kit which is taken to a crime scene.

Sketches and diagrams

Legally, for a sketch or diagram to be admissible in court, it (1) must be part of some qualified person's testimony; (2) must recall the situation—the preparer must have seen the area; and (3) must express it (the place or scene) correctly.

Purpose of Sketch A sketch is made for several reasons, viz., to refresh the memory of the investigator; to reflect the precise

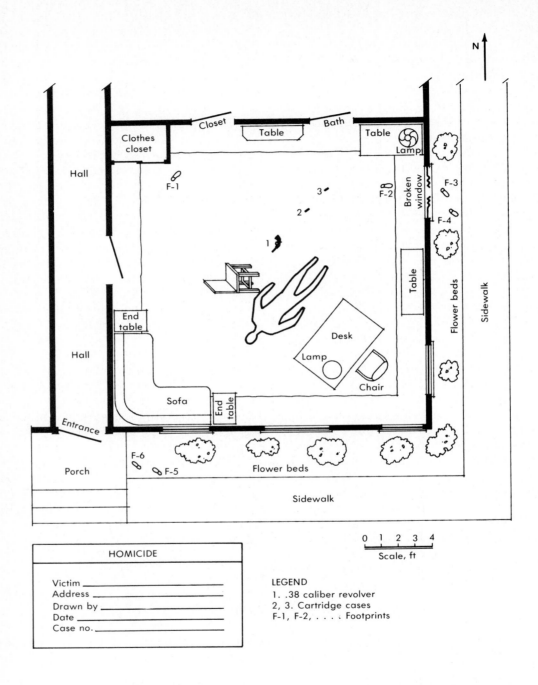

Figure 3-2. Homicide scene. The sketch depicts the location of the victim, gun cartridge cases, and footprints.

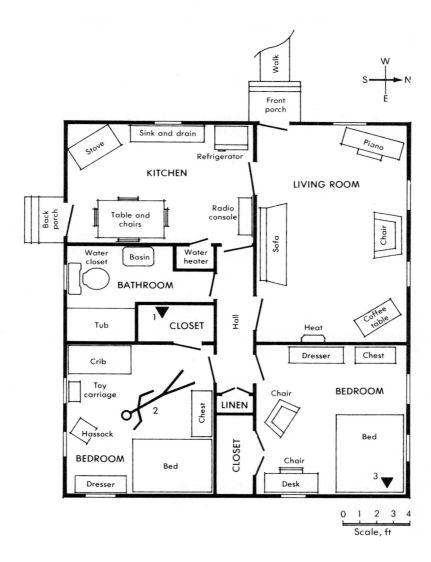

Figure 3-3. Sketch of the floor plan of a suspect's residence. The drawing shows a closet (number 1) in the southeast bedroom from which the first suspect emerged and attempted to kill the officer searching the room. Number 2 shows the position of the first suspect on the floor after being wounded by the officer in a scuffle. Number 3 shows the location of the bed in the northeast bedroom under which a second suspect was found.

location of objects and their relationship to other objects and surroundings; to assist the prosecutor, judge, and jury in understanding conditions at the crime scene; to help correlate a witness's testimony; to provide a record of conditions at the crime scene; to supplement photographs; and to assist in the questioning of witnesses and suspects. (See Figure 3-2.)

Preparing the Sketch A sketch need not be artistically perfect. A simple line drawing with accurate measurements is sufficient. It must relate to the case only. Some outdoor measurements may be paced off, measured by use of the automobile speedometer, or estimated. However, precise measurements should be made at the crime scene. Prior to drawing a sketch, the area should be looked over first to get a general picture. Then, it should be decided what to include or exclude in the sketch as well as the scale to be used. The largest scale possible should be used; that is, $1'' - 4'$ or $1'' - 10'$. Graph paper makes it easier to draw to scale. All sketches should include a compass with an arrow indicating the direction north; a legend to explain the letters or numbers used in the drawing; and the scale used. (See Figures 3-2 and 3-3.)

Locating Points on a Sketch The location of objects by use of a sketch is generally done in several different ways. Some of these ways are rectangular coordinates (Figure 3-4a); triangulation (Figure 3-4b); base line method (Figure 3-4c); compass point (Figure 3-4d); and sketch in cross projection (Figure 3-5).

Rectangular Coordinates This method requires two reference lines at right angles to each other and thus is often used to locate objects in a room. Two walls of the room serve as the lines and distances are measured from the object to each of the walls

along a line perpendicular (at right angles) to the wall. (See Figure 3-4a.)

Triangulation This method requires two fixed reference points X and Y to locate the position of objects. This method may be used indoors or outdoors. However, if the objects to be located are within a room, the corners of the room are convenient points. Objects are located and recorded simply by the distance from the two points. For example, in Figure 3-4b, object A is 4 feet [1.2 meters] from Y and 8 feet from X.

Base Line Method This method requires measurements to be taken along and from a single reference line, called the base line. This line should be established by use of a string, chalk line, or some convenient means before any measurements are made. Often the line is established between two objects (tree and rock) or between two corners of a room (see Figure 3-4c). One end of this line is selected as the starting point. Objects are located by giving the distance from this starting point along the base line to a point opposite to the object, and then from the object to the base line along a perpendicular line to the base line.

Compass Point This method requires the use of a protractor, or some method of measuring angles between two lines. One point, often the corner of a room, is selected as the origin. A line going from the origin is the axis line from which angles are measured. For example, object A in Figure 3-4d, is located as being 10 feet [3 meters] from the origin X and at an angle of 20 degrees from the vertical line through point X.

Cross Projection In this procedure, the crime scene sketch takes on the appearance of a box opened out. The ceiling opens up like the lid of a hinged box with the four walls opening outward. This method is an effective way to portray evidence found on the walls or ceilings of rooms. (See Figure 3-5.)

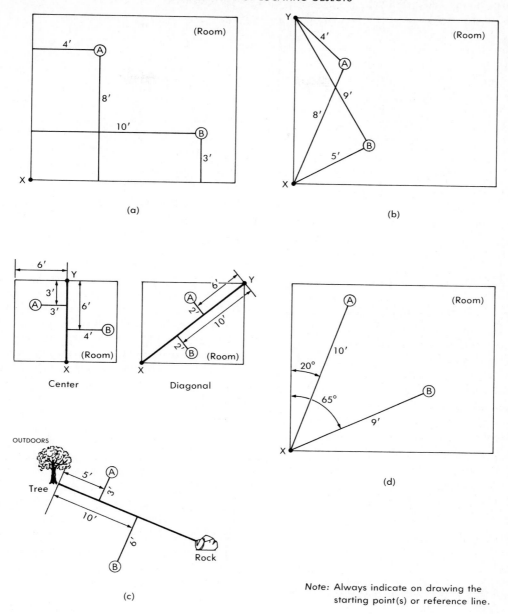

Figure 3-4. (a) Rectangular coordinates. (b) Triangulation. (c) Base line. (d) Compass point (this last method requires a protractor).

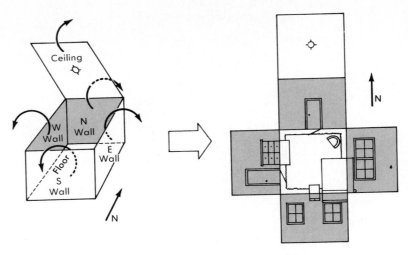

Figure 3-5. Sketch in cross projection.

PROCEDURES FOR COLLECTING, PRESERVING, AND TRANSPORTING COMMON TYPES OF PHYSICAL EVIDENCE

Bloodstains

In cases where bloodstains are involved, a complete search of the scene should be made. Submit all bloodstained articles to the laboratory immediately. Obtain blood samples from both victim and suspect and submit them along with the other evidence in order that comparison tests may be made. A blood specimen or sample should only be drawn by an authorized person.

Types of cases in which bloodstains may be of value

Abortion   Blood may be found on bedding, towels, garments, and instruments.

Assault   Blood may be found on both victim and suspect. Clothing, weapons involved, and fingernail scrapings are common sources for this type of evidence. Rags, handkerchiefs, towels, tissues, toilet paper, rugs or other materials that suspect may have used to wipe off hands or the weapon are sources of bloodstains. In investigations of crimes of violence or death, blood may be found in sink traps, floor cracks or crevices. If offense occurred out of doors, vegetation or soil in crime area may contain blood.

Burglary   The possibility that bloodstains are present should be kept in mind, especially when glass has been broken or when extensive hammering might have resulted in injury to the burglars.

Hit-and-Run   The points of impact and the undercarriage of the vehicle should be examined for any suspicious stains.

Investigation of Death   (See "Assault" above.)

Rape   (See "Assault" above.) Particular attention should be directed to the examination of the undergarments of both victim and suspect. If crime was committed outdoors, soil in area of the attack may reveal blood-stains.

Collecting, preserving, marking, and transporting bloodstains

Bloodstains on Clothing and Other Textile Material   Submit the entire garment or article to the laboratory. Never cut out a portion of a stain. Do not package evidence while a stain is still wet. If garments are wet or damp, allow them to air dry before packing. Do not put them in a draft and do not use either a fan or artificial heat of any type to dry them. Mark each item of clothing directly on the material. Attach an identifying tag to each article of evidence. If more than one article is to be submitted, fold them in clean sheets of paper and wrap separately in order to prevent contamination of one piece by the other. Place them in a larger container, preferably a stout cardboard box, seal, label, and forward to the crime laboratory.

Bloodstains on Small Movable Objects   Submit all small movable objects such as weapons, pieces of glass, wood, or paper to the laboratory with the stains intact. Mark each item carefully in order that the identifying mark does not interfere with the processing of the article. The materials should be packaged in such a manner that the stained area will not rub against any other surface. Guard against contamination. Seal and forward to the laboratory.

Bloodstains on Large Immovable Objects   Note size, shape, and location of blood spots. Flake off particles of the dried stain with a clean knife or other instrument. A different knife should be used each time if more than one source of the blood is suspected. A scraping (using a clean instrument) should be obtained from the unstained area near the actual bloodstain. If clean pillboxes or glass vials are not available, an

adequate alternative is to place each sample in a separate sheet of clean paper, folded carefully. The pillbox, glass vial, or folded paper should be sealed, labeled, and thereafter placed in a more substantial container. The outer container should be identified in the same manner as the inner package. Transmit all materials to the laboratory.

Blood Traces from Fingernail Scrapings   Take scrapings from both victim and suspect. Use either a clean knife or other instrument such as a nail file or toothpick. Do not use the same instrument for more than one person. Place the scrapings from each hand in separate pillboxes or vials. As an alternative, the scrapings may be placed in a folded paper and placed within an envelope. Label, seal, and transmit to the laboratory.

Freshly Drawn Blood Samples for Blood Grouping Purposes   Have the blood sample drawn under the supervision of a licensed physician or another authorized person. Place 1 cc of blood in a clean glass vial and add a few crystals of anticoagulant. Keep the specimen as cool as possible, preferably in a refrigerator. Do not freeze. Seal the container tightly, label appropriately, package in a more substantial container, and transmit to the laboratory.

Results possible from laboratory examination of bloodstains

From the laboratory examination of bloodstains there are three primary questions that can be answered.

1. Is it blood? (If not, what is it?)

2. Is it *human* blood? (If not, from what animal did it come?)

3. If human, to what blood group does it belong?

Do the position, size, and shape of the blood spots answer any of the following questions:

From what approximate *angle* did blood spurt or fall?

From what approximate *height* did blood fall?

From which *direction* did blood come?

Seminal Stains

Handle suspected seminal stain areas as carefully as possible. Rough treatment will break up spermatozoa so that a positive identification may be impossible. Submit all articles for seminal stain examination to the laboratory immediately. Do not neglect to submit all swabs, smears, and stains removed from the person of the victim by the examining physician.

Types of cases in which seminal stains may be of value

Investigation of Death The possible presence of seminal stains should never be overlooked in homicides and suicides. The victim's body and clothing, as well as bedding, towels, and other articles at the scene may be sources of such stains. Other good sources could be suspects and their surroundings, such as clothing, handkerchiefs, and automobiles.

Rape and Other Sex Offenses Seminal stains are often, although by no means always, found as physical evidence in sex offenses. All clothing of both victim and suspect, as well as other articles in the immediate vicinity, may be a source of such stains. The victim should be examined for seminal stains, particularly in the genital area.

Collecting, preserving, marking, and transporting seminal stains

Seminal Stains on Clothing and Other Textile Materials (Refer to "Collecting, preserving, marking, and transporting bloodstains.")

Seminal Stains on Small Movable Objects Submit all small movable objects such as paper, wood, and sanitary napkins to the laboratory with the stains intact. Mark all objects for future identification and label completely. Package in such a manner that the stained region will not rub against any other surface. Guard against contamination. Seal and forward to the crime laboratory for examination.

Seminal Stains on Large Immovable Objects Note size, shape, and location of the stains. Cut around the entire stain and remove it intact, including a portion of the unstained area. Place in a clean box or preferably in a glass container. Label, seal, package in a more substantial container, and transmit to the laboratory.

Seminal Stains on Victim or Suspect Have the examining physician or autopsy surgeon note the presence of any stains in the genital area. Such stains on thighs and legs can be removed by transferring them onto filter paper or other absorbent paper moistened with distilled water. Hairs that might bear seminal stains can be clipped or pulled. Have the physician obtain a vaginal smear as soon as possible if applicable. Use a long pipette with a rubber bulb or cotton swab. If fluid is present in the vaginal tract, have him prepare smears and preserve the remainder of the fluid in a tightly stoppered small vial. Place soaked-off stains in a clean powder box or envelopes after they have been air-dried. Place hairs in pillboxes or glass vials. Package cotton swabs in a test tube after air-drying, or in a clean glass cigar container. Slides bearing smears are best transported in special cardboard mail holders. Label all containers completely, seal, and transmit to laboratory.

Results possible from laboratory examinations of seminal stains

Does the stain contain human seminal fluid? If spermatozoa are not found but acid phosphatase is demonstrated, the presence of semen can be established with a very high degree of probability. Can the blood group (A, B, O, AB) of the seminal stain be determined? If so, what is it?

Hair

The possible presence of hair evidence in any type of crime should never be overlooked. Hair is often valuable as a means of personal identification or as an investigative aid. It may be found on articles of furniture, in hats, on clothing, and on the body of a victim. Collect, but do not cut hair samples for submission to the laboratory for comparison purposes.

Types of cases in which hair may be of value as evidence

Assault   Hair might be found from both victim and suspect. Clothing and weapons involved are common sources for this type of evidence. Strands or tufts or hair may sometimes be found in the grasp of the victim.

Hit-and-Run   The points of impact and the undercarriage of the suspected vehicle should be examined for the presence of hair. When a vehicle comes into contact with a person, hairs and fibers are often found in the areas of fresh damage, torn fenders, loose chrome, and bug catchers. If hair is firmly attached to a removable part of the vehicle, remove the part from the vehicle, if possible, rather than the hair from the part.

Investigation of Death   (See "Assault" above.) As a matter of routine, a sample of head hair from the deceased should be collected in all cases of sudden or unusual death. In those cases involving sex offenses, a sample of pubic hair should also be collected.

Rape   (See "Assault" above.) Particular attention should be directed towards the examination of the undergarments of both victim and suspect for the presence of pubic hairs. Blankets, sheets, and seat covers are among the other sources of hair evidence in sex crimes.

Collecting, preserving, marking, and transporting hair

Objects on Which Hairs Are Visible and Appear To Be Firmly Attached (as with Dried Blood)   In this situation, leave hair intact on the object. Draw a diagram showing the position and amount of hairs. Label object and package in such a manner that the hair cannot become dislodged in transit to the laboratory. If the object is immovable, such as a wall or certain parts of an automobile, carefully remove the hairs with fingers and place them in a pillbox or glass vial. If neither of these two types of containers is available, folded paper may be used. Seal and label appropriately.

Objects on Which Hairs Are Visible and Not Firmly Attached   Collect and handle as set out above.

Articles on Which the Presence of Hair Is Suspected   On articles such as clothing, blankets, seat covers, and other items, wrap the object separately in clean paper; label accurately. The wrapped article should then be placed in a large container and identified as to contents, stamped with the word "evidence," and transmitted to the laboratory. Never place the clothing of the victim in the same container with the clothing of the suspect.

Comparison Samples—Collection Procedure[1]   If injuries to a victim suggest a point of origin, secure hair specimens from

[1]*Physical Evidence Manual,* State of California, Department of Justice, Division of Law Enforcement, Investigative Services Branch, March 1976.

as near this location as possible. When the point of origin is unknown, secure samples from various locations and keep samples separate; record area from which the sample was obtained. Whenever possible, obtain large samples from each area. It is desirable that at least several dozen hairs be obtained. Attempt to pull out standard samples that will be used for comparison purposes. If this is not possible, samples may be collected by running a clean comb through the hair. If possible, obtain hair samples from all individuals involved. Place hair samples in pillboxes, glass vials, or folded pieces of clean paper. Label completely, seal, and transmit to the laboratory.

Results possible from laboratory examination of hair

Is the hair sample animal or human? If animal, from what type of animal did it most likely come? Is it a fur hair? If human, from what part of the body did it originate? Are there any indications of the characteristics of the individual from which it came? Could the hair have come from a specific individual; and, if so, what is the probability of common origin? Did the hair fall out naturally, was it pulled out, or was it cut by a sharp instrument? Are there any foreign substances adhering to the hair; for example, dye, blood, or grease?

Fibers

Textile fibers probably occur more frequently than any other type of microscopic evidence. Yet this type of evidence is often overlooked by investigating officers. With the advent of modern synthetic fibers, this type of microscopic material has taken on added significance as a source of corroborative evidence. Fibers are examined microscopically to determine the type of fibers and the distribution of the various accidental characteristics. Such examination may iden-

tify the type of garment or fabric from which they came. A most important point in collecting and transporting fiber evidence (especially clothing) is to wrap each item separately and to guard against possible contamination.

Types of cases in which fibers may be of value as evidence

Assault   This type of crime usually involves personal contact of some sort: e.g., aggravated assaults. Therefore, clothing fibers will be interchanged (transferred) between victim and suspect; i.e., fibers from the victim's clothing will be found on the suspect's clothing and vice versa. Weapons and fingernail cuttings also may be important sources of fiber evidence.

Burglary   Clothing fibers will almost always be found at the point where the burglar may have been forced to crawl through a window or other opening.

Investigation of Death   (See "Assault" above.) If entry was effected by climbing through a window or by other means similar to those used in burglary, important fiber evidence may be found.

Rape   The nature of this crime results in the cross-transfer of fibers from the clothing of the victim, the clothing of the suspect, and such articles as blankets or automobile seat covers. Weapons and fingernail scrapings may also be sources of fiber evidence.

Collecting, preserving, marking, and transporting fiber evidence

Objects on Which Fibers Are Visible and Appear To Be Firmly Attached Leave fibers intact on the object. Draw a diagram showing the position and amount of fibers. If the object is immovable, such as a window sill, door of an automobile, or wall, record the exact location of the fibers. Carefully remove fibers with fingers or tweezers. Place fibers in a small pillbox, glass vial, or other tightly capped container. Label the container with identifying data. Seal and transmit to the laboratory. If the fibers are too small to be handled with fingers or tweezers, use the adhesive tape technique described below.

Fibers That Are Visible on Objects and Not Firmly Attached   Carefully remove fibers with fingers or tweezers and package by placing fibers in a small, round pillbox, glass vial, or other small, tightly capped container. Label the container with appropriate identifying data, seal, and transmit to laboratory.

Fibers Not Readily Visible but Presence Is Suspected   In those instances where it is believed that fiber evidence may be present, for example, on a window sill or automobile bumper, the *adhesive tape technique* may be used. Using an ordinary transparent adhesive (cellophane tape), cover the area to which fibers may have adhered. When the tape is pulled off, any fibers will adhere to the sticky surface. Attach tape, sticky surface down, to a clean, smooth, nonabsorbent surface (glass, plastic, cellophane wrapping from package of candy or cigarettes). Be careful not to contaminate the tape with fibers from your own clothing. It is important to note that although no fibers are apparent to the naked eye, microscopic examination of the tape often reveals the presence of a number of fibers. Place in a small envelope, pillbox, or glass vial. Label completely, seal, and transmit to the laboratory.

Fibers Possibly Transferred to Clothing of Victim or Suspect   If clothing of more than one person is involved, keep each set of clothing separate from the other. Avoid possible contamination. Do not wrap on the same table. Take special care to avoid disturbance of soil, dust, blood, seminal stains, or other foreign material that might be adhering to the fabric. Place an identifying mark on each item of clothing; ink or indelible pencil may be used. Take care not to interfere with any stained areas.

Fibers Possibly Transferred to Other Fibrous Materials   Where there is a possibility that fibers may be transferred to such materials as blankets, seat covers, towels, keep all items separated from the clothing of the victim or suspect. Avoid contamination. Avoid disturbing soil, dust, blood, seminal stains, or other foreign material that might adhere to the fabric. Place an identifying mark on each item. Ink or indelible pencil may be used. Be careful not to interfere with any stained areas. Wrap each article separately. New paper bags are suitable for this purpose. Label and seal the individual packages. They may now be placed in a larger container for transmission to the laboratory.

Fingernail Scrapings   From both the victim and the suspect, scrapings should be taken; cuttings are preferred. If scrapings are to be taken, a clean knife, fingernail file, or toothpick may be used for this purpose. Do not use the same instrument for more than one person. Place the scrapings or cuttings from each hand in separate pillboxes, glass vials, or other tightly capped containers. Label, seal, package in a more substantial container, and transmit to the laboratory.

Results possible from laboratory examination of fiber evidence

What type of fiber is it (wool, cotton, rayon, nylon)?

Is it a fiber "match" when compared with the clothing of the victim (or suspect)?

Is it the same type of fiber?

Is it the exact same shade of color?

Are there any other points of similarity?

Fiber evidence can be a corroborative aid in establishing such facts as whether one person has been in contact with another (rape, assault); whether a suspect has climbed through a particular window (burglary); or whether a weapon (gun, knife) has been carried in the pocket of a suspect (homicide).

Glass

The value of glass fragments as evidence is not always fully recognized. As a general rule, criminals are unaware of its importance in the field of crime detection. This fact, together with the ability of the laboratory to prove identity between glass samples with high probability, often enables glass to play an important role in the solution of a crime. In cases where glass fragments are suspected of being present on clothing, shoes, tools, or other objects, submit the articles to the laboratory as soon as possible in order to prevent any further loss of the glass fragments.

Types of cases in which glass may be of value as evidence

Burglary Burglars are often forced to break a window while effecting entry into or exit from the scene. It is known from experience that any person standing in close proximity to glass when it is broken will invariably pick up several fragments of the broken glass, particularly on his clothing. Consequently, the clothing of burglary suspects, in cases where windows have been broken, will almost always carry a large number of microscopic glass fragments.

Hit-and-Run Frequently, as a result of hit-and-run accidents, headlight lenses are broken. Less common, but also possible, is the breaking of windshield glass. Therefore, both the scene of the accident and the clothing of the victim can be expected to be sources of glass fragments.

Collecting, preserving, marking, and transporting glass

Fragments of Microscopic Size Glass fragments of microscopic size are usually found on articles of clothing, including shoes. The items of clothing should be wrapped separately. Attach an identifying tag to each article wherever possible. Shoes and other solid objects, such as tools and bullets, which are suspected of carrying glass fragments should be placed in the smallest container in which the object will fit. For example, bullets can be placed in small pillboxes and shoes in shoe boxes. Do not pack with cotton or other protective material. To prevent rattling, objects may be fastened to the bottom of the container with cellophane tape. Seal completely, leaving no holes through which the glass particles may be lost, should they become loose. Label container and transmit to the laboratory.

Large, Visible Glass Fragments (Collection Procedure) Where there are large, visible glass fragments, there is a chance that physical matching ("jigsaw" type) may be accomplished with the fragments. Protect thin protruding edges against damage by imbedding them in modeling clay, putty, or some similar substance. Thereafter, place the fragments in small pillboxes or similar boxes with a tight-fitting lid. Do not use glass or paper containers. If glass is submitted for the purpose of determining *direction of impact* of a bullet or other fracture analysis, record which side of the glass was on the outside of the window, and which side was on the inside.

Comparison Samples The laboratory examination of glass fragments is almost exclusively a process of comparison. For this reason, a sample of the broken glass, at least the size of a quarter, must always accompany the rest of the evidence submitted. Samples should be obtained from the area near the point of impact. Keep the comparison samples separate from the questioned fragments. Place in separate containers and label accurately.

Results possible from laboratory examination of glass

The laboratory can fit pieces of glass from a broken window or headlight lens together and make a positive identification Even if the glass fragments are smaller than the head of a pin, identity between two samples can be proven with high probability.

If a window has been hit with a blunt instrument such as a rock, stick, or fist, it is possible to determine the side from which the blow was struck. Where a bullet penetrates a window, it is possible to determine the direction from which it was fired. If two or more bullet holes are in close proximity, it is possible to determine the sequence of firing.

Paint

Paint will normally occur as physical evidence in three different forms: (1) chips or flakes, such as may be found adhering to clothing or at the crime scene; (2) smears, either from fresh or old "chalking" paint; and (3) intact, on objects such as tools or automobiles. Do not use the same instrument to obtain both the questioned and comparison samples. Keep samples separate at all times. The paint fragments should not be placed in ordinary envelopes or other loose containers from which the sample may be lost in transit.

Types of cases in which paint may be of value as evidence

Burglary Paint fragments, often of microscopic size, may be found adhering to the tools used in the commission of a burglary or on a vehicle into which a safe was loaded. Paint fragments from the scene may have lodged in the clothing of the burglar.

Hit-and-Run The clothing of the victim, upon microscopic examination, will often yield the presence of minute paint fragments resulting from the impact with the automobile. In collisions between automobiles there invariably will be a considerable amount of paint interchanged.

Paint Fragments on Clothing (Collection Procedure) Wrap each item of clothing separately. Clean paper or polyethylene bags are satisfactory for this purpose. Mark each item in an inconspicuous place. Label the individual package completely and seal. Place the articles in a larger container and transmit to the laboratory.

Paint Fragments on Small Portable Objects (Firmly Attached) If the paint fragments are on such objects as tools or headlight rims, submit the entire object. Record the exact position found. Mark the object containing the paint fragments or smears. Wrap carefully, or place in clean paper bags. Tools may be wrapped so that the portion bearing the paint fragments (usually the end of the tool) is in a clean paper bag. Protect the area bearing the foreign smear. Seal the package, label completely, and transmit to the laboratory.

Paint Fragments on Large Nonportable Objects Scrape the paint fragments off carefully using a clean knife or similar instrument. Try to dislodge the fragments onto a clean piece of paper by tapping the object. Record the exact location and describe the apparent amount, nature (smear, particles, flakes), color, and type of surface paint was on. Place the paint specimens in pillboxes, glass vials, or other small, tightly capped containers. If paint fragments have been scraped from two or more different places, put the paint from each location into separate containers. Do not place paint fragments in ordinary envelopes or other loose containers from which the sample may be lost in transit. Seal, label the container, and transmit to the laboratory.

Liquid Paint and Wet Smears Place liquid paint samples in widemouthed tins, glass bottles, or jars. Let wet paint smears on cloth, wood, metal, or glass dry completely before preparing for shipment. Seal tightly, label, and transmit to the laboratory.

Comparison Standards Remove the comparison paint sample from an area near apparent damage. If there is more than one location bearing damage, collect additional samples from areas near each. Put paint from each separate location into individual containers. Always flake the complete paint sample off; i.e., get down to bare metal. For example, in securing samples of paint from a suspect's vehicle, the paint should be chipped off the surface rather than shaved or scraped off. A sample that is chipped off to the base metal represents all the layers of paint which were applied to the vehicle surface. If the suspect suggests a source of paint smears to substantiate his alibi, get a paint sample from that source for elimination purposes. Place specimens in pillboxes, glass vials, or other small, tightly capped containers. Seal, label, and transmit to the laboratory.

Matching Flakes of paint may be shown to fit together along a common fracture edge in the manner of a jigsaw puzzle. Such matching would indicate a conclusive identification of source. If the fragments consist of several layers, identity of source can be established with a high degree of probability. If the paint fragments are present in minute amounts or as a single-layered, common variety, evidence of a corroborative nature can be provided.

From the paint found at the scene or recovered from the victim's clothing, the laboratory (subject to certain limitations if an original and not a refinish paint is in question) may narrow down the types of automobiles from which the questioned paint could have originated.

Firearms

Every effort should be made to submit the firearms involved in a crime situation to the laboratory. Without the questioned weapon, bullet comparisons, functioning tests, powder pattern examinations, and other tests cannot be conducted. Moreover, fingerprints or adhering material such as blood, hairs, or fibers might be a significant aid to an investigator.

Types of cases in which firearms may be of value as evidence

These are crimes against persons, such as aggravated assaults and homicides. Stolen, found, or confiscated weapons should be submitted to the laboratory for test firing and for comparing with evidence in pending cases.

Collecting, preserving, marking, and transporting firearms evidence

Where fingerprint evidence on a gun is of importance to a case, do not unload the weapon, but deliver it in person to the laboratory just as it was found. Never submit a loaded gun to the laboratory unless delivered in person. Do not clean the gun.

Fibers, hairs, or other microscopic evidence may be found adhering to the suspected gun and may be matched with similar material in the suspect's pocket. Do not fire test shots. All test shots from suspected guns must be fired in the laboratory. Ammunition of the kind under suspicion should be submitted. Identification scratch marks should be placed on the frame, side of barrel, or some other part of the gun not readily removed. Record the make, type, caliber, and serial number. Retain this information in your personal records for future court use.

If a gun is to be shipped to the crime laboratory, *unload* it before packing. If an autoloading pistol is involved, remove the clip and cartridge from the chamber (if the gun was loaded). If the weapon is a revolver, remove all cartridges from the cylinder, both fired and unfired. However, notes should be made of the exact position of each cartridge and the chamber from which it was removed. This information should be furnished to the laboratory.

To prepare firearms for shipment, place the gun on its side on the bottom of a strong corrugated cardboard box. Lace the gun in place by punching holes around it and sewing it down with strong twine. Place the gun in a larger carton, or place a lid on the one used and wrap securely with heavy paper. Seal, label, and transmit to the laboratory. Be sure to include a copy of the request for examination within the package. Rifles and shotguns may be dismantled in order that they may be more conveniently shipped.

Fired Bullets   Bullets embedded in material such as wood or plaster should be removed by cutting out a portion of the material in which the bullet is embedded. Send the piece containing the bullet intact to the laboratory. Do not attempt to dig a bullet out. Removal of an evidence bullet from the body of a deceased person should be done by a physician. The doctor performing the autopsy should be instructed to use special care

in recovering the bullet in order not to damage the delicate markings essential for laboratory identification. Rubber-tipped forceps should be used in extracting the bullet. Never probe for a bullet.

Fired bullets should be marked on the base ends, never on the sides. If this is not possible, mark the bullet on the tip or nose. Each specimen should be wrapped separately and individually in soft tissue paper. Handle as little as possible. Bullets should not be placed loosely in pockets along with objects like keys or coins. They should be placed in pillboxes, glass vials, or small envelopes and packed tightly with cotton or tissue paper to prevent motion within. Label, seal, place in a more substantial container, and transmit to the laboratory. Do not clean or wipe off bullets. Protect any blood, hair, fibers, or other material that may be adhering to the bullet.

Shot Pellets   Pellets embedded in material such as wood or plaster, should be handled in the same manner as bullets embedded in solid objects. If it is not possible to submit material in which pellets are embedded, they may be dug out with a knife or other instrument. Care should be taken not to mutilate them any more than is absolutely necessary.

Whenever it is necessary to remove pellets from the body of a deceased person, they should be removed by a physican. The doctor should be instructed to use special care in recovering the pellets so that there will not be undue damage to them. Rubber-tipped forceps should be used. Wrap collected pellets in soft tissue paper or cotton and place them in a glass vial, pillbox, or small envelope. Label, seal, package in a more substantial container, and transmit to the laboratory.

Shot Wads   Search for wadding at the crime scene and in the victim's clothing or body. When a shotgun is fired, the wads travel along with, or behind, the shot charge for a short distance; then they trail along in the wake of the charge for a few feet, and drop to the ground. Inscribe marks of identification on wads using ink or indelible pencil. Place wads in a glass vial, small pillbox, or small envelope. Label, seal, package in a more substantial container, and transmit to the laboratory.

Empty Cartridge Cases Make accurate measurements of exact location where cartridge cases were found. If found in the revolver, note the chamber location in which each cartridge was located. The cases should be marked by scratching initials or code numbers on the *inside* of the open end. Never mark the closed end. Package cases in the same way as fired bullets, viz., by placing in pillboxes, glass vials, or small envelopes packed tightly with cotton or tissue paper to prevent motion within. Label, seal, package in a more substantial container, and transmit to the laboratory.

Loaded Shells or Cartridges Make accurate notes of the number, location, and manufacturer's designation of cartridges found (e.g., Rem — UMC, .38 S & W). Initials should be scratched on the sides of brass cartridges. Have the cartridges processed for fingerprints if it is deemed advisable. Boxes of ammunition should be marked on the side of the box with ink or indelible pencil. Large quantities should be placed in a cardboard box or wooden container. Label, seal, and transmit to the laboratory.

Shot or Powder Patterns If the victim's clothing contains powder burns, it should be cautiously removed to prevent any loose powder particles from being dislodged. Identification should be placed on the garment with an indelible pencil or pen and ink in such positions that will not interfere with the wound area. Keep the clothing as flat as possible and under no cirsumstances fold the garment. Do not attempt to cut out suspected areas. Submit the entire garment or garments to the laboratory. If personal delivery of the clothing is not necessary, place a clean sheet of paper on each side of the cloth in the vicinity of the bullet holes. Then, place the clothing and paper between two pieces of heavy cardboard and tape firmly in place. Label, wrap in a substantial container, and send to the laboratory. Always enclose (within the outside wrapper) a letter requesting the examination desired.

In cases where there is a gunshot wound on an unclothed portion of the body, a scaled photograph of the wound area should be taken. This photograph should be taken before any attempt to clean around the wound is made. A second scaled picture should be taken after the wound area has been cleaned. Mark the margin of the photographic negative for identification purposes.

Results possible from laboratory examination of firearms

From what type or make of firearm was the fatal bullet fired?

Was the fatal bullet fired from the suspect's gun?

Was the discharged cartridge case fired from the suspect's gun?

Were two or more bullets fired from the same gun?

Were two or more cartridge cases fired in the same gun?

What was the gauge of the shotgun used?

What size shot was used?

How far from the victim was the gun held?

Is there any foreign material attached to the bullet that would indicate its path of flight?

Was this gun carried in the suspect's pocket?

What were the serial numbers which have been ground off this gun?

Has the gun ever been used in the commission of an offense not yet solved, in which bullets or cartridge cases were previously submitted?

Flammables

The basic principle of arson evidence collection is to prevent the volatile liquid from evaporating. In some instances it may be possible to collect the substance as is by sealing the original container and thus avoid having to pack it in another sealed metal container.

Types of cases in which flammables may be of value as evidence

Arson Flammable liquids may be suspected as the cause of a fire either because of the nature of the fire, or because of the absence of a natural cause. The most common liquids encountered are gasoline, kerosene, and paint thinner. Less frequently encountered are isopropyl (rubbing) alcohol, charcoal lighter, or a variety of petroleum base liquids.

Theft The siphoning of gasoline from automobiles and/or the theft of petroleum products from storage locations are examples of other cases in which flammables may be significant physical evidence.

Collecting, preserving, marking, and transporting flammables

Liquid in Container Often a container (can, bottle) is found at the scene, or in the possession of the suspect, still containing some undistributed liquid. If the container is a gasoline can or jar, close the top and seal it with tape. An identifying sticker or tag should be securely affixed to the container and include an item number and a description of the liquid. It should tell where it was obtained, the date it was obtained, collector's name, position, badge or serial number, and case identification. Handle all containers so as not to destroy fingerprints that may be on the container.

A bottle (Molotov cocktail, see Chapter 19) or can without a top should be sealed with a cork, or a portion of the liquid should be transferred to another clean container that can be securely sealed. Label with identifying data such as described above. A chemical analysis should be made as soon as possible.

Liquids Distributed at Scene Occasionally, suspected flammable liquids may be pooled at a location at the scene. These liquids should be transferred to clean glass containers and securely sealed. Usually, however, the liquid will be distributed in some porous material and will tend to gravitate downward. Thus, it will often be found below the point of the fire. The probable location of these liquids may be determined by odor, discoloration, or inference from the nature of the fire (see Chapter 19).

Soil If a liquid is thrown on a structure or vehicle, it will often settle in the soil. Collect the most likely soil areas in new, clean 1-gallon paint cans (with metal lids) or clean 1-gallon pickle jars. At least 1 gallon of soil is needed for laboratory analysis. Secure the paint-can lids completely. If pickle jars are used, seal the lid with electrician's plastic tape.

Upholstery Collect the upholstery and stuffing of furniture (or automobile seat) where indicated. Again, seal in paint cans or gallon jars.

Flooring and Carpeting In fires set inside a dwelling, the carpeting or wood flooring may soak up the flammable liquid. Section (cut out section of flooring or carpeting) and seal material in airtight containers. If the necessary tools for sectioning are not available, wrap the material in question in several layers of plastic sheeting and deliver to the laboratory as soon as possible.

Rags Occasionally, rags soaked with flammable liquid are found at the scene. The suspect rags should be placed in airtight paint cans or gallon jars and taken to the laboratory for examination.

Glass Broken bottles suspected of having contained a flammable liquid are often found at the scene. Glass is nonporous, so the fragments do not usually retain identifiable traces of the liquid. However, since they may be connected to a suspect, they should be preserved.

Clothing Flammable liquids rapidly dissipate from clothing. Often a suspect is arrested with an odor of some flammable about his person, but no trace is found when the clothing reaches the laboratory. However, if the clothing is obtained quickly, and securely sealed in cans or jars, the laboratory may be able to confirm the presence of the flammable.

Comparison Samples Samples for comparison with flammable liquids should be collected as soon as possible and securely sealed. Each sample should be specifically identified as to nature of contents, location where obtained, date, and name of officer submitting specimen. If a specific service station is suspected as the source, collect *all* grades of gasoline sold at that station and determine the date of delivery of each grade to that station.

Results possible from laboratory examination of flammables

Confirm Corpus Delicti The laboratory can isolate the flammable liquid from the fire debris and determine whether it is gasoline, kerosene, or some other kind. Thus, such examination can furnish some evidence from which the jury may infer that the fire was of incendiary origin.

Connect Flammables with a Source Available to the Suspect If the liquid has not appreciably evaporated (e.g., if it is present in a can left at the scene or well soaked into an unburned material), the laboratory can compare it to material available to the suspect. The liquid might come from a drum of paint thinner in the suspect's garage or be gasoline from a service station.

Explosives

When dangerous explosives are believed to be involved, immediately clear the area for a reasonable distance. Notify the crime laboratory. Do not try to disarm, move, or transport explosive material unless directed to do so by explosive experts (see Chapter 19 and Figure 3-6).

Corrosive Materials (Acid or Alkaline)

These kinds of liquids require special handling and containers. Consult and follow the advice of a laboratory expert prior to handling, preparing, or transporting any such liquids.

Narcotics

All suspected narcotic evidence must be submitted to the laboratory for chemical analysis. Whenever narcotic substances (powders, capsules, pills, tablets, etc.) are found, the officer finding the suspected narcotic should place such substance in an evidence envelope, seal with sealing wax, and place his or her thumbprint impression in the wax. The identifying tag or envelope should contain the following data: case number, suspect's name, charge, place, date, and time material found, identity of the officer, and name of the laboratory analyst who received the evidence. A receipt signed by the person accepting the evidence should be obtained in order to maintain the *chain of possession*. Thereafter, should the narcotic

tioned and exemplary handwriting as is possible to obtain. The suspect's exemplary writing should include the written or printed material appearing on the questioned document. It is impossible to make a comparison of value between dissimilar written letters or numbers. For example, little is gained in comparing capital "F's" with capital "G's," small "h's" with small "a's," or number "7's" with number "6's." Photostatic or photographic copies of documents should be submitted only when originals are unobtainable.

Cases in which documents may be of value as evidence

Questioned Documents   Documents of this type may play an important part in the investigation of almost every type of offense. For example, an anonymous letter could be important in the investigation of a death, or the comparison of handwriting on a hotel register might lead to the conclusion that a suspect was in the vicinity on the night of a burglary.

Collecting, preserving, marking, and transporting document evidence

Documents Requiring Handwriting Examination   This type should be handled carefully. Regardless of who touched the document before the arrival of the investigator, immediate steps should be taken to protect such items for possible latent fingerprint processing. Do not staple, date stamp, or mark the face of the document. Mark the paper in question on the reverse side in the lower left or right corner. Determine whether or not any portion of the check, for example, was written by a sales clerk or other person in the store where it was cashed. Indicate to the handwriting examiner which writing is in question. When forgery is suspected, submit known genuine

Figure 3-6. A type of protective equipment used by some police agencies in handling packages suspected of containing explosives.

evidence be taken from the laboratory for any purpose, a record should be made in order that there is an exact accounting for that evidence up until the time it is presented in court.

If the suspect narcotic is a liquid, it should be placed in a bottle. The cap of the container should be sealed and identified. A property tag should be securely attached to the suspected substance and contain the identifying data set out above. If marijuana cigarettes are found, place identifying data on the paper wrapper of *each individual cigarette* before placing them in evidence envelopes. Identify the envelope.

Documents

In cases where a document examination is deemed advisable, submit as much ques-

writing of the person on whom the document is forged (in addition to the suspect's writing) so that forgery can definitely be established. Place the document in an envelope, being careful not to add any new folds or creases. Do not attempt to repair damaged documents. Any specific comparisons or other special information that is desired should be made clear at the time the documents are submitted for examination. If any suspects are available, exemplars of their writing should be taken and submitted with the documents.

Documents Requiring Other Examinations (Erasures, Obliterations, Ink, Typewriting, etc.) Keep in mind the possibility that latent fingerprints may be present. As with all document evidence, handle carefully and as little as possible. Identify the document on the back side in the lower left or right corner. Do not circle or otherwise mark any particular word or area on the document. Place the document in a manila or cellophane envelope and transmit to the laboratory.

Results possible from laboratory examination of document evidence

Was a particular document written by a particular individual?

Is a particular writing forged?

What was the make, model, and approximate age of the typewriter used?

Was a particular typewriter used to type a particular document?

Was a particular check protector used to make a particular imprint?

What is the context of an erased, obliterated, eradicated, indented, altered, or written-over writing or typing?

What differences are there, if any, between inks in one or several documents?

Which stroke was written last, when two strokes of writing cross one another?

Did two pieces of paper originate from the same source?

Do uneven edges of torn paper match to prove that several pieces originally formed a whole document?

Do perforated edges of check, receipt, or stamp match with corresponding checkbook, receipt book, or sheet of postage stamps?

Will the creases and folds in the document aid in determining the place where it has been, as, for example, in a particular billfold?

What is the context of writing or printing on burned or charred paper?

Procedure for obtaining handwriting comparison standards

Submit as much exemplar (known original writing) as is possible to obtain. Original documents, if they can be obtained, should always be submitted rather than photocopies of them.

Check Cases Samples should be collected in the following manner: use blank check forms of the same size as the check in question. Have the suspect write (at your dictation) the material appearing on the worthless check. Do not assist him with form, spelling, or punctuation. Do not allow the suspect to see the questioned check during the procurement of the sample writing. Use the same type of writing instrument as was used on the fraudulent check. Obtain at least six samples, preferably more, removing each specimen from the suspect as he completes it. In addition to the check forms, it is also advisable to obtain known genuine standards of the subject's writing from other sources such as letters, legal documents, or employment records. If this is not possible, obtain additional samples by following the procedure set forth below.

Cases Not Involving Checks In cases not involving checks, samples should be collected as follows. Place the suspect in the writing position that would be comparable to that under which the suspected document was written. If any doubt exists as to the position of the writer at the time of the offense, endeavor to place the suspect in a comfortable writing position. Provide the writer with paper similar to the questioned document in texture, ruling (lined or unlined), and size. Require the style or method appearing on the questioned document. For example, when the questioned writing consists of hand-printed capital letters, the exemplary writing should also consist of hand-printed capital letters. The officer requesting the hand-writing might *dictate* the wording of this letter.

Friday
September 29, 19 —

Dear Mr. Morales:

Well, the old class of 19__ is through at last. You ask where the boys are to be. Victor and Zach Brown go on the 24th to Harvard for Law. Don't forget to address them as "Professor." Ted Peterson takes a position with the New York and New Haven Railroad, 8726 Ladd Avenue, Fall River, Massachusetts, and Jack Queen with the Central Pump and Power Company at Jersey City, New York, 400 East 6th Street. William Fellows just left for a department position in Washington: his address is 735 South G Street. At last account, Dr Max King was to go to Johns Hopkins University for advanced study in X-Ray analysis. Think of that! Elliot goes to Toledo, Ohio, to be a Y.M.C.A. secretary. I stay here in San Bernardino, California, for the present. What do you do next? How about Idaho?

Sincerely,
Raymond Sanchez

This sample letter should be written at least three times on three different sheets of white paper. As each specimen is completed, remove it from the view of the suspect. Names or ordinary words should not be spelled out by the investigator. Have the suspect use the same type of writing instrument as was used on the questioned document. In addition, numerous words and phrases similar to those appearing in the questioned writing should be dictated to the suspect. Do not assist the writer with form, spelling, or punctuation. Obtain samples with both the right and left hand, rapidly, slowly, and at varied slants.

If a questioned signature is also involved, obtain *ten* or *fifteen* samples of the signature, each written on a different piece of paper. Remove each signature from the suspect's view as it is completed. Witness each sample on the back side, never on the front. It is advisable to obtain known genuine standards of the suspect's writing from other sources, such as letters, notes, or legal documents. These specimens must have been written at about the same time as the suspected document. After dictating each sample, the officer should number each sample and, as indicated above, initial and date each sheet on the back side of the paper. The procedure suggested herein for obtaining handwriting specimens is also applicable in obtaining handprinting samples.

Procedure for obtaining typewriter comparison standards

Type the specimens on paper similar in surface texture to the questioned document. If in doubt, use standard typewriter paper. Type the questioned document at least three times. Obtain a full word-for-word text of the message in question, copying the document exactly (form, spacing, spelling). If the document in question is too lengthy, specimens of the first page or two may suffice.

It is also desirable to make a direct carbon copy impression of all type characters on the suspected machine. In making a carbon specimen, lay a sheet of carbon paper over a sheet of bond paper, set the machine on stencil, and type directly on the carbon paper. The typewriter ribbon may be removed.

Submit the ribbon, as well as the typing specimen, to the laboratory.

Record on each sheet of exemplary typewriting the following data: (1) when, where, and by whom specimens were taken; (2) the make, model, and serial number of the machine used (for example, Smith-Corona, Standard Super-Speed, serial number LA 212686); and (3) initial and number each sheet on the back in the lower left or right corner.

Example of some common letter groups that should be included in the standard typewriting to be used for comparisons are:

ing, act, at, al, ed, it, ar, in, ten, es, ies, eis, est, art, ord, que, quo, che, chi, men, man, ain, tion, the, thi, er, ion, ent, ry, pe, pi, pos, poi, te, ta, po, ple, pia, ew, we, wa, wo, tr, oy, king, rot, rat, rut, boy, ad, aid, af, go, age, bad, dab, able, fall, fix, just, sta, sti, gun, ill, igo, get, gone, hun, hut, hob, had, his, ape, sh, fu, lu, roc, run, muk, ac, ck, ek, cu, he, bid, bex.

Make at least three impressions of each type-face, spaced as follows

```
2  3  4  5  6  7  8  9  0  -
q  w  e  r  t  y  u  i  o  p  ½
a  s  d  f  g  h  j  k  l  ;  ¢
z  x  c  v  b  n  m  ,  .  /
"  #  $  %  _  &  '  (  )  *
Q  W  E  R  T  Y  U  I  O  P  ¼
A  S  D  F  G  H  J  K  L  :  @
Z  X  C  V  B  N  M  ,  .  ?
```

The Crime Laboratory

Inasmuch as the very essence of the work involved in the collection and preservation of physical evidence often involves scientific examination, no treatise would be complete in this field without a discussion of the crime laboratory. Scientific examination plays a vital role in the successful prosecution of criminal cases, particularly in view of the many legal decisions that have curtailed investigative methods and procedures.

The crime laboratory is normally represented on television and in detective fiction by someone wearing a white laboratory coat looking through a microscope for a brief moment at a single hair recovered from the scene of a crime. Before long the lab technician turns to the detectives who are waiting for an answer and says, "Folks, the person you're looking for is white, male, American, 6'2", weighing 194 pounds; he is left-handed, works as an accountant, and at this very moment you'll find him in a hotel in Chicago." Unfortunately, the large majority of the examinations carried out by a crime laboratory do not lead to such astounding conclusions. However, a laboratory can and does provide valuable services to the investigator and to the courts. It may help the officer evaluate leads or eliminate some suspects; it may help the court establish certain facts or corroborate the stories of witnesses or, by itself, establish certain facts.

The single hair mentioned above could, for example, be compared with hairs from the heads of three suspects; and two might be conclusively eliminated. In short, *the purpose of a crime laboratory is to carry out a scientific examination of physical evidence recovered at the scene of a crime and to report the results of such examinations to the investigators concerned or to the courts by means of expert testimony.* Physical evidence can be anything. Glass, paint, soil, bullets, blood, handwriting, paper, capsules, and knives are a few examples. In size, physical evidence may range from a battleship to a pollen grain; from an apartment building to a sample of air.

The types of examinations carried out in the laboratory can be expressed in just two words, viz., *identify* and *compare*. An unknown white powder contained in a capsule taken from a suspected dope addict is identified as heroin; or a reddish stain in the

POSSIBLE SOURCES FOR HANDWRITING AND TYPEWRITING COMPARISON STANDARDS

Administrator, estate	Express companies	Neighbors
Answers to decoy letters	Family	Newspaper reporters
Applications for licenses	Fraternities	Notaries
Assignees	Furniture contracts	Official positions
Athletic contests	Gas company	Order blanks
Auctions	Guardian	Passports
Auto owner's or driver's license	His office	Pension records
Autograph albums	Home	Political organizations
Bail bonds	Hospitals	Postal cards
Bank accounts	Hotel registers	Prescriptions
Bankruptcy proceedings	Incorporation papers	Probation and parole office
Baptismal records	Installment companies	Professional rolls
Bible, family	Institutions	Public library
Chattel mortgages	Insurance companies	Railroad passes
City clerk's office	Janitor (waste paper)	Receipt books
Civil Service examinations	Job applications	Receipted bills
Clubs and lodges	Jury records	Receipts for pay
College records	Labor union records	Registered letter receipt
Copyright applications	Leases	Safe-deposit company
County clerk's office	Legal papers	School examination papers
Courts	Letters	Shipping records
Credit slips	Loan companies	Societies
Criminal records	Luncheon clubs	Tax departments
Death certificates	Marriage certificates	Telephone company
Department records	Messenger receipts	Time cards
Draft boards	Military records	Title companies
Electric company	Mortgages	Tradesmen in neighborhood
Employment bureaus	Motel registers	U.S. Veterans Bureau
Executor	Municipal records	Valentines and greeting cards
Exhibitions	Naturalization records	Voting records

trunk of a murder suspect's car is identified as human blood, type B. This same murder suspect may also have a bloodstained hatchet on the end of which a hair is adhered. This hair may be compared with the hair from the head of the victim. The handwriting on the face of a check may be compared with exemplary handwriting obtained from a suspect.

The crime laboratory not only assists in convicting the guilty but often helps to protect the innocent. Whether a victim is interested in seeing that the person who burglarized his or her home or business establishment is apprehended and successfully prosecuted or whether the issue is protection from a false charge of forgery, the crime laboratory stands ready to assist the investigator and the courts in presenting data.

Many of the larger police and sheriffs' departments and state law-enforcement agencies have crime laboratories staffed by competent personnel who are constantly performing valuable services in criminal investigations. The FBI laboratory is likewise available on a national scale to provide laboratory examinations of the most sophisticated type to all law-enforcement agencies. A major crime laboratory is actually a large group of laboratories under one roof, each specializing in its own branch of science, and yet intimately related to each other. For example, certain criminalists will specialize in blood examination; others document examination; still others will be involved in the sciences of ballistics, hairs and fibers, petrographic analysis, etc.

Scientific crime laboratory equipment

Among the sophisticated equipment and techniques that a major scientific crime laboratory may use in processing physical evidence are

Microscopes There are many microscopes used in a crime laboratory. These include bullet comparison, tool-mark and fiber comparison, polarizing, surgical, vertical illuminating, and stereoscopic microscopes. The usual working magnification of an optical microscope ranges up to 1000 times, with an upper limit of 2000. Each instrument performs a specific function. Examples are isolation and identification of plant material, hairs, fibers, paint and other trace material; determination of the metallic composition of questionable materials; the study of color and coloring agents; the identification of certain compounds as narcotics; the analysis of crystalline substances.

Scanning Electron Microscope (SEM) The scanning electron microscope has an attached x-ray spectrometer. (See Figure 3-7.) The SEM is a much more powerful instrument than conventional light microscopes and provides very high magnification (over 100,000 times), greater resolution and depth of field, and an additional elemental analysis capability in the form of an x-ray microprobe. This versatile instrument has been used in such examinations as

Figure 3-7. Police laboratory technician conducting an examination of evidence with the aid of a scanning electron microscope.

analysis of glass fragments from break-ins (burglaries); identification of human hairs, counterfeit money, and paint scrapings from the scene of hit-and-run auto accidents; and the tracing of cutting tools from markings made by the tools. It has also been used in identification and comparison of bore striations on bullets, markings on cartridge cases, gunshot residue cases, and numerous other examinations of microscopic evidence.

Atomic Absorption Spectrometer The atomic absorption spectrometer is used for the quantitative analysis of most elements and for the detection of trace metals in biological and other physical evidence. Atomic absorption spectrometry is an extremely sensitive technique that can be used for quantitative determination of trace amounts of sixty-seven different metallic elements. It is among the most sensitive techniques available for bulk analysis of these elements. Yet it is one of the easiest and least costly methods. It is well suited to automatic sampling and recording. Because it can be used for the determination of almost any metal, it has become a standard analytical method for elemental analysis. It is an improvement over neutron activation analysis because it is sensitive to lead as well as antimony and barium, and also because it eliminates the necessity for radiochemical separations. In addition, it removes the need for sending the samples to a central facility where a nuclear reactor is located. Instead, the equipment required for atomic absorption spectroscopy can be purchased by many of the larger laboratories. Thus, the analysis can be performed locally.[2]

X-ray Diffraction Spectrometer One of the most important uses made of x-ray radiation is that of identifying crystalline substances by use of an instrument known as the x-ray diffraction spectrometer. X-rays are passed through an unknown crystalline material and are diffracted with the diffraction spectrometer. By recording the diffraction pattern it is possible to identify a substance by reference to known diffraction patterns. It is thus possible not only to differentiate between two white crystalline materials, one of which may be sugar and the other a deadly poison, but also to identify the poison.

Gas Chromatography This process is used for the separation and identification of chemical mixtures encountered in drug, alcohol, toxicology, and petroleum analyses. The gas chromatography/mass spectrometer combination is used for the separation and identification of microgram quantities of drugs and related materials.

Laser Emission Spectrograph The laser emission spectrograph is used to determine the trace metallic content of minute particles of soil, glass, oil, paint and metal fragments.

Refractive Index and Light Dispersion Apparatus This apparatus is used to measure and compare the physical properties of liquids and microscopic glass particles.

Neutron Activation Analysis (N.A.A.) N.A.A. is used to compare, identify, and measure the elements in a specimen. In neutron activation analysis a sample of unknown material is irradiated with neutrons (nuclear particles). Some of the irradiated atoms in the unknown material are thereby made radioactive and begin to disintegrate (radioactively) with the emission of gamma rays. The energy of these gamma rays is measured with a gamma ray spectrometer. These energy values are then used to identify the element in the original material. Quantitative measurement of the elements present can be made by comparing the radioactivity of the elements in the evidential material with the radioactivity of known amounts of these elements.[3]

Voice Spectrograph (Voiceprint Identification) Voice recognition rests upon the supposition that each person's voice pattern is unique. Voiceprints are graphic representations of sound vibrations which occur when a person speaks. The visual impressions of voice patterns are usually identified as grams. They are produced by running a magnetic tape recording through the sound spectrograph. The spectrograph analyzes the three basic voice characteristics: frequency, time and loudness. Although voiceprint is not presently a positive means of identification, it does have good probative value. It is considered a good investigative aid and definitely useful in the investigation of such crimes as obscene telephone calls, extortion threats, kidnapping cases, bomb threats,

[2]G.M. Wolten and G.L. Loper, "Detection of Gunshot Residue Status and New Approaches," *Journal of California Law Enforcement,* vol. II no. 3, p. 106, January, 1977.

[3]"Neutron Activation," *FBI Law Enforcement Bulletin,* November 1972, p. 25.

and many others. Personal identification through the use of voice spectrograms was introduced into criminal justice in 1962 by Lawrence G. Kersta of the Bell Telephone Laboratories, Murray Hill, New Jersey.[4]

Ultraviolet Light Ultraviolet light is sometimes called "black light." It consists of radiations of shorter wavelength than those forming the violet end of the visible spectrum. Radiations of still shorter wavelengths are known as x-rays. Radiations longer in wavelength than the red end of the visible spectrum are called infrared. Those of still longer wavelength are used for radio broadcasting and are known as radio waves. Ultraviolet light is used primarily for the detection of fluorescent materials not visible under ordinary light. It also frequently reveals, in ordinary materials, differences that are not apparent under ordinary light. These differences include those among various inks, papers, watermarks, pieces of cloth, colors, and glass. Ultraviolet light can be used to show up invisible characteristics such as the location of stains or secret writing; invisible laundry marks; check alterations; erasures; fingerprints in processing a multicolored surface; and markings on gems.

Although ultraviolet light itself is invisible, it can produce a visible phenomenon known as luminescence; that is, it can cause a great number of materials to give off wavelengths of visible light. Ultraviolet light is often used by criminal investigators to identify specific articles, like money, which they had previously treated with fluorescent powders in order to trap a criminal suspect. For example, the marked or treated money that is the object of a theft is left as a "plant." Thereafter, the person taking the money will have the powder on his or her hands and clothing, which powder will fluoresce under ultraviolet light treatment. Fluorescent powders have also been useful in such cases as narcotics, extortion and kidnapping.

Infrared Photography Examinations of evidence by infrared radiation have been made possible through the use of photographic plates and film which are sensitive to this radiation. Many materials exhibit characteristics of transmission and reflection of infrared rays which are different from those in visible light. Thus, with infrared, it may be possible to distinguish between two dyes which appear identical in ordinary light. Other infrared photography uses include detection of altered serial numbers; differentiation among inks, dyes, and pigments which seem to be visually identical; detection of forgeries and erasures; and detection of writing on charred documents. Infrared photography also helps to make visible bleached or written-over writing, invisible ink, markings of identification on leather goods, development of faded laundry marks, and clothing stains. With suitable infrared light sources it is possible to photograph rooms, objects, or persons in almost complete darkness. Electronic equipment is available which permits observation of a location in total darkness by the use of infrared light.

Criminalistics Laboratory Information System (CLIS) This computerized information system, when it is developed and implemented, will collect and disseminate forensic science data for law enforcement throughout the United States. Through it, information will be identified, collected, and stored for on-line retrieval via National Crime Information Center (NCIC) telecommunications lines. The information will be centrally stored at FBI headquarters. The FBI Laboratory will maintain the files and perform related quality-control tasks. A

[4]*Voice Identification Research,* U.S. Department of Justice, Law Enforcement Assistance Administration, National Institute of Law Enforcement and Criminal Justice, February 1972, p. 65.

CLIS committee will develop operational policy for this sytem. It is composed of seven members: four from member laboratories of the American Society of Crime Laboratory Directors and one each from the Bureau of Alcohol, Tobacco and Firearms; the Drug Enforcement Administration; and the FBI.

—— SOME CONSTRUCTIVE CRITICISMS LEVELLED AT POLICE BY JUDGES AND PROSECUTORS CONCERNING PHYSICAL EVIDENCE AND COURT TESTIMONY ——

Lack of scientific evidence at the time police ask the district attorney's office for a criminal complaint.

Failure to protect the crime scene. Improper movement of physical evidence before it has been carefully noted, photographed (if possible), and roughly sketched with accurate measurements, distances, and dimensions.

Need for more scientific evidence. This can speed up trials and often alter the verdict of a given case.

Overlooking total physical evidence. For example, after finding narcotics in the jacket pocket of a suspect during an arrest, officers fail to book the jacket itself as evidence.

Failure to take fingerprints of a possible defendant. For example, in a case where a husband and wife were charged with possession of marijuana for sale, the packaged kilos were not processed for fingerprints. Failure to process packages made it difficult to refute wife's claim of ignorance of the marijuana being in the residence.

Freehand drawings on court blackboards. These are often not drawn to scale. They result in extended arguments about the location of physical evidence that the drawings portray.

Failure to make detailed laboratory tests of blood at rape scene. For example, this can be of help in a case where the victim scratched the assailant and drew blood.

Poor tape recordings, or failure to make a tape recording at all.

Lack of preparation. For example, officers may fail to read over their reports prior to trial.

Failure to take sufficient photographs (particularly color photographs) in sexual and other assault cases. The victim may have received many bruises, but evidence of the bruises could have been healed over by the time the case went to trial.

Failure of officers to take photographs of injection marks in narcotic cases.

Insufficient observation. For example, officers on the witness stand can make such statements as "I don't remember" when asked specific questions concerning the finding of physical evidence. The court may feel then that it is difficult to have confidence in such an officer's testimony.

Officers' hostility to cross-examination of their actions at a crime scene. Officers should not take such questioning as an affront to their integrity. A reaction like this creates a negative reaction on part of jurors.

Unlawful searches and seizures. These have resulted in many motions to suppress physical evidence.

Failure to interview all possible witnesses. For example, a homicide occurred across the street from a party attended by forty people. Only two of those people were questioned. Perhaps some of the other thirty-eight people attending that party could have furnished some valuable information had they been questioned.

Failure to gather available physical evidence. For example, officers sealed off the place of a crime and did not complete their search for physical evidence. Upon their return days later, they learned the landlord, thinking the officers were not coming back, threw out or destroyed valuable physical evidence.

Lack of an overall case report. This should set forth a well-organized, indexed, and complete file that contains the original report; the results of interviews with the suspect; the suspect's identification record; statements of witnesses; a list of physical evidence; and results of laboratory examinations. Photographs of the crime scene, victim, and suspect; prosecutive action to date; and any other relevant material of possible assistance should be included.

CONDENSED PHYSICAL EVIDENCE COLLECTION GUIDE

EVIDENCE SPECIMEN	IDENTIFICATION/PACKAGING	NOTEBOOK RECORD
Ammunition: Fired bullets	Scratch identifying mark on base of bullet with knife or scriber. Wrap each bullet separately in soft tissue or cotton. Pack in small container, seal and label with case identifying data. If more than one bullet, use item number to designate.	Record date, time, case number, recovery location, type of identification mark placed on specimen and location of mark, witness to recovery, and disposition. Sketch recovery area and show relationship to other evidence at scene.
Fired metallic cartridge cases	Scratch mark on inside of open end, or identify on outside near top with initials and date. Handle evidence and packaging as suggested above for fired bullets.	Same as above.
Loaded metallic cartridges	Scratch identifying mark or initials and date on side of case near top. Wrap and package as indicated above for cartridge cases, bullets.	Same as above
Loaded shotgun shells	Place initials and date on side of shell in ink or indelible pencil. Wrap shells separately and package as noted above for fired bullets.	Same as above.
Fired shotgun shells	Same as above.	Same as above.
Shot pellets	On outside of container indicate nature of contents, date and place obtained, name of officer, and case identifying data. (Place pellets in cotton or tissue).	Notes should include date, time, location and method of recovery, witness to recovery, how packaged, and disposition. Make small sketch of recovery area.

EVIDENCE SPECIMEN	IDENTIFICATION/PACKAGING	NOTEBOOK RECORD
Shot wads	Place date, initials on wad with pen and ink or indelible pencil. Put in glass vial, small envelope, or pill box. Seal, label with identifying case data.	Notes similar to above.
Firearms: a) handguns serial number	Scratch identifying mark on the frame, side of barrel, cylinder, or other part of gun not readily removed. Attach a reinforced tag to the trigger guard. On tag record make, type, model, case identification data, officer's identity, and date. Place weapon in polyethylene bag, plastic pouch, or manilla evidence envelope. Seal container and label appropriately. If gun is to be unloaded, record the position of the fired/unfired cartridges in the gun's cylinder. Deliver in person.	Include make, type, caliber, barrel length, color and all numbers showing on weapon. Also, date, time, how gun identified, witness to recovery and disposition of weapon. Draw small sketch of recovery area and relationships to other items of evidence. Include measurements.
b) rifles/shotguns	Scratch identifying mark on an inconspicuous part of the barrel or other major component of weapon. Attach a reinforced tag to trigger guard containing identifying data of make, model, caliber, serial number, place of recovery, officer's initials, and date. Package as for handguns. Deliver in person. If gun is to be unloaded, identify position of ammunition in gun and clip using a numerical figure to represent each round.	Same as above
Acids/alkalies/ blasting caps	CONSULT CRIME LABORATORY FOR ADVICE	
Blood: Liquid	Place identifying data on adhesive tape affixed to outside of sterile test tube containing specimen. Seal and deliver to laboratory as soon as possible. If delay is involved, refrigerate but do not freeze.	Include date, name of victim or suspect, case identification, identity of doctor who obtained specimen, location where obtained, and disposition.

EVIDENCE SPECIMEN	IDENTIFICATION/PACKAGING	NOTEBOOK RECORD
Liquid recovery at crime scene	Place identifying data on adhesive tape attached to sterile glass test tube containing specimen.	Record date, time, recovery location, name of victim/suspect, method of collecting specimen and identification, disposition, and case number. Sketch recovery area, indicate measurements.
Bloodstains: a) On small objects	Place initials and date on object away from stain area. Package in appropriate-sized container so that stain will not rub against surfaces. Seal and label package with identifying case data.	Same as above.
b) On large, immovable objects	Cut out portion around stain and remove intact. Place initials and date on material away from stain. Place in container, seal, label with identifying case data. If stain portion cannot be cut out, scrape or chip off specimen into clean glass vial, seal, label appropriately.	Same as above.
c) On clothing and other textile materials	Mark each item directly on the material away from stain area. Also tie a tag to article with identifying case data thereon.	Notes should contain data as to date obtained, kind of article, location of recovery, type and place of stain, how identified, disposition.
d) In soil	Place identifying data on adhesive tape affixed to glass jar containing the soil specimen. Seal jar and deliver to laboratory.	Record date, appearance of stain, location, amount, relationship to fixed objects, and disposition. Make sketch, include measurements.
Clothing	Mark identification directly on clothing items in an inconspicuous place. Wrap each item separately, seal and label with identifying case data. Date and initial.	Record date, case identification, type of article, place of recovery, how identified, disposition and case number.

EVIDENCE SPECIMEN	IDENTIFICATION/PACKAGING	NOTEBOOK RECORD
Documents: Checks, anonymous threatening letters, demand notes, ransom letters, suicide notes	Place initials and date on reverse side in lower right or left corner. Place item in cellophane or plastic envelope. Seal and label with identifying case data.	Notes should include date and title of case, type of document, identity of person furnishing item or place where obtained, and disposition.
Charred or burned paper	Place charred material on top of loose cotton and then in a card-board container. Seal, mark "frag-ile," and deliver to laboratory. Show date, case identification data, and initials of officer.	Same as above.
Drugs: a) powders, capsules, pills, tablets	Place date, initials and case number on container. Leave drugs in container and place in special sealing envelope. Identify enve-lope with pertinent case data.	Record date, place of recovery, suspect's name, method of mark-ing, witness to recovery and dispo-sition. Make sketch of recovery area. If more than one item, use an item number sequence.
b) liquids	Mark and date bottle(s). Seal tightly and place in evidence en-velope. Label appropriately.	Same as above.
Fibers/hairs	On outside of container indicate type of material, place of recovery, date and initials of officer, and case number.	Same as above.
Glass fragments	Place in small plastic box or glass vial, seal and label with identifying case data. Package glass from different area separately and indi-cate location.	Notes similar to above.
Paint: a) liquid	Place in clean, unused paint can. Seal and label appropriately.	Same as above.
b) solid (paint chips or scrapings)	On outside of pill box or glass vial affix a label which should contain case identifying data, place of re-covery, date and officer's initials.	Notes should be similar to those made for glass fragments and liq-uid paint as noted previously.

EVIDENCE SPECIMEN	IDENTIFICATION/PACKAGING	NOTEBOOK RECORD
Rope, twine, cordage	On tag or container, type of material, date, officer's name, and case identification data.	Record date, place of recovery, type of material, how identified and disposition. Make sketch.
Safe insulation, soil	Place in plastic box, glass vial or clean jar. Seal and label with identification case data.	Record date, time, title of case, type of material, recovery area, how collected and identified, and disposition. Sketch location where obtained and relationship to safe.
Seminal stains	Identify and package in the same way as set forth above for blood-stained clothing.	Same as above.
Tools	Identify on tools or use string tag. Cover ends with soft paper and place in evidence envelope. Record case identifying data on label. Wrap tool carefully to prevent shifting.	Notes made should be similar to above for safe insulation/soil.
Toolmarks	Cut out portion containing impression or marks. Identify on portion away from impression itself. If unable to obtain portion of material, take photographs and make cast.	Same as above.

NOTE: In each case involving the recovery of evidence and where necessary, obtain adequate standards of material from the crime scene for later comparison with similar materials found on the person, clothing, shoes, car, tools, etc., of a suspect who may be apprehended the day of the crime or later.

SUMMARY

Each day the value of science as one of law enforcement's most potent weapons is proved in the scientific crime laboratory. Analysis of drugs, stains, hair, fragments of glass, vegetable debris, toolmarks, firearms, questioned documents, fingerprints, and other tasks are performed there. Any of these elements may provide the essential piece of evidence that links criminal to crime or clears an innocent person.

Recognizing, collecting, and preserving evidentiary materials are most essential to the work of every criminal investigator. The custodial chain of evidence must also be maintained. Officers must know where to look and what to look for; practical methods of collecting evidence; how and where to identify it; and methods of packaging and disposition. In addition, they should know the value of microscopic evidence and what scientific examinations could be applied to the evidence recovered. They must also be familiar with the kinds of assistance that crime laboratories can provide.

The decision to request the assistance of the crime laboratory depends on the relative degree of expertise and special equipment required and the seriousness of the offense.

REVIEW QUESTIONS

1. What does the laboratory examiner consider to be the important steps in the collection and preservation of evidentiary materials?
2. In general, what are the three main sources from which physical evidence is obtained?
3. What is meant by the term "physical evidence"?
4. Of what value to an investigator is the sketch of a crime scene?
5. Explain the base line method for locating objects at a crime scene.
6. What are some of the results possible from a laboratory examination of bloodstains?
7. Why are items of evidence found at a crime scene packaged separately?
8. What is meant by "trace evidence"? What is "transfer evidence"?
9. Name two types of cases in which glass may be of value as evidence.
10. What is a good method for preparing a firearm for shipment to the laboratory?
11. Where should a lead bullet be marked? Where should an empty cartridge case be marked?
12. If marijuana cigarettes are found in a crime scene search, how should they be identified by the finder?

WORK EXERCISE

Crime Scene—collection and preservation of physical evidence

From the facts of the following hypothetical case, prepare a paper on (or discuss) the physical evidence that you would collect during your investigation. Indicate the areas you would process, types of physical evidence you would look for and collect, and the methods you would use in collecting, identifying, and preserving the evidence gathered. What type of scientific laboratory examination would you request?

Facts

At 0900 hours the suspect entered a neighborhood grocery market. He then took a shopping cart, and was observed by the lone store employee to proceed up and down the store aisles selecting grocery items. At the time there were three other customers in the store. The suspect, just prior to the attempted robbery and aggravated assault, was observed at the magazine rack near the front of the store. He was reading a magazine, and was apparently in no hurry.

Shortly thereafter the suspect approached the checkout counter with several items in his cart. At that time he was the only customer in the store. As the store employee began ringing up the suspect's purchases on the cash register, the suspect drew a blue short-barrel revolver from beneath his brown sweater. He leaned far over the counter and stated, "Give me all your bills. Make it fast or I'll kill you."

The husky clerk pretended to comply and then made a lunge at the suspect. During the ensuing struggle, the suspect hit the clerk with the barrel of the gun, inflicting a deep cut on the left side of the clerk's head. The wound bled. The impact of the blow also caused the gun to discharge. A bullet grazed the forehead of the clerk and became imbedded in the west wall of the market. During the struggle the clerk managed to tear a piece from the brown sweater of the suspect. The suspect's gun, a .38 caliber B/S revolver with a 2-inch barrel, fell from his hand behind the counter. He then ran without the gun toward the front door.

In fleeing, the suspect also dropped his hat and his tortoise shell prescription-type eyeglasses. The suspect ran into the front door of the store's main entrance. He hit the glass on the door panels with both hands, apparently unaware that the door opened inwardly. The impact shattered one of the glass panels. The suspect fled and was observed by the store clerk and an arriving customer to run to the dirt alley behind the market. There he disappeared from view. Shortly thereafter, a car believed to be a late-model red Datsun of the hatchback type left the alley in a westerly direction at a high rate of speed. Neither the clerk nor the arriving customer were able to observe the license number of the speeding car.

In the shopping cart left at the checkout counter were the following items: a copy of a current *Playboy* magazine; a loaf of Weber's sandwich bread wrapped in cellophane; a large bottle of Coca Cola; a large can of Del Monte sliced pineapple; a package of Wheaties; and two Everglow flashlight batteries, size "D."

The suspect was described as a white male, twenty-five to twenty-eight years old, 5'9-5'10", 165 pounds, long brown shoulder-length hair, wearing solid brown slacks, a brown sport shirt, and brown loafer-type shoes.

CHAPTER 4 — *Modus Operandi*

Modus operandi (M.O.) is a Latin term for mode, or method, of operation. In police work, it is used in connection with the activities of the criminal. The first published material dealing with modus operandi appeared in 1913, written by Major Sir Llewelyn W. Atcherley, then Chief Constable of the West Riding Constabulary, Yorkshire, England.[1]

During a visit by the author to New Scotland Yard's famed headquarters and in conversations with officials of the CID (Criminal Investigation Department), the success of many of the "Yard's" (as it is commonly referred to) investigations was attributed to the continued importance placed on the *method index*, as it is known.

Scotland Yard's M.O. file is an index of methods used in the perpetration of crimes with additional indices on deformities and characteristics, stolen property, and other data. The criminal's peculiarities, methods, techniques, descriptions, tools used, etc., are carefully reported, recorded, and indexed for reference purposes. It is such attention to detail and the recording of all facts in a case which permit successful solutions by the Yard in criminal investigation.

---

[1] *Modus Operandi and Crime Reporting Manual*, State of California, Department of Justice, Division of Criminal Law and Enforcement, Bureau of Criminal Identification and Investigation, Sacramento, 1964.

In the United States, the establishment of the modus operandi and its modifications are attributed to August Vollmer, former Chief of Police, Berkeley, California.

Theory of Modus Operandi System

The theory upon which the M.O. system has been developed is that the criminal, like all human beings, is a creature of habit. As we all know, a habit may be started intentionally or accidentally. After a thing has been done once, memory will then assist and will determine whether or not the previous action will be repeated. This, of course, will be dependent upon the success or failure of the previous act or the sensation of pleasure or displeasure which was incurred when it was committed. If we are successful in doing something for the first time, we are likely to repeat the act in the same way, possibly making what we believe to be minor improvements. Generally speaking, if the criminal, on the first attempt at burglary, has been successful in using a ½-inch [12-millimeter] "jimmy" on a rear bedroom window, continued use of the same or a similar tool on a rear bedroom window is likely. If the crime is successful during the early morning hours, the burglar is likely to continue using the same hours. Habits or methods will always be more or less influenced by success or failure. It cannot be said that a criminal will always use the same methods and tools or will confine attacks to the same type of building or against the same class of people, but the habitual criminal is inclined to follow the same pattern often enough to assist the investigator in identification and apprehension.

The method of operation of a criminal includes individual peculiarities, methods, techniques, tools used in committing the crime, and the physical conditions at the crime scene. The M.O. is a means whereby a particular burglar may be set apart from other burglars, or a con artist or a fictitious check passer set apart by a particular habit or method. The method of operation may be established by a single act or by a combination of acts. It includes those acts of a suspect that are unrelated but form a behavior pattern for that particular individual. In most instances, it is the seemingly insignificant detail in a criminal's method of operation which results in identification and apprehension. In one instance, it may be the time element; in another, it may be the property that was taken. In some cases, the characteristics of the criminal are outstanding, while in others a thorough investigation is required to determine them. By the use of M.O. data, burglary operations, for example, can be forecast in advance in terms of hour, the day, the month, and geographic location throughout the city.

Factors Influencing Modus Operandi

Criminal acts are usually products of an improper exercise of the will and several other factors. Law-abiding citizens provide for their needs according to the rules of society; criminals do so by ignoring these rules. All crimes are motivated by the combination of two factors: (1) *opportunity,* whether accidental or created, and (2) *need,* whether real or imaginary. These two factors are set into action by *desire,* whether normal or abnormal. The means of satisfying the desire are referred to as motive or intent, which, coupled with opportunity, result in the act's commission.

Whenever any of the factors (opportunity, need, desire, motive, or intent) are dissimilar from those of the criminal's last crime, the result of the present combination of factors will be different from the past. Also, the modus operandi pattern of the type of crime often will be different. For example, a known burglar, who gained his living by theft, committed a rape in response to a desire for sexual gratification. In another case, a thief when in the U.S. Army had no need for gaining a living by theft. His method of operation then changed to attacking and raping women pedestrians and also robbing them. When his need to make a living became more pressing, his modus operandi changed again. Opportunity brought about a different combination of factors in another case. In that instance, the opportunity to obtain money by a safe burglary at night was not available since the money obtained by the bank during the day was used to cash payroll checks that same day. Thwarted in the safe burglary, the criminals resorted to armed robbery, kidnapping, and murder.

These are offenses that are termed *crimes of opportunity*. These need little or no planning and therefore have no consistent M.O. Even in these cases, however, there still are perceptible similarities in the "trademark" used by the individual offender.

Knowledge is another factor acquired by criminals to aid them in their crimes. Information is obtained by study, associating with other criminals who pass along their techniques, or by experience. In one state prison, a pamphlet on methods of attacking safes was confiscated. This treatise was compiled surreptitiously by an inmate who rented it to neophytes.

Experience gained in criminal activities also controls the method of operation of some criminals who learn by past mistakes and are able to avoid making the same errors in their next crimes. One burglar, unsuccessful in attacking a burglar-resistive safe, invested $300 and bought a similar safe. He took the safe apart at his home and learned how it could be most successfully attacked.

Experience lawfully gained may also determine the type of tools used by the criminal. For example, in one case a suspect was employed as a forklift operator. He stole a forklift and a truck and used the equipment to load a safe onto the truck. Some convicts who learn to use an acetylene torch in prison apply this knowledge to "burning" safes when released.

Conditions sometimes affect the method of operation in a case. For example, barred windows may cause a criminal to select other means of entry. The unusual conduct of victims in protecting themselves or their property may also make a change in planning.

From the examples cited above, it is apparent that an officer cannot solely rely on a criminal's method of operation. The M.O. is only an *aid* in an investigation. It is recognized, however, that all acts committed at a crime scene are important facets of an M.O. Information obtained through interrogation regarding the suspect's activities (legitimate and illegal), associates, family, personality, intelligence, reputation, etc., is of tremendous help to an analyst in the identification of criminals.

Deductions from Modus Operandi Data

The M.O. file is an orderly method of recording and coding information designed to reveal habits, traits, or practices of criminal suspects. The trained analyst, as well as the investigator, should be able to see beyond the physical aspects of how a crime is committed in order to determine why it was done in such a manner. M.O. leads should be weighed according to the degree of probability. Some of the deductions that may result from a review of M.O. data are

A theft by stealth rather than by violence or fraud may indicate not only that the criminal is physically unaggressive or lacks confidence in his or her powers of persuasion, but also that the object of attack might be more easily obtained by stealth.

A theft by stealth may mean the thief is known to the victim or intends to remain in the community and might be recognized later should contact be made with the victim during the crime.

Well-planned crimes generally eliminate the emotionally unstable suspect.

A certain type of premises might be selected not only because of the type of business conducted but also because the criminal is familiar with the victim's habits and manner of conducting business.

A knowledge of the activities of persons who frequent the area at a certain time (the victim, neighbors, police, etc.) and an indication of the probable whereabouts of the people living on the premises may result in burglarizing a residence.

Crimes committed in areas frequented only by persons working or living in that vicinity usually indicate a local criminal.

The occupation or previous experience of the criminal may be indicated by the tools selected for the crime as well as the skill with which they are employed.

The point of entry (window, rear door, roof, etc.) may result from an observation of a burglar alarm system outside the premises.

Prior "casing" of the victimized premises was necessitated due to the conditions of the location or precautionary measures taken by the management.

The selection of a certain victim may be the result of his or her discussing business in public places, keeping large amounts of money at the place of business, hiring transients, employing persons with undesirable associates, etc.

A suspect with physical disabilities may be eliminated where the type of crime calls for an agile person, unless evidence of a more physically fit accomplice is developed.

Burglars known to be adept in the handling of certain tools can be eliminated as suspects where investigation shows that such equipment was used unskillfully.

Uses of Modus Operandi Data

One segment of a suspect's M.O. can have greater value than another for purposes of identification, apprehension, or repression. The use of M.O. information furnished by witnesses in several robberies can aid in the *identification* of a suspect by compiling the information on physical characteristics recurring in descriptions of suspects, such as facial features, scars, marks, deformities, height, weight, and other data. Even a nickname (unless used as decoy) may materially assist in an identification of a suspect.

The method of operation can assist the police in the *apprehension* of a suspect by pinpointing certain operational patterns of a check passer. For example, the type of business establishment victimized, locality, time, day of week, type of purchase made, dress, conversation, and identification used by the passer of the check permit the police to counterattack by alerting merchants in projected areas, placing stops, and using special check bulletins as well as other aids.

As a means of *repression*, M.O. data can indicate the time and location of occurrences. For example, in a series of prowler complaints, the M.O. data obtained from the reports of several preliminary investigations reflected that the incidents occurred generally between 9:30 P.M. and 11:30 P.M. in a certain seven-block section. A concentrated patrol in the involved section during the above times resulted in a sharp drop-off of prowler calls.

In addition to the uses of M.O. data for the purposes set forth above, there are other ways in which the information obtained in investigative reports is applied. For example, in the interrogation of a suspect, it is possible to clear related cases. Leads are furnished to the investigator in identifying suspects who have used the same M.O. The administrator can use this information in the assignment of personnel and equipment in places where surveillances are needed. M.O. data are an excellent means of identifying criminals who move about the state or even the nation.

The Modus Operandi Parts of a Report

These are generally broken down into nine or more major subdivisions. Crime report forms may vary in different law-enforcement agencies with regard to the format, but the modus operandi data are generally obtained from the following bits of information.

1. Time of attack or date and time committed: The exact time the offense was committed should be reported if it is known. If the time and date are unknown, then the entire period should be noted in reporting, e.g., "May 8, 9, 7:00 P.M. to 5:00 A.M." Many suspects will operate between specified hours, for instance, between 9:00 P.M. and 11:00 P.M. Some commit their crimes only on a particular weekday or weekend, and thus the time becomes an identifying trait.

2. Person attacked (type of victim): This subdivision is used because the criminal often picks persons of a particular occupation or class as victims. The information wanted here is the *type* of person attacked, e.g., liquor store owner, bank messenger, jewelry seller, high school girl, doctor. The name of the victim is not used.

3. Property attacked, or type of premises entered: Describe here the place in which the offense was committed. The meaning of "property attacked, or type of premises entered" will be clear if the officer asks, "Where was the property or person attacked?" For example, in liquor store robberies, the suspect may rob only those places situated on a corner. Therefore, in reporting this type of store location it should be listed as "liquor store — corner." In reporting other types of premises attacked, they should be accurately listed. For example, we might find the descriptions "one-story, six-room stucco dwelling," "hallway, third floor," "eight-story office building," "drugstore on ground floor of office building," "bank, midblock." For reporting purposes under this section, street, alley, sidewalk, highway, vacant lot, or field may be considered "property attacked."

4. How attacked (point of entry): This section requires information as to how the offense was committed and how it was made possible. The type of information is determined by the class of crime that was committed. For example, in robbery cases show what induced the victim to hand over the property. The "how attacked" might be "beaten," "threatened," "bound and gagged," etc. In fraudulent-check cases, the "how attacked" may be "forged signature," "forged endorsement," "signed fictitious name and address," "used counterfeit payroll checks," etc. In burglary cases, the method of attack refers to the place of entry and the manner by which entry was effected. If a safe is burglarized, the investigator should also indicate whether the safe was attacked by drilling, explosives, burning, peeling, punching, pulling, haul-away, etc. In sex crimes, the method would be what made the victim do the act — promise of marriage, articles of value, threat, and others. In "bunco" cases the "how attacked" might be introducing a companion to the victim as a prominent person in political, business, mining, racing, or other fields.

5. Means of attack (tools or equipment used in the commission of the crime): The instrument used to gain entry should be reported first as to size and then as to type; for example, in a burglary case,

"¾-inch drill," "hook and line," "glass cutter," "½-inch jimmy," ".38 caliber nickel-plated revolver." Means of attack may also be "bodily force." In the body of the report, the marks left by the instrument should be described in detail.

6. Object of attack (why the crime is committed or attempted): For example, the object might be to obtain money, jewelry, furs, stamp or coin collection, narcotics, firearms, cigarettes, etc. (any item, regardless of value). In crimes against the person, the "object of attack" or reason the crime was committed may be ransom, revenge, or perpetration of another crime such as homicide. The object of attack in a homicide case might be robbery or rape. In another homicide case, it might be to prevent witnesses from testifying, to secure an estate or inheritance, to gratify sexual desires, etc. Identifiable property listed in a report as stolen and later found in possession of a suspect tends to connect that person with the crime.

7. Trademark or peculiarity: These are personal habits shown by the criminal, e.g., "ate food during crime," "wore gloves," "lowered window shades," "left note behind," "malicious damage done to property," "pretended to be a customer," etc. Some criminals while committing a robbery, for example, say very little and are cool in their operations; others appear excited and talk more than necessary. Some criminals perform sadistic or perverted acts that establish their "trademark." Generally speaking, the more unusual the trademark is, the greater it is of value in identifying the offender. However, all crimes will disclose to the diligent investigator some individual characteristic that will assist in identification of a suspect. The trademark may occur before, during, or after the commission of the crime.

8. What suspect said: Quote verbatim if possible. In the investigation and reporting of any crime such as robbery, "bunco," check cases, and others where the victim had conversation with the criminal, particular attention should be paid to what the suspect said and did, as well as to the physical description. The suspect may mispronounce a particular word or use a peculiar expression, mannerism, or dialect which will assist in identification. Speech habits seldom change, especially while the individual is under tension, and such commands as "Get 'em up," "I'll blow your guts out," "Reach," or "This is a stickup," soon unconsciously become a part of the criminal's modus operandi.

9. Transportation used or observed: Include year, make, model, color, license number, and unusual features if a car was observed arriving at or leaving the scene. Descriptive data such as type of tires, seat covers, emblems, exhaust pipes, spotlights, antennas, are helpful in identifying a car. Any other mode of transportation or travel used should be reported.

Example of reporting modus operandi data

The facts in a burglary case are: A series of nighttime burglaries occurred in a certain section. The suspect's M.O. was to enter medical office buildings via the fire escape and through an open or unlocked window. Access was gained to medical and dental offices by using a 2-inch jimmy bar with a V notch in the blade. Money, narcotics, and prescription forms were taken, and the burglar left the premises via the fire escape. The M.O. data obtained from the above burglaries would be recorded as follows:

Time of attack	Nighttime, 0100. (If the exact time of occurrence is not known, the dates during which the offense took place should be recorded. For example: 6–8 Jan. '79, 1700 Sat/0800 Mon.)

Type of crime	Burglary.
Location of crime	The specific address of the medical building involved.
Property attacked or type of premises entered	Medical and dental offices in six-story medical building.
How attacked	Climbed fire escape and entered building through an open or unlocked window.
Mean of attack	2-inch jimmy bar with a V notch in blade.
Object of attack	Money, narcotics, and prescription forms.
Trademark or peculiarity	Enter and leave premises by use of fire escape; pry open medical and dental office doors with 2-inch jimmy bar with V notch in blade.
Transportation used	Unknown.

The body of the report should contain a complete chronological narrative of all the facts obtained during the investigation including an explanation of the M.O. factors. Any detail that might be connected with the crime should be set forth. Information that is not strictly part of the suspect's method of operation (physical description, or description of property stolen) includes such acts as: lying in wait, luring the victim, drugging the victim, detouring a vehicle, casing by observation, establishing confidence of victim, or purchasing or acquiring equipment. Such procedures as developing contacts, gaining employment with ulterior objective of theft, procuring accomplices, securing market for disposal of loot, wiping off fingerprints, wearing mask, ignoring valuable property, setting fire to destroy evidence, abandoning tools, searching particular places, overlooking valuable items, and post-

ing lookouts, should also be part of a complete report.

The maintenance of M.O. files is dependent upon two general types of information: (1) that pertaining to crimes committed by unknown suspects and (2) that concerning known suspects arrested for specific crimes. All data from reported crimes that pertain to the modus operandi are coded on computer cards. Desired information is obtained by running the cards through a tabulating machine and making an analysis of pertinent cards identified by the machine. It is important, therefore, that investigating officers know what specific information should be secured during an investigation in order to prepare their crime reports. They should pick out the unusual features that are most likely to recur from one crime to the next and tend to establish the suspect's method of operation.

Modus Operandi Conclusions on Reported Crimes

When every act of a crime is reported, the investigator should determine such factors as:

How was the crime committed?
What was the motive for the crime?
What knowledge was needed by the criminal?
What were the criminal's habits?
What opportunities were available?
What was the criminal's personality?
How was the crime planned and what was the selection or arrangement of circumstances most appealing to the criminal?

Legally, the modus operandi can be used only as an investigative lead and only introduced in court as evidence to show the common purpose and design of the criminal when a series of crimes has been committed and the defendant is charged with more than one of the crimes. Otherwise, enough evidence, real or circumstantial, must be obtained to prove a specific case against an arrested person.

SUMMARY

Modus operandi is a Latin term for mode or method of operation. The modus operandi is the manner in which a suspect committed a crime. The M.O., as it is known, may be established by a single act, but it is usually established by a combination of acts. Factors such as the trademark (peculiar characteristics) of the suspect, exact type of crime, time element, location, person or property attacked, object of attack, method of attack, means of entry, words spoken, personal description, and type of car used represent important M.O. information. Other factors may also be important M.O. information, depending upon the resources and facilities of the police agency which maintains the data. Habitual criminals, upon release from confinement, often revert to the behavior patterns they established in the commission of earlier crimes. Although these individuals refine their criminal methods, there is often sufficient carryover from their original M.O. to permit their identification.

The M.O. data are compiled by the officer or investigator who examines the crime scene and interviews witnesses. As important as the M.O. is, officers should not rely solely on a criminal suspect's M.O., since this may be affected by such factors as opportunity, need, desire, motive, or intent. The primary purposes of the modus operandi system are the identification of an unknown criminal before arrest and the clearing up after arrest of all cases which that person is responsible.

REVIEW QUESTIONS

1. To what does the Latin term *modus operandi* refer?
2. Who was the first person to devise a system for using modus operandi data?
3. What are the modus operandi parts of a report?
4. What are some uses of M.O. data?
5. Under what circumstances can the modus operandi of a defendant be used against him or her in court?
6. When is an M.O. report prepared?
7. Under what circumstances might a criminal change an M.O.?
8. How can M.O. data be used as a means of repression by police?
9. Give an example of how the method of operation can assist the police in the apprehension of a subject.
10. What aspects of a criminal's activities are referred to as the trademark?

Set forth below is a hypothetical case involving the robbery of a motel, followed by a modus operandi section of a crime report. After reading the facts of this robbery, discuss what data you would list under the appropriate headings in Figure 4-1.

Facts

On 2/15/79 at 0900 hours, reporting person (RP), the night clerk, was working behind the registration desk just inside the front entrance of the Firefly Motel, 1525 Dixon Highway located on the north edge of Center City. Suspect #1 (S#1) entered and asked, "Do you have a room for two?" RP said yes and placed a registration card on the counter. S#1 reached under his jacket at the waist and drew out a 4-inch B/S revolver. S#1 stated, "Turn around and don't look at me. Keep still and we'll have no trouble." S#1 reached up and removed RP's eyeglasses and threw them on a nearby desk. S#1 directed RP to the back room, bound RP's hands behind her back with 2-inch wide white adhesive tape, and then bound her ankles together. A piece of tape was placed over RP's mouth, eyes, and around her head. S#1 removed RP's wallet containing $40 from her purse, which had been on a shelf in the back office. The money was removed, and the wallet and other contents of the purse were thrown on the floor.

MODUS OPERANDI (SEE INSTRUCTIONS)
39. DESCRIBE CHARACTERISTICS OF PREMISES AND AREA WHERE OFFENSE OCCURRED
40. DESCRIBE BRIEFLY HOW OFFENSE WAS COMMITTED
41. DESCRIBE WEAPON, INSTRUMENT, EQUIPMENT, TRICK, DEVICE OR FORCE USED
42. MOTIVE - TYPE OF PROPERTY TAKEN OR OTHER REASON FOR OFFENSE
43. ESTIMATED LOSS VALUE AND/OR EXTENT OF INJURIES — MINOR, MAJOR
44. WHAT DID SUSPECT/S SAY - NOTE PECULIARITIES
45. VICTIM'S ACTIVITY JUST PRIOR TO AND/OR DURING OFFENSE
46. TRADEMARK - OTHER DISTINCTIVE ACTION OF SUSPECT/S
47. VEHICLE USED – LICENSE NO. – ID NO. – YEAR – MAKE – MODEL – COLORS   (OTHER IDENTIFYING CHARACTERISTICS)

48. SUSPECT NO. I (LAST, FIRST, MIDDLE)	49. RACE - SEX	50. AGE	51. HT.	52. WT.	53. HAIR	54. EYES	55. ID NO. OR DOB	56. ARRESTED YES☐ NO☐
57. ADDRESS, CLOTHING AND OTHER IDENTIFYING MARKS OR CHARACTERISTICS								

58. SUSPECT NO. 2 (LAST, FIRST, MIDDLE)	59. RACE - SEX	60. AGE	61. HT.	62. WT.	63. HAIR	64. EYES	65. ID NO. OR DOB	66. ARRESTED YES☐ NO☐
67. ADDRESS, CLOTHING AND OTHER IDENTIFYING MARKS OR CHARACTERISTICS								

REPORTING OFFICERS	RECORDING OFFICER	TYPED BY	DATE AND TIME	ROUTED BY

Figure 4-1.

As S#1 was blindfolding RP, RP heard the front office door of the motel open and close. The sound of footsteps and drawers being opened indicated to RP that someone was searching the front office behind the registration counter. RP said she heard someone moving in the area of the TV set, and then she heard the front door opening and closing. RP stated that, soon after this, S#1 walked out of the office through the front door. According to RP, the suspects never spoke to each other and no car was heard. RP advised that it took her about five minutes to work free and call the police. She discovered that $600 was missing from a box in the bottom right desk drawer and $145 from the motel's cash register.

Investigating officer CHARLES BOOVER responding to the call did not see any vehicles leaving the scene. In the front office he observed open drawers and scattered papers on the desk and floor. In the back room on the floor, wadded pieces of tape and an empty Johnson & Johnson 2-inch tape spool were found. The spool had a Thrifty Drug Store price tag on it. The tape was not from the motel. Identification Officer MARIANNE MORRIS processed the crime scene and filed a separate report on her findings. Guests at the motel were questioned but were unable to furnish any information of value.

Interviews and
CHAPTER
5—Interrogation

Basically, an interview is a conversation with a purpose, motivated by a desire to obtain certain information from the person being interviewed as to what was either done, seen, felt, heard, tasted, smelled, or known. Inasmuch as interviewing takes place between human beings, it cannot be reduced to a fixed formula nor can rules be made to cover all situations. Each interview is an individual endeavor, a search for the truth. The technique of interviewing can be acquired by careful study and practice. Questions must be asked if information is to be gathered. An officer cannot assume that persons interviewed will furnish complete information.

Witnesses, for example, may have mental reservations with regard to furnishing information. They withhold bits of valuable information for many reasons. They may consider their information unimportant or insignificant; may be fearful of repercussions or retaliation against themselves or their children; may feel that they are or have been involved in some way; may not trust the police; or may be afraid of ensuing publicity. Best results are usually obtained by conducting these conversations in a courteous, friendly, sincere, and straightforward way. Every effort should be made to establish as pleasant a relationship as possible. The effective investigator should ask questions in a probing, penetrative, and exhaustive way so that all pertinent information in possession of the witnesses may be elicited. An officer's value is dependent upon interviewing ability.

A good interview is an ideal public relations project in that a police officer is constantly selling himself or herself and the department. Knowledge and confidence are both essential in a successful interview. However, in expressing personal confidence, the interviewer should not adopt an egotistical or overbearing attitude. Interviews should be conducted in a face-to-face, courteous, attentive, and sincere manner. With few exceptions, no one is legally obligated to provide information to the police. However, by law, drivers in some types of automobile accidents must make reports to proper police authorities; also, sex delinquents and ex-convicts upon conviction and release must register and furnish certain information to the police agency in the area in which they reside.

The words "interview" and "interrogation" have similar meanings in police work. In an interview, questions are asked for the purpose of securing specific information; there is the implication that the desired data will be voluntarily furnished. Interrogation, on the other hand, goes a step further. Questions are also asked, but there is an implication that resistance will be met in endeavoring to secure the information. Interrogation is a technique of investigation.

Complaints

Complaints are generally classified under two headings: (1) specific and (2) nonspecific. The determination as to which of these two categories the information furnished by a complainant would come under is dependent upon the facts that person furnishes. If there is a criminal offense involved and supporting data furnished, the matter would be considered specific. However, if no basis in fact exists to justify police action, the matter would be considered nonspecific and no official action would be justified. In some instances, however, the complainant may be referred to the department or agency having an interest in the specific matter.

Specific complaints

Whenever complainants provide information of a possible crime, they should be interviewed thoroughly for all available facts. This is the first step in an investigation. The initial interview with the complainant should be as exhaustive as possible, as the key to many investigative approaches that will be considered after the information is processed may be furnished. After determining that the matter in question is within the jurisdiction of the police, the information secured from a complainant should include such data as

Identity of complainant—name, address, telephone number(s), occupation.
Time and specific location of occurrence.
Nature of offense.
Number and description of suspect(s) if known—race, age, height, weight, build, color of hair and eyes, complexion, scars, marks, oddities in appearance, clothing.
License number and description of automobile if one is involved—year, make, model, color, accessories, dents, and other means of identification.
Direction taken by suspects when leaving the scene.
Present location of suspects and where last seen.
Description of property taken—quantity, kind, physical description, material, color, identifying data, value.
Whether suspects are armed—type of weapons.
Identity of any witnesses.

The success of most investigations is dependent to a great extent upon obtaining complete information at the outset from the complainant. In a hypothetical complaint, Ms. "A" of a certain address and telephone number advises the police that she has good reason to believe that an extensive gambling operation is being carried out at a certain designated location. This type of complaint would constitute a possible criminal violation. In order to ascertain the basis of her complaint, the following searching types of questions should be propounded to Ms. "A."

Why does Ms. "A" suspect gambling is being conducted at the designated residence?

How did Ms. "A" first learn of these activities? What brought this matter to her attention?

What did Ms. "A" observe or hear that convinced her that gambling was being conducted at this address?

What words, terminology, or expressions were overheard by Ms. "A"?

Where are the suspected premises in relation to Ms. "A's" residence?

Is Ms. "A" familiar with gambling games generally?

Has Ms. "A" ever participated in a gambling game at this address?

Who or how many people occupy the suspected premises? For how long?

What is the name of the landlord or manager of the residence of suspect?— obtain both identities.

Does Ms. "A" know the landlord? How well? How did they become acquainted?

Is the landlord or manager aware of the suspected activities?

What specific gambling games are being conducted?

How long has Ms. "A" been aware of the alleged gambling activities?

Can Ms. "A" describe the interior and exterior of the premises including exits, fire escapes, windows?

When are the gambling games conducted? Day, night, or both?

When do the games begin? When do they end?

How many individuals generally participate in the games?

Does Ms. "A" know the identity of any of the people who frequent these premises? Can she furnish descriptions?

How do the alleged players enter the premises? Singly? In pairs? Through the front, rear, or side door?

Is any system used to announce the arrival and identity of the participants at this location? What type of knocks, rings, or words are used?

Where do the visitors park their automobiles? Do they park in front of the suspect premises, at the rear, or a block away? Do they arrive by taxis?

What type of cars to do these persons drive?

Do the same cars usually show up at this address?

Can Ms. "A" furnish any information concerning car descriptions and license numbers?

Does Ms. "A" have access to the suspect premises? Does she know anyone who does?

Who else is aware of the activities at this address besides Ms. "A"?

Would these people cooperate with the police?

Would complainant be willing to assist the police further if needed?

After receiving answers to the above and other pertinent questions, the information obtained should be transmitted to the vice detail for the necessary follow-up action in this instance. The way an officer conducts this interview will make a favorable or unfavorable impression. If all the pertinent information in possession of the complainant is not obtained at the outset, valuable time will be lost in many instances and a reinterview necessitated before proper evaluations can be made and procedures adopted.

Nonspecific complaints

This type of complaint is probably the most frequently placed. Complaints of this kind have no real basis in fact and are often generalizations. A nonspecific complaint might be, for example, a call where a person complains to the police that he or she has a strong suspicion that a person residing across the street is believed to be engaged in criminal activities. The person advises that the suspect does not appear to be gainfully employed; wears expensive clothes; drives a late model luxury automobile; keeps late hours; and does not associate with anyone in the neighborhood. In addition, the complainant says that the suspected person just looks and acts suspiciously and ought to be investigated. No specific criminal activities of the unknown subject could be recalled by the complainant. The information received from this caller concerns only suspicion, not facts. The officer should carefully explain to this person that no police action is possible since no law has been violated. The appreciation of the police department should be expressed to the caller for reporting this matter. A brief record of the complainant's information should be made for future reference in the event additional data is received which would indicate a violation of a law.

Complainants

Complainants come from all walks of life. They are generally persons who have a personal interest in the case and are invariably ready and willing to furnish all the information desired. Data furnished by a complainant to an officer may appear trivial at times but are considered very important to the complainant. Thus the handling of this sort of information tends to mold public opinion of police. The Los Angeles Police Department's motto—"To Protect and Serve"—reflects a noteworthy approach to police service. The impression of the treatment received by a complainant in a contact with the police is a lasting one. An officer has the opportunity to make a friend of the complainant by treating that person in a courteous, civil manner, or to make an enemy by uncivil, discourteous treatment. Complainants are police clients.

A complainant should be allowed to tell the story in his or her own words prior to being questioned. Officers should use the five W's and how of journalism, i.e., *who* [identity of subject(s)]; *what* (occurrence); *when* (time); *where* (place); *why* (motive); and *how* (circumstances of case). Primarily, an officer should be concerned about whether a criminal violation has been committed. Complaints involving civil or private matters are generally of no concern to the police other than as referral of the complainant to the appropriate agency, if warranted.

Mentally deficient complainants occasionally furnish valuable information. However, in those instances where it is determined that the complainant's statements have no basis in fact, the interview should be terminated as soon as possible. A typical example of the information received from a person in this classification might be a report that radar waves have been set in motion through the body of the complainant by foreign agents. The complainant may then ask the police to apprehend the spies responsible. An index card bearing the complainant's name, address, date of call, and nature of the complaint should be prepared and filed so that no more time than necessary is wasted on future calls or visits of this complainant to the department.

Alcoholic and psychotic complainants contacting the police from time to time furnish information of a real or imaginary nature. Complainants in these two classes should never be disregarded. A person under the influence of alcohol may desire to report something that has been preying on his or her mind. In some instances, depending upon the nature of the information furnished, a reinterview may be warranted when the complainant is sober. Psychotics, who may appear perfectly normal to the interviewer, often make statements that are pure fancy to give themselves a feeling of importance. Whenever psychotic complainants become repeaters, their names should be placed on a 3-by-5 inch file card and maintained in an index near the complaint counter or information desk.

Witnesses

The solution to many cases is obtained as a result of talking to people and obtaining information as to what they saw or heard. Knowledge concerning the victim's background, habits, associates, and enemies is also helpful. Descriptions of cars, objects, and suspects provide other pertinent data. During the questioning of witnesses, the officer should anticipate the questions which the defense will put to each witness at the subsequent trial of the case. Questions asked will be directed by the defense at the credibility of the prosecution's witnesses to determine such factors as their physical or mental condition, emotional state, experience, and education. Witnesses do not have to be advised of their constitutional rights; however, no threats or promises of any kind should be made to them to obtain statements. In view of the United States Supreme Court restrictions on the questioning of suspects under arrest, it is now vitally necessary for the officer to extract as much information as is available from witnesses.

Witnesses are often interviewed at the scene of a crime immediately after the reported violation. At that time, these witnesses are interviewed hurriedly in order to obtain information that might lead to the immediate apprehension of the perpetrator. Whenever the suspect has fled the scene, the information furnished by the witnesses is broadcast to other police units to facilitate the apprehension of the responsible party. Thereafter, and following the action set forth above, the investigating officer conducts a more extensive questioning of the victim and witnesses in order to obtain additional information. In some cases follow-up interviews are conducted with witnesses based on new information developed or for clarification purposes. Formal interviews with witnesses differ from on-the-scene interviews in that they are often conducted without urgency. The investigator in these instances can review file data, plan the time, place, and approaches as well as determine the identity and relationship, if any, between the suspect and witness.

Basic guides for interviewing witnesses

Except in those instances where direct action is necessary following the commission of a crime and where time is of the essence, the investigating officer achieves success in interviewing witnesses by considering ten basic rules.

1. Plan the interview. Make whatever appointment is needed, particularly with business and professional people, as it permits an alloted time to be given the officer. If circumstances necessitate a change, notify the person at the earliest possible moment.

2. Arrange for some degree of privacy; avoid places where conversations are overheard, interrupted, or other distractions prevail.

3. Identify yourself properly.

4. Have all available facts at hand when beginning the interview. Such preparation will prevent important points from being overlooked and save time.

5. Know what you are after. Be aware of the object of the interview.

6. Conduct the interview as soon as possible after the incident, while the information is fresh in the mind of the witness.

7. Encourage the witness to do most of the talking.

8. Be a good listener. Permit the witness to tell what happened before questioning.

9. Govern the interview in accordance with the conditions under which it is conducted, such as the place, type of person, or environment.

10. Be courteous, efficient, and friendly; always strive for the true facts.

Persons being interviewed should be addressed as Mr., Mrs., Sir, Ms., or Miss, rather than by first name. Familiarity breeds contempt and could affect the results of an interview. On one occasion, an investigator contacted a business executive in connection with a highly important case without the courtesy of making an appointment or ascertaining the reputation of the official. Stopping by the executive's office unannounced and after the usual introduction preliminaries, the officer advised the executive that the interview was strictly confidential and proceeded to close the door leading to the adjoining outer office where the secretary was located. As the officer was in the process of closing the door, the executive shouted, "Leave that door alone, this is my office and if there are any doors to be closed around here, I'll close them." In this instance the officer obtained only limited information. It is a little thing like this that can defeat the entire purpose of an interview.

In another case involving an interview with a bartender, the officer, walking in "cold" and seeking information pertaining to a certain person, came away without obtaining anything. It is obvious that a bartender in such an interview setting is not going to advertise in front of customers that the law is told everything about the customers; the bartender is not anxious to chase away business. Such an interview puts the bartender on the proverbial spot when the officer flashes a badge or credential at the bar in front of everyone. Even taking the bartender down to the end of the bar would not be any better since this would excite the curiosity of anyone on the premises and cause them to suspect that something was amiss. It would be more productive to consult the manager or owner of the bar privately and get his or her cooperation—away from the business premises. A private meeting with the bartender or other employee could be arranged by telephone with the ensuing meeting held at some agreed-upon location. The facts of each case should dictate the proper approach.

Police function in the questioning of witnesses

The police officer's job in the questioning of witnesses is to obtain the truth about the matter involved. The investigator should never lose sight of the fact that all information gathered, to be admissible in court, must conform to the rules of evidence—competent, material, and relevant to the matter involved. Meticulous care should be exercised in ascertaining details and relationships from witnesses as to: (1) *Things of importance,* such as the identification of physical evidence with the crime scene and with the suspect; ownership and exact locations, distances, lighting, visibility, weather, shots, screams, sounds, voices, odors, car noises, writings. (2) *Places of importance,* such as the location of the crime, weapons, victim, subject, car, meeting places, avenues of approach and escape, concealment, other pertinent areas. (3) *Persons of importance* in regard to identities, number, positions, where seen, dress, conduct, actions, topic of conversation, words used. (4) *Times of importance* to establish a timetable of movements of witness, victim, suspect, time of observation, accountability for time lags.

In obtaining this information, the officer should seek answers from all possible sources.

When talking to witnesses, the following things should be paramount in order to evaluate properly the information they furnish: *physical defects* —limitations of sight, color blindness, hearing, or other physical handicaps; *emotional barriers* —love, jealousy, hate, revenge, prejudice; *personal problems* —dislikes, possible involvement, sympathy, or reluctance to furnish complete data; *educational limitations* —language difficulties; *intelligence level* —ignorance, illiteracy; *lying* —motives, reasons for covering up for associates, friends, or other reasons.

Investigating officers often have to rely upon their ingenuity in devising methods to induce witnesses to furnish the desired information. In extremely confidential or important cases, it may be advisable to learn something about the individual to be interviewed before attempting interrogation. The officer will then be in a better position to approach the witness properly and the results will be much more productive. Previous knowledge concerning the witness's past activities may be an advantage in connecting her or him with the crime or with the person under arrest. The witness may fear that he or she is also under suspicion, and this will cause the person to speak freely to avoid any implication.

Prosecution and defense witnesses should be interviewed if possible. Defense witness statements furnish the prosecutor with indications of the type of testimony that will be offered at a subsequent court proceeding and may suggest the need for additional investigation that will assist in the successful prosecution of the case. The statements obtained can be used to monitor the testimony of a witness.

In conversations with witnesses, an investigating officer should keep in mind the many defenses a defendant may interject at a subsequent trial. These include intoxication, self-defense, provocation, alibi, coercion, mitigation, necessity, insanity, or entrapment. For example, in checking against the possibility of a defense of intoxication in a crime where a specific intent is required, information should be gathered during interviews with witnesses as to whether they observed anything unusual about the defendant: how did the person talk, act, walk. How did the witness form the opinion that the subject appeared intoxicated? Where self-defense may be a defense, inquiry should be directed at witnesses to establish answers to such questions as the following: What precipitated the argument? Where were they standing? What was said and by whom? Who struck the first blow? Who can identify the weapon? Who else was present at the time? Who can corroborate these facts?

Types of witnesses

Willing Witnesses   Persons in this category generally cooperate with the police and furnish all information they possess concerning a given incident. These witnesses either seek out the police to furnish their information, or cooperate fully when located and interviewed. They may be reliable or unreliable. When witnesses testify exactly alike, there is a possibility that they may have been talking with one another and comparing notes. Some witnesses have a tendency to minimize their testimony; that is, they make it less strong against the defendant than it should be. Other people go to the opposite extreme and exaggerate the data furnished. The fact that witnesses are cooperative, however, is a sort of "voice of confidence." In the event that there is no bias on the part of such willing witnesses in furnishing information, their cooperation should be gratefully accepted.

Eyewitnesses An eyewitness to a crime is frequently a most important witness. Permit such persons to state in their own words what happened rather than asking them a lot of questions. When the witness has related the information, then the officer should ask questions to cover specific points that have not been mentioned.

In testing a witness's knowledge, observation, and memory, the investigator may wish to ascertain how well the witness is acquainted with the specific subject matter. Questions pertaining to the descriptions of various details, location of objects, and where they were with reference to each other and with reference to other objects might be asked. Such questions as the following can also be asked: What first called your attention to the incident? When did you arrive there? What were you doing there? In what position were you standing? Were you with anyone? Did you talk to anyone about the case prior to this questioning? With whom? Answers to these and other questions can convince the officer of the real value of a particular eyewitness. In some types of cases the officer may want to have the eyewitness repeat the story to see how the second version differs from or resembles the first version. Questions of the above type will be the sort of queries that the witness will be confronted with should the case go to trial.

Unwilling or Reluctant Witnesses
Witnesses of this type are reluctant to furnish information to the investigator for many reasons, such as hostility toward police, stubbornness, fear, indifference, or relationship to the subject. A reluctant witness represents one of the most difficult problems an officer has to contend with in an investigation. Patience, tact, and persuasiveness should govern the officer's conduct during this type of interview. Information that a witness of this leaning possesses may be the link needed to convict or clear the suspect of the crime charged. The effort expended by the interviewer in these instances may be very rewarding.

When a person refuses to become involved or is hesitant to discuss information he or she is known to possess, the reason should be ascertained. Is the person afraid of retaliation from the suspect or friends of the accused? Is there a personal reason, as in a sex case, to avoid publicity? Is there a distrust of the police or some business connection? Appeals to the witness's pride, civic, duty, personal interest in justice, family, race, and other reasons have been successfully used in obtaining the cooperation of this kind of witness.

Sound logic and a reasoning approach are probably the best techniques an officer can use in these situations. For example, a witness should be convinced that if his or her own son, daughter, spouse, relative, or friend were attacked, beaten, robbed, raped, kidnaped, or murdered by a criminal suspect — or if the witness were the victim — the witness would surely want to see the perpetrator brought to justice. If a moral issue is involved where a witness questions an individual's right to pass judgment on others, the officer might explain the jury system, the fact that the jury questions the credibility of each witness and passes judgment on the testimony presented.

Those witnesses who are afraid or do not want to miss work should be put in the position of the victim. Make them realize the importance of their testimony. Explain how the trial cannot go on without their testimony.

In conversations with unwilling or reluctant witnesses, the officer should refrain from giving the impression that the witness will be compelled to furnish information; nor should any threats or promises be made. Whenever the above types of appeals fail, the witness may be persuaded to furnish the requested information on a confidential basis. A conference with the local prosecutor regarding the information in possession of a reluctant witness may provide helpful suggestions to the investigator.

Unreliable Witnesses People in this classification may be mentally deficient persons, publicity seekers, children with vivid imaginations, or pathological liars. By allowing witnesses to talk freely, obvious discrepancies in their statements can be called to their attention. To establish the reliability or unreliability of statements furnished by such a witness, the officer should endeavor to ascertain knowledge, opportunity of observation, memory, interest, possibility of remembering the particular facts, veracity, credibility, personal feelings, contradictions, or honestly mistaken impressions. In the case of a pathological liar, bring forcibly to the person's attention the fact that he or she is lying and the seriousness of the situation.

Frightened Witnesses Persons of this kind fear that suspects or their associates will seek revenge should they cooperate with the authorities. They honestly believe that someone is lying in wait to harm them, and they suffer loss of sleep and appetite. In discussions with such witnesses, try to assure them that retaliation is extremely rare and that they should immediately notify the police of any threats received. Endeavor to gain the confidence of these witnesses and remind them that law and order prevails.

Biased Witnesses Persons in this group willingly furnish information to law enforcement officers. However, the statements given are often favorable or unfavorable toward the suspect or victim and may be prejudiced in some way. Witnesses are sometimes biased and inclined to exaggerate or minimize something. A close relationship between a witness and the party with whom he or she sides is an influence that tends to bias the statements furnished. A desire to wreak personal vengeance is often very strong. The officer during interviews with biased witnesses should consider the witness's manner of conversation, the inherent probabilities of the story, the amount and character of the contradictory information furnished and the nature and extent of interest in the case. Ascertain how long the witness has known the various parties in the case. Seek corroboration of all statements.

Hostile Witnesses These witnesses, who are not disposed toward furnishing any information to the police, are antagonistic, and resist any form of questioning. The officer should not allow a hostile witness to know from the manner of the interview, that there is resentment of the attitude shown by the witness. Try to determine the reason for such hostility. If the witness explains the reason, the officer can carefully correct any misunderstanding. Make a person of this frame of mind feel that the information given is greatly appreciated. Appeals to civic duty, racial pride, religion, decency, family, or justice may be helpful in these instances. Efforts expended in trying to win over the cooperation of hostile witnesses may ultimately provide the margin of proof necessary for the successful prosecution of a suspect.

Timid Witnesses When witnesses are self-conscious, uneducated, or have other limitations, the officer should make every effort to put these persons at ease. Conversations with these individuals should be conducted in a slow, relaxed manner, questions should be asked in a simple matter-of-fact way to offset any feelings of inferiority they may have.

Deceitful Witnesses When persons of this kind are encountered, the officer should listen attentively to the narration of their story. Questionable aspects of their statements should not be immediately challenged. Do not let such witnesses know by your conduct that you disbelieve them. Permit these witnesses to recite many falsehoods before confronting them with the questionable aspects of their remarks. Inform them of each false statement made and remind them of the serious consequences involved in offering perjured testimony before a court of law. Tape recordings and a playback of the false statements offered can induce most witnesses to recognize the futility of deception.

Children as Witnesses Information furnished by children is often unreliable. Corroborative testimony should be obtained. Judges or juries realize that children are very very imaginative. They are therefore hesitant to convict a suspect merely upon the testimony of a child. Children confuse fact with fancy. In one case, an elderly man purchased some ice cream in a park and gave it to a young girl. Later the child fell down, injured her leg, and tore her new dress. The mother of the youngster, noting the condition of the child's dress, questioned the girl as to whether she had been molested by anyone. The child had previously heard about "bad men" and falsely admitted that an elderly man had bought her some ice cream and attacked her. A careful interview by police and examination of the child by a doctor resulted in the admission by the child that the story was fabricated to prevent a scolding by her parents for her torn dress. Officers must be exceedingly careful about putting words in a child's mouth; leading questions should be avoided. For the most part, children observe well and often remember things that would not register with adults.

Some children may be helpful in such areas as mechanical equipment. Others can be of assistance in observations regarding clothes, appearances, and neighborhood gossip.

Young Adults People in this age bracket, whether married or single, are not as good witnesses as mature persons. They are usually preoccupied with their own problems.

Mature Adults These people possess a fuller appreciation of police responsibility and are generally more dependable witnesses. Their opinions are more apt to be reserved; their personal adjustments have been made and social experiences have been widened. The powers of observation and retention of these adults are usually at their peak.

Loquacious Witnesses These persons are eager to talk a lot and relate what they know in answer to a single question. Witnesses in this class should be handled very carefully. Only short, simple questions that call for short, simple answers should be asked. Efforts should be made to have such witnesses confine their answers to the questions asked. The officer should explain why only specific answers are in order. If this approach fails to control the talkativeness of these individuals, allow them to complete their statements and thereafter attempt to fill in the gaps.

Taking notes in the presence of witnesses

When to take notes during witness questioning is a controversial issue. It is suggested that at the beginning of the interview a notebook should seldom be displayed. Let the witnesses tell their stories in their own words. Size up witnesses and use the notebook to record only proper names, addresses, telephone numbers, or other specific data. Whenever the officer senses that the use of a notebook would make the witness reluctant to talk, it is preferable not to take any notes. The officer should do this immediately following the interview and before the information is forgotten. These notes can be made in the police unit, away from the place of the interview, or at headquarters. Whether to take notes, then, depends upon the individual witness. Some people have a horror of anything being recorded. The main objective is to obtain all the desired information and record it accurately.

Pretext Interviews

Investigators from time to time utilize a pretext interview technique to protect their official identity or to conceal the real reason for the interview with someone. The person being interviewed is led to believe that the interviewer is interested in some particular person, situation, or object. Pretext interviews have been used successfully to identify a person; locate an individual; view a premise or situation closely; obtain specimens, photographs, or other evidence; make recordings in surveillances; and for other miscellaneous reasons. Telephonic pretext interviews have also been used to establish identities; make voice recordings; establish the presence, absence, or whereabouts of specific individuals; and to obtain positive or negative information regarding a person's occupation, hobbies, background data, employment, and other useful information. An important thing to consider when using a pretext interview is to know in detail all available facts—be conversant with the occupation or thing you are representing.

Interrogation of Suspects and Subjects

There is no "slide rule" that an officer can use to conduct a successful interview, nor is there a guide to say when and how to interrogate suspects. In interrogation, no one set of rules, regardless of the rigidity to which it is held, can guarantee that a person will admit knowledge of or participation in a crime. Interrogation is a technique that employs psychological principles without assurance

that any one approach will work at all times. In this chapter, interviews of subjects and suspects are discussed with reference to custodial interrogation.

The word "interrogation" appears to be on the road to extinction. This may be partly due to the failure of investigators to realize the full potential of the interrogation technique. Interrogation is not and never has been a weapon to get a guilty person to break down and confess. It is actually a procedure to obtain the truth. If suspects being questioned can prove their innocence and lead to other areas of investigation, it has served its professional purpose.[1]

During the initial phases of interviews, subjects must be informed of their legal rights under the rules established by the Miranda decision,[2] namely, "Prior to any questioning, the person must be warned that he has a right to remain silent, that any statement he does make may be used as evidence against him, and that he has a right to the presence of an attorney, either retained or appointed. The defendant may waive effectuation of these rights, provided the waiver is made voluntarily, knowingly, and intelligently."

When these rights are expressly waived by a suspect, the interviewing officer during the course of the interrogation must *first* decide whether or not to confront that person on his first lie and each succeeding falsehood. If so, the officer may use the falsehoods as a weapon to make the suspect realize the importance placed on truthful answers. Such direct confrontation by the interviewer can

---

[1] Rudolph R. Caputo, "Notes on Criminal Investigation," *The Bulletin,* Society of Professional Investigators, October 1964. Mr. Caputo is coauthor of *Interrogation for Investigators* (William Copp & Associates, New York, 1964) and *Criminal Interrogation* (Charles C. Thomas, Publisher, Springfield, Ill., 1965); he is a retired Special Agent of Naval Intelligence and a member of the police science staff, Brooklyn College, N.Y.

[2] *Miranda v. Arizona*, 384 U.S. 436, 444 (1966).

so impress subjects that they will be prone to tell the truth. A *second* decision the officer should make in the early stages of the interview is whether or not to hear suspects out without interruption — to listen to what they have to say. This approach is based on the theory that if subjects are interrupted while voluntarily telling a story, they may refuse to continue. In addition, subjects sometimes trap themselves if they think their stories are believed. By permitting suspects to relate the facts they wish to present, investigators may gain new knowledge.

As a general rule, the officer should display no signs of surprise, joy, or disappointment. At the conclusion of the statements furnished by the subject, the officer should be in a good position to compare the known facts of the case with those furnished by the subject. Valid decisions can then be reached as to the suspect's veracity. It is important to remember in any conversation with a suspect that everything said or left unsaid may figure in the investigator's decision as to that person's involvement. Close attention should likewise be directed to each reaction, emotional outburst, facial expression, voice inflection, time delay in response, nervous behaviorism, indication of surprise, sorrow, regret, or embarrassment on the subject's part. Careful observations of this kind should assist the interviewer in arriving at conclusions as to the probable guilt, implication, or innocence of an accused.

The interrogation of subjects is an extension of the art of interviewing complainants, victims, and witnesses. It is a process of probing and gathering available data in crime solving. Effective interviewers must be good listeners. They must try to obtain all possible data from a suspect and yet give out a minimum of information themselves. A suspect should be convinced that the officer is sincerely trying to establish truth rather than trying merely to elicit a confession to a crime.

Interrogation Objectives

The investigator should understand the objectives of an interrogation in order to achieve maximum results. The aims or goals include such objectives as

Learning the truth.

Obtaining an admission of guilt.

Ascertaining the identity of participants, principals, and accessories.

Recovering evidence and property.

Discovering crimes in which the suspect is or has been involved.

Eliminating suspects.

Obtaining all the facts, method of operation, and circumstances of the crime in question.

Gathering information enabling the investigator to arrive at logical conclusions (to corroborate or disprove some fact).

Recording, reporting, and furnishing the results of interviews to the prosecutor's office for prosecutive opinion or court action.

Developing intelligence information that might uncover unlawful activities and identify persons and criminal groups.

Legal Aspects of Police Interrogation

In 1963, the United States Supreme Court in *Escobedo v. Illinois*[3] held that a suspect in police custody, upon whom an investigation has focused and who is being interrogated concerning involvement in a crime, must be advised of the constitutional right to remain silent and must be provided with assistance of counsel when requested. The Escobedo decision was extended by the California Supreme Court in *People v. Dorado* in 1965[4] in

---

[3]*Escobedo v. Illinois*, 378 U.S. 478 (1963).
[4]*People v. Dorado*, 62 Cal. 2d 338 (1965).

which it was held that a suspect who is to be interrogated by the police need not specifically request counsel, but must be expressly informed of the right to counsel and must intelligently and knowingly waive constitutional rights before his or her statements can be admitted into evidence.

The Supreme Court of the United States, in *Miranda v. Arizona* et al.,[5] eliminated for all practical purposes the use of interrogation as a reliable means for the investigation of crime. The opinion was written in response to four cases which were all decided on June 13, 1966. Each of the four cases was based primarily upon the same issue, the right of the accused to have the assistance of counsel during custodial interrogation.

In the Miranda decision, the Supreme Court reaffirmed the rulings of Escobedo and Dorado and extended them by holding that suspects must be informed that if they cannot afford counsel, legal help will be provided free of charge prior to any questioning. In addition, the Miranda decision requires affirmative proof from the police that the defendants clearly understand their rights and that they expressly waive each of these rights before their statements can be introduced in court.

Each of the four cases decided in the Miranda decision involved confessions which were obtained without advising the defendants of their right to consult with counsel; the right to have counsel present during interrogation; the right to remain silent; and that any statements made could be used against them. The high court in the Miranda decision indicated that the prosecution may not use statements, whether inculpatory (incriminating) or exculpatory (to clear one from blame), stemming from custodial interrogation unless it demonstrates the use of safeguards against self-incrimination. The foremost requirement upon which later admissibility of a confession depends is that a *fourfold* warning be given to persons in custody before questioning: (1) that they have a right to remain silent; (2) that anything they say may be used against them; (3) that they have a right to have an attorney present during the questioning; and (4) that indigent persons have a right to a lawyer without charge. To forgo these rights, some affirmative statement of rejection is required, and threats, tricks, or cajoling to obtain this waiver are forbidden. If before or during questioning the suspect seeks to invoke the right to remain silent, interrogation must cease; a request for counsel brings about the same result until a lawyer is produced. (See Figure 5-1.)

The California Attorney General's office, in advising law enforcement officers of procedures that may facilitate compliance with the requirements of *Miranda v. Arizona* et al., opined that all statements, whether confessions, admissions, incriminating statements, or exculpatory statements, are subject to the Miranda warnings before they are admissible evidence except (1) in an ordinary traffic citation; (2) when a person walks into a police station and states that he or she wishes to confess to a crime; and (3) when an officer is engaged in general on-the-scene questioning or other general questioning of citizens in the fact-finding process.[6]

The California Attorney General's office stated that in matters other than the exceptions described in 1, 2, and 3 above, if the warnings are not given, not only the statements themselves but evidence obtained through such statements might be inadmissible. Regardless of the defendants' knowledge of these rights, they must be given the warnings. If a suspect understands the warning and still wishes to talk without consulting counsel and having the lawyer

---

[5]*Miranda v. Arizona,* 384 U.S. 436 (1966).

[6]*Journal of California Law Enforcement,* California Peace Officers' Association, October 1966.

SPECIFIC WARNING REGARDING INTERROGATIONS

1. You have the right to remain silent.

2. Anything you say can be used against you in a court of law.

3. You have the right to talk to a lawyer and have him present with you while you are being questioned.

4. If you cannot afford to hire a lawyer, one will be appointed to represent you before any questioning, if you wish one.

Signature   Date

Witness   Time

☐ Refused signature

WAIVER

After the warning and in order to secure a waiver, the following questions should be asked and an affirmative reply secured to each question:

1. Do you understand each of these rights I have explained to you?

2. Having these rights in mind, do you wish to talk to us now?

Figure 5-1. A type of warning-waiver form used by many police departments before interrogation of an in-custody suspect. This form complies with the requirements of the U.S. Supreme Court decision *Miranda V. Arizona,* 384 U.S. 436 (1966).

present, the statement should be immediately taken. If it is possible to have it tape-recorded, this should be done. If not, a hearing reporter should be used if available. The person's present and the time should be set forth in the statement. If possible, the suspect should be requested to date and sign the statement. If a waiver is secured, affirmative evidence of the waiver should be placed in the arrest report along with an evaluation of the suspect's background if known, age, experience, and anything that would tend to show the suspect knew what he or she was doing when agreeing to talk to the law-enforcement official. This would be evidence to corroborate a knowing and intelligent waiver.

General Guidelines in Interrogations

The following interrogation guides are a compilation of suggestions that every interrogator should consider before and during an interrogation.

Recognize legal rights and ethical and humanitarian principles. Threats or promises of any kind are not an acceptable part of an interviewing procedure.

Have a plan of interview. Carefully review all material pertaining to the crime and statements of witnesses and victims prior to beginning a conversation.

Try to interview as soon as possible.

Do not wear a side arm or other police weapon when questioning a suspect at a police facility.

Never lose your temper. Nothing is gained by being hostile, belligerent, or sarcastic.

Avoid a cocky, arrogant, or hard-boiled attitude.

Recognize individual differences of social, economic, and intelligence levels. Adjust your vocabulary to the level of the subject.

Endeavor to establish good rapport with the subject.

Be a good listener. If subjects want to talk, let them do so without too frequent interruption.

Try not to begin the interview with pertinent questions; irrelevant opening questions serve as an adjustment period.

Size up the subject during the initial stages of the interview prior to using a particular interrogation technique.

Constantly observe the subject's actions, reactions, breathing, eyes, mouth, tone of voice, time lags in answering questions, legs, unnatural emphasis on answers, evidences of embarrassment, forced humor, offers to help solve case, assurances of truth telling, and other symptomatic expressions.

Be frank. Do not give the impression of being cagey; this serves to build up a defense mechanism within the subject.

Keep in mind that the object of the interview is to learn the truth. No case is ever important enough to justify falsification.

Avoid leading questions unless used for motivating purposes. Do not phrase two questions as one.

Ask a lot of questions. Inquiries must be made if answers are sought. Have a reason for every question asked.

Ask important questions as though they were unimportant.

Do not express surprise, joy, hatred, or disappointment at information received unless you have some particular reason for reacting in a particular way.

Do not divulge previously acquired information that would allow the subject to become aware of the extent of the information you possess concerning the case unless such a disclosure is an interviewing tactic.

Make appeals to common sense founded on factual analysis.

Do not use bluffs, trickery, or deceit; this is risking disaster and is frowned upon by the courts.

Never lose confidence, patience, or perseverance.

Always terminate an interview so that it might be reopened at a later time should it be necessary.

Tape-record interrogations wherever possible.

Prepare an interview log showing name of person interviewed, date, place, time interview began, time suspect was advised of constiutional rights, identities of persons present, nature and time of such interruptions as for eating and rest, and time interview was concluded.

Consideration of Crime, Suspect, and Victim in Interrogations

In preparing for an interview, the results are proportionate to the efforts the interviewer expends on planning. Each case must be judged by the conditions present. Reviewing all available data in a case permits the questioning of a suspect to be more efficient, systematic, and exhaustive. Information concerning the *crime*, the *suspect*, and the *victim* should be carefully reviewed.

The crime

Prior to conducting interrogations, officers should make certain they know the elements of the offenses under investigation. In addition, all material in the case file (if any) should be reviewed. Physical evidence, crime scene, and method of operation likewise must be noted. Uncleared crimes involving a similar pattern of activity should be reviewed for possible tie-ins.

The suspect

Available material on the suspect should be examined. Such data may include personal property, background, relationship to the victim, motive, alibi, and opportunity to commit the crime. Other items are identification record, previous employment, occupation, associates, family, hobbies, hangouts, type of automobile suspect drives or has access to, and financial status.

The victim

Information pertaining to the victim that should be scrutinized includes marital status, reputation, financial situation, employment, and leisure activities. In addition, personal habits, associates, places of amusement frequented, and other activities should be looked into. This procedure is recommended particularly in those cases where there appear to be discrepancies in the victim's account of the reported incident. Alleged victims in robberies, burglaries, kidnapings, rapes, and arsons have been known to report fictitious crimes.

Although this preparatory interview procedure appears to be very time-consuming, it actually takes only minutes. It will enable the interviewer to have the benefit of the material listed above. In some cases, only limited information will be available. However, experienced investigators seldom engage in an interrogation without first going through as much of this process as time permits.

Preparation of Outline For Use in Conducting Interviews

In preparing for an interrogation, the interviewing officer may find it helpful to prepare an outline of the topic areas to cover in his interview. Such a guide enables the interviewer, particularly the inexperienced officer, to conduct a more thorough interview. The wording or makeup of the outline can be as brief or as long as the interviewer desires in the particular case. For example, suppose a suspect committed an armed robbery of a Food Mart at 5 P.M. on a certain date and obtained $1500 by forcing the manager to open the cash register. Twelve customers browsing around the store at the time were unaware of this robbery. In this case the accused was apprehended two hours after the robbery, at which time identifiable money from the crime was found on his person. The suspect's legal rights (see the Miranda warnings, above) were explained to him and a knowing waiver of these rights was obtained.

In the above hypothetical case, a quick preparatory outline of things the interviewing officer wanted to be sure to cover and to get complete information on might include

Explanation of rights—obtain waiver.
Introduction of persons present in interview room or place.
Identifying data—background of suspect.
Ascertaining of activities just before crime and establishing presence at scene.
Identity and location of victim store.
Reason for choosing this store.
How long was crime planned?
Plans made for robbery.
Time, date, places where activities took place.
Others involved?
Car used—description.
Method of operation used in committing crime.

Weapon—describe—disposition?

Customers present.

Description of store manager.

Words used in robbery.

Amount of money obtained: type and denominations.

Place money was taken from in store.

How loot was carried from premises.

Method of entrance to store; exit and getaway route.

Place of concealment after crime.

Disposition of property taken.

Present location of property.

Reading of statement.

Additions—deletions—corrections.

Signature of suspect.

Witnesses—date—badge or serial number.

Participation in other crimes? Get details.

Interrogation Approaches

There are many interrogation approaches; several volumes could be written on this aspect of criminal investigation. Any remark or gesture made to suspects in an effort to make them tell the truth could be considered an interrogation approach. For example, saying to a suspect "Well, I guess you know why you're here," or "You sure did a foolish thing" could fall into this category. Two interrogation approaches that Rudolph R. Caputo,[7] noted authority on the subject of criminal interrogation, considers to be applicable to the greatest number of suspects are (1) the *logical approach* and (2) the *emotional approach*.

The logical approach

The use of a logical approach in the interrogation of suspects is one that is based upon common sense and sound reasoning. It assumes that the person interviewed is

[7]Rudolph R. Caputo, op. cit.

reasonable and rational and there is considerable evidence available. In addition, it assumes that the suspect has knowingly and intelligently waived legal rights and agrees to be interviewed. Prior to using this approach, or the emotional approach discussed below, the interrogator must assess the suspect's personality and character traits and decide which approach is best. The logical approach is used more often against suspects with prior criminal records, educated people, mature adults, and others where there appears to be good rapport between the officer and suspect. When using a logical approach, the interviewing officer must confront the suspect with convincing evidence and overwhelming proof—pointing out all the specific elements that prove the suspect's involvement.

One approach of this kind is made in the following manner: the officer draws a comparison between the suspect's activities and gambling. The officer explains how the suspect played the cards to win; that the suspect played the game knowing full well what the consequences would be; that, unfortunately, the suspect lost; and that since the suspect was brave enough to get involved, he or she should face the fact that justice has won. The suspect should be encouraged to settle the debt to society.

Other interrogators using a different logical approach feel that no one will argue with physical evidence such as a sales slip, a hat, a handwritten item, a pawn ticket, or a copy of a latent fingerprint lifted from the crime scene. They think the accused cannot but be impressed with the futility of denying the guilt. The officer in this instance can further impress the accused by such comments as "I suppose you have seen this item or these things before? . . . none of us like to admit failure but this evidence tells your story." This approach, together with the additional use of other select items of circumstantial evidence, can be helpful in obtaining a true statement.

In another logical approach the officer might show evidence of the suspect's guilt by making positive factual statements of which the interviewing officer is certain. Remarks such as "We found your fingerprints at the scene; you were observed looking the place over; one of your fingerprints was found on the weapon; we have a witness who saw your car at the crime scene" can often bring about the cooperation of a suspect and an admission of guilt.

Factual remarks such as those set out above make it hard for an accused person to deny involvement with any amount of conviction. A criminal commits a crime with the hope that no clue is left behind. If, however, information of the above-mentioned type is not available, any reference to such a positive factual statement when such evidence does not actually exist may expose the officer's weak case to the suspect. For example, if the officer remarks that the suspect's license number was taken down at the crime scene by a witness when in fact the suspect used a borrowed automobile, the accused person would recognize the bluff. Should the officer indicate to the suspect that the suspect's fingerprints were found at the scene when the accused knows that gloves prevented the leaving of such evidence, the interrogation would expose the lack of any real incriminating evidence. Bluffing therefore is a weak technique and is fraught with danger; it should be used very cautiously.

Should the subject furnish an *alibi* during an interrogation process, the interviewing officer should go over the story carefully with the person several times in minute detail. Thereafter, by meticulous questioning, numerous discrepancies can be uncovered in "manufactured" statements. The theory of this procedure hinges upon the fact that a suspect in these situations has two stories to remember—the true account and the fabricated tale. The accused person should be challenged on each and every inaccuracy in order to demonstrate the untenable nature of this position.

The emotional approach

An emotional approach is one in which the interviewing officer, in seeking the truth, appeals to a suspect's sense of honor, righteousness, decency, morality, family pride, Christian beliefs, justice, fair play, restitution, or other honorable reasons for disclosing the truth. This discussion presupposes that the arrested suspect has waived legal rights not to be interviewed and consents to an interview confrontation— possibly in the mistaken belief that he or she can outwit the police. It can be said at the outset that emotions are a part of the makeup of every person. Some people, however, are more expressive than others. The use of this approach is generally most successful with first-time violators who become involved with the law because of a careless criminal act committed because of anger, passion, or other emotional reasons.

Prior to determining to use an emotional approach, the officer should have a preliminary conversation with the subject. The person being interviewed quite often outwardly expresses nervousness, tenseness, and embarrassment. Other symptomatic reactions are troubled conscience, perspiration, heartbeat, and, failure to look an interviewer in the eye. The crime itself has a direct bearing on this approach. Murder, for example, will have a greater emotional impact on a suspect than petty theft.

Calm confidence and understanding can help the officer communicate with the accused. The interviewee can be reminded of the strong evidence against him or her. Some of the facts indicative of the suspect's involvement can be pointed out in explanation. The person questioned should be informed of such things as the officer's interest in knowing the suspect's motivations and the necessity for obtaining the whole truth of the matter. It should be carefully explained that the officer has no desire to trick the suspect into admitting to something she or he did not do; that the officer will work just as hard to prove the accused innocent as to establish that person's guilt. The following types of remarks have been used successfully in conjunction with the emotional approach.

"You're not the first person who has gotten into trouble; however, I see no reason to lie about it."

"Society can forgive people for their mistakes, but will not condone lies, hypocrisy, or cowardice."

"All of us have made mistakes, but the least a person can do is to try to rectify them."

"It takes courage to tell the truth. Do not compound your crime with lies.

"Truth is the only thing that all of us want and understand—why not clear your conscience and have peace of mind?"

"Many decent people get into trouble but they do not lie about it."

In every interrogation the officer should, at opportune times, call the attention of the accused to any obviously untruthful answers which are contradicted by the facts. With experience, the interviewer will recogize that there is a certain time in talking with suspects when a direct accusation should be made. The person interviewed is then confronted with undeniable evidence of guilt.

On-the-Spot and Formal Interrogations

Two of the more common types of interrogation procedures used in day-to-day criminal investigation are (1) *on-the-spot,* or *at-the-*scene,* as it is also called, and (2) *formal interrogation*. The determination as to when either of these interviews should be used is the decision of the investigating officer. It should be based upon a consideration of the facts as they exist at the particular time.

On-the-spot interrogation

Following the commission of a crime, a suspect who has been apprehended in connection with that particular crime often condescends to be interviewed in expectation of providing adequate answers to police questioning. Constitutional rights are readily waived by the suspect who tries to project an aura of innocence. It is somewhat like a poker game in that the suspect tries to bluff the arresting officer(s) with an attitude of cooperation, hoping to convince "the law" that they have the wrong person. In these situations the interview takes on the appearance of a cross-examination in a courtroom. Questions asked by the interrogator should be short, simple, direct, and businesslike. One case in point involved the robbery of an ABC market. Following the robbery, a suspect resembling the description of the robber was located a few blocks from the victimized location as he was making his way back to his parked automobile. Just prior to that time, he had hurriedly hidden the proceeds of the robbery, together with his hat, dark glasses, gun, jacket, and tie. He rolled these items into a bundle which he hid in a thick green hedge while fleeing the area in hopes of returning after dark. Two detectives cruising the area in answer to an emergency broadcast observed and apprehended a shirt-sleeved suspect. Taken into custody on suspicion of robbery, the suspect was quickly searched for any weapons. Before any interrogation was conducted, one of the officers informed the suspect of his legal rights in accordance with the guidelines established by the Miranda decision, proceeding as follows:

Mr. "X," I would like to ask you some questions. Before I do so, I want to be sure that you understand what your rights are. I wish to advise you that you have a right to remain silent, that you do not have to answer any of my questions, and that whatever you say can be used against you in a court of law. I also want to advise you that you have a right to consult with an attorney of your own choosing before answering any of my questions; that if you have no money to employ an attorney, one will be appointed to assist you without cost to you. Do you fully understand each of these rights? Knowing these rights, are you willing to answer my questions?

After the officer completed the above recitation, the suspect acknowledged the fact that he fully understood these enumerated rights and was willing to waive them and answer any questions proposed to him. No threats or promises of any kind were made to Mr. "X." It was apparent to the officers that since this suspect did not have any of the proceeds of the robbery nor other identifiable items on his person, he felt confident in his ability to foil detection by a pretense of complete cooperation. He was immediately escorted to the unmarked police car where the following on-the-spot interrogation followed.

What is your name?

Where do you live?

May we see your identification?

What are you doing in this area?

Where did you park your automobile?

Why were you hurrying so?

Why are you so scared—so nervous?

Where is your jacket?

Do you know why you are under arrest?

Why did you rob the ABC Market?

You might be interested in knowing that two witnesses observed your flight from the market.

We are sure that you want to get this matter cleared up. Let's get the money and take it back to the market. Your gamble just did not pay off.

The suspect, thwarted in his efforts, frustrated by defeat, disillusioned in his get-rich attempt, and exposed by witnesses as a thief, confessed to his crime and led the officers to the location of the hidden articles which he voluntarily turned over to them. This type of straightforward interview usually occurs when the subject involved is a prime suspect and often takes place shortly after the individual's arrest. The interview may be conducted at the place of arrest, in the police car, at the suspect's residence, or other locality. Questioning should pertain to the crime and answers sought as to *who, what, when, where, how,* and *why* as well as the identity of any associates and involvement in other crimes.

It is to be noted that court decisions regarding the interviewing of suspects have emphasized the requirement that an accused be taken before a magistrate for arraignment without "unnecessary delay." However, just what is meant by unnecessary delay is fraught with legal terminology and is confusing. No single description of this term would satisfy all incidents of arrest.

Formal interrogation

Interviews of this type presuppose that the in-custody subject has waived the constitutional right not to be interviewed. The interview generally takes place at police headquarters in a room free from any distracting articles or objects. Although suspects should generally be interviewed as soon as possible after their apprehension, interrogations at headquarters are more convenient for officers than on-the-spot confrontations. Procedure in a formal interrogation at the police facility permits privacy, planning, preparation, recording or stenographic assistance, availability of files and supplies, and an atmosphere conducive to obtaining truthful answers.

Things that should be taken into account prior to the interrogation of suspects include a review of available file material on the case; a review of similar unsolved crimes; the identification record of the suspect; a scrutiny of personal property taken from the suspect at the time of booking—names, addresses, telephone numbers, receipts, pawn tickets, sales slips, etc.; examination of physical evidence; and a review of witnesses' statements. Also of importance are the interrogation approach considered and a list of key points to which answers are sought or which should not be overlooked in questioning.

Persons present during a formal interrogation should be kept to a minimum; as a general rule, two officers should be present. The officers can combine their talents and expertise in conducting such interviews. However, only one of the officers present should actually do the questioning. The second officer may question the accused regarding specific points or omissions after the original interviewer has exhausted a line of questioning. There may be occasions when both officers may wish to inject pertinent questions at appropriate times as long as there is no conflict in the control of the interrogation. The advantages of having two officers present at an interview safeguards against unfounded allegations of misconduct, unethical tactics, false charges, or other complaints that a suspect might make.

The demeanor of the interrogator during the interview should be one that expresses a calm, confident, self-assured, and businesslike attitude. Never underestimate the intelligence of the accused. One case, for example, involved the arrest of a suspect for numerous robberies involving markets, liquor stores, and financial institutions. Following his voluntary confession he made the remark, "You know, I can always tell when the police have got nothing on me, they get mad and excited and shout at me. When they have a good case against me and evidence to

Figure 5-2. A simulated interview setting.

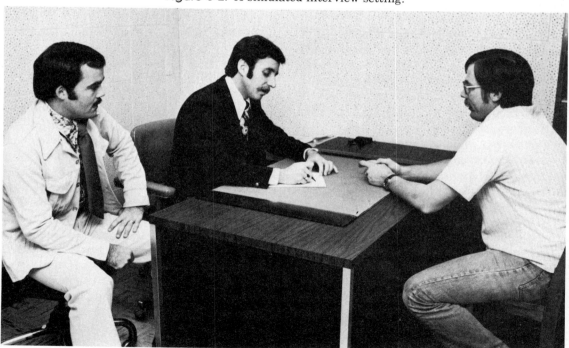

support their charge, they talk to me in a nice, easy way; they are polite, and extend me many courtesies."

If the subject of the interrogation is a female, it is advisable to have more than one officer present, and, if possible, one should be a female. An accurate record of the time spent in every interrogation procedure should be maintained as part of the case file. This record can be of value in refuting allegations of lengthy questioning. Officers should be ever mindful that any person present during an interview is subject to examination in court.

Interrogation of Juveniles

Legal aspects

In 1967, significant changes in juvenile law resulted from the U.S. Supreme Court Gault decision.[8] This Arizona case involved a fifteen-year-old boy, Gerald Gault, who was taken into custody by a deputy sheriff, following a verbal complaint made by a female neighbor. The neighbor alleged that the youth had made indecent phone calls to her. The youth was placed in a children's detention home. The following day, a petition was filed in juvenile court asking for a hearing regarding the care and custody of Gault. The petition gave no factual basis for the judicial action it initiated but recited that Gault was under the age of eighteen and in need of the protection of the juvenile court. The petition also stated that Gault was a delinquent minor. Gault's parents neither were served with nor saw the petition; no witnesses were sworn at this hearing nor at the second hearing a week later. No transcript or recording was made at either hearing. Information as to these hearings was based entirely on the testimony of the juvenile court judge, the probation officer, and the boy's parents, and was given at a

habeas corpus proceeding held two months later. The complaining witness attended neither hearing. At the conclusion of the second hearing, the judge committed Gault as a juvenile for the period of his minority — for six years. In this instance, if Gault had been eighteen years or over, the maximum penalty for making vulgar, abusive, or obscene calls would have been a $50 fine or two months imprisonment.

As a consequence of the Gault case, the new Supreme Court ruling obligates a police officer or probation officer to advise the minors upon taking them into custody that they have a right to remain silent, a privilege against self-incrimination and a right to be represented by counsel retained or appointed — at every stage of the proceedings. The Court held that the juvenile is entitled to equal protection of the law, termed *due process*. The Court stated that the language of the Fifth Amendment, applicable to the states by operation of the Fourteenth Amendment, is unequivocal and without exception — and the scope of the privilege is comprehensive.

In the Gault case, Associate Justice Abe Fortas in a majority opinion stated, "We conclude that the constitutional privilege against self-incrimination is applicable in the case of juveniles as it is with respect to adults. We appreciate that special problems may arise with respect to waiver of the privilege by or on behalf of children, and that there may well be sound differences in techniques — but not in principle — depending upon the age of the child and the presence and competence of parents. The participation of counsel will, of course, assist the police, juvenile courts, and appellate tribunals in administering the privilege. If counsel is not present for some permissible reason when an admission is obtained, the greatest care must be taken to assure that the admission was voluntary, in the sense not only that it has not been coerced or suggested, but also that it is not the product

---

[8]*Gault v. Arizona*, 875 U.S. 1428 (1967).

of ignorance of rights, or of adolescent fantasy, fright, or despair."

Factors to consider in the interrogation of juveniles

In view of the Court's ruling in the Gault case and other decisions, once a minor has been taken into custody for an offense, the youth must be afforded the opportunity of exercising legal rights as set forth in the Miranda and Gault decisions. Should the minor be unable to knowingly and intelligently waive these rights because of his youthfulness, these legal rights to silence, to freedom from self-incrimination, and to counsel must be explained to the parents or legal guardian prior to conducting any interrogation of the juvenile. The parents should, in this instance, exercise the waiver on behalf of the child.

Preparation for an interview with a juvenile should be as thorough as time will permit. Important facts, details of the offense, and significant knowledge about the juvenile should be reviewed prior to any questioning. The interviewing officer should display a friendly attitude, discuss a common interest such as a sport or other activity, and make every effort to gain the juvenile's confidence. If the interview is conducted with sufficient personal interaction, it is possible to get an understanding of the juvenile's inner thoughts, ambitions, and frustrations. The youth should be encouraged to do most of the talking. In this way the officer can learn more about the problems with which the minor is faced. The interviewer should also be a good listener. The juvenile likes to know that the officer is deeply concerned. Questions should be worded to encourage more than a yes or no answer and to tell all the facts: "Tell me about it." "Help me to understand." "Then what happened?" "Explain what you mean." Such phrases can help the youth relate the story.

In juvenile interviews, the youth should be given a chance to "save face." Rather than point out instances of lying, the officer should give the youth an opportunity to restate the facts. A review of the facts as the officer knows them can help the juvenile admit participation in the offense. Pointing out discrepancies and being factual also helps. Efforts might also be made to get juveniles to think through plans so that they learn to be responsible for their own conduct. The officer should be aware of what the juvenile does not tell. This may throw light on sensitive areas that are avoided but that are important in understanding the minor's problem. The youth's failure to mention a certain member of the family may reveal hostility toward that person. After a youth has admitted to the offense, he or she should be encouraged to clear up any other offenses. In those instances where female juveniles, particularly those under eighteen years, are interviewed regarding sex offenses, a policewoman should conduct the interrogation. If this is not possible, a female employee of the police department should be present.

The use of profanity or vulgarity in dealing with a juvenile should always be avoided. Epithets such as "liar," "thief," "burglar," should never be used. Language of this type used against juveniles is a reflection upon the character and intelligence of the officer. The officer should not get angry. Lying to gain a point with a juvenile is likewise considered inadvisable and risks disaster. Physical force of any kind in handling juveniles only tends to develop greater hostility.

It is sometimes helpful when interviewing a juvenile to have the youth write down the story given. Whenever written statements are taken from a juvenile there is no difference between the kinds of evidence that are admissible in juvenile court and adult criminal courts. A tape recording of the statements made by a juvenile in an interview is very impressive with the juvenile court or with a jury in those instances where a minor is tried in general court. In any statement taken from a juvenile, the officer should be sure to incorporate all the elements necessary to substantiate the elements of the offense as he would if it were an adult case.

Legal Aspects of Confessions and Admissions

Early court cases excluded confessions where they were involuntarily obtained because it was felt that they might be false. The Supreme Court first banned physical violence and then prohibited the more subtle police processes. Beginning with the McNabb decision in 1943,[9] involving a delay in arraignment, the Court became largely concerned with protecting the personal rights of the defendant and with curtailment of illegal police practices. As a result of the numerous decisions considered by our highest court, it has been noted that the law is not so concerned with whether or not the confession of a subject is true and whether or not the defendant was actually guilty. Instead, the law is concerned with extending to a subject the *due process* theories of the Constitution, and guaranteeing civil rights. In the confession area, the Court tried for a long time to work with the standard—was it voluntary? It dealt with each defendant's psychological makeup, education, language difficulty, and any other factors that are relevant to psychological susceptibility to coercion. This resulted in an individualistic approach requiring that every case had to go to the Supreme Court to be settled. This was not a good guideline for trial courts to decide specific cases. It was productive of appeal.

From a review of some of the decisions handed down by the Court since the McNabb

ruling, confessions of defendants have been excluded on such grounds as: psychological pressure; overborne will and lengthy questioning; psychological and physical duress; failure to arraign promptly; totality of circumstances; right to remain silent; and denial of counsel. The aftermath of excluded confessions brought about a new set of requirements, applying the guarantees embodied in the Fifth and Sixth Amendments to the United States Constitution and making these guarantees applicable to the states as well as to federal officers. The new requirements (guidelines) for the admissibility of confessions, admissions, incriminating statements, or exculpatory statements were furnished to law enforcement in the landmark Miranda decision.[10] The Miranda ruling is primarily important because it establishes that warning and waivers are prerequisites to the admissibility of statements obtained during custodial interrogation. If the government seeks to introduce a confession or admission made during custodial interrogation by an accused without counsel, the government has to meet the burden of establishing that the accused knowingly and intelligently waived rights. The theory of the cases that led to the exclusion of statements is important because, by understanding the basis for the Court's actions, the officer can see the trend of the law.

Distinctions between confessions and admissions

In accordance with the Supreme Court ruling in the Miranda case, it is important to note that all statements, whether admissions or confessions, are subject to the requirements laid down in that case before they are admissible as evidence. A *confession* is a voluntary statement, either oral or written, made by a person charged with the commission of a crime to another person

---

[9]*McNabb v. U.S.*, 318 U.S. 332 (1943).

[10]*Miranda v. Arizona*, 384 U.S. 436, 477 (1966).

wherein the suspect admits participation or commission in the criminal act. It is considered an exception to the hearsay rule when the person to whom the confession was made tries to relate it on the witness stand. An *admission* differs from a confession in that an admission is a statement by the accused of facts pertaining to the crime. It tends, in connection with proof of other facts, to prove the suspect's guilt. To be received into evidence, an admission must relate to relevant and material facts. Admissions may not necessarily incriminate the accused person. In an admission, the accused is not confessing the commission of the crime but merely admitting certain facts. For example, if a defendant, upon being shown a certain knife states, "Yes, that is my knife, I killed him," this would be a confession because it admits the main fact at issue. If, however, a defendant says, "Yes, that is my knife, but I was not present when he was killed," this would be an admission only to the fact of possession of the knife. The admission of this fact, together with other evidence showing that the suspect was present at the time of the killing would go toward proving the main fact, i.e., that the defendant was guilty of the slaying. Admissions are competent evidence where they are pertinent to the issue and where they tend to incriminate and connect the accused with the crime charged.

Confessions as an aid in prosecutive action

The primary purpose of all confessions or statements obtained is the use of them in a judicial proceeding. The Miranda decision did not abolish the use of confessions; in fact, the Court specifically pointed out that confessions remain a proper element in law enforcement. The taking of a voluntary written statement from a suspect can assist the prosecution in several ways: (1) by making a permanent record of the oral testimony furnished; (2) by discouraging the suspect from subsequently changing an account of the incident; (3) by permitting the prosecutor to refresh the memory of the person who made the statement; and (4) by acting as a basis for impeachment in legal proceedings. The burden of proving that the confession or statement was obtained in a legal manner rests with the state. A confession cannot, however, be admitted into evidence without first proving the corpus delicti of the crime charged.

Corroboration of confessions

Confessions in and of themselves cannot support a conviction unless there is other, independent evidence that, standing alone, proves every single element of the crime charged. In other words, even though the suspect has confessed to every detail of the crime charged, it is absolutely necessary to have other evidence that will of itself show that the crime charged has been committed.

Rudolph R. Caputo graphically describes a written confession as a document that actually serves as a map for backtracking from the final deed to the intent or initial step of the crime.[11] Mr. Caputo aptly points out that if a confessed murderer reveals where the murder weapon was purchased, where that murderer stopped for a drink prior to confronting the victim, and where gas was bought for the car, it becomes necessary for the interrogator or the participating investigators, to confirm each detail of the confession. The seller of the weapon, if possible, must be questioned, as must the bartender and the gas station attendant. Signed statements obtained from the witnesses interviewed are valuable documents and help convince the court that what the confessed killer revealed in the confession did not originate in the mind of an overly imag-

---

[11] Rudolph R. Caputo, "Notes on Written Confessions," *The Bulletin*, Society of Professional Investigators, New York, February 1966.

inative and smoothly persuasive law-enforcement officer.

Crime reenactments accomplished with movie cameras, tape recorders, and qualified technicians have been suggested by Mr. Caputo. The written confession is used as the script. In this procedure the officer should make certain that the action follows the details of the crime as reported by the accused. Such a reenactment procedure will serve to strengthen the prosecutor's case and serve to convince the jurors that the accused, whose face is seen on the screen, was not handicapped by any physical abuse or sinister psychological influence. Evidence of this type is admissible provided some person can testify that the contents of the recording or of the film and sound track are an accurate reproduction of what actually took place and the recording is authentic.

Judicial and extrajudicial statements

Confessions are divided into judicial and extrajudicial statements. A judicial statement is a court proceeding in which the defendant makes a confession in court and under oath. The statement is actually a preliminary hearing with the defendant being the sole witness to testify. In order for a defendant to make a judicial statement, he or she must be willing to waive an attorney; must actually tell the court that the right to remain silent is waived; and request the opportunity to take the witness stand and tell about the offense. Officers who desire a judicial statement from a suspect should contact the district attorney's office and arrange for a time for the court to take such a statement.

An extrajudicial statement is one that is made by a suspect elsewhere than in a court and not made in the course of judicial examination. Inasmuch as this type of statement is taken by police officers outside the court-

room, it is subject to severe scrutiny by the court before it becomes admissible evidence.

Written Statements and Confessions

Guidelines in taking confessions

There is no magic formula for the taking of confessions or statements. Officers are more or less on their own and are held strictly accountable by the courts for everything they do. Remember, the courts look at the transaction after it has occurred rather than during the time that it happens. This puts a large burden on the officer to use great care in the obtaining of any statement. The following suggestions are set forth to assist the officer in understanding the basic considerations involved in the taking of statements.

1. The form of the confession is immaterial; it may be oral, narrative, question-and-answer, or combination question-and-answer/narrative type.

2. The suspect should not be placed under oath; such precaution reflects a possible form of compulsion.

3. Confessions may be handwritten (pen and ink but not pencil) by the officer or suspect and prepared in the first person; that is, it should be written in the language of the defendant. They may be typewritten, recorded by a stenographer and transcribed into written form for the suspect's signature, or tape-recorded. The additional factor of taking movies during the confession in some select cases is of added value. However, the possibility exists that the defense may question the failure of the police to use movie/tape recordings in all their cases, contending that such failure implies the possible use of improper methods that they did not want to show on video.

4. A tape recorder, if used, should not be turned on until the officer is ready to obtain a concise statement from the suspect.

5. When suspects confess orally to a crime, a written statement should be immediately prepared for their signature. Delays or postponements in obtaining a written confession may result in a change of attitude in an otherwise cooperative suspect.

6. The basic guidelines, laid down in the Miranda decision, of advising the suspect of rights before any questioning or the taking of statements or confessions should be followed. This procedure should be adhered to even though the required warnings of this famous case had been previously given to the same suspect at the time of his arrest.

7. Statements should begin with the recitation of the suspect's legal rights and be followed by questions designed to bring out identifying data relating to the suspect: the type of crime involved; the name of the person being questioned; the date, time, place statement was taken; and the introduction of all parties present.

8. The number of persons present at the taking of a confession should be kept to an absolute minimum. The implication of coercion or duress becomes a factor when several officers are present either as interviewers or as curious observers.

9. Questions should be asked in the shortest and simplest manner so that they are easily understood by the suspect. This manner of questioning brings out all the facts in the most effective way.

10. Clarify all indefinite answers given by a suspect to questions asked during the taking of the statement. This is accomplished by asking specific questions of the suspect as to the identity of a particular person, exact location of a place, meaning of terminology used, specific time, date, etc. For example, such expressions as "hot car," "junkie," "pad," should be explained.

11. Statements should not include any crime other than that for which the suspect is charged unless it is tied in closely with that particular case. For example, where a suspect burglarized a residence and thereafter raped an occupant at the same location, both the burglary and rape offense could be included in the same confession. If the suspect was involved in another burglary a block away prior to committing the above burglary-rape offenses, then two separate statements would have to be taken.

12. In complicated cases, consideration should be given to having the suspect visit the crime scene so that movements before and after the commission of the offense can be clarified. Of course, this assumption hinges upon the voluntary cooperation of the suspect.

13. Confessions should be as brief as possible and commensurate with all the relevant details involved. There is no minimum length for a statement. The inclusion of details assists the officer in corroborating the statements of the suspect.

14. When alterations, changes, corrections, or erasures are necessitated in a statement, they should be made in the suspect's own handwriting or made by the officer and initialed by the accused to show that the accused is cognizant of them. This procedure prevents the claim that other pages were added to the statement.

15. Each page of a statement should be initialed or signed by the subject unless, of course, the subject writes out her or his own confession.

16. In the narrative portion of a confession, whether it be a narrative statement or a question-and-answer/narrative type of format, the suspect should be permitted to relate the complete story with a minimum of interruptions unless clarification is needed.

17. The concluding paragraph of a statement should say in the suspect's own handwriting that the statement has been read and is acknowledged to be true. Each officer present should witness the statement with signature, date, and identity of department.

18. A confession should appear as a complete unit, independent of any previous questioning, and not look forward to any future questioning.

19. All statements made by the suspect (entire contents) should be thoroughly checked to determine their accuracy.

20. Where a confession involves more than one crime, separate statements should be taken for each offense. (See number 11).

21. The suspect's identification record should never be included in his confession.

22. Statements should not be mutilated by punching holes, stapling, stamping, or adding any case file numbers.

Construction of Statements

Essential parts

The general format of a statement taken from a suspect should include the following three main parts: (1) heading or introduction, (2) body of statement, and (3) ending.

Heading   The heading of every statement must contain several things. Of primary importance is the fact that the suspect must be fully informed of legal rights and voluntarily exercises a waiver of them. The suspect's age, date and place of birth, residence, marital status, and educational attainment should also be part of this section.

Body of Statement   This section is devoted to the presentation of information designed to present a complete, factual, and chronological account of the crime, incorporating the elements of the particular offense.

Ending   The ending portion of the statement (last paragraph) should contain an acknowledgment in the handwriting of the subject to the effect that "I have read the

above statement consisting of—pages and wish to state that it is true." Thereafter the interviewing officer and other officers present should sign the statement as witnesses. Each page of the document should be signed or initialed by the confessor. If corrections in the statement are requested by subject, they should be made in the subject's own handwriting followed by her or his initials to attest the change.

Methods of Obtaining Statements

There are several methods used in obtaining confessions from a suspect. Statements in the context of this chapter are synonymous with confessions. They may be taken from a suspect in one of the following ways: (1) oral, (2) question-and-answer, (3) combination narrative and question-and answer, and (4) narrative.

Oral statements

A voluntary oral confession by a suspect made after he or she has exercised a waiver of legal rights is competent and legal evidence. However, it is generally agreed that a statement of this kind is less desirable than a written statement to the prosecution. During the trial of a suspect, the question as to the credibility of an oral confession often creates controversy. Many times suspects have a change of heart and deny having made statements attributed to them, contending that the police are misquoting them; that the police misunderstood what they said; or, that they never made such statements. When this happens, the judge and jury have a problem in credibility. They do not know whether to believe the version of the officer or the subject's denial. Testimony of any witnesses to the oral confession of the accused can be helpful to the prosecution in proving the validity of the statements in question. It is advisable, therefore, that in every instance in which a suspect has voluntarily furnished an oral confession of guilt to an officer, that such confessions be immediately reduced to writing and the confessors' signatures be obtained wherever possible. A *tape recording* of the oral statements of suspects during the interrogation is strongly recommended and highly desirable.

Question-and-answer statements

This method for obtaining a statement from a suspect is the type most prevalently used. It is one in which the officer asks a question and the subject responds. The ability to ask questions properly can bring out the details of the offense as well as incorporate the elements of the crime into the statement. When this method is used, the questions should be clearly organized, short, and simple. Questioning should proceed logically and cover a period of time immediately prior, during, and following the offense.

In the question-and-answer type statement, *leading questions* should be avoided. These are questions that lead the suspect into the desired answer. For example, in a robbery case involving the loss of $800, a question such as, "Did you obtain $800?" should more properly be asked, "Did you obtain any money in this robbery?" If the answer is affirmative, then the next question should be, "How much money did you obtain?"

Sample Format of a Question-and-Answer Statement

Opening remarks. Miss Doe, I would like to ask you some questions. Before I do I want to advise you that you have a right to remain silent. Anything you say can be used against you in a court of law. I also want to advise you that you have the right to talk to a lawyer of your own choice and have the lawyer present with you while you are being questioned. If you cannot afford a lawyer, one will be appointed to represent you by the court at no cost to you.

Q. Do you understand each of these rights I have explained to you?

A. Yes sir.

Q. Having these rights in mind, do you wish to talk to us now?

A. Yes sir, I do.

[Heading of statement to be dictated to stenographer] This is a statement of Jane A. Doe taken at the Los Angeles County Jail on October 19, 19—, at 8 P.M., concerning a robbery which occurred at the Acme Variety Store, — — West Temple Street, at approximately 5 P.M., on the above date. Present at this interview are Detectives John W. Smith and Sally B. Jones, and Mr. Stephen Howard, stenographer; questioning by Detective Smith.

Q. What is your full name?

A. Jane Alice Doe.

Q. Would you please spell your last name?

A. D O E.

Q. What is your present address?

A. 1246 North Maple Avenue, Long Beach, California.

Q. What is your present age?

A. Twenty-seven years.

Q. What is your birthdate and place?

A. August 20, 19—, Haverhill, Massachusetts.

Q. How far did you go in school?

A. Eighth grade.

Q. Did you graduate?

A. Yes sir, I did.

Q. Do you have any trouble with reading, writing, or understanding English?

A. No sir.

Q. What is your occupation?

A. Typist.

Q. Where are you employed?

A. I am unemployed, sir.

Q. Miss Doe, since you have been positively identified as the person responsible for the robbery of the Acme Variety Store today, are you willing to tell us about it?

A. Yes sir, I will.

Q. In giving us this statement have any promises or threats of any kind been made to you?

A. No sir, none whatever.

Q. Are your statements being given freely and voluntarily?

A. Yes sir.

[Body of statement] From this point on, questions should be asked to bring out all the details concerning the subject's involvement and activities in a step-by-step way. Following the completion of the necessary questioning, the interrogator might ask:

Q. Is there anything else at this time that comes to your mind that you would like to tell us about?

A. No sir.

Q. When this statement is typed and you find it to be accurate, will you be willing to sign it?

A. Yes sir.

[Ending] Following the typing and reading of the statement by the suspect and her confirming its accuracy the suspect should be asked to write the following paragraph in her own handwriting: "I have read the above statement consisting of — pages and wish to state that it is true"

Witnessed: Signed: _____

John W. Smith, Detective

_____ Police Dept.

Serial No. _____   Time: _____

Sally B. Jones, Detective

_____ Police Dept.

Serial No. _____

Narrative and question-and-answer (combined)

Many prosecuting attorneys feel that the combination of narrative and question-and-answer statements together produces a more accurate confession. In this type of statement, before any questioning takes place, the suspect must be advised of legal rights (as enumerated in the Miranda decision). Following the explanation of these rights by the officer to the suspect and obtaining a knowing and intelligent waiver of them from him, the interview can proceed.

The opening remarks should be of an introductory nature in which the interviewing officer and an associate if one is present are introduced. The secretary should be introduced if one is present. The initial questions should be specifically directed to ascertaining the suspect's true name, age, date and place of birth, residence, occupation, place of employment, and educational background. After this identifying data is obtained, the suspect is then questioned about activities just prior to the alleged crime. Thereafter, the suspect is questioned with the purpose of placing him or her at the crime scene. At this point in the questioning, the officer asks the subject to tell the story in her or his own words. The question-and-answer statement now changes to a narrative type as the suspect relates the story in narrative fashion.

When the accused has completed the narration of the crime, specific questioning should begin again (based on the suspect's narrative account) in order to clear up any questionable aspects of the story. When specific questioning has been completed, the statement is typed and handed to the suspect to read and check for accuracy. If the statement is considered all right, the suspect should be asked to write the following paragraph: "I have read the above statement consisting of — pages and wish to state that it is true." The suspect is then requested to sign the statement. Thereafter, the interviewing officer and the other officer present should sign the document as witnesses. It may be noted that it is preferable to have the suspect initial or sign each page of the statement to reflect the fact that every page has been read. Should corrections of any kind be desired by suspects, such changes should be made in their own handwriting followed by their initials at the location where the correction is made.

Narrative statements

This type of statement is one in which suspects tell the story in their own words. The Miranda warnings must be given to the accused before any questioning can take place. A waiver of the suspects' legal rights must be exercised by them. Statements of this type can be either written out in longhand by suspects, typed out by them, or dictated to a stenographer if interviewees prefer. Usually, however, it is prepared in the language of the defendant by the interviewing officer and in that officer's handwriting (or typing). If stenographic assistance is available to the interrogator, he or she may wish to dictate a statement, using the notes made in the oral interview with the suspect as the source material. The stenographer transcribes the statement which is then given to the accused for reading, corrections (if any), and signature.

If the statement meets with the suspect's approval, she or he is asked to write the following paragraph at the end of the statement: "I have read this statement consisting of — pages and it is true and correct." The statement should then be signed by the suspect and witnessed by the officers present. Each page of the statement should be signed or initialed by the confessor to attest the fact that the material has been read. If corrections are requested by subjects, they should be made in suspects' own handwriting and initialed at that corrected place in the statement.

Sample Format of a Narrative Statement

DATE:_____

[Heading] "I [name of accused] make the following voluntary statements to officers [name of officers conducting the interview] who have identified themselves to me as members of the _____ Police Department. I make these statements without any threats or promises being made to me. I have been advised of my rights to remain silent and that any statements I do make can be used against me in a court of law. I have also been advised of my right to

consult with an attorney of my choice and to have this attorney present during any police questioning of me. I have been told that if I could not afford an attorney, that an attorney would be provided for me without cost. I wish to state that I understand my rights. It is my desire to waive these rights.

I wish to state that I am ___ years of age, my birthdate and place being July 2, 19___, Chicago, Illinois. I reside at 2800 North Broadway, San Francisco, California. I am single and am presently employed by the XYZ Corporation, San Jose, California, as a computer programmer. I am a graduate of Clearwater High School, San Francisco.

[Body of statement] Details of the offense should be set forth here and contain a chronological narrative account of all the circumstances connected with the suspect's activities shortly before, during, and immediately after the crime.

[Ending] Have the suspect write: "I have read the above statement consisting of ___ pages and wish to state that it is true."

Witnessed:_____   Signed:_____

Unsigned statements

In some instances suspects may refuse to sign prepared statements even though they orally admit their truthfulness and accuracy and where all legal requirements had been complied with. In instances of this kind, the officer should make a record of the fact that the suspect read the statement; that the suspect acknowledged it to be a truthful account; and the reasons given for not signing the document. This record should be made in the officer's report immediately after the unsigned statement. Even though the suspect refuses to sign the statement, the witnesses should place their signatures and identifying data (rank, department, and serial number) on the statement following the word "witnessed." There are some jurisdictions that will admit unsigned statements after consideration of the totality of circumstances under which the confession was obtained.

The Polygraph (Lie Detector)

Principle, operation, and use

Earl L. Lorence is a former detective sergeant with the Erie County Sheriff's Department, Buffalo, New York. He is an instructor and a polygraph expert who has written a very informative article concerning the basic principles involved in the mechanics of the polygraph instrument (lie detector), its method of operation, and application.[12] Mr. Lorence discusses this important topic in layman's language which should assist the police science student in understanding this highly important aid in criminal investigation. (See Figure 5-3).

Figure 5-3. A demonstration of the use of a polygraph instrument.

---

[12]Earl L. Lorence, "The Polygraph—Its Effectiveness as an Investigative Aid," *The Bulletin*, Society of Professional Investigators, New York, February 1966.

The polygraph is based on the scientific fact that when a person lies in response to relevant or important questions, his fear of detection has an effect on his nervous system. Certain physiological changes occur uncontrollably when the subject lies. There is an increase in his pulse rate or blood pressure, and a change in his breathing and skin resistance, or sweat gland activity.

These responses, in effect, record on the polygraph chart the subject's own evaluation of the truthfulness or falsity of his replies. A competent examiner then analyses the chart and interprets the recordings. There is no discomfort to the subject in obtaining any of these readings.

The Keeler polygraph is recognized worldwide as one of the leading instruments in the field. It has a recording chart and three marking pens. The pens are actuated by three units which are attached to the subject; a chest tube for recording changes in breathing, a blood pressure cuff, and a hand electrode for sweat gland activity.

The examiner can adjust the instrument to accommodate individual differences and to establish a normal recording pattern. In other words, anyone who is nervous by nature is apt to be nervous during the examination; the dials help the examiner make allowances for this. Once the examiner adjusts the instrument, he is then concerned **only** with deviations from the individual's norm.

The only persons who are unfit subjects for the polygraph are those who are mentally disturbed, or suffering from a serious physical disorder, or under the influence of drugs at the time of the examination.

The polygraph is effective only when the examination is given in a quiet room, preferably one that has been stripped of all wall pictures and other distractions, and with no one present other than the examiner and the subject. And even then, of course, only when relevant questions are asked.

How is the polygraph examination conducted? First, the examiner explains to the subject the nature of the test; that is, the crime or incident being investigated, why the subject is being asked to take the test, the type of questions that will be asked, and what the polygraph instrument is designed to do. The examiner also reminds the subject of his right to refuse the test if he chooses to do so, and that his refusal would not constitute an admission of guilt. The subject is then asked to sign a statement of his voluntary submission to the examination.

Before the instrument is attached to the subject, he is questioned by the examiner. This pretest interview is a crucial part of the examination — so much so, in fact, that examiners in some instances have obtained confessions from subjects before using the polygraph instrument itself. The primary purpose of the pretest interview is to help the examiner establish rapport with the subject and create an atmosphere in which the subject is encouraged to speak freely. The examiner also formulates the relevant questions to be asked on the polygraph, and elicits a direct verbal statement from the subject as to his truthfulness or deception regarding the crime or incident in question.

The instrument is then attached to the subject, who is instructed to answer all questions either yes or no. He is also avised that he will be given an opportunity to explain after the examination in any instance where a clarification is necessary.

The number of questions asked on the polygraph varies with each test, depending on the nature of the investigation. On the average, however, about twelve questions are asked during each polygraph test (which takes about four or five minutes). If deception is detected, the examiner then conducts a posttest interrogation of the subject and attempts to elicit a confession. Usually, it is during this posttest interrogation that the subject who is attempting deception confesses to the crime or subterfuge.

. . . The polygraph is a scientific diagnostic instrument on much the same order as the x ray, the stethoscope, and the electrocardiogram. None of these instruments can diagnose anything by themselves, or in the hands of the unskilled. Through proper use of the polygraph, the skilled examiner can diagnose truth or deception, just as the skilled physician or cardiologist can diagnose a physical ailment or disease. Obviously, then, the controlling factor regarding the reliability of the polygraph examination is not the instrument itself. It is the ability, education, training, experience, and integrity of the examiner.

Naturally, when we are dealing with physiological phenomena, and when the interpretation of these phenomena is undertaken by a fallible human being, there is always the possibility of an imperfect conclusion being reached, whether it be in the field of practical medicine, cardiology, or polygraphic investigations. However, a diagnosis of truthfulness or deception is made **only** after careful analysis of the subject's polygraph chart. Since the action of all three marking pens on the chart cannot be controlled, it is practically impossible to deceive a competent examiner. In the hands of a skilled examiner, the results of the polygraph examination are extremely accurate.

Moreover, the polygraph is the quickest, most inexpensive, and accurate means of verifying information devised. Its reliability is recognized by many Federal agencies, law enforcement departments, and businesses of every type and size all across the country.

. . . Police Departments throughout the country are using the polygraph not only as an aid to criminal investigations but also for the preemployment screening of police applicants. In the fields of commerce and industry, thousands of pilferage-plagued firms, from industrial giants down to retail stores and service stations, now use the polygraph as an integral part of their personnel procedure and for specific loss investigation.

. . . It is our opinion, as well as the opinion of many others close to this subject, that the polygraph can be far more helpful to the truthful or honest person than virtually any other type of investigative aid. We have found also that once employees and other people understand the nature of the examination and know that the issues will be limited to the incident under investigation, they are usually more than willing to take the test.

Use of polygraph in investigations

Results from lie detector examinations, when conducted by competent personnel, can assist law-enforcement agencies and industrial security personnel in many areas of crime solving and prevention. Some of the ways this instrument can be of service is by helping to

Determine whether the suspect is telling the truth
Develop leads in a case
Verify information
Verify suspicion
Aid in interrogation
Obtain confessions
Assist in clearing unsolved crimes
Exonerate suspects
Aid in locating stolen property
Discover wanted persons
Expose security risks
Detect subversives
Screen applicants
Aid in probation, parole, and rehabilitation investigations

Admissibility of polygraph test results

Prior to administering a voluntary polygraph examination, a suspect under arrest should be fully apprised of her or his legal rights. These are the right to remain silent; to have the services of an attorney retained or appointed during questioning; and to know that any statement he or she makes can be used against the suspect in a court of law. These rights must be expressly waived by the suspect. Court testimony regarding polygraph examination or the examiner's diagnostic opinion is not generally admissible. In some instances where the prosecution and defense have stipulated upon the admissibility prior to the administration of the test, the results of such examination may be received at the trial.

Truth Serum and Hypnotics in Lie Detection

The use of truth serums such as scopolamine (also known as hyoscine), sodium pentothal, sodium amytal, phenobarbital solution, or other types of drug injections that produce a narcosis have not achieved scientific acceptability as a reasonable and accurate means of establishing the truth in lie detection. The theory in the use of such drugs is that the subject is relieved of inhibitions and will make true statements while under the influence of the drug. Where a truth-serum test is given, it should always be administered by a physician under controlled conditions. Interviews with a person in a drugged state should be conducted in the presence of an attending medical doctor. The administering of a truth serum presupposes that a signed waiver was obtained from the subject who was fully advised of legal rights as laid down in the Miranda decision. Declarations by the accused or other persons while asleep, hypnotized, or otherwise unconscious are likewise not admissible.

SUMMARY

The ability of an interviewer to obtain complete information from complainants, victims, and witnesses is essential to the success of any investigation. This information is often the beginning of a case. Without receiving all the data from complainant, victim, and witnesses, proper decisions cannot be made, time is lost, energy and equipment are wasted.

Reinterviews may be necessary. During this delay the suspect may be given extra time to escape or to plan an alibi or cover-up.

A good interview is a public relations project. The interviewer must be able to sell himself or herself and the department. Courtesy, sincerity, professionalism, fairness, patience, and tolerance are needed. The interviewer must be a good listener and conversationalist and must never be overbearing. There is no formula for the technique of interviewing. The necessary skills are acquired by practice. The interviewer must continually seek the truth by asking enough questions in a probing, exhaustive way.

The interrogation of criminal suspects is an extension of the art of interviewing complainants, victims, and witnesses. Proficiency is acquired by practice and experience. In any custodial interrogation, it is imperative that the interviewing officer comply with the prerequisites laid down in the now famous landmark Miranda decision. The Miranda ruling excludes all confessions, admissions, and incriminating statements unless the prosecution can show that the accused knowingly and intelligently waived the Miranda rights. A U.S. Supreme Court ruling in 1967 *(Gault v. Arizona)* now obligates a police or probation officer to advise a minor of legal rights as indicated in that decision and the Miranda ruling (both of which are discussed in this chapter).

Prior to the actual interrogation of a suspect, the officer should be thoroughly familiar with the available facts of the case, have knowledge of the corpus delicti of the crime involved, know as much as possible about the suspect's background (including any criminal record), and have some knowledge of the victim. The interrogation should have the objective of obtaining a confession or sufficient information to clear the suspect of any criminal involvement in the case.

Written statements (confessions) should be as brief as possible and commensurate with all the relevant details involved. The polygraph is regarded as an aid in an investigation. It can help investigators eliminate suspects or pinpoint a strong suspect. However, court testimony regarding polygraph examinations or the examiner's diagnostic opinion is still not generally accepted as evidence.

REVIEW QUESTIONS

1. What approach would you use in an interview with a hostile witness?
2. Should witnesses in an investigation be advised of their rights (as set forth in the Miranda decision)? Discuss.
3. In questioning a witness, what things must an officer observe about that person in order to evaluate the information received?
4. What is the purpose of a pretext interview? Give an example of a type of situation in which you would use such an approach.
5. What are the provisions of the Miranda decision?

6. What interrogation approach would you use in the questioning of an experienced criminal who is a suspect?

7. What are the two interrogation approaches that are applicable to the greatest number of suspects?

8. What does the U.S. Supreme Court decision in the *Gault v. Arizona* case represent in regard to juvenile offenders?

9. What is the difference between an admission and a confession?

10. What is the difference between a judicial and an extrajudicial statement (confession)?

11. In discussing the general format of a statement (confession) when taken in writing or dictated, what are the three main parts of the statement?

12. Must a confession, in order to be valid, be in writing? Discuss.

13. What are two methods of taking statements (confessions)?

14. Why are written statements obtained from a criminal suspect of assistance to the prosecution?

15. Why are Miranda rights not given to a subject of a field interview?

16. In an interview of a criminal suspect, a leading question should not be asked by the interviewer. Give an example of a leading question.

17. What information should be recorded in an interview log?

18. Should a polygraph be used to screen applicants for police positions? Should it be used to screen applicants for positions in any large company?

19. What physiological changes are generally recorded by a polygraph?

WORK EXERCISE

Based upon the following abbreviated facts involving a bank examiner swindle (a bunco game), you are to interview your instructor, who will act out the part of the victim. Obtain from your instructor all the necessary information pertaining to suspect's M.O. and a complete description.

Abbreviated facts:

ROGER MASON posed as a bank examiner from the Last Frontier Bank in which the victim has an account. He talked the victim into withdrawing $4000 from her bank account in order to "trap" a dishonest bank employee of the Last Frontier Bank who allegedly had been tampering with the victim's bank account as well as with the accounts of other bank customers. The victim withdrew $4000 from her savings account and turned this money over to the alleged bank examiner at the victim's home, as an act of cooperation. Later, the victim became suspicious and checked with the bank. She learned that the suspect was not an employee of the bank and was unknown to the other bank employees.

Research Paper

Prepare a research paper on the polygraph instrument and its use in crime detection. Include any limitations on its use as well as advantages. In addition, discuss the legal aspects of its acceptability in either criminal or civil court proceedings.

CHAPTER
6——Fingerprints

The purpose of this chapter is to give the reader a basic knowledge of fingerprints, their use, and application. It is intended to provide an understanding of what is involved in the study of fingerprints themselves rather than their classification. Fingerprint classification other than the primary classification is not discussed herein.

The study of fingerprints is recommended for every officer.[1] Frequently the principal

evidence found at a crime scene is a latent fingerprint which becomes the key to the perpetrator's identification and conviction. Of all methods, only fingerprint identification has proved to be infallible. It must be noted that classification of fingerprints is not the same as identification of fingerprints. Classification is a method by which impressions are transposed into a formula in order to facilitate the filing and searching of them. Identification, on the other hand, is the comparing of the fingerprints of a suspect with any latent ones obtained at the scene to determine whether an identification can be made. (See Figure 6-1.) Latent prints are generally invisible fingerprints left on an object or surface by the person touching that

---

[1] For an exhaustive treatise on fingerprints, refer to either of the following books: *The Science of Fingerprints,* Federal Bureau of Investigation, Washington, D.C., 1957; B. C. Bridges, *Practical Fingerprinting,* Funk & Wagnalls, New York, 1963.

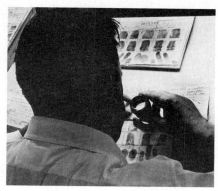

Figure 6-1. Fingerprint examiner checking fingerprint card.

surface. The fingerprints are made by the perspiration on the top of the ridges of the fingers.

One of the prime functions of a police agency is the identification of people. The most accurate way of making an identification is through the use of fingerprints, which is law enforcement's most powerful weapon. Footprints can be substituted for fingerprints as an identification medium. Likewise, palm prints may also serve as a means of identification. The ridge characteristics in palmar impressions are used as the basis of identification in the same way as fingerprint identification.

History of Fingerprint Science

In tracing the origin of fingerprint science[2] and the recognition of finger impressions, one must draw a distinction between the realization that the tips of the fingers bear diversified ridges, and the application of this knowledge to the problem of personal identification. Unquestionably, awareness of the patterned ridges on the fingers and palms predates the Christian era by many cen-

[2]*Fingerprint Identification,* Federal Bureau of Investigation, Washington, D.C., 1954.

turies and has been evidenced in varying degrees by successive civilizations. On the face of a cliff in Nova Scotia, for instance, prehistoric American Indian picture writing of a hand with crudely marked ridge patterns has been found. Scholars refer to the impression of fingerprints on clay tablets recording business transactions in ancient Babylon and to clay seals of ancient Chinese origin bearing thumbprints. Some of these clay seals can be seen in the Smithsonian Institution, Washington, D.C. Chinese documents identified with the Tang dynasty (618– 907) refer to fingerprints being impressed upon business contracts. It is conjectural as to what extent these earlier instances of fingerprinting were intended for actual identification of the persons impressing the prints. Certainly in some cases the object was simply to add more or less superstitious solemnity to business contracts. There is evidence, however, that the fact of the individuality of fingerprints, though not put to practical use, dawned recurrently through the ages.

Professor Marcello Malpighi, an Italian anatomist, in 1686 commented in his writings on the elevated ridges on the fingerprints and alluded to divers figures on palmar surfaces. He perceived the ridges to be drawn into loops and spirals at the end of the fingers. However, it appears that he did not pursue these observations.

In 1823, Johannes Purkinje, a Czechoslovakian professor of anatomy at the University of Breslau, published a treatise in which he commented upon the diversity of ridge patterns on the tips of the fingers. He evolved a vague differentiation of fingerprint patterns into nine varieties. Purkinje's paper was intended only as a scholarly treatise and had no practical application to the problem of identification.

Sir William James Herschel, British Chief Administrative Officer, Hoogly District of Bengal, India, in 1858 began the first known official use of fingerprints on a large scale. Herschel used fingerprints in India to prevent fraudulent collection of army pay accounts and for identity on other documents. He did not, however, develop a method of classification suitable for general use.

In 1880, Dr. Henry Faulds, an English doctor stationed at Tokyo, Japan, wrote a letter to the English publication *Nature* (Oct. 28, 1880) on the practical use of fingerprints for the identification of criminals. He recommended the use of a thin film of printer's ink as a transfer medium, as is generally used today. Faulds conducted experiments which established that the varieties of individual fingerprint patterns were very great and that the patterns remain unchangeable throughout a lifetime. Faulds also demonstrated the practical application of his theory by establishing through greasy fingerprint marks the identity of a person who had been drinking some rectified spirits from the laboratory—one of the earliest latent fingerprint identifications of modern times.

Also in the 1880s, Sir Francis Galton, a noted British anthropologist and a cousin of Charles Darwin, began observations which led to the publication in 1882 of his book *Finger Prints*. Galton's studies established the individuality and permanence of fingerprints. Galton devised the first scientific method of classifying fingerprint patterns.

In 1882, the first authentic record of official use of fingerprints in the United States reveals that Gilbert Thompson of the U.S. Geological Survey, while in charge of a field project in New Mexico, used his own fingerprints on commissary orders to prevent forgery.

In 1883, an episode in Mark Twain's *Life on the Mississippi* relates to the identification of a murderer by his thumbprint. Mark Twain further developed this theme eleven years later in 1894 with the publication of *Pudd'nhead Wilson*, a novel based on a dramatic fingerprint identification demon-strated during a court trial. His story pointed out the infallibility of fingerprint identification.

Juan Vucetich, an Argentinian police official, in 1891 installed fingerprint files as an official means of criminal identification. Vucetich based his system on the patterns identified by Sir Francis Galton. The Vucetich system is the basis of those systems presently used in most Spanish-speaking countries of Central and South America. Vucetich also claimed the first official criminal identification by means of fingerprints left at the scene of a crime. In 1892, at La Plata, Argentina, a woman named Rojas, who had murdered her two sons and had cut her own throat, though not fatally, blamed the attack on a neighbor. Bloody fingerprints on a doorpost were identified by Vucetich as those of the woman herself and led to her confession.

The year 1901 marked the official introduction of fingerprinting for criminal identification in England and Wales. The system was developed from Galton's observations and devised by Edward Richard Henry, then Inspector-General of Police in Bengal, India, and later Commissioner of London's Metropolitan Police. Henry simplified fingerprint classification and made it applicable to police indentification. His system and the one devised by Vucetich form the basis of all modern ten-finger fingerprint identification. The basic Henry System, with modifications and extensions, is used by the FBI and law-enforcement agencies throughout the United States today.

In 1902, Dr. Henry P. deForest, Chief Medical Examiner of the New York Civil Service Commission and an American pioneer in fingerprint science, installed the first-known systematic use of fingerprints in the United States for the New York Civil Service Commission to prevent applicants from having better-qualified persons take their tests for them.

New York State Prison at Albany, New

York, in 1903, claims the first systematic use of fingerprints in the United States to identify criminals. Captain James Parke of that institution installed the identification system. Fingerprints of prisoners were taken and classified, and the fingerprint system was officially adopted on June 5 of that year. Today, New York State uses the American System which is similar to the Henry System and represents the system initiated by Captain Parke in 1903.

Leavenworth Penitentiary at Kansas together with the St. Louis Police Department inaugurated fingerprint bureaus in 1904, which were followed by the adoption of a fingerprint system by the U.S. Army in 1905, the U.S. Navy in 1907, and the U.S. Marine Corps in 1908. The Identification Division of the Federal Bureau of Investigation was established in 1924, after J. Edgar Hoover was appointed Director. The fingerprint records both of the National Bureau of Criminal Identification of the International Association of Chiefs of Police and of Leavenworth Penitentiary, totaling 810,188 sets of fingerprints, were consolidated to form the nucleus of the FBI fingerprint files at Washington, D.C. The FBI's identification files are rapidly approaching 200 million sets of fingerprints — the largest collection in the world.

Legality of Fingerprinting

In 1911, an Illinois court in the case of *People v. Jennings*[3] was the first appellate court to pass upon the admissibility of fingerprint evidence. In that case, fingerprint evidence was admissible as a means of identification. It was also held that persons experienced in the matter of fingerprint identification may give their opinions as to whether the fingerprints found at the scene of the crime correspond with those of the accused. The court's conclusions were based on a comparison of the photographs of such prints with the impressions made by the accused, there being no question as to the accuracy or authenticity of the photographs. It was stated that the weight to be given to the testimony of experts in the fingerprint identification is a question for the jury. Other cases have supported the value of fingerprint evidence since the Jennings case.

Following the Illinois case was one in New Jersey, *State v. Cerciello*, in which fingerprint evidence was permitted to be introduced. In the Cerciello case the defendant argued that it was an error to allow testimony by experts explaining the comparison of fingerprints obtained from the defendant voluntarily with those fingerprints found upon a hatchet near the body of the deceased. The New Jersey Court of Errors and Appeals held "in principle its admission as legal evidence is based upon the theory that the evolution in practical affairs of life, whereby the progressive and scientific tendencies of the age are manifest in every other department of human endeavor, cannot be ignored in legal procedure, but that the law in its efforts to enforce justice by demonstrating a fact in issue, will allow evidence of those scientific processes, which are the work of educated and skillful men in their various departments, and apply them to the demonstration of a fact, leaving the weight and effect to be given to the effort and its results entirely to the consideration of the jury."[4]

In the case of *State v. Connors*[5] it was held competent to show by a photograph the fingerprints upon the balcony post of a house entered, without producing that post in court, and to show by expert testimony that the fingerprints found on the post were similar to the fingerprints of the defendant.

[3]*People v. Jennings,* 252 Ill. 534; 96 N. E. 1077 (1911).

[4]*State v. Cerciello,* 86 N.J.L. 309; A. 1112 (1914).
[5]*State v. Connors,* 87 N.J.L. 419; 94 A. 812 (1915).

Again, in the case of *Lamble v. State*[6] which involved the discovery of fingerprints on the door of an automobile, the court was of the opinion that it was not necessary to produce the door in evidence. The court stated that a photograph of the fingerprints noted on the door would be sufficient along with the identification of the fingerprints by an expert to show similarity of the fingerprints with those of the defendant. The court referred to the previous decided case of *State v. Connors*.

In the case of *Commonwealth v. Albright* a fingerprint expert testified that the fingerprint on a piece of glass, established to be from a pane in a door that had been broken to effect entrance to the house, was the same as the impression of the defendant's left index finger. In addition, the expert explained in detail the points of identity which led him to that judgment. In the Albright case, the court stated, "It is well settled that the papillary lines and marks on the fingers of every man, woman, and child possess an individual character different from those of any other person and that the chances that the fingerprints of two different persons may be identical are infinitesimally remote."[7]

In a California case, *People v. Corral*, the court stated, "It is completely settled law that fingerprints are the strongest evidence of the identity of a person."[8] This doctrine was reasserted in another California case, *People v. Riser*, in which the court stated, "Fingerprint evidence is the strongest evidence of identity, and is ordinarily sufficient alone to identify the defendant."[9]

The U.S. Supreme Court in the case of *Schmerber v. California*,[10] held that the introduction into evidence of fingerprint impressions taken without consent of the defendant was not an infringement of the constitutional privilege against self-incrimination. The Court held that it is constitutional to obtain real or physical evidence even if the suspect is compelled to give blood in a hospital environment; *submit to fingerprinting*; photographing, or measurements; write or speak for identification; appear in court; or stand or walk. It also held that it is constitutional to compel a suspect to assume a stance or make a particular gesture; put on a blouse that fits; or exhibit his or her body as evidence when it is material. The Schmerber case points out the fact that the privilege against self-incrimination is related primarily to "testimonial compulsion."

Uses of Fingerprints

Fingerprint identification (dactylography) has long been regarded as the greatest contribution to law enforcement. This science provides a distinct service in the administration of justice and many other areas where positive identification is of paramount importance. Some of the uses of fingerprinting include

Identification of criminals whose fingerprints are found at the scene of a crime.

Identification of fugitives through a comparison of fingerprints.

Assistance to prosecutors in presenting their cases in the light of defendants' previous records.

Imposition of more equitable sentences by the courts.

Assistance to probation or parole officers and to parole boards for their enlightenment in decision making.

Exchange of criminal-identifying information with identification bureaus of foreign countries in cases of mutual interest.

[6]*Lamble v. State*, 96 N.J.L. 231; 114 A. 346 (1921).
[7]*Commonwealth v. Albright*, 101 Pa. Sup. Ct. 317 (1931).
[8]*People v. Corral*, 224 Cal., 2d 300 (1964).
[9]*People v. Riser*, 47 Cal.2d 566 (1956).
[10]*Schmerber v. California*, 384 U.S. 757, 763–764 (1966).

Identification of persons.

Identification of unknown deceased persons.

Recognition by the government of honored dead.

Prevention of hospital mistakes in the identification of infants.

Identification of persons suffering from amnesia.

Identification of missing persons.

Identification in disaster work.

Identification of unconscious persons.

Identification in licensing procedures for automobiles, firearms, aircraft, and other equipment.

How to Take Inked Fingerprints

Materials needed

The materials needed for the taking of inked fingerprint impressions are readily available (Figure 6-2) and consist of the following items:

Tube of printers ink (a black, heavy paste)

Glass inking plate (¼ inch thick, 6 inches wide, 14 inches long [½ × 15 × 35 centimeters])

Rubber roller to spread ink

Stand on which inking glass can be placed (height sufficient to allow subject's forearm to assume a horizontal position when the fingers are being inked)

Supply of 8- by 8-inch fingerprint cards

Can of noninflammable cleaning fluid or denatured alcohol for cleaning purposes

Cloth to clean fingers, roller, and inking plate

Procedure

1. Place several small daubs of printers ink on inking glass and thoroughly roll with the rubber roller until a very thin, even film of ink covers the entire surface. The use of too much ink will obliterate or obscure the ridges of the fingerprint pattern. Too little or insufficient ink will produce ridges that are too light and faint to be counted or traced.

2. Have the subject being fingerprinted stand in front of and at forearm length from

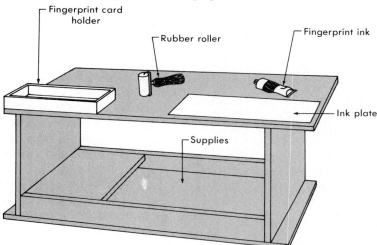

Figure 6-2. Fingerprint stand.

Figure 6-3. (a) Police science students learning methods of fingerprinting. (b) Fingerprinting

the inking plate (see Fig. 6-3). The subject should be told to relax and refrain from helping the operator in any way.

3. Hold the subject's right hand so that the right thumb is first rolled on the inking plate (the whole area from the tip to below the first joint). The side of the bulb of this right thumb is placed upon the inking plate and the finger is rolled to the other side until it faces in the opposite direction. Inasmuch as the classification of fingerprints involves differentiation by patterns, ridge counting, and ridge tracing, each finger must be *fully rolled* in order to obtain the entire contour of the pattern. Figure 6-4a shows a fingerprint that is only partially rolled. Such a fingerprint impression would indicate that particular fingerprint to be a tented arch. Figure 6-4b depicts the same finger fully rolled, which supports the classification of the pattern as a composite or whorl (an entirely different pattern). In addition, the

Figure 6-4. (a) Partially rolled fingerprint. (b) Same print, fully rolled.

fully rolled impression affords the expert a greater number of points of comparison.[11]

4. Press the right thumb lightly on the card, rolling from one side to the other to get the complete pattern of the fingerprint (delta and core).

5. Ink and roll the right index finger on the fingerprint card; then ink and roll the right middle, the right ring, and right little finger.

6. The same procedure as outlined above for the right hand should be followed for the left hand. Begin with the left thumb; then ink and roll the left index finger, left middle finger, left ring finger, and left little finger. *Note:* It is often considered desirable to ink all fingers before rolling.

In the process of rolling the fingers onto the fingerprint card, the thumbs should be rolled toward and the other fingers away from the center of the subject's body. This procedure relieves strain and leaves the fingers relaxed upon the completion of rolling so that they may be lifted easily from the card without danger of slipping, which smudges and blurs the prints.

7. The four fingers of the right hand (excluding the right thumb) should be extended straight out, inked, and pressed lightly upon the inking plate. Thereafter,

Figure 6-5. Left middle finger being rolled on a fingerprint card.

press simultaneously upon the lower right-hand corner of the 8- by 8-inch fingerprint card in the space provided.

8. Proceed similarly as in number 7, using the left hand.

9. Have the person fingerprinted sign his or her name on the fingerprint card, in your presence. As the person who took the fingerprints, sign the card in the appropriate place. Completely fill in all spaces on the fingerprint card with the descriptive data called for. See the specimen of a fingerprint card in Figure 6-6.

10. Clean the inking plate and rubber roller thoroughly.

11. Exceptions: In the event of an amputated or missing finger, leave a space or gap where the finger would ordinarily be placed had the finger not been missing. Temporary disabilities affecting an individual's hand, such as fresh cuts, wounds, or

---

[11]*The Science of Fingerprints,* Federal Bureau of Investigation, Washington, D.C., 1957.

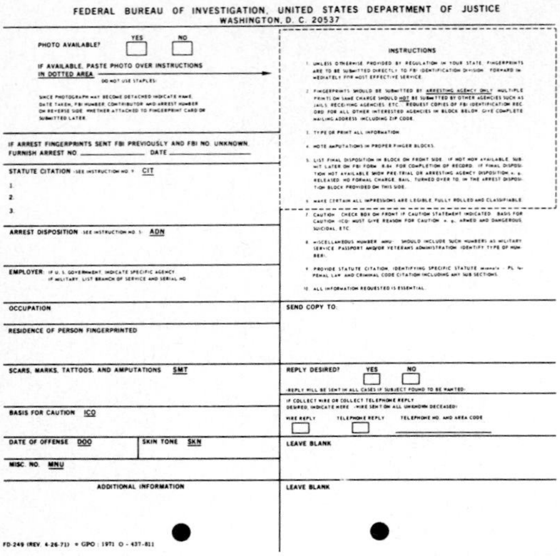

FEDERAL BUREAU OF INVESTIGATION, UNITED STATES DEPARTMENT OF JUSTICE
WASHINGTON, D. C. 20537

PHOTO AVAILABLE? YES NO

IF AVAILABLE, PASTE PHOTO OVER INSTRUCTIONS IN DOTTED AREA
(DO NOT USE STAPLES)

SINCE PHOTOGRAPH MAY BECOME DETACHED INDICATE NAME, DATE TAKEN, FBI NUMBER, CONTRIBUTOR AND ARREST NUMBER ON REVERSE SIDE WHETHER ATTACHED TO FINGERPRINT CARD OR SUBMITTED LATER.

INSTRUCTIONS

1. UNLESS OTHERWISE PROVIDED BY REGULATION IN YOUR STATE, FINGERPRINTS ARE TO BE SUBMITTED DIRECTLY TO FBI IDENTIFICATION DIVISION. FORWARD IMMEDIATELY FOR MOST EFFECTIVE SERVICE.
2. FINGERPRINTS SHOULD BE SUBMITTED BY ARRESTING AGENCY ONLY. MULTIPLE PRINTS ON SAME CHARGE SHOULD NOT BE SUBMITTED BY OTHER AGENCIES SUCH AS JAILS, RECEIVING AGENCIES, ETC. REQUEST COPIES OF FBI IDENTIFICATION RECORD FOR ALL OTHER INTERESTED AGENCIES IN BLOCK BELOW. GIVE COMPLETE MAILING ADDRESS INCLUDING ZIP CODE.
3. TYPE OR PRINT ALL INFORMATION.
4. NOTE AMPUTATIONS IN PROPER FINGER BLOCKS.
5. LIST FINAL DISPOSITION IN BLOCK ON FRONT SIDE. IF NOT NOW AVAILABLE, SUBMIT LATER ON FBI FORM R-84 FOR COMPLETION OF RECORD. IF FINAL DISPOSITION NOT AVAILABLE SHOW PRE-TRIAL OR ARRESTING AGENCY DISPOSITION, e. g., RELEASED, NO FORMAL CHARGE, BAIL, TURNED OVER TO, IN THE ARREST DISPOSITION BLOCK PROVIDED ON THIS SIDE.
6. MAKE CERTAIN ALL IMPRESSIONS ARE LEGIBLE, FULLY ROLLED AND CLASSIFIABLE.
7. CAUTION: CHECK BOX ON FRONT IF CAUTION STATEMENT INDICATED. BASIS FOR CAUTION (ICO) MUST GIVE REASON FOR CAUTION, e. g., ARMED AND DANGEROUS, SUICIDAL, ETC.
8. MISCELLANEOUS NUMBER (MNU) SHOULD INCLUDE SUCH NUMBERS AS MILITARY SERVICE, PASSPORT AND/OR VETERANS ADMINISTRATION. IDENTIFY TYPE OF NUMBER.
9. PROVIDE STATUTE CITATION, IDENTIFYING SPECIFIC STATUTE, PENAL LAW AND CRIMINAL CODE CITATION INCLUDING ANY SUB SECTIONS.
10. ALL INFORMATION REQUESTED IS ESSENTIAL.

IF ARREST FINGERPRINTS SENT FBI PREVIOUSLY AND FBI NO. UNKNOWN, FURNISH ARREST NO. ________ DATE ________

STATUTE CITATION (SEE INSTRUCTION NO. 9) CIT
1.
2.
3.

ARREST DISPOSITION (SEE INSTRUCTION NO. 5) ADN

EMPLOYER: IF U. S. GOVERNMENT, INDICATE SPECIFIC AGENCY. IF MILITARY, LIST BRANCH OF SERVICE AND SERIAL NO.

OCCUPATION

RESIDENCE OF PERSON FINGERPRINTED

SCARS, MARKS, TATTOOS, AND AMPUTATIONS SMT

BASIS FOR CAUTION ICO

DATE OF OFFENSE DOO | SKIN TONE SKN

MISC. NO. MNU

ADDITIONAL INFORMATION

SEND COPY TO:

REPLY DESIRED? YES NO
(REPLY WILL BE SENT IN ALL CASES IF SUBJECT FOUND TO BE WANTED)

IF COLLECT WIRE OR COLLECT TELEPHONE REPLY DESIRED, INDICATE HERE. (WIRE SENT ON ALL UNKNOWN DECEASED)
WIRE REPLY TELEPHONE REPLY TELEPHONE NO. AND AREA CODE

LEAVE BLANK

LEAVE BLANK

FD-249 (REV. 4-26-71) ☆ GPO : 1971 O - 437-811

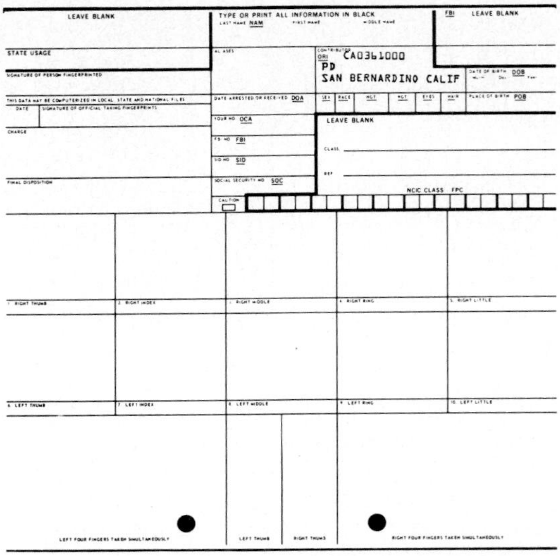

LEAVE BLANK

TYPE OR PRINT ALL INFORMATION IN BLACK
LAST NAME NAM FIRST NAME MIDDLE NAME

FBI LEAVE BLANK

STATE USAGE

SIGNATURE OF PERSON FINGERPRINTED

ALIASES

CONTRIBUTOR ORI CA0361000
PD
SAN BERNARDINO CALIF

DATE OF BIRTH DOB Month Day Year

THIS DATA MAY BE COMPUTERIZED IN LOCAL, STATE AND NATIONAL FILES
DATE | SIGNATURE OF OFFICIAL TAKING FINGERPRINTS

DATE ARRESTED OR RECEIVED DOA

SEX | RACE | HGT | WGT | EYES | HAIR | PLACE OF BIRTH POB

CHARGE

YOUR NO. OCA

FBI NO. FBI

SID NO. SID

SOCIAL SECURITY NO. SOC

CAUTION

LEAVE BLANK
CLASS
REF
NCIC CLASS - FPC

FINAL DISPOSITION

1. RIGHT THUMB | 2. RIGHT INDEX | 3. RIGHT MIDDLE | 4. RIGHT RING | 5. RIGHT LITTLE

6. LEFT THUMB | 7. LEFT INDEX | 8. LEFT MIDDLE | 9. LEFT RING | 10. LEFT LITTLE

LEFT FOUR FINGERS TAKEN SIMULTANEOUSLY | LEFT THUMB | RIGHT THUMB | RIGHT FOUR FINGERS TAKEN SIMULTANEOUSLY

Figure 6-6. (a) Front and (b) rear sides of a standard 8- by 8-inch criminal-identification card.

bandaged fingers, cause problems. Indicate these cases on the fingerprint card with expressions like "fresh cut," or "bandaged." These fingerprints should be taken after the injury has healed.

In occupational cases such as those of bricklayers, carpenters, and others where the friction ridges are less pronounced or calloused, the use of softening agents (oils and creams) will make it possible to obtain legible inked impressions. In these cases, a very small amount of ink is used.

Where excessive perspiration exists, wipe the fingers with a cloth, then immediately ink and roll them on the card. Alcohol, benzine, or a similar fluid can be used as a drying agent.

If a person is born without a certain finger or fingers, the notation "missing at birth" should be inserted in the proper space. In those cases where all the fingers are amputated, inked footprints should be obtained. Special inking devices are used for taking the prints of bent or crippled fingers and of deceased individuals. In these cases, each crippled finger is taken as a separate unit with the use of a spoon or curved instrument and then the fingers are block pasted on a fingerprint card in their respective order.[12]

Nature of Fingerprints

A fingerprint is a composite of the ridge outlines which appear on the skin surface of the bulbs on the inside of the end joints of the fingers and thumbs. These ridges are commonly referred to as papillary or friction ridges. The ridges have a definite contour and appear in several ridge formations or patterns, each possessing definite individual details by which positive identification can be made. Ridge characteristics are formed prior to birth and remain constant throughout life except for growth and deep scarification. Skin conditions such as warts and blisters or temporary impairments caused by certain occupations, e.g., bricklaying and carpentry, have no permanent effect and the

[12] Ibid.

individual characteristics revert to their natural alignment once the temporary skin condition has been corrected. In ordinary usage, the skin surface is inked and the ridge outlines are transferred to a standard 8- by 8-inch card form which then serves as the basic document utilized in the maintenance of the fingerprint files.

From a law-enforcement viewpoint, fingerprints serve an additional purpose. Since the ridges on the skin surface emit a film of perspiration or oily matter, there is a tendency for the ridge impressions to adhere to nonporous objects that a person may touch. Such fingerprints may be rendered visible by various powders and chemicals used for this purpose. When latent impressions discovered at a crime scene during an investigation are searched against the fingerprints of a suspect and a positive identification is made, these latent fingerprints are admissible as evidence in a court of law.

Permanency of the ridge characteristics, plus their unique distribution by type, location, and direction provides the basis for the premise that no two fingerprints are the same except when taken from the same finger of the same person. Generally the courts set twelve characteristics as the minimum number of matching characteristics required to establish identity. The actual determination as to whether identity exists is dependent upon the matching of the individual minute ridge characteristics. Figure 6-7 shows the type of ridge characteristics which are used for comparison purposes. If a fingerprint is clear, it is not unusual to be able to find thirty or more characteristics which can be used for identification purposes.

Fingerprint Patterns

Fingerprints may be resolved into three large general groups of patterns and divided further into subgroups as follows:

DIVISION OF FINGERPRINT PATTERNS

ARCH	LOOP	WHORL
Plain arch	Radial loop	Plain whorl
Tented arch	Ulnar loop	Central pocket loop
		Double loop
		Accidental whorl

Definitions and interpretations

In order to understand differences between the general and subgroupings of fingerprints, the following classifications are set forth (see Fig. 6-8):

Arches

Plain Arch   In a plain arch the ridges enter on one side of the impression and flow or tend to flow out the other side with a wave in the center. Arches have no delta formations.

Tented Arch   In this type of pattern most of the ridges enter upon one side and flow or tend to flow out the other. However, the ridge or ridges at the center have a decisive upward thrust.

Loops   In loop patterns at least one ridge, and usually many more, enter from one side, recurve in the form of a hairpin turn, and exit on the side from which they entered. At least one ridge must follow this course and pass between the delta and the core. A loop has one and only one delta. Loops are divided into radial and ulnar on the basis of the way that they flow on the hands and not according to the arrangement on the fingerprint card.

Radial Loop   In this loop pattern the ridges slant toward the thumb or radius bone of the forearm.

Ulnar Loop   Ridges in this pattern slant toward the little finger or ulnar bone of the forearm.

Whorls   Whorl patterns are of four types, namely, plain whorl, double loop, central pocket loop, and accidental (Figure 6-8). In whorl patterns at least one ridge must make

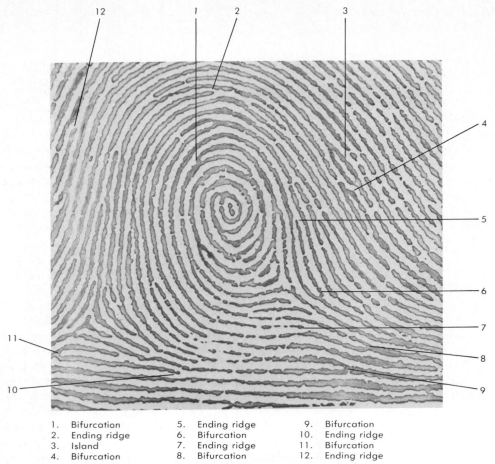

1.	Bifurcation	5.	Ending ridge	9.	Bifurcation
2.	Ending ridge	6.	Bifurcation	10.	Ending ridge
3.	Island	7.	Ending ridge	11.	Bifurcation
4.	Bifurcation	8.	Bifurcation	12.	Ending ridge

Figure 6-7. Enlarged, inked fingerprint showing the location of twelve ridge characteristics.

a complete recurvature about the core or center. This recurve may be in the form of a spiral, circular, oval, or any variant of a circle and make at least one recurve in front of each delta. (Whorls have two or more deltas—one at the right side and one at the left side.) They are subclassified by ridge tracing. (See Figure 6-9a, b, and c.)

Plain Whorl The plain whorl is the simplest form of whorl construction and the most common of the whorl subdivisions. It has two deltas and at least one ridge that makes a complete circuit, which may be spiral, oval, circular, or any variant of the circle. An imaginary line drawn between the two deltas must touch one of the recurving ridges within the inner pattern area.

Double Loop (Whorl Pattern) This type of finger impression consists of two loop formations with two separate and distinct sets of shoulders and two deltas. Both *twinned loops* and *lateral pocket loops* are considered to be under the double-loop pattern.

Central Pocket Loop (Whorl Pattern) In a central pocket loop most of the ridges take the form of a loop. However, one or more ridges recurve at the core to form a pocket. There are two deltas. An imaginary

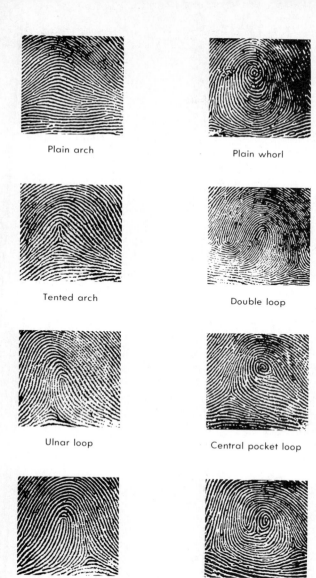

Plain arch	Plain whorl
Tented arch	Double loop
Ulnar loop	Central pocket loop
Radial loop	Accidental

Figure 6-8. The basic fingerprint patterns.

line drawn between the two deltas must not touch or cross any of the recurving ridges within the inner pattern area.

Accidental (Whorl Pattern) An accidental is a combination of two or more different types of patterns (not including the plain arch) and is referred to as a freak pattern. This type of pattern may possess

two, three, or four deltas. In tracing this pattern, only the extreme left delta and the extreme right delta are used.

Cores and Deltas The *core*, as the name implies, is the approximate center of the finger impression. The *delta* in loops, whorls, and composites may be nontechnically defined as the first ridge formation nearest the center of divergence of two type lines.

Pattern area and type lines

The *pattern area* is that part of a loop or whorl in which appear the cores and deltas. It is the only part of the finger impression with which we are concerned in regard to pattern interpretation. The pattern areas of loops and whorls are enclosed by type lines as defined below. In arch-type patterns it is impossible to define the pattern area.

Type Lines These lines may be defined as the two innermost ridges which start parallel from the lower corner of the pattern, flow inward, diverge, and surround or tend to surround the pattern area. Everything which is needed to interpret a fingerprint pattern will be found inside these basic boundary lines. The type lines may be continuous or broken. If broken, the ridge just outside the break is taken as its continuation.

Ridge Counting

Ridge counting is a process of counting each ridge that touches or crosses an imaginary straight line drawn between the core and the delta of a loop. Neither the core nor the delta is included when counting. Figures 6-10a, b, c, and d illustrate ridge counting. The dashed line *AB* shown in this illustration is the imaginary line between the core and delta. It may be noted that ridge counting is used *only* for loop patterns. To be a loop, a

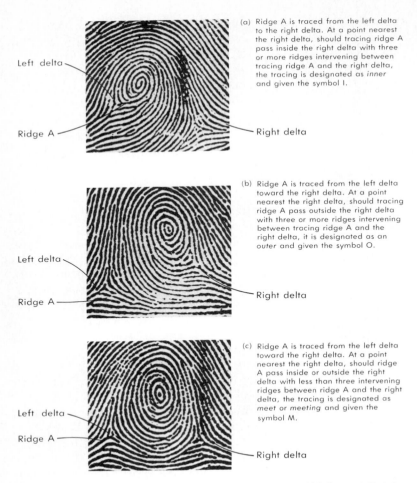

(a) Ridge A is traced from the left delta to the right delta. At a point nearest the right delta, should tracing ridge A pass inside the right delta with three or more ridges intervening between tracing ridge A and the right delta, the tracing is designated as *inner* and given the symbol I.

Left delta

Ridge A

Right delta

(b) Ridge A is traced from the left delta toward the right delta. At a point nearest the right delta, should tracing ridge A pass outside the right delta with three or more ridges intervening between tracing ridge A and the right delta, it is designated as an *outer* and given the symbol O.

Left delta

Ridge A

Right delta

(c) Ridge A is traced from the left delta toward the right delta. At a point nearest the right delta, should ridge A pass inside or outside the right delta with less than three intervening ridges between ridge A and the right delta, the tracing is designated as *meet* or *meeting* and given the symbol M.

Left delta

Ridge A

Right delta

Note: If the ridge being traced bifurcates (forks), the lower branch of the fork is followed; should the ridge being traced end, drop to lower ridge and continue tracing.

Figure 6-9. Ridge tracing. (a) Whorl-type pattern designated as an inner tracing—I; (b) Whorl-type pattern designated as an outer tracing—O; (c) Whorl-type pattern designated as a meet tracing—M.

pattern must have a ridge count of at least one, although the count may be as high as twenty-five or thirty.

If the imaginary line, as described above, passes through a bifurcation (fork-type ridge), both branches of the fork are counted. If there is an island (enclosure), both sides of the island are counted. See Figure 6-7 for examples of bifurcation and an island. Fragments and dots are counted as ridges only if they appear to be as thick and heavy as the other ridges in the immediate pattern and, of course, touch the imaginary line mentioned above. Ridge endings — , bifurcations (forks) ⌐ , and islands ⌐○ are the most common ridge characteristics. These characteristics have to be pointed out as the identifying features to prove that two fingerprint impressions are, or are not, the same.

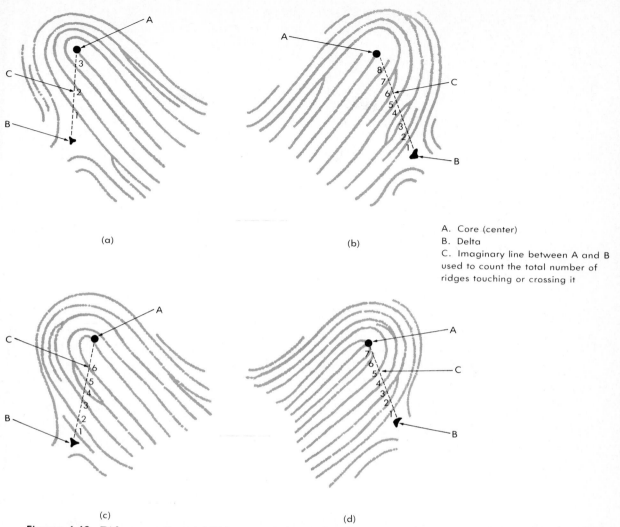

A. Core (center)
B. Delta
C. Imaginary line between A and B used to count the total number of ridges touching or crossing it

Figure 6-10. Ridge counting. (a) Ridge count three; (b) ridge count eight; (c) ridge count six; (d) ridge count seven.

Whorl Tracing

This aspect of fingerprint classification and interpretation pertains *only* to whorls. Since whorls are subclassified by ridge tracing as shown in Figure 6-9, the first examination of a whorl fingerprint impression is the determination of the pattern itself. The fingerprint impression being observed must have two or more deltas to be classified as a whorl.

Once the deltas are located, the process of ridge tracing involves the tracing of the ridge that emanates from the lower side of the left delta toward the right delta until the point nearest or opposite the extreme right delta is reached. The number of ridges intervening between the tracing ridge and the right delta is then counted.

If the ridge traced passes inside of the right delta and three or more ridges intervene between the tracing ridge and the delta, the tracing is said to be an "inner," and therefore given the symbol I. (See Figure 6-9a.) If the ridge traced beginning with the left delta passes outside or below the right delta and three or more ridges intervene between the tracing ridge and the right delta, the tracing is designated as an "outer" and given the symbol O as shown in Figure 6-9b. If the tracing ridge beginning with the left delta and traced to a point inside or outside the right delta is noted to be less than three ridges, it is called a "meet" or "meeting" whorl tracing and is designated by the capital letter M. (See Figure 6-9c.) Actually, all whorl tracings other than "inner" or "outer" are "meeting" tracings.

The Primary Classification

The primary classification of fingerprints deals with *whorls only*. It is not a positive identification of the person bearing the prints. But this aspect of the fingerprint classification system performs a great service for the officer by helping to eliminate a subject who has a physical resemblance to a wanted person or one having a similar name. Every officer should know how to compute the primary classification. The most important aspect of determining the primary is the officer's ability to distinguish between fingerprints of the whorl type and those of the nonwhorl type. The whorl-type patterns include plain whorls, central pocket loops, double loops, and accidentals. (See Figure 6-8.) The nonwhorl-type patterns include arch and loop patterns. In distinguishing fingerprint patterns, it must be recognized that whorls have two or more deltas, whereas loop patterns have only one delta, and arch patterns have no deltas.

The value of the primary classification is that it is simple, fast, requires little training, and can be done without the aid of special equipment. The officer away from the office may easily determine the primary classification of a subject and transmit this information to headquarters as an aid in the search of the department's records. If the record indicates that two people have the same name and approximate physical description, the primary classification will usually distinguish one subject from the other. A positive identification must be made, however, by an examination of the individual fingerprint characteristics of the suspect.

How to obtain the primary

For the purpose of obtaining the primary classification, numerical values are assigned to each of the finger spaces beginning with the right thumb. (See Figure 6-11.) The presence of *whorls* in any of the ten finger impressions is used as the basis for the determination of the primary classification. Wherever a *whorl* appears in the ten finger spaces, it assumes the value of the space in which it is found. Beginning with the right thumb and using odd-numbered fingers of both hands (1, 3, 5, 7, 9), the number in the corresponding space is added each time a *whorl* appears. This sum, plus 1, is the *denominator* of the primary classification. Starting with the right index finger and using even-numbered fingers of both hands (2, 4, 6, 8, 10), the numbers in the corresponding finger spaces are added each time a *whorl* appears. This sum, plus 1, is the *numerator* of the primary classification. Should an arch or loop pattern appear in any of the ten finger spaces on a fingerprint card, they are disregarded, as they are not used in this method of classification.

Primary classification guide

This guide (Figure 6-11) sets forth the formula and the numerical values which are assigned to each of the ten finger spaces. It is noted that the values are assigned in pairs and in the order in which they appear on the fingerprint card. The first pair, right thumb

$$\frac{N}{D} + \frac{1}{1} = \text{Primary classification}$$

	Thumb	Index	Middle	Ring	Little
R I G H T	Denominator 16	Numerator 16	Denominator 8	Numerator 8	Denominator 4
L E F T	Numerator 4	Denominator 2	Numerator 2	Denominator 1	Numerator 1

Figure 6-11. Primary classification guide. Numerical values are assigned to whorl patterns *only* when computing the primary. Where loops, arches, and tented arches appear, no numerical value is given.

and right index, is given a value of 16; the second pair, right middle and right ring fingers, is given a value of 8; the third pair, right little and left thumb, a value of 4. The left index and left middle are given values of 2 each, and the left ring and left little are given values of 1 each.

The method of obtaining the primary can probably be shown best by Figure 6-12.

In this example, it is noted that *whorl* patterns appear on fingers 1 (right thumb), 4 (right ring finger), and 7 (left index finger). In accordance with the fixed formula (Figure 6-11), add the values of whorls appearing in the fingers to ascertain the primary. Disregard patterns other than whorls.

In determining the *numerator*, we examine the finger impressions of the even fingers (2, 4, 6, 8, 10). Only one whorl is evident in the above example—namely, on the right ring finger (finger 4), which always carries a fixed value of 8. In accordance with the formula, we add 1, making a total for the numerator of 9.

In determining the *denominator*, we again examine the finger impressions of the odd-numbered fingers (1, 3, 5, 7, 9). In Figure 6-12, we note that whorls appear on fingers 1 (right thumb) and 7 (left index) only. Adding the fixed values assigned to these fingers, we add 16 (value assigned to the right thumb) and 2 (value assigned to

Figure 6-12. Hypothetical problem. Sketch of fingerprint patterns of right and left hand to ascertain the primary.

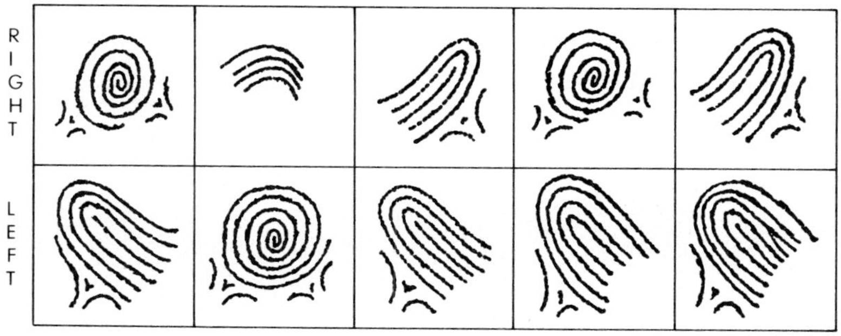

the left index finger) to obtain 18. To the sum of 18, we add 1, in accordance with the formula, making a total of 19 for the *denominator*. The *primary classification* in this example would therefore be 9 over 19.

The *Henry System* of fingerprint classification involves the classifying of a person's fingerprints into various divisions and expressing the result in a formula. Each segment of the classification formula has a particular meaning and definite rules which must be followed to determine its value when classifying a set of prints. One should keep in mind the fact that the main purpose of the classification formula is to systematically divide and subdivide a large number of fingerprints into small compartments so that they can be filed and retrieved with reasonable case.

The primary classification is called the first or main classification because it is the key to all fingerprint classification and filing. The other divisions of classification explained here are merely subdivisions of the primary. The primary classification, which is the first segment in the fingerprint classification as indicated above, divides the fingerprints into 1024 groups[13] on the basis of whorl- or nonwhorl-type patterns on each of the ten fingers. The primary ranges from nonwhorl patterns in all ten fingers to whorl-type patterns in all ten fingers, including all combinations in between. An example of how a classification formula and the positions in the classification line might appear on a fingerprint card is shown in Figure 6-13.

For this illustration, representing a modification and extension of the Henry System, the primary classification would be represented by the *first numerical fraction* in the fingerprint formula (encircled). The first

---

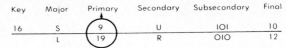

Figure 6-13. A classification formula and the positions in the classification line.

complete numerical fraction in our example is 9 over 19 and therefore it would represent the primary classification. The number 9 in the numerator would indicate that the person had a whorl pattern on the right ring finger; the number 19 in the denominator would indicate that the individual had whorl patterns in two fingers, viz., the right thumb and the left index finger.

The fraction (representing the primary) may be located first, second, or third along the line; but it will be the only group of numbers standing both above and below the line. Other examples of how the total classification may appear on a fingerprint card appear in Figure 6-14.

Interpretation of Fingerprint Classification Segments

Although the classification of fingerprints is not discussed in this chapter, a capsule de-

Figure 6-14. A total classification on a fingerprint card.

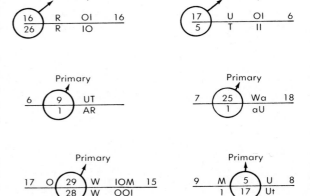

scription is provided of all the segments in the classification formula, with extensions, as used in a large identification bureau. (See Figure 6-15a.) For information purposes only, Figure 6-15b shows the method used in classifying fingerprints for entry into the Wanted Persons File of the National Crime Information Center (NCIC) at FBI headquarters, Washington, D.C.

Methods of Processing Fingerprints in An Identification Bureau

The purpose of this section is to explain the ways in which fingerprints are processed in a large identification unit. After fingerprints have been classified, they are processed by three methods: (1) by hand (manual search); (2) by card-sorting machines; and (3) by computers.[14] In each method, the basic concept of the Henry System is used. However, the classification formula that is derived to describe each set of fingerprints may vary somewhat from method to method.

Manual search

When a set of fingerprints is received at the identification unit, the first attempt to effect an identification is a search of the name index file. Before the name search is made, a fingerprint classifier determines the primary fingerprint classification in order to assist in distinguishing between people with the same name. If one or more possible matches are made in the name index file, the case jacket folder number or the master fingerprint classification is recorded so that the incoming fingerprints can be checked with the prints on file. If the fingerprints are positively identified, the appropriate information will be sent to the requestor. The reason for making the name search first is

that it is a much faster operation than that of completely classifying the fingerprints and then searching the main fingerprint file.

Those fingerprints that are not identified during the name search must be fully classified, including any reference classification, before they are searched against the main fingerprint files. Each fingerprint classification formula identifies a particular compartment within the main file. The person conducting the search makes a visual comparison between the set of prints being searched and the fingerprints field in the identified compartment. All of the visual matches that are made by the searcher must be visually verified before the processing can continue. If the fingerprints are identified, the desired information is returned to the requestor. If the fingerprints are not identified, the requestor will be notified that there is no record. The unmatched arrest/identification prints are then added to the fingerprint base file. In the event that the prints are to be added to the latent print file, they must be classified a second time according to the latent print classification system that is used by that identification unit. The reason for this is that the main fingerprint file and the latent print file are separate entities.

Card-sorter search

In order to search arrest/identification prints against a main file with card-sorting equipment, the classifier must determine the manual classification in the usual way. In addition, the classifier must record the pattern type and ridge count for every one of the ten fingers. The processing of an arrest/identification unit that uses card-sorting equipment is similar to that in a unit that employs a manual search in that a name search is made before the main fingerprint file is searched. If a tentative identification is made in the name file, then the subsequent processing is as that of a manual search.

---

[14]*New York State Identification and Intelligence System Status Report,* October 1965.

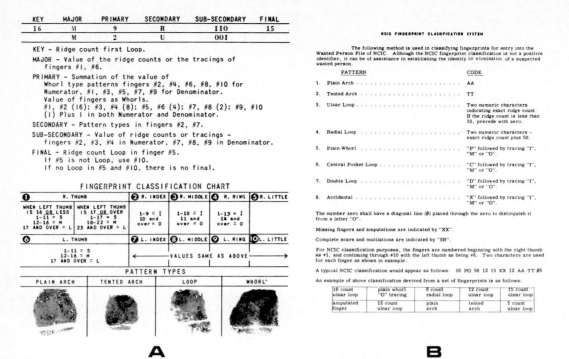

Figure 6-15. (a) Interpretation of fingerprint classification segments. (b) Interpretation of the method used in classifying fingerprints for entry into the Wanted Persons File of the National Criminal Information Center (NCIC).

There are two files in a card-sorting system. One file contains the actual fingerprint cards which are filed in sequence by a fingerprint identification number. The second file is composed of punched cards that contain the machine classification formulas. The files are cross-referenced through the fingerprint identification number. The punched cards are filed by primary, secondary, and final classification, within sex and date-of-birth groupings. The machine operator uses the fingerprint classification (i.e., the primary, secondary, and final classification), as well as the sex and age grouping, of the person whose fingerprints are being searched to select the desired set of punched cards from the punched-card file. These cards are inserted into the card sorter. Before starting the search, the operator adjusts a set of dials on the machine so that it will search for ridge counts that correspond to those contained in the set of fingerprints to be searched. The machine compares the ridge counts of all ten fingers on the punched cards with the ridge counts that have been set on the machine. If the two sets of ridge counts agree within the allowable tolerances, the card sorter prints out the fingerprint identification number on the punched card.

After the machine search is completed, the searcher uses the fingerprint identification numbers that have been listed by the machine to extract the fingerprint cards from the fingerprint file. A visual comparison is then made to determine if any file prints belong to the person whose print is being searched. If so, the match is verified and the appropriate information is sent to the records and administrative processing. If the machine does not select any candidate prints, or if the visual comparison of the selected candidate prints proves to be negative, then it is assumed that the print being searched is not in the main file. In this case, the incoming set of fingerprints must be added to the fingerprint card file and a punched card must be prepared and filed.

Computer search

The classification that is used in those identification units that have the capability to search arrest/identification fingerprints by computer is very similar to that used in the card-sorting systems. The primary difference is that the information that is normally stored on the punched card is stored on some computer storage device such as magnetic tape or magnetic discs. When the decision has been made to search the computer fingerprint file (i.e., the initial name search has failed), a computer operator enters the fingerprint search request into the computer. The search request contains the fingerprint classification, the ridge count of every finger, the date of birth, and the sex of the individual. The search request can be keypunched into a card and then read into the computer by a card reader, or it can be entered directly by an input/output (I/O) typewriter. In either case, the computer takes this information and searches through its base file, selecting as candidates those fingerprints that fall within the tolerance allowed by the search. At the end of the search, the computer prints out a list of candidate prints that are identified by a fingerprint identification number. A fingerprint expert extracts the candidate fingerprints from the fingerprint card file and makes a visual comparison to determine whether the search prints can be matched with any of the candidate prints. If a match is found, the desired information is sent to the requestor. If the computer does not select any candidate prints, or if the candidate prints that are selected cannot be matched with the search prints, then it is assumed that the unit does not have a record of this individual. The incoming set of prints must then be added to the fingerprint base file and possibly to the latent print files. The procedure for doing this is exactly the same as that for a card-sorting system except that the punched cards are put into the computer for storage.

TYPES OF FINGERPRINT IMPRESSIONS FOUND AT THE CRIME SCENE

Fingerprints found at the scene of a crime are known as chance impressions. These impressions may be visible, plastic, or latent.

Visible Prints

Impressions that are visible are fingerprints a person with soiled or stained fingertips or palms would leave, particularly on a white or light-colored surface, or in dust. Prints of the visible classification are often observable on many surface areas touched. Materials that have been carried usually bear visual prints of fingertips or palmar surfaces. Finger images of this kind may or may not have identification value depending upon the distinctive characteristics of the friction left on the surface of the material or object touched.

Plastic Prints

These are found on plastic-type surfaces such as soap, butter, wax, soft putty, tar, grease, or other materials that form a mold of the fingerprint when touched. Plastic impressions should not be dusted with fingerprint powders. Such prints should be photographed with the aid of direct or side lighting. The use of side or oblique lighting highlights the ridges, causing the furrows to show up as shadows in the photograph. A fingerprint camera (Figure 6-16) can be useful in photographing prints in these conditions. This specialized camera has its own light source and fixed focus, and photographs fingerprints in their natural size. In photographing plastic prints, two of the four bulbs contained within this camera may be loosened on one side so that they will not light. The light given off by the two remaining bulbs is directed so as to pass at right angles across the ridges of the embedded print. The exposure time should be adjusted to compensate for the low lighting, type of film used, and the color of the object upon

which the impressions have been found. Prior to the actual photographing, it is recommended that a slip of paper containing identifying data be placed near the suspect print. The identifying data should include the date, initials of the officer, and an identifying or case number. Notes taken during the photographing process should include such data as time, date, type and make of camera, place from which the fingerprints were obtained. Information such as the kind of lens, lens opening, shutter speed, and chain of custody of the photographic film should also be noted. Whenever plastic prints are located, processed, and photographed, it is a highly desirable practice to prepare a simple sketch showing where the prints were located.

When using a fingerprint camera it is recommended that two or three exposures of varying lengths be taken to ensure a good picture. Since the fingerprint camera is a fixed-focus camera, it is limited to surfaces against which the front of the camera may be placed.

The fingerprint camera has many other uses in addition to photographing fingerprints. This camera can be used for photographing serial numbers, handwriting, signatures, engravings, check stubs, receipts, jewelry, and other evidence. Photographs of latent fingerprints can also be taken by this camera after development by powdering or chemical methods, described later in this chapter. In those instances where latent fingerprints are found on clear, transparent glass (a drinking glass, for example), such prints can be powdered with black or gray powder. Prior to lifting the prints from the glass, however, it is suggested that they be photographed. A fingerprint camera can be used in photographing latents on such surfaces. In photographing such prints, a black or white piece of paper should be inserted within the drinking glass or behind the transparency in order to provide a good background contrast.

Figure 6-16. Fingerprint camera.

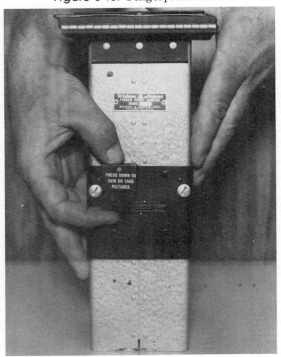

Latent Prints

These are impressions that are not readily visible; they are hidden or concealed. Fingerprint powders and chemical sprays or solutions are needed to develop latents (make them visible) so that they may be preserved and used for identification purposes and in court trials. Methods involved in the processing of latent prints will be discussed later in this chapter. A latent fingerprint consists of perspiration (98.5 to 99.5 percent water and 0.05 to 1.5 percent solid). The solids include inorganic matter (mostly salt) and organic substances (urea, volatile fatty acids, acetic acid, and traces of other substances). When an object or other surface is touched, a film of moisture may be deposited. Fingerprints may also be transferred in combinations with oil or grease from preparations on the hair or skin to an object, or from oily tools handled. The fingerprints left by virtue of this touching with the fingertips are called latent prints. Not all people leave latent prints; for example, people with dry hands do not. Weather too is a factor; in cold weather, pores close. Gloves worn during the commission of an offense will likewise prevent the transfer of a latent impression. However, despite the fact that the perpetrator appeared to wear gloves, a search should be conducted for latent prints. Suspects have been known to remove their gloves during the period involved in the crime. Photographs of glove prints will, in addition to furnishing the type of weave or pattern in the glove, help to connect that suspect with other cases in which similar prints were found and will also help to furnish possible investigative leads.

Latent impressions may be found at a crime scene on *nonporous articles* such as glass objects, tableware, polished metal surfaces, finished wood, unfrosted electric light bulbs, doorknobs, window moldings, telephones, enameled surfaces, finished leather, and plastic. Innumerable other nonporous, nonabsorbent, hard, smooth surfaces are possible sources. Finger impressions may also be obtained from many *porous materials* such as paper, cardboard, unfinished wood. Identifiable latent impressions have been successfully obtained from such porous materials as closely woven textiles (sheets, handkerchiefs, tablecloths, shirts), smooth plaster walls, fruit peelings, shoes, guns, and shell casings.

The sole purpose in developing latent fingerprints is to make them visible so that they may be preserved and compared with fingerprints from suspects believed involved in that crime. During an investigation, discovery of latent impressions on crime-scene-related objects is not uncommon, and, if identified against inked impressions, are admissible evidence in a court of law. The expert in latent fingerprints makes a comparison between the latent prints found at the crime scene with the known prints of criminal suspects or other persons who might have left the latent print on the object under examination. This comparison takes into consideration the same ridge detail in both the latent and the known prints. If a sufficient number of points of similarity are noted between the latent and the known prints, an identification is made. Should twelve ridge characteristics be found (of the type shown in Figure 6-7) common to both the latent and the fingerprint of a suspect, this identification would place that suspect at the crime scene and be acceptable in court as proof of identity. Courts generally require the prosecution to identify twelve or more characteristics. There have been cases wherein less than twelve points of similarity have been admitted to prove the identity of a suspect based on clearness, shape, ridge characteristics, and pores. In cases where only a partial fingerprint is obtained at a crime scene, such a print can often be compared with a known suspect's fingerprints. One-fourth or one-fifth of a fingerprint, if located, can be sufficient to establish identity.

Where fragmentary fingerprint impressions are found at a crime scene, an identification may require the application of *poroscopy*. Poroscopy involves the study, analysis, and comparison of the size, shape, number, and position of the pores on the ridges of the partial fingerprint with those of a suspect's finger impressions. The science of identification by the study of pores was originated by Edmond Locard, a French criminologist.

Searching for latent fingerprints

An investigator searching a crime scene for possible latent fingerprints should carefully examine objects or suspect areas that may have been touched by the perpetrator. Latent fingerprints can often be detected by the use of a flashlight played over the surface of an object or placed at an angle. Sometimes prints can be detected by blowing on the surface of an object believed to contain latent prints. In most instances, however, suspect areas must be processed by dusting with a contrasting colored fingerprint powder to bring out latent prints.

The search for latent fingerprints should be conducted in a systematic manner. When considering the possible areas to examine for fingerprints, the probable movements of the intruder through the house or building should be considered. Points of break-in or entry such as doors and windows, and objects disturbed or likely to have been touched should be examined. In cases involving a stolen unlocked car, the only exterior fingerprints will probably be on the door handles or outside mirror unless the license plates were tampered with. If the car was locked and force used to gain entry, a search for latent impressions should be made around the area of the break-in. If the investigator thinks that the car was hot wired, an examination under the hood or inside the car around the ignition should be made, depending on the location of the hot wiring. In addition, such items as the rearview mirror, seat adjustment lever, registration certifi-

cate or holder, doorsill on driver's side, steering wheel, chrome buckle on seat belt, the glove compartment and contents, and the trunk area should be checked. The location of the search for latent impressions will vary with the design of the car itself and likely metal gadgets or surfaces touched.

When latent fingerprints have been detected, a record of the exact location of the print on the object and the object itself should be made. After making adequate notes (including measurements and compass directions), the fingerprints should be photographed, if possible, on the original object before any attempt is made to lift the print or to have chemical processing done. It should be stressed that taking a picture is preferred to risking the destruction of the evidence by employing powders or vapors. A sketch of the particular room should likewise be made. The sketch should depict doors, objects, windows, and pieces of furniture where the latent prints were obtained. A good reason for taking photographs of the latent fingerprints found is that they will show the relationship of the latent impression to other objects at the crime scene.

Powdering and lifting latent impressions

In the search and detection of latent fingerprints, many different types of powders and chemicals may be used. A black or gray fingerprint powder is adequate in most instances. The determination to use black or gray powder is dependent upon the color that will contrast with the material on which the latent was left. For example, a black powder should be used for white or light backgrounds and gray powder for black or dark backgrounds. Gray powder would also be used on mirrors or reflecting surfaces inasmuch as it photographs black. Other fingerprint powders that can be used include aluminum powder (which may be substituted for gray powder), gold or red-bronze powders on light-colored surfaces (photographs dark), and dragon's blood (a neutral powder that may be dusted on either a light or dark surface). Anthracene, a fluorescent type of powder, is used for the development of latent fingerprints found on multicolored backgrounds. A powder, such as anthracene, fluoresces vividly while the colors in the background remain only faintly visible.

During an examination for latent fingerprints, a contrasting fingerprint powder should be applied with a camel's hair brush or brush made of feather down. The camel's hair brush should have hairs 1½ or 2 inches (4 or 5 centimeters) long. Prior to using, the hairs of the brush should be fluffed out by rolling the brush back and forth between the palms of the hands. Thereafter, dip the brush lightly into the powder or pour out a small portion of the powder onto a piece of clean paper. Tap the handle of the brush with a finger to knock off excess powder. Sweep the brush back and forth across the surface where you think latent prints might be. As the powder begins to stick to a fingerprint, stop and examine the print to see which way the ridges flow. Thereafter, brush in the general direction of the ridges. For example, arches should be brushed from side to side; whorls in a circular motion; and loops from the top of the loop to the exit of the loop ridges. Add more powder if necessary to improve the development of the print. An atomizer is often used for blowing powder onto a latent fingerprint inasmuch as powder tends less to bunch up than when it is dusted. A basic rule to remember when using any fingerprint powder is that it is better to use too little powder than too much.

If an officer is not sure what powder to use, it is well to place a fingerprint of her or his own on an area away from the suspect latent and experiment with the powder thought to be best — a sort of trial-and-error process. By noting the results of this experiment, the officer will have the necessary confidence to process the suspect latent prints.

Magnetic Brush and Powders In addition to the conventional brushes (camel's hair, squirrel's hair, fiber glass, and feather dusters) used in the application of fingerprint powders in developing latent fingerprints, identification officers also use a device called a magnetic brush or wand as part of their kits. The magnetic brush is effective only with magnetic powders, which are manufactured in many colors (gray, black, jet black, red, yellow, silver, and others for multicolored surfaces). The brush attracts the powders magnetically for clean dusting of latent fingerprints. The brush is a magnetic rod which is pushed in or out of a small cylinder, causing the magnetic powder to be attracted to the magnetic field. This magnetic field causes the metal powder to appear as a brush and allows the officer to process the crime-scene areas. A magnetic brush and attracting powders are very useful in dusting overhead and slanting surfaces for latents. This brush can be used in searching for latent impressions on paper, tissue, light wood, leather, cardboard boxes, glass, plastics, wax drinking cups, and other materials.

Lifting Latent Fingerprints Two things that should always be kept in mind with regard to powdering and lifting fingerprint impressions are (1) do not powder a print unless it is necessary to do so. Photograph it before and after powdering. And (2) do not lift a latent impression unless necessary. Bring all portable objects or articles to the crime laboratory for processing. Photographing the latent print is strongly suggested because of the possibility of destroying the print by lifting it.

Whenever latent prints are powdered and lifted, the examiner is provided with a second method of preserving the latent images. There are two types of lifting mediums employed in latent fingerprint work: (1) transparent cellulose tape in 1½- or 2-inch (4- or 5-centimeter) width rolls or in pre-assembled, assorted-size lifters, and (2) opaque rubber lifters.

Transparent Cellulose Lifting Tape
This type of tape is used by many fingerprint technicians because it may be used for all powders, is economical, easy to work with, and offers some advantages in making immediate comparisons with inked fingerprints. Fingerprint supply firms sell rolls of cellulose tape of the office variety in 1½-inch and 2-inch (4- and 5-centimeter) widths for this purpose. A dispenser greatly facilitates the handling of this tape. Transparent lifts made with this tape should be mounted on a good grade of card stock.

To use this type of tape, pull off sufficient tape from the roll to adequately cover the powdered print. Fold over one end of the tape about a quarter of an inch to use as a tab; this prevents the end of the tape from sticking to one's fingers and leaving a finger impression in the adhesive. Press the tape down at one end as an anchor. With the tape held taut, slide an index finger or thumb along the tape until the tape completely covers the powdered latent print. Make sure that no air bubbles form under the adhesive. Care should be taken not to touch the gum

Figure 6-17. Latent fingerprint transfer card. This type is used for backing latent prints that have been lifted with transparent tape. Space is provided for investigation information.

File	Dept.	Date
V-		L-
Prints Log.		

side of the adhesive area you plan to press over the print. Thereafter, pull the tape off the surface and carefully transfer the lifted tape to which the latent has been transferred, to the latent transfer card. (See Figure 6-17.) After the latent print is transferred onto the transfer card, cut off the piece of tape used from the roll; trim off any surplus tape. Thereafter, fill out the data required on the transfer card and include the number of the particular lift, place obtained, and the initials of the officer.

The transfer card (front and back) might contain a small sketch depicting the area from which the print was obtained and the measurements of the area. Additional notes should be made by the investigating officer for report and court purposes. In some instances an officer at the scene of a crime may choose to cover the latent impression with transparent tape after powdering the prints, rather than attempt to lift them onto a transfer card. This procedure serves to protect the print and leaves the additional processing to the crime laboratory experts. Care should be exercised in lifting latent prints from some kinds of materials, such as paper and painted surfaces, with the above type of cellulose tape lest portions of the paper or paint cling to the adhesive upon lifting. In questionable cases where this possibility may exist, the officer might place his or her own finger impression on the surface of the suspect material away from the particular area. Therefter, by trial and error, the officer can decide whether to make a lift attempt.

Transparent Preassembled Black or White Lifters   These lifters are available in sizes 1½ by 1½ inches, 2 by 4 inches, and 4 by 4 inches (4 by 4, 5 by 10, and 10 by 10 centimeters). The use of individual transparent lifters eliminates cutting and extra handling. In the use of the above individual lifters, it is only necessary to peel away the separator to expose the adhesive side; place the adhesive over the powdered print, press gently and evenly across the lifter to make sure that no air bubbles form under the adhesive, lift the print from the surface or object, and then fold the hinged flap over the print to permanently seal and protect it. The lifted latent impression should be identified. Where several latents appear to have been made simultaneously, they should be lifted as a unit on a large-size lifter. (See Figure 6-18.)

Opaque Rubber Lifters This type of lifter is similar in appearance to an ordinary tire patch — having an adhesive surface which is protected by a celluloid cover. (See Figure 6-19.) Lifters of this type come in 4-by 9-inch [5- by 23-centimeter] size and in two colors, black and white. Latent impressions developed with black powder should be

Figure 6-18. Preassembled white and black transparent hinged lifters (various sizes) for use in lifting powdered latent prints. The lifter has a separation that is pulled away to expose the adhesive side. After the print is lifted, the clear viewing flap is replaced to seal the print in. The lifter is marked on one side to indicate viewing position.

Figure 6-19. Rubber fingerprint lifters, black or white. A color that will contrast with the powder should be used. The print on the rubber tape is in reverse position for comparing. To compare, photograph and reverse.

lifted with white tape; prints developed with gray or aluminum powder should be lifted with black tape. Gold-bronze and red-bronze powders photograph darkly and should be lifted on white rubber tape. Dragon's blood powder (a neutral powder) may be lifted on either black or white tape. Opaque lifters are used to lift latent fingerprints from all types of surfaces (curved, uneven) and are considered an excellent transfer medium.

In lifting a latent print, a piece of rubber tape large enough to cover the impression is cut from one of the sheets with an ample margin. The celluloid cover is then carefully peeled from the piece of rubber lifter that is about to be used. The adhesive side of the rubber tape is then applied to the powdered print. The tape should be pressed evenly to the latent to ensure a good contact and prevent air bubbles from forming. Thereafter, peel the rubber lifter from the surface. The print will then come with it. A small piece of paper bearing identifying data should be placed under one corner of the celluloid cover, away from the lifted print. Notes made by the officer should indicate the number of the lift, officer's initials, and date. Identifying data may be placed on the back of the white tape. Complete data on each lifted print should, of course, be written in the officer's notebook. Whenever latent prints appear to have been made simultaneously, such prints should be lifted as a unit on a single piece of tape.

Chemical methods of developing latent fingerprints

There are many different chemical methods that have been successfully used in the development of latent fingerprints. Four of the more widely known chemical liquids or vapors used in this process are (1) iodine, (2) silver nitrate, (3) Ninhydrin (Sirchie Finger Print Laboratories, Moorestown, N.J.) and (4) Chem Print (Criminalistics, Inc., Opa-Locka, Fla.).

Iodine Method   In this process, iodine crystals, heated or cold, are used. The fumes which the crystals give off develop the latents. When iodine crystals are heated, much more rapid latent print development occurs. The iodine fumes react with the perspiration and fatty matter. These fumes are absorbed by fatty or oily matter with which they come in contact. The result is that the print is made visible by the absorption of the iodine fumes and ridges of the print appear yellowish brown or brownish against the background.

All latent impressions on an object will not be developed by the iodine process. Only those containing fat or oil will. Iodine prints are not permanent and begin to fade once the absorption stops unless a fixative is used or the print is lifted with a silver transfer sheet. A silver transfer sheet is a transfer medium that, when applied directly to the latent image produced by the iodine fuming process, permits the lifting of that fingerprint image. The lifted latent when exposed to direct sunlight or heated by means of a photoflood bulb will darken and become permanent. The latent print will appear as a black image upon the silver. The latent fingerprint image may necessitate additional iodine fuming in some instances if the latent is too faint or strong. It is possible to make several transfers from the same latent. Prior to using the transfer sheet, it is always a good practice to photograph the developed latent when it appears. The exposed silver transfer sheets should be placed in an envelope, appropriately identified, and filed.

In the iodine fuming process, a fuming cabinet, a box or container, or an iodine fuming apparatus is used. If a fuming cabinet is used, a hole in the bottom of the cabinet permits the insertion of an evaporating dish containing the iodine crystals. The cabinet floor should be raised to permit the placing of a small alcohol burner (used to heat the iodine crystals) beneath the floor of the cabinet. The use of heat is referred to as the *hot iodine method*. A glass-type enclosure permits observation of the development of the latents. A removable top permits access to the specimens and closer inspection if desired. The paper or material being treated is hung from a sort of clothesline within the box or container.

Latent prints can be made visible by exposing suspected materials to unheated crystals. This process is known as the *cold iodine method*. The suspect specimen should be placed face down above the evaporating dish containing the iodine crystals—preferably about 2 or 3 inches (50 or 75 millimeters). As the crystals reach room temperature, the gas given off develops the prints in a brownish color. The use of the cold iodine process takes longer to develop latents. Old prints may require an hour of exposure to the iodine gasses. Tongs, tweezers, or gloves should be used at all times in handling materials during iodine processing. The fumes from iodine crystals should be avoided since they are considered harmful and should not be breathed.

Another method in iodine fuming, as previously indicated, is the use of an iodine fuming gun or apparatus. This apparatus is a cylindrical, hollow, glass tube with a rubber tube affixed at one end and a nozzle at the other. Within the main glass section of this apparatus are iodine crystals and calcium chloride separated from each other by glass wool. In using this piece of equipment the operator blows through the rubber tubing. The iodine vapor flows out through the nozzle at the opposite end and can be directed at the paper, wood, or other surface to be processed. The calcium chloride within the apparatus removes the moisture so that dry heat vaporizes the iodine. Any latent prints present will appear. Once the print appears and the image is sufficiently clear, the latent should be photographed or lifted with silver transfer sheets. The iodine fuming apparatus has the advantage of being able to control the iodine vapor and apply it only where necessary on a given object. In the event the fingerprint image is not photographed or lifted, there are many types of commercial fixatives available which can be used to fix the prints raised through the iodine fuming process.

Iodine fuming apparatuses also come in heat-resistant glass filter beakers that can be used in fuming operations. The top of the fuming beaker has an airtight stopper through which a fuming funnel projects. The neck portion of the beaker has a horizontally protruding outlet. A rubber squeeze bulb is attached to it. When using this beaker, a capsule of iodine crystals is emptied into the beaker, which contains glass wool. The beaker is then heated with a match or lighter. The resultant iodine vapors are dispersed from the beaker by compressing the rubber bulb, causing the fumes to flow through the fumer funnel onto the surface of the suspected area at which the funnel is directed. This action results in the development of any latent prints present.

Iodine fuming processes have been successfully used in developing latent impressions on greasy surfaces, paper, documents, cardboard, wood surfaces, metal, and other materials. Iodine fuming should be applied before using the silver nitrate process described below.

Silver Nitrate Method   The silver nitrate method (also referred to as the silver chloride process) of developing latent fingerprints on paper, documents, currency, unpainted wood, and other porous substances has been used by crime laboratories for many years. The development is dependent upon the fact that sodium chloride (common salt) is present in the perspiration. Sodium chloride forms the ridges in most latent impressions and reacts with the silver nitrate solution to form silver chloride. Silver chloride is an unstable white substance which darkens when exposed to light, breaking down into its components, silver and chlorine. The ridges of the fingerprints developed in this manner appear reddish brown against the background.[15]

There are several silver nitrate processes used for the development of latent prints. One of the processes commonly used in fingerprint work employs the use of a 3 percent solution of silver nitrate. Other silver nitrate solutions ranging from 3 to 10 percent are used in this developing process. The 3 percent solution is prepared by dissolving 4 ounces of silver nitrate crystals in 1 gallon of distilled water. If a stronger mixture is desired, a 5 percent solution may be obtained by adding 6⅔ ounces of the silver nitrate crystals to a gallon of distilled water. A 7 percent solution is made by adding 9⅓ ounces of crystals to a gallon of distilled water. A 10 percent solution is obtained by adding 13⅓ ounces of the crystals to a gallon of distilled water. Prepared solutions may be used several times before losing their strength. When not in use, the solution should be kept in a brown bottle away from light in order to retard deterioration. An alcohol solution may be preferred. This is prepared by mixing 4 ounces of silver nitrate crystals, 4 ounces of distilled water, and 1 gallon of 190 proof grain alcohol. The alcohol solution dries faster and, when treating paper bearing ink, it is less likely to cause the ink to run. A glass or porcelain tray approximately 18 by 12 by 5 inches (45 by 30 by 13 centimeters) is a convenient size for use with the above solutions. The silver nitrate process should be used in subdued light.

To use silver nitrate solution, pour a quantity in a tray. Immerse the paper or other porous material with suspect prints in the solution. This is called "silvering." The

---

[15]*The Science of Fingerprints,* Federal Bureau of Investigation, Washington, D.C., 1957.

paper is then taken out of the solution, placed between two clean, white photo-blotting papers to remove the excess solution, and dried. The specimens should be reasonably dry before exposing the paper to light—the next step. The document is exposed to a strong light source, such as a photoflood bulb, an ultraviolet lamp, a carbon arc, or even bright sunlight coming through a windowpane, until any developing fingerprints have darkened sufficiently. Latent prints become visible as dark brown outlines against the lighter background of the article. As soon as the latent fingerprint image is sufficiently clear, the paper should be removed from the light since continued exposure will darken the paper and the contrast will be lost. Photographing the suspect prints is recommended at this time.

Prepared silver nitrate solutions and atomizer-type spraying devices are commercially available for use in spraying questionable materials for latent prints.

Items such as cardboard cartons, newspapers, road maps, wrapping paper, or smooth, unpainted wood surfaces that are too large for dipping may be treated by brushing the silver nitrate solution over the surface with a paint brush. Wet paper should be carefully handled to prevent tearing.

Photographs, photostats, and blueprints of any value should not be treated with silver nitrate since the developed fingerprints or stains cannot be removed without destroying such documents. Rubber gloves should be worn in working with silver nitrate solutions, and tongs should be used in handling the specimens. Avoid spilling the solution on hands or clothing as it will cause brown stains. If removal of silver nitrate prints (called "desilvering") is desired, the material is dipped in a 2 percent solution of mercuric nitrate and thereafter washed in distilled water. It should be reiterated here that both the silver nitrate and iodine method can be employed on the same article provided the iodine method is used first.

Ninhydrin Method This process is considered a highly effective way of developing latent fingerprints, particularly in the treatment of documents. It is also effective on such porous items as writing paper, wallpaper, envelopes, bank notes, blotting paper, some types of fabrics. Older latent fingerprints appear to be more responsive to Ninhydrin than to silver nitrate. Trikeotohydrindene hydrate, trade named as Ninhydrin, reacts to the longer-remaining amino acids in human perspiration rather than the fleeting salt deposits. The reaction of Ninhydrin to the amino acids causes purple-reddish-brown stains. Methods of using Ninhydrin involve the use of Ninhydrin powder in a volatile substance such as ethyl alcohol, acetone, or ether. The most frequently used proportion is that of 1.5 percent (1.5 grams of Ninhydrin in 100 cc of ethyl alcohol or acetone). The solution is applied to the document or surface to be processed in one of several ways, viz., by means of an atomizer spraying device, by immersion in a developing tray, by painting the solution on with a brush, or by swabbing the suspected material with a cotton ball. Ninhydrin fingerprint spray can be obtained commercially in aerosol containers that require no mixing or preparation. To prevent staining of the hands when using Ninhydrin, rubber gloves should be worn in addition to protective clothing. Tongs should be used in handling suspect materials during processing or after treatment with Ninhydrin. In other words, avoid all skin contact with articles treated with this chemical solution.

Materials treated with Ninhydrin solution should be permitted to dry at room temperature. When latent fingerprints are present on a paper surface, Ninhydrin stains the fingerprint pattern and renders visible the latent image. Visible prints generally appear within three to five hours after application of the developing reagent and may continue to appear for about twenty-four hours or longer in some instances. Prints have been known to appear as late as ten days after application of Ninhydrin. Experiments with Ninhydrin have been successful in raising latent fingerprints as old as ten to fifteen years. The development of latents after so many years is mentioned only to point out the value of this process.

To hasten the development of latent fingerprints, a dry, treated document can be heated at 220°F (100 to 105°C) in an oven for two or three minutes or the document can be exposed to an infrared lamp or hair dryer. The "slow cure" at room temperature is preferable unless time is of the essence.

In view of the occasional "running" of writing on documents treated with Ninhydrin, the effect of highly volatile solvents used to dilute Ninhydrin powder is a factor that is carefully considered by the fingerprint technician before a decision to use Ninhydrin is made. Precautions against carelessly oversaturating a document with Ninhydrin should always be taken since this causes distortions of paper fibers. As a result, the diffusion of written or printed traces, ink bleeding, and spreading, as well as other obscurities, makes it impossible for a document examiner to conduct a proper examination. Whenever a handwriting examination is desired, that examination should be conducted prior to any processing with Ninhydrin solutions. Practice and experience with experimental latent fingerprints impressed on various materials can provide valuable training in the proper technique needed in the application of the Ninhydrin method.

Chem Print Method   Chem Print, a trade name, is a chemical solution that has been successfully used by many police agencies in the development of latent fingerprints on cardboard and all other paper products, wood, fabrics, and other materials. Chem Print solution is marketed commercially in an aerosol-type container for ready use. In the application of this reagent, the suggested method is to spray all sides of the suspected material until reasonably wet by holding the dispenser approximately 8 inches (20 centimeters) from the evidence surface. Thereafter, the treated material should be permitted to air dry. Following the drying process, the treated document or other material should be subjected to heat of approximately 200°F (94°C) at which time the latent prints will develop readily. The heat source should not be open flames. It should not be applied directly to the surfaces processed. If it appears desirable, questionable areas may be retreated to obtain additional contrast. The latents may continue to develop for several hours after the above-mentioned processing procedure.

When time is not of the essence, the suspected material may be sprayed as suggested above. The treated material should be permitted to air dry for twenty-four hours at 75 to 110°F (24 to 43°C). In this instance, the latent images, if present, will appear within a few hours. For the best results, twelve hours should be allowed for the full reaction of Chem Print on latents that may be three to six months old; fresher prints will become visible more quickly. All latents developed by the above processes will remain stable for three to six months. It is recommended that a photograph be taken of the developed latent images as soon as possible. Chem Print spray should be used in a ventilated area and not inhaled.

Latent fingerprint classification

The method employed in the classification of single fingerprints will not be presented here. However, a few general remarks about this specialized system will be of assistance to the police science student in understanding this phase of fingerprint identification. The fundamental difference between an arrest/identification, classification system and a latent fingerprint classification system is that there are ten fingerprints with which to work in the former and only one in the latter. In other words, latent fingerprint classification uses only a *single finger* in its system of classification. The formula for the single fingerprint classification is not related to the ten finger formula. The primary, secondary, and subsecondary classification, etc., of the Henry System cannot be used to classify latent prints since the Henry System is based upon ten fingers; all ten fingers are considered as a unit in arriving at the classification. The primary object of a single fingerprint classification system is to file criminal fingerprints in such a manner that accidental or latent fingerprints, such as those found at the scene of a crime, may be searched against the file in an effort to identify them.

One of the well-known systems of classifying single fingerprints is the Battley System used extensively in Great Britain. This system was devised by former Chief Inspector Harry Battley of New Scotland Yard, London, England. The fundamental principles of the Battley System, with modifications and extensions, have been utilized by many of the larger identification bureaus in this country. The Battley System classifies each finger according to type of pattern, ridge count or ridge tracing, type of core, and location of the delta. This system is gradually falling into disuse in the United States because it is cumbersome and entails considerable maintenance and searching. Other types of single fingerprint classification systems have been devised and are now used in this country. Experimental research projects are continuing in high-speed computer analyzers that will have the capability of analyzing a single fingerprint in fractions of a second. High-speed computer analyzers are expected to identify fingerprint ridge characteristics (ridge endings, bifurcations, islands, and others) and to convert such data into digital information.

The purpose of a single fingerprint file is to identify a suspect from one latent finger-print or fragments of a print. Many police agencies maintain single fingerprint files of local suspects who have been involved in such felonious crimes as burglaries, robberies, auto thefts, and sex crimes, as an aid in crime solving. After a latent fingerprint is obtained at a crime scene, the fingerprint expert classifies the print according to the latent fingerprint classification system that is used in that particular identification unit. When the classification is completed, the expert searches the latent fingerprint base file for an identification. If the print is not identified it is added to the file of unidentified prints. Fingerprints from any suspects in the case in question would be checked against the latent prints found at the scene.

The single fingerprint file of the FBI was installed in February of 1933. This single fingerprint file is confined to certain classes of criminals: bank robbers, bank burglars, kidnapers, extortionists, gangsters, and other selected criminals. After the inauguration of this single fingerprint file it became possible for the FBI to receive latent fingerprints obtained at the scene of one of the above enumerated crimes or other major felonies and make a tentative identification. After classifying, searching, and filing unidentified latent prints found at the scene of major felonies, it is possible to connect certain criminals with particular crimes.

Elimination prints

When police officers search for latent prints at the scene of a crime, they may find several. Some of the latents may belong to persons who had a legitimate reason for being (at one time or another) at the scene of the crime. Before searching these latents against the latent fingerprint file, the officer will fingerprint those persons who had a lawful reason for being at the crime scene and then will compare the latent prints against these inked prints. The inked prints that are taken for this purpose are called elimination prints.

Fingerprint Kit

Some of the items that a minimum portable field fingerprint kit might contain include

Flashlight
Tongs or tweezers
Thin cloth gloves
Large cellophane envelopes and polyethylene bags
Evidence stickers
Notebook and pencil
Roll of transparent lifting tape 1½ or 2 inches (4 or 5 centimeters) in width
Transparent hinged lifters, assorted sizes
Black and white opaque rubber lifters
Scissors and magnifying glass
Small ruler and measuring tape
Fingerprint powders (black, gray, dragon's blood, bronze, and various other colors)
Fingerprint brushes, several
Latent transfer cards, 8 by 8 inch (20 by 20-centimeter) standard fingerprint cards

8- by 8-inch (20 by 20-centimeter) plain white cards for taking palm prints
Ink pad, small tube of fingerprint ink, and 2- or 3-inch (5- or 7.5-centimeter) rubber roller
Fingerprint card holder
Cleaning fluid and paper towels or cheesecloth
Fingerprint camera and film

Automated Fingerprint Scanner

The feasibility of using computerized optical scanning equipment to rapidly identify and record fingerprint characteristics from inked fingerprint cards has been demonstrated.[16] The FBI is well on its way toward its goal of using computer technology to speed up the entire identification process. As the operations of the FBI Identification Division become fully automated, the identification services provided will add immeasurably to the efficiency of criminal justice agencies throughout the United States.

---

[16]*FBI Law Enforcement Bulletin,* July 1977, p. 6.

SUMMARY

Criminal identification by means of fingerprints is considered to be the greatest contribution to law enforcement. Of all the methods of identification, fingerprinting alone has proved to be infallible. Fingerprint identification makes it possible for police, probation departments, parole boards, courts, and other authorized agencies to determine whether or not the person fingerprinted has any prior arrests, convictions, or is wanted by a police agency.

The use of fingerprints for identification is based upon distinctive ridge outlines which appear on the bulbs inside the end joints of the fingers and thumbs. These ridges have definite contours and appear in several general pattern types, each with general and specific variations of the pattern. The Henry system and the one devised by Juan Vucetich, an Argentinian police official, form the basis of all modern ten finger identification.

Fingerprints found at a crime scene may be visible, plastic, or latent. Visible prints are those left on such places as light-colored materials or surfaces from soiled hands. Plastic fingerprints are those left in soap, wax, grease, etc. Latent (invisible) prints require development by fingerprint powders, chemical sprays, or solutions. Investigators are constantly on the alert for any physical evidence which might assist them in the solution of a crime. If latent fingerprints are found, notes should be made of the location. The print(s) should be processed with chemicals or fingerprint powder designed to give maximum contrast. Scaled photographs should be taken of the developed print, and the print(s) should be lifted with a transparent pressure-sensitive tape or rubber lifter. Footprints and palm prints can be substituted for fingerprints as identification media.

REVIEW QUESTIONS

1. In addition to fingerprints what other parts of the body may also serve as a means of identification?
2. What is dactylography?
3. Who devised the first scientific method of classifying fingerprint patterns?
4. What contribution did Sir Edward Richard Henry make to the science of fingerprinting?
5. Where is the largest collection of fingerprints in the world maintained?
6. Fingerprints serve many useful purposes. Name six.
7. Fingerprint patterns are divided into three large groups of patterns and divided further into subgroups. Name the three main groups and their subdivisions.
8. In obtaining the primary classification, what is the only type of fingerprint pattern that is considered?
9. What is the formula for obtaining the primary in a set of ten fingerprints?
10. One type of fingerprint impression found at a crime scene is called a "latent impression." What are the other two types of chance impressions that are sometimes found?
11. What is the approximate percent of water contained in secretion from sweat pores on the fingertips?
12. What is the sole purpose of developing latent fingerprints?
13. What is the highest primary classification a set of fingerprints can have? What is the lowest?
14. In the search and detection of latent fingerprints many different types of powders and chemicals are used. What are two basic types of powders that are adequate in most instances?
15. How many points of identification are generally required in presenting a fingerprint comparison to a court?

1

2

3

Figure 6-20.

16. Name four chemical methods of developing latent fingerprints.
17. What is meant by "elimination prints"?
18. How many deltas does a loop pattern have? How many does a whorl pattern have?
19. What percent of all fingerprint patterns are loop patterns?
20. How many fingerprints are necessary for a complete fingerprint classification?

--- **WORK EXERCISE** ---

Each separate set of ten fingerprints in Figure 6-20 represents the prints of the right and left hand of an individual. You are to obtain the *primary classification* for each set.

In the following work exercise, you are given the primary classification. In addition, the box-like diagrams below each contain ten empty spaces. The five spaces on the top are for the right hand, representing the right thumb, right index, right middle, right ring and the right little fingers; the five spaces on the bottom represent the corresponding fingers of the left hand. On a separate sheet of paper, draw duplicates of these diagrams and fill in the proper space with the letter "W" (representing a whorl pattern) in accordance with the primary classification formula set out in this chapter.

Example: $\frac{18}{11}$

Rt.T	Rt.I W	Rt.M W	Rt.R	Rt.L
Lt.T	Lt.I W	Lt.M	Lt.R	Lt.L W

1. $\frac{22}{15}$

2. $\frac{29}{28}$

3. $\frac{16}{18}$

4. $\frac{20}{13}$

5. $\frac{25}{17}$

Surveillance and Stakeouts

CHAPTER
7

Surveillance

"Surveillance" is a French word meaning (to) "watch over." In police work, surveillance can be described as a discreet observation of a person, group, place, or vehicle. Surveillance activity is a valuable investigative tool, one that depends upon alertness, ingenuity, and experience of officers. Officers engaged in this type of assignment must be patient, resourceful, versatile, alert, and keenly observant. They must also possess a good memory for faces, names, streets, and other related data. Since notes cannot be made at all times, surveillant officers must recollect events, names, and other information correctly for their report. A surveillance log (running account of all observable activities) is a necessary part of this investigative activity. All observable activities of the subject should be in this log. It should include dates, times of arrival and departure, physical descriptions, types of activities noticed, dress, vehicles, license numbers, whether photographs were taken, and other observations of possible value. Prior to change of shifts, a careful review of this log together with a briefing of relief officers permits a smooth continuity of operation.

In surveillance, unlike most other investigative techniques, the initiative is held by the subject. Without advance knowledge of the subject's plans, officers must be governed by the subject's movements. In other words, the officers react rather than act. The initiative can be seized only by determining in advance the subject's plans. This knowledge might be ascertained through the use of a reliable informant. A surveillance that discloses the activities and associates of a subject quite often means very little unless such activity and relationships are understood. An informant in some instances can be of value in interpreting surveillance information for the police. Hard and fast rules cannot be set forth for the procedures to be used in surveillance work.

Inasmuch as surveillances are expensive in personnel and equipment, each case should be individually considered. Surveillance is not an end in itself, it is simply another method of obtaining information and evidence. It differs from undercover work in that when engaged in undercover work the investigator uses an assumed identity to make direct contact with the subject. In surveillance work, officers avoid direct contact with a subject.

Purpose of surveillances

The purposes or objectives of surveillances are many. In some cases, a great deal of information is sought; in others, perhaps only minor details are desired in order to clarify some phase of the investigation. The attempt to discover a crime may take one or several weeks; in some instances, only a few days. Officers should always keep the purpose of the surveillance in mind in order that the objectives of the particular case may be met. Some of the reasons a surveillance is undertaken are

To detect and prevent crime.
To locate a wanted fugitive by observing known hangouts and associates.
To learn contacts and movements of a particular suspect or group.
To learn the identity of confederates.
To secure probable cause for issuance of a search warrant.

To determine activities and movements of suspected individuals.
To recover stolen property.
To intercept crime before its commission.
To develop intelligence information to justify or confirm suspicion.
To identify people and their affiliation with a person under investigation.
To obtain information for use in interrogation.

Preparation for surveillance

The success of any surveillance operation depends upon coverture. Preparation for such undertaking should be as thorough as time will permit. Consideration of personnel (active and relief), together with the equipment needed, must be decided in advance. The use of code words, methods of summoning aid, methods of entrance and exit from the surveillance location, and dress should also be discussed. Prior to beginning a surveillance, each participating officer should become familiar with all available facts of the case and the purpose of the surveillance. She or he must also understand the assignment and have a knowledge of the planned communication methods. Although dependable and rapid communication for surveillance teams is essential, a system of prearranged hand signals is often valuable in situations where a radio cannot be used or is inoperable.

It is important that the officers involved know the subject's full name, nicknames, and aliases; residence and business addresses and telephone numbers; and complete physical description including age, height, weight, hair, eyes, complexion, build, and posture. Information regarding walking habits, mannerisms and peculiarities, types of clothing, color preferences, jewelry, smoking habits, haunts, and daily routine are also important. The identities and descriptions of friends, associates, doctors, dentists, as well as their business and telephone numbers, can be of assistance. In addition, dining and recreation preferences are activities that, if known, can help in reestablishing the location of a suspect should the officers lose the suspect during the surveillance.

Another important item to consider is the identity of the types of vehicles the subject drives or has access to. Information such as the following should be known: license number, make, model, color, individual characteristics, type of seat covers, dents, and accessories. The subject's driving habits—slow, fast, reckless, changing lanes frequently, route of travel, and parking preferences—are also pertinent. Familiarization with street names, locations, traffic signals, one-way streets, types of neighborhood, inhabitants, and transportation facilities is desirable. Prepared fictitious credentials and plausible stories often prove to be of value in protecting the secrecy of a surveillance.

Preparation for surveillance entails the use of equipment; the type needed varies with each case. Among the items to be considered in surveillance operation are

Automobiles (inconspicuous type) with three-way communication of car to car and car to station
Unregistered license plates
Extra supply of gasoline
Binoculars or spotting scope
Camera with telephoto lens and a miniature camera
Communication equipment including miniature transmitters and receivers
Tape recorder (electric or battery operated)
Luggage, dummy packages, uniforms
Vehicles such as panel trucks, taxis, and other vehicles of a commercial nature
Fictitious credentials
Any other specialized equipment

It is imperative that a complete inventory of all equipment used on a surveillance be made prior to and at the time the surveillance is ended. No scrap of paper or other material should be discarded or left behind that could reflect in any way on the nature of the investigative operation.

Types of surveillance coverage

In the technique of surveillance operations, there are two general types of coverage: (1) *fixed* (from a "plant") and (2) *moving* (following a subject on foot or in an automobile).

Fixed Surveillance In police terminology a fixed or stationary surveillance is known as a *plant*. A plant may be established to initiate a *tail* of a subject or vehicle. A "tail" or "tailing" is the close observation of any individual or vehicle in movement from place to place. "Tailing" has the same connotation as "shadowing." In those instances where the purpose of a fixed plant is such that only *temporary* coverage is necessary, an outside plant is usually sufficient. This temporary coverage may be conducted from an unmarked police car, truck, or other camouflaged vehicle, or the surveillance can be carried on by standing in an inconspicuous place in the area. Moving to a different vantage point or substituting personnel can be helpful in keeping the surveillance inconspicuous. A fixed surveillance may sometimes require a ruse. Surveillance officers may assume such temporary occupational roles as gardener, plumber, or painter as a means of carrying out a fixed surveillance in a particular area. Other pretenses are limited only by the imagination of the officers.

Where advance information is received regarding a contemplated robbery, burglary, theft, or other crime, a fixed surveillance or *stakeout* is established in order to apprehend the suspect involved. In such instances the same precautionary measures applicable to any surveillance should be utilized, viz., concealment, adequate observation, sufficient personnel, dress, equipment, and communication arrangements. In cases of robberies, burglaries, and other felonies, suspects may try to shoot their way out of a prearranged police trap. In these instances, a basic axiom all officers should keep in mind is that the protection of life always comes before the protection of property.

In those situations involving a *lengthy surveillance*, considerably more planning is necessitated. Naturally the first requirement of any fixed surveillance is observation—having good visibility· of the place or area under investigation. The purpose of the surveillance and the physical setup of the premises to be observed will determine the number of personnel needed to maintain the operation. Establishing a fixed location involves reconnaissance and strategy. This means that before a fixed surveillance is put into operation at one or more points, a survey is conducted of the particular area involved. This survey takes into account such considerations as the identity of the residents located in that zone, their businesses, occupations or employment, business and social affiliations, and reliability and trustworthiness. Information of this kind can be obtained from various sources such as file checks, directories, retail credit bureaus, employment records, contacts with social clubs, church and school officials, and many other sources that are known to the policing agency. The results of such a survey may disclose the identity of a resident living close to the subject. This resident will thereafter be contacted and his or her cooperation solicited. In such instances, it is not desirable or necessary to reveal all the facts of a case to secure the cooperation of persons contacted. However, when any person is taken into police confidence, the confidential nature of the activity should be emphasized.

In some instances, depending upon the objectives and length of the surveillance, a room or apartment may be rented, thus obviating the necessity of taking anyone into police confidence. If appropriate space for an indoor plant is available, it should be rented under an assumed identity or possibly a fictitious firm name depending upon the type of premises involved and the location of the surveillance. However, should the area be a residential one, the procedure set out must be initiated in order to find a reliable and cooperative individual.

Moving Surveillance Following a subject on foot may involve close or loose surveillance. A close tail is necessary where there is a heavy flow of pedestrian traffic or where it is imperative that a subject's presence be known at all times. In a loose foot surveillance the subject is followed in such a way that the surveillance may be discontinued to avoid detection by the subject. A loose surveillance can be picked up at another time and place depending upon the surveillance pattern developed.

In a foot surveillance, the number of officers needed may vary depending upon the amount of pedestrian traffic or the locale of the surveillance—downtown, residential, or rural. Surveillance operations can be conducted by two officers working as a team. In such instances, concealment is difficult for any length of time. Foot surveillances are best accomplished with a three- or four-person operating unit. When three officers are used on a foot surveillance as noted in Figure 7-1, one officer, "A" follows the subject closely (depending upon the existing conditions); a second officer, "B," follows behind "A" either to "A's" inside or outside and at varying distances in order to keep "A" within sight at all times; the third officer, "C,"participates in the observation from across the street. In accordance with prearrangements made among the three-man surveillance team, "A" can exchange positions with "B" or "C"; or "C" with "A" in order to cover the movements of the subject, thereby making it difficult to observe any

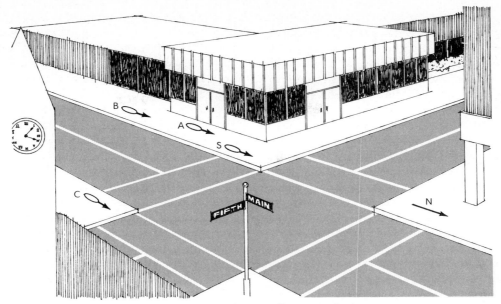

Figure 7-1. ABC surveillance method.

one of the surveillance team for any appreciable length of time. In this type of surveillance procedure, "B," instead of following "A" on foot, may follow in an unmarked automobile ready to assist both "A" and "C" should the suspect board a taxi or other commercial vehicle.

Variations of the above three-person pattern of operations may place "A" behind the suspect, "B" *preceding* the suspect, and "C" observing from a position across the street. The three-person surveillance operation is often referred to as the *ABC method*. However, it is most advantageous to have a fourth person in a mobile unit for transportation emergencies that might arise. Should the identities of any of the surveillance team be in jeopardy, that individual member can be replaced in order to avoid exposure of the surveillance. In such instances, depending on the direction in which the suspect is proceeding, it is often possible to anticipate the destination, based on established patterns of behavior. Whenever a suspect under surveillance makes a contact with another person who appears to have significance, every effort should be made to identify this contact and photograph the meeting if possible. A complete description of the contacted person should be made.

A surveillance will often develop patterns of activity for the subject—things done, places stopped, places frequented, times, routes, etc. A knowledge of these patterns can be used in anticipating his movements in order to set up advance checkpoints and fixed plants where needed.

Automobile surveillance

As in a foot surveillance, the officers should be as close as they can without being conspicuous. The cars used should be of a nondescript type with unregistered plates. Prior to commencing the surveillance, each car should be serviced and its communication equipment checked out. Generally a mobile surveillance operation requires two or more vehicles. Extra automobiles permit one of the units to drop out of an operation should it become necessary to avoid detection. Some of the cars used should contain a foot officer who can be dropped off at any given point to observe the suspect or to identify any person who is a contact of the suspect.

In automobile surveillance, the "perimeter box" surveillance has been used by many departments in both downtown and residential areas. In one variation, four cars are used, with at least two of them carrying an extra foot officer. In this procedure, one car stays ahead of the subject's car, one car follows it, and the other two units maintain position on parallel streets. Thus it is possible to cover any turns made by the suspect and to maintain coverage should the subject cross an intersection when the traffic light is amber or red. (See Figure 7-2.)

Moving surveillances can also be conducted with two or three units. In a procedure with three cars, two cars follow the subject's car changing their distance and positions frequently as existing conditions dictate; the third car travels ahead of the subject and maintains contact and observation by use of radio communication and rearview mirror. At least two of the surveillance cars should have a foot officer who can be dropped off wherever needed to maintain the surveillance and identify the subject's contacts if desirable.

In an automobile surveillance with only two units available, both cars can follow the suspect's car at varying distances and positions or one can be positioned ahead of the suspect's car and endeavor to keep the subject under surveillance from there with the use of radio communication and rearview mirror. With only two cars available, the risks of detection are greatly increased.

Figure 7-2. "Perimeter box" method of surveillance. The sketch shows the positions of police cars 1, 2, 3, and 4 in relation to subject's car S. This method permits coverage of all turning movements that the subject could make.

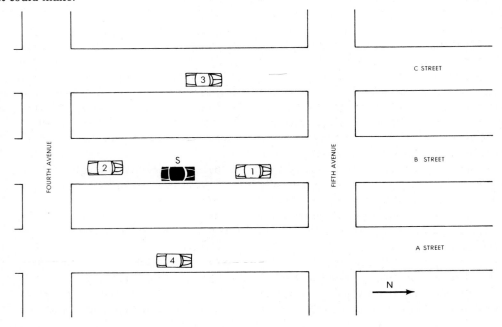

Additional officers in both police units permit necessary coverage of the subject as well as availability to check on contacts made. In any event, the type of subject, availability of officers and cars, as well as the importance of the case itself should dictate the operational plan needed.

Suggestions for surveillance operations

Constant vigilance must be maintained inasmuch as changes may occur suddenly. Inattention or laxity even for brief moments can result in losing the suspect or following the wrong person or automobile. Be very observant of any actions on the part of the suspect which may indicate communication with a confederate. On these assignments be sure you are not being followed. Suspects have been known to use a "convoy" (associate) to tag along behind them, follow from a position across the street, or follow in another car to detect a surveillance of their confederate. In other words, the quarry may initiate a countersurveillance on the police. Of course, the police can do likewise. As a means of determining whether a surveillance is being maintained on their residence and activities, suspects have been known to use an associate or spouse to drive around the area of their residence in an effort to detect a surveillance car.

Prearranged signals among the observing officers preparatory to initiating the surveillance can be very helpful. Signals may be given with a magazine, newspaper, handkerchief, hat, hands, or any other agreed-upon method. In the event of an equipment failure or other mechanical difficulty, signals can be used to implement existing devices. It is a good practice to avoid open recognition of surveillant partners.

Suspects quite often try to detect a surveillance. They have used many methods to uncover a tail. An officer, by becoming familiar with countermeasures used by subjects, can avoid exposure of surveillance. The following techniques have been used: driving down a deadend street; speeding up or slowing down; doubling back after rounding the corner of a building; making a U-turn in the middle of a street; running a red traffic light; discarding a piece of paper or other object and observing whether anyone attempts to pick up the item; and frequently changing traffic lanes. Other methods that have been used are riding backwards up an escalator, riding an elevator to the top floor of a building or to the second floor and returning, jumping on and off buses or rapid transit railway cars as the vehicle is about to move, and stopping to talk with anyone and observing if that person is subsequently contacted regarding the nature of the conversation. Subjects have been known to use a telephone booth as a stall to size up persons in the immediate area who later might be recognized at a subsequent place. Suspects may drive through an alley, enter a building, and remain just inside the door to view persons entering the lobby in pursuit. The methods used vary with the suspect, gang, criminal activity involved, and the nature of the case itself.

Officers on surveillance should try to blend in with the people and activity in the vicinity. Clothing should be appropriate to the locale. A surveillant officer in order to allay suspicion might buy a newspaper, talk with someone, carry a bag of groceries, window shop, or do anything that the "natives" in that area do. It is advisable to try and create the impression of transacting business in a particular area. Methods of concealing a surveillance operation are limited only by the ingenuity of the surveillance officers themselves.

In business areas, an officer might enter a store and make a pretense at purchasing some item; enter an establishment and make an appropriate inquiry; use the guise of a vendor or taxicab driver; walk a dog or ride a bike; or employ other pretense normal to the particular environment.

In the event that a subject makes a telephone call, sends a telegram, or purchases a ticket on a common carrier, an officer should try to stay as close as possible to the subject in order to observe or overhear the transaction. Should this proximity not be advisable, a request for a ticket to the "same" destination might give you the desired answer. Should the subject enter a hotel, the cooperation of the manager or security officer or other employee (if considered reliable) can be of considerable assistance in checking the subject's phone calls, types of correspondence, possible contacts, trash, comings and goings, and other activities of possible value.

When suspects accost surveillant officers, the officers should never conclude that they have been uncovered. The fear of being "made" (identified as an officer) is often one of the biggest mistakes an inexperienced officer makes in surveillance work. The fact that a suspect looks directly at you or in your direction does not mean that he or she has uncovered your identity. Experience has shown that a suspect looks inquiringly at many people and quite often suspects innocent people of following him or her. A suspect in trying to identify a "tail" may walk up to anyone, including the surveillant officer, and ask directions, request a match, ask for the correct time, etc. In surveillance operations it is always well to have a plausible story ready for such a confrontation. Should a suspect under surveillance accuse the officer of following him or her, the officer should act surprised, answer the question with a question, claim to know the suspect, be insulted or outraged, or plead mistaken identity. In any event the officer should emphatically deny following the suspect. Of course this surveillant officer should drop out of the surveillance and be replaced by another officer.

If the surveillance is lost, it may often be reestablished by a review of the surveillance log and study of patterns developed in the case. These surveillance patterns disclose the suspect's habits, routine, places frequented, relatives, friends, employment, likes, and other activities. By noting the time of day and spot-checking the likely places suspects visit, it is often possible to locate their whereabouts. Sometimes the suspect's location is ascertained by contacting certain favorite places and asking for the subject by name. Failure to locate a subject's whereabouts through the above checks may necessitate posting surveillants at locations where the suspect can be expected to appear. In the event the suspect jumps into a taxicab and surveillance is momentarily lost, the cab number should be noted as well as the time and location of the cab taken by the suspect. Thereafter, a contact with the taxicab dispatcher or a check of trip sheets of the particular driver can reveal the subject's destination or location where alighted.

Act naturally at all times during a surveillance assignment. Try to adapt to local conditions and customs; stop and talk to somebody; appear to be waiting for a bus; examine your watch frequently to create the impression you are waiting for someone. If in a store, examine merchandise; if in a restaurant, purchase food or a soft drink, always paying when served so that you can be ready to leave at a moment's notice.

Avoid disclosing identity or activity by "Hawkshaw" leering, peeking from behind a pole, or out of a doorway. In addition, standing on an automobile fender, bumper, or other object or getting out of position to view a particular location in an effort to check a suspect's activities are not desirable. Do not dash for a taxi when the suspect does. Park properly; do not park in a no parking zone. Change positions behind the suspect, varying your distance. A pretense of looking at window displays is a normal behavior and useful in observing a suspect. Have a supply of small change for phone calls, tips, and other expenses. Wear ordinary clothing; change license plates on your automobile;

and never assume the suspect is aware of being followed.

Stakeouts

A stakeout is a form of surveillance. It is an investigative technique just as are interviews, crime scene searches, collection of evidence, and other police methods. A stakeout is a procedure of waiting and watching a person, place, vehicle, or object for a particular purpose. A stakeout is considered a hazardous assignment requiring constant vigilance since an officer may, in some instances, have to open fire at an armed suspect in self-defense, defense of others, or to prevent a felon's escape. An officer engaged in this type of assignment must contemplate every likely situation and be psychologically ready for immediate action.

Stakeouts are usually limited in duration. For example, where there is a series of crimes that appear to be the work of one person and where certain neighborhood types of businesses are the favorite victims, a temporary stakeout can result in the apprehension of the person responsible and thus close out the investigation. Stakeouts may be initiated merely to identify a suspicious individual or a vehicle in areas of high crime frequency. A watch may be instituted because of a contemplated robbery, burglary, narcotic operation, or other criminal activity reported to police by an identified or unidentified complainant. In some instances the identity of the suspect is known; in others, the identity of the suspect is not known until he or she appears on the crime scene or commits an overt act.

Stakeouts, although planned by a staff officer, are conducted by either plainclothes or uniformed officers. Some departments have identification vests or other regalia with distinctive police markings which readily identify plainclothes officers as police in any confrontation situation. The success of stakeouts depends upon how well the participating officers have prepared for and understand their assignment. It is generally not necessary for the detective division to handle stakeouts unless there is a shortage of patrol personnel. If a watch will not be depleted of its personnel, uniformed patrol officers may be assigned. The criteria in stakeouts should be that once in the position of surveillance, the officer should be able to establish her or his identity without having to say, "I am a police officer." Plainclothes officers must identify themselves. They should fasten their badges on the outside of their jackets. An identification card is not sufficient.

Reasons for stakeouts

To observe a payoff in an extortion case

To identify contacts and movements of suspects in narcotics cases

To detect a bookmaking operation

To identify prostitutes, pimps, and procurers in prostitution activities

To determine the associates and activities of burglary suspects

To detect and apprehend criminal suspects in those instances where advance information is received concerning robbery, burglary, larceny, or other criminal violations

To identify suspected receivers of stolen property

To detect and apprehend suspects in an area where "mugging" (aggravated assault), molesting, purse snatching, or a confidence operation has been occurring

To identify suspects frequenting pawnshops where questionable transactions have been reported

To identify contacts or meetings of known or suspected hoodlums

To observe operations of garages, or auto repair or auto paint shops suspected of automobile theft ring operations

To gather intelligence about the activities of criminal suspects

To obtain background information preparatory to an interrogation procedure

To provide a basis for a search warrant

Preparation for stakeouts

Each participating stakeout officer must understand the part he or she is to play. Officers must dress for the location, eat in advance, and attend to other duties of a personal nature prior to arrival on such assignment. The officers must have a good description of the suspect, her or his automobile, activities, method of operation, and all other available information. In addition, each officer should be familiar with any special equipment or firearms that may be required. Other preparatory considerations should include a knowledge of the physical characteristics of the stakeout site, places of concealment, lighting, visibility, entrances, and exits. Dress, inconspicuous automobiles, and communication arrangements are necessities.

In a stakeout of a store or market, for example, officers should carefully look over the premises to determine the accessibility of rear exit, visibility within the store, and appropriate vantage points. The employees in a store should understand the elements of robbery and not confuse a shoplifter with a robbery suspect. Where employees are taken into confidence they should be advised that some holdup men call the prospective scene of a robbery, burglary, or other crime and ask to speak with an officer. The caller uses this means to ascertain if police are staking out the premises. Therefore it is advisable to give the employee your name, obtain theirs, and explain the telephone procedure. On burglary stakeouts it is suggested that ring signals and call-back procedures be used. Should code words or signs be agreed upon at a stakeout location, such activity should be simple and understood by all parties.

In the above type of stakeout, officers should assure people working in a store that the subject will not be fired upon if gunfire would be dangerous to others. Also, advise employees to act normally and go about their business within the store as though they were unaware of any expected occurrence. In the event a robbery actually occurs, an officer should summon aid by radio to supporting units. One officer should, if possible, exit from the rear of the store to an outside vantage point, being particularly alert for any possible lookouts or getaway vehicles. The inside officer, after giving the other officer an opportunity to leave the store, should chamber a round loudly in the shotgun, use available cover, and make a verbal arrest. *Caution:* The improper use of a weapon may lead to serious consequences. It may not only injure or kill any suspect but may result in injury to an innocent person or unnecessary property damage. If a weapon is to be used at all, it must be done with the intention of taking a life in order to protect others. The weapon must be aimed at the suspects, not over their heads.

When the arrest is consummated, the suspects must be handcuffed and searched for dangerous weapons, advised of their rights, and taken to the station. Thereafter, an in-custody teletype should be prepared and sent with the approval of the watch commander. Record checks should be made at headquarters. Teletype inquiries should likewise be made to each suspect's city of residence, the county sheriff's office, state identification bureau, and the National Crime Information Center (NCIC), FBI headquarters, for any wants that may be outstanding for the suspects.

If a suspect is shot in a stakeout operation, an officer should ride in the ambulance to the hospital since the suspect is a police prisoner. It is possible that the suspect, when advised of rights, may wish to make a voluntary statement. Should an officer or civilian be shot in a stakeout operation, another officer should ride in the ambulance to the hospital and obtain a dying declaration (statement made in expectation of death). No matter how badly injured persons appear, they sometimes rally about thirty seconds before they die and make a statement that will lead to a successful prosecution.

After any apprehension is made in connection with a stakeout assignment, it is advisable to check for any accomplice who may be lurking in the vicinity as a lookout or driver of a getaway automobile parked nearby. Such persons should be approached cautiously and taken into custody whenever possible. A search of the immediate vicinity for the car used by the apprehended suspect should likewise be conducted. It is also advisable to continue the stakeout of a suspect's room after an arrest since a confederate may appear and another good arrest follow. A search should be made for physical evidence in accordance with legal provisions. Latent fingerprints obtained from a stolen car found abandoned near the scene of a holdup may be identified with those of the suspect.

On a stakeout for a specific suspect, do not rule out the possibility of other suspects appearing on the scene who may differ in race, age, size, weight, and other physical characteristics from that of the subject. In one particular case, the police were plagued by a series of over thirty-five armed robberies of markets, motels, cleaning establishments, and other businesses. The armed robberies were considered to be the work of one man who was variously named "The Cleaner Bandit," "The Motel Bandit," and "The Black-Gloved Bandit." After reviewing the pattern of this elusive suspect's operations, stakeouts were put into operation at twenty selected motels for several nights during the period the suspect was known to operate. At approximately 6:40 P.M., on a Sunday night, the "Black-Gloved Bandit" entered one of the staked motels. In a confrontation with police, the suspect fired one shot at the officers from his .357 magnum revolver before being felled by the stakeout officer's bullets. Before dying, this suspect admitted the commission of numerous robberies and the burglary of a gun shop from which he had obtained the magnum revolver taken from him.

Of particular interest in the above motel stakeout operation was the fact that three robbery suspects, none of whom was identical to the suspect, were apprehended by surveillant officers. Had not the stakeout officers been continually observant of all people entering the motels under surveillance during this period, the three robbers would probably have gone unnoticed, which would have resulted in a most embarrassing situation for the assigned officers.

Avoid stakeout positions that confine officers in such small areas that they cannot draw weapons or are cramped to such an extent that they are unable to pursue the subject. In one particular stakeout, a bandit fired a shotgun twice at stakeout officers whose positions were discovered. The shotgun blasts fortunately went between the officers. In that instance, the cramped position of the stakeout officers delayed their physical efforts to return the bandit's fire. However, the suspect was killed by the officers before he was able to fire a third shot.

Every likely approach by a suspect should be contemplated. For example, in one robbery stakeout operation two uniformed officers in an unmarked police car were watching a drive-in restaurant in an attempt to intercept a robbery suspect. While the officers were conducting this vigil, two suspects quietly walked up behind the police unit and attempted to ambush the two officers, firing a shotgun and carbine rifle at them. One of the officers was hit by shotgun pellets. Both officers succeeded in jumping from the police vehicle and returned the fire. In the shooting exchange, the officers managed to kill one of the suspects. Prior to being fatally wounded, one of the suspects fired several shots from his war surplus carbine into the police car before the rifle jammed. The second suspect escaped, but was later apprehended when he sought medical help at a hospital for wounds he received in the exchange of gunfire at the stakeout scene.

Nothing should be taken for granted by stakeout or surveillance officers. In a case involving an extortion payoff in a large Eastern city, the payoff spot was designated as a window receptacle on the first floor of a large office building in a busy downtown area. The package containing the extortion money was placed in this container as per instructions. The area was placed under intensive surveillance. Shortly after the placing of the money into the above-mentioned box, the surveillance officers were amazed at the sight of the payoff package being pulled up the side of the office building on a piece of thin string. The package was seen to disappear into one of the windows several floors above street level. An intense investigation in the area of this building resulted in the location of a known gambler and con artist whom one of the alert officers recognized mingling with the crowd. This suspect was noted to be carrying a shopping bag containing a variety of grocery items. However, beneath these articles the officers discovered the payoff package.

As a further example of not taking things for granted, an extortionist in another case directed the victim to place a package containing $10,000 at the base of a certain state highway signpost on a certain date and time. Coverage of the particular spot was initiated. As the surveillance officers maintained their watch, a late-model car containing a young man and woman was observed apparently stalled near the payoff location. The male was noted to be pushing the car. The female was at the wheel. It was an obvious effort to get the motor to start. The stakeout officers were amused at the apparent predicament of this young couple. However, the officers failed to note the license number of this car. In that instance no one attempted to pick up the extortion package. Several days later, at a newly designated payoff spot, a young man was apprehended as he attempted to retrieve the money package. During the subsequent interview with the arrested extortionist, that individual volunteered the information that he simulated car trouble on a previous attempt to obtain the extortion package but became suspicious of a possible police trap and decided against going through with the recovery of the money. He stated that he simulated car trouble as a means of trying to determine whether any police were in the immediate area. Had the officers checked on the license number of the "stalled car" they would have undoubtedly identified their man since this suspect had a criminal record. Handwriting examination would have cinched their case.

Electronic Surveillance

Electronic devices capable of eavesdropping on anyone in most any given situation are now available. They are to be distinguished from wiretapping, which is confined to the interception of telegraphic and telephonic communications. The general rule prohibiting unauthorized electronic surveillance is that eavesdropping and wiretapping are permitted only with probable cause and court authority.

In December 1967, the United States Supreme Court in the case of *Katz v. United States*[1] ruled that the Constitution protects private telephone conversations, even though made from a public telephone booth, from unauthorized government wiretapping. The Supreme Court in the Katz case abandoned its "trespass" doctrine, the view that privacy is not violated unless there is a physical trespass. The Court took the posi-

---

[1]*Katz v. United States,* 389 U.S. 347 (1967).

tion that the Fourth Amendment protection against unreasonable search and seizure pertains to people and not just places. In other words, as Justice Potter Stewart put it, "What a person knowingly exposes to the public, even in his own home or office, is not a subject of the Fourth Amendment protection. . . . But what he seeks to preserve as private, even in an area accessible to the public, may be constitutionally protected. . . . Wherever a man may be, he is entitled to know that he will remain free from unreasonable search and seizure. . . ." Justice Stewart significantly asserted that a judicial order could have accommodated the "legitimate needs of law enforcement" by authorizing the careful, limited use of electronic surveillance. The government could have eavesdropped on Katz, according to Stewart, if it had told a magistrate why the eavesdropping was necessary and outlined a limited area of surveillance. Because it did not, Stewart said the government's activities "violate the privacy upon which he [Katz] justifiably relied while using the telephone booth."[2]

The Katz decision involved a Los Angeles racetrack handicapper, Charles Katz, who phoned betting information to Miami and Boston (transmitting bets in interstate commerce in violation of U.S.C., title 18, sec. 1084) from two public phone booths located on Sunset Boulevard in Los Angeles. Unknown to Katz, FBI agents had taped a recorder and microphones to the top of the booths. These instruments recorded several of the conversations Katz made in interstate commerce.

In June of 1968, the Congress of the United States enacted legislation[3] outlawing wiretapping and all electronic eavesdropping. However, a provision for closely supervised, court-approved electronic eaves-

dropping by federal investigative officers to combat certain serious criminal activity (primarily organized crime) was included. This provision permits both wiretapping and electronic eavesdropping by federal agents under strict federal court supervision. The Crime Control Act of 1968 provides that federal law-enforcement officers may tap wires when authorized to do so by a federal judge in certain types of serious criminal cases. The application to the judge must justify the procedure fully, including a showing of "probable cause" to indicate that the serious offense is being committed and that messages regarding it will be obtained through the tap. In addition, it must be shown that "normal investigative procedures have been tried" and are too dangerous or unlikely to succeed. In emergencies involving national security or organized crime, messages may be intercepted without prior court order, but in those instances application must be made to the judge within forty-eight hours.

The Crime Control Act of 1968 also authorizes state and local officers to tap wires under similar circumstances and conditions, if the state has a statute authorizing such procedures. In the absence of an authorizing statute, it is both a federal and state offense for police officers to participate in wiretapping. In addition, the Crime Control Act deals with eavesdropping other than by wiretapping. Eavesdropping may be authorized by a federal judge upon showing of probable cause, as in the case of wiretapping, or by a state judge if there is an authorizing state statute. Suppression of evidence obtained in violation of the Fourth Amendment can be successfully argued only by those whose rights were violated by the search itself, not by those who are aggrieved solely by the introduction of damaging evidence.

Title III of the Omnibus Crime Control and Safe Streets Act of 1968, which governs the use of electronic surveillance, has had an

---

[2] Ibid.
[3] Omnibus Crime Control and Safe Streets Act of 1968.

impact on law-enforcement agencies. Title III accomplished the following:[4]

1. Prohibited nonconsensual private wiretapping and bugging.

2. Permitted private intercepts with the consent of one party to the conversation if not done to commit a tort or crime and not prohibited by state law.

3. Permitted interceptions by communications common carriers (including firms which conduct major portions of their business by telephone) if necessarily incident to the rendition of services or the protection of rights or property of the communications common carrier.

4. Set up a federal court order system for wiretapping and bugging to obtain evidence of specified offenses.

5. Set similar standards for an optional state court order system for wiretapping and bugging.

6. Prohibited federal nonconsensual law enforcement wiretapping and bugging except under court order.

7. Prohibited state nonconsensual law enforcement wiretapping and bugging unless authorized under a state statute providing a court order system at least as restrictive as the federal system.

8. Permitted federal law enforcement intercepts with the consent of one party to the conversation.

9. Permitted state law enforcement intercepts with the consent of one party to the conversation unless prohibited by state law.

10. Expressly disclaimed any intent to regulate federal wiretapping or bugging in foreign or domestic security cases.

11. Authorized recovery of civil damages for unauthorized wiretapping and bugging.

12. Required annual reports for federal and state court-ordered wiretapping and bugging.

In the interpretation of terminology used in Title III, "electronic surveillance" and "wiretapping" are sometimes used interchangeably. *Wiretapping* generally refers to the interception (and recording) of a communication transmitted over a wire from a telephone, without the consent of any of the participants. *Bugging* generally refers to the interception (and recording) of a communication transmitted orally, without the consent of any of the participants. *Consensual surveillance* refers to the overhearing, and usually recording, of a wire or oral communication with the consent of one of the parties to the conversation. *Electronic surveillance* carried out with the consent of one of the parties to the conversation is not a search for criminal conversations within the meaning of the Fourth Amendment and therefore does not require court authorization. Its basic use is to corroborate conversations, thereby improving the accuracy of evidence for use in court. The Federal Wiretap Act, enacted as Title III of the Omnibus Crime Control and Safe Streets Act of 1968, was an attempt to reach a compromise of all the conflicting views.

TV Surveillance

Closed-circuit TV (CCTV) surveillance is a widely accepted investigative procedure employed by law-enforcement agencies, industrial facilities, stores, banks, correctional institutions, hospitals and other places where this type of coverage is considered desirable. Surveillance cameras placed at vantage points are very effective in those criminal situations where the physical surroundings do not permit concealment of officers (extortion cases, kidnap for ransom, espionage activities, etc.). Video recording equipment can record a suspect's photograph and activities, which in turn can be used in the identification and prosecution processes.

---

[4]Ibid.

Many cities are continually experimenting with closed-circuit TV as a method of patrolling certain sections of a community where crime hazards exist. Several segments of major freeways and expressways in the United States, England, and France are now monitored by closed-circuit TV in order to control the flow of traffic and traffic problems.

Camera equipment designed to provide surveillance coverage is now available to accomodate many problems. For example, sound survey cameras operate upon the contact of sound. The sound mechanism is adjusted to the level of sound desired. Touch survey cameras are designed to operate when an object is touched, permitting a series of photographs to be taken. Button survey cameras are made operative by merely pressing a remote-control button or by a wireless activator.

Closed-circuit TV surveillance enables investigators or security officers to see around corners, behind walls, and scan several different places at a time. It permits the detection of unauthorized persons entering restricted areas, enables operators to check identification passes at remote gate locations on industrial plant premises, and allows one guard to perform the security function of several employees.

Prior to using camera surveillance equipment, a careful check of all the facts and circumstances of the particular case should be made. In theft cases, for example, the following information should be taken into account: time of losses, particular section or area where thefts are occurring, the specific property taken, and the location where the TV monitor is to be positioned. In this regard, the concealment of the camera by constructing dummy facilities that appear normal is suggested in order to allay suspicion. Lighting problems as well as type of film are other considerations. Closed-circuit TV surveillance coverage of crime and other problems is a valuable adjunct to other proven investigative techniques and procedures. (See "Surveillance Photography in Robbery Investigation" in Chapter 12.)

SUMMARY

The surveillance of persons, places, groups or vehicles is an important investigative technique of law enforcement. Inasmuch as criminal suspects do not "advertise" their activities, it is a function of police agencies to uncover criminal acts and operations by the use of discreet operations. Surveillance operations must include several considerations to be successful. Among these are total secrecy, careful planning, type of coverage, objectives, selection of personnel, length of surveillance, procedures, materials, specialized equipment, communication methods, clothing and vehicles. These considerations depend upon the nature and purpose of the surveillance. A stakeout is a form of surveillance that is usually done from a fixed post. It is done for a specific purpose and is of relatively short duration.

In the Omnibus Crime Control and Safe Streets Act of 1968, the Congress of the United States enacted legislation stating that where none of the parties to the communication has consented to the interception, an electronic surveillance should be allowed only when authorized by a proper court and should remain under the control and supervision of the authorizing court. In addition, the interception of wire and oral communications should further be limited to certain major types of offenses and specific categories of crime. Title III denies to nonfederal law officers the right to make use of electronic surveillance of conversations unless there is a state statute permitting it. Today, less than half of the states have statutory procedures for the interception of wire or oral communications. For those states that permit court-ordered electronic surveillance, Title III establishes minimum standards which all state statutes must meet. States, however, are free to establish even more restrictive standards.

REVIEW QUESTIONS

1. Discuss the qualities which you believe would be useful in the selection of surveillance personnel.
2. What type of data should be included in a surveillance log?
3. List five purposes of surveillances.
4. In the preparation for a surveillance operation, what considerations should be taken into account?
5. What are the two general types of coverage used in a surveillance operation?
6. What is the minimum number of officers that is generally used on a moving surveillance?
7. Discuss the ramifications of the ABC method of a moving surveillance.
8. What precautionary measures must an officer on a stakeout take?
9. When a suspect is taken into custody as a result of a stakeout, what considerations must be taken into account?
10. Prepare a list of the types of equipment that should be considered for use in a moving surveillance.

WORK EXERCISE

Law library assignment

Review and prepare a brief résumé on the facts of the cases involving *Katz v. United States*, and *Berger v. New York* (citations set out below). Include for each case the Supreme Court ruling, majority opinion, and the impact these rulings have made on law-enforcement procedures involving the use of electronic eavesdropping. *Note:* These cases provided the guidelines for Title III of the Omnibus Crime Control and Safe Streets Act of 1968.[5]

Citations: Katz v. United States, 389 U.S. 347, 88 S.Ct. 507, 19 L.Ed.2d (1967).
Berger v. New York, 388 U.S. 41, 87 S.Ct. 1873, 18 L.Ed.2d 1040 (1967).

---

[5]"Electronic Surveillance," NWC Report, U.S. Government Printing Office, Washington, D.C. 1976, p. 38.

CHAPTER 8

Sources of Information

This chapter is not intended to be an exhaustive treatise on the topic "sources of information" but rather a summary of reference sources that are often resorted to in day-to-day investigations. Police cannot function without sources of assistance. There are literally hundreds of persons, places, indexes, directories, file systems, places of business, organizations, newspapers, libraries, municipal, county, state, federal, and miscellaneous other records that are available to an investigator, and that can furnish useful information. Source references are to an investigator as a library is to a student. The more sources of information a police department has, the easier the work will be in the investigative area. Information obtained through investigative resources can cut short an investigation by days or weeks. Early solutions in an investigation result in quick apprehensions, recovery of property, and savings in personnel use, investigative time, and money. The effectiveness of an investigator is directly proportionate to the ability to utilize information from every available source. As a general rule, an officer cannot be forced to disclose a confidential source of information, as it is against public policy to force such disclosure.

Source-of-Information Filing

Sources of information are maintained by some police agencies in a 3- by 5-inch (7.5- by 13-centimeter) card filing system similar to Figure 8-1. Such a card filing system contains an alphabetical listing by subject matter of various reference sources. Some source listings are airlines, apartments, auto agencies, auto rentals, bank-loan companies, bus companies, and credit associations. Behind each of the source listings, cards are filed alphabetically in order to facilitate the location of a particular agency, company, organization, or other record. The index cards prepared for this kind of source-of-information file should contain the name, address, and telephone number of the source, the identity and position of the person to contact, type of information available, and any security notations regarding the use of information furnished.

Some police agencies use a more extensive breakdown in source-of-information filing procedures. A filing system similar to that employed by a library is used. Cards are prepared and filed under three separate headings as in Figure 8-2: (a) alphabetically by the name of the person who can supply the information; (b) by type of information; and (c) by name of the agency, company, organization, or place. Each of the index cards prepared for the files depicted in Figure 8-2 should contain sufficient information to enable the searcher to locate information where there is only a name, type of activity or occupation, or the name of an agency, company, organization, or place. The index cards prepared for the type of filing system shown in Figure 8-2 should contain such information as: name, address, and telephone number of the person to contact, method of contact, place of contact, type of information the reference source can furnish, and any other notation or security limitation believed necessary in order to safeguard the particular source of data.

In practice, when an investigation is initiated and resource information is needed

Figure 8-1. A 3- by 5-inch source-of-information file showing the breakdown of reference sources.

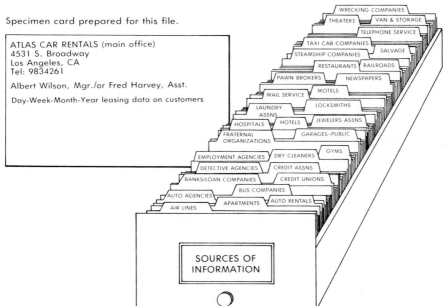

Specimen card prepared for this file.

ATLAS CAR RENTALS (main office)
4531 S. Broadway
Los Angeles, CA
Tel: 9834261

Albert Wilson, Mgr./or Fred Harvey, Asst.

Day-Week-Month-Year leasing data on customers

WRECKING COMPANIES
THEATERS
VAN & STORAGE
TELEPHONE SERVICE
TAXI CAB COMPANIES
STEAMSHIP COMPANIES
SALVAGE
RESTAURANTS
RAILROADS
PAWN BROKERS
NEWSPAPERS
MAIL SERVICE
MOTELS
LAUNDRY ASSNS
LOCKSMITHS
HOSPITALS
HOTELS
JEWELERS ASSNS
FRATERNAL ORGANIZATIONS
GARAGES–PUBLIC
EMPLOYMENT AGENCIES
DRY CLEANERS
GYMS
DETECTIVE AGENCIES
CREDIT ASSNS
BANKS/LOAN COMPANIES
CREDIT UNIONS
BUS COMPANIES
AUTO AGENCIES
AUTO RENTALS
AIR LINES
APARTMENTS

SOURCES OF INFORMATION

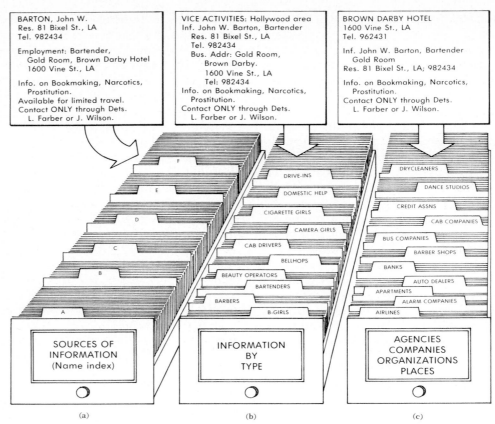

BARTON, John W.
Res. 81 Bixel St., LA
Tel. 982434

Employment: Bartender,
Gold Room, Brown Darby Hotel
1600 Vine St., LA

Info. on Bookmaking, Narcotics,
Prostitution.
Available for limited travel.
Contact ONLY through Dets.
L. Farber or J. Wilson.

VICE ACTIVITIES: Hollywood area
Inf. John W. Barton, Bartender
Res. 81 Bixel St., LA
Tel. 982434
Bus. Addr: Gold Room,
Brown Darby.
1600 Vine St., LA
Tel: 982434
Info. on Bookmaking, Narcotics,
Prostitution.
Contact ONLY through Dets.
L. Farber or J. Wilson.

BROWN DARBY HOTEL
1600 Vine St., LA
Tel. 962431

Inf. John W. Barton, Bartender
Gold Room
Res. 81 Bixel St., LA; 982434

Info. on Bookmaking, Narcotics,
Prostitution.
Contact ONLY through Dets.
L. Farber or J. Wilson.

F
E
D
C
B
A

SOURCES OF
INFORMATION
(Name index)

(a)

DRIVE-INS
DOMESTIC HELP
CIGARETTE GIRLS
CAMERA GIRLS
CAB DRIVERS
BELLHOPS
BEAUTY OPERATORS
BARTENDERS
BARBERS
B-GIRLS

INFORMATION
BY
TYPE

(b)

DRYCLEANERS
DANCE STUDIOS
CREDIT ASSNS
CAB COMPANIES
BUS COMPANIES
BARBER SHOPS
BANKS
AUTO DEALERS
APARTMENTS
ALARM COMPANIES
AIRLINES

AGENCIES
COMPANIES
ORGANIZATIONS
PLACES

(c)

Figure 8-2. A 3- by 5-inch source-of-information filing system showing three separate files. (a) Alphabetical name index; (b) type of information index; (c) alphabetical listing of agencies, companies, organizations, places. Preparation of cards for each of these files enables a searcher to locate necessary information.

from some specific agency, association, transportation company, hotel, or other source, the investigator checks the source-of-information file to determine whether or not there is a contact at that particular place. Should there be a reference source on file, the index card would list the identity of the person to contact, the method of reaching that person, and the type of information that that source can furnish. This check is made prior to leaving headquarters. At other times when an investigator is away from headquarters, a check of the source-of-information file may be requested in order to determine whether there is a contact listed in the file for a particular place. If so, the listed person is contacted and the information obtained. If, however, there is no information listed in the source-of-information file, an inquiry is made by the investigator at the particular place. In those instances where the individual contacted is cooperative, and in a position to furnish resource data, a card is subsequently prepared for the file listing the person's name for future contacts. Obviously many persons contacted will not be in a position to be of assistance, some reluctant to furnish information, and still others unwilling to cooperate for one reason or another.

Information Sources

Sources of information fall into three groups: (1) information obtained from persons, (2) information obtained from physical properties, and (3) information obtained from books, records, and other sources.

Information from persons

Police obtain information from victims, witnesses, suspects, other police officers, and people from all walks of life. Some people furnish information voluntarily whether or not their identity becomes known. In those instances where the confidential character of information is not a real concern, the furnishers of the data should be considered merely sources of information. However, there are other individuals who furnish information of a semiconfidential or confidential nature, who specifically request that their identity be kept secret. People in this category request anonymity for any one of several reasons: their particular job, profession, occupation, affiliation, residence, status, or other personal reasons. They are often referred to as "confidential sources." These persons may be paid or furnish information for one of several reasons set forth below. The word of the officer in such confidential relationships should never be broken. In order to protect the identity of a confidential source, police departments assign a fictitious name, number, symbol, letter, or code word to the particular individual. The index file containing confidential sources is maintained under strict security conditions within an agency, under the control of a high-ranking police official. Many police agencies maintain a separate file on confidential sources and permit only limited access to such a file.

Index cards prepared for the source-of-information name index (Figure 8-2a) should contain such information as name, alias or other designation, place and manner of contact, telephone number, pretexts to be used if any, alternate officer who can contact the source, and a notation as to whether the individual is available for travel. Wherever possible it is a good practice to obtain a copy of the confidential source's fingerprints, palm prints, specimen of handwriting, and a voice recording.

Reasons People Furnish Information
Information is furnished to the police for a variety of motives. Some of the more common reasons people reveal information are

- To cooperate with police for patriotic or civic reasons
- To obtain money or a reward
- To expose a criminal due to his or her illegal wealth
- To obtain revenge for some previous act committed by the suspect that affected the informant or an associate
- To satisfy a dislike for a criminal confederate
- To expose persons engaged in certain types of illegal activities such as prostitution, child molesting, strong-arm tactics, kidnaping, and other crimes of which the source disapproves
- To seek favor of police under guise of cooperation
- To furnish information out of fear, avoidance of punishment, repentance, egotistical reasons, or other dissatisfaction

A confidential source of information may be a public official, an executive, member of the arts or sciences, a hoodlum, or one of a number of "John Doe" citizens. Many important arrests are made because a confidential source contacted a trusted officer and furnished information concerning the identity and location of the perpetrator of a robbery, theft, burglary, or other crime.

Potential Sources of Information
The following types of individuals are potential sources of information because

of their occupational status, profession, or other proclivity. Persons in these categories often furnish useful information to a police agency.

Actors and entertainers
Apartment house managers
Bank and financial institution employees
Barbers
Bartenders
Beauty shop operators
Bond posters
Boxers
Building employees
Cabdrivers
Cigar stand operators
Credit officials
Dock workers
Door openers
Elevator operators
Ex-convicts
Garage operators
Hat-check clerks
Hotel employees
Janitors
Locksmiths
Musicians
Pawnshop proprietors
Public utility employees
Racetrack habitues
Restaurant employees
Truckdrivers
Union officials

DON'TS in Handling Confidential Sources of Information In view of the vital importance attached to the subject matter of handling criminal sources of information, the following rules are set forth to ensure that all precautionary measures are considered when dealing with such persons.

Don't use an informant if you can get results by any other means.

Don't divulge any more information than necessary.

Don't use a form of communication that can be traced to police.

Don't use the right name of a confidential source—use some cover name or alias.

Don't put entire confidence in information furnished by an informant.

Don't make any promises or "deals" with an informant that cannot be fulfilled.

Don't meet a confidential source at police headquarters, on the street, at a bar, or other place where the element of exposure is great. Extreme care should be exercised when communicating with sources of this kind.

Don't use "informant," "stoolie," "pigeon," or other such terms in the presence of a confidential contact.

Don't fail to consider the motive and interest of the informant when estimating reliability.

Don't permit the informant to break the law.

Don't make payments to a confidential source until the information rendered has proven of value. Make sure the source understands the arrangement of payments; be exact in all financial transactions; and obtain a receipt for all payments. If no receipt is desired, have someone witness the payment to the informant.

Don't fail to take notes or make a tape recording of information. It is even more desirable to have the informant submit written reports.

Don't fail to verify all information received. Insist on accuracy.

Don't adopt low standards if your informant has them. Bring the informant up to your standards.

Don't permit the informant to take charge of any phase of the investigation. She or he should be warned to never disclose the fact of working for the police.

Don't fail to show appreciation for information received.

Information obtained from physical properties

Resource information is obtained from things as well as people. The scene of a crime or accident is usually the starting point of an investigation. It is here that physical evidence or traces of the criminal are often located by investigators that help to identify or link a suspect with the crime, the place, or the geographical area. Items found may include discarded wearing apparel, fibers, hair, blood, tissue, fingerprints, and tool marks. Other possible traces are glass fragments, paint chips, soil particles, metal filings, tools, weapons, and safe insulation. Comparison and identification of articles, materials, or substances of the type set out above can provide valuable information to an investigation. In addition to finding physical evidence at the scene of the crime, evidence may be found on or in a suspect's person or environment, or on or about the victim in crimes involving contact. Crimes such as rape, aggravated assault, homicide and hit-and-run often involve a transfer of materials or substances between persons or objects. The collection, identification, and preservation of physical evidence and the role of the laboratory in examinations are set forth in Chapter 3.

Information obtained from books, records, and other sources

Seeking information on a particular individual, place, company, or corporation may involve the research of one or several reference sources. In many instances the necessary data are located by examination of available city, county, state, federal, and private records, as well as books and documents. Records maintained by the sources above are, for the most part, public records, and are available for reference purposes. Private records, directories, and publications are generally obtainable in public libraries. An awareness of the type of information available through the above sources can be of valuable assistance to the investigator. The following records are usually available to a police investigator:

Police Records and Reports

Master name index
Incident or offense reports
Arrest records
Identification records
Modus operandi files
Photo albums
Traffic and accident reports
Location files (accident and crime)
Sources of information
Sex offender registrations
Missing persons reports
Field interrogation reports
Juvenile records
Oddity file (scars, marks, amputations, deformities)
Warrants
Pawnshop records
Gun registration records
Lost and stolen property indexes
Intelligence files
Correspondence files
Wanted bulletins and other specialized files
Prison releasees' albums
Dispatcher's log

City and County Sources of Information

Assessor's Office Contains records of persons taxed within the city or county geographical areas as to real and personal property, deeds, transfers, and mortgages.

Building Department Has records of building permits, blueprints, and diagrams showing construction details, building inspections.

Civil Service Contains personnel history statements, employment records, efficiency reports, liens filed against employees, and other personal data.

Coroner Maintains autopsy reports, inquest reports, names and descriptions of deceased persons, causes of death, dates of inquest, testimonies taken, lists of witnesses, property found on deceased persons, and disposition of same.

County Clerk Has records on naturalization applicants, passports, marriage licenses, adoptions, register of doctor certificates, fictitious names, corporations, and businesses. The Civil File Division has information on civil suits, damages awarded, judgments, attachments, changes of name, insanity hearings, liens, intemperance records, and divorce proceedings. The Criminal File Division has information on actions heard in superior court (criminal complaints, rulings of court, findings of courts or juries, probation officer's reports).

County Recorder Keeps records of judgments, trust deeds, mortgages and chattel mortgages, bankruptcy filings, notary public commissions, wills admitted to probate, notice of mechanics liens, records of marriages, births, and deaths except those occurring in the city.

County Treasurer Has information on payment to all county employees, schoolteachers, welfare recipients, and other specialized district employees including retired employees. The county treasurer issues tax bills and collects taxes levied on lands, improvements, and personal property, and collects special district taxes and assessments.

Credit Unions Have records of loan applications, cosigners, payment records, reasons for loans, and savings accounts.

Fire Marshal Has records of building and premise inspections.

Health Department Keeps data on vital statistics (birth and death certificates and other health records).

License Bureau Maintains information on all business licenses and permits issued in the city.

Sanitation Department Contains a list of garbage and trash subscribers.

Schools (Boards of Education) Have personnel records of teachers and students.

Street Department Has maps of the city, correct street numbers, alleys, easements, and former street names.

Tax Collector Has names and addresses of assessees, amounts of assessed valuation, and legal descriptions of property.

Voter Registration Has a roster of voters, affidavits of registrations, names, addresses, occupations, places of birth, places of naturalization. For naturalized citizens, it has places of previous registration, party affiliations, specimens of registrants' handwriting, and nomination papers of candidates for county offices.

Welfare Department Has records containing information on persons involved in public assistance programs. It maintains background data and social history.

State Agencies as Sources of Information The administrative system of various states have certain offices in common, such as Lieutenant Governor, Secretary of State, Treasurer, Auditor or Controller, Attorney General, Superintendent or Commissioner of Education. Some of the many state agencies that can provide information to an investigator are criminal identification bureaus, motor vehicle departments, parole boards, departments of fish and game, etc. It is important to the success of any investigator to know of these sources and others in the area in which he or she is employed. The investigator should know the exact name and address of the agency, the telephone number, the identity of the person to be contacted when checking with that particular source, and the type of information that can be provided. As an example of the type of services provided by a state agency, see Figure 8-3.

Federal Sources of Information

Federal agencies operate within specified areas of responsibility and authority. It is important for each officer to know where information from federal sources can be obtained. The departments or agencies set forth below were created for the purpose of enforcing laws that extend beyond the investigative jurisdiction of state and local agencies. The following are but a few of the numerous government agencies and bureaus which have records that may provide useful information.

National Personnel Records Center Has all permanent noncurrent military records of the Army, Navy, Marines, and Air Force. These can be located at the National Personnel Records Center (NPRC), Military Personnel Records, St. Louis, Missouri 63132. In addition, the records of retired enlisted personnel, enlisted reservists not on active duty, and deceased enlisted personnel can be found there.

Army Has records of current enlisted personnel, enlisted reservists on extended active duty, WACs, and deserter records. These can be located at Fort Benjamin Harrison, Indiana 46249. Records of officer personnel (including WACs), regular army, reservists on extended active duty, army nurses, and retired officers can be located by writing c/o The Adjutant General's Office, Hoffman Building Number 2, 200 Stovall Street, Alexandria, Virginia. Records on discharged officers, deceased officers, reserve officers not on active duty, and warrant officers can be located at the National Personnel Records Center mentioned above. U.S. Army Reserve records are maintained under the U.S. Army Administrative Center (USAAC), also located at the NPRC above.

Navy Has records on both currently enlisted and inactive personnel, and Reserve Corps personnel. These can be located by writing c/o U.S. Navy Annex, Arlington, Virginia. Records on retired enlisted personnel and deceased enlisted personnel can be located by contacting the NPRC (National Personnel Records Center) at the address given above.

Air Force Has records of currently enlisted personnel, enlisted reservists on extended active duty, WAFs, persons missing in action, and prisoners of war. These can be located at the Randolph Air Force Base, San Antonio, Texas. Records of retired enlisted personnel and those serving sentences in disciplinary barracks, can be located at the NPRC. Records of civilian employees of the Air Force can be located at the NPRC, Civilian Personnel Records, St. Louis, Missouri 63132.

Marine Corps Has records of current enlisted personnel and enlisted reservists on extended active duty, AWOL ("absent without leave") personnel, deserters, and enlisted reservists. These can be located by writing c/o U.S. Navy Annex, Arlington, Virginia. In addition, records of enlisted personnel in temporary disability retired status, and officers in active duty may be obtained through the above U.S. Navy address. Retired enlisted personnel and deceased enlisted personnel records are located at the NPRC.

Coast Guard Has records of enlisted personnel on active duty. These can be located by writing c/o Coast Guard Headquarters, 400 Seventh Street, SW, Washington, D.C. 20590. In addition, records of discharged, retired, or deceased personnel can be found there.

Merchant Marine Has records which can be located by writing c/o National Personnel Records Center, Civilian Personnel Records, St. Louis, Missouri.

Merchant Seamen Has personnel records which can be located at the Coast Guard Headquarters, 400 Seventh Street, SW, Washington, D.C. 20590.

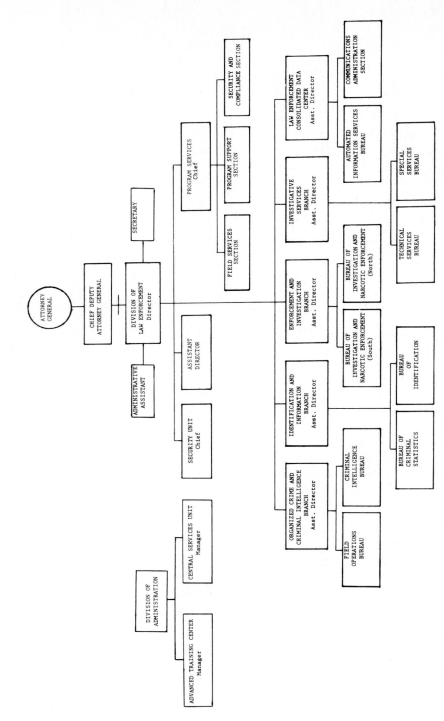

Figure 8-3. Organization chart showing functional relationships of the various services provided by the division of Law Enforcement, California Department of Justice.

National Guard Maintains records at state capitals.

Veterans Administration Has records of active personnel which can be located at the local office covering the residence of the veteran. Inactive files can be located through the Veterans Administration Record Processing Center, Post Office Box 172, St. Louis, Missouri 63132.

Federal Aviation Administration (FAA) Has pilot certification and medical records and aircraft registration and history records. These can be located by writing c/o FAA Airmen's Certified Branch, Aeronautical Center, Oklahoma City, Oklahoma; or by contacting FAA Aircraft Registration Branch, Aeronautical Center, Oklahoma City, Oklahoma.

Civil Service Commission Has records of civil service employees employed by the federal government. These can be located by writing c/o National Personnel Records Center, Civilian Personnel Records, St. Louis, Missouri 63132. In addition, inactive

personnel files of all federal agencies are maintained.

Department Of Justice The investigative agencies under the U.S. Department of Justice include the Federal Bureau of Investigation (FBI), the Immigration and Naturalization Service (INS), and the Drug Enforcement Administration (DEA). The FBI is the principal investigative arm of the Department of Justice and is charged with investigating all violations of federal laws with the exception of those which have been assigned by legislative enactment or otherwise to some other federal agency. (See Figure 8-4.)

Federal Bureau of Investigation (FBI) Can provide information regarding stolen property involving six categories through the National Crime Information Center (NCIC), a computerized criminal justice information system. The categories are vehicles, license plates, missing or recovered guns, securities, boats, and identifiable articles. In addition, information on wanted per-

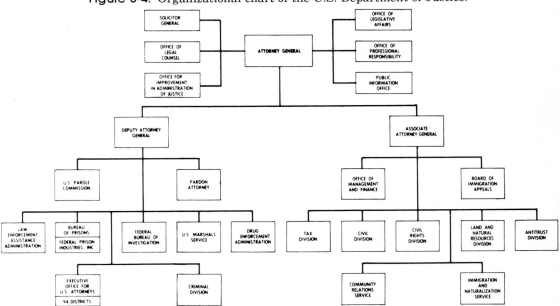

Figure 8-4. Organizational chart of the U.S. Department of Justice.

sons, criminal histories, and missing persons can be obtained. Through remote terminal network devices located in state and metropolitan police agencies throughout the United States, vital information concerning crime and criminals can be obtained in a matter of seconds. (See Figure 8-5.)

A case that illustrates the value of the NCIC as an aid to law enforcement involved a crime in which four victims were viciously murdered in the course of a robbery committed by four subjects at a savings and loan association in a large Ohio city. Shortly thereafter, two persons were arrested and data on the other two suspects were placed with the NCIC. Four days later, in the early morning, the state police in New Mexico made a routine check of three persons asleep in a vehicle parked on a highway. Inquiries were made by radio relay from the patrol car to the NCIC terminal at the State Police

Figure 8-5. A section of the Los Angeles County Sheriff's Department communications bureau, which serves ground and air units by providing local, state, and federal criminal identification data within seconds, as well as handling many other miscellaneous police service functions.

headquarters. No record was located for the driver of the car; however, the wanted status of the two hitchhikers present in the car was obtained through the NCIC. This instantaneous response from NCIC and the subsequent arrest of the two subjects ended a four-day nationwide search which extended approximately 1,500 miles from the scene of the crime. Since its inception in 1967, NCIC has aided the apprehension of badly wanted criminals, the recovery of stolen property, the saving of investigative effort, the personal safety of law enforcement personnel, and the prevention of crime. In addition, it has resulted in substantial savings to police agencies.

The Identification Division of the FBI makes its criminal arrest records available to all police agencies. The FBI laboratory is also available to all duly constituted law-enforcement agencies on a cost-free basis. Scientific examinations and expert testimonies are provided. Within the laboratory is a large reference collection which is also available to police. The reference files include such collections as national fraudulent check file, automotive paint file, firearms collection, tire tread file, typewriter standards file, watermark file, and hair and fiber file. The bureau also has a bomb data program which compiles and disseminates information to law-enforcement agencies concerning improvised explosive devices. In addition, it offers training relating to bombing investigations and bomb technology.

Drug Enforcement Agency (DEA) Investigates violations of narcotic laws and keeps records of all licensed handlers of narcotics such as physicians and druggists.

Immigration and Naturalization Service (INS) Has records on aliens which are maintained at regional and district offices. Where an alien's address is unknown, a record may be on file at the central office of INS, 425 I Street, NW, Washington, D.C. 20536.

Information from Private Organizations, Businesses, and Other Sources
In addition to the information available in city, county, state, and federal records, there are a number of private organizations, businesses, directories and other sources that provide information to an investigator. The number of investigative resources is limited only by the inquisitiveness of the officer. Reference sources cannot be ranked in the order of importance. The following sources of information (many of which can be found in public libraries) are set forth as an indication of some of the types of data available.

Auto Rental or Leasing Companies Have records on persons renting cars, operator's license information, make, model, mileage traveled, license, and other descriptive data on cars rented.

Bankers' Directory (The "Bankers' Blue Book") Lists banks in the United States by American Bankers Association (ABA) routing numbers. It is published by Rand McNally & Company, Chicago, Illinois 60680.

Banks, Loan Companies, and Finance Companies Contain records on bank accounts and deposit and loan transactions. These companies also have records on credit information, safe deposits, and loan transactions.

Better Business Bureaus Have information on the reputation of businesses and firms, rackets, and confidence game operators.

Cumulative Book Index Lists all the books in the world that are published in English.

Chambers of Commerce Have information regarding the reputation of businesses and operators. Chambers of Commerce also have libraries of back issues of city directories.

City Directories List individuals alphabetically by name, and include residence, occupation (sometimes place of employ-ment), and firm. Separate sections of these directories list all streets alphabetically and give street numbers as well. These directories are useful in obtaining or verifying such information as old addresses, occupations, and relatives of subjects under investigation. Old issues may be found in public libraries. City directories are published by private companies.

College and University Records Contain background information on students. Handwriting specimens, educational achievements, and other data are included.

Congressional Directory Includes biographies of the president, vice president, cabinet members, senators, representatives, and state governors. It also lists administrative assistants, secretaries, and accredited reporters, photographers, and correspondents. A guide to persons high in the federal government, it is published annually and is available in public libraries.

Corporations: Poor's Register of Corporations, Directors and Executives Includes listing of executives, corporations, firms, and products. This directory is a roster of 37,000 leading American and Canadian corporations. It is published by Standard and Poor's Publishing Company, 345 Hudson Street, New York, New York 10014. It is available in public libraries.

Credit Associations Maintain credit files on persons who have applied for credit or use credit in transacting business. Their records contain data on former residences, sources of income, bank accounts, tangible assets, references, other charge accounts, and personal history.

Dun & Bradstreet Has records on businesses including financial data, credit data, and organizational structure. Dun & Bradstreet, Inc. is a national business reporting agency located at 99 Church Street, New York, New York 10007.

Express Companies Maintain records of shipment of goods, number of pieces, weight, contents, and value if insured, destination, and consignee.

American Insurance Agency (formerly National Board of Fire Underwriters) Can furnish good assistance on arson cases and thefts of valuable insured items.

Hospitals Have records of patients' illnesses and injuries.

Hotel Associations Maintain files on criminals, bad checks, gamblers, and con artists. Many hotels have a security officer who can furnish desired information.

Housing Projects Have records of present and former tenants and personal data.

The New Jersey State Police Identification Bureau (Jewelry Identification) Maintains one of the largest files on jeweler identification scratch marks in the United States. This file represents thousands of coded marks obtained from jewelers in most Eastern states and several in Arizona, California, and Colorado. The jeweler's scratch mark, as identifiable as a fingerprint, is etched or scratched on the backs of watches and other expensive jewelry. It is a combination of digits and letters which are generally discernible only with a jeweler's magnifying glass. This mark corresponds to a ledger kept by the jeweler, recording the name and possibly the address of the customer. Though it is rare when two jewelers have the same mark, each can identify his or her own mark at a glance. The Bureau is located in Trenton, New Jersey. The National Crime Information Center (NCIC) also is worth a check where stolen identifiable property is involved.

American Medical Directory Lists doctors by states and cities in the states, U.S. possessions and territories, and Canada. It is published by the American Medical Association, Chicago, Illinois. The American Dental Association publishes a similar directory.

Laundry and Dry Cleaning Sources Maintain records on laundry and dry cleaning marks.

Lawyer's Directory Lists lawyers by state, city, and alphabetically by name. Background data on attorneys is included. *The Law Directory* is published by Martindale-Hubbell, Summit, New York.

Thomas Register of American Manufacturers Lists the manufacturers of most products. The guide is published by Thomas Publishing Company, 461 Eighth Avenue, New York, New York 10001.

Moving Companies Provide the destination of persons using movers.

Newspapers Maintains a list of subscribers in their circulation departments. Newspaper libraries contain such items as back issues and photographs. Newsclipping services are other good sources of information.

Directory of Newspapers and Periodicals Can provide interviews of out-of-town suspects. It is a guide to newspapers and periodicals printed in the United States and its possessions.

Port Authorities Provide information on ship arrivals.

Public Utilities Maintain records of applications for service and some background information on subscribers. Information is usually filed according to address rather than by name. In addition, the name of the person who had service previously at the same address is listed. Gas, electric, and water companies generally have a special agent's office through which investigative information is handled. The method of keeping files depends upon the office procedure of the particular company.

Telegraph Companies Have records of transmitted messages and money order information. In some instances it is possible to obtain writing from a pad used by a subject. Names and addresses are often provided.

Telephone Companies Have records of names and addresses of subscribers, long distance calls, lengths of telephone service, previous service, and locations. Telephone information should be obtained through the special agent's office of the telephone company or through the local manager. Telephone directories list subscribers alphabetically with their addresses. For assistance call "Information." Frequently the information operator may have a removal slip which will disclose the subscriber's forwarding address. Reverse directories (not available to general public) list telephone subscribers by street and number. This information is valuable in making background or neighborhood checks. The *Telephone Number Directory* (not available to public) lists all telephone numbers in local areas followed by the name of the individual subscriber.

Religious Directories Include membership of clergy. The directories can help to locate a pastor or minister. Many religious denominations issue them.

Real Estate and Rental Agencies Have records of residents and former tenants of rental property, business and character references, and handwriting exemplars.

Taxicab Companies Maintain records of trips kept by drivers on each fare. Trip sheets list the time, location from which cab was taken, and destination. Checks of trip sheets for fares picked up in a specific zone often provide leads in investigations.

Theatrical Publications Furnish information on show people, circuses, carnivals, vaudeville, nightclubs, and orchestras. *Variety* and *Billboard* magazine are among the best known.

Travel Agencies, Railroads, Airlines, Steamships Have records of the names and addresses of passengers, dates of travel, and points of disembarkation. Information on reservations made ahead for hotel accommodations or land transportation, passenger lists, baggage information, beneficiaries, and itineraries are also available.

U.S. Government Manual Lists all United States government branches, departments, bureaus, agencies, and the location of each office. It is published by the Government Printing Office, Washington, D.C. 20408.

Who's Who in America Includes alphabetical list of all men and women in the nation who have attained distinction. Each entry includes biographical data, educational information, membership in societies and organizations, religious and political affiliations, marital status, and family. Other information includes former spouse, date of divorce, death, publications by subject, occupation and previous positions, hobbies, and other personal data. It is published every two years by A. N. Marquis Company, 200 East Ohio Street, Chicago, Illinois 60611. The Marquis Company also publishes a *Who's Who* for the South, Southwest, West, East, and Midwest. It also publishes *Who's Who in Science*.

The International Who's Who Has biographical data on leading personalities in almost every sphere of human activity. It is published by Europa Publications, Ltd., 18 Bedford Square, London, W.C. 1, England.

In addition to the above sources, there are many other references that may be considered on a local or regional level such as truck or van rentals, private airplane rentals and services, bonding companies, credit card companies, union hiring halls, fraternal organizations, and refuse collection departments.

SUMMARY

An investigator cannot function without sources of assistance. In fact, an officer's effectiveness is related to the ability to get information. There are innumerable persons, places, indexes, directories, file systems, organizations and departments (city, county, state, and federal) that are at the immediate disposal of an officer. However, in checking sources, the investigator must know when, where, how, and whom to contact. The officer must also be aware of the limits of confidentiality that must be exercised. Savings in personnel, investigative time, and money are the by-products of an effective source-of-information system.

REVIEW QUESTIONS

1. Into what three general groups do sources of information fall?
2. List four precautions an officer should take in handling confidential criminal sources of information.
3. What types of records may an officer hope to find in a police agency? List ten.
4. What types of records would you expect to find in a county clerk's office? What type of information would you find in a voter registration file?
5. The NCIC computer system of the FBI contains many types of records available to a police agency. What types of information would you expect to obtain through NCIC?
6. What news sources would an officer consult to obtain theatrical information on show people, nightclubs, orchestras, or circuses?
7. Name five reasons people furnish information.
8. One type of resource is physical evidence found at the scene of a crime such as a hit-and-run, or felony case, an aggravated assault, or a homicide. These crimes may involve transfer evidence. What is meant by "transfer evidence"? Give an example.
9. Under what U.S. government department is the Drug Enforcement Agency (DEA)?
10. Where are the permanent noncurrent military personnel records of the Army, Navy, Marine Corps, and Air Force located?

WORK EXERCISE

Prepare a paper or discussion on how you, as an investigator, would attempt to develop a confidential source of information at the following location. Indicate your procedures, considerations, precautionary measures, etc.

The Lion's Den is a restaurant and bar located in a one-story brick and stucco building. It is in the center of a small shopping area consisting of six other miscellaneous stores. The Lion's Den employs fifteen people (seven men and eight women). Four female and two male employees work in the bar area. The restaurant and bar is frequented continually by a variety of criminal characters. The manager is a member of the local Rotary Club.

CHAPTER 9

Report Writing

A report, oral or written, is a communication of information set forth in an accurate, concise, clear, and complete manner serving as a record of a given incident. A report may also be defined as a written account of something seen, heard, read, done, or considered. Police reports are official records of the activities of a governmental agency and are used in a wide variety of circumstances. Reports are as vital to a police department as is blood to the human body. A department without a healthy circulation of information is inefficient and ineffective. Every investigation should be complemented by an accurate report. Reports are a necessary part of an officer's job. The results achieved by the FBI are due largely to the complete reports made by its agents.

Reports provide the starting point for all further action on a case. When an original report is not complete, the reporting officer has to be contacted, witnesses must be reinterviewed and supplemental reports made out. Reports are necessary to law enforcement at every level—supervisory, administrative, prosecution, and the courts. In a court of law, the burden of proof falls on the district attorney's shoulders. Reports are the ammunition needed to build the case. The district attorney has to depend on them. If statements in a report are inaccurate or incomplete, the obvious result will be an acquittal for the accused.

Reports are one of the principal sources of information in conducting any type of investigation and are often the only sources of information for the disposition of a case. They tell whether the offender should be prosecuted or subjected to other measures of control. Reports convey to other persons what has been ascertained, observed, or done. Police reports often mean the difference between a person's freedom or confinement and, in some cases, even the right to live. Material set forth in a report should be presented in a functional rather than a literary style. One district attorney was asked how he would like the facts set forth in a report. His answer was, "Your report must have a definite purpose in mind. It must contain all the elements of the crime by time, location, circumstances, and, if possible, the motive. As to where these facts appear in the report is immaterial, if the report is written in a clear, concise narrative."

Tests of a Report

1. Is is complete, concise, clear, accurate?
2. Will a verbal explanation be required in addition to what is already included in the report?
3. Can what you say in the report be proven?

Value of Reports

Reports provide a department with essential data that are necessary to the apprehension of criminals and solution of crime. Advances made in recent years clearly indicate that one of the most effective new tools available to law enforcement is the ability to communicate information at the very high speeds now possible in processing reports with electronic equipment. Many of the larger departments tabulate data from reports in their planning and research division. Reports are valuable to a department and its officers in the following ways:

Provide a written record and a readily accessible memory bank of police business and information.

Refresh an officer's memory regarding further investigation and administrative handling.

Provide a method and means of controlled communication throughout the police department and its associated agencies.

Furnish a base of accurate statistical information upon which decision and policy may be based.

Aid in detection of wanted persons and suspects.

Aid in identifying crime hazards, distribution of manpower, and in the analysis of operations.

Indicate unusual or periodic difficulties.

Offer main contact between the follow-up investigator and the field officer.

Assist in the formulation of budget requests.

As a basis for compiling local, state, and FBI national crime statistics.

Provide one of the vital tools used by the department to carry out its many and varied objectives.

Account for adequate and accurate information for prosecutive action where violations of law are indicated.

In addition to the above residual benefits, reports permit accountability upward and outward for police activities, administrative control, and justification of its program. In reporting upward and outward, the police agency must report information concerning progress, future needs, plans, and decisions. It must also take into account the police organization itself, the city manager, mayor, city council, and the general public.

Reports inform downward within the police organization concerning policies, programs, organization resources, procedures, and all other matters concerning the work in the agency. In reporting downward in the organization, the department must take into consideration all of the levels of responsibilities and any special units or personnel that need to be kept informed of matters contained in a given report. In any of these situations a report may serve the useful purposes of interpreting facts, transmitting information, analyzing problems or situations, and educating employees and others according to superior authority or policy within the department itself.

Characteristics of a Good Report

The principal characteristics of a good report are completeness, conciseness, clearness, and accuracy. They are the requisites of a police report.

Completeness

Reports should be complete in all necessary details. Partial facts may create a false picture. Completeness means that the report must contain all necessary information and omit what is not needed. Include negative results as well as positive. If you search a suspect's room and find nothing, report it. It may save an investigator's time in duplicating your work. Let another officer read your report to see if questions are unanswered. What did you do with the car? Where did you locate the gun? Was the victim alone when this happened? Does the victim want to sign a complaint? Unanswered questions raise questions for a person who was not at the scene. Consider the follow-up investigator. Will she or he have to call you in the morning to get the meaning of the report? Will the follow-up investigator be duplicating any of your work because you did not report it? Will the names and addresses be correct and the phone numbers reported?

Conciseness

Reports must be as brief as is consistent with the setting forth of their essential features in an understandable manner. Eliminate unnecessary words, technical phrases, clauses, and sentences. Express as much as possible with a minimum number of words. Use short simple sentences—long sentences are confusing. Do not use meaningless words when a concise word will do. For example, "I observed the car pass the intersection 'at a high rate of speed.' " It is better to write "at a speed estimated to be in excess of 70 mph." The inexperienced report writer should make it a practice to write a composition of at least seventy-five words on some police topic at every opportunity. The composition should then be corrected and condensed. Advice should be sought from experienced report writers as to how the reports might be improved.

Clearness

A report must clearly explain to the reader what you saw, heard, and did. Short sentences lead to clear meanings. Plan what you want to say before you write it out or dictate it. Never leave your reader in doubt about what you mean. Clarity is best accomplished by the use of good sentence structure; correct word usage, punctuation, spelling, and capitalization; proper paragraph arrangement; and other elements of good language. Words and phrases should be used so that the reader will readily comprehend the contents of the report. Always be specific in your choice of words. Avoid the use of unnecessary words and technical phrases.

Accuracy

Accuracy cannot be emphasized too strongly. Reports must demonstrate exactness to be valuable. Restrict the report to facts. Do not confuse fact with hearsay information. Information reported must relate only to those things that have transpired and that have been verified by investigation and not the conclusions at which the officer has arrived. Since decisions must be made and in many cases certain action must be taken immediately which will be based solely upon a report, the necessity for absolute accuracy is essential. Exactness should be demonstrated in such things as correct times and dates, names of all persons, complete addresses and phone numbers, descriptions of suspects and crime scene, items of evidence, and proper identification. An example of inaccuracy is recalled in which an officer, in filling a descriptive form, reported "no scars or marks." In a subsequent report involving the same suspect, a half-dozen scars or marks were listed. Errors or omissions in reports raise doubts as to the thoroughness, accuracy, reliability, and the personal ability of the reporter. An individual's fate often hinges upon the accuracy and completeness of the information that the officer has compiled in a given case.

The When, Who, Where, What, How, and Why Formula of Reports

Basically, all reports are answers to six questions: when, who, where, what, how, and, sometimes, why. Answers to these questions will constitute the elements of the case and give the information that any interested person will want to know. If the investigating officer will keep these questions fixed in mind and devote attention to securing satisfactory and accurate answers to them, the reports are certain to be acceptable. The application of these questions may be clarified as follows.

When?

When did the incident occur? What was the time of day, the day of the week, the month? When was this matter discovered?

In brief, any information that has to do with the fixing of time may properly be given under the answer to the question *when?* and given in such detail as the purpose of the report demands.

Who?

Who were the persons concerned? Who were the principal persons involved in the case? For example, who was the complainant in a felony or misdemeanor? Who was the victim of an accident? Who was a suspect or offender? The *who* is the principal or title of the case. Information concerning these persons, their friends, associates, habits—all it is possible to secure should be obtained. *Who* will vary somewhat in accordance with the nature of the report. For example, a dog, the property of Mrs. John Doe, 250 Adams Street, is run over and killed. The principal purpose of making such a report is to have the dead dog removed from the public highway. In a report such as this, only the information absolutely necessary should be recorded or a complaint or incident report. But suppose that Doe is involved in a felonious hit-and-run auto accident, or some other serious crime and has not been arrested. Now it becomes necessary that as much information concerning Doe, her friends, associates, habits, etc., as it is possible to secure be obtained in order that Doe might be located.

Where?

Where did the incident happen? Correct address and name of the street, type of building, house, apartment, store, service station, etc., should be noted. Where in the building did it occur—bedroom, hallway, front office? Any information that has to do with the location of places, persons, or objects connected with the matter under investigation should be given under the question *where?* If it occurred outside, give the exact location. Pinpoint the exact location where the offense took place. Use stationary objects when taking measurements ("12 feet west of the west curb"). The correct listing of the *where* will aid in further investigation and presentation of evidence and testimony.

What?

What is the crime? What happened? Describe in such detail as may be necessary for the purpose of the report. In the case of a person found injured on the street, the *what* would be the circumstances of the injury. Exactly what took place? This too will vary according to the purpose for which the report is made. The investigator should be able to report such information as the actions of the suspects, what evidence was obtained, what knowledge, skill, or strength was needed to commit the crime, what was reported but did not occur, what was done with the evidence, what further action is needed, what the witnesses know about it, etc.

How?

How was the event accomplished? Under this heading should be included all the information obtainable which will tend to show exactly how the occurrence took place; also the method of operation used by the suspect(s). Answers should be sought to such questions as How was the crime committed? How did the suspect get to the scene? How were the tools obtained and used?

Why?

In addition to the above questions, reporting officers also seek answers to the question *why?* The *why* covers the motive involved in the complaint. Motives are usually nothing more than deductions. However, the *why* should not be overlooked. The investigator should consider such things as the following: Why did so much time elapse before the crime was reported? Why were the witnesses so anxious to point out the guilty party? Why were the witnesses reluctant to talk? Why did the suspect commit the particular violation against a particular person, mar-

ket, messenger, premises? In cases of burglary, robbery, or larceny, for example, generally the *why* is answered by the crime itself, as it is presumed that the suspect committed the crime to gain possession. However, it is always worthy of consideration to determine why a suspect chose one particular victim, premise, market, etc., over some other. In traffic cases there is seldom a motive. In homicide cases the motive may take a considerable amount of work to develop and it may not be possible for the reporting officer to bring it out at the time of the report. Nevertheless, the *why* is still there and has to be considered by the investigator.

The above six questions (when, who, where, what, how, and why) can be used to the officer's advantage in conducting inquiries of suspects and witnesses. Questions should be worded according to these six inquiries. Such questioning forces the person being questioned to think more: "What do you think?" "How did it happen?" "Why did you do it?" "Where were you during the incident?," etc. Questions prefaced by these words (when, who, where, what, how, and why) call for definite information and will often result in positive answers. The sequence in which these questions are to be asked will vary in accordance with the nature of the report. In some reports it may not be necessary to obtain answers to all of these questions. In no case will the questions and answers be written down in the report. The questions are merely intended as a guide so that the person making a report will know what information to obtain and include in the report.

A brief first paragraph that contains a synopsis of the entire report in the when, who, where, what, how, and why order serves as the completed report for 80 percent of misdemeanor crimes reported. For longer reports, the elements of the crime should be organized. Such organization eliminates the possibility of forgetting an essential element of the report and serves as an important organizational tool for long narrative reports. A good introduction makes a report seem clear and meaningful even if it is otherwise poorly organized.

A résumé of investigation set forth in the table below can be used as an aid in report writing. This resume is a "checklist" for the reporting officer and helps to determine whether all the essential information called for in order to make a satisfactory report has been covered.

In report writing, as in all other phases of police work, common sense, good judgment, and especially a good working knowledge of police procedure are required. The officer making the report should know the purpose for which it is intended and the channels through which it will go. The advice of those members of the department who are proficient in making reports should be sought whenever an inexperienced officer must file a report on an unfamiliar matter. An officer must know and understand the elements of

RESUME OF INVESTIGATION

When	Time of crime	Arrest of perpetrator
	Date of crime	Trial
	Discovery of crime	
	Identification of victim	
	Identification of property	
Where	Crime	Reported
	Approach to	Arrest made
	Escape from	Trial
	Place of discovery	
	Loot recovered	
Who	Victim	Relatives of perpetrator
	Discovered	Friends of perpetrator
	Reported	Accomplice
	Witnesses	
	Perpetrator	
What	Elements of crime:	
How	Description of scene	Vehicle
	Means of entry	Odd and unusual acts
	How entered	Alias or nickname
	Loot	
	Associates	
Why	Motive (sometimes good to establish if possible)	

the crime reported, since each element must be proven for a successful prosecution of the case. For example, in grand theft, a purse snatch is not the same as strong-arm robbery of a purse. In every department, reports that have been properly prepared by proficient report writers on a variety of cases are available for review. A review of these cases can enhance the report writing abilities of an inexperienced officer. The range and scope of the subjects to be covered in written reports is so broad and inclusive that there is scarcely anything that may not at some time become the subject of a written report.

Mechanical Elements of Writing Police Reports

In police reporting, the last name should be capitalized and set forth in reports first, followed by first and middle name. For example, WILSON, John Edward. Capitalization of surnames in a report assists a reader in locating names readily. In the details of a report, many departments capitalize all names, e.g., JOHN HENRY WILSON.

The designations of Mr., Miss, Ms., or Mrs. are not used as a prefix when setting forth a name in a report. For example, it would not be proper to state *Mr.* John Paul

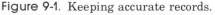

Figure 9-1. Keeping accurate records.

SMITH or *Mrs.* John Paul SMITH. These two names would more properly be listed as: SMITH, John Paul, or JOHN PAUL SMITH; or SMITH, Mary Jane (Mrs.), or MARY JANE SMITH (Mrs.) It is preferable to always use the full middle name of a person rather than listing a middle initial. If the middle name is an initial only, surround the initial in quotes: MOORE, Alice "P"; or ALICE "P" MOORE. If the first and middle names are initials only, surround both the initials in quotes. If the subject has no middle name, indicate that: MOORE, Alice (NMN), or ALICE (NMN) MOORE.

The first time a witness, for example, is referred to in the body of a report, the full name, JONES, Robert Edward; or ROBERT EDWARD JONES is indicated. Thereafter, JONES is identified by the word "witness" followed by the last name, i.e., witness JONES. The first time a suspect appears in a report, the full name should be set forth: ADAMS, Barbara Joan, or BARBARA JOAN ADAMS. Thereafter in the report it would only be necessary to identify ADAMS as suspect ADAMS.

Similarly, the first time a victim's name appears in a report, the full name (last, first, middle) would be set forth in lower case letters, or the first, middle, and last in capital letters. Thereafter reference to this victim would begin by indicating victim DOE, or whatever his or her name might be. If there is more than one victim, suspect, subject, or defendant, and all their names are known, they should be used in the body of the report as noted above, preceded by the proper qualifying term, such as suspect, BROWN, witness SMITH, defendant ADAMS.

An alias (an assumed name) is reported, if known. An alias can be a different spelling of the same name: MAIER, John, aka (also, known as) MEYER, John. An alias may be a maiden name or the name of one of a succession of husbands. An alias may be an often-used nick-name or a phony name used to

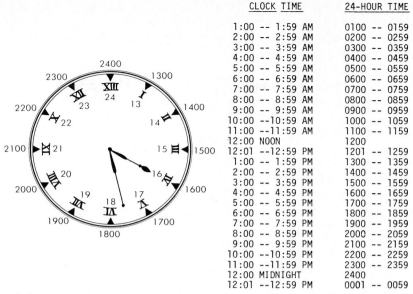

CLOCK TIME	24-HOUR TIME
1:00 -- 1:59 AM	0100 -- 0159
2:00 -- 2:59 AM	0200 -- 0259
3:00 -- 3:59 AM	0300 -- 0359
4:00 -- 4:59 AM	0400 -- 0459
5:00 -- 5:59 AM	0500 -- 0559
6:00 -- 6:59 AM	0600 -- 0659
7:00 -- 7:59 AM	0700 -- 0759
8:00 -- 8:59 AM	0800 -- 0859
9:00 -- 9:59 AM	0900 -- 0959
10:00 --10:59 AM	1000 -- 1059
11:00 --11:59 AM	1100 -- 1159
12:00 NOON	1200
12:01 --12:59 PM	1201 -- 1259
1:00 -- 1:59 PM	1300 -- 1359
2:00 -- 2:59 PM	1400 -- 1459
3:00 -- 3:59 PM	1500 -- 1559
4:00 -- 4:59 PM	1600 -- 1659
5:00 -- 5:59 PM	1700 -- 1759
6:00 -- 6:59 PM	1800 -- 1859
7:00 -- 7:59 PM	1900 -- 1959
8:00 -- 8:59 PM	2000 -- 2059
9:00 -- 9:59 PM	2100 -- 2159
10:00 --10:59 PM	2200 -- 2259
11:00 --11:59 PM	2300 -- 2359
12:00 MIDNIGHT	2400
12:01 --12:59 PM	0001 -- 0059

Figure 9-2. A 24-hour clock. Time is based on four digits; used in report writing.

conceal true identity. If a name was previously recorded wrongly, and the true name becomes known, the report should reflect the person's true name followed by the letters TN (true name). It is not uncommon for a suspect to use many aliases in an attempt to avoid detection. In report writing the suspect's true name is listed first, followed by his many aliases. For example, CLARK, Howard Robert, was (with aliases) Howard Donlon, Harry Emerson, George Lewis, Robert Stone, "Howie," "Steelhead."

The word "criminal" should not be used in reports. In its place the word "suspect" is used before a warrant is issued. The designation "defendant" is used after a warrant has been obtained. "Subject" is used when a person is not involved in criminal charges or is a juvenile.

Military time is now used by many departments in their reporting procedures. Military time is based on a twenty-four-hour clock. (See Figure 9-2.) The only exception to this would be in reporting the exact words of a witness or suspect in a direct quote regarding time.

Common, popular abbreviations may be used in report writing, viz., R. R., Inc., Misc., Dr., FBI, N.Y., Calif., etc. Do not make up your own. Your report will be read and acted upon by other persons who may not understand your abbreviations. Do not abbreviate terms common to police work in official reports. POI (point of impact), POE (point of entry), and HDB (had been drinking) would be proper on an interoffice memorandum, but would be meaningless to a city insurance clerk or a new city prosecutor. Long titles that are necessarily repeated in a report may be abbreviated after first using the full name and then placing the abbreviation to be used in parentheses—for example, Central Intelligence Agency (CIA), Immigration and Naturalization Service (INS).

Reports requiring statements of witnesses, victims, or other persons are understood to contain the substance of their story or testimony, not a direct quotation. Quota-

GUIDE TO THE SYSTEM OF REPORTING

STAGE	ITEM	DETAILS	STAGE	ITEM	DETAILS
1	Day, date, time, and place	Opposite number (if on premises include description of premises, e.g., dwelling house, etc.). Name of occupier, name and address of owner.	5	Statements	Person concerned. Police witnesses. Other witnesses. In exact words used by the speakers.
2	Person concerned	Name, address, apparent age, and occupation. Where applicable, full description of occurrence and injuries complained of.	6	Additional particulars	Friends informed (show by what means—if personally—the time must be shown). In cases of dead bodies or unconscious persons who are unidentified, include a full description of the person, dress, and property. How property disposed of. Advice given to complainants. Names and addresses exchanged. Expenses incurred. Condition of footwear or roadway. Time absent from beat. Station officer informed.
3	Ambulance	Time called. Time of arrival. Hospital to which person was conveyed.			
	Police action	Include full details of investigation in case of complaints.			
4	Damage to property	(Any kind.) With all particulars of owner.			

(London Metropolitan Police Cadet Training School — Hendon)

tion marks are not used. A judge or jury may doubt your ability to remember the exact words of a statement beyond "yes" or "no." Limit your use of direct quotes to short, vital responses that you can substantiate in court. Be sure to show that the statements were legally obtained; a report of arrest must demonstrate a legal arrest.

Profanity is not used in reports even when it is vital to the elements of the crime. Profane words should be kept in the officer's notebook. Blanks may be used in direct quotes in rare cases. For example, "Yes, I killed the _____ (profanity)." Never use abbreviations such as SOB or other such epithets. It is nearly always sufficient (a capital crime could be an exception) to state, "SMITH called JONES a profane name and was struck in the mouth" or "JONES was yelling loudly and profanely at officers." Record the exact words used by JONES in your notebook. If the suspect goes to court the judge may want to hear the exact words used by the defendant.

Personal opinions should be avoided. They lessen the value of a report. If a personal opinion is expressed, it should be labeled as such—"It is the opinion of reporting officer that. . . ."

The number of copies required for each report will vary depending upon uses and distribution. Each squad room is usually equipped with a prominent chart of the number of copies for each report. Check each report after you begin writing to determine if the last copy is being clearly reproduced.

Correct your own errors. The last mechanical step in report writing is to read your report before submitting it for approval. Evaluate your report. Determine how you can improve it. Does it meet with departmental standards? Does the report meet your personal standards? If the answers are no, revise the report.

Preparation for Report Writing

The first phase of report writing is preparation. In this step, all the available data in the case should be gathered. Both the writer's notes and the material of other officers who have worked on the case should be assembled. Tape recording and stenographic assistance are methods of information gathering. If such methods are available and the officer intends to use the recorded information as evidence, then, at the beginning of the tape of dictation there should be an introduction of persons present, witnesses, suspects, time, date, place of recording, advice as to legal rights, and an express waiver by the suspect should be given.

The data that may be gathered for reports includes the victim's statement, statements of witnesses, laboratory reports, investigative activities, statement obtained from suspect(s), arrest data, district attorney's prosecutive opinion, filing of the complaint, identification record of suspect(s), and any other miscellaneous information of value. In addition, it is imperative that all pertinent names obtained during the investigation be checked through the department's records and identification division for any reference material, wants, or prior records.

The second phase of report preparation should be to review all notes, sort the information gathered, then study and rearrange the material in the order that it will be set out in the report. Make sure all the material is understandable. If some items need clarification, this should be done. If need be, witnesses should be recontacted, the crime scene revisited, or whatever else is necessary in the interest of clarity and accuracy.

During an overseas Criminal Justice Practicum in the summer of 1970, sponsored by Michigan State University in cooperation with the London Metropolitan Police Department, the author, as a participant, visited the various training facilities of that police agency. While visiting the Metropolitan Police Cadet Training School at Hendon, the above report writing guide was noted to be one of the many instructional aids used in their cadet training process. (See p. 180.)

Responsibility for Reporting Crimes

In many states specified reports (felony, vehicle, fingerprints, etc.) are required to be forwarded to their respective state identification bureaus. By law, California makes it the duty of all sheriffs and chiefs of police to furnish daily to the Division of Law Enforcement, the Identification and Information Branch, reports on all felonies and certain misdemeanor sex crimes committed in their respective jurisdictions. In addition, they must submit reports concerning any lost, stolen, found, pledged, or pawned property. Reports of the above types, when processed at state headquarters, make it possible to identify criminals from a study of their methods of operation; they also aid in the recovery of identifiable property.

The sheriff or chief's legal responsibility regarding the submission of reports is delegated to each officer who has the legal duty to the individual state, and as a moral duty to the sheriff or chief, to report any crimes that come to the officer's attention. Deliberate failure to report is a dereliction of duty and may be grounds for suspension. Making a false report or knowing the report to be false is also cause for suspension or dismissal from duty.

Crime reports are taken when it is brought to the attention of the department that within the city or county, a misdemeanor has been committed, a felony has been committed, or a felony is believed to have been committed. When officers are directed by radio to investigate crimes, they are responsible for making crime reports when they determine that crimes were committed. The unit within whose beat boundaries a crime occurs is generally responsible for the crime report if that unit is present at the crime scene. In those instances where the police unit of the beat of occurrence is not available for a radio call, the first unit dispatched by radio to the scene is ordinarily the unit responsible for the report if a crime has occurred. An officer who determines that a crime has occurred becomes responsible for the report since she or he has the necessary information for the report forms. An assisting officer may, when so authorized, make the crime report. Some incidents that come to the attention of police are not recorded because they are considered of insufficient importance, such as, for example, violations observed by police requiring only "warning" or "party advised." However, all such incidents should be recorded on a Daily Log Sheet or Daily Activities Report.

Reporting Methods

In the early pioneering days of law enforcement, a few short words or sentences constituted a law-enforcement officer's report. The "story" is told of a Texas Ranger's report submitted in a homicide case. The following is alleged to represent the report made in that case.

NAME	Big Nose Smith
CRIME	Homicide
DISPOSITION	Mean as hell, had to shoot him

There are, of course, many report writing systems employed by police agencies in the United States. For example, some departments have officers in the field telephone in to headquarters and dictate their reports. In this type of reporting, the officer should be sure to include all necessary identifying data. This procedure minimizes the report writing time required at the end of each shift. Other departments require officers to complete all reports at headquarters prior to going off duty.

A system employing the use of dictating equipment within the police car if away from headquarters is utilized by other departments. Reports are recorded on a plastic belt and subsequently transcribed by a clerical employee onto a report form. This type of reporting permits the investigating officer to remain in the field and be available for call. When dictating on recording equipment, the officer reporting should make sure to identify the heading of the report correctly, enunciate distinctly, spell out all names, and adhere to all the other principles of good report writing.

Some departments use a reporting system that utilizes modern duplicating machines in combination with old-fashioned handwriting or handprinting. Reproduction of reports and their distribution are accomplished with minimum effort. During the course of their watch, officers carry blank report forms into the field, usually in a briefcase or attaché case. Thereafter, when officers have to write reports, they use the proper forms in recording specific offenses or complaints. In this way information that is initially recorded in the field is recorded (handprinted or written) directly onto the appropriate form, thereby completing the report at the scene. In many instances the report is finished by the time the officer leaves the victim's premises. On some occasions, officers make additional comments on the report after leaving the scene; however, this can be accomplished while the officer remains on the beat. When reports are made in the field, officers can remain visible to persons passing through their beats. In addition, officers can remain available for radio calls while they write their reports. Exceptions to preparing reports in the field are usually permitted when the report is several pages long or highly detailed, or when a typed report is required and the supervisor authorizes same. With experience, the officer becomes adept at putting the information down on the form in a style that is satisfactory as a finished product. Field reports are often printed on NCR paper (no carbon required). However, when using NCR paper, it is essential that the metal backing plate be used to produce clear copies. A medium ball-point pen should be used. Care should be taken to ensure that the last duplicate copy is readable.

Handprinted capitalization of all words in reports ensures uniformity, legibility, readability, and the elimination of mistakes of capitalization. Numbers should be clearly printed with sharp angles to avoid mistake. In the narrative portion of the report, words are used for numbers below a hundred (one, two, eighty-eight) and numerals are used for 100 and above (101, 188, 275). Dates and addresses should be printed in numbers. When officers complete and turn in their reports, a supervisor reviews and signs them if they are prepared properly. In some agen-

cies the supervisory officer may indicate the routing of the report and the number of copies needed. The report is also cleared or assigned for follow-up by the detectives. It is then reproduced on a copying machine by the records section. Some departments require all reports to be typed by either the officer making the report or a clerical employee.

The reporting procedure in many departments often begins with the recording of a complaint on the complaint form. Thereafter, the complaint is assigned to a particular officer or unit for appropriate handling. The matter is investigated and a report submitted as soon as possible. If the offense is determined to be a felony, the initial complaint form would contain only the necessary identifying information in the form section. Under details, a notation would be made *"see crime report."* Thereafter, all information obtained in that case would be reported on a crime report used for felony reporting.

The Format of a Report

Reports and reporting forms used by police agencies throughout the United States vary considerably. Differences in reporting forms are the result of department needs, requirements, or particular preferences. Despite the variances in reporting forms, the type of information sought by officers the world over is essentially the same in regard to the detection and apprehension of criminals, crime solving, and the rendering of police service. The form or composition of many of the report forms used by police agencies basically contains two reports. (See Figure 9-3.)

The *form* or first section of most police reports varies in length and content. The format of the form section consists of fill-in blocks and blank spaces that call for specific responses by the reporting officer. These

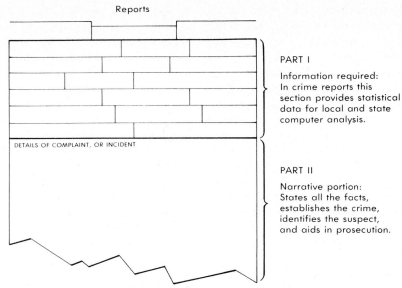

Reports

PART I

Information required:
In crime reports this
section provides statistical
data for local and state
computer analysis.

DETAILS OF COMPLAINT, OR INCIDENT

PART II

Narrative portion:
States all the facts,
establishes the crime,
identifies the suspect,
and aids in prosecution.

Figure 9-3. Two major sections of reports.

blocks are identified as a guide to ensure that vital information is not excluded from the report. Also, the fill-in portion of the report forms is designed to facilitate the rapid transfer of the report data to computer punch cards for electronic analysis of crime and suspects. Part I includes M.O. data.

The type of information required in the form section of the report generally consists of such data as case or file number, date and time of report, type of offense and classification if applicable, date and time reported, victim or source of complaint, addresses, telephone numbers, description of suspect(s) and vehicles. It is extremely important that all the boxes in this form section of the report be properly and completely filled in. Whenever the required information is not known, but appropriate to the crime, the space is left blank, or the word "unknown" or abbreviation "unk" can be used. If the reported matter or crime occurrence involves a felonious offense, a felony crime report is used. A felony crime report format has a longer and more detailed form section em-

phasizing the method of operation of the suspect.

The *narrative* or second part of a report format is the body of the report and sets forth the *details*—in other words, the story of what happened. Many officers find it easier to make a report by beginning with the suspect's first known act and recording successive acts in the sequence of occurrence. Describe exactly what the witness saw, heard, or did. In the *narrative* portion of the report, refer to individuals as suspects, witnesses, and victims. Refer to, for example, witness JONES, suspect SMITH, defendant ADAMS, or victim WILSON.

The details of a report should describe any physical evidence obtained, location of evidence, who found it, how identified, and disposition. For example, describe a heel print found on top of a counter near bank manager's desk, lifted by identification officer R. L. Mason. All other details that might be connected with the crime or incident should be set forth. Property taken should be itemized, described completely and accurately, and the value of property listed (owner's estimate). Wherever possible, a complete physical description of the suspect(s) should be made.

Some departments require a *synopsis* (summary) in felony cases. The synopsis would appear as the first item in the report under details of case. A synopsis is a clear and concise account, in chronological order, of the important facts contained in the report—a condensed version of the report's substance. The synopsis is designed to save the reader's time if it is well stated. Statements in the synopsis *must* be substantiated by information set out in the subsequent details.

Types of Reports

Reports and reporting forms vary considerably in local, state, and federal agencies. Variances occur because of such factors as the responsibility and jurisdiction the particular department has, the peculiar needs of a department, the nature of the subject matter, and individual agency preference. Regardless of these differences, police agencies concern themselves with the following types of reports: (1) internal business reports which relate to the management of the agency, for example, personnel reports, equipment reports, correspondence, property maintenance, purchases, financial, and similar matters; (2) technical reports relating to any specialized subject, viz., electronic equipment performance and capabilities, video file system, building specifications, and other matters relating to proper functioning of police management; (3) summary reports which furnish intelligence information necessary to the solution of crime, accident, and police administrative problems (summary reports serve the useful purpose of keeping executive and legislative authority and the general public informed as to problems, progress, and needs of the par-

ticular agency); (4) operation reports which relate to the reporting of police incidents, investigation, arrests, identification, traffic, and a number of other items necessary to the conduct of police operations. Operation reports are the raw material from which administrative reports are derived. Inasmuch as *operation reports* are the type most officers are primarily concerned with, the following types of reports shall be discussed: misdemeanor and/or miscellaneous reports; felony reports; follow-up reports; arrest reports; and vehicle accident reports.

Misdemeanor and/or miscellaneous reports

This kind of report is used to record all misdemeanor crimes and incidents of a miscellaneous nature. The form is known by other names, e.g., complaint report, incident report, complaint and/or incident report, etc. The report, when filled out, includes such identifying data as the nature of the complaint, code violation if applicable, file number, date and time received, location, name of victim, witnesses, suspects, addresses and telephone numbers, and descriptions. There is generally sufficient space on the form under the heading Details of Crime or Incident to report the results of the investigation and the action taken. If there is need for additional space to complete the record of a particular incident or offense, the reverse side of the form, a blank piece of paper, or some form of a continuation sheet can be used as the second or accompanying page. Whenever a second page is used, however, the added page should contain a heading with identifying data listed such as file number, type of crime, victim's name, in order to connect the page with the proper report to which it pertains.

All misdemeanor offenses are reported by the responsible officer if the crime has a victim. Note that all misdemeanors against persons or property will have a victim against whose person or property the crime was directed. Many victims of minor crimes do not want a report made and indicate that they would not sign a complaint even if the suspect were identified and arrested. When the victims are unwilling to sign complaints on misdemeanors, usually because they "don't want to cause any trouble," it is vital that the information be recorded for the following reasons.

> In order that the detectives and supervisors are kept up to date on crime.
> Victims may discover additional loss or damage, or change their minds for other reasons and decide to report crimes at a later date.
> Their insurance agents will tell them they cannot make claims until they have made police reports.
> Known suspects of unreported crimes may be sought for similar crimes on reported cases.

Many times officers are sent to take a report where investigation determines that a crime may have occurred but it cannot positively be established; or, that a misdemeanor crime is determined to have occurred, but the victim does not desire to make a complaint. Some examples of these cases are

> Money is missing from a purse in a locked house, but "no one in the family could have possibly done a terrible thing like steal from the family."
> A door is found open that was probably locked by the victim, and there is no evidence of any loss or forced entry.
> Victims report the loss of an item from their garage, but a friend may have borrowed it for a vacation without telling them.
> A screen that looks freshly cut may have been cut by the last tenant who one day lost the house key and had to break into the house.

> "I know the Smith kids are the ones that got into the garage and stole the tools, but I don't want you to arrest them. I have to live here, you know."

When a misdemeanor report is first recorded on a misdemeanor and/or miscellaneous type form (or similar complaint report form), and it is subsequently determined that the reported offense is a felony, or attempted felony, or a type of crime that requires a felony crime report to be filed, the misdemeanor and/or miscellaneous report, under Details of the Report, should contain the notation, *"see crime report."* The crime report (felony report) would thereafter be completed, together with any follow-up reports, and would represent the case file on that offense being investigated. A completed misdemeanor and/or miscellaneous report, involving a prowler complaint, showing the type of information needed is shown in Figure 9-4.

Felony reports

Crimes of a felonious nature are reported on a felony crime report form. The exception of not preparing a felony report would be made in those cases determined by policy to be of such a nature that the knowledge of a specialist is required, e.g., narcotics and vice offenses. The information required in a felony report form is much more detailed than that required in a lesser crime such as a misdemeanor or noncriminal matter. Many law-enforcement agencies have specially printed felony crime report forms which contain all the method of operation factors and additional information as required by the particular agency. It is important that every officer understand the specific information that must be secured during an investigation to prepare a crime report that emphasizes the modus operandi of the criminal.

It is not feasible to discuss here the many different police report forms and reporting

MISDEMEANOR and/or MISCELLANEOUS REPORT

CRIME OR INCIDENT: 647g PC PROWLER (hypothetical)   FILE NO. 79-224

STATION Central   DATE RECEIVED 2-6-79   TIME 2215   RECEIVED BY Sgt. J.R.Brown
                             LAST   FIRST   MIDDLE

INFORMANT'S NAME PALMER, Helen   Marie (Mrs.)   TELEPHONE 88-55441
                                  STREET
    ADDRESS 567 Maple St., Apt. "C" Center City, California
                  LAST   FIRST   MIDDLE

VICTIM'S NAME Same as above
(IF DIFFERENT
FROM INFORMANT)   STREET   TELEPHONE
    ADDRESS Same as above   CITY

LOCATION 567 Maple St., Apt. "C"
                                        DATE OCCURRED 2-6-79   TIME 2210

SUSPECT   Unknown Suspect

ADDRESS   -   TELEPHONE

	SEX	RACE	AGE	HEIGHT	WEIGHT	HAIR	EYES	DIST. MARKS
DESCRIPTION	M	W	17-19	5'10-6	150-160	Dk.Brn	Unk	High cheek bones/large eyes

OTHER DESCRIPTION Long Dk.Brn.Hair, shoulder length, parted in center;

VEHICLE   small frame silver rimmed glasses; lt.tan windbreaker jacket;
(none seen) yellow sport shirt; blue jeans   LICENSE NO.

DETAILS OF CRIME OR INCIDENT:

Advised by radio, 2217 hours this date to contact female victim of a
Peeping Tom, at Apt. "C", 567 Maple St.; suspect scared away. Last
observed fleeing north on Maple St.

Apt. located mid-block on W side of Maple; 3-story white stucco; Caucasian
middle-class neighborhood. Apt. set back about 30' W of sidewalk line.
A 6' wood fence borders property on both sides and rear. Victim, WFA,
age 42, resides on first floor.

Victim advised that she was sitting alone in her living room which fronts
on Maple St., watching TV at 10:10 p.m. 2/6/79, when she heard a noise outside
ground floor window on E side of her apartment. She stated that she looked
out her apartment window but saw no one. Victim said that 10 minutes later
she again heard noises outside the same window and proceeded to the window
to draw the shade. On approaching this window victim observed above-
described young man peering into her window. She stated that suspect fled
as soon as he realized he had been seen; running north on Maple St.

Victim stated that she resides alone and has been bothered on three previous
occasions by a suspect of similar description. Mrs Palmer mentioned that
due to the poor lighting in her room her description of the suspect is not
too accurate.

Several overlapping footprints noted outside victim's front window; one clear
shoeprint located; cast made. Neighbors contacted and area cruised with
negative results. Shoe design set forth -

Follow-up investigation to be conducted.

15 – 7205 – 401   INVESTIGATING OFFICERS Wilson #34/Brown #8 SUPERVISOR Lt.Moore

Figure 9-4. Misdemeanor and/or miscellaneous report.

procedures used by police agencies throughout the United States. However, it is important to emphasize one of the most vital aspects of felony crime reporting—the modus operandi (M.O.) of a suspect. A detailed review of modus operandi factors and the use of M.O. data is explained in Chapter 4. As it has been stated, the M.O. factors include the following: (1) date and time committed; (2) person attacked or type of victim; (3) property attacked or type of premises entered; (4) how attacked (point of entry); (5) means of attack: weapons, tools, or physical force involved; (6) object of attack: reason crime is committed or attempted; (7) trademark or peculiarity; (8) what the suspect said; and (9) transportation used.

Any analysis of the modus operandi used must take into consideration variables in time, type of premises attacked, and other circumstances that influenced the criminal in the particular offense reported. Whether or not a burglar alarm system could be observed from the outside of the premises might have been the determining factor in whether the point of entry was a window, a rear door, or the roof. Conditions in the victimized premises may have been such that prior "casing" of the location was necessary. Thefts in which some of the property stolen (object of attack) might superficially indicate those responsible were juveniles, may in fact turn out to be the work of known, experienced adult burglars when all aspects of the case are observed, reported, and analyzed.

Figure 9-5 illustrates the hypothetical facts in a specimen case involving an armed robbery. This sample crime report is set forth to demonstrate the proper recording of the modus operandi factors and the details of a crime occurrence.

The crime report illustrated in Figure 9-5 is designed to include the information that the officer should obtain in order that the report may be properly classified, searched, filed, and retrieved, according to the modus

operandi used by the responsible suspect. Emphasis is placed on the importance of determining and reporting the method of operation of the criminal as well as including an accurate and detailed description of all suspects and stolen property.

Attached to the crime report (Figure 9-5), or submitted separately, are reports captioned *property report* and *evidence report* (as shown in Figure 9-6a and b). The property report and evidence report would be recorded on a *continuation form,* the same as that used for pages 2 and 3 of the sample McDaniel's Market crime report illustrated in Figure 9-5.

As *follow-up* or *supplementary* reports are submitted in the above McDaniel's Market case, for example, they would be written up or typed on the same *continuation form* as that used to record the *property report* and *evidence report* (Figure 9-6a and b), but the form would have a caption *follow-up* or *supplementary report* (Figure 9-6c).

Single and multiple crimes

Insofar as it is possible, each crime report should describe only one offense. However, in connection with multiple crimes, for example, robbery, rape, and kidnaping, committed against the same victim and constituting what might be considered as one continuous action, one report is sufficient. It must be recognized, however, that robbery, rape, and kidnaping are each separate and distinct offenses. If two or more types of crime arising out of the same incident are described in one crime report, the most serious offense would be listed first.

In offenses against the person such as homicide, rape, or aggravated assault, a separate crime report is generally prepared for each person against whom the crimes were committed or attempted. In thefts, a report is made for each separate and distinct operation undertaken or attempted. A robbery report is prepared for each separate robbery case. Each offense or attempt is

```
SAMPLE REPORT - Robbery                                        I. CASE NO.
Original Form 8-1/2 X 11                                        78-1024
                           CRIME REPORT

                      BLANK POLICE DEPARTMENT
                      BLANK, CALIFORNIA        CA5200
```

2. CODE SECTION	3. CRIME	4. CLASSIFICATION	5. REPORT AREA
211a PC	Armed Robbery	Market w/revolver	5

6. DATE AND TIME OCCURRED - DAY	7. DATE AND TIME REPORTED	8. LOCATION OF OCCURRENCE
12/29/78 0700 Friday	12/29/78	100 North "C" St., San Bernardino

9. VICTIM'S NAME LAST, FIRST, MIDDLE (FIRM IF BUSINESS)	10. RESIDENCE ADDRESS	11. RES PHONE
McDaniel's Market		

12. OCCUPATION	13. RACE - SEX	14. AGE	15. DOB	16. BUSINESS ADDRESS (SCHOOL IF JUVENILE)	17. BUS. PHONE
Grocery Store				Same as 8	632-1505

CODES FOR BOXES 20 AND 30   V=VICTIM W=WITNESS P=PARENT RP=REPORTING PARTY DC=DISCOVERED CRIME

18. CHECK IF MORE NAMES IN CONTINUATION X

19. NAME - LAST, FIRST, MIDDLE	20. CODE	21. RESIDENCE ADDRESS	22. RESIDENCE PHONE
McDaniel, John Joseph	RP	1234 Elm Avenue	632-3210

23. OCCUPATION	24. RACE - SEX	25. AGE	26. DOB	27. BUSINESS ADDRESS (SCHOOL IF JUVENILE)	28. BUSINESS PHONE
Owner	MWA	54	9/9/24	Same as 8	632-1505

29. NAME - LAST, FIRST, MIDDLE	30. CODE	31. RESIDENCE ADDRESS	32. RESIDENCE PHONE
Johnson, Mary Lois	W	955 North "C" San Bernardino	632-1433

33. OCCUPATION	34. RACE - SEX	35. AGE	36. DOB	37. BUSINESS ADDRESS (SCHOOL IF JUVENILE)	38. BUSINESS PHONE
Housewife	WFA	48	12/12/30	None	

MODUS OPERANDI (SEE INSTRUCTIONS)

39. DESCRIBE CHARACTERISTICS OF PREMISES AND AREA WHERE OFFENSE OCCURRED
Large groc. mkt in downtown area next to hotel. Alley in rear, Pkg.lot on E.side

40. DESCRIBE BRIEFLY HOW OFFENSE WAS COMMITTED
Climbs fire escape on adjoining hotel, jumps to roof of mkt, drills out 20" hole in roof, lowers self via rope to floor of store, waits till opening, forces mgr. to open safe, locks victims in walk-in cooler, leaves through rear alley exit.

41. DESCRIBE WEAPON, INSTRUMENT, EQUIPMENT, TRICK, DEVICE OR FORCE USED
2" B/S Rev. 1-1/4" drill, chisel, hammer, rope

42. MOTIVE - TYPE OF PROPERTY TAKEN OR OTHER REASON FOR OFFENSE
Money & Checks

43. ESTIMATED LOSS VALUE AND/OR EXTENT OF INJURIES - MINOR, MAJOR
$8,110.

44. WHAT DID SUSPECT/S SAY - NOTE PECULIARITIES
"This is a robbery, behave and you won't get hurt. Get over here 'fass',"

45. VICTIM'S ACTIVITY JUST PRIOR TO AND/OR DURING OFFENSE
Opening Store

46. TRADEMARK - OTHER DISTINCTIVE ACTION OF SUSPECT/S
Ate on premises, drank Vodka

47. VEHICLE USED - LICENSE NO. - ID NO. - YEAR - MAKE - MODEL - COLORS (OTHER IDENTIFYING CHARACTERISTICS)
None seen

48. SUSPECT NO. 1 (LAST, FIRST, MIDDLE)	49. RACE - SEX	50. AGE	51. HT.	52. WT.	53. HAIR	54. EYES	55. ID NO. OR DOB	56. ARRESTED
S-1 Name Unknown	WMA	30-35	6'	200	blk	brn		YES ☐ NO X

57. ADDRESS, CLOTHING AND OTHER IDENTIFYING MARKS OR CHARACTERISTICS
Work clothes, wore flashy ring with large brilliant stone

58. SUSPECT NO. 2 (LAST, FIRST, MIDDLE)	59. RACE - SEX	60. AGE	61. HT.	62. WT.	63. HAIR	64. EYES	65. ID NO. OR DOB	66. ARRESTED
S-2 Name Unknown	NMA	30-35	5'8'	180	blk	brn		YES ☐ NO X

67. ADDRESS, CLOTHING AND OTHER IDENTIFYING MARKS OR CHARACTERISTICS
Work clothes, Army type boots, small blue dot left cheek under eye

68. CHECK IF MORE NAMES IN CONTINUATION ☐

REPORTING OFFICERS	RECORDING OFFICER	TYPED BY	DATE AND TIME	ROUTED BY
Smith #18/Jones #35	Jones	mmk	12/29/78 1300	Owens

FURTHER ACTION	COPIES TO:		
X YES	X DETECTIVE	X CII	
☐ NO	☐ JUVENILE	☐ PATROL	
	X DIST. ATTNY	☐ OTHER ____	
	X SO./P.D.	☐ OTHER ____	

REVIEWED BY	DATE
Moore, R.L. Lt.	12/29/78

Figure 9-5. A completed, three-page hypothetical felony crime report. This form, which emphasizes the suspect's method of operation, is used widely in California.

SAMPLE REPORT - Robbery (2)
Original Form 8-1/2 X 11

69. CASE NO.
78-1024

BLANK POLICE DEPARTMENT
BLANK, CALIFORNIA   CA5200

70. CODE SECTION	71. CRIME	72. CLASSIFICATION
211a PC	Armed Robbery	Market w/revolver

73. VICTIM'S NAME - LAST, FIRST, MIDDLE (FIRM IF BUS.)	74. ADDRESS RESIDENCE [X] BUSINESS	75. PHONE
McDaniel's Market	100 North "C" St.	632-1505

W-2 RENTSTROM, Josephine Mary, Rm 410 Shasta Hotel, 632-1349
Beauty Operator, WFA, 52, 2/18/25, Classic Beauty Salon, 10th and K Sts.
Phone 632-1010

12/29/78 0700 RP after unlocking front door of store, proceeded to the back
storeroom where he was confronted by two unknown suspects. S-1,
the taller of the two, pointed a 2" B/S revolver at RP stating -
"This is a robbery, behave and you won't get hurt, get over here
fast (the word fast slurred to sound like 'fass')." S-2, a negro,
short and stocky, did not speak. At that time W-1 entered the
market at which time S-2 escorted her to the rear of the store
where RP and S-1 were standing.

S-1 then ordered RP into rear office where he commanded RP to open
the floor safe (combination Mosler) and get the money. $8,110 in
used currency and checks given to S-1. (Three $100 bills, two $50
bills and about 20 checks were included).

Thereafter, S-1 ordered RP and W-1 into the walk-in refrigerator
at which time the door was closed, the outside strap latch locked,
and a stick of wood put in the hasp to secure the lock. After
about 24 minutes, RP succeeded in opening the door.

Entrance to the market was determined to have been gained by cutting
a 20" square hole through the roof. A series of holes were cut through
the tar paper and wood with a 1½" bit. Some holes overlapped. Where
they did not, the wood between the holes appeared to have been cut
with a chisel. Two sets of shoeprints were observed to lead from the
edge of the roof to the hole, but did not return. It was noted that
the Shasta Hotel is located adjacent to this market, which hotel has
a fire escape opposite the edge of the roof where the shoeprints start.
In the market attic, trails in the dust led from a point just below
the hole in the roof to a trap door in the store ceiling. The trap
door, which had been closed at the end of the previous business day,
was open. From this point there was noted to be a 12' drop to the
open storeroom floor below. Dust, scuff marks and partial shoeprints
of the same pattern which appeared on the roof, were observed on the
linoleum floor just below the trap door.

Two 1/2" holes, 4'8½", and the other 5'2" above floor level had been
drilled through the storeroom wall which faces the front of the store.

REPORTING OFFICERS Smith #18/Jones#35	RECORDING OFFICER Jones	TYPED BY mmk	DATE AND TIME 12/29/78	ROUTED BY Owens

FURTHER ACTION [X] YES [ ] NO

COPIES TO: [X] DETECTIVE [X] CII [ ] JUVENILE [ ] PATROL [X] DIST. ATTNY. [ ] OTHER [ ] S.O./P.D. [ ] OTHER

REVIEWED BY Moore, R. L. Lt.   DATE 12/29/78

SAMPLE REPORT - Robbery
Original Form 8-1/2 X 11   (3)

69. CASE NO.

78-1024

BLANK POLICE DEPARTMENT
BLANK, CALIFORNIA   CA5200

70. CODE SECTION 211a PC	71. CRIME Armed Robbery	72. CLASSIFICATION Market w/revolver

73. VICTIM'S NAME - LAST, FIRST, MIDDLE (FIRM IF BUS.) McDaniel's Market	74. ADDRESS 100 North "C" St.	RESIDENCE	[X] BUSINESS	75. PHONE 632-1505

Fresh sawdust and plaster was found on the floor on both sides of the wall just below the holes. Remnants of three packages of Gallo salami, three empty milk cartons, a half-pint of Samarov Vodka and a brown plastic satchel were found in the storeroom. The satchel had a 16" length of 1/2" hemp rope tied to it's handles and contained the following tools: wood brace, four wood bits, a carpenter's hammer, wood chisel, linoleum knife, 12" crow bar, pair of side cutters, and a keyhole saw. The tools, satchel, and rope were foreign to the crime scene and were not recognized by anyone who had legal access to the property.

W-2   a guest of the Shasta Hotel, reported that about 0200 hours she got up to take an Alka-Seltzer and saw a black man and a white man ascending the fire escape of the hotel. She stated that she returned to bed and did not notify anyone. W-2 advised that she did not believe she could identify either of these suspects.

- PROPERTY REPORT ATTACHED.

Identification Officer LEE JENKINS processed the crime scene.
SEE EVIDENCE REPORT BY JENKINS.

Investigation continuing.

REPORTING OFFICERS Smith #18/Jones #35	RECORDING OFFICER Jones	TYPED BY mmk	DATE AND TIME 12/29/78	ROUTED BY Owens

FURTHER ACTION [X] YES [ ] NO   COPIES TO: [X]

[X] DETECTIVE   [X] CII
[ ] JUVENILE   [ ] PATROL
[X] DIST. ATTNY. [ ] OTHER
[ ] S.O./P.D.   [ ] OTHER

REVIEWED BY Moore, R. L., Lt.	DATE 12/29/78

CAL. JUS. C? #2

(CONTINUATION FORM)

SAMPLE REPORT - Robbery Original Form 8½ X 11 (hypothetical)	69 CASE NO 78-1024

BLANK POLICE DEPARTMENT CA5200
BLANK, CALIFORNIA

70 CODE SECTION 211a PC	71 CRIME Armed Robbery	72 CLASSIFICATION Market w/revolver		
73 VICTIM'S NAME - LAST, FIRST, MIDDLE (FIRM IF BUS.) McDaniel's Market		74 ADDRESS ☐ RESIDENCE ☒ BUSINESS 100 North "C" St.		75 PHONE 632-1505

PROPERTY REPORT

ITEM	DESCRIPTION	VALUE
1.	Currency in denominations of $1. 5, 10, 20's; 3 - $100's; 2 - $50.'s; and approximately 20 checks. (Owner's estimate). Checks taken were personal type checks under $50 and drawn on the Bank of America or Wells-Fargo National Bank.	$8,110.00

REPORTING OFFICERS Smith #18/Jones #35	RECORDING OFFICER Jones	TYPED BY mmk	DATE AND TIME 12/29/78 1300	ROUTED BY Owens

FURTHER ACTION ☒ YES ☐ NO
COPIES TO: ☒ DETECTIVE ☐ JUVENILE ☒ DIST. ATTNY. ☐ S.O./P.D.
☒ CII ☐ PATROL ☐ OTHER ☐ OTHER

REVIEWED BY Moore, R. L., Lt.	DATE 12/29/78

CAL. JUS. CR #2 △ OSP

Figure 9-6. Three continuation forms. (a) Property report; (b) evidence report; (c) follow-up report that would be submitted in conjunction with the sample felony crime report shown in Figure 9-4.

(CONTINUATION FORM)

SAMPLE REPORT - Robbery Original Form 8½ x 11 (hypothetical)				69 CASE NO 78-1024
	BLANK POLICE DEPARTMENT	CA5200		
	BLANK, CALIFORNIA			

70 CODE SECTION 211a PC	71 CRIME **Armed Robbery**	72 CLASSIFICATION Market w/revolver		
73 VICTIM'S NAME - LAST, FIRST, MIDDLE (FIRM IF BUS) McDaniel's Market		74 ADDRESS | RESIDENCE | X BUSINESS 100 North "C" St.		75 PHONE 632-1505

EVIDENCE REPORT

ITEM   DESCRIPTION

1.   One, brown satchel (plastic material), 18" x 14" x 8",
      with a 16' length of 1/2" hemp rope tied to its
      handles. Contents of bag included: 1-wood brace (red
      in color), 4-1¼" bits, carpenter's hammer, wood chisel,
      linoleum knife, 12" crowbar, side cutters, keyhole saw.

2.   3-empty pint milk cartons (Arden Farms Dairy).

3.   **Remnants** of 3 packages of salami (Gallo brand).

4.   One-half pint empty bottle of vodka (Samarov label).

   The above items were collected and marked for identification
by Identification Officer JENKINS #63, with the initials "L.J."
and maintained by him until delivered to Lt. JOHN WILSON, Police
Crime Laboratory on 12/29/78. Specimens of tar paper, insulation
material, wood chips, and ceiling plaster were obtained by Officer
JENKINS from area of roof breakthrough, for possible future
comparison purposes. Ten photographs of shoeprints taken from
the surface of the market roof, the attic, and from the area
below the trap door of the market ceiling were also obtained
by Officer JENKINS for comparison with the footwear of suspects
developed in this investigation.

REPORTING OFFICERS Lee Jenkins #63	RECORDING OFFICER Jenkins	TYPED BY mmk	DATE AND TIME 12/29/78 1400	ROUTED BY Owens

FURTHER ACTION [X] YES [ ] NO   COPIES TO: [X] DETECTIVE [ ] JUVENILE [X] DIST. ATTNY [ ] SO./P.D.   [X] CII [ ] PATROL [ ] OTHER [ ] OTHER

	REVIEWED BY Moore, R. L., Lt.	DATE 12/29/78

CAL. JUS. CR #2

SAMPLE REPORT - Robbery
Original Form 8½ X 11
(hypothetical)

69. CASE NO.
78-1024

BLANK POLICE DEPARTMENT
BLANK, CALIFORNIA   CA5200

70. CODE SECTION	71. CRIME	72. CLASSIFICATION		
211a PC	Armed Robbery	Market w/revolver		

73. VICTIM'S NAME - LAST, FIRST, MIDDLE (FIRM IF BUS.)	74. ADDRESS RESIDENCE X BUSINESS	75. PHONE
McDaniel's Market	100 North "C" St.	632-1505

<u>**FOLLOW-UP or SUPPLEMENTARY REPORT**</u>

(For reports made subsequent to the initial report)

REPORTING OFFICERS	RECORDING OFFICER	TYPED BY	DATE AND TIME	ROUTED BY

FURTHER ACTION ☐ YES   COPIES TO ☐ DETECTIVE ☐ CII
☐ NO   ☐ JUVENILE ☐ PATROL
☐ DIST. ATTNY ☐ OTHER _____
☐ SO./PD. ☐ OTHER _____

REVIEWED BY   DATE

CAL JUS CR #2   △ OSP

considered only one case even though there were two or more victims. In burglaries of hotels or rooming houses, any single operation, despite the fact that more than one room was burglarized, is considered one case for reporting purposes. Burglaries of apartments or separate dwelling units are reported as separate cases for each premise entered. Crime reports are taken in felony cases even though many victims of such crimes do not want a report made and refuse to sign a complaint—despite the fact that the suspect was identified and arrested.

Descriptions in Report Writing

Descriptions of persons

Although the first page of many felony crime report forms does not provide sufficient space for a detailed description under *"suspects,"* the following information, if available, should be included under *"details of crime"*:

Name, including aliases and nickname
Address, present and past
Telephone number
Sex
Race
Age, birthdate, and place
Height
Weight
Hair color
Hair characteristics
Eyes, color
Build
Complexion
Beard
Marks, scars, birthmarks, tattoos, limp, amputations
Teeth
Unusual mannerisms or voice accent
Dress habits
Education

Occupations, present and past
Hobbies
Parents, brothers, sisters
Relations, associates, friends
Military service, ID number
Social security number
Marital status, wife's maiden name
Other information

Description of property

The more accurately the article is described, the easier it will be to locate. Wherever information is available, the minimum description of an article listed in a crime report should cover

Quantity of article
Kind of article
Physical description (model, style, design, shape, size)
Material (gold, silver, wool, white metal, gold color, etc.)
Color
Condition (include age)
Value (market value of property at the time report is submitted; indicate method of determining value, e.g., owner's estimate, jeweler's appraisal, property receipt, etc.)
Trade names
Identifying numbers, initials, marks
Serial numbers

In describing and listing stolen property, list items bearing identifiable numbers together in one grouping; list property with personal names or initials in another separate grouping; and items without identifiable numbers or markings, together in another separate grouping. When listing in a report stolen or missing property, assign a number to each article in the list, describe the article in another column, and in a third column list the value of the item. For example:

ITEM	DESCRIPTION	VALUE
1	One (1) woman's size 6, YG wedding ring, orange blossom design, engraved on the inside with initials "J.R. to M.R. 6/1/71."	$50
2	One (1) man's YG ring, fleur-de-lis carving on both sides of setting. Setting of black onyx stone, 1 inch long by 1/2 inch wide, size 9. And so on.	$125

Vehicles Whenever a vehicle is material to a report, a description of it should contain at least the following information:

Year manufactured
Make
Model and body type
Color
License number
Motor number or vehicle identification number (VIN)
Accessories, distinguishing marks, or characteristics including upholstery, interior of vehicle (dashboard), seat covers, etc.
Registered owner
Legal owner

Description of Real Property All pertinent data should be included such as dimensions, topography, vegetation, and the type of structure, including such information as composition, size, and height in stories.

Firearms Indicate the type, such as revolver, semiautomatic pistol, rifle, or shotgun; the manufacturer's name and code mark; the caliber or gauge and barrel length; the serial number and, if one has been assigned, the city or state registration number. Also describe the finish such as

nickeled or blued and whether the stock or grips are bone, wood, metal, plastic, pearl, or ivory. Other identifying marks such as initials and engravings must also be shown. For example:

Revolver, Colt "Cobra" .38 caliber, 2 inch bbl, standard sights, blued finish, stag handles, serial number 1841-IW, initials "J.J.H." scratched on frame under the grips, two years old, good condition. Value $60.00.

Since different manufacturers produced models of Colt, Smith and Wesson, and other makes for the armed forces during the war, duplication of serial numbers frequently occurred. Therefore specific information concerning the name of the manufacturer and the owner's identifying marks cannot be overemphasized. Particular care should be taken in the description of foreign and souvenir guns, many of which are brought home by members of the armed services. Frequently these guns have no serial or other numbers and an exact description is necessary for identification.

Watches Show the type such as wristwatch, lapel watch, pocket watch; whether it is a man's or woman's timepiece; the manufacturer's name; the description, type of metal or material, and size of case; the description of the face; whether the case and/or face is set with stones, such as diamonds or rubies, and the number and color of the stones; the movement and case numbers; and the number of jewels. Also describe all initials, monograms, and identifying marks. For example:

Man's wristwatch, Bucherer, chronometer, Incablock, automatic, round white gold-filled case, raised black Arabic numbers on round open satin finish white gold face, black luminous hands with silver sweeping second hand, twenty-one jewel, movement number 154325, case number 43670, the initials "R.A.H." engraved in English script on the back of case. White gold-filled expansion bracelet, two years old, good condition. Value $100.

As the movement and case numbers are usually the most important features of the description, they should be obtained, whenever possible, from the owner or his jeweler. Also, jewelers and watchmakers ordinarily place "scratch marks" in the case of watches they repair. These marks are helpful in identifying such property and owner. Furthermore, they provide background information concerning the customer.

Rings Specify whether it is a man's, woman's, or child's ring; the kind of metal or material including the karat; the type of mounting and setting; whether plain or engraved; the kind, number, size, and weight of stones; the jeweler's or manufacturer's code marks; and whether engraved with initials or inscriptions or identifying marks; and value. For example:

Man's yellow gold Masonic ring, white gold top and Masonic emblem, .60 karat, blue white rose-cut diamond set inside of square and compass, shrine and commandery emblems in white gold inset on side of band, names "Arthur from Margie 4/19/72" inscribed on inner surface. Value $250.

Other Jewelry Indicate the name of the article; the manufacturer's name; the kind of material, size, color and shape; the kind, number, size, and color of stones; the type of setting and design; the initials, engravings, or other inscriptions; and, the unusual marks or deep scratches which might help identify the article.

Silverware Show the kind and number of articles; whether complete or part of a set; the design; the manufacturer's name, code, and trademark; whether sterling silver, plated, or stainless steel; and the engraving, initials, monograms, or inscriptions.

Cameras Give the type and model; the manufacturer's name, code, and trade name; the film size; serial and model numbers; the kind and color of materials; and the identifying marks including initials and inscriptions. As the lens is generally the most valuable part of a camera and can be removed and sold as a separate unit, when possible obtain the type, manufacturer's name (when not the same as the camera manufacturer), size and serial number, and all other data that usually appear on a lens mount. All camera accessories should likewise be described.

Clothing Designate the kind of clothing, such as a suit, dress, hat, shoes, overcoat, topcoat, or blouse; whether it is for a man, woman, boy, or girl; the manufacturer's name, code, and trade name; and, the size, material, color, and age. Also state whether any repairs or alterations have been made.

Laundry or cleaner's marks are very important. If their existence is doubtful, the cleaner or laundry concerned should be contacted. Many cleaners use an invisible dye mark which fluoresces and appears under ultraviolet light. This possibility should be considered when no cleaner's or laundry marks can be found in the clothing.

Miscellaneous Describe the article as completely as possible with emphasis on special features of identification including the manufacturer's name, code name, and trade name; serial and model numbers; kind and color of the material; and size. Usually all data appearing on a nameplate should be included in the description. For example:

3/4 horsepower Craftsman electric motor, serial number 56213, described as high speed (3450 rpm), single phase (110 V) with five-step pulley attached to the shaft (5/8-inch diameter). Frame of motor is painted gray with chrome-aluminum band running around diameter of motor, snap-type electric switch on base of motor, same side as the nameplate, three years old, fair condition. Value $15.

Follow up or supplementary reports

A follow-up report, or a supplementary report as it is also known, is a report made subsequent to the initial report. This type of report is made by an investigating officer or any other officer who obtains information bearing on a case under investigation. In felony cases particularly, there may be several follow-up reports written, since many investigations extend over several days or weeks. Whenever an officer rechecks any offense previously reported, she or he should fill out a supplementary report of what was discovered or of any additional property recovered.

In most instances this follow-up report will be made out by the officer assigned to the particular case. However, if other officers do receive information regarding the particular case, they too should make a follow-up report giving all details of any information obtained. For example, a patrol officer during a tour of duty may recover some of the stolen property in a burglary case, or may learn from a confidential source that a recent robbery was committed by a certain individual. This information should be submitted on a follow-up report.

Follow-up reports always carry the same case number as that given when the case was originally started regardless of the number of reports that are prepared in that case. Figure 9-7 is an example of a completed follow-up report prepared a few days after the burglary of a jewelry store. The report presupposes that an initial report was prepared on this hypothetical case when it was first brought to the attention of the police agency.

Arrest reports

The arrest report is used to report the circumstances of the arrest or detention of persons by a police agency. The purpose of the arrest report is to serve as a basis for court prosecution. Before an arrest report can accomplish its purpose, the report must meet two qualifications: (1) the report must demonstrate a legal, proper arrest justified by probable cause to make the arrest; and (2) the report must be complete and correct to serve as an adequate guide for follow-up investigation.

The effectiveness of the prosecution is generally equal to the effectiveness of the arrest report. Evidence located by follow-up investigation does not carry the same "weight of evidence" as facts and evidence discovered at the time of arrest. The defense attorney may ask the court or jury, "Why did not the officer who made the arrest find this damaging bit of evidence?" Many cases are lost in court because of poor investigations, but more are lost because evidence was not properly reported. An officer may demonstrate the most commendable skills possible in using initiative and intelligence in making an arrest, but will fail in the final test of the accomplishment in court if the report of arrest fails to meet any of the above qualifications.

Arrest reports are generally completed by officers immediately upon making an arrest, with or without a warrant, for any of the following reasons: a misdemeanor or a felony; arrest for mental commitment or on warrants served; desertion, AWOL, or other military personnel arrested by officers; or when another agency makes the arrest and transfers custody of a suspect to the police or sheriff's office.

The arrest report form, like most other reports, has a form and narrative section. The form section consists of a group of fill-in boxes which the arresting officer is required to complete. The information sought calls for such identifying data as date, crime, booking number, case number, defendant's identity, description, address, place of arrest, arresting officer, time of arrest, division or station,

	69. CASE NO.
	79-313

BLANK POLICE DEPARTMENT
BLANK, CALIFORNIA   CA5200

70. CODE SECTION	71. CRIME	72. CLASSIFICATION		
459 PC	**Burglary**	**Commercial - Jewelry Store**		

73. VICTIM'S NAME - LAST, FIRST, MIDDLE (FIRM IF BUS.)	74. ADDRESS	RESIDENCE	X BUSINESS	75. PHONE
Leighton's Jewelry Store				883-56432

.FOLLOW-UP REPORT (hypothetical)

On 2/27/78, 1030 hours, WALTER J. SMITH, Mgr., Fidelity Loan Co., 208 S. Spring Street, telephonically advised the writer that an unknown individual had tried to pawn a lady's W/G diamond ring, set with a 1/2 karat diamond in a basket setting, engraved "J.A.". Mr. SMITH stated that he did not like the looks of this suspect and refused to take the items. The unknown person left the store and walked south on Spring St., according to SMITH. Suspect was described as M/W/A, 35-38 yrs, 5'7-9", 160-170, wearing dark trousers, faded blue shirt with white square-shaped buttons; long dk.brn.hair- neck length; dk.sun glasses.

Since the above jewelry fit the description of some of the property taken in the burglary of the LEIGHTON'S JEWELRY STORE on 2/25/79, reporting officer proceeded to S. Spring St., where an individual similar to the person described by Mr. SMITH, was observed walking south on the east side of Spring St. Suspect was placed under arrest by reporting officer at 1040 hours. At this time Officer_____ informed suspect that he had a right to remain silent and that any statement he did make could be used against him as evidence in a court of law. He was advised that he had the right to speak with an Attorney of his own choice and to have the attorney present during questioning; that if he so desired and could not afford one, an attorney would be appointed for him without charge. At this time suspect stated that he understood his rights but was willing to make a statement.

A search of suspect's person disclosed several articles of jewelry similar to the items taken in the LEIGHTON store burglary as well as an eight-inch screw driver. The screw driver tip appears similar to the tool impression left on the window ledge of victim jewelry store.

Suspect was identified as HARRY AMES, 405 Maple St., San Francisco, California, and claimed he had just been released from Soledad Prison on 2/19/79, where he had served four years on a burglary conviction. He was booked at Central Jail on suspicion of Burglary, Booking #6345k.

ROBERT B. LEIGHTON, owner, Leighton's Jewelry Store, identified the three rings found on suspect's person, and the lady's Bullova Watch, as being part of the stolen jewelry taken in instant case on 2/25/79

(Include in report)
SUSPECT: (description)
PROPERTY RECOVERED: (list of items, description, value)
ARREST REPORT: (attach copy of arrest report)

REPORTING OFFICERS	RECORDING OFFICER	TYPED BY	DATE AND TIME	ROUTED BY
Moore, Robert L. #436	Moore	mmk	2/27/79	Miller

FURTHER ACTION	X YES	COPIES TO:	X DETECTIVE	X CII			
	NO		JUVENILE	PATROL			
			X DIST. ATTNY.	OTHER			
			SO./P.D.	OTHER		REVIEWED BY George Aplin, Capt.	DATE 2/27/79

Figure 9-7. A completed follow-up report.

and warrant information. Generally the arrest report will be typed, but in emergencies and in certain circumstances when the arresting officer does not have the opportunity to type the report it may be handprinted or handwritten.

Under *details* in the body of the arrest report, the circumstances of the arrest and the corpus delicti of the crime should be set forth. The report should describe what happened in chronological order, beginning with the first act of the suspect. It should relate what was said and by whom, and include statements of witnesses to confirm or deny allegations. Statements made by the arrested party should be recorded with as much accuracy and detail as possible.

If there is any physical evidence associated with the arrest, such evidence should be itemized, the location where found and by whom, date, and the final disposition indicated: e.g., .45 caliber Colt "Gold Cup" auto pistol, serial number 1642310, found by Officer Jones under right front seat of defendant's car. Delivered to property room by Jones, property tag number 1335.

In some cases where arrests are made and large amounts of loot recovered, it is not possible to itemize such property on the arrest report because of the limited space on the form. In instances of this kind it is proper to itemize all the evidence, where found, and disposition, on a separate continuation sheet entitled *Evidence Report,* arrest of JOHN RAYMOND DOE, 459 PC (burglary), booking no. 624814k, case no. 79-6641. Attach the evidence report to the arrest report. The arrest report would bear the notation, *"see attached evidence report."*

The following is an example of an arrest report made after the commission of a hypothetical burglary. This example illustrates the narrative account only.

On 2/10/79, at 0150 hours, officers received a radio all-units call "459 there now" at 640 East Baseline, Apt. 6.

Officers interviewed the victim who stated that at approximately 1:45 P.M. she awoke when she heard a noise at her bedroom window. She saw the defendant crawl through the window and watched him for several minutes while he ransacked the dresser drawers. The victim screamed and the defendant fled from the apartment through the back door. Victim gave officers a description of the male person she observed in her apartment.

Officers searched the immediate vicinity of the building and observed the defendant running from one of the garages behind the victim's apartment. The defendant was pursued and apprehended by the undersigned officers who noted that he closely resembled the person described by the victim.

Defendant was advised by Officer _____ that he had a right to remain silent, that any statement he did make could be used in evidence against him in a court of law. He was advised that he had the right to speak with an attorney and to have the attorney present during questioning, that if he so desired and could not afford one, an attorney would be appointed for him without charge. At this time the defendant stated, "I know all my rights. This is not the first time I've been busted. I don't want a lawyer. I can handle my own affairs."

Officers then asked the defendant what he was doing in the garage and he replied, "What difference does it make; you caught me this time. Next time you won't be so lucky."

Officer _____ searched the defendant and found a 4-inch screwdriver in the defendant's right front pants pocket. When asked about the screwdriver, the defendant stated, "I never saw the screwdriver before; it's not mine." Officer _____ found a woman's white metal ring containing three clear white stones in the defendant's left coat pocket. The initials "A" "B" "L" were observed on the inside of the ring, which were the initials of the victim.

Defendant was transported over to headquarters where he was booked as above on the advice of Sgt. _____. The screwdriver and ring were marked and booked as evidence by Officer _____ under the above case number.

Figure 9-8 shows an example of a completed arrest report. This specimen report demonstrates sufficient facts to establish the basis for an arrest and detention of a robbery suspect.

Injuries Associated with an Arrest Persons arrested are sometimes injured during the process of the arrest or have been injured in fights or accidents prior to the arrest and, as a result, special attention is required for the protection of the prisoner and the police agency. The injury or illness noted should be described and set forth in the report, and the medical or first aid treatment listed. If the injury was the result of force used in overcoming resistance to the arrest, outline the details of the force and the resulting injury in the narrative part of the arrest report. As soon as possible after the injury has been discovered, and if not of a minor nature, the prisoner should be examined by a licensed physician since officers are not capable of determining the extent of serious illness or injury. Photographs of any visible marks or bruises are desirable. Some departments have a special form for reporting injuries. The recording of injuries serves two purposes: it protects prisoners as it assures them of adequate medical examinations, and it protects the police agency by recording the approval of a competent medical authority that the prisoner may be incarcerated.

Property or Evidence Held in Connection with Arrest In those cases where evidence is held or property impounded, all items should be accurately identified and described so that such items can be properly released to a suspect or victim when no longer needed. Property receipts are issued wherever possible. If property taken from an arrestee is identifiable by number or inscrip-

tion, it should be checked against the stolen property file of the arresting agency or through other state and federal agencies when so warranted. A list of property taken from a prisoner, when checked, may serve to connect the arrestee with unsolved or uncleared crimes. In arrests where the suspect has a vehicle, the disposition of the car should be shown in the report, e.g., released to witness JONES, left at scene, Bates towing, "held for processing." Impound form reports are prepared by many agencies to show the condition of vehicles at time of impounding.

Vehicle accident reports

The vehicle accident report form is a basic form in any report system. If executed properly the form will furnish all necessary information needed for engineering, enforcement, and education as well as assisting in other major areas such as the enactment of laws and ordinances, court adjudication, driver's license administration. Hydraulic brakes, safety glass, better visibility, shock-absorbing driver compartments, and seat belts are among the many safety advances that have developed because of accident-investigation reporting and crash research. Accident reports are absolutely necessary to an intelligent, efficient program of accident prevention. The reports, made as a result of accident investigation, are the only source of complete unbiased information that is available for interested parties. In civil cases resulting from accidents, courts have come to rely upon vehicle accident reports for unbiased and reliable testimony.

Some of the purposes of accident reporting are to

Show the problem
Indicate methods of correction
Measure the results of prevention efforts
Classify vehicle accidents by the degree of seriousness and type

SHERIFF'S DEPARTMENT

SAMPLE ARREST REPORT
Original 8-½ X 11
(hypothetical case)

ARREST INFORMATION

Booking # **65432k**
File # **79-305**
S.S. # **555-44-3210**
DDL # **Y-12992**

Defendant

Last	First	Middle
DAWSON,	Richard	Joseph

Date of Report **2/11/79**
Crime **211 PC, Robbery; 12025PC**
Carrying Concealed Weapon;
Warrant #_____

Description:

Race	Sex	Age	DOB	Ht.	Wt.	Hair	Eyes
Cauc./	M /	36 /	1/25/43 /	5'10 /	165 /	Brn. /	Brn.

Address **1331 Taylor St., R'm 15, (Apache Motel)** Phone # **982-3042**

Time at Above Address **1 day** Time in State **1 month** Marital Status **Single**

Dependents: No. **0** / Ages _____ Employment **Unemployed** How long **-**

Place of Arrest **Alley, (across street from 4489 Fairview)** Court _____

Arrested by **Jones #109/ Roberts #155** Date **2/11/79** Time **1420**

No. Prior Arrests **3** No. Misc. Convictions **1** No. Felony Convictions **1** X-Con **Yes**

Is Defendant Currently On: **No** Parole **No** Probation _____ Bail _____ O.R. Release _____

Holds: **None** Location of Vehicle **Wilson's Garage**

DETAILS OF ARREST

On 2/11/79, 1345 hours, Officers JONES and ROBERTS were S/B on Fairview
Ave when they observed an unknown person seated in a 1975 Ford 2-Dr.
Lt. Blue/White, Colorado Lic. SUZ038 which was parked in a no parking
area in the alley across the street from HENRY'S LIQUOR STORE, 4489 Fairview. The car was facing the liquor store headed east. Officers had
been advised at roll call on 2/10/79 that a B/W Ford with a partial
license S----38, possibly Colorado, had been used in a robbery of the
ACME LIQUOR AND DELICATESSEN STORE (File 79-313) on 2/9/79. Above
Colorado License SUZ038 was checked through NCIC with negative results.

Because of several recent liquor store robberies in this section of
the city between 1300 and 1400 hours, and the similarity of the above
B/W Ford with that of the car used in the ACME LIQUOR STORE robbery on
2/9/79, officers drove around the block and parked where they could
observe the defendant and vehicle. During this observation suspect
was noted to glance furtively all around and to be particularly watching
HENRY'S LIQUOR STORE. On two separate occasions during this surveillance
suspect leaned forward in the front seat of his vehicle (below the
window ledge of the door), to apparently avoid being observed by
pedestrians who passed close to his car.

At approximately 1420 hours, both the undersigned officers approached
the suspect and requested him to get out of his vehicle. Officers

Signature of Arresting (or Transporting) Officers **/s/ M. R. Jones #109; J. J. Roberts #155**

15-6554-401 Rev. 11/69   Approved by **/s/ Lt. R. L. Smith**

Figure 9-8. A completed arrest report. The form itself is one of several types used by police agencies.

ARREST REPORT
DAWSON, Richard Joseph

noted that suspect was extremely nervous and closely
resembled the description of the suspect involved in
recent liquor store robberies. A quick search of suspect's
person was made by Officer ROBERTS but no weapons were found.

Suspect was asked what he was doing in the area. He replied,
"I'm just waiting for a friend who lives near Fairview Ave
and Taylor St." He refused to disclose the name or specific
address of the "friend" for whom he was waiting. Suspect
also was unable to explain why he was at this location when
his alleged friend lived several blocks south of this address.

When officers asked if they could search his vehicle, the
suspect consented but was noticeably nervous. Officer JONES
searched the vehicle and found a .38 cal. B/S automatic,
serial #123561, under the front seat on the driver's side,
which gun was fully loaded (including one round in the chamber).
On noting the found gun, subject remarked - "I keep it there
for protection." He was advised by Officer JONES that he was
under arrest.

At this time the following statement was read to the arrestee
by Officer JONES - "You have the right to remain silent. If
you give up the right to remain silent, anything you say can
be used against you in a court of law. You have the right to
speak with an attorney and to have the attorney present during
questioning. If you so desire and cannot afford one, an attorney
will be appointed for you without charge before questioning."

Following the reading of the above admonition to suspect, he
was then asked by JONES whether he understood these rights.
To this question suspect replied - "I am well aware of my
rights, I don't want an attorney, I'll tell you guys what you
want to know." Officer JONES then asked the suspect - what
do we want to know? Suspect replied - "about that ACME LIQUOR
STORE job the other day, it's the only place I've hit."

Suspect was transported to headquarters where he was booked
by Officers JONES and ROBERTS on the above charges, per Desk
Sergeant HUNT #305.

The .38 cal. automatic (Colt) and cartridges (9), were identified
by Officer JONES with the initials "J-R", and booked by Officer
JONES at headquarters crime lab., property tag No. 6642L.
Suspect's vehicle was impounded at WILSON's GARAGE - "Hold
for Detectives."

Attach responsibility to drivers and pedestrians

Direct engineering, enforcement, and education activities

Collect statistics for remedial measures and enlistment of public support

Vehicle accident reports are valuable because of the facts that can be determined from them, that is, the number of people killed or injured, where they were killed or injured, the cause of the accident, the responsibility of driver or pedestrian, and necessary action for reduction of accidents.

Policies, laws, and ordinances will dictate whether a written report must be made on every traffic accident that comes to a police department's attention. Most police agencies require a written report in accidents involving appreciable property damage, but do not require a report covering minor damage such as a slightly dented fender. However, damage does not have to exceed a specified amount to make an accident constitute a traffic accident. The investigation and reporting of all known vehicle accidents that occur in public places is suggested, since the only difference between a fatal accident and one involving property damage alone is a matter of chance, a small difference in position, time, or a slight variation in speed. Information in a vehicle accident report must be so written that anyone who refers to the report will have as much knowledge of the circumstances as the investigator does. The report must contain all knowledge of the accident.

A vehicle accident report form generally is a face sheet in which a detailed framework is supplied. The officer completes the form by merely filling in the blank spaces with the required information and placing X's in the appropriate boxes. Additional information as to details or summary is recorded on supplementary sheets which are attached to the face sheet (front page). The vehicle accident form provides the recording of essential information and serves basic purposes, viz., a reminder to obtain certain necessary information, an indicator of matters that might be sufficiently important to bear investigation, the report of the officer who investigated the accident, and a supplier of information necessary to the formulation of a program of traffic control and regulation.

The table below is an interview and investigation guide that can be used as an aid in the investigation and preparation of vehicle accident reports. (See p. 211.)

The following completed vehicle accident report (Figure 9-9) demonstrates the use of the above interview and investigation guide in a hypothetical vehicle accident situation.

Inasmuch as diagrams are generally required on reportable accident investigations, the selection of symbols to portray various items oftentimes presents a problem. A list of accident diagram symbols (Figure 9-10) are used by many departments for this purpose.

Reporting Hints

Since actions of the officer at the scene often determine whether the victim will prosecute the suspect or even furnish the necessary information for completion of the report, it is important to observe the following:

Do not be influenced by information received before you arrive at the location. Be guided by the facts or information you receive at the scene.

Determine the type of report to be taken at the scene.

Learn to listen and observe. Allow the complainants to tell the story in their own words. Interrupt only when necessary and then ask questions that tend to guide them in the desired direction.

Stick to the conditions concerning the report. Do not engage in useless or rambling conversation.

TRAFFIC COLLISION REPORT   (HYPOTHETICAL ACCIDENT)

PAGE 1 OF 5

| SPECIAL CONDITIONS | NO. INJ.
1 | H & R FELONY ☐ | CITY
Upland, Ca. | JUDICIAL DISTRICT | No. |
| | NO. KILLED
0 | H & R MISD ☐ | COUNTY
San Bernardino | REPORTING DISTRICT | BEAT
5 |

LOCATION

| COLLISION OCCURRED ON | | | | MO. DAY YR.
1 24 79 | TIME(2400)
0800 | CII NO. | OFFICER I.D.
1408 |

☐ AT INTERSECTION WITH
☐ OR: **40** FEET/MILES **S** OF **"A" Street**

INJURY, FATAL OR TOW AWAY ☒ YES ☐ NO   STATE HWY ☐ YES ☒ NO

PARTY 1

| NAME (FIRST, MIDDLE, LAST)
Robert Edward Young | STREET ADDRESS
845 Taylor St. |

DRIVER ☒   PEDESTRIAN ☐   PARKED VEH. ☐   BI-CYCLIST ☐   OTHER ☐

| DRIVER'S LICENSE NO.
D543104 | STATE
Ca | BIRTHDATE MO. DAY YR.
4 8 12 | SEX
M | RACE
C | CITY
Ontario, | STATE
Ca. | PHONE
982 4543 |

| VEHICLE YR.
1972 | MAKE
Chev. | LICENSE NO.
129 SUZ | STATE | OWNER'S NAME ☒ SAME AS DRIVER |

DIRECTION OF TRAVEL **N**   ON/ACROSS (STREET OR HIGHWAY) **2nd Street**   OWNER'S ADDRESS ☒ SAME AS DRIVER

| SPEED LIMIT
35 | DISPOSITION OF VEHICLE
Towed to Wise's Garage   ☐ BY DRIVER   ON ORDERS OF Driver | VEHICLE DAMAGE EXTENT ☐ MINOR ☒ MOD. ☐ MAJOR ☐ TOTAL   LOCATION
R.F.Fender | VIOLATION CHARGED
2 |

PARTY 2

| NAME (FIRST, MIDDLE, LAST)
Walter Joseph Murray | STREET ADDRESS
643 Broadway |

DRIVER ☒   PEDESTRIAN ☐   PARKED VEH. ☐   BI-CYCLIST ☐   OTHER ☐

| DRIVER'S LICENSE NO.
W533421 | STATE
Ca. | BIRTHDATE MO. DAY YR.
9 15 50 | SEX
M | RACE
C | CITY
Ontario, | STATE
Ca. | PHONE
982 24321 |

| VEHICLE YR.
1972 | MAKE
Ford | LICENSE NO.
155 OLC | STATE
Ca. | OWNER'S NAME ☒ SAME AS DRIVER |

DIRECTION OF TRAVEL **W**   ON/ACROSS (STREET OR HIGHWAY) **Private Drive to 2nd St.**   OWNER'S ADDRESS ☒ SAME AS DRIVER

| SPEED LIMIT | DISPOSITION OF VEHICLE
Cared for   ☒ BY DRIVER   ON ORDERS OF | VEHICLE DAMAGE EXTENT ☐ MINOR ☒ MOD. ☐ MAJOR ☐ TOTAL   LOCATION
L.F.Fender | VIOLATION CHARGED
21804a VC
2   26483 VC |

PROPERTY

DESCRIPTION OF DAMAGE

OWNER'S NAME   ADDRESS   NOTIFIED ☐ YES ☐ NO

INJURED/WITNESS

WITNESS ONLY	AGE	SEX	EXTENT OF INJURY				INJURED WAS (check one)					IN VEH. NUMBER
			FATAL INJURY	SEVERE WOUND DISTORTED MEMBER	OTHER VISIBLE INJURIES	COMPLAINT OF PAIN	DRIVER	PASS.	PED.	BI-CYCLIST	OTHER	
☐			☐	☐	☐	☒	☒	☐	☐	☐	☐	2

NAME **Walter Joseph Murray**   PHONE **982 4321**
ADDRESS **643 Broadway, Ontario, Ca.**   TAKEN TO (INJURED ONLY) **Refused medical care**

| ☐ | | | ☐ | ☐ | ☐ | ☐ | ☐ | ☐ | ☐ | ☐ | ☐ | |

NAME   PHONE
ADDRESS   TAKEN TO (INJURED ONLY)

| ☐ | | | ☐ | ☐ | ☐ | ☐ | ☐ | ☐ | ☐ | ☐ | ☐ | |

NAME   PHONE
ADDRESS   TAKEN TO (INJURED ONLY)

SKETCH

(INDICATE NORTH)

(see page 3)

MISCELLANEOUS

Suggested:

Vehicle Description
    and
Driver Description

(put in this section)

| VEHICLE TYPE | | |
| PARTY 1   01 | PARTY 2   01 | |

ROAD TYPE	
	A CONVENTIONAL, ONE WAY
X	B CONVENTIONAL, TWO WAY
	C EXPRESSWAY
	D FREEWAY
	E OTHER (EXPLAIN IN NARRATIVE)

555 (REV.11-71)   9   57698 - 456 555 Rev 11-71 500M OSP

Figure 9-9. Completed traffic collision report (hypothetical accident).

COLLISION NARRATIVE

SUMMARY: Veh. #1 was proceeding N/Bound on 2nd St., S/ of "A" St. Veh. #2 proceeding W/Bound on a private driveway E of 2nd St. Veh. #2 failed to stop for Veh. #1, in violation of Sec. 21804(a) V.C. Veh. #2 also had defective brakes, viol. Sec. 26453 V.C.

PRIMARY COLLISION FACTOR (2)

A	VC SECTION VIOLATION __21804a__
B	OTHER IMPROPER DRIVING*
C	OTHER THAN DRIVER*
D	UNKNOWN*

WEATHER

X A	CLEAR
B	CLOUDY
C	RAINING
D	SNOWING
E	FOG
F	OTHER

LIGHTING

X A	DAYLIGHT
B	DUSK - DAWN
C	DARK - STREET LIGHTS
D	DARK - NO STREET LIGHTS
E	DARK - STREET LIGHTS NOT FUNCTIONING

ROADWAY SURFACE

X A	DRY
B	WET
C	SNOWY - ICY
D	SLIPPERY (MUDDY, OILY, ETC.)

ROADWAY CONDITIONS (MARK ONE TO THREE ITEMS)

A	HOLES, DEEP RUTS
B	LOOSE MATERIAL ON ROADWAY
C	OBSTRUCTION ON ROADWAY
D	CONSTRUCTION-REPAIR ZONE
E	REDUCED ROADWAY WIDTH
F	FLOODED
G	OTHER
X H	NO UNUSUAL CONDITIONS

RIGHT OF WAY CONTROL

A	CONTROLS FUNCTIONING
B	CONTROLS NOT FUNCTIONING
C	CONTROLS OBSCURED
X D	NO CONTROLS PRESENT

TYPE OF COLLISION

A	HEAD-ON
X B	SIDESWIPE
C	REAR END
D	BROADSIDE
E	HIT OBJECT
F	OVERTURNED
G	AUTO/PEDESTRIAN
H	OTHER

MOTOR VEHICLE INVOLVED WITH

A	NON-COLLISION
B	PEDESTRIAN
X C	OTHER MOTOR VEHICLE
D	MOTOR VEHICLE ON OTHER ROADWAY
E	PARKED MOTOR VEHICLE
F	TRAIN
G	BICYCLE
H	ANIMAL
I	FIXED OBJECT
J	OTHER OBJECT
K	OTHER

PEDESTRIAN'S ACTION

A	NO PEDESTRIAN INVOLVED
B	CROSSING IN CROSSWALK AT INTERSECTION
C	CROSSING IN CROSSWALK - NOT AT INTERSECTION
D	CROSSING - NOT IN CROSSWALK
E	IN ROAD - INCLUDES SHOULDER
F	NOT IN ROAD
G	APPROACHING/LEAVING SCHOOL BUS

TYPE OF VEHICLE

		1	2	3	4
A	PASSENGER CAR (INCLUDES STATION WAGON)	X	X		
P	PASSENGER CAR W/TRAILER	X			
C	MOTORCYCLE/SCOOTER				
D	PICKUP OR PANEL TRUCK				
E	PICKUP OR PANEL TRUCK W/TRAILER				
F	TRUCK OR TRUCK TRACTOR				
G	TRUCK OR TRUCK TRACTOR W/TRAILER(S)				
H	SCHOOL BUS				
I	OTHER BUS				
J	EMERGENCY VEHICLE				
K	HIGHWAY CONSTRUCTION EQUIPMENT		X		
L	BICYCLE				
M	OTHER				

OTHER ASSOCIATED FACTOR (MARK ONE TO THREE ITEMS)

		1	2	3	4
A	VC SECTION VIOLATION				
B	VC SECTION VIOLATION 26453		X		
C	VC SECTION VIOLATION				
D	VC SECTION VIOLATION				
E	VISION OBSCUREMENTS	X			
F	INATTENTION		X		
G	STOP & GO TRAFFIC				
H	ENTERING/LEAVING RAMP				
I	PREVIOUS COLLISION				
J	UNFAMILIAR WITH ROAD				
K	DEFECTIVE VEHICLE EQUIPMENT	X			
L	UNINVOLVED VEHICLE				
M	OTHER*				
N	NONE APPARENT				

MOVEMENT PRECEDING COLLISION

		1	2	3	4
A	STOPPED				
B	PROCEEDING STRAIGHT				
C	RAN OFF ROAD				
D	MAKING RIGHT TURN				
E	MAKING LEFT TURN				
F	MAKING U TURN				
G	BACKING				
H	SLOWING - STOPPING				
I	PASSING OTHER VEHICLE				
J	CHANGING LANES				
K	PARKING MANEUVER				
L	ENTERING TRAFFIC FROM SHOULDER, MEDIAN, PARKING STRIP OR PRIVATE DRIVE		X		
M	OTHER UNSAFE TURNING				
N	CROSSED INTO OPPOSING LANE				
O	PARKED				
P	MERGING				
Q	TRAVELING WRONG WAY*				
R	OTHER				

SOBRIETY - DRUG - PHYSICAL (MARK ONE TO THREE ITEMS)

		1	2	3	4
A	HAD NOT BEEN DRINKING	X			
B	HBD - UNDER INFLUENCE				
C	HBD - NOT UNDER INFLUENCE				
D	HBD - IMPAIRMENT UNKNOWN*		X		
E	UNDER DRUG INFLUENCE				
F	OTHER PHYSICAL IMPAIRMENT*				
G	IMPAIRMENT NOT KNOWN				
H	NOT APPLICABLE				

INVESTIGATED BY	I.D. NUMBER	INVESTIGATED BY	I.D. NUMBER	REVIEWED BY
J. L. Moore	1408			R.A.Jones

*EXPLAIN IN NARRATIVE

SKETCH - NARRATIVE CONTINUATION

No.

ALL MEASUREMENTS ARE APPROXIMATE AND NOT TO SCALE UNLESS STATED (SCALE = *NONE*

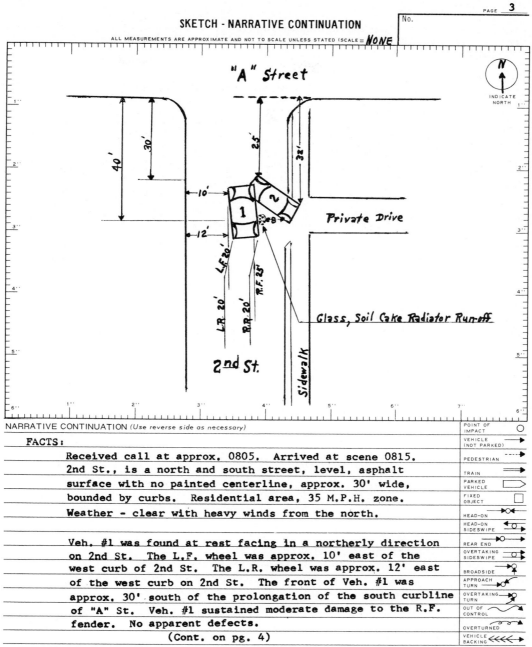

"A" Street

N

INDICATE NORTH

Private Drive

Glass, Soil Cake Radiator Run-off

2nd St.

Sidewalk

NARRATIVE CONTINUATION *(Use reverse side as necessary)*

	POINT OF IMPACT	○

FACTS:

Received call at approx. 0805. Arrived at scene 0815.
2nd St., is a north and south street, level, asphalt
surface with no painted centerline, approx. 30' wide,
bounded by curbs. Residential area, 35 M.P.H. zone.
Weather - clear with heavy winds from the north.

Veh. #1 was found at rest facing in a northerly direction
on 2nd St. The L.F. wheel was approx. 10' east of the
west curb of 2nd St. The L.R. wheel was approx. 12' east
of the west curb on 2nd St. The front of Veh. #1 was
approx. 30' south of the prolongation of the south curbline
of "A" St. Veh. #1 sustained moderate damage to the R.F.
fender. No apparent defects.

(Cont. on pg. 4)

556 (REV.10-71)

VEHICLE (NOT PARKED)
PEDESTRIAN
TRAIN
PARKED VEHICLE
FIXED OBJECT
HEAD-ON
HEAD-ON SIDESWIPE
REAR END
OVERTAKING SIDESWIPE
BROADSIDE
APPROACH TURN
OVERTAKING TURN
OUT OF CONTROL
OVERTURNED
VEHICLE BACKING

CHECK ONE		DATE OF ORIGINAL INCIDENT			TIME (2400)	(FOR STATE USE ONLY)	ORIGINAL NO.
	SUPPLEMENTAL	MO. DAY YR.					
	SUPPLEMENTS FORM 555 TRAFFIC COLLISION REPORT	LOCATION/SUBJECT					CITATION NO.
	OTHER:						BEAT
X	FORM 555 NARRATIVE CONTINUATION ONLY	CITY	COUNTY			REPORTING DISTRICT	

Veh. #2 was found at rest facing in a north-westerly direction
partially on 2nd St., with the rear on the sidewalk. The
R.F. wheel was approx. 7' west of the east curb on 2nd St.,
and approx. 25' south of the prolongation of the south curbline
of "A" St. The R.R. wheel was approx. 32' south of the prolongation of the south curbline of "A" St. Veh. #2 sustained
moderate damage to the L.F. fender. Upon checking brakes of
Veh. #2 found pedal went to floorboards on first application;
three applications necessary to obtain approximately 1/2"
brake pedal.

Physical Evidence: Veh. #1 left the following locked wheel
skids prior to impact: L.F. 20', R.F. 25', R.R. 20' and the
following skids after impact: L.F. 10', L.R. 11', R.F. 10'
R.R. 11'. Veh. #2, no skid marks. Headlamp glass, soil cake,
and radiator run-off were found approx. 8' west of the east
curb of 2nd St., and approx. 40' south of the prolongation
of south curbline of "A" Street.

Driver #1 - No injuries apparent
Driver #2 - H.B.D., field sobriety test was given.
             Complained of pain in left side but refused medical
             aid.

STATEMENTS:
      Driver #1 (Mr. Young) - "I was driving north on 2nd St., about
      20 to 25 M.P.H. following another car. Suddenly this car
      swerved to the left. I applied my brakes but was unable to
      avoid hitting the Ford."
      Driver #2 (Mr. Murray) - "I was coming out of my girlfriend's
      driveway. I didn't see any cars coming. Suddenly this car
      came out of nowhere. It must have been going 60 M.P.H. I
      applied my brakes but couldn't stop in time."

                        (Cont. on page 5)

PREPARED BY	I.D. NUMBER	PREPARED	REVIEWED - APPROVED BY	I.D. NUMBER	DATE
NAME/RANK		MO. DAY YR.	NAME/RANK		MO. DAY YR.
J. L. Moore	1408	1 24 79			

| | | | ORIGINAL NO. | | |

CHECK ONE		**SUPPLEMENTAL**	DATE OF ORIGINAL INCIDENT		TIME (2400)	(FOR STATE USE ONLY)	
			MO. DAY YR.				
		SUPPLEMENTS FORM 555 TRAFFIC COLLISION REPORT	LOCATION/SUBJECT				CITATION NO.
		OTHER:					BEAT
X		FORM 555 NARRATIVE CONTINUATION ONLY	CITY	COUNTY		REPORTING DISTRICT	

Q - What condition are your brakes in?

A - My brakes need a pint of fluid every other day

Q - What have you had to drink?

A - Two beers this morning.

OPINIONS AND CONCLUSIONS:

    Driver #1 was driving north on 2nd Street at approximately 25 M.P.H. when Driver #2 pulled partially onto 2nd St., from a private driveway. Both drivers applied brakes but Driver #2 was unable to stop his vehicle due to faulty brakes. Driver #2 passed the field sobriety test.

    Point of impact was approx. 40' south of the prolongation of south curbline of "A" Street and approximately 8' west of the east curb of 2nd Street. Established by skid deviation, broken glass, and radiator water.

    Driver #2 caused T.C. by entering through highway from a private driveway in violation of Section 21804a V.C. Violation of right-of-way. Also, Veh. #2 had defective brakes in violation of Sec. 26453 V.C.

    Complaint to be filed.

RECOMMENDATIONS: None.

PREPARED BY	I.D. NUMBER	PREPARED			REVIEWED - APPROVED BY	I.D. NUMBER	DATE		
NAME/RANK		MO.	DAY	YR.	NAME/RANK		MO.	DAY	YR.
J. L. Moore	1408	1	24	79	R. A. Jones, Lt.	652	1	24	79

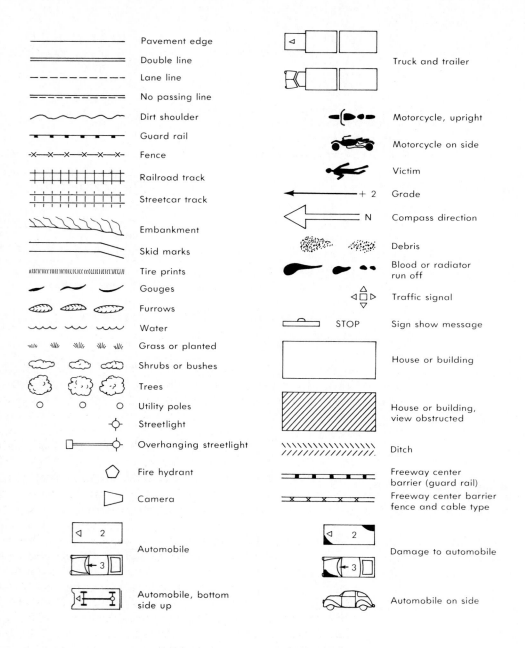

Figure 9-10. Accident diagram symbols used as aids in preparing drawings of accident scenes.

INTERVIEW AND INVESTIGATION GUIDE:
VEHICLE ACCIDENT REPORT*

Facts	1. Time of call and arrival
	2. Description of highway and scene
	3. Vehicle no. 1
	   a. Location and position
	   b. Damage
	   c. Defects
	   d. Information on driver or occupants when applicable (repeat sequence for other vehicles)
	4. Other property damaged
	5. Physical evidence
	   a. Skid marks and tracks
	   b. Debris
	   c. Vehicle parts

Statements	1. Verbal statements made by principals and witnesses should be written as nearly verbatim as possible 2. If the statement is obtained by asking a series of questions, the questions should be shown in the report.
Opinions and conclusions	1. Directions of travel 2. Resultant collision and POI (point of impact) 3. How vehicles came to point of rest 4. Violations committed 5. Comment on prosecution
Diagrams	Required on all reportable accidents and those property damage accidents that result in criminal prosecutions. **Draw items** in proper proportion to one another

*Used by the California Highway Patrol in their reporting procedure.

Check the condition of the scene yourself. Do not take someone else's word for it—get inquisitive, ask questions, see for yourself.

Do not use words unless you know the meaning of them. Consult the dictionary if you do not understand a word that you feel is needed in your report.

Do not use words that have a double meaning.

Do not use more words than are necessary to express one thought.

Avoid rambling and confusing sentences.

Avoid making a social event out of taking a report. Refrain from smoking or accepting alcoholic drinks.

Remember that your report is written for the other person. Do not make it impossible to understand.

Avoid personal opinions as they lessen the value of a report and should not be included. Personal opinion and preconceived ideas of the reporter or the complainant are often detrimental.

Use only standard abbreviations that everyone recognizes; do not make up your own.

Do not use slang or profanity unless it is absolutely necessary in the report. When it is included, be sure to employ the use of quotation marks. Profane or slang expressions may be used only if they have modus operandi or investigational value.

Get all the facts while you are at the scene. Make a habit of writing a rough draft of the report at the scene. Include sketches.

Preserve your notes even after the report has been completed. Such notes will be useful in refreshing your memory when preparing for and testifying at a trial. Do not mix these notes or memos with notes of other investigations.

Your signature and title must be on a report. Without them, it is a piece of paper with no value.

The Completed Report

When a written report is prepared, it is reviewed by the officer's immediate superior and thereafter may possibly pass through critical appraisals from many persons, including

The bureau head
The division head
Other division and bureau heads
The deputy chief or undersheriff
The chief or sheriff
The record division
The court officer
Other police agencies
The deputy district attorney
The clerk who draws up the complaint
The grand jury, in some instances
The jury
The defendant
The trial judge

The prosecuting attorney, defense attorney, and higher court officials

Since reports carry the information necessary for sound decisions affecting the public and private parties, they must be accurate and sufficiently authentic to withstand attacks by anyone. Reports are the professional tool of law enforcement necessary to carry out the administration of justice.

Abbreviations

Abbreviations should be of such character that the intended meaning in reports will be readily conveyed to persons reading the report. When there is doubt as to the understandable abbreviation of a word, do not abbreviate. The Table shows some of the abbreviations used by many police agencies:

ABBREVIATIONS COMMONLY USED BY POLICE AGENCIES

Also known as	Aka.
All points bulletin	APB
Apartment	Apt.
Approximate	Approx.
Arrest	Arr.
Attempt	Att.
Attention	Attn.
Avenue	Ave.
Black	Blk.
Broadcast	B/C
Booking	Bkg.
Boulevard	Blvd.
Brown	Brn.
Building	Bldg.
Burglary	Burg.
Caucasian	Cauc.
Chief of police	COP
Citation	Cit.
Citizen	Citz.

Date of birth	DOB
Dead on arrival	DOA
Defendant	Deft.
Delinquent	Del.
Department of motor vehicles	DMV
Descent	Desc.
Description	Descr.
Division	Div.
Double	Dbl.
Drunk	Drk.
East	E
Eastbound	E/B
Emergency	Emer.
Estimate	Est.
Evidence	Evid.
Expire	Exp.
Felony	Fel.
Female	F
Field interview	FI
Freeway	Fwy
Green	Grn.
Hawaiian	Haw.
Hazel	Haz.
High school	Hi. Sch.
Hit and run	H & R
Hospital	Hosp.
Hour	Hr.
Identification or identity	ID
Information	Info.
Injury	Inj.
Intersection	I/S
Investigation	Invest.
Japanese	Jap.
Juvenile	Juv.
Latin	Lat.
Left front	LF
Left rear	LR
License	Lic.

Lieutenant	Lt. or Lieut.
Light	Lgt.
Location	Loc.
Male	M
Malicious mischief	Mal. Mis.
Market	Mkt.
Maximum	Max
Medium	Med.
Mexican	Mex.
Miles per hour	MPH
Miscellaneous	Misc.
Month	Mo.
Motor	Mtr.
Motorcycle	M/C
North	N
Northbound	N/B
Observe	Obs.
Officer	Ofcr.
Operator's license	Op. Lic.
Passenger	Pass.
Pedestrian	Ped.
Penal Code	PC
Point of impact	POI
Point of rest	POR
Possible	Poss.
Private	Pvt.
Probable	Prob.
Property	Prop.
Received	Recd.
Registration	Reg.
Report	Rpt.
Residence	Res.
Right front	RF
Right rear	RR
Section	Sect.
Sergeant	Sgt.
South	S
Southbound	S/B
Station	Sta.
Street	St.
Subject	Subj.

Suspect	Susp.	Warrant	Warr.
		Week	Wk.
Temporary	Temp.	West	W
Traffic	Traf.	Westbound	W/B
Traffic accident	T/A	Witness	Wit.
Traffic collision	T/C		
Trailer	Trlr.	Year	Yr.
		Yellow	Yel.
Unknown	Unk.		

SUMMARY

Reports are the professional tools of law enforcement and are necessary to carry out the administration of justice. They are the sources of information required to expedite the official business of the department at every level. The information contained in reports assists the prosecutor in trying his case. Inasmuch as the prosecuting attorney depends upon the information set forth in a report, the reported data must be clear, concise, accurate, factual, and complete. The crime report furnishes answers to the question who, what, when, where, how, and, sometimes, why. Reports also serve as a tool of supervision, provide crime statistical data, identify crime hazards, and assist the officer in court testimony.

REVIEW QUESTIONS

1. What are the characteristics of a good report?
2. Reports are valuable to a police department and its officers for many reasons. Name five.
3. What is the purpose of a synopsis if used in a report? Where in the report should the synopsis be placed?
4. Before submitting a report in a given case, what is the last mechanical step an officer should take?
5. When are crime reports taken?
6. Operational reports are the type of report which most officers are primarily concerned with. What are the various types of operational reports?
7. Before the actual writing or dictation of a report, what preparation is suggested?
8. In listing stolen or missing property in a report, the more accurately the article is described, the easier it will be to locate. Describe how you would list the data if your own watch or ring were stolen from you.

9. If the Moonstone Bar was robbed and the two bandits involved obtained $195 from the cash register and $68 from the wallets of four patrons who were there at the time, who would be considered the victim(s) in this case?

10. After submitting a report, the reporting officer discovers a minor error made in the report. The officer believes that this error will have little effect on the total information set forth. This single error is the only mistake in the lengthy report. It is the officer's opinion that this lone error should be overlooked in the interest of expediency. Discuss your approval or disapproval of the officer's position.

WORK EXERCISE

Set out below is an unacceptable report concerning a robbery of the proprietor of the Lamplighter Motel, Center City, on October 26. This report contains many unnecessary words and sentences and is obviously poorly written. You are to rewrite this report, correcting all errors. Use good sentence structure, punctuation, and proper paragraph arrangement.

Armed robbery at the Lamplighter Motel (hypothetical)

Facts

It was a cold rainy day in the fall season when on October 26, at 1130 hours, the proprietor of the Lamplighter motel at Center City, Mr. John A. Fisher, was preparing to depart from his living quarters at the motel for an extended vacation in Florida. He was planning to make the trip in his new Datsun 210 Hatchback, light brown in color, a very pretty car. This was the first Datsun Mister Fisher ever owned, having traded in a Toyota on it several days before. The Lamplighter Motel was planned and built by Mr. Fisher and his brother Walter who recently died of a heart attack. When Walter died, John became the sole owner of the motel. Mr. Fisher heard a knock on the door to his apartment, number 8 at the motel, and when he opened it an unknown white man quickly stepped inside and pointed a blue steel revolver toward Mr. Fisher's head and ordered him to open the wall safe located behind an oil painting on the west wall located behind an oil painting of the Timeaco mountains, an excellent painting, and considered priceless to Mr. Fisher. The living room of this motel room is small but the furniture and wall-to-wall carpeting expensive. Mr. Fisher stated that the bandit told him: "Hurry up, I've been watching you for several days, I have nothing to lose if I have to kill you." Mr. Fisher stated he opened his safe and gave the bandit all the contents which he said included $2,500; one man's white gold ring with initials JAF on an onyx setting valued at one hundred and fifty dollars; and one string of pearls valued at $800. The pearls were an heirloom and handed down to Mr. Fisher by his mother Nellie Fisher who died three years ago. He was planning to give the pearls to his only niece, Miss Helen Fisher for a wedding gift. Helen is engaged to marry a childhood sweetheart on November 26 which is Thanksgiving day. The robbery loss totaled $3450 plus the $185 the robber got from a small cigar box located beneath the reception counter. Mr. Fisher felt quite elated over the fact that he was fully covered by insurance which he obtained only a month previous to this robbery. The bandit placed the loot in his topcoat pocket and ordered Mr. Fisher to "face the wall and stay there for ten minutes or I'll blow your damned head off." "I'll be watching you." Mr. Fisher stated the bandit then left by the same door and about two minutes later Mr. Fisher heard a car speed away from the parking lot of the motel. Not knowing whether this was the bandit's car, he waited for about three more minutes, then he telephoned the police department and reported the robbery. Mr. Fisher is a very industrious man and he has'nt missed a days work for several years. Mr. Fisher was noted to work hard for every thing he has. However, Mr. Fisher was noted to be under medical treatment for arthritis for the past three years although this has not caused him to miss any work. Prior to this affliction, Mr. Fisher had been in excellent health and was the captain of his football team in his senior year at college ten years ago. Mr. Fisher described the bandit as follows: 5'5" to 5'7", 165–170 pounds, stocky build, twenty-eight to thirty years old, ruddy complexion, blond hair and blue eyes, wearing olive green felt hat, dark brown gaberdine topcoat, brown leather gloves, and oval shaped gold cuff links. The pistol was in his, the bandit's hand at all times. Mr. Fisher stated the bandit held the gun in his right hand. It was Mr. Fisher's opinion that the bandit was probably driving a new car because of his neat and prosperous appearance. Mr. Fisher further stated he doesn't think the bandit was a professional hold-up man because he did not look like a criminal. Other than Mr. Fisher, no one could be found at the motel who had noticed any suspicious person or car. We called the Radio Dispatcher and requested that the bandit's description be broadcast then we asked Mr. Fisher to accompany us to police headquarters to observe our mug file for possible suspects. He was unable to make any identification.

    Investigation will continue.

   /s/ Thomas A. Novice
(Signature of Officer Writing Report)

Auto and Motorcycle Theft

─────── **AUTO THEFT** ───────

Auto theft has long been a major law-enforcement problem. It represents personal loss and inconvenience to owners, over a billion dollars in monetary loss, and higher insurance premiums. Methods used to steal cars and frauds connected with stolen and missing cars have become increasingly diverse and complex. Cars are stolen from almost every conceivable place: homes, shopping centers, streets, parking lots, business establishments, and new and used car lots. The high cost of auto repairs and shortage of parts have made car and parts theft a most profitable business. For example, an auto that sells for about $12,000 can be chopped up and its component parts sold for over $20,000.

According to federal authorities and the insurance industry, thousands of passenger cars are stolen in the United States each year by professional car thieves who are paid a fee for their services. These cars end up in "chop shops" (garages where the bodies of stolen cars are dismantled and parts sold on a nationwide black market). Methods of taking apart cars differ from garage to garage. One of the methods used is to remove all flammable material from inside of the car, remove the doors and then, using a circular saw and blow torch, cut the roof into two major segments. In this process the valuable body parts—the front and rear assemblies—are salvaged. A late model "nose clip" (grill, lights, front assembly, and bumpers) ordered from a manufacturer would cost between $800 and $1000. A parts thief can provide this same equipment for a few hundred dollars. The "chop shops" deal with only parts that contain no identification numbers. Parts like the engine and transmission are discarded, shredded into scrap, or shipped out of state, where numbers are removed and parts filtered back into the market. Once a stolen car has been reduced to its parts, it is no longer identifiable. It is for this reason that there is a dire need for the provision of identification numbers for all body components. The more identification numbers cars have, the better chance law enforcement has of identifying parts and furnishing proof in prosecution proceedings. Presently, the vehicle identification number (VIN) represents the true identification of an automobile. A check of the license number of a suspected stolen car is generally not sufficient, as it takes only a few minutes for a thief to change a license plate.

Types of Auto Theft

Auto thefts can be broken down into two general categories: (1) joyriding or thefts for transportation and (2) commercial thefts or thefts for profit.

Joyriding

Most car thefts are perpetrated by joyriding youngsters. The cars are usually found abandoned within a few hours and often in the same vicinity. The recovery rate is high, although the cars when recovered are often damaged.

Thefts for transportation

This type of offense generally involves transients, hitchhikers, runaways, service personnel, and criminals. The cars are abandoned when their trip is finished or when they run out of gas. Often, the thief will steal a second vehicle in the same vicinity where the first car was abandoned.

Commercial thefts, or thefts for profit

Thefts of this type are the greatest auto theft enforcement problem. In stolen car cases, you cannot distinguish between so-called "joyriding" offenses and theft for profit solely on the basis of the complaint. The apprehension and conviction of a professional auto thief is difficult to obtain as a car stolen by a criminal of this type is not likely to be recovered as quickly, if at all. Most of the unrecovered cars have undoubtedly been handled by the professional thief and although some of the cars may have been completely stripped down, many of them are probably being operated today with fictitious numbers, under good titles, or under counterfeit or fraudulently obtained titles. There is no doubt that there are numerous stolen automobiles being operated by innocent purchasers who have no idea that they are driving stolen cars. Thieves are continually contriving new methods to beat the law, and, in order to combat them, police must know as much as possible about the following methods they use in concealing the identity and disposing of stolen vehicles.

Stripping   The unlawful taking of automobiles for the purpose of stripping is a continuous problem. The thief will hunt for a particular make and model. If the keys are in the car, it will be driven away. If not, the ignition wires are short-circuited to start it or it is towed away. The stolen car will then be taken to a garage or an isolated locality, stripped of parts wanted, and then the chassis or unwanted parts are abandoned. Accessory and parts theft rings operate for the sole purpose of stripping the stolen vehicle and selling parts such as wheels, tires, batteries, and radios. Thieves involved in this type of theft often use a tow truck and may wear mechanic's uniforms to disarm suspicion. Suspects might be teenagers, hot-rodders, persons in their early twenties, students, or mechanics. Offenses such as stripping account for the complete disappearance of many stolen vehicles.

Dismantling and Illegal Wrecking   In this operation a car is stolen and taken to an open area where it is cut up and sold to scrap metal dealers; salable parts are sold to automobile wrecking yards. Parts of stolen cars are traded and often reappear in many of the same make of car. Upon questioning, the individuals involved will produce some type of bill of sale. This bill might be written on a scrap of paper, in pencil, and is generally illegible. Frequently a case is solved from information furnished by the victims or their "dragster" friends.

In one stolen parts case, a victim received information that his car might have been taken by a youth in another city. The victim and a friend proceeded to the suspect's home and arrived just as the youth drove up in the stolen car. The police were called and the suspect arrested. His garage was checked and found to be full of auto parts. Many of the parts were identified as stolen and subsequent investigation led to the arrest of two accomplices. The case resulted in the identification of seven cars, partial recovery of three more, and information that led to the arrest of a second group of hot-rod auto thieves. Investigation of the second gang resulted in the recovery of several additional cars. A bill of sale produced by suspected auto thieves is worth no more than the paper it is written on unless one can go back to the seller for verification. A thief will buy one auto part and will then exhibit the same bill of sale for a dozen similar parts.

Salvage Racket   This is probably the oldest and most prevalent racket used by the commercial thief. It is a difficult case to combat. In cases of this kind the thieves acquire titles to late model cars that have been wrecked or burned. They dispose of the salvage as scrap metal but retain the license plates, registration cards, ownership certificates, and serial number plates. They will then steal cars of the same year and model on which they will install the salvage serial plate, restamp the motors to agree with the salvage documents, and attach the salvage license plates. The serial number plate and license plates from the stolen vehicles are then disposed of. The identities of the vehicles thus changed become the ones which were wrecked or burned. Only an expert in the identification of vehicles would be able to identify them as the cars that were stolen.

The National Automobile Theft Bureau (NATB), combating this type of theft, receives reports from all of its member companies on all cars sold as salvage. Stop cards are then filed with state motor vehicle departments. Should the car be reregistered, a representative of the NATB, assisted by the police, will inspect the car to determine if it is the salvage car rebuilt or if it is a stolen car. The police, by observing discarded late model wrecked and stripped automobiles with vehicle identification numbers removed, can, with the assistance of the NATB, identify the vehicle through confidential numbers or by restoring obliterated numbers.

The National Automobile Theft Bureau is a service organization maintained by a number of insurance companies to assemble and disseminate reports of stolen automobiles and to assist law-enforcement agencies in their identification and recovery. This auto theft agency has branches throughout the United States staffed by special agents who are experts in the detection of theft rings, methods used, and the identification of automobiles. As one of its services, the NATB, as it is referred to by officers, annually publishes a booklet entitled *Manual for the Identification of Automobiles*. This manual is distributed to police agencies throughout the respective states and is valuable in making identifications of suspected stolen automobiles. This booklet contains information which can be of extreme value in determining the true identity of automobiles involved in thefts or arson investigations. There is no expense to law enforcement for the services rendered by the NATB.

Vehicles Stolen for Resale Cars in this category may involve rental cars, cars secured on contract by means of a bad check, or out and out thefts. These cars are sold without benefit of title, duplicate title, altered title, counterfeit title, or salvage title. A fictitious bill of sale will be executed and a registration certificate will be secured, usually in a nontitle state. The registration certificate is then presented in a state where a title to the car is obtained. A common practice is to use salvage vehicles where the title, license, and vehicle identification from a total collision or total fire loss is used to dispose of a stolen car.

Counterfeit and Forged Certificates of Ownership Documents of this type are often prepared by auto theft rings to show ownership. Blank titles my be stolen from motor vehicle departments in some states and subsequently filled out to match the description of a stolen car which is then sold under the prepared papers. Detection of the suspected certificate can be made by comparing with genuine documents or by laboratory examination.

Insurance Fraud This is used by dishonest car owners who take their vehicles to remote areas, remove saleable parts in some instances, and burn the remains. Thereafter, the owners file theft reports and collect from the insurance companies with whom their cars are insured. In other instances, the owner purposely burns the car, attributing the cause to a short in the wiring. Defective wiring is the most common excuse given for the origin of an automobile fire. It is to be noted that the chance of a modern automobile developing a fire from a short in the wiring sufficient to destroy it is almost negligible.

Fictitious License Plates These are often used by automobile thieves. In one case, a thief stole a Cadillac for his personal use. He then stole a registration certificate from a Cadillac of similar make and model. Thereafter, he changed the vehicle identification number of the stolen Cadillac to conform to that appearing on the registration certificate. A license plate was then made from two plates to match that of the certificate. The "phony" plates were not discovered until the police called the registered owner and advised him that his car was impounded. The owner stated that his car was in his garage and the license plates were on his car. The officers then rechecked and found the "phony" plates.

Methods of Auto Theft

Various methods of operation are used by auto thieves to enter and steal cars. Some thefts are made possible by the carelessness of owners in leaving their cars unlocked and a key in the ignition. If the car is unlocked and there is no ignition key available, several types of jump wires can be employed by thieves to bypass ignition switches. The use of such wiring is a popular method employed by "joyriders" and professional thieves. Hairpins, paper clips, coins, steel wool, or other metal objects can also be placed between the terminals of the ignition switch, permitting the current to flow into the electrical system. "Hot wiring" the automobile under the hood of the car by connecting a wire from the battery to the coil is also used in stealing cars. Prying open the trunk compartment and entering the car through the rear seat, forcing door handles with pieces of pipe, breaking or prying the wind wing with screwdrivers or other tools, using can openers and long pieces of wire with bent, hooked ends have likewise been employed by car thieves to gain access to locked vehicles. Other innovations in tampering include the removing and replacing of ignition switches, making duplicate keys, or obtaining the number from the original key and having a duplicate key made.

With the introduction of locking devices on steering columns in newer cars, thieves now use long thin saws that can be slid into the steering column to break the lock. Some use "slam hammers" to strip an ignition key system with one jolt and then replace it with a new ignition and key. Others use cranes to simply lift a car up and place it on a truck — and then drive off.

In one case a flapping furniture pad partially covering a Corvette became the key to breaking up an auto theft ring. In this instance, alert patrol officers stopped a pickup truck hauling an auto trailer carrying several cars. Subsequent investigation resulted in the location of several garages where numerous cars and motorcycles were recovered as well as a large number of component parts. In addition, "shopping lists" of wanted cars and motorcycles were recovered. As a bonus, the officers also found a large quantity of dangerous drugs as well as uncovering a prostitution ring. The members of this theft ring included the ring leader (a pimp), a bank teller, a loan company manager, two school teachers, and a reserve deputy sheriff.

The use of subterfuge in obtaining cars has also been employed on many occasions. The thief visits a new or used car lot and shows an interest in one of the vehicles. The salesman, intent on making a sale, permits the prospective purchaser to take the car off the premises for a demonstration ride, often without requiring any identification. Thereafter, the alleged customer will have a duplicate ignition key made and will return the car. Later the car is taken by using the duplicate ignition key.

Use of fictitious checks

In securing automobiles, thieves have been known to issue fictitious checks particularly after banking hours. Since it is not possible to cash the checks, the thieves have several hours head start on the police before the loss is discovered. In some cases the thief will answer an advertisement in the newspaper regarding a car for sale by a private owner. After some discussion with the owner regarding the price and condition of the car, the thief will write out a check for the price of the vehicle and in return receive a clear title. The thief is then in a position to resell the car before the victim realizes she or he has been swindled.

Auto Theft Investigation at the London Metropolitan Police

During the summer of 1970, the author had occasion to study the Metropolitan Police of London, England. One of approximately twelve specialist branches of CID (Criminal Investigation Department) of Scotland Yard is known as C_{10}. C_{10} is the Stolen Vehicle Investigation Branch which concerns itself with auto theft. A CID Inspector mentioned that this branch has two sources of business, viz., cars that were stopped by policemen on the streets of London and elsewhere and suspected of being stolen, and cars that had been crashed, junked, repaired, or reregistered. It was indicated by officials that C_{10} did not particularly look for stolen cars but meticulously checked those suspect cars that came to the attention of this branch. The work of the officers assigned to C_{10} provides the necessary expertise in testimony and available evidences in court presentations. The C_{10} officers (counterparts of our own detectives) were said to trace "the origin of each bit" of a suspect stolen car in an effort to determine ownership and/or when and where it came from. Car thieves in London are called "ringers" because they "ring the changes" on stolen cars. It was noted that one of the methods employed by car thieves in England was to cut a stolen vehicle directly in half and thereafter weld the cut half to a second stolen vehicle which also had been cut in half (or other various proportions) in order to confuse the identity of the automobile and escape detection. (See Figure 10-1).

Car Theft Prosecution

Every state has a law relating to the theft of automobiles. The federal law prohibiting the interstate transportation of a stolen motor vehicle or aircraft is found in United States Code, title 18, section 2112—enforced by the FBI. In addition, in U.S. Code, title 18, section 2313, receiving, concealing, storing, bartering, selling or disposing of a stolen motor vehicle or aircraft which is moving in interstate or foreign commerce, knowing it to have been stolen, constitutes theft.

Figure 10-1. Officers receiving instruction in auto theft investigation at the Metropolitan Police Training School at Hendon in London, England.

Under United States Department of Justice guidelines for interstate car thefts (the Dyer Act), only car ring cases are now prosecuted federally. Individual violations are referred for state and local action.

State law

Prosecution in auto theft cases varies in many states with regard to what may constitute a grand theft violation. In California law, prosecution in auto theft cases may be done under section 10851 of the California Vehicle Code or under section 487.3 of the California Penal Code. Section 10851 differs from the larceny of an automobile under 487.3 in that the intent to permanently deprive the owner of property, a necessary element of the corpus delicti of larceny, is not essential. It is sufficient if the intent be merely to temporarily deprive the owner of the possession of the car. In view of this difference, many police departments in California charge auto theft suspects under the California Vehicle Code section 10851. California Penal Code section 499b (misdemeanor) is sometimes used to charge persons who unlawfully take a motor vehicle, bicycle, motorcycle or other vehicle, or motorboat or vessel for temporary use.

Automobile Investigation

The first report of the theft of an automobile is usually an oral statement made by the victim that his or her automobile has been stolen. Inasmuch as this theft complaint is generally made by telephone, proof of ownership of the vehicle and the signing of a formal report by the complainant is required by some departments prior to issuing a theft broadcast. Other departments make this theft information immediately available to all patrol units in the area, prior to obtaining the above formally signed report. However, in this instance, the fact that a report has not been signed should be stressed in any broadcast regarding the stolen vehicle. Where a telephonic auto theft complaint is received, an officer is dispatched to interview the victim in order to obtain the facts and signature of the victim on a report. Completeness and accuracy in reporting auto theft data are essential to protect fellow officers in the field who will be looking for the wanted car. The investigating officer should obtain the following descriptive data on the stolen vehicle (for police radio dispatcher):

> Make
> Year
> Color(s) (list top or front color first)
> Model
> License number
> Owner
> Address
> Vehicle identification number (VIN)
> Location and time of theft
> Distinctive characteristics

If the license and vehicle identification numbers are unknown, the victim may obtain them by referring to such things as the car's insurance policy, gasoline sales slips, and repair bills. Inquiry of the state motor vehicle registration department will also provide this information if needed. Other information pertaining to the stolen car that would be of benefit to all officers would be such things as damage, dents, tires, equipment, accessories, tools, types of upholstery, tears, spots, paint scratches, seatcovers, and contents of the glove and rear compartments.

The initial investigation should be concerned with the gathering of such information as date, place, and hour of the theft, identity of the last person who drove the vehicle, evidence of ownership (registered and legal owner), whether car payments are delinquent, and the identity of the persons who have keys to the car as well as the names of the persons who drive it. Other

data to be gathered includes name of insurance company with which it is insured, whether ignition key was in the vehicle at the time, whether doors were locked or unlocked, what person last saw vehicle, and the name and description of any suspects. The possibility that the car has been misplaced, of the victim giving a false report (generally a penal code violation), of a family dispute, of the involvement of the car in a hit-and-run accident, or of it being reported stolen to serve as an alibi should also be considered.

Identification of Automobiles

There are five general methods by which automobiles can be identified: (1) license or registration number; (2) motor number; (3) vehicle identification number (serial number); (4) general description and personal identification; and (5) hidden numbers or component part numbers.

License number

The first step in checking any vehicle is to obtain the license number of the car if the plates are attached. From this number it is possible to ascertain who is the registered owner of record. The license number is the means by which most stolen automobiles are recovered. In recording the license be sure to note the location of dashes, stars, or other methods of separation of license numbers. Some states designate the county by the prefix of the license number and the balance of the number may be repeated in each county. In checking a license number it should be remembered that license plates can be changed. It is therefore of little value for identification unless the plates are on the vehicle to which they belong. The vehicle identification number, or motor number, should always be checked if possible. License plates should also be examined to determine if they are genuine plates. In one case, one of the plates examined reflected that the number "3" had been painted so that it looked like an "8." Thieves have also been known to weld parts of two plates together to make a third number. The work in one case was so well done that it could not be detected except by feeling for the weld marks on the back of the plate.

Motor number

The engine number is a die-stamped number appearing on the engine block generally on a smoothed raised boss, although on a few models the number is die-stamped into the rough cast surface of the block. In any event, the motor numbers are always indented, not raised. Manufacturers often place raised numbers on the engine or chassis, however, the raised numbers are parts or casting numbers and are of no value in identifying a motor. Motor numbers are sometimes difficult to locate as they may be covered by dirt and grease.

When a motor number is to be checked, the following equipment will assist the investigating officer: (1) a pair of work gloves; (2) a rag to wipe off dirt and grease; (3) a solvent (paint thinner, typewriter cleaner, gasoline); (4) a flashlight; and (5) a wire brush and piece of emery paper. The location of the motor number can be determined by reference to the *Manual for the Identification of Automobiles* distributed by the National Automobile Theft Bureau.

After locating and cleaning the area where the motor number is located on the automobile, the examiner should check the number closely to determine if it might have been ground or altered. The separate digits should be checked to determine if a factory die was used in stamping the number. If the investigating officer is not familiar with the type of die used, a check of the number of a car of the same make will assist in any comparison made as to size and style.

After this examination the number should be checked to determine if it is correct for that particular make and model of car. This information is set forth in the *NATB Manual* referred to above. As it is possible to obtain factory style dies, the surface upon which the number has been stamped should be checked. Again you will probably have to refer to a vehicle of similar make to compare surfaces. Look for file marks, gouges, grind marks, signs of heating, etc. If the number appears to have been ground or tampered with, the original number can usually be restored. Number restoration should be done by an expert who is familiar with the restoration of numbers.

Wherever there is evidence of tampering, detailed impressions should be made by an expert. In the process of obtaining motor numbers in tampering cases, various methods are used. Successful lifts have been made by the use of a surface replica plastic in which the area surrounding the motor number is dammed with putty and liquid plastic poured directly into the impression. When it hardens, the plastic forms an effective lift which can be used as evidence if needed. Lead sheets that can be cut into small squares and applied to the questioned number by applying a sharp blow with a punch have also been used to obtain impressions. Other material, such as a plastic with a metal backing that, unlike sheet lead, can be struck a number of soft blows to force the plastic into the motor number impressions has been used. Whenever any of these methods are used, two impressions should be made, either using lead or plastic, as the first impression serves to clean out microscopic debris that might not have been otherwise removed.

The FBI maintains a National Automobile Altered Numbers File which is a central depository for lead impressions of altered or fictitious automobile identifying numbers. This file is a reference collection and is maintained for the purpose of comparing lead impressions from altered numbers to determine if the same dies made both sets of impressions. Successful identifications made from searches of this file have resulted in a considerable number of cars being identified as having been handled by different auto theft rings. In one particular case, successful identifications were made of a total of 122 automobiles.

Other methods used to bring out tampered motor numbers in order that they might be photographed and recorded include the use of (1) heat treatment, (2) acid (muriatic) used in proper strength and *not* on aluminum cast motors, and (3) heat and acid.

The most common procedures of number restoration are (1) the electrolytic acid process and (2) the heat process. The use of both these procedures involves considerable skill. As a general rule the electrolytic acid process should be used first. *Caution:* The electrolytic acid process should *not* be employed on motorcycle blocks or on engine blocks made of aluminum. The die-stamping of the number on a cast-iron block or on a steel frame compresses the molecules to a depth below the actual indentation of the number. When an etching solution is applied to the surface on which the number has been removed, it will react more rapidly on the area surrounding the location where the numbers were stamped, thereby causing them to reappear in a lighter shade of color.

The heat process is a method of heating the number boss with an acetylene torch. As with the electrolytic acid process, the surface reacts differently to the heat at the location where the numbers were previously stamped, resulting in their reappearance in a lighter shade of color.

If a motor number appears to have been tampered with by grinding, drilling, defacing, etc., the National Auto Theft Bureau representative or other police specialist should be consulted in order that expert assistance be utilized in identifying a suspect or a possible car theft ring.

Carbon paper (soft) can be used to process motor numbers in conjunction with transparent tape. Paper of this type is rubbed across the motor or serial number leaving fine deposits of carbon on the numbers. A strip of transparent tape is then placed over the numbers, gently rubbed, and removed. The lifted serial numbers or engine numbers are then transferred to a 3- by 5-inch plain white card. The card containing the motor or serial number is thereafter identified with the date, initials or name of the officer involved in the lifting of the numbers, place from which taken, and case number, if available. The person using this method might leave a fingerprint impression on one or both ends of the cellophane tape to act as additional identification for court purposes.

Vehicle identification number (VIN)

Since January 1, 1955, the vehicle identification number plate has replaced the engine number for registration and recording purposes and is now referred to as the permanent identification number. The metal plate is die-stamped and has a high resistance to water, rust, and fire. The *Manual for the Identification of Automobiles* published by the National Auto Theft Bureau should be referred to for the location of the vehicle identification number plate.

When checking the VIN, look for signs that would indicate that the metal plate has been changed or disturbed as it is almost impossible to remove this metal plate from a vehicle without some mutilation or telltale sign of alteration. When a VIN plate is taken from one vehicle and attached to another, it is often not affixed firmly and often is replaced in a different manner from that used by the manufacturer. Any vehicle from which the VIN plate has been removed or where numbers have been altered or tampered with should be impounded for further investigation. The state vehicle code generally has a section pertaining to alteration and tampering.

For information purposes, the data on the metal plate of a Chevrolet for example, includes the "Mfg. Symbol," "Car Line Series," "Body Type Symbol," "Engine Code," "Model Year," "Assembly Plant," and "Production No." In a Chevrolet, the Vehicle Identification (1972 to present) would appear as: 1D35H3K401527

1	Mfg. Symbol
D	Car Line Series
35	Body Type Symbol
H	Engine Code
3	Model Year
K	Assembly Plant
401527	Production No.

It is imperative that the number (1D35H3K401527) is correctly noted since a transposition or an incorrect digit will lead to information on an altogether different vehicle. Care should be taken so that an "S" is not mistaken for a "5," or a "2" for a "Z." In writing always use written style for letters "S" and "Z." The innovation by some automobile companies of locating the automobile vehicle identification number on the top surface of the vehicle instrument panel, visible from the outside, is of considerable assistance to police in checking and recovering stolen cars.

Description and personal identification

Although numbers are very important, vehicles can be identified without them. Vehicles should be inspected carefully and in detail. Look under floor mats and seats for pieces of paper with names, addresses, or other identifiable data. The owner will undoubtedly be able to identify many points on the car such as scratches, damage, tears in upholstery, and other minor defects. Personal identification in court has been used many times when numbers have been removed and where it is not desired to disclose the location of confidential numbers on a car.

Hidden numbers or component part numbers

Through the cooperation of automobile factories, hidden numbers are stamped on cars. Factories keep records of assembly information on cars which are made available to the National Automobile Theft Bureau. This information is confidential and is not published.

It is also possible to identify a vehicle by the *lock numbers* since manufacturers assign numbers to most of the various locks on a car and keep records of them. Some manufacturers identify high-performance engines and transmissions with a traceable number.

Stolen Car Records

After the identifying VIN, motor, or license numbers have been obtained from a vehicle being checked out as possibly stolen, it is necessary to find a theft report on the car and locate its owner. To do this, officers depend on the stolen automobile records maintained locally by the police department, or on state and federal records.

At a national level, the National Crime Information Center (NCIC) headquartered in the FBI, Washington, D.C., is a nationwide computer network that provides, within seconds, pertinent information to police departments. Data on stolen automobiles, wanted persons, stolen guns, and other identifiable property, is supplied on a twenty-four-hour, seven-day-a-week basis. The NCIC complements the electronic information systems of metropolitan police and state agencies.

Commercial Vehicle Thefts

Whenever a *commercial* vehicle is reported to be stolen, the investigator should obtain all of the modifications that the owner has made to the vehicle, i.e., extra equipment, types of tires, type of trailer or truck body, etc. Many truck parts have identifying numbers of which the truck manufacturer often keeps records. The vehicle may be identified by these part numbers or it can be shown that the part originally belonged on a stolen vehicle. Identification numbers on trucks and trailers may be found in various locations on either the body, engine, or frame. There is no standard location for these numbers. However, the identification number location may be found by referring to the *Manual for the Identification of Automobiles* published by the National Auto Theft Bureau. When inspecting the registration of a commercial vehicle, be aware that commercial vehicles may be registered by either the motor number or identification number if registered prior to 1959. All 1959 and subsequent models are required to be registered by identification number.

Recognizing a Stolen Car

There are no foolproof methods of "spotting" stolen vehicles. However, some of the suspicion arousers that should cause officers to check a particular automobile include such things as

License plate irregularities
A new license plate on an old car or an old plate on a new car or the location where the plate is attached should arouse curiosity and a quick check of a suspected vehicle. Missing plates, front and rear license plates that do not match, plates that are loosely attached, or one plate over another, certainly suggest that an immediate verification is called for. Alteration of license plate or numbers, new bolts on old plates, torn holes around the bolt area, or a combination of shiny and rusty nuts would indicate the investigation of the particular car. A bent license plate covering a portion of the license number, a local automobile dealer license frame mounted on an out-of-state plate, color differences or misalignment of the license numbers likewise warrant a check of the vehicle.

Damage indicating forced entry
A vehicle that has damaged ventilators, broken car windows, or new vent glass replacements should be checked to see whether there is a stolen report outstanding. A new car with dented fenders or other signs of neglect also suggest that a status check to see if it is wanted is called for. A check of cars with such noticeable things as a broken door handle, bullet hole, punched-out trunk lock, partial stripping, or missing accessories might result in the location of a stolen vehicle.

Location of vehicle
A check of cars parked in unusual locations, improperly parked vehicles, or those parked in yellow, red, or white zones has often resulted in the location of a missing car.

Suspicious behavior of driver
Careful observation of any furtive actions on the part of drivers or occupants of vehicles has resulted in the location of stolen cars. Suspicion might be aroused by the age, poor dress, and nervousness of the driver of an expensive automobile; evasive answers to questions; attempts to evade arrest; driving without lights; apparent unfamiliarity in the manipulation of the car's equipment; reckless driving; etc. Other observation of a vehicle's contents (evidence of eating and sleeping in the car), car registration documents on cheap paper stock, a General Motors key in a Ford product, etc., may furnish reasonable cause to suspect the possibility of a stolen car.

Stakeout indicators

When a wanted car is located, consideration should be given to observing the vehicle in order to apprehend the thief.

One of the following circumstances could justify a discreet observation of a suspected car: a warm radiator, motor, or exhaust pipe; a recent write-in on the "hot sheet" (list of current stolen and wanted cars); weapons or valuable articles left in the car. Also, the location of the car near a stadium, school, or any residence may justify watching the vehicle for a period of time. In each case, however, the urgency and nature of the investigation dictate the desired action.

Examining Stolen Vehicles

In the recovery of a stolen automobile, the immediate area where the car is recovered is the crime scene. On stripped recoveries it should be noted whether the vehicle was on the street, in an alley, on a vacant lot, etc., and the direction the vehicle was pointing, where pertinent; in addition, check for oil trails. Property left in the abandoned vehicle should be carefully processed; items with serial numbers should be checked if they were unknown at the time a report was taken. The area surrounding the vehicle should be carefully checked for physical evidence or other identifying data that might lead to the identification of the thief. A recovered car should be processed for evidence of fingerprints left by the perpetrator in order to place her or him in the automobile. This processing should be done prior to conducting a search of the vehicle.

Latent fingerprints are most likely to be found on rearview and outside mirrors, edges of the door, door posts, door handles, steering column, steering wheel hub, knobs on dashboard panel, area around the glove compartment, objects in the glove compartment, and plastic registration slip holder. Other places are windshield area, seat ad-justment lever, edges around the license plates, trunk handle, and gasoline and water pressure caps.

Fingerprints sometimes can be seen by close observation and the use of oblique lighting (holding a flashlight so that its light beam falls across the suspected area at a sharp angle). If indentifiable latent prints are located on the stolen automobile, they should be photographed, if possible, and lifted from the place found. The fingerprints found should be preserved for future comparison with those of any suspects involved in the case. A set of fingerprint impressions should be obtained from the car owner and drivers having access to the vehicle. These fingerprints are called *elimination prints* and are taken in order to eliminate them from other fingerprints found on or in the car.

Search of stolen automobile

After processing for latent fingerprints, a thorough search should be undertaken of the vehicle's contents for any information that might suggest the identity or whereabouts of the suspect involved in the theft. In searching a car, consider such factors as the known cleverness of the suspect and the size, shape, and weight of a particular object being sought in relation to the possible hiding places in the car, e.g., guns, checks, narcotics, jewelry, etc. In some cases (homicide, kidnaping), only crime laboratory specialists should search the suspected automobile. In any search conducted of an automobile, do not discard anything—small scraps of paper, burned matches, identification cards, lube stickers and receipts, or any other property that might lead to the identity of persons responsible. State inspection decals, safety inspection decals, and other such items are often good sources of information as the decal number can be traced back through the state and important information often can be obtained regarding the vehicle and owner. Make notes of all physical evidence found. Include location, date, initials of officer, and case number if known. Searches of stolen cars have produced evidence of narcotics on floor mats, marijuana cigarettes in ashtrays, bloodstains on upholstery, traces of paint from burglarized safes in the trunk or rear seat section, and other helpful materials leading to solutions of other crimes.

Where narcotics, jewelry, money, or other small valuable articles are believed to be concealed in a vehicle, the search may include the following areas: air cleaner and oil filter; dashboard section—behind this area, above car radio, compartment cowling; and inside door and body panels. The ashtray, sun visor, area under seats, cushions, under floorboards, floor mats, and vent ducts should be checked. Places of concealment such as the inside of a flashlight, beneath the horn plate on some cars, underside of the clutch, brake, and accelerator pedal should not be overlooked. The trunk compartments, spare tire, and tube, and special compartments in the radiator or gasoline tanks should be scrutinized carefully. The outside of the vehicle should be examined, particularly the hubcaps beneath door frames, behind chrome strips, headlights, beneath fenders, behind bumpers, and containers wired to frame.

The following case illustrates the importance of seemingly insignificant evidence found in the search of a recovered car in one of the Western cities. An alert NATB representative, during the processing of a suspected stolen car, picked up a small piece of paper rolled into a sort of "spitball." Unravelling this insignificant ball, it was noted that it was a torn piece of a nickel money wrapper from an agency in the Portland, Oregon, area. Contact with the Portland authorities ascertained that there had been a safe burglary in Portland in which coin wrappers of this kind were involved. Further investigation by the FBI and police disclosed that the stolen car had been taken from a parking lot in a Missouri city by escapees from a county jail. Investigation conducted thereafter resulted in the solution of numerous burglaries by these suspects during their visit to the West Coast.

Impounded, Recovered, or Stored Vehicle

There is a difference between stored and impounded vehicles. If a car is to be processed for fingerprints, searched, or checked for possible evidence, it is impounded. However, when a person is driving a vehicle at the time of arrest and the vehicle is not needed as evidence, the car is stored for safekeeping. An impounded vehicle cannot be released without an official impound release form filled out and signed by the police agency involved. A stored vehicle can be released by the storage garage to anyone who has an interest in the vehicle. Whenever a vehicle is impounded, the investigating officer should make sure that a complete inventory of the contents of the car is taken and the tow truck driver has signed for the inventory at the scene.

In those cases involving embezzled cars, a report is generally not taken by many police departments until, for example, several days have elapsed, the victim's signed complaint is on file with the local district attorney's office, and a warrant is issued. At this time, a radio broadcast, teletype, or other bulletin is initiated by the auto theft detail. Commencement of an investigation in embezzled car cases is governed by the policy of the district attorney's office in the area involved.

Whenever a vehicle is recovered, the investigating officer should make sure that the registered owner is notified of the location of the car and of its condition, whether it is driveable or not, and the name and address of the garage where the vehicle is stored. In addition, pertinent information, including data on the suspect involved, should be disseminated to interested agencies. The officer's report on the recovered vehicle should include any case in which the located car may have been involved. All stops placed against the recovered car *must* be removed immediately.

A dozen don'ts to remember when the car is in the hands of a suspect claiming ownership:

1. *Don't* permit suspect to enter building or any other place unaccompanied, for the purpose of procuring title papers or documents to prove a claim to ownership.

2. *Don't* permit suspect to enter a room in a house or any building alone, under any pretext.

3. *Don't* permit suspect to enter car or reach into glove compartment, trunk, or any part of car under investigation, before the vehicle has been legally searched.

4. *Don't* permit suspect to visit restroom unaccompanied.

5. *Don't* permit suspect to stroll away or get out of reach for arrest.

6. *Don't* permit suspect to gain an advantageous position between investigating officers and their vehicle, which as a rule has the motor running or the keys in the switch.

7. *Don't* permit suspect to drive the car under investigation to a garage or police station, either accompanied or unaccompanied.

8. *Don't* permit one or more suspects to ride in an investigating officer's car unhandcuffed, when the investigation is conducted by a single officer. The automobile seat belt can help secure the handcuffed suspect. Units having a caged rear passenger section have distinct advantages in transporting suspects.

9. *Don't* leave your vehicle exposed to theft by chasing a suspect who has fled on foot while you were questioning several other suspects.

10. *Don't* make snap judgments in taking the word of suspect or accused against complainant or informant.

11. *Don't* attempt to check the motor or serial number of a car while suspect is in it.

12. *Don't* put your head under the hood of car or attempt to check the motor, beneath the seats, the trunk, or underside of car while suspect is close at hand and unguarded.

Sources of Information in Automobile Thefts

There are many excellent sources of information available to police agencies in car theft cases. A partial list of potential sources would include the following:

Complainant
Owners and operators of wrecking yards
Used-car lot operators
Auto auction sale lots
Garages
Auto paint shops
Body and fender shops
Insurance company claim adjusters
Service station attendants
Parking lot employees
State criminal identification and investigation bureaus
State motor vehicle departments
State highway patrols
Checking stations
Automobile Manufacturers Association, Detroit, Michigan
National Automobile Theft Bureau
FBI National Crime Information Center (NCIC) and specialized files maintained by this agency
Border patrol officers
Criminal informants and sources of information
Other sources

── MOTORCYCLE THEFTS ──

One of the most effective tools that an officer has to combat motorcycle theft is a thorough familiarity with the traffic laws and motorcycle equipment requirements of his or her particular state. Good traffic law enforcement permits the officer to determine the status of the motorcycle, the rider's right to possession of the vehicle, proper registration, licensing, and identification of the rider.

The three popular makes of motorcycles most often stolen are the Harley-Davidson Model 74 (United States), the Triumph (English), and the BSA (English). These motorcycles are popular makes and have interchangeable parts from one year to the other. A large number of disreputable motorcycle clubs use Harley-Davidson motorcycles. This is generally the members' most prized possession. The method by which they come into possession of these motorcycles or components is often questionable.

Harley-Davidson

In California, the Harley-Davidson motorcycles are registered with the State Department of Motor Vehicles by the *engine number* in contrast to all other types of motorcycles which are registered by *frame number*. Model 74 Harley-Davidson motorcycles have remained essentially the same in structure and parts; there are sixteen models of this motorcycle. The accessories on the "full-dress" model 74 Harley-Davidson are the ones that are continually the subject of thefts. A full-dress motorcycle has the standard handle bar, fenders, tanks, saddlebags, stoplights and foglights. A so-called "chop-job" motorcycle usually has high handlebars, chopped fenders (fenders partly cut off), custom tanks, and a lot of extra chrome.

The *engine number* on the Harley-Davidson models 74, 61, Sprint, and Sportster are located on the left half of the engine case, on the left side, under the front cylinder. The frame numbers of the Sprint and Sportster models are located on the right side of the steering head and are identical to the engine numbers. Model 61 and the Sprint are two Harley-Davidson motorcycles quite often found among motorcycle riders. The model 61 is similar to the model 74 mentioned above in both size and weight and is designated by the letters "EL" in the engine number. The Sprint model is comparable in size and weight to the Triumph and the BSA motorcycles. The frame numbers of the Sprint and Sportster models are located on the right side of the steering head and are identical to the engine numbers. A sample engine number on a Harley-Davidson motorcycle would appear as 69FL5449.

69	Denotes the year of manufacture
FL	Denotes the model (in this case, the Harley-Davidson model 74)
5449	Represents the engine number (four or more numbers)

Assembly numbers

In addition to the vehicle identification numbers on a Harley-Davidson, there is a series of numbers located on the bottom of both engine cases. A complete engine crankcase consists of two halves, one right and one left, which are bolted together. These will be referred to as left case and right case. Numbers on the cases are not available at motor vehicle departments. Assembly numbers normally consist of three numbers, a dash, and four production numbers. This number normally will not match the production or engine boss number.

Altered numbers

There are numerous methods of altering the identification numbers on Harley-

Davidson motorcycle engines. This is primarily true because the cases are molded from soft aluminum alloys. Some of the factors that indicate an alteration has occurred include the following:

1. An obvious removal of the identification numbers by grinding or filing.

2. An overstamp which gives the appearance of superimposed numbers. This is normally obvious as numbers are difficult to distinguish and are not clear-cut.

3. A ground surface that contains identification numbers and other numbers subsequently stamped on.

4. Engine boss completely removed by grinding and then sandblasted and restamped.

5. Engine boss ground off and the surface of the boss built up by heliarc welder.

6. Weld marks on the sides of the raised engine boss.

7. A merging or partial merging of the engine boss with the upper horizontal ridge. This indicates a welding process has been applied.

8. Pits (holes) on the flat surface which are caused by air bubbles forming at the time of the welding.

9. An improper numbering process used at the time of restamping a case. Since 1960, serial numbers start with an even number in even years and an odd number in odd years.

10. A distinct difference in the texture of the surface where the number is located and on the surrounding surfaces (the texture should be the same, as the engine cases are produced in a mold when manufactured).

Common terms

These are used by members of disreputable motorcycle clubs when referring to Harley-Davidsons and component parts:

Hog. Term used to denote a Harley-Davidson motorcycle. This is due to its bulk and size in relation to other motorcycles.

Garbage wagon. Denotes a full-dress Harley-Davidson, especially one that is equipped with numerous accessories.

Tin can. A term given to overhead-valve Harley-Davidson engines. "Tin can" refers to the thin metal valve covers on the engine heads, first used in 1948 and still being used to date.

Chopper. A Harley-Davidson motorcycle that has been stripped to its essential parts, and sometimes lowered. Parts such as the gas tank, rear fender, forks, handlebars, etc., are then modified to suit the owner.

Knucklehead. Term given to a Harley-Davidson motorcycle manufactured prior to 1948. Following 1948 only the "tin can" was made. The only models were the 74 cubic inch and the 61 cubic inch. They can be identified by the large cuts on the right side above the cylinders.

Parts. Denotes engine and chassis accessories found on Harley-Davidson motorcycles. These are prized by members of disreputable motorcycle clubs, particularly because of the difficulty in identifying the parts or their source.

Other terms. "Ape hanger" refers to high handlebars. "Sissy bars" refers to the high bar placed on the rear of the motorcycle (usually the passenger uses this as a back rest). "Flat held" refers to the type of engine in which the valves are not activated by overhead rocker arm systems.

BSA

The BSA (English) motorcycle, manufactured by the Birmingham Small Arms Corporation, Birmingham, England, is one of the most popular English motorcycles used for pleasure and racing. It is much lighter than the Harley-Davidson. Two of the BSA models that are very prevalent in this country are the Starfire Scrambler (one cylinder) and the BSA Twin (a two-cylinder motorcycle also called the "Super Rocket"). The *engine number* of the BSA is stamped in sand casting (never on a smooth surface) on the left side of the crankcase below the cylinder. The *frame number* is stamped on a diagonal bar below the steering head, on the left side. There is no connection between the frame and the engine number (prior to June 1966.). After June of 1966, the engine number and frame numbers are the same. It is to be remembered, however, that this motorcycle is registered by frame number. Alterations of numbers become apparent when the front corner loses its roundness or a portion of the cylinder is smoother. Usually the file grinding marks will indicate the area altered. The BSA has parts that are interchangeable with the *Triumph* motorcycle.

Triumph

The Triumph motorcycle is similar to the BSA in size, weight, and appearance. The engine number on the Triumph is located on the left side of the crankcase below the cylinder and is the same as the frame number. The frame number is stamped on an angle on the lower portion of the steering head, forward of the gas tank on the left side (same as last five or six digits of the engine number).

Alterations of numbers on the Triumph are most common to the engine number. Since the engine is cast in one piece, the consistency of the metal to the engine number is the same as elsewhere on the casting. Look for file marks and sharp corners at either end of the engine number. The shape of the engine casting at either end of the numbers is a rounded curve. When filing off the number there will be left, in most cases, a sharply defined edge to the roundness of the casing. In altering the frame

number, it would be necessary to grind down into the frame and either fill the depression or grind down the surrounding area, which will leave grind marks on the frame.

Honda

The Honda (Japanese) is another popular motorcycle. There are twenty-one models of this motorcycle distributed in this country. Honda motorcycles are registered with the Department of Motor Vehicles (California) by frame number. The frame number on the Honda is located in one of four locations: (1) on the frame directly in front of the left side cover; (2) on the left side of the head stock, directly in front of the gas tank; (3) on the left side of the frame behind the rear crankcase bolt; and (4) on the left side to the rear of the left side cover.

The engine number on the one-cylinder Honda is located on the left lower side of the engine, to either the front or the rear. On the two-cylinder engine the number will be found on the top left side.

Altered numbers

A Honda engine number is one of the most difficult to alter without detection. The single engines have a recessed area where the engine number is stamped. Surrounding the recessed area is a raised border. The larger two-cylinder engines have a distinctive engine number that is stamped into a raised knurled area surrounded by a raised lip. Any attempt to alter this number would necessitate the removal of the knurled surface and probably disturb the surrounding lip, thus making the alteration apparent.

Frame numbers are frequently altered on Honda motorcycles. Grind marks, unlevel and irregular surfaces, evidence of welding, unusually heavy paint, or unevenly stamped letters or numbers are indications of alteration. If the engine number appears unaltered and the frame number appears to be altered, compare the two. They should be similar in size and style. Several of the Honda numbers are distinctive and difficult to duplicate. The numbers 9 and 4 are probably the most distinctive.

Other Motorcycles

The Yamaha motorcycles are also a product of Japan. They are registered through the Department of Motor Vehicles in California by the frame number. The frame numbers on all Yamahas are stamped on the left side of the gooseneck, except for the model 100, which is stamped on the right side of the gooseneck.

The engine numbers of the Yamahas are stamped on a corrugated boss located on the left side of the top of the engine. One of the unique features of the engine boss is that its surface is corrugated. The absence of these corrugations would suggest an alteration.

Suzuki motorcycles are also a product of Japan. They are registered through the Department of Motor Vehicles by their frame number. The frame number is stamped on a plate on the left-hand lower frame member next to the engine; from 1968 on, it has been stamped on the gooseneck. The engine number on this vehicle is stamped into the top left-hand engine case.

The location of the engine and frame numbers on any motorcycle not mentioned above can be obtained by consulting the vehicle identification manual on file at most police departments or through the cooperation of the National Automobile Theft

Bureau field representative. It may be noted that many of the above-mentioned motorcycles can be altered by an owner or thief so that they resemble each other. Exhaust systems are changed, handlebars replaced, gas tanks, fenders, frames, and forks are substituted to make identification of the motorcycle difficult to trace.

Modus Operandi of Motorcycle Thieves

Motorcycle thieves often use a pickup or panel truck to conceal and transport a desired vehicle. After the theft, the motorcycle is taken to a prearranged location where it is stripped, altered, and parts stored or sold. Often, the frame numbers are punched out and the frame discarded. Engine numbers are ground off, polished, a new number stamped on the engine, or the motor block is itself discarded. When the original number is ground off, it leaves a portion of the engine block smooth, which, upon careful inspection, will be observed to be different from the rest of the case. If the vehicle identification number is stamped on a smooth surface, it probably is a restamped number. Restamped numbers are not as deep as the original number, due to inferior dies used by the thieves.

Another method used by thieves is to have two persons ride a motorcycle to the motorcycle to be stolen. One of the riders gets off and rides the wanted motorcycle away to a prearranged location where it is altered, and its parts are stored, sold, exchanged, and the like.

SUMMARY

Auto theft is a major-law enforcement problem, ranking high in frequency among all felonies committed in this country. Although a large percentage of stolen cars are recovered, only a small number are retrieved in their original condition. This crime is often committed by persons under twenty-five years of age. A large portion of this group is under eighteen. Many of the youthful offenders steal cars for transportation or excitement, although some of them strip the cars or use them in the commission of other crimes.

Generally three-fourths of the professional thieves are parts strippers and salvage switchers; the remainder are those who use stolen, altered, counterfeit, and non-title states' registration documents as their primary modus operandi.

Many crucial problems associated with titling and licensing procedures provide opportunities for professional thieves to legitimatize or otherwise dispose of stolen vehicles and thereby realize significant profits from their illegal activities. Motorcycle thefts present an increasing problem due to the volume of sales and the ease with which they can be stolen, concealed, and disposed of. Inasmuch as identifying numbering standards for motorcycles are virtually non-existent, engine and other components may be more easily made to appear legitimate. Many of the motorcycles are not used on public roads and are not registered.

REVIEW QUESTIONS

1. Why is strict traffic law enforcement one of the most effective means the police have of combatting the auto theft problem?
2. Auto thefts generally are broken down into two broad categories. What are these two?
3. The National Automobile Theft Bureau is not an agency of the federal or state government. What is the status of the Bureau and how is it supported?
4. What are five general methods by which an automobile can be identified?
5. Whenever there is indication that a motor number has been tampered with, there are several methods that can be used to bring out the true engine number. Name three.
6. What information is contained in the *Manual for the Identification of Automobiles*? Who publishes this manual?
7. What are some of the ways that commercial thefts, or thefts for profit, are committed?
8. While there are no foolproof methods for spotting stolen automobiles, there are several suspicion arousers that help police to locate them. Name at least eight things that might cause an officer to check out a car to determine whether it may be stolen.
9. In processing a stolen car for fingerprints, what areas of the vehicle are likely to contain a suspect's fingerprints?

10. When a stolen motor vehicle or aircraft is transported across a state line or in foreign commerce, what federal agency would be involved in the case?

11. When a stolen car is located, what criteria would govern whether or not a stakeout of the car is warranted?

WORK EXERCISE
---

1. Research crime statistics on auto theft for the past ten years. Prepare a chart showing the fluctuation and/or growth of the theft problem during this period.

2. Prepare a paper on the antitheft devices that are now available to car owners. Include those which are built in by car manufacturers and others which are commercially available.

11———Burglary

Burglary is a crime against property and is one of the most difficult crimes to solve and prove because the perpetrator(s) are seldom seen. The proof of the corpus delicti (essential elements) in this crime generally rests on circumstantial evidence. In view of this, an investigator should have a basic knowledge of the legal aspects of this crime before conducting a proper investigation. The laws regarding burglary vary from state to state. In common law, this offense consisted in the breaking and entering of the dwelling house of another in the nighttime with intent to commit a felony. The common law conception of burglary was based on the idea of the protection of habitation and therefore was confined to dwelling houses or the buildings appurtenant to or included within the enclosure, if there were any. The breaking was construed to include the exertion of the slightest force. Constructive entry into a dwelling house was interpreted in those cases where any or all of the burglar's body was inserted into a window, such as reaching through with an arm; also, where a stick or pole was used as an extension of one's arm to obtain property from within a room. All our state laws are in general agreement that the act of burglary includes breaking and entering to commit a criminal act. Many modern statutes have eliminated the requirement of both breaking and entering by eliminating one of the two and in specifying degrees of burglary.

California law effects the following departure from common law burglary, greatly widening the scope of the nature of the criminal act. It eliminates the requirement of any breaking, abandons the concept of dwelling house, and makes the intent requirement the specific intent to steal or commit any felony. The elements of burglary under California law consist of (1) the entry of a building (or one of the other places listed below) and (2) the specific intent at the time of entry to commit grand or petit larceny or a felony.

The crime of burglary is completed the moment entry is made. It is not necessary that the person actually steal something. To constitute an entry, it is not necessary under California law that the entire body or a part thereof should actually enter the building; e.g., the use of a pole with a hook on the end would constitute entry.

DEGREES OF BURGLARY (CALIFORNIA)

First degree	Entry of inhabited dwelling at night
	Entry of inhabited building or trailer coach at night
	Committed by an armed person, day or night
	Committed by a person who arms himself or herself during a burglary
	Assault of any person during burglary, day or night
Second degree	All other kinds of burglary

Investigation of Burglaries

A thorough knowledge of the methods used by burglars is essential in order to conduct a good investigation. The uniformed officer is generally responsible for all preliminary investigations within a police department. Because of this, it is imperative that she or he have a basic knowledge of criminal investigation. This phase of police work should be conducted by an officer who not only knows what to do, but what not to do in a given incident.

In the conduct of a burglary investigation, officers are seeking evidence to show

1. That the suspect was actually in the building

2. That the suspect was in the vicinity at the time the burglary was committed

3. That the suspect has loot from the burglary

The first is the most difficult to prove. However, in the absence of fingerprints or palm prints, the presence of building materials such as roofing material, plaster, plasterboard, concrete mortar, brick, glass, cement, paint, wood, metal, lath, or tar substances on clothing, tools, or the suspect's vehicle can place a suspect at a particular location.

It must be borne in mind that some types of evidence will bear additional evidence, possibly latent or microscopic, which is of greater evidential value. For example, a gun found a short distance from the body is important as the possible lethal weapon, but a fingerprint on the weapon or an ejected cartridge may be of greater importance. A sledge hammer found among the effects of a suspected safe burglar would be very important as a possible safe-opening tool, but of greater importance is the insulation or paint on the head of the hammer. A bit and brace in possession of a burglary suspect may be very good evidence, but more important would be the contents on the bit should it have a half circle of wood matching a roof burglary case.

Precautionary measures in responding to a call

In responding to burglary calls, the siren should be used discriminately in order not to alert suspect(s). Officers should be particularly alert for lookouts, e.g., persons standing around, seated in cars, loitering or walking in the vicinity, sounding horn, whistling as if signalling, simulating car repair, carrying packages, fleeing scene, etc. Also, officers should be observant of lights, movements, actions, and vehicles in the immediate area and at the actual location.

Precautionary Measures upon Arrival At this stage of the investigation, some important things to consider include not parking police car directly in front of location; keeping conversation low and to a minimum; opening and closing car doors quietly; removing ignition key; using flashlight sparingly and away from the body (gun drawn but not cocked); and preventing keys and other equipment from jingling or reflecting light. Particular observance of roofs, trees, and unusual locations at the scene should be made.

On *alarm* calls, the inside of the building should be searched after a representative from the alarm company opens the building. On *nonalarm* calls, the exigencies of the case should dictate the procedure required as to whether entry of the building should be made. Whenever there is indication of *forced entry,* a search for the suspect(s) should be undertaken. The searching officers should try to determine whether the burglar(s) have left the premises. This might be determined through interviews with witnesses and by searching the premises to see if any valuable items still remain. In all instances, however, *never take anyone or anything for granted at the scene.*

Conduct of the investigation

This will include (1) apprehension of suspect(s), (2) protection of the scene, (3) search for evidence, (4) determination of the method of operation, and (5) identification of witnesses.

The first officer at the scene of the burglary should take' a vantage point and wait until requested assistance arrives.

Thereafter, the desired deployment procedure will depend on the facts, circumstances, personnel and equipment available.

Two officers at a burglary should use *diagonal deployment,* as shown in Figure 11-1, so that the four exterior sides of the building are covered visually and the suspect(s) are contained pending the arrival of additional unit(s). The assigned car should conduct the search of the building for the burglar(s) while the other officers guard the premises to prevent suspects escaping. In diagonal deployment, one officer is positioned at the northeast corner of the building so that the north and east sides of the building can be observed. The other officer takes a position diagonally opposite his partner, at the southwest corner of the building to observe both the south and west sides of the premises.

Before the actual search, however, the light switches in the building should be located and turned on if possible in order to aid the searching officers. The search should be carried out in all possible places of concealment, searching in, around, under, and through objects and places of possible hiding, always in anticipation that the suspect(s) may be hiding and armed.

In one case, officers responding to a silent alarm at a tavern in the early morning hours succeeded in apprehending a burglar as he was about to depart the premises with

Figure 11-1. Diagonal deployment.

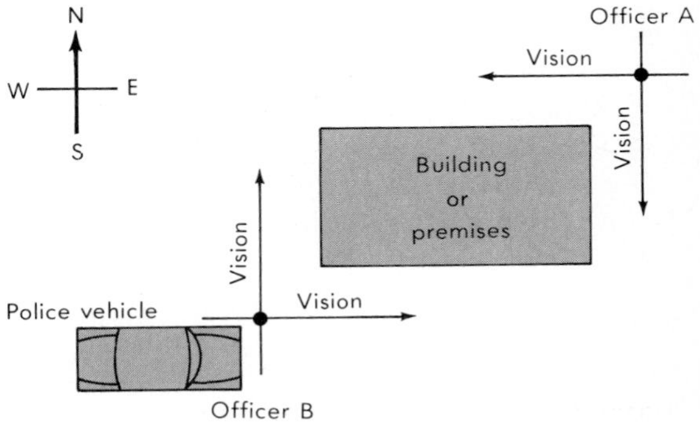

considerable loot. A search of the building for evidence and additional suspects by the investigating officers met with negative results. However, as the officers were completing their report prior to departing, one observed what appeared to be something protruding just under the lower section of a pool table located at one end of the room. Following through on his curiosity, the officer approached the pool table for a closer look. This resulted in the location of a second suspect hiding beneath the cushion of the pool table. This suspect, by stretching out his arms and legs, had braced himself just under the pool table against the sides and legs in an effort to conceal himself. The initial search in this case had not been sufficiently thorough.

In another instance, officers on night patrol responded to a silent alarm at a market. One officer covered the front of the building while his partner quietly went to the rear, awaiting an additional unit that had been dispatched as a backup. As the officer reached the rear of the market, he heard someone trying to open the rear door of the store from the inside. The officer, on hearing this noise, backed across the darkened alley into the shadows along a concrete wall. From alongside on the other side of a wooden gate in the wall, the officer was startled to hear a voice state, "Drop the gun cop, or die with it in your hand."

At that point the officer took a quick glance and observed a lookout (accomplice) 10 feet away [about 3 meters] staring at him over the top of the gate, holding a gun pointed at him. Reacting swiftly, the officer wheeled around and fired three shots in rapid succession into the gate. At that time, the officer at the front of the store came running to the aid of his fellow officer. A crash of glass was heard at the front of the store as the inside burglary suspect fled via the front window.

Both officers cautiously proceeded through the gate where they found the burglary accomplice lying wounded on the ground with a loaded Walther P-38 in his hand. The officer's three shots had found their mark. In view of the suspect's condition, a dying declaration was taken from him in which he admitted the identity of his confederate. For his bravery in the line of duty and under extreme circumstances, the officer was awarded the medal of valor.

In searching the scene of the burglary, look for the manner and method of entry as well as exit (Figure 11-2). The method of entry may be by cutting a hole in the roof or wall; prying open a bathroom window or rear door; sawing the hasp; breaking the glass in a window; or using a passkey or shim, Channel Lock pliers, knife, pry bar, etc. Do not draw conclusions or opinions as to the method used to gain entry if not discernible. If unknown, it should be so indicated in the report. Reconstruct the crime as it occurred in a step-by-step manner. Record only those facts that can be substantiated through knowledge, physical evidence, or statements made by victims or witnesses. A thorough neighborhood investigation may enable the investigator to locate witnesses

Figure 11-2. Deputy sheriff examining a broken lock during a preliminary burglary investigation.

who may have heard identifiable sounds such as those of an automobile, barking dogs, breaking of glass, etc., thereby helping to fix the approximate time of the crime as well as furnishing other possible leads. The investigator should seek answers to the following questions:

Who discovered the offense?

Who is the last person to secure the premises?

How did the thief reach the point of breaking in?

What articles were used to reach that point?

Is there any indication of the thief's concealment prior to burglary?

Is the property that was taken insured? For how much? When was insurance taken out?

Who has keys to the premises and how accessible are they?

Are fingerprints or footprints available at points of entry or exit?

What valuable property was not taken?

Did the thief limit the crime to one kind of property stolen, or was anything taken?

How did the burglar gain access to cupboards and dressers? By force? By keys?

Was the search haphazard or systematic?

Did the suspect do anything besides search and steal?

Where was the property usually kept by the owner?

When was the property purchased? Where? Receipts?

When was the property last seen? By whom? Where? In whose possession?

Can the owner furnish a complete list of the stolen property?

How can the owner identify the property? By serial numbers? By other marks or identification?

If it was a business burglary, were any checks stolen from checkbooks?

Are there any fingerprints inside or outside the house that will need processing? If so, are they being protected?

Does the victim suspect anyone?

Can the victim point out the "disturbed areas" of his premises?

Can the victim identify or eliminate items found at the scene?

Whenever property is taken from the location, list all articles and their quantity, description, and value. Include small articles such as jewelry, coins, and other souvenirs as these possibly could be found on a suspect at a later date. If tools are found, do not place a suspected tool in an impression to make a comparison, as this might affect the case when that evidence is introduced in court. The size and type of the instrument used can be estimated by measuring the mark or injury on the door, window, or other surface, and recording the imprint with such notes as, "probably ¼-inch screwdriver" or "probably ¾-inch pry bar or jimmy." If photographs, casts, neoprene lifts, or latent fingerprint processing is desired, most departments utilize a specialist from their identification bureau or a detective specialist. A search for latent fingerprints is usually made in residence burglaries; however, there is little use in searching for latent prints in a business burglary except in cases when you know what the suspect has handled or the areas she or he traversed. Circumstances of each case, however, will dictate the extent of the latent fingerprint search.

If the property taken is in excess of $5000 and has been transported in interstate or foreign commerce, there may be a possible violation of U.S. Code, title 18, section 2314, Interstate Transportation of Stolen Property. The elements of this violation are (1) property was stolen, converted, or taken by fraud; (2) property valued at $5000 or more was transported in interstate or foreign commerce; and (3) the transporter had knowledge that property was stolen, converted or taken by fraud.

Apprehension of burglary suspects

Whenever burglary suspects are apprehended, they should be immediately advised of their right to remain silent, that any statements they make can be used against them in a court of law, that they have a right to have an attorney and to have the attorney present during any questioning, and that if they cannot afford an attorney, one will be appointed without charge. The fact that the suspect was so advised should be included in the investigator's report. Following the above admonitions, other considerations should include

Seizing of all wearing apparel including shoes for examination

Reviewing of each and every item of property in suspect's possession

Search of suspect's vehicle (search warrant may be needed)

Determining names and addresses of all of suspect's associates

Recording all facts and obtaining statements if possible

Checking of record bureau, teletypes, and other sources for related crimes and connections

Dispatching all-points or regional broadcasts

Following up on items like suspect's past activities and whereabouts on questionable dates and times

Fingerprinting, palm printing, photographing, and obtaining handwriting specimens

Setting forth any necessary leads based on the above

If a search is to be conducted of a suspect's residence, a waiver of search must be obtained from him, or her, or a search warrant issued. Whenever suspects voluntarily give officers consent to search their own premises, this consent should be reduced to writing. The following suggested *waiver of search form* may be written or typed for the suspect's signature:

I, _____, having been informed of my constitutional right not to have a search made of the premises hereinafter mentioned without a search warrant and of my right to refuse to consent to such, hereby authorize _____ and _____, officers of the _____ Police Department, to conduct a complete search of my residence located at _____. These officers are authorized by me to take from my residence any letters, papers, materials which they find, and which they have reasonable cause to believe would be evidence in a criminal proceeding.

This written permission is being given by me to the above named officers voluntarily and without threats or promises of any kind.

WITNESSED:_____   SIGNED:_____
                     DATE:_____
                     PLACE:_____

With regard to the above suggested form the local district attorney's office should be consulted regarding its acceptability.

Methods of Operation Used in Burglaries

In the perpetration of burglaries, suspects operate in many ways. Examples of types of burglary operations include

Party Burglar Burglarizes bedrooms or other areas of a household where guests leave their valuables.

Telephone Burglar Calls a residence. If no one answers, proceeds to the residence and rings the front doorbell. If someone answers the door, the burglar hands the person a household sample or handbill and leaves. If no one answers, the burglar signals an accomplice who picks the lock and they burglarize the residence.

C.O.D. Burglar Rings doorbell of victim. If no answer, picks lock. If someone answers the door, the burglar asks for the addressee on the package and leaves.

Residence Burglar Burglarizes apartment houses, private residences, and vacant houses. Different methods are used to ascertain if the occupant is home. Residences are picked because of their apparent emptiness. Many of these burglars take advantage of the carelessness of occupants in leaving keys in such places as under the doormat and in the mailbox. In burglarizing apartments, some burglars place a form letter in victim's mailbox and carefully watch while a partner perpetrates a theft. Should the occupant unexpectedly return and take the letter from the mailbox, the lookout buzzes the apartment or uses another electronic device to warn the confederate.

Tunnel Burglar Tunnels through roof, wall, basement, or from above or below business premises to burglarize them.

Hideout Burglar Enters business establishments during regular business hours and remains hidden until all employees have left, at which time the perpetrator proceeds with the burglary of the premises.

Opportunist Burglar Drives around and notes homes where outward appearance indicates victims are away, such as uncut grass, shades drawn, newspapers scattered about, accumulated mail, milk bottles stacked on front porch, and air-conditioning units turned off in hot weather.

Window Smashers While an accomplice waits at the wheel of a getaway car, burglar smashes the window, grabs jewelry or other merchandise, and flees. Generally committed by young men.

Research-Minded Burglar Obtains likely "prospects" from such activities as studying local newspapers to note which prominent citizens are taking trips or attending social functions; reads news items and ads such as those placed by coin collectors; reads biographical data in social registers; checks license plates and registration for addresses of persons driving expensive cars; uses accomplices in hotels such as room cleaners to obtain the names and activities of potential victims.

Simulated Burglary "Victim" reports fraudulent burglary to conceal some financial loss or theft. Generally in these cases, a careful investigation will disclose inaccuracies in the victim's account of the theft, particularly in method of operation, which will be unlike that of a burglar's.

Dishonest Bellhops, Janitors, and Maintenance Employees Because of their access to keys and knowledge of intimate details of business and financial operations, they either commit burglaries themselves or furnish keys to accomplices who then burglarize the premises or businesses.

A case involving a burglary and forgery ring reflects the careful planning and ingenuity employed by members of that group who victimized banks of the amount of approximately one quarter of a million dollars. The M.O. peculiar to this gang's activities involved the commission of an undetected burglary of a large business company's office wherein three or four company checks were taken from the back of its checkbook which went unnoticed for several days. In addition, cancelled checks and bank statements from the burglarized company were obtained so that perusal by the gang enabled them to ascertain the financial condition of the company. During the burglary, the company's typewriter was used to make several checks using the company's business procedure and duplicating the signature of a company official. Varying amounts of several hundred to several thousand dollars were filled out. In some cases, these suspects would telephone the company on the following day posing as local members of the press and inquire if there had been a recent burglary, to determine if the theft had been discovered.

In conjunction with this operation, accounts were opened by this burglary gang at victim banks, using the name of fictitious or newly formed companies. Thereafter, the company's bookkeeper, a gang member, made a few deposits in this account to establish it. In a few days, this "bookkeeper" would appear at the victim bank and present a teller with a large check made out in four figures. Because the size of the check, the bank teller would seek the approval of a bank official who would in turn call the office of the legitimate business firm to verify the check.

However, just prior to the "bookkeeper's" check transaction, a gang member climbed a telephone pole near the legitimate business company's address and informed the company's switchboard operator that he was working on the telephone line and told the operator to disconnect the telephone trunk lines for a short while. At the time that the bank called the legitimate company to verify the check, the call was intercepted by the gang member on the telephone pole. When the bank official, believing that he was in communication with a legitimate company official, was assured that the check' was "perfectly all right," he then approved the check. The "bookkeeper" obtained the money and departed. The money was thereafter dropped into a mailbox and delivered to a post office box in a distant city.

An example of one of the methods used by experienced burglars can serve as a learning experience for investigators. In this particular instance a burglary gang known as the "Cat Burglars" committed numerous burglaries in several states. This group travelled extensively and usually stayed in the best hotels. Expensive late-model cars were used for transportation. In most instances gang members were armed.

Their burglaries were most often committed in affluent residential areas. Suspects usually parked their cars a few blocks from their victim's residence. They approached the residence chosen by going over fences and through rear yards to remain out of view from the street. On occasion, they burglarized several houses in a given area during one operation. They usually worked in pairs or threesomes, operating between 2 A.M. and 5 A.M.

Channel Lock pliers or pipe wrenches were carried to the location attached to the frame of their vehicle. Entry into residences was sometimes made by using these tools to twist the doorknob until the mechanism broke. At other times, they slipped the lock with the aid of a shim. Money, jewelry, and furs were their chief objectives. Purses, wallets, and jewel boxes were discarded outside the victimized premises. The jewelry obtained was placed in a man's sock. If occupants were awakened during the burglary, the suspects would threaten them with a gun and thereafter cut or pull out the telephone cord and tie the victims' hands and feet.

Thumbtacks were sometimes thrown on the floor to assist in escape. Loot often was stashed in shrubs or bushes near the victimized residence in order to eliminate the possibility of their possessing stolen property should they be stopped by police patrols. Later, the suspects would check the area to determine if the coast was clear and, if so, would pick up the stolen loot.

This group of burglars was very alert to police surveillance and checked extensively to determine if they were being followed. At times these thieves hid the stolen jewelry in their vehicle behind the bumpers, radiator grill, inside the taillight, in windshield washer bottles, in air vents, and in flashlight cases. Cars were replaced every few months. A break in this came when an armored car driver became suspicious of a vehicle he believed to be following his vehicle and jotted down the license number.

Burglar's Notebook

A search of the personal effects of a thirty-seven-year-old West Coast burglar following his arrest disclosed a personal notebook into which he had jotted down random thoughts, observations, and ideas as they presented themselves to him. This individual, who was regarded as a real professional, had held only one legitimate job for a period of three weeks during his life. Some of his entries read as follows:

Clothes express and accentuate a person's personality and station in life. Wear good clothes in order to be inconspicuous. Live in best hotels, so I won't be noticed going and coming at odd hours.
Always carry the daily paper when on the prowl early in the evening—or a magazine. It looks like a person coming home from the office. Better still, carry a briefcase.
It takes an amazing amount of cunning to master crime.
Wear headphones attached to microphone or electronic magnifiers to pick up sounds of breathing, etc., more clearly.
Use bulb in toilet bowl to hide diamonds or cash.
Check to see if a town has an opera house or concerts on certain nights of the week. That's where rich people congregate. Watch newspapers for names of people attending these.
Gambling diverts a man faster than lechery.
Bend the end of small screwdriver to get between glass and putty in window.
Bartenders, cabbies, fences, and women are stools. Frequent high-class places where cheap stools and detectives can't go.

A woman alone at a bar usually expects to meet someone—anyone. Most nice girls don't drink alone at bars.
Walla Walla, Washington, is a good joint.
Patience excels science.
Notice if garage is empty and lights out in home. Then people are out.
Leave phoney coat button at scene.
Few people can remember accurately what they see or hear under emotional pressure.
I must not lose the sense of danger when prowling by thinking I'm too clever.
I don't have to prove my innocence. The police must prove my guilt beyond a reasonable doubt.
Be audacious, have a gentleman's taste in clothes, be a good liar. Have no scruples against shooting a person or slugging a person. It's just as easy to steal a fortune by being audacious and creating a front to blend with an exclusive section. Good car, good clothes, etc. Spot big estates in country with large lawns, and Cadillacs, Lincolns, etc., in driveways. Prowl when occupants are giving bridge parties or dinner parties. Ransack second stories.
In most cities the police have abandoned the foot patrolman and put in his place the squad car—especially cities of 30,000 and over.
On the day a criminal decides he is smarter than the police, he moves that much closer to the moment of his capture. Don't belong to the egocentric class of criminals. Thieves who are so egotistical as to think they can't be caught are the ones who get caught.

The notebook entries above illustrate the thinking of one confirmed adult burglar. Inasmuch as crime and criminals must be studied from the viewpoint of the criminal, the philosophy, procedures, and inhibitions of the above subject are of interest.

In another case, a West Coast burglar was apprehended after committing over 800 burglaries. During the many conversations this burglar had with the police investigators before his profitable operation ended, he made many observations of interest to the field policemen. This individual advised that he always had a plan of action figured out before starting "an operation." He spent many hours "casing" his victims and/or locations, recalling that "for those times I was successful, my success was due to figuring what the police would probably do and I would do the opposite—you might call it logic." In discussing his illegal nocturnal activities, this burglar revealed the following insight into his operations:

Clothing worn. I always dressed nice so I wouldn't look out of place in a neighborhood. I carried a pair of women's gloves with me and wore them at work as they fit my hands snug. Of course, I always wore dark clothing at nighttime. Usually, my prowl shoes were thick-soled rubber and a couple of sizes too big, so I wore up to three pairs of socks to fill them.

Tools. I never carried any tools except a three-bladed pocketknife and a small flashlight. That's all you need. My knife had one heavy blade which was a fair pry, a medium-sized blade for cutting screens, and a small blade for working locks.

Vehicles used. I had numerous stolen cars at my disposal at all times. I had a "personal" car and others were "work" vehicles. The Lincoln stolen in _____ was my "personal" car for nearly a year and I never used it on jobs. Work cars were Fords and Chevies. I kept them out of circulation until they were off the hot sheet before I would use them. I seldom changed plates on cars as it was too much trouble. It takes twenty minutes to change a set of plates. I did have cold plates on hand for emergencies, for I sometimes stole cars that had no plates. My supply of cold plates was obtained by stealing plates and holding them for a long period before using them. If I could, I got them from vehicles where they might not be reported for a long time. I usually fixed the radio to get police calls in the area I worked.

Selecting victims. I didn't care much for places like _____ for people might have a lot of money "on paper" but very little in the kick. In just average nice residential areas where the people worked in _____ plants and such you could always figure on some cash laying around. Friday night was particularly good and it wasn't unusual for them to have $200 in their poke. By Monday night, however, it was usually gone, so I had to hit these sections on weekends. I believed in eight hours of work so I would enter numerous houses. Generally, I could pick up several hundred dollars, which you can't do in rich sections. Many times I picked the street by following a resident to it. If he looked like the type that might have dough around the house, I just saw him home. If his house and the rest of the neighborhood looked good, I noted it and eventually included it on my schedule.

Casing the victim. Generally, my hours were 8 or 9 P.M. to daylight. If the house appeared unoccupied, I tried the garage or basement first. If there was an extension phone, I would dial the ring-back number and see if anyone answered. If not, I assumed the coast was clear. If it was a warm night and windows were open, I might detect snoring. I didn't worry about people who were steady snorers. Generally, I operated in only the "living area" and not the sleeping area of a house, but I believe I could have moved the bedroom furniture out of some of those places and never awakened the people. Once inside a house, I always listened for sleepers. I didn't enter if a dog was barking. If the dog was asleep, however, I didn't worry about him, but just didn't disturb him.

The crime. I varied my points of entry, oftentimes in the belief that it changed my luck. I liked glass patio doors best, other doors next, and then side windows. However, my knife would easily open the average locked door. Once inside, and if the weather was cool, I would turn up the thermostat. The popping and cracking would cover up my noise and was normal and unnoticed by the residents. I was always careful to turn it back to its original setting just before I left. Usually, I checked every house in the block and such loot as I selected was piled near the curb or sidewalk under bushes. Small items like purses and wallets I occasionally put in trash barrels. When I was done for the night I would walk to my car, drive back, and load it in. Only once did I have to abandon my loot stored at the street front.

The flight. When I was discovered and the police started moving in, I would go up the nearest tree or get on a flat roof. When I had to flee an area on foot, I never used streets or alleys. I would go over fences and hedges for blocks, always paralleling the streets being searched. When I had to cross a side street to continue my backyard flight, I would wait and listen first. I could usually figure that all of the cars on a call would go to the source, then fan out. This gave me a big edge. It takes about ten minutes to go ten blocks on foot without running. I could be three or four miles away in the car without breaking any traffic laws. If I figured the car I had was too hot, I would dump it and get another one.

Burglary tools

The tools selected by burglars usually depend upon the entry to be effected and the type of burglary contemplated—a residence or a safe, for example. Eighteen- to thirty-inch [45- to 75-centimeter] jimmies are used for doors or windows; a hacksaw to cut bars; and braces and bits where the entrance is to be made from floors above and through the ceiling, or from the floor below. Interior metal ceilings are usually cut with tin snips carried by the burglar. Tools of a safe burglar range anywhere from relatively few, as in Figure 11-3, to a complete, elaborate set like those in Figure 11-4.

Types of tools found on burglars include such items as celluloid strips, lock picks (see Figure 11-3), electric drills, stiff pieces of wire, gloves, heavy rope with knots, hooks, glass cutters, screwdrivers, crowbars, and penlight flashlights. Others are pipe wrenches, adhesive tape to tape windows so

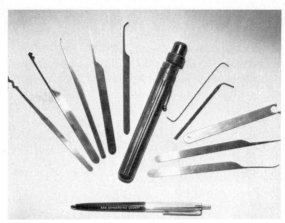

Figure 11-3. Lock-picking tools.

that glass won't shatter and fall when broken, water pistols (with ammonia) to ward off watch dogs, Channel Lock pliers, Vise-Grip pliers, passkeys, chisels, punches, saws, heavy jacks to break through floors or spread

Figure 11-4. Elaborate set of burglar's tools found in the luggage of a burglar.

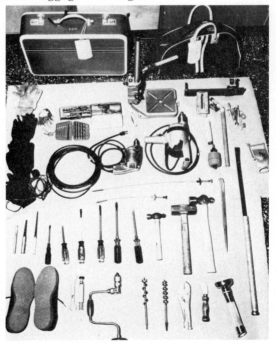

door frames, spotter-scope or field glasses, etc. Many of these tools may be concealed in such containers as salesperson's kits, shaving kits, music cases, handbags, paper bags, overnight suitcases, suspended from trouser belt, or hidden in vehicle.

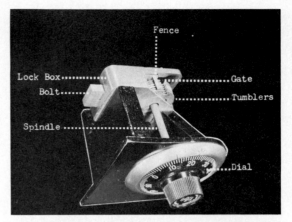

———— SAFE BURGLARIES ————

Safes in General

A safe may be described as a container designated to keep articles secure from fire or burglary attacks. It is usually equipped with a combination locked door. For the purpose of law enforcement, safes may be divided into two general classifications.

1. Fire-resistive or fire boxes. This type of safe is designed primarily to resist fire and consists of a thin metal shell filled with a fire-resistive insulation.

2. Burglar-resistive or money chest. This type of safe is constructed for the primary purpose of offering resistance to burglarious attack and consists of laminated or solid steel.

The burglar-resistive safe is a container having a 1½-inch [4-centimeter] steel front plate and a 1-inch [2½-centimeter] steel plate on all sides; it is equipped with a combination or time locking device; and it may be attached to the floor, or be in concrete. Figure 11-5 depicts the component parts of a safe dial mechanism (front and rear).

Although numerous businesspersons and other individuals use safes, most people are unaware that most of the safes in use are constructed for the purpose of protecting valuables against fire and not against theft. Although not required by underwriter's specifications, safe manufacturers are now building modern safes of the fire-resistant classifications with relockers, in order that burglary attempts by the punch method

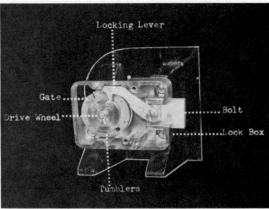

Figure 11-5. (a) A safe dial and component parts of a locking mechanism. (b) Component parts of a safe dial locking mechanism as viewed from the rear.

(discussed below) may be thwarted. However, because of the light metal used in the construction of some safes, they can be easily ripped or chopped open. Safes are built with a white, fire-proofing substance between their walls in order to be heat resistant. Safes that do not have fire-proofing material between their walls have heavy lamination of metal and are constructed largely to resist burglary attempts.

Old safes, like those of the old "T"-handle type, are all susceptible to entry by the punch method unless they have accessory relocks installed that would give the safe added protection against unlawful entries. Most safes are built to last for years and years, unlike other furniture or equipment. Because many of the safes are old and still in use, many of them can be entered by burglars equipped with ordinary tools, such as a hammer, punch, chisel, wrecking bar, or heavy screwdriver, in a very few minutes.

Safe classifications

By Underwriters' Laboratories, Inc. (ULI) and Safe Manufacturers National Association (SMNA), safes are classified for insurance purposes according to their ability to resist fire and/or burglarious attacks. In general these classifications are as follows:

nize the various burglarious attacks on safes; to evaluate them, and intelligently describe the attack in the report and communications with other police agencies.

Punch

The dial knob of the safe is broken off and a punch placed on the exposed spindle. The spindle is then driven back with sufficient force to break the lock box loose from its mounting. Thereafter the handle can be turned and the door opened. Modern safes now have an adequate relocking device. The burglar's M.O. may be established by the type of tool used; the method by which the dial knob was broken; and by examination of handle and hinges, and by looking for other peculiarities. (See Figure 11-6.)

CLASSIFICATION	DOOR	WALLS
"B" (Fire-resistive)	Steel less than 1 in [2-1/2 cm] thick	Body of steel less than 1/2 in [1-1/4 cm] thick
"C" (Burglar-resistive)	Steel at least 1 in [2-1/2 cm] thick	Body of steel at least 1/2 in [1-1/4 cm] thick
"E" (Burglar-resistive)	Steel at least 1-1/2 in [4 cm] thick	Body of steel at least 1 in [2-1/2 cm] thick

The above chart is not intended to be all-inclusive as to ULI and SMNA specifications for various classifications. In addition, the ULI and SMNA have higher classifications, but these will not be mentioned since the vast majority of burglarized safes fall into the "B" through "E" classes.

Methods of Attacking Safes

The purpose of discussing safe attacks in this chapter is to give the investigator a working knowledge of the various methods used by safe burglars to attack safes. This knowledge will enable the officer to recog-

Figure 11-6. Safe dial removed, leaving exposed spindle.

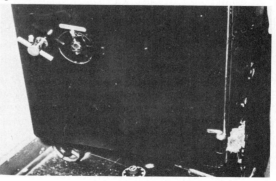

Carry out (haul-away)

This method is one frequently used, by those burglars who are not well enough acquainted with safes to effect an entry while on the premises. (Most safes could be opened in less time than it would take to remove them from the building.) The thieves thereafter take the safe to some secluded spot in order to have as much time as necessary to open it.

The method of operation may be established by consideration of the type of premises attacked, method of entry and exit, type of vehicle used to transport safe, location of recovery, and method used to gain entrance to the safe.

Rip or peel

This method is used on fire-resistive safes because of the lightweight metal used in their construction. In these cases the door plate is peeled off with a bar, or the sides ripped. Ripping or peeling a safe is accomplished similarly to opening a can of sardines, starting at one corner and ripping metal loose from its rivets. The *peel* is an attack on the door of a fire-resistive safe. Its counterpart is the *rip,* which is an attack on a portion of the safe other than the door.

The purpose of the peel is to expose the boltwork. It is frequently used after an unsuccessful attempt to punch the safe. Once the boltwork has been exposed it can be pried until the bolts are withdrawn, or the lock box and relocking device can be pried loose so that the bolts can be withdrawn in much the same way as they would be if the handle was turned. To facilitate the peel, the safe burglar will generally, but not always, knock off the dial and handle since they tend to hold the door plate in place. The dial being knocked off indicates the possibility that an attempt was first made to punch the safe. The spindle should be examined to determine if this is the case.

The method of operation may be noted by determining the starting place of the peeling or ripping, the type of tool used, and other observations of the handle, knob, hinges, bolts, etc. (See Figures 11-7, 11-8, and 11-9.)

Hinge Attempts Sometimes the removal of hinges makes a peel attack easier as it enables the burglars to remove the entire face of the door when the safe is properly peeled. It can generally be assumed that when the hinges of a safe have been tampered with, it was an amateur attempt.

Chopping

In this method, the bottom metal plate and fireproof material are chopped out of a safe with a sledge hammer, chisel and hammer, hand axe, etc. A hole large enough to insert one's hand, or larger, is made and money or other valuables are removed.

The method of operation may be noted by determining the location of the hole, the tools used, the amount of damage, and other

Figure 11-7. Rip attack on a portion of a safe other than the door.

Figure 11-8. Peel attack on a fire-resistive safe.

Figure 11-9. Rip attack on a burglar-resistive floor safe.

peculiarities observed in the injury to the safe. (See Figure 11-10.)

Drag

In this method a drag plate (heavy metal plate with three or more adjacent bolts) is used. Force is applied by gradually tightening the bolts, which in turn pulls the knob and spindle out of the safe. This method accomplishes the opposite of a punch job.

The method of operation may be established by obtaining accurate measurements of the spacing of the bolt impressions left on the safe door. This method is rather obsolete today. (See Figure 11-11.)

Torch or burn

The oxyacetylene cutting torch is one of the most effective tools used by safe burglars. The small-size acetylene tanks in use today make this equipment easily concealable. The acetylene torch is used to burn a hand-size hole through the side of the safe,

similar to chopping, or to burn around the edge of the door to sever the bolts at their locked position, thereby permitting the door to be opened. Burglars frequently fill the compartment with water to prevent the burning of the money. This method is used on those round, lug-type door, burglar-resistive safes, to cut the one locking bolt at its place of locking.

The method of operation can be noted by a careful examination of the specific area burned, the extent of burning and damage,

Figure 11-10. Chop or rip attack on the bottom of a fire-resistive safe.

and other peculiarities observed. (See Figures 11-12 and 11-13.)

Drill

This method is used in conjunction with other tools. In order to be successful, however, the burglar must be acquainted with the construction of a safe. In these cases, the thief, knowing where the safe bolt is located, finds the exact spot to drill in order to strike the bolt. A high-carbon drill equally as large as the bolt is used. If the bolt is only partially drilled, it is then broken with a center punch and hammer; the door then unscrewed and removed.

The method of operation can be established by determining the size of the drilled hole, location and amount of damage to other parts of the safe, as well as a close study of any other peculiarities. Figure 11-14 shows a drilled safe.

Explosives

The use of nitroglycerin by safe burglars is almost a thing of the past, as it is dangerous to handle and because of the noise involved. Should a burglar contemplating the use of nitroglycerin be scared off prior to

Figure 11-11. The "drag" or "knob-puller" is a special tool used to pull the knob off a safe dial. It is now rather obsolete in view of modern lock construction.

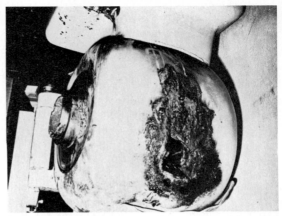

Figure 11-12. Burn attack on the side of a burglar-resistive safe.

setting off the explosive charge, the safe would be considered "loaded" and be very dangerous to the person discovering the attempted burglary. Indication of this dangerous potential would be soap or soap paste; putty or wax smeared around the lock, door handle, or door seams; or a jelly-like substance (nitroglycerin in its most dangerous state) near or on the safe. A faintly acidic odor or a bitter taste in the mouths of persons in the area (caused by the nitroglycerin fumes) are also indications of nitroglycerin.

Whenever explosives or indication of explosive materials (nitroglycerin, trinitrotoluene (TNT) blocks, dynamite in gelatin form, explosive cord, blasting caps, or detonators) are noted on or near a safe, the crime laboratory should be immediately advised and their instruction followed meticulously. *Do not* attempt to neutralize or destroy explosives; *Do not* walk or step on suspected explosive materials.

When nitroglycerin is used, two of the common methods employed by safe burglars in "blowing" a safe are the *lock shot* and the *door shot* discussed below.

Lock Shot The explosive is placed in a drilled hole above and left of the dial. A piece of cotton or cloth is wrapped around an

Figure 11-13. Burn attack on a burglar-resistive floor safe. The bolts were burned off through an access hole and the door was then lifted out.

Figure 11-14. A floor safe drilled through the lip at the position of the locking bolts.

explosive cap and saturated with nitroglycerin. It is then gently forced through the hole with a glass rod or wooden pencil to avoid sparks. Connecting wires are then run off to a distance of about 15 feet [4½ meters] and the caps discharged by use of batteries, by placing the wire ends in an electric plug, or by a discharging box such as miners use. Some burglars place the explosive in a finger stall and insert it into the drilled hole near the locking mechanism in order to destroy the locking device.

Door Shot   The door seams are packed with clay, putty, or brown kitchen soap. An opening is left at the top where a cup is formed, and at the bottom. Nitroglycerin is dropped into the cup with a hypodermic syringe and allowed to seep around the door. When the nitro appears at the hole at the bottom, the hole is sealed and an explosive cap is sealed into the cup at the top. Thereafter the cap is discharged by batteries or by placing the wire ends in an electric plug, and the door is blown off the safe.

The method of operation can be established by determining the amount of damage done to the safe, type of cap used, probable method of exploding cap, type of safe attacked, whether safe was covered with soaked blanket to muffle noise, etc. If the safe was not covered, the walls and ceiling will be spotted with soap, putty, or other sealant.

Sawing

In this method a high-speed power saw equipped with a carborundum blade or a diamond-edge blade is used in safe attacks. The saw is used to cut a hole through the chest large enough to insert the hand and take out the valuables.

Force

This is a crude, noisy, but effective method of opening a fire-resistive safe and, as in the peel and rip attacks, is possible because of the light construction of this type of safe. The object of this attack is to force the cabinet away from the door. It is accomplished usually by hammering on the safe

Figure 11-15. Fire-resistive safe opened by force.

until a bulge appears between the cabinet and the door. Pry bars are then used to force the cabinet back far enough to withdraw the bolts from their recesses in the cabinet, permitting the door to be opened. (See Figure 11-15.)

Manipulation

No single type of safe burglary has been more publicized than the fine art of safe manipulation as practiced by the legendary Jimmy Valentine with the sandpapered fingers. Manipulation refers to opening of a safe by using the combination dial without having any knowledge of the proper combination. In order to accomplish this an individual must apply an intimate knowledge of safe-locking mechanisms to the coordinated uses of sight, sound, and touch. A safe can be manipulated, but there are relatively few persons in the country, and this includes legitimate safe mechanics, capable of performing this feat. In addition, this type of safe opening is extremely time-consuming, and modern safes are equipped with manipulation-proof locks.

When a visit to the scene of a safe burglary reveals that the safe was opened by finding the combination, the investigator may safely assume that the burglar chanced on the combination or memorandum, or found the safe open, or a possible dishonest employee or former employee "had a hand in the theft."

Safe Burglary Investigation

Safe burglars usually work in groups of two to five. They are adept at obliterating all traces of their identities at the scene of a crime. They wear gloves to eliminate the risk of leaving fingerprints. They time their operations with the precision of airlines dispatchers. Safe burglars "case" their jobs with an eye to detail worthy of research technicians. Prior to committing a safe burglary, these thieves seek information such as the make and size of the safe; its exact location on the premises; its possible cash contents; the habits of the manager and other personnel; the type of people in the neighborhood; the police patrol patterns; and the habits of guards and passersby.

During the casing of the place to be victimized, gang members visit the establishment and observe, among other things, whether or not there is an alarm system on the premises. Sometimes, the tools to be used in the safe burglary will be hidden near the building in advance. Assignments of gang members, communication equipment, lookouts, transportation, etc., are all taken into account during the planning stage. Weekends are often favored because safe entries may take considerable time.

Many of the suggestions concerning burglary investigation set forth earlier in this chapter apply to safe burglary investigation. All of the suggested investigative steps set forth below will not be used in every case, as each situation is unique. Investigations of safe burglaries generally will follow the investigative procedures set forth below.

Procedures at the scene

Apprehend suspect if still at scene. During the premises search for suspect, guards should protect the perimeter.

Prevent unauthorized persons from entering the location.

Make a check of the premises (inside and out) to locate the point of entry and to determine suspect's *modus operandi*. Victim or employees may help by pointing out the disturbed areas (articles moved, items missing, condition of windows, doors etc.). Exercise caution when walking in critical areas to avoid destruction of evidence.

Endeavor to reconstruct the activities of the burglar(s).

Call headquarters if technical assistance needed.

Take scale photos of the damaged safe and other areas. Sketch the location, including relationship of physical evidence to the safe. Pry marks on the safe and at point of entry should be photographed, or castings made.

Collect such types of physical evidence as: fingerprints, palmprints, gloveprints, heelprints, shoeprints, safe insulation material, metal fragments, paint chips from safe, broken/damaged parts of safe, discarded tools or parts thereof, broken glass, bloodstains, clothing fibers, soil particles, cigarette butts, burnt matches, samples of wall board, plaster, paint chips, building insulation, wood core left by tool bit and any other materials foreign to the premises. All evidence should be carefully collected, identified, packaged separately, labeled, and the chain of custody maintained.

Interview person(s) having access to the safe; also, the last person leaving the premises, the night guard, janitor or other persons having access to the location. Note the procedures used to secure the premises.

Determine the make of the safe, size, weight and serial number.

Check areas adjacent to victim premises for possible shoeprints, tireprints, or discarded items.

Canvass the neighborhood for any information of value.

If a suspect is arrested, request that his clothing be taken from him at the jail. Have such items processed by the laboratory. Inventory all property taken from suspect after his arrest.

If suspect is in an auto when apprehended, impound the vehicle and consult the prosecuting attorney relative to search.

Complete the crime report.

After the immediate investigation described above, the following additional investigative steps should be undertaken:

Have identifiable stolen property indexed in the records bureau.

Place stops with other identification bureaus—local, state, and the National Crime Information Center (NCIC), if deemed advisable.

Review pawnshop and secondhand store records following burglary, as sometimes stolen items are pawned.

Area or regional teletypes should be sent to alert police agencies of the missing identifiable items.

Informants should be alerted as to the missing property so that they might be on the lookout for it.

Whereabouts of known burglars should be determined, particularly those whose M.O. is similar—specifically as to where they were during the pertinent period of the burglary.

Consideration should be given to the advisability of preparing a confidential bulletin to supplement the original teletype.

Liaison should be maintained with burglary details of adjacent communities in order to identify possible suspects.

Recovery of safes

Whenever a safe is recovered in carry-out cases, it should be photographed at the place of recovery. A thorough crime scene investigation should be made in the recovery area for possible evidence. This investigation should include a search for fingerprints, shoe prints, heel prints, tire marks, discarded items, and miscellaneous debris that might furnish leads. Persons residing in the area of the abandoned safe should be contacted for possible leads. Plaster casts should be made of any tire prints found near the abandoned safe. The safe itself should be preserved as evidence in order that a comparison of tools and safe insulation materials found in the possession of suspects might be made by the crime laboratory specialists.

Security Devices and Systems in Crime Prevention

All security alarms are made up of three parts: the detector or sensor, the control unit, and the alarm itself. The detectors or sensors are electronic or electromagnetic devices that register the presence or action of an intruder. Many homes and commercial facilities use a wide variety of alarm services. They are all designed to detect intrusion. Among the many types offered are the following:

Audio monitoring devices. Can detect sounds associated with any type of forced entry. Sonic audio range motion detection is designed to pick up reflected sound caused by motion of intruders.

Capacity alarms. Have wires that continuously radiate an electrical field tuned to a set frequency. Capacitance wires can't be cut or tampered with, as any damage to them will set off an alarm.

Closed-Circuit TV (CCTV). Has variations. Video monitors scan specific areas such as bank lobbies, corridors, elevators, tunnels, traffic segments, stairways or other specific coverage desired.

Doors and window switches. Have switch sensors. Electromagnetic devices installed at all points of entry can be reached from the ground. Alarm is triggered when a door or window is opened.

Foil tape. Is used to detect glass breakage. Tape is placed on windows and glass portions of door. Should anyone attempt to open one of the doors or windows containing this tape, one of the closed-circuit contacts would be opened and the alarm set off.

Infrared detectors. Project an infrared light beam between two points. Any interruption of the beam triggers an alarm. The sensors can be connected to a control unit by direct wiring or a wireless system. The roofs of some business premises are now protected by a system of cross-beam, infrared, motion detectors which are armed twenty-four hours a day. The instant anyone steps onto any portion of the roof, the detector flashes a signal and an alarm is sounded.

Photoelectric cells. Have electrical properties which are changed by the action of light. Alarm systems may be based upon the interruption of light rays. When used with infrared ray light filters, the light cannot be seen, thus making finding and avoiding it impossible.

Motion detection devices. Are ultrasonic. They are designed to detect motion. Devices fill a room with sound waves too high for most people to hear. Any movement in the room disturbs the pattern and sounds the alarm. This device can be adapted to exclude such movements as those made by animals, wind, or falling objects.

Seismic intrusion detectors. Are buried beneath the ground. Sensitive enough to pick up footsteps or any ground disturbance caused by intruders.

Treadle switches or pressure mats. Are a series of contacts placed under a rug or doormat so that pressure establishes contact and causes an alarm.

Trip wires. Are strung across a given area which, when disturbed by any contact, activitate electric switches. The switches, in turn, sound an alert.

SUMMARY

Burglary is a crime against property and one of the most common felony crimes. Since burglars operate most often under cover of darkness and are seldom seen, the lack of witnesses makes detection difficult. Successful prosecution usually depends upon circumstantial evidence to prove entry, intent, and also to connect the defendant with the offense. The location and recovery of physical evidence during the initial investigation is a most important phase of these cases.

A thorough knowledge of the modus operandi employed by burglars is essential to an investigator in order to conduct a successful investigation. Of great aid to the police is the burglar's adherence to a certain method or technique. Generally, burglars fall into two categories: the casual or amateur burglar who takes advantage of an opportunity for a burglary where the premises are easy to attack and there is little chance of being detected or apprehended; and the professional burglar who carefully plans the crime and relies heavily on the use of proper tools and equipment. One of the primary requisites of a burglary investigation is to obtain a complete list of the property taken. Stops placed against identifiable stolen property in both the local, state, and federal stolen property files have been the means of locating considerable stolen property as well as identifying criminal suspects.

REVIEW QUESTIONS

1. What are some of the precautionary measures an officer should take in responding to a burglar alarm call?
2. Explain the difference between burglary and robbery.
3. Name seven examples of methods used by burglars to gain entrance.

4. What types of physical evidence are frequently found near the point of entry in a burglary case?

5. What is the legal definition of a burglary-resistive safe?

6. What is the most positive means of placing a burglary suspect at the scene of a particular burglary?

7. Safe burglars attack safes in many ways. Name eight methods of attack.

8. When explosives or explosive materials are found during the preliminary investigation of a safe burglary, what should be done?

9. Why is burglary a difficult crime to solve?

10. List four types of alarm systems that are designed to detect intrusion.

WORK EXERCISE

Set out below is an account of a reported burglary. Prepare a concise teletype setting forth the pertinent facts of the case. In addition, write a paper or prepare a discussion on each of the items of physical evidence that you feel should be collected; the relative importance of each item; and what assistance the laboratory might be able to furnish.

Facts

At 0900 a call was received from the manager of the Bestway Market, 608 Washington Street, stating that his store had been burglarized. The loss was said to be around $8600 in currency, silver, and checks. Other miscellaneous papers were said to have been lost. On arriving at the market, you observe the following: an approximately 30-foot [9-meter] long brown twisted ½-inch [1¼-centimeter] hemp rope dangling from the skylight; a 500-pound [225-kilogram] Mosler burglar-resistive safe ripped open in the rear of the store; fireclay strewn on the floor near the front and sides of the safe; a 16-inch [40-centimeter] arm-type hatchet with claw on top of safe; possible blood-stains on lower portion of rope as well as on the front top edge of the safe; and a fabric glove print on top of the safe toward the front and in the center. In front of the safe, four cigarette butts (Kent brand) and several burned matches have been noted. A broken piece of a screwdriver blade approximately ¼-inch wide, and one white square shirt button have also been found. Twenty-four footprints were observed on the polished floor of the market and appear to have been made by three different persons. One set of footprints is that of the manager (the last person out and the one who locked up the store), and the other two sets lead from the area of the safe to a rear exit. Two identifiable tire prints have been noted in the vicinity of the rear exit on the north side of the loading platform. A further check of the premises shows that the unknown suspects apparently reached the roof of this building by climbing a large tree on the northwest side and making their way on to the roof via an overhanging limb. Thereafter, the suspects chopped an 18- by 24-inch [45- by 60-centimeter] hole through the roof. They tied the rope, mentioned above, to a roof ventilator to lower themselves to the market floor. The only result of a neighborhood check by one of the officers was a statement by a neighbor that he had heard his dog barking shortly after midnight.

12 ——————Robbery

Robbery is one of the leading forms of major crime with which a police officer must deal. The perpetrators of robberies encompass every age group, occupation, social strata, race, and sex. The only characteristic in common is the desire to get money without working for it. In the investigation of robbery, all methods of police science may be useful. Fingerprints may be found on stolen cars and on other paraphernalia. On discarded firearms, filed-off numbers may be revealed by number restoration, thereby disclosing the original owner. Palm prints, footprints, heel prints, and tire impressions found at the scene may furnish valuable information. Even in seemingly hopeless cases, a careful investigation will almost always reveal some physical evidence to track the criminal.

An interesting historical reference to the crime of robbery, reported in the *Sacramento Bee,* one of California's leading newspapers, dated October 24, 1860, reads

Never was high crime rifer in California than now. Highway robbery and open murder are an everyday occurrence. A strict enforcement of the laws may check this, but we consider the laxity of the courts and indifferences of prosecuting officers and jurors in such cases as the immediate cause which led to many of the crimes now being committed against life and property.

Again historically, between 1902-1913, a young Bolshevic named Joseph Stalin, nee Iosif Vissarionovich Dzhugashvili (who subsequently rose to the position of Russian Communist dictator), was five times arrested by the czarist police and escaped each time. He allegedly took part (1906) in a bank robbery at Tiflis in his native Georgia in order to replenish the funds of the revolutionists.[1]

When a robber is convicted and incarcerated in a penal institution, the fact of being a robber quite often is a status symbol in the eyes of fellow inmates. Unfortunately, there are those who even admire a robber. Some convicted criminals imprisoned for less popular crimes such as theft, sex offenses, auto theft, forgery, etc., resolve that "the next time they are busted" it will be for robbery, despite the fact that for the most part it is an unprofitable crime.

In a shooting incident in Chicago, two of the armed members of a gang were killed while resisting arrest. Ironically, one of the slain bandits had among his possessions a little newspaper article entitled "My Wish in Life" which read in part

I wish I now were old enough
To give some sound advice
To make each person weigh his thoughts
And turn them over twice
I wish my eyes had seen enough
So I could make him see
The way impressions in this life
Can fool us easily.

Legal Aspects

Robbery is defined as the taking of personal property of another from her or his person or immediate presence, against the victim's will, by means of force or fear. *Force* must be more than just enough to remove the property. It must be the additional force required to overcome even a slight degree of resistance. *Fear* must be present at the time the

offense occurred, and may be (1) fear of an unlawful injury to the person or property of the person robbed, or to a relative or member of the victim's family; (2) fear of an immediate and unlawful injury to the person or property of anyone in the company of the person robbed at the time the offense occurred.

The corpus delicti of robbery is the same as that required for the crime of larceny, but with two additional elements: the taking is by force or fear and the taking is from the person or in the presence of the owner. Robbery is divided into degrees by many statutes in accordance with the violence used or threatened. In California law, all robbery which is perpetrated by torture or by a person armed with a dangerous or deadly weapon, and the robbery of any person who is performing duties as operator of any motor vehicle, streetcar, or trackless trolley used for the transportation of persons for hire, is robbery in the first degree. All other kinds of robbery are of the second degree.

The federal law regarding bank robbery, bank burglary, and bank larceny is found in United States Code, title 18, section 2113. Bank robbery is both a state and federal offense. The FBI has primary federal investigative jurisdiction for the investigation of violations of this section.

The term "bank" as used in the above federal statute means any bank, banking association, trust company, savings bank, or other banking institution organized or operating under the laws of the United States, and any bank, the deposits of which are insured by the Federal Deposit Insurance Corporation (FDIC). A savings and loan association which comes under the above federal section means any federal savings and loan association and any insured institution as defined in section 401 of the National Housing Act, as amended, and any "federal credit union" as defined in section 2 of the Federal Credit Union Act as amended.

---

[1] *Columbia Encyclopedia,* 2d ed., Columbia University Press, New York, 1950.

Robbery Methods

Classification of robberies

While robbers do not always use the same method of operation, confine their attacks to one kind of victim or type of premises, or overlook those crimes that are crimes of opportunity, there often may be perceptible similarities in the type of victim or premises attacked. By correlating the facts and method of operation of unsolved robberies with other police agencies and through the use of electronic data equipment, it is often possible to identify the perpetrator.

The type and classification of robberies is often an indication of an individual's peculiar attraction for certain types of victims or premises. Various types of robberies are generally classified in reporting in the following ways: Robbery—Market, Robbery—Liquor Store, Robbery—Bank, Robbery—Savings and Loan Association, Robbery—Armored Car, Robbery—Jewelry Salesman, Robbery—Petting Party, Robbery—Alley, Robbery—Street, Robbery—Private Residence, Robbery—Hotel, Robbery—Transit Lines, etc.

Planning of robberies

Some robberies require very little planning on the part of the criminal. Others, due to protective measures taken, require careful planning and precise timing. Precautionary measures used include

Survey of the premises and neighborhood
Study of the individual(s) to be attacked
Study of police patrols and procedures in area
Consideration of the most opportune hour
Maps or sketches of area or location
Organization and assignment of participants to act definite parts
Location of cars and places of abandonment of stolen cars
Transportation by means of theft of car and/or license plates

Weapons
Masks or other forms of disguise
Phony identification
Equipment
Meeting places, before and after
Study of traffic flows and impediments in the area

Use of disguises

Face masks of all types are used by some robbers to prevent identification. Disguises are often in the form of Halloween masks (comic or grotesque coverings), silk stockings, adhesive tape, gauze, ski hoods, handkerchiefs, scarfs, paper sacks, etc. Makeup materials are preferred by others. Such preparations as pancake makeup; faked collodion scars, dots, moles; cotton placed in cheeks, upper lips, or nostrils to distort appearance; dyed hair; hairpieces; faked charcoal sideburns or mustaches; brown or blue contact lenses to alter color of eyes; and other disguises are used. Shoe polish and hair dyes to color face and hair, wigs to cover bald pates, false noses, etc., have also been used.

Clothing

Articles of clothing have often been used to throw off suspicion. Look-alike suits, hats, and other attire; extra sets of clothing to discard following the commission of robbery; lifts placed on the inside of shoes to give added height; padding to simulate weight; and other things have been tried as means of deception.

Uniforms have aided robbers on many occasions, particularly clothing that is readily recognized by most people, such as that of a police officer, mail carrier, or Western Union employee. Painter's, carpenter's, and other forms of regalia are worn by some thieves to foil detection. One notorious bank robber wore police, mail carrier, and Western Union uniforms in his robbery sprees. When asked why he favored these forms of disguises, he stated that he felt that it was an intellectual game—something like chess—matching wits against bank officials and their protective devices.

A "uniform" might be a pair of pajamas and bathrobe to simulate the appearance of a patient, which one robber used in an unsuccessful attempt to rob a hospital business office. After gaining entry into the business office dressed in a patient's attire, this suspect pointed a pistol at the financial counsellor and demanded all the money. As this subject was trying to find out where the money was, three other women happened on the scene. All four women were herded into an inner office and securely bound. The robber fled, however, when one of the women screamed. He left the safe open and several thousand dollars untouched.

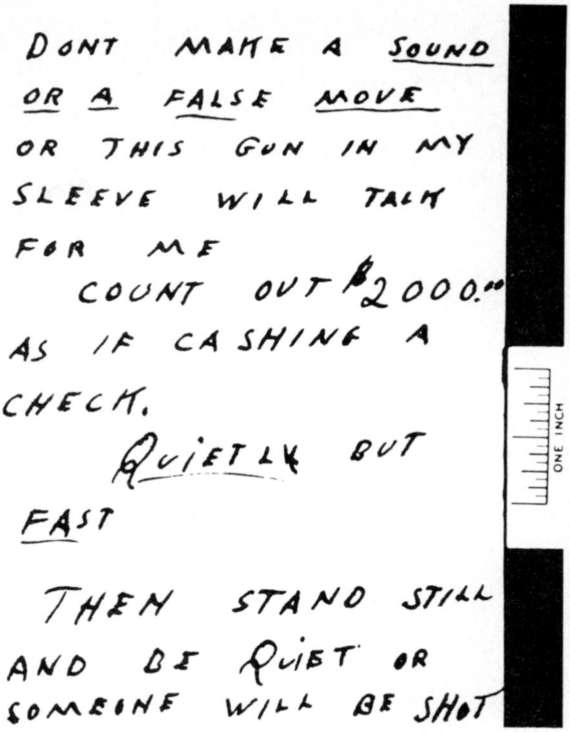
DONT MAKE A SOUND
OR A FALSE MOVE
OR THIS GUN IN MY
SLEEVE WILL TALK
FOR ME
COUNT OUT $2000.00
AS IF CASHING A
CHECK.
QUIETLY BUT
FAST
THEN STAND STILL
AND BE QUIET OR
SOMEONE WILL BE SHOT

Figure 12-1. A robbery demand note.

Weapons

Most robbery offenders use weapons of some kind. Pistols, revolvers, shotguns, rifles, machine guns, toy guns, air pistols, knives, razors or other cutting instruments, explosives, tear gas, acid, and other forms of dangerous articles have been used. In one case, a robber (construction engineer by trade) used a black mechanical pencil as a weapon in committing several robberies before being apprehended. This bandit removed the cap and eraser from the mechanical pencil and wrapped several layers of black friction tape around the shiny exposed metal which housed the pencil eraser. Thereafter the edges of the tape were tucked into the eraser socket to give the appearance of the barrel of a gun. The top edge of the tape was pinched to form a front sight. The prepared pencil was then placed inside the coat sleeve of this suspect and affixed to his wrist by rubber bands. The bandit chose female employees to victimize. His method was to present a hand-printed note as shown in Figure 12-1. After obtaining money, the above subject would flee the scene, slide off and discard the black friction tape from the end of his pencil, replace the eraser and pencil cap, and run to his car parked away from the crime scene. Thereafter, he would disappear into the heavy traffic.

The type of gun used in a robbery is an important element of a robber's method of operation and often connects the bandit to other robberies. The most commonly used guns are depicted in the drawings in Figure 12-2.

Vehicles

Automobiles play a peculiar and important part in the plans of many robbers. Some robbers show partiality to certain makes of cars and colors and steal them from parking lots, shopping centers, airports, or industrial plant areas where they are aware that the owner will not miss the car until his or her particular work shift is over. Robbers have

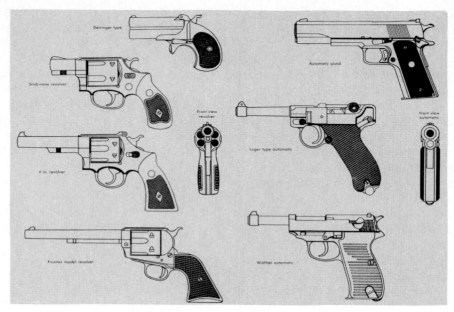

Figure 12-2. Guns most commonly used in robberies.

been known to use their own car with or without license plates, or with stolen license plates; to use a rented car with stolen plates; to use a stolen car and stolen plates; to use a friend's car with or without license plates, or any combination which it is felt will prevent identification.

Since planning quite often plays an important role in the perpetration of a robbery, some criminals steal and store cars for days or weeks prior to committing a robbery. During this period of concealment, the stolen car is disguised by painting and other forms of alteration such as removing the radio antenna or changing it to another location on the car, removing or adding other accessories, etc. Following the commission of the particular robbery, the car is either abandoned or sometimes hidden again for use in additional crimes.

In one case, a robber used a green Plymouth (a car which he favored) and after committing a robbery, hid this car in a vineyard between rows of grapes in the belief that the police helicopter patrol would

not spot his getaway car because of the color blend with the grapevines.

The extent of the problem

In the commission of crimes, state or national boundaries present no barrier for the robber. In one case, two bandits, following their arrest, were found to have committed several robberies in Canada, three in the United States, and many in Germany. In the robbery of a German bank (the last of their robberies), these subjects, one of German and the other of English origin, moved all the customers into one of the bank's rooms. The bandits made the customers face the wall with their hands in the air. As one of the bandits covered the employees, the second subject removed money from the tellers' cages and safe placing it in a briefcase. During this robbery, one of the bank officials managed to release the alarm which summoned the police. As German police arrived at the bank, they were met at the door by the departing bandits. A gun battle ensued which resulted in the killing of one of the officers and serious injury to another. In the shootout, one subject was hit by bullets in the face and left hand. Both subjects managed to escape in a previously stolen automobile, but were apprehended later that same day in another part of Germany. Both subjects were tried and convicted in Germany of murder and armed robbery and sentenced to penal servitude for life. Their subsequent appeal was rejected.

Following these subjects' arrest, investigation linked them to a Los Angeles robbery through stolen identification one of the subjects had among his effects. Stolen miscellaneous identification cards, a discharge paper, and a driver's license were determined to have been obtained from one of the patrons of a cocktail bar that was robbed. All customers and the bartender were forced at gunpoint to turn over their wallets and property. The suspects were identified by the FBI and Los Angeles Police as the perpetrators of a bank robbery in Los Angeles in which the same method of operation was used as those employed by the subjects in their German bank robbery. Fingerprint examination by the FBI linked one of the suspects with a bank robbery in the Midwest. Several other crimes in Canada were determined to have been committed by one or both of those individuals.

Investigation of Robberies

When the police are informed that a robbery has occurred, this triggers the response of many units. Time becomes a critical factor. Each minute lost lessens the chance to apprehend the suspect. Experience has shown that *speed* and *personnel* are essential to the successful solution of this crime. Solutions are proportionate to effort expended. The chance that an officer might become involved in a shooting while handling a robbery call is greater than in most crimes. Regardless of the type of robbery, extreme caution should be used in approaching and deploying at the scene.

Time and distance are extremely important factors in robbery investigations. Research has shown that the average time elapsed from the time the robbery occurred until the officer(s) receive the radio call is close to five minutes. Thus a fleeing suspect will be at least two miles or so from the scene if driving a vehicle and will increase this distance by ½-mile or more per minute when using surface streets at average speeds. If a suspect chooses to take a freeway, the distance would be much greater. If subjects are on foot, it is reasonable to assume that they could be a mile [1½ kilometers] from the scene in approximately ten minutes if walking and about seven minutes if running.

Response and approach to robbery scene

Due to varying circumstances, any procedure and techniques relative to robbery calls must necessarily be flexible. A robbery notification ("all-units") call justifies an emergency response. All-units broadcasts are justified by police incidents that involve violence, physical danger, or the presence of a felony suspect at the scene. The basic purpose of an all-units call is to get police units to the scene as expeditiously as possible with safety. The job of the radio dispatcher is to direct sufficient units to the scene. The nearest unit or units to the victimized location are immediately dispatched to handle the assignment. A speedy response is essential in order that the safety of the victim may not be jeopardized. Excessive speed in response to a robbery can impair an officer's ability to observe while on the way to the location. During the approach to a crime scene in which the fleeing suspect may be encountered, the streets, sidewalks, doorways, and automobiles should be scanned looking for suspects or cars. Particular observance should be made of any evasive action on the part of drivers or pedestrians that would indicate possible implication in the robbery. The license numbers of vehicles that arouse suspicion, but not sufficient to warrant stopping en route, should be jotted down. It is a good practice to "cut" the siren and red light when a sufficient distance from the scene so that suspects will not be warned. An exception to this could be made when an officer is in difficulty.

In responding to robbery calls a course of action to take upon arrival at the location should be considered. A decision as to where to stop, who will cover the rear, the best way to approach, and other safety procedures should be contemplated. The location of the robbery, type of structure, number of doors, parking lots, alleys, adjacent businesses, crime hazards, etc., should be mentally reviewed. Whatever action is decided upon, it should be a team operation and deployment procedure.

Sometimes an exact address is not broadcast because the witness is excited, or an address is transposed. A person across the street in a business equipped with a silent alarm may have set it off when a crime in progress was observed.

Officers should be careful of driving up in front of the entrance or windows of a business to which they have been called. Suspects observing the arriving police may shoot down the officers as they step from their vehicle. Additional caution should also be taken for an *ambush* situation in which there is no robbery but a trap engineered by a vindictive person(s) to kill an officer.

As additional officers become available for assignment, they are deployed wherever they are most needed. If a suspect is known to be afoot in the vicinity, the immediate thrust would be to "flush out" that person. If witnesses observed the suspect's getaway in a vehicle, the patrol cruising units would have the greatest opportunity of intercepting the wanted car. Freeway on-ramps and key intersections should be considered in deploying units.

Arriving at scene

On arrival at the location, a few moments of time are required to consider all possible consequences. This interval may require only fifteen or twenty seconds but may save an officer's life. The attitude to take in robbery calls is to assume that an actual emergency exists and that the suspect is still at the scene. The officer should keep uppermost in mind the thought that the robber is just inside the door waiting to injure, kill, or take a hostage. In other words, don't walk into a trap.

Investigating officers should be alert, curious, and identification conscious until the true situation is determined. A person may call out, "Everything is OK, officer!" But is it? The helpful person may be the subject. The bandit may be wearing a distinctive clerk's garb. Maybe a subject has forced an employee to make that statement. It may be appropriate to call persons from where they are and talk to them alone in case they are being covered by a suspect. Any strange actions on the part of the employee at a robbery scene should be cause for suspicion.

To illustrate how the unexpected can happen at a crime scene the following case is presented. Officers received a radio call, at approximately 10 P.M. saying that a robbery had occurred at a local hotel. On entering the hotel through the front door the officers found the lobby empty with no guests or hotel employees in sight. One of the two officers walked toward the hotel registration desk to make an inquiry as his partner trailed slowly behind. At a point about 10 feet [3 meters] from the desk a suspect "popped up" from behind the counter, pointed a gun at the lead officer and proceeded to disarm him. At that time the other officer, on glancing down a hallway to his right, observed a second suspect covering twelve hotel guests with their hands in the air. The second police officer, on observing the plight of his partner, retreated out of the hotel lobby to a vantage point just outside the main entrance. The first bandit on observing the actions of the second officer took the victim officer hostage with a gun at his back and proceeded toward the front entrance in an effort to make his escape. The second bandit "ran out" on his partner making his exit through a rear door of the hotel.

As the bandit and officer reached the front door, newly arriving officers took cover behind hotel entrance pillars in an effort to effect the release of their fellow officer and to apprehend the bandit. As the bandit and hostage officer proceeded out of the entrance in the direction of a getaway car, the hostage officer suddenly whirled around, causing the bandit to change his position and expose his body to covering officers. One of the officers, taking advantage of this turn of events, shot the robber in the back, enabling the hostage officer to wrestle the bandit's gun from him. The second bandit was located a few blocks from the hotel.

Duties at scene

The order of investigative preference in robbery cases is dictated by the facts of each situation. In all crimes, however, patrol officers, who are usually the first to arrive at the scene, have certain responsibilities, namely, to apprehend the suspect; to secure the name, address, and telephone number of all witnesses as soon as possible; and to safeguard the evidence. The first unit arriving at the robbery scene should conduct brief interviews with the victim or available witnesses and transmit the *initial broadcast* data as expeditiously as possible. This is one of the most important aspects of a robbery investigation since a suspect's car travelling at 40 miles [65 kilometers] per hour will cover nearly 1½ miles [2½ kilometers] in

two minutes. The information needed for the broadcast is

Type of crime
Type of premises
Location of occurrence
Time of occurrence
Number of suspects
Sex of suspects
Race of suspects
Direction suspects left scene
How suspects departed, foot or auto
Was a car seen
Description of car, if used
Weapon used

Below is an example of an initial broadcast:

Attention all units—robbery—liquor store, 1300 West Adams Boulevard, 8:45 P.M., this date, by one male, white, suspect. Left scene driving east on Adams in a 1979 dark green Pontiac four-door sedan, no license plate. Suspect used a .38 caliber blue steel, short barrel revolver.

Immediately thereafter, a *supplemental broadcast* is made giving a detailed description of the suspect, clothing worn, and any equipment carried. The vehicle is described as completely as possible. In addition to the color, year, make, body type, and license number, other identifying data such as emblems, stickers, cracked windows, type of seat covers, presense of a trailer hitch, etc., are furnished.

A *physical description* and the order in which it is generally broadcast is set out below:

Sex
Race
Age
Height
Weight
Color of hair
Color of eyes

Clothing: hat, coat, shirt, jacket, trousers, shoes

Other outstanding features

(When an item of this description is negative or unknown, it should be so stated: for example, "race unknown," or "no hat,")

An example of a supplemental broadcast follows:

Robbery—liquor store, 1300 West Adams Boulevard, at 8:45 P.M., this date, by one suspect, male, white, twenty to twenty-five years, five feet six to eight inches, one hundred sixty pounds, dark brown, thick wavy hair, neatly combed, parted left side, brown eyes, no hat wearing dark gray jacket with white and black specks, white shirt, yellow tie, charcoal pants, color of shoes unknown. Suspect carrying brown plastic zipper briefcase approximately twelve by sixteen inches. Wore a large white metal ring with red-colored stone on left hand. Suspect left scene driving east on Adams in a 1979 Pontiac sedan, dark green, no license plates, right rear fender had noticeable shallow approximate twelve-inch dent. Suspect used a .38 caliber blue steel, short-barreled revolver. Amount taken unknown but believed in excess of $1000, mostly small bills.

It is a good practice to listen to the radio transmission to see that it is correct in every detail. As additional pertinent information is obtained in the case, it should be made the subject of a supplemental broadcast in order that all field units are kept advised.

Witness' descriptions of bandit

In order to expedite the obtaining of information from witnesses at the scene of a robbery, some police agencies use a *form* to record witness data. Whenever a form is used, however, it is not designed to take the place of a face-to-face interview with witnesses, but is a means to quickly obtain information, particularly when personnel is short and witnesses many. This form is shown in Figure 12-3.

Preserving and searching the scene

Preservation of the crime scene is the responsibility of the first officers who arrive (usually patrol officers). It is most essential that all available evidence be safeguarded from employees and curious spectators, to prevent destruction, alteration, or contamination. Only those officers whose presence is necessary should enter the crime scene. The relationship of all items to the case can provide investigating officers with a frame of reference with which to conduct interviews with the victim and witnesses, to help reconstruct the crime, and to do the robbery report. It also is important that officers try to connect any physical evidence obtained with the suspect during interviews with victim and witnesses. Officers collecting evidence should avoid moving any items of physical evidence until notes are made, photographs taken where necessary, sketches prepared, and measurements recorded.

Inasmuch as eyewitness testimony changes, the search for physical evidence must be thorough. Fingerprints are often easier to locate in a robbery than in a burglary. The nature and extent of the search, however, are governed by such considerations as type of property, place of occurrence, type of area, and articles or materials involved. In a bar, for example, the officer would be interested in where the suspects sat, what they handled; in a restaurant, the cup used, salt and pepper shakers, and menu card used might provide fingerprint evidence. Binding materials (rope, adhesive tape, wire, etc.) would be valuable evidence in other cases. All physical evidence must, however, be collected in accordance with acceptable practices in order that the crime laboratory examiners can conduct whatever examinations are suitable. It is a

Name of witness: _____

Address: _____

Telephone No. _____

Please complete this form and return it to an officer before leaving the scene. Record only your own observations. Thank you.

DESCRIPTION
Sex
Race
Age
Height _____ feet _____ inches
Weight
Build: *Circle one* Slender, Medium, Heavy, Stocky, Very Heavy, Very Thin
Color of hair
Color of eyes
Complexion: *Circle one* Dark, Fair, Pale, Freckled, Pimply, Ruddy
Scars or Marks
Outstanding features
Voice (tone, accent, speech)
Weapon (type)
In what hand was gun held?
Glasses (type, color of rims?)

CLOTHING (indicate style and color)
Hat
Coat
Shirt
Tie
Jacket
Trousers
Shoes
JEWELRY

METHOD OF ESCAPE
On foot

Vehicle
        Make & model
        Color
        License No.
        Other identifying data:
           Accessories
           Emblems
           Stickers
           Dents
           Seat Covers
           Trailer hitch

COMMENTS: (use other side if needed)

Figure 12-3. Witness's description-of-bandit form.

good procedure to have evidence booked by the finding officer to ensure an unbroken chain of possession.

All witnesses must be interviewed in detail and statements obtained wherever possible since every item of information can help in solving a case. The cardinal rule in interviewing witnesses is that they be separated and questioned individually. This separation may be accomplished at the time persons are identified as witnesses. The victim and witnesses should be questioned about any specific oddities, conversations, unusual method of operation, and characteristics of the suspect(s); also, the identities of customers or persons observed in the vicinity during or just prior to the incident. Persons known only by first or last name, nickname, residence, or occupation should be listed. Following the questioning of witnesses, the investigating officers should be able to piece together and reconstruct the events as they occurred. Chapter 5 of this text discusses the subject matter of interviews with witnesses in detail.

Neighborhood investigation

Innumerable cases have been solved because of the excellent work officers have done in this important phase of criminal investigation. In this type of assignment, officers are searching for (1) the suspect and (2) evidence to indicate such data as previous casing of victim or location, additional witnesses, accomplices, getaway route, evidence of suspect residing in area, and discarded items (clothing, weapons, demand note, etc.).

Following the commission of a robbery, suspect(s) may try to avoid detection by hiding in the immediate vicinity. A neighborhood investigation involves the interviewing of persons residing in the area of the robbery occurrence to determine if they saw or heard anything that might assist in locating the suspect. A physical search to locate the subject is also part of this assignment. Residents may recall seeing a person acting suspiciously on the day of the robbery or previous day; they may have heard or seen someone run through their yard, climb over their fence, or heard the dog barking to signal an intruder. Investigation may reveal the identity of a parolee residing in the area who may warrant checking. Neighbors may know of a young person residing in the area who is engaged to someone who "has been in trouble with the police."

In addition to talking with residents in the vicinity of the robbery, all possible hiding places should be carefully checked for the bandit. Suspects may hide in such places as

Underneath or within cars parked nearby the robbery location
In garages, sheds, trash containers
In trees and on flat roofs
In churches located close by the location
In rest rooms of service stations where they may change clothes
In bars, bowling alleys, and restaurants
In nearby department stores
In barbershops, getting a shave or haircut
In nearby business offices posing as a potential customer
In motels, hotels, or rooming houses in area
In private residences or apartments where occupants are held hostage
Hailing a bus or taxi

Quite often a check of the license numbers of the parked cars in the vicinity may uncover the suspect's vehicle, which for some reason may not have been used to make a getaway from the scene. A check of parking tickets issued for overtime parking may produce the identity of a suspect. Investigation may reveal that the suspect commandeered a passing automobile to escape from the area.

Other investigation

Among the many investigative steps to take on the day of the robbery and thereafter (in addition to the above suggestions) are the following:

Search for stolen and abandoned cars.

Check "hot sheet" (list of stolen cars) for similar stolen automobiles.

Inquire of storage garages and check parking lots.

Conduct field interrogation of all logical suspects.

Alert informants and sources of information for possible suspects they might be able to suggest.

Check taxi companies for pickups in the crime scene area.

Check bus drivers to see if a bus passed by the crime scene around the time or after commission of the robbery.

Check hotels, motels, bus depots, train depots, airports, bars, etc., to the extent deemed advisable, depending on the circumstances of case.

Return to the scene of the crime at different times on subsequent days to locate additional witnesses.

Check new and used car lots, giving consideration to suspects who may have "tried out" a car for the alleged purpose of buying.

Prepare Ident-a-kit sketch or artist sketch and special bulletins.

Place stop notices with identification bureaus where facts warrant.

Perform other investigation suggested by any peculiar facts of this case or evidence recovered.

Robbery in progress

When officers discover a robbery or some other serious crime actually in progress, their actions will be dependent on the circumstances of each case. It is well to remember that the protection of life comes before the protection of property in all situations. Action must be taken to protect an innocent person. It may be necessary to fire without warning to save an innocent person's life, or to fire to save an officer's own life. Good decisions are based on correct facts. The senses must perceive a situation before an evaluation can be made. Rushing blindly into a dangerous situation can only result in needless loss of life. Knowledge of one's limitations must be a consideration in the method used to handle emergency situations. Probably the best tactic for an officer in these circumstances to use is to take a vantage point affording the greatest cover where possible, e.g., behind a car, building, pole, or other available shelter, and wait for the suspect to leave. Radio control should be alerted to the situation and the necessary personnel and equipment summoned.

Consideration in these cases should be given to sealing off the scene to protect pedestrians and motorists from possible gunfire. The officer at the scene should direct the responding officers to the most advantageous positions and warn them of any hazards. Suspects should be kept penned in without firing if possible. Innocent persons' lives must not be jeopardized if they are in the officer's line of fire. If the suspect runs out, the officer has the advantage. If the suspect's car can be identified, it should be disabled. Plainclothes officers should team up with uniformed officers so they will not be mistaken for the suspect. Officers should not bunch up or get in another officer's line of fire. If possible, officers should position themselves so as to catch the suspect(s) in a cross fire. A roof or second-story window may afford an excellent vantage point.

If officers must enter a critical area to protect innocent persons, they should take advantage of cover along the side of the entrance, crouch down to present a smaller target, and utilize any available cover within the building. A logical appeal to a contained criminal suspect might persuade her or him to surrender or a statement, "This is the police, the building is surrounded, come out the front door with your hands up" might help. If possible it may be desirable to telephone the premises and talk with the suspect, or use an electric megaphone.

Aid to injured
In crime situations in which a victim is injured, the investigating officers have a further responsibility to aid the injured. An ambulance should be called as soon as it is ascertained that its services are necessary. If the condition of the victim is such that there is a possibility of death, the officers should endeavor to obtain a *dying declaration.*

A dying declaration, verbal or written, is the act of a deceased person, made under a sense of impending death, about the cause of death. It may be apparent to the officer that the victim has received a fatal injury. However, the officer should ask how the victim feels and if she or he realizes he may die. The most essential question to ask the victim is, "Who did it?" The next question is, "Why?" On arrival at the hospital, the doctor may confirm the officer's opinion that the victim is dying and may so inform the victim. After this, the victim may spontaneously express "a sense of impending death" to the doctor or officer. A police officer may then take a dying declaration. The dying victim's statement must meet the same legal requirements as those of any other person. Clergymen and doctors are permitted to approach dead or dying persons but should be cautioned to avoid destroying any evidence.

Wounded suspect
The prime concern to all officers in all situations should be their own safety and the safety of others. Dangerous criminals become even more dangerous when they are wounded. Officers should remain under cover and reload their weapons if necessary before approaching a wounded suspect. Suspects should be covered at all times until they are thoroughly searched and handcuffed. Even though officers know the suspects are wounded, they should not relax. The hands of a suspect lying face down should be checked. Whenever one weapon is recovered, the suspect should be carefully searched for "hideouts" (extra weapons).

A poignant example of the dangerousness of a wounded suspect is exemplified in the following incident involving a New York police officer. The officer, while directing traffic at a major intersection in New York City, observed a man running from a jewelry store nearby. The officer gave chase at which time the unknown man fired at him. The officer returned the fire. The fleeing suspect threw down his gun and fell to the street. The officer went to give the suspect first aid and to get him to the hospital. As the officer leaned over the fallen robber, the wounded bandit drew a second gun and shot the officer through the heart.

In the interrogation of wounded suspects, interviewing officers (after carefully explaining suspect's constitutional rights and obtaining their consent to be interviewed) should ask how many other crimes the suspects have committed, who their accomplices are, where they are living, and where any stolen property is hidden. At least one officer should continuously remain with the wounded prisoner during medical treatment since it is the responsibility of the police to protect the ambulance attendant, the nurses, and the doctors. The guarding of the prisoner is maintained until the prisoner is incarcerated.

Surveillance photography in robbery investigation

Photography is becoming an important tool in crime detection. Regulations issued by

Figure 12-4. Photographs taken with hidden cameras at various banks.

federal banking supervisory agencies to implement the Bank Protection Act of 1968 require banks to consult with local law-enforcement officers and to install the degree of protection dictated by the incidence of crimes in the area. The provisions of the act are designed to discourage bank robberies, burglaries, and larcenies and to assist in the identification and apprehension of persons who commit these crimes. In January 1970, banking institutions were required to have a security program that included the installation of a vault area lighting system, tamper-resistant exterior door and window locks, an alarm system, and other devices. Every bank and savings and loan association under the Bank Protection Act must comply with the regulations issued by one of the four banking supervisory agencies, the Federal Reserve System, the Comptroller of Currency, the Federal Deposit Insurance Corporation, and the Federal Home Loan Bank Board.

Hidden surveillance cameras have been of particular assistance to law enforcement in solving robberies, provided the cameras have been installed and positioned properly. The area must also have appropriate lighting. Photographs taken with hidden cameras at scenes of bank robberies are shown in Figure 12-4.

SUMMARY

Robbery is the most frequent crime of violence. Perpetrators encompass every race, age group, sex, occupation, profession, and social strata. All have one desire—to obtain money or other valuable property. Victims of robbery include a wide range of subjects. Business establishments are the most frequent targets. Some robberies require little planning and usually are of the "hit-and-run" variety. Others take on varying degrees of preparation, including the use of disguises, communication equipment, transportation (stolen, rented, or personal cars), stolen license plates, knowledge of victim, getaway routes, police patrol patterns, etc.

In the absence of physical evidence, the modus operandi of robbers is most important. The type of robbery, victim, time, location, method of attack, weapon used, object of attack, physical characteristics of suspects, what suspects said, vehicle used, and other characteristics all play vital roles in robbery solutions. As in all serious crimes, immediate response; broadcasts of descriptive data; coordination and deployment of personnel; collection of physical evidence; interviews with victims, witnesses, and neighbors; exhibition of mug books of known robbers to witness; and follow-up of all leads are key ingredients to successful detection and apprehension.

REVIEW QUESTIONS

1. How would you distinguish robbery from larceny, since they are both thefts?
2. In responding to a robbery call, what considerations should you take into account?

3. How much descriptive data should be obtained from the victim and/or witnesses before the initial broadcast is dispatched?

4. What element in the crime of purse snatching can change that offense to robbery?

5. Suppose a person puts harmless, colored mouthwash in a test tube. Later, when committing a robbery, that person advises a victim that the tube contains nitroglycerin. The suspect says that if the victim fails to comply with demands, the suspect will blow the victim "sky-high." With what degree of robbery should suspect be charged? Explain.

6. In the absence of physical evidence, what is the next most important type of information that can be of assistance to robbery investigators?

7. Is the crime of robbery a crime against persons or against property?

8. J. B. Smith is employed as the assistant manager of Farmer's Market. The establishment was held up by a lone bandit armed with a blue steel, short-barreled revolver. Four customers (A, B, C, and D) were in the market at the time. No one was hurt. The bandit obtained $945 from the cash register. Who would be considered the victims in this robbery? Explain your answer. How many reports would be written in this case?

9. How is robbery different from extortion if a victim is threatened in an extortion case?

10. The police have a robber trapped inside a medium size market. About ten or twelve customers are in the store. You have the place surrounded and are the officer in charge. What exactly would you tell the bandit over a bullhorn? Suppose the contained robber refuses to comply?

WORK EXERCISE

1. Research the crime statistics on robberies and burglaries during the past ten years and prepare a chart showing the comparative annual increase or decrease in these offenses.

2. You and your fellow officer have just responded to a robbery call at a supermarket. While conducting an immediate investigation, you are confronted by a robbery suspect who has surprised and disarmed your partner. The suspect loudly demands that you drop you gun and threatens to kill your partner. Confronted by this extremely critical situation, how would you react? Explain.

3. At 2100 hours, you are off duty, unarmed, and about to enter a drug store to make a purchase, when you observe that four of the customers in the store have their hands in the air. You also notice a bandit with a revolver in hand. The robber does not see you. What action would you take? Explain.

4. You and your partner are assigned to cover the inside of a variety store whose manager has been tipped off that the store is going to be robbed between 6 P.M. and 7 P.M. that night. The manager asks you what to do. What advice would you give? What arrangements would you make with the store manager?

Theft and Receiving Stolen Property

Theft

This chapter, of necessity, is limited in scope to specific types of theft with which the student of police science should become familiar. It is hoped that it may serve as a refresher for the line officer. It is by no means an exhaustive treatise of this subject area, in view of the many kinds of theft and the ways it can be committed.

G. K. Chesterton, the English essayist and novelist famous for his crime fiction with the much beloved detective, Father Brown, once wrote

> Thieves respect property. They merely wish the property to become their property that they may more perfectly respect it.

Theft is the most common of the crimes for gain. It is generally a crime of opportunity and one against property. The problem of identifying a thief from any other person is a complex one. A thief may be young or old; rich or poor; an employee or an executive; or of any occupation, race, or social status. From an investigator's viewpoint, it requires an ability to distinguish the law-abiding citizen from the one with criminal intent. Unfortunately there is no slide rule that an officer can use. The professional thief feels contempt for law, police officers, prosecutors, and judges. Thieves feel that law impedes their behavior. They take pride in their reputations as criminals. Some, of course, do not conceive of themselves as criminals.

Business crime in the United States is an offense of major proportions. In terms of dollars and number of people involved, it far exceeds crime in the streets. From internal theft and outside theft, criminals are said to be draining off cash and goods at the unprecedented rate of almost 40 billion dollars a year.[1] There are many specific types of thefts, however, wherein the criminal works by design, e.g., shoplifting, purse snatching, bunco-fraud cases, auto theft, burglary, forgery, and others. The range of property crimes, the techniques used in such crimes, and the type of persons involved in such acts are very diverse. Many states, including California, have merged larceny, embezzlement, and bunco crimes—sometimes classified as "larceny by trick" or "confidence games"—into the one crime of *theft*. It is interesting to note that the three categories of offenses against property (burglary, larceny, and auto theft) account for the greater part of all serious crimes reported to the police. These crimes are included in the seven-crime classification index which is used to measure the trend and distribution of crime in the United States. The crimes are murder, forcible rape, robbery, aggravated assault, burglary, larceny-theft, and auto theft.

The term "theft" is not the technical name of any common law offense. It is a popular name for larceny and used as a synonym for the word larceny. In the ancient Saxon laws, larceny was divided into two sorts, simple larceny and grand larceny. If the value of the property was above the value of twelve pence, the offense was grand larceny and subject to the death penalty. Criminals under early law were permitted to redeem their lives by pecuniary ransoms, but, in the ninth year of Henry the First, this power of redemption was taken away, and all persons guilty of larceny above the value of twelve pence were directed to be hanged.[2] The above distinction between simple and grand larceny was subsequently abolished.

Modern statutes very generally retain the classification of grand and petty larceny with different penalties and different values arbitrarily set as the dividing line. Grand larceny is a felony and petty larceny a misdemeanor under most modern statutes. Many states frequently include larceny of a motor vehicle, certain domestic animals, and other specific articles as grand larceny. What might be grand larceny in one state may be only petty larceny in another. Brief definitions and examples of larceny, embezzlement, obtaining property by false pretenses, and obtaining property by trick or device are given below.

Larceny   The felonious taking and carrying away of the personal property of another with a specific intent to permanently deprive the owners of her or his property. Examples are shoplifting, pocket picking, and thefts from autos.

Embezzlement   The fraudulent appropriation to the criminal's own use or benefit of personal property or money entrusted to him or her by another in a relationship of trust. For example, an employee takes money entrusted to her or him by an employer, intending to restore it at a later date to the employer.

Obtaining Property by False Pretense   Designed misrepresentation of existing facts or conditions whereby a person obtains another's money or goods. For example, a doctor falsely states that a person has an ailment that can be cured if certain sum of money is paid.

---

[1] *U.S. News and World Report,* February 21, 1977, p. 47.

[2] John C. Devereux, *Blackstone's Commentaries on the Law of England,* Baker, Voorhis & Co., New York, 1915.

Obtaining Property by Trick or Device A form of swindle in which, by trick, device, fraud, or artifice, false and fraudulent representation is held out to victim in the promise of financial or other gain. Examples are bunco or confidence games ("badger game," "pigeon drop," "handkerchief switch," etc.).

Note: It is often very difficult to distinguish the offense of obtaining property by false pretenses from larceny by trick. The *distinction* turns on the intent of the property owner. If the owner intended to pass *both* title and possession to the accused, then it is obtaining by false pretenses; if the owner intended to pass possession only (retaining title), it is larceny by trick.

Embezzlement (theft)

The offense of embezzlement is being discussed herein in view of the fact that this type of theft commands more attention than most crimes. The individual involved is usually highly placed, trusted, and frequently a member of the middle or upper class. Embezzlement, fraud, and forgery are sometimes referred to as the "big three" of white-collar crime. White-collar crime is a non-legal term referring to certain criminal acts committed by salaried or professional workers whose jobs generally do not involve manual labor. Bailees, cashiers or tellers of banks, clerks, public officers, agents and employees of corporations, bookkeepers, and all persons entrusted with the care of money or property belonging to others, who fraudulently appropriate that money or property to their use are embezzlers. Embezzlement is frequently not reported when restitution is possible or if the amount involved is small. Sometimes the crime is not discovered.

The embezzler's rationale is the expressed belief that she or he is only "borrowing" the money and will eventually return it; that he or she is using the money to get a start in life and not really stealing. As far as friends, employers, and neighbors are concerned,

embezzlers' honesty is above reproach until they are exposed. They may feel they are too clever to get caught. An embezzler may be employed in any business, industry, or financial institution, or be a public official. The reasons embezzlers steal are many—gambling, drinking, living beyond income, adultery, drug addiction, and other personal problems. This offense might also be brought about by financial hardship, heavy expenses, or extended illness in the subject's family which may have resulted in the depletion of her or his life's savings. One embezzler, upon apprehension, attributed his downfall to "fast women and slow horses."

In cases where millions of dollars are involved in bank embezzlement, as in one Eastern case, the thief originally never intended to embezzle the funds. All he wanted to do was "borrow" the money and speculate with it. He felt he had access to the money, that he was in charge of its administration, that he would put back whatever he took, and that, therefore, he had a right to use it. He simply did not count on losing.

A president of a bank with forty years experience in the banking business, in discussing his crime theory, stated that "a thief steals because he thinks he's entitled to the spoils." The veteran banker told of interviewing a bank officer whose speculations over a period of time finally came to light. The exposed bank officer felt he was justified in doing what he did, stating, "Look at the overtime hours I put in, the hotel bills I paid myself, and the meals I paid for out of my own pocket. . . ." The bank president remarked that in every case of bank fraud, misappropriation of funds, or forgery that has come to his attention, the crime was committed because the thief was able to rationalize in the above way.

Investigation of Embezzlement Cases

In checking the subject involved in an embezzlement case, of particular concern to the investigator would be the following types of data:

The results of a complete audit of any records maintained by a subject during the course of employment in order to establish the extent of embezzling activities.

Details of a subject's employment, i.e., exact duties and accessibility of funds, keys, and other valuables.

The identity of the person who recommended the subject for employment in order that this individual might be interviewed concerning the subject.

The reason the subject chose this particular employer.

All positions of trust held by the subject and a review of activities in each position.

Prior employment, reason for leaving, reputation for trustworthiness, honesty, and veracity in former jobs.

Background: criminal and credit information.

Determination of checking, savings, and safe deposit holdings.

Major purchases: nature, extent, amount, and type of payments.

Activities of the subject when away from employment as to unusual spending, habits, gambling, stock speculation, vacation locations, etc.

Identity of friends and associates and their general reputations, occupations, and activities.

Theft and Embezzlement of Government Property (U.S.C., Title 18, Sec. 641)

Whoever embezzles, steals, purloins, or knowingly converts to his use or the use of another, or without authority, sells, conveys, or disposes of any record, voucher, money, or thing of value of the United States or of any department or agency thereof, or any property made or being made under con-

tract for the United States or any department or agency thereof; or

Whoever receives, conceals, or retains the same with intent to convert it to his use or gain, knowing it to have been embezzled, stolen, purloined, or converted.

Penalty—fine not more than $10,000 or imprisonment not more than ten years or both; if value does not exceed $100 the fine is not more than $1,000 or imprisonment not more than one year or both.

Other Possible Federal Violations

In property thefts, when property taken is of the value of $5000 or more and there is reason to believe the goods are taken across state lines, the FBI generally is involved under two possible federal statutes: (1) Interstate Transportation of Stolen Property (U.S.C., title 18, sec. 2314) and (2) Receiving Stolen Property (where goods are transported in interstate or foreign commerce) (U.S.C., title 18, 2315).

Types of Theft

Pickpockets

This type of thief works alone or in groups of as many as five persons. The word "pickpocket" describes a theft of property from the person. The property must be: (1) on the body, (2) in the clothing being worn, or (3) in a receptacle *carried* by such person.

Professional pickpockets are expert in human nature, in every trick of distraction, and in the knowledge of physical reflexes. They are highly skilled in maneuvering a victim into a position to remove a wallet or money. Pickpockets are nonviolent. They use psychology in their work, physiology in body contact, and strategy in maneuvering victims into position to distract them from their money. Oftentimes they will let prosperous victims go rather than arouse suspicion or call attention to the thievery. The average citizen has no defense against nimble-fingered pilfering except an aware-ness that he or she could have his or her pockets picked in a crowd.

It is impossible to distinguish between a pickpocket and an honest citizen by appear-ance. They often appear to be busi-nesspersons or everyday shoppers, having dressed so as not to be obvious. Pickpockets move smoothly and blend into any crowd with great skill. They are difficult to observe and remember. Frequently their clothes are of good quality so that the average person has difficulty imagining that a person of such appearance could be guilty of trying to steal a pocketbook.

Pickpockets operate in many different ways. The theory behind pocket picking is, "You can't steal people's money if they have their minds on it." The theft is timed when the victim shifts interest; for instance, op-portune places are often a fire or an accident, ticket lines, depots, markets, and theaters. The pickpocket may engage in a conversa-tion with the intended victim, gain her or his confidence, then steal his or her wallet.

The average pickpocket usually uses an object (such as a newspaper or a coat over the arm) to hide actions or to dispose of the wallet when taken. Pickpockets are known by such terms as a cannon, dip, wire, mechanic, clipper, tool, or hook. Pickpockets work alone, in pairs, or sometimes in groups of more than two. One does the picking while the others act as stalls to maneuver victims into position and to distract them so their pockets can be picked. Valuables taken are transferred from the pickpocket to a confed-erate known as the "tail." Members separate and meet later to split the loot.

Pickpockets are considered to be among the most skilled types of mechanical crimi-nals. They utilize many different proce-dures. Some of the more common approaches

Pickpockets who work in crowds.
"Jug mobs" who seek their victims in banks.

"Choppers or slitters" who work all-night theaters using taped razor blades to cut pockets.
"Spitters" who sneeze on a victim and pick his pocket while cleaning him off.
"Short workers" who concentrate their activities on public transportation.
"Hugger-muggers" who are prostitutes who generally work in pairs while operating on a "trick."
"Toilet workers" who operate in public restrooms.
"Moll buzzers" who are thieves who open a purse while the victim is carrying it.
"Sleepers" who open a purse that has been laid aside.
"Ticket-line operators" who work ticket lines at depots, markets, theaters, and amusement centers.
Pickpockets who use a hot cigarette or cigar close to the victim's ear. In the confusion, a confederate moves in to lift the victim's wallet.

The "Ochos," an international pickpocket gang from Colombia, periodically frequents Southern California, generally during the holiday season. "Ocho" (meaning "eight" in Spanish) refers to the number usually operating in each group. The gang is very clever, well schooled, and goes through ex-tensive training in special schools in Tijuana and Colombia. Members of the gang dress well, stay in the best hotels, and are always amply supplied with funds. Distraction is their greatest ally. In their method of opera-tion, the number 1 "Ocho" will sit or stand next to a victim in a bus or public gathering and carry a coat draped over an arm. The thief often wears a loose-fitting jacket and slips the left arm out of the sleeve. Number 2 acts as a shield or lookout for number 1. Number 1, using the left arm, reaches be-hind the back and into a purse or rear pocket of a victim to extract money or property. Members of this group sometimes carry a briefcase and carry it on a bus so that it hovers over a victim's leg. When the bus lurches or something else distracts the victim, the suspect "lifts" the wallet or other property of the victim.

Investigation of Pickpockets Pickpockets can generally be located wherever there are people: shopping crowds, crowded streets, parades, sporting events, amusement centers, transportation facilities, railroad stations, airports, bus terminals, carnivals, all-night theaters, etc. Investigators assigned to this detail should be most observant of the activities of suspects in the above situations. Recognition of known pickpockets and a "mug" file (photograph album) of these thieves is most essential. In the detection of pickpockets one should be particularly observant of such activities as

Individuals moving from place to place for no apparent reason.

Persons carrying a jacket or coat over an arm, or a newspaper in hand, in close quarters.

Groups that huddle, split up, and thereafter board the same bus separately.

Persons who show no interest in the event taking place.

People whose behavior is unnatural.

Individuals constantly moving from one place to another.

Persons who edge close to people dozing or intoxicated when there is plenty of other seat space available.

Individuals who drop something (an object or loose change, for example) or create a situation that lends itself to pocket picking.

Suspects whose eyes seem to constantly shift from one person to another or in a searching manner to see if they are being observed.

Observe a basic rule: Don't stare or stalk a suspect in a way that would disclose the officer's status.

Shoplifters

A shoplifter is one who steals goods from the shelves or displays of a retail store while posing as a customer. This type of thief may be male, female, child, minor, college student, homemaker, a person of any occupation, customer, or employee. Shoplifters are commonly known as "boosters." It should be noted at the outset that shoplifting is a crime, the same as any other larceny. It can be petty theft or grand theft depending upon statute provisions, and, in some cases, burglary—if it can be shown that the person entered the store for the purpose of stealing.

The objective of shoplifting is "to get away with it if possible." The prime targets for shoplifters are department stores, variety stores, and self-service markets. Shoplifters fall into several categories: the amateur, the professional, the narcotics addict, and the kleptomaniac.

The Amateur The amateur often steals on the impulse of the moment without premeditation. In some instances he or she may not even need the item, e.g., a teenager stealing six cigarette lighters and not being a smoker. Amateurs steal for many reasons, including hardship, personal need, thrill, dare, envy, and peer status. A great many law-abiding citizens are overcome with the urge to get something for nothing.

The method used by the amateur operator to conceal merchandise is predictable, although there is no obvious way to predict who will shoplift. The amateur shoplifter usually stuffs stolen wares into shopping bags, purses, and pockets, or hides things under jackets or coats, in trouser cuffs, inside bras, socks, shoes, up sleeves, etc. In some instances they simply don garments that are taken into dressing rooms and wear them out of the store under their clothes. Persons with merchandise beside their handbags in the baby seats of shopping carts are prime suspects in supermarket thefts. Other types of shoplifting revolve around such methods as switching price tags or removing tags and claiming articles were a sale item, changing higher-priced items from their original containers to a different container priced lower, putting extra accessories in with products purchased, returning merchandise for refund without sales receipt, and using a child to steal articles and, if caught, pretending to scold the child for wrong-doing.

The teen-age juvenile female shoplifter will most frequently steal phonograph records, slacks, bathing suits, sweaters, blouses, costume jewelry, cosmetics, sundries, hosiery, and underwear. In most instances, the items are stuffed into her purse and carried from the store. Clothing of various sorts oftentimes is donned under street clothes. In one case, a juvenile thief was apprehended after leaving a department store with ten bikini bathing suits worn under her dress. Teen-age boys most frequently steal long-playing records, small appliances, tools, jackets, and sophisticated toys. They usually place these items in their trouser pockets, within notebooks, and inside their shirts or trouser belt areas.

In one case when a minor was taken into custody for shoplifting, she had in her purse a "shopping list" of ten items ranging from hosiery to pillowcases. She had already stolen the first six items on her list. The last item on this list read "anything to make the apartment more beautiful." Teen-age shoplifting is a tremendous policing problem. Young people seem to think "everyone else does it, so it's OK." In college bookstores, a student will often purchase books for $20 or $30 and carry off $2 or $3 worth of small stuff as a "little dividend."

To cope with juvenile and amateur shoplifting, many police agencies and security personnel have sponsored lectures and handed out printed materials in which they place emphasis on the dangers of shoplifting practices, reminding the shoplifter that this type of thievery is a criminal offense, and that this crime may well limit job opportunities for them in the future.

The Professional Professional shoplifters are often more imaginative than amateur ones are. Their motive is profit or resale; their specialties are clothing, furs, jewelry, or other expensive items. They are successful because they are clever. This thief generally makes a study of the victim premises, security measures employed, and the physical layout prior to any shoplifting attack. He or she may work alone or with one or more confederates as a team. When working as a team, one of the group creates a diversion so that a confederate can go undetected. One member of the group occupies a salesperson's attention or shields a confederate while another team member does the "lifting." If observed, members of the group will huddle around the particular display and the goods taken are put back.

The professional often uses sophisticated equipment, mechanical devices, or "made-to-order" wearing apparel. Hooks on retractable springs to seize and retrieve merchandise, special harnesses or belts with hooks on which to hang stolen items, and other ingenious contrivances are popular. Hollowed-out books, wrapped cylindrical tubes or "booster boxes" have also been used with success. Such "packages" give the appearance of being merchandise neatly wrapped and tied, when in reality one end has a spring door to permit a suspect to stuff articles within the box. The "booster box" gimmick appears to be on the wane since it is now a dead giveaway to alert store detectives when carried by "prospective store customers." Clothing with tier pockets, use of large safety pins to pin items to the inside of clothing, zipper briefcases, umbrellas, concealing articles under armpits, and other methods of hiding merchandise are used.

Experienced women shoplifters often practice walking with thick telephone directories held between their legs to strengthen their thigh muscles. Thereafter these thieves are able to shoplift such items as canned hams, roasts, cartons of cigarettes, portable typewriters and cases, and other expensive merchandise beneath their skirts. They are referred to as "crotch carriers." Some professional female thieves wear special bloomer pants in which to conceal merchandise. In one particular Ohio case, a young twenty-three-old professional shoplifter, following her apprehension, was found to have $63,000 in her bank account. She admitted that she had stolen as much as $200,000 worth of merchandise a year. This thief supplied stolen-to-order merchandise at half the retail price to hundreds of customers. She claimed that she learned how to steal when she was nine years old from her mother.

The Narcotics Addict Drug addicts are crime-prone persons. Many shoplifters are desperate drug addicts capable of stabbing or slugging a detective and then escaping into crowds of passersby. Inasmuch as addicts spend between $50 and $175 per day for a twenty-four-hour supply of heroin, and since they cannot legitimately earn this amount, they turn to crime. In many cases they will steal property anywhere. Addicts working alone or in teams steal thousands of dollars worth of merchandise from food markets, department stores, warehouses, and distributors. They quite often "shop" for merchandise with a high resale value. The addict generally peddles stolen loot to a "fence", or receiver, who pays less than one-third the value of the merchandise. The "fence" knows that addicts are desperate and in no position to bargain, and consequently takes advantage of them.

The Kleptomaniac Kleptomania is an irresistible urge to steal—sometimes as a result of an emotional condition. The defense of kleptomania is frequently used to describe any kind of excessive, repetitive, and apparently unreasonable stealing. Cases involving shoplifting by a kleptomaniac represent a very small percentage of larcenies. One suspect, when taken into custody for shoplifting (with a long background of this offense) told the judge she was forced to steal by an inner drive that came upon her at the full of the moon. A true kleptomaniac has a psychiatric problem and should be given adequate psychiatric treatment.

Investigative Aspects of Shoplifting In an effort to curtail shoplifting, retail stores utilize a variety of protective devices. Security measures include the use of security officers and such equipment as convex overhead mirrors; silent alarm and light warning systems; self-operated cameras; hidden movie cameras to record acts of pilferage; observation posts behind one-way glass; two-way communication equipment; telescopes; and photo-scan or other types of closed-circuit television as illustrated in Figure 13-1. Some police departments have shoplifting patrols that circulate in stores as a selective enforcement tactic.

Electronic wafers securely fastened to expensive coats, garments, or other valuable items have been used with success as a preventative method. A salesclerk using a special tool removes the wafer when a customer buys the high-priced merchandise. Should a person attempt to leave the store without having paid for the article to which the wafer is attached, an alarm is sounded and the security officer intercepts the suspect.

One veteran detective in giving advice as to his success in spotting shoplifters, stated, "Watch a suspect's eyes—the way they flick back and forth taking in everything. Watch his hands. If he is going to pocket something he will fold it up small, even if it's small already; just a habit."

Figure 13-1. The photo-scan camera (closed-circuit television) is a type of security measure used to detect thefts in large retail stores.

It is recommended as a good policing procedure, and before an arrest is made, that the officer know where the stolen merchandise is on the subject's person, concealed or otherwise. A constant surveillance of the suspect, from the time the merchandise is taken until the arrest, should be undertaken. Extreme care should be taken in arrest situations since in most shoplifting cases the officer is dealing with a misdemeanor. Arrest made without the merchandise can make subsequent prosecution very difficult.

The reason for being certain as to the location of the suspect and merchandise at all times is to establish beyond all doubt the intent to steal the articles in question. Therefore constant surveillance of the shoplifter is a must. Should the suspect be even momentarily out of sight, it affords that person the opportunity to dispose of the property. Of course, additional acts of pilferage observed would make a case that much stronger.

In instances where a suspect has a confederate, there is always the possibility of passing the merchandise to the associate. The policy of many city and district attorneys is to recommend that shoplifting arrests be made outside the store. While there is no requirement that a suspect must leave the store before apprehension,[3] the district attorney's office (handling felonies) and the city attorney's office (handling misdemeanors) generally do not accept shoplifting cases unless the arrest is made outside the store with the merchandise. Prosecutive opinions should be sought from the local city and district attorney's offices in these cases.

In many cases, the suspect will claim that she or he intended to pay for the items. If, during the interview or the actual arrest, it is determined that the suspect did not have enough money to pay for the item taken, this fact should be included in the narrative portion of the police report. Devices used such as "booster boxes" or other contrivances, as well as special clothing, may well establish the intent necessary for the crime of statutory burglary in some states.

Purse snatchers

This crime is closely akin to the crime of robbery. The element of force used is the determining factor as to whether a crime is a robbery or a purse snatch (theft). Because of the possible robbery aspect in these cases, larger departments often assign this criminal violation to the robbery squad. In California law, any theft from the person [pickpocket, purse snatch, drunk roll (stealing from an intoxicated person)] constitutes grand theft if the property has marketable value.

[3]*People v. Thompson,* 158 CA. 2d 320, 1958.

Purse-snatching thieves usually operate around shopping areas, retirement centers, theaters, and residential areas. They work alone or in pairs. In most cases the thief is a juvenile. His or her usual method is to approach a victim from the side or rear, grab the purse, and run. Thereafter any monies in the purse are taken and the purse discarded nearby as soon as possible. Suspects working in pairs will drive up near a likely victim, grab the purse, run to the waiting automobile, and make a getaway. The radio broadcast following a purse snatch should include the following:

Description of the suspect(s) in detail

Complete description of the purse and identifying contents

Method used to approach the victim and the direction taken on leaving the scene

Description of the vehicle, if one used, and direction taken

Actual location of the victim

Window smashers

In this type of theft the display window of a jewelry store, or a store displaying furs, clothing, or other valuable merchandise, is broken. Then the thief reaches in, grabs as much merchandise as possible, and flees in a waiting car driven by a confederate. They operate in late or early hours when stores are closed and very few persons are about. Usually the window is broken with a brick or stone wrapped in paper or cloth, or any other available object. In one case, for example, within one minute, thieves using this method of operation smashed a men's clothing store window, scooped up sixty suits and a number of sport coats, and fled before sheriff's deputies arrived in answer to the store's silent alarm.

Jewelry thieves

This crime is usually committed by armed robbery, burglary, or larceny. A professional thief, in committing an armed robbery, usually robs around opening or closing time when valuable jewelry tray displays are being put in or taken out of a jewelry store's window. The better-class store is generally selected.

Jewelry thieves spend long hours of planning and following a jewelry salesperson, looking for an opportunity to steal valuables. In one case, for example, a jewelry salesperson drove fifty miles before he discovered that he had left $50,000 worth of jewelry on the sidewalk. In another instance a jewelry salesperson left his jewelry case in the back of his car while he went to get change for a parking meter. Needless to say, such opportunities are welcomed by thieves. Jewelry is also taken from hotel rooms and residences of wealthy guests or celebrities whose activities, including travel, are followed closely by professional thieves.

Thieves are ever cognizant of the high value of jewelry and the ready market for it. It is a commodity that is relatively easy to dispose of through "fences" who often discount the "stuff" at fractions of the actual worth. Following a jewelry theft, the property taken is often sent to another distant state where valuable stones are cut up, remounted in different settings, and resold. A 2-karat diamond resold in a different setting is oftentimes hard to identify unless the diamond is unique.

Hotel thieves

Guests, dishonest room cleaners, bellhops, and other employees having access to rooms may be found among this class of thieves. The method is much the same as with any other type of dishonest employee. During employment they are constantly on the lookout for an opportunity to steal.

The professional hotel thief registers at first-class hotels or resorts under a phony name. She or he arrives at the hotel with expensive luggage and sometimes with a confederate of the opposite sex and a small child to allay suspicion. During his or her stay, this thief makes a survey of the hotel, elevators, stairways, hallways, etc., and makes a particular study of the habits of other guests. The thief enters rooms at opportune times by using the fire escape, a duplicate key, a lock-picking aid, or force. Following the theft of desired items, the thief will check out of the hotel before the loss is discovered. Many hotel thieves register at numerous hotels in order to make a collection of keys or to make duplicates for possible future use. A hotel thief can get in and out of a room with the loot in a minute or two. On some occasions passkeys are obtained or duplicates are made with help of dishonest hotel employees. Modern hotels may have adequate locks on their doors and windows but are unable to cope with crooked guests who make duplicate keys for use in subsequent thefts by themselves or a confederate.

Mailbox thieves

These criminals focus on certain areas of a city, stealing from apartment building mailboxes, especially seeking U.S. Treasury checks and major credit cards. For stolen mail to be considered a postal offense, the theft must occur after the letter is mailed, but not after its recipient has taken it from the mailbox. If stolen after receipt, it becomes a local matter involving petty theft or grand theft depending on the amount involved. In California law, the value of the item taken must (with exceptions) exceed $200 to constitute grand theft. In instances where a U.S. government check (Treasury check) is taken from the mails, the U.S. Secret Service would have jurisdiction over this violation. In other matters not relating to coins, obligations, and securities of the United States and of foreign governments, the postal inspectors would have jurisdiction.

A method some mail thieves use is to extract a monthly bill from the letter box and thereafter call upon the recipient pretending to be a representative of the particular store or company and endeavor to collect payment on the account. This method is used particularly around the first of the month when bills are sent out by the various creditors. Some thieves obtain monthly bank statements from the mails at which time they are able to observe the current balance of the particular account. Thereafter the subject forges the victim's signature to a check.

Theft or Receipt of Stolen Mail Matter Generally (U.S.C., Title 18, Sec. 1708)

Whoever steals, takes, or abstracts, or by fraud or deception obtains, or attempts so to obtain, from or out of any mail, post office, or station thereof, letter box, mail receptacle, or any mail route or other authorized depository for mail matter, or from a letter or mail carrier, any letter, postal card, package, bag, or mail, or abstracts or removes from any such letter, package, bag, or mail, any article or thing contained therein, or secretes, embezzles, or destroys any such letter, postal card, package, bag, or mail, or any article or thing contained therein; or

Whoever steals, takes, or abstracts, or by fraud or deception obtains any letter, postal card, package, bag, or mail, or any article or thing contained therein which has been left for collection upon or adjacent to a collection box or other authorized depository of mail matter; or

Whoever buys, receives, or conceals, or unlawfully has in his possession, any letter, postal card, package, bag, or mail, or any article or thing contained therein, which has been so stolen, taken, embezzled, or abstracted, as herein described, knowing the same to have been stolen, taken, embezzled, or abstracted, shall be fined not more than $2,000 or imprisoned not more than five years, or both.

Hijacking thieves

Thefts from shipments involve hijacking with the use of force or violence, burglary, robbery, embezzlement, fraud, and petty and grand larceny. This crime is generally committed by gangs, many of whom specialize in this field only. Shipments may be household appliances, television sets, liquor, clothing, drugs, cigarettes, metals, etc. A lot of the hijacked items are stolen "on order," often in collaboration with receivers who make their wants known to these thieves. Hijackers are meticulous in plotting a theft. Prior to a theft, hijacking gangs ascertain, through bribery or surveillance, the truck's departure, exact time and route, as well as the security measures employed by the trucking company. Armed with this information they are able to rob or steal cargoes at opportune times. One Chicago gang used "consultants" to tip them on movements of valuable cargoes. The gang used custom-built "work cars" equipped with police radios, high-powered engines, and switches to turn off rear lights. A "crash car" containing armed gang members instructed to "take out any heat" caused by police during an operation was part of the planning.

Hijack gangs operate in and around major freight centers. Trucking associations in many states have banded together in programs called "Hijack Alert" and "Radio Alert" as a means of self-protection. This alert is similar to a chain-letter type of operation in that dispatchers, upon being notified of a truck theft, alert other dispatchers, and through broadcasts to association members often are able to locate trucks and cargoes.

On a smaller scale, thieves follow delivery trucks of all kinds, particulary into alleys where deliveries are generally made. During unguarded moments or carelessness, thieves enter these trucks and steal whatever the contents might be. Bolt cutters are used to cut chains or locks if necessary. These thieves need only minutes to operate. Confederates drive a car alongside the truck at which time merchandise is hurriedly transferred from the truck to the thieves' car and the criminals speed off. Trucks and/or contents are also stolen from insecure parking areas or stopping places during stops or at other unguarded times.

Federal laws relating to thefts from interstate shipment cover not only the theft or embezzlement of goods or chattels moving as, or a part of, an interstate or foreign shipment, but the obtaining of such items through fraud or deception (U.S.C., title 18, sec. 659). The unlawful breaking of a seal or lock, the entering with intent to commit larceny of a conveyance containing such shipments in transit is also a violation (U.S.C., title 18, sec 2117). A federal crime is also committed in cases involving the purchase, receipt, or possession of such goods by any person with knowledge of its stolen character (U.S.C., title 18, sec. 659).

Confidence Games, or Bunco

Confidence games are generally classed as the "short con" or the "long con" ("big con"). The "short con" game is generally one involving a short, speedy bunco attack with little or no preparation. This confidence game generally employs one or two operators, many of whom are content with small profits. These operators are known as "mass-production" con artists compared with the thieves who work the "long con" for big profits. In the "short con" the operator makes a quick "score" and promptly disappears. In the "long con" bigger profits are the goals. The "long con" operators regard the "short con" bunco artists as the "punks" or "pikers" of the confidence "profession." The "long con" operation requires a buildup of the victim's confidence, which may take several days or weeks. In a well-managed confidence game, swindlers may outnumber their victim by three, four, or five to one. The "long con" is now running afoul of stricter interstate laws, income taxes, and gambling permits.

In combatting the con artist, who on many occasions operates throughout the United States and in foreign countries, the bunco squads of major police agencies are in regular contact with one another around the country and, through *Interpol,* with agencies in other nations. Interpol (International Criminal Police Organization), with headquarters at St. Cloud, on the outskirts of Paris, acts as a clearinghouse for information on international criminal activities. A special bureau has been created within the U.S. Treasury Department and is responsible for maintaining daily contact with the General Secretariat of Interpol and with the other 104 affiliated foreign countries.

Bunco or confidence games are swindles *(thefts)* in which a person is cheated at gambling, persuaded to buy a nonexistent, unsalable, or worthless object, or otherwise victimized. Bunco includes the use of false pretenses, tricks, or devices intended to swindle or defraud. Con artists try to avoid arrest by selecting their victims carefully, proceeding with great caution, and, at the critical moment, modifying the basic scheme to avoid discovery. There is often a fine line separating civil disputes that are not bunco cases from criminal fraud. The difference lies in the intent of the suspect. For example, if "A" sells "B" something and then can't deliver the goods, "B" can sue to recover the loss. It's a private matter. But if from the beginning "A" never intended to deliver, this would constitute criminal fraud.

The characteristic that distinguishes the confidence game from any other fraud is that there is generally no product or service involved. The confidence game plays upon superstition, greed, or ignorance. A *bunco* game, which is a form of confidence game, often involves a false or inferior product or service. For example, crankcase oil may be used to resurface a driveway or to oil a roof instead of a good bona fide oil. Bunco may involve a misrepresentation of price or contractual obligation. For example, the bunco artist on selling the victim a fertilizer compound of supposed standard formula, uses instead a fertilizer compound composed of 96 percent sawdust and 4 percent steer manure. The original quoted price is always far from the final price demanded by the bunco operator. The terms "bunco" and "confidence game" or "con game" are often used interchangeably in discussing thefts involving either a bunco operation or a confidence game.

Basic ingredients of the confidence game

The confidence game has three basic ingredients

A conversation or approach designed to determine if the victim has enough money to make it worthwhile.

An offer of something for nothing or an appeal based on superstition.

Getting the victim to physically exhibit money.

The con artist's business is to so stimulate the interest and greed of the victim that conscience, logic, and judgment are overwhelmed. The emotional rapport between the victim, referred to as the "mark," and the con artist is used to serve this purpose. Bunco operators are high-pressure salespersons, good actors, congenial people with a good knowledge of psychology and human nature. They know how to approach a victim, how to determine financial status, and when the "sucker" is ripe for the take. The philosophy expressed in many confidence games is that there is "larceny in everyone's heart." The victim believes what the swindler says only because it coincides with her or his inner wishes—the eternal hope of getting something for nothing.

Victims in these swindles may be educated or uneducated, wealthy business or professional people. Many times they are elderly. It is estimated that only a fraction of bunco cases are reported to the police. The reason is that victims are aware that they are doing something dishonest and generally want to avoid the attendant public embarrassment and ridicule. These types of thefts are reported in some instances, however, since one cannot collect insurance for losses resulting from crime that is not reported. Swindles involving elderly victims who lose their life savings to a con artist are also reported.

An effective investigator is familiar with the many types of bunco thefts set forth below. There are many variations of these swindles.

Phony Bank Examiner Swindle This scheme is operated by three or more persons posing as bank examiners. They avoid arrest by carefully selecting their victims, proceeding with great caution, and, at the critical moment, modifying the basic scheme to avoid discovery. An elderly person is observed conducting routine business at a bank. Older people are chosen because some con artists think that they are more gullible than younger people. The victim is followed home by one of the con artists. The operator learns the victim's identity. Then the con artist phones the victim's home posing as a bank examiner investigating alleged embezzlement at the victim's bank. In the conversation with the victim, the operator succeeds in obtaining the amount the victim has in his or her account and other information. The con artist tells the victim that a withdrawal had been made from her or his account and requests cooperation to trap the dishonest employee. The caller suggests that the victim withdraw a sum from his or her account, an amount under her balance, and turn it over to another "examiner" who will redeposit it after noting the serial numbers

on the withdrawn bills. The caller warns the victim to keep the entire matter confidential and not to disclose the matter to anyone, not even bank officials since they may be involved in the "embezzlement." The victim is promised a reward of $500 or more for cooperation and assistance.

After the victim has withdrawn the money, a confederate of the caller, posing as a bank examiner, contacts the victim and takes the victim's money for checking. This contact is made either inside the bank or elsewhere as the second con artist acts as a lookout for police or bank officials. It is the last the victim sees of her or his money.

In a period of a few weeks two different gangs using the above bunco operation succeeded in swindling seven persons out of an estimated $50,000. In this instance the con artists talked their victims into withdrawing their sayings "so the money could be fingerprinted." The members of both groups were arrested, however, after their cars and license plates were described by their victims.

Pigeon Drop This bunco game is said to be one of the oldest on record. The bunco operator is usually neatly dressed and gifted with convincing conversational qualities. Upon sighting a potential victim (pigeon), bunco operator 1 will "find" a previously planted wallet in a place where the victim can observe the operator picking it up. The con artist, on opening the wallet (within the hearing of the victim), expresses surprise at its contents. Bunco operator 1 will then turn to find the victim watching and ask whether the victim saw him or her pick up the wallet. The victim will, of course, reply in the affirmative. Bunco operator 1 will then tell the victim that the wallet contains a large sum of money and will show the contents briefly.

The contents will be either counterfeit bills or some genuine bills mixed with fake currency totaling several thousand dollars. About this time, bunco operator 2 happens by posing as an uninterested person. After being consulted, bunco operator 2 will offer the suggestion that both parties attempt to find the owner and to wait twenty-four hours. The victim and bunco operator 1 are asked to put up a specified sum of money as security and good faith. Victim and bunco operator 1 are advised that if they are unable to locate the owner they are to return in twenty-four hours and collect their security and half of the money in the wallet. When the victim leaves, the bunco operators get together at a prearranged location and split the victim's money.

Pigeon Drop: Two Female Operators In this case the victim is stopped on the street and engaged in conversation by bunco operator 1, usually about the high prices of merchandise or about family problems. Bunco operator 1 tells the victim that her husband or child was killed and that she has just settled with the insurance company for a large amount of money. She also tells the victim about a woman to whom she had just been talking who had just found a large amount of money in an envelope on the street. She adds that it must have been lost by a gambler as it contained betting markers as well as money.

Bunco operator 2 arrives and acts disturbed with bunco operator 1 for telling the victim about the money. Bunco operator 2 then states that she works in the vicinity and that she will go and ask her boss what to do with the money. Bunco operator 2 leaves and returns in a few minutes and states that her boss had counted the money and that there was $10,000 (this amount varies) in the envelope along with the betting markers. She says that her boss would be afraid to claim it, as the money undoubtedly belonged to a gambler. Bunco operator 2 states that her boss told her to share the money with everybody who knew of the find. But first, the boss said, these people must show money of their own to show that they know

how to handle money (also to show good faith).

One of the bunco operators then goes with the victim to her or his bank, where the victim withdraws cash and returns to the place where the other bunco operator is waiting. Bunco operator 2 then sends bunco operator 1 to a fictitious address to see her boss to get her share of the money, after showing her own money. Bunco operator 1 returns in a short time, excited, and shows bunco operator 2 what appears to be a large amount of money as her share. Bunco operator 2 then asks the victim for her money to show the boss. Bunco operator 2 leaves with the victim's money and returns shortly, telling the victim that it will be necessary for her to go after her own money. The victim is instructed to go to a certain address and ask for a certain person and receive her share of the money. He or she goes to the location given, but is unable to locate the address or the person. When the victim returns to where the bunco operators were, they are gone and so is the money.

In one case the victim, accompanied by a con artist, withdrew cash from her Seattle bank. An alert teller, sensing a possible swindle, switched on the bank's hidden camera. Seattle police immediately obtained photographs of the suspect the same day and forwarded copies airmail to the Los Angeles police as a routine matter. The following day the Seattle bunco operator was apprehended in Los Angeles trying to commit the same bunco game and wearing the same dress! It appeared that the photograph and the bunco thief may have arrived in Los Angeles on the same plane.

Latin American Charity Switch This bunco game is conducted by a Mexican, South American, or Latin American. They always speak Spanish. Victims are Spanish-speaking Americans. In this racket the victim is stopped on the street by bunco operator 1 and asked if he or she speaks

Spanish. If the victim replies, "Yes," bunco operator 1 engages the victim in conversation in Spanish and asks for assistance in locating a fictitious person (usually a real estate agent or attorney).

At this time, bunco operator 2 joins the conversation as if also trying to locate the fictitious person. Bunco operator 1 then reveals that her or his father is dying in Mexico (or from wherever he or she alleges to be). The operator says that years ago the father stole a large sum of money in the U.S.; and that when he returned to his native land, he became very rich. The dying father had gone to a priest and confessed the theft. The priest insisted that before he could give the father absolution, it would be necessary to return the money to the United States and distribute it to charity. Bunco 1's father told her or him to locate the fictitious person and give that person the money to distribute for him.

At this time, bunco 1 displays what appears to be a large amount of money and states that it is $10,000 or $15,000. Bunco 1 then asks the victim and bunco 2 if they will assist him or her to return to the father before he dies and tell him of his successful mission. Bunco operator 1 then tells the victim and bunco 2 that if they can show that they have money of their own, she or he will give them all the money for them to distribute to charity. The bunco operators then ask the victim to obtain money to show good faith. One of the bunco operators goes to the bank with the victim.

Afterwards, the bunco operators will suggest that they all go to the nearest church and pray. When they get to the church, bunco 1 takes the victim's and bunco 2's money and places it in a handkerchief with his or her money, tying it up in a bundle with tight knots. All three go into the church to pray. While they are in the act of praying, handkerchiefs are switched. The victim is given the switched handkerchief. When the victim opens the handkerchief she

or he finds folded newspapers. The bunco operators, meanwhile have departed.

Jamaican Bunco This bunco game is operated by two male blacks (bunco operator 1 uses a phony foreign accent). Victims may be men of all races and ages. In this scheme bunco operator 1 approaches the victim on the street (or in a store or bus depot, for example) and tells him that he is a sailor off a boat. This boat has just arrived from Jamaica, West Indies, or from another foreign port. The bunco operator tells the victim he is looking for a hotel and gives him the name of a nonexistent hotel. The second bunco operator walks by and bunco operator 1 tells the victim to ask him about the hotel. The victim calls bunco operator 2 over and bunco operator 1 gives him the name of the hotel, stating he is looking for that hotel because there is a woman there to whom he has already given $50 for a "party." Bunco operator 1 then displays a large roll of what appears to be money and says he wants to have a good time. Bunco operator 2 tells bunco operator 1 he should put his money in a bank before someone robs him. Bunco operator 1 says his captain on ship told him not to put money in the "white man's bank" because it was a "one-way deal" in this country—a black can deposit money but cannot draw it out.

This statement puts a white victim on the defensive and he will usually reveal the location of his bank account and attempt to convince bunco operator 1 that his captain's advice is erroneous. In the case of the victim being a black, all three may berate the white race; however, the black victim becomes vulnerable because he wants to prove that he, as a black, can conduct business the same as a white can. Often bunco operator 2 tells the victim that bunco operator 1 is ignorant and will lose his money, and suggests that they (victim and bunco operator 2) could get some of his money if the victim would bet bunco operator 1 that he could withdraw money from the "white man's bank," and draw money out to prove this to bunco operator 1. The black victim often "bites" on this.

In the case of the white victim, bunco 1 bets him a considerable amount that he cannot withdraw cash from his account. In both cases, after the victim has withdrawn his cash, bunco operator 2 tells bunco operator 1 that he will take him to see some women, but he had better leave his money with the victim while they are gone, because the women are dishonest.

At this point, bunco 2 sometimes tells the victim to keep all of bunco operator 1's money and that he will meet him later to split the money. If the victim does not seem to have enough of a larcenous inclination for that approach, the "safekeeping" angle is used. The victim is to keep bunco operator 1's money until they return. In either case, bunco operator 1 demands that the victim put his money in also. Bunco 1 then folds the bag and, at this time, a "switch" is made and a bag containing pieces of newspaper is will receive his "winnings" for proving he could withdraw money.

Bunco operator 1 produces a bag and places his roll in the bag and has the victim put his money in also. Bunco 1 then folds the bag and, at this time, a "switch" is made and a bag containing pieces of newspaper is handed to the victim. Both bunco operators then leave agreeing to meet the victim later, after they "see the women."

In some cases, a particularly larcenous victim who is willing to gamble is talked into shooting dice after he withdraws his money. (Sometimes bunco 2 and the victim agree to cheat bunco 1 in a dice game.) On the last roll, the victim loses but operator 2 suggests he write a bum check, which is gambled against bunco operator 1. The victim loses. Bunco operator 1 goes into a store to cash the check and comes running out shouting, "He's calling the police. Run!" All three run.

Handkerchief Switch　This bunco operation is often performed by fortune-tellers, card readers, palmists, and others of similar ilk. The victim first has his fortune told for a nominal fee. By skillful interrogation the operator is able to learn about the problems the victim may have and if the victim is a person of means. The operator assures the victim of the power of prayer, offering to pray and to burn candles for a price which depends upon how large a candle the victim wishes to burn. The victim is told that there are evil spirits within her or his body which cause problems and these evil spirits are caused by money. To confirm his supernatural prowess, the operator may perform a practical demonstration by having the victim bring in a raw egg and produce a black mass within the egg (by sleight of hand) representing the evil spirit. Or the operator may produce a skull within a tomato, also representing an evil spirit. After the victim is convinced his or her body does contain evil spirits, which have caused problems, the rest is easy. It is impressed upon the victim that money is the source of the trouble and that only by removing the money can she or he be rid of the evil spirit.

The victim is then told to bring in a large amount of money, the larger the bills the better. The operator takes the money and tells the victim either that it will be flushed down the toilet, thrown in the ocean, or buried in a cemetery. Occasionally the operator will ask the victim to throw the money in the ocean after placing the money in a cloth bag and sewing the ends. While the victim's attention is distracted, the bag is switched.

Diamond Switch　This type of theft is usually perpetrated by one or more persons who will enter a jewelry store pretending to be interested in the purchase of a diamond. While the salesperson's back is turned or he or she is otherwise distracted, the thief will substitute a worthless ring or stone for a genuine one. In most instances, the substitution is not discovered until after the "potential buyer" has departed.

In one case involving two separate Fifth Avenue New York jewelry stores, a well-dressed thief visited the first store to price a diamond ring, an $18,000 item. After examining the ring, she decided it was too costly. Using the diamond-switch method of operation she handed the clerk back a facsimile of the $18,000 diamond worth only $7500 and left the store before the clerk discovered the switch. Shortly thereafter, the same thief, using the same approach, visited another nearby jewelry store as a prospective customer. After looking at a $35,000 diamond she cleverly switched the $18,000 diamond which she had acquired at the previous jewelry store, for the $35,000 stone and again departed before the switch was noted.

Coin Matchers or Coin Smack This confidence game is perpetrated by two or more confederates. The confidence of a victim is gained by striking up a conversation, usually around transportation facilities After a short conversational period, bunco 1 suggests they match as to who buys a round of drinks. Other coin matching takes place at which time bunco 2 eases into the scene and all three continue to match coins. The victim is allowed to win for awhile as the stakes are steadily increased. Thereafter, when the stakes are high, the victim continually loses due to the collusion of both bunco operators.

In a variation of the above scheme, as the two bunco artists and the victim are matching coins, bunco operator 2 leaves the game to go to the rest room. While bunco 2 is gone, bunco 1 suggests to the victim that they conspire to "take" the "sucker" by always having their coins match. When the absent bunco 2 rejoins the game the new scheme is worked for a period of time. Thereafter, the second operator accuses bunco 1 and the victim of cheating and threatens to call the

police. The first operator offers $100 or whatever amount they hope to get from the victim, to the "sucker" to forget the whole thing. The victim usually comes through with something to avoid an arrest.

Short-Change Artists This type of bunco involves the manipulation of currency. A suspect hands a cashier a large bill with a request to be given change in certain denominations. After receiving the money, the operator will change her or his mind and request a different form of change. In the transfer a small bill is substituted for one of the larger ones and the complaint made that the clerk gave the bunco operator the wrong change.

A case in point involved two bunco operators who drove into a city gas station. One got out of the car and asked for a quart of oil for a lawn mower, giving the attendant a glimpse of a $10 bill. He then replaced the bill in his hand (out of sight of the attendant) and gave the victim a $1 bill. The attendant gave him $9.40 in change. The suspect then produced another $10 bill and a second $1 bill and asked for a $20 bill. The attendant gave him a $20 bill and then realized that he was being short changed. The suspect insisted he gave the attendant two $10's and left without returning the money. A check of the register revealed the loss.

Till Tap This type of larceny is generally committed by two or more "customers" on a retail business (service station, variety store, dry cleaning shop, supermarket, or other store). The method of operation may vary somewhat but usually a theft is committed in those locations where there is limited personnel. One of the suspects usually diverts the clerk or employee's attention with a request for assistance. While the clerk is assisting the "solicitous customer," a confederate of the suspect seizes this opportunity and proceeds to the location of the cash register and steals from the "till." In this operation, the suspect may either open the cash register, take the money, and run, or wait for the clerk to open the register and then take the money and run.

Art Fraud In this fraudulent scheme the bunco artists, operating under a veneer of culture and respectability, deal in art works they claim are legitimately worth millions. Paintings are forged and passed off as originals by famous artists. The ring follows two ploys: sale of fake or misrepresented art to individuals, and the use of similar items as collateral to secure loans from financial institutions.

Three-Card Monte This ancient bunco game is also known as "three-card trick" or "find the lady." It is a short confidence game played with three cards—quite often two aces and a queen. The operator first shows the bystanders these three cards and their relative positions in his right hand, with the backs of the cards toward his palm. The operator then lays them out on a flat surface, face down, and moves them around rapidly. Thereafter the operator asks someone to bet on the location of the queen. Even skilled gamblers can be beaten by the speed at which the operator moves the cards about (or palms the queen).

The operator, in some variations of this game, works with a confederate who helps to attract bettors by apparently beating the operator. The confederate bends one corner of the queen card, which permits her or him to pick the queen and "beat" the operator at this game. This induces bystander bettors to place bets on an apparently "sure thing." The operator however, with the little finger, straightens out the corner of the queen card and bends the corner of one of the other two cards. The victim places his bet on the newly bent card only to discover that the bent-cornered card is not the queen.

Shell Game In this bunco operation, three hollow halves of English walnuts are most often used with a small rubber ball or pea. It is similar to the three-card monte game in operation. The ball is placed under one of the shells. Thereafter the shells are moved around so speedily that it is not possible to keep sight of the key shell. A bet is then made as to the location of the ball. The ball is often not under any of the shells when the bet is made. After the victim has made his bet, however, the ball or pea is cleverly replaced under one of the two shells that the victim did not bet on. Again, like the three-card monte bunco, the operator may work with an accomplice. The accomplice may "con" the bettor into "taking" the operator. In such cases, the operator permits the accomplice and victim to win and when the stakes are sufficiently high, the operator can palm the ball or pea and beat the bettor.

In both the shell game and three-card monte, the shells or cards are carried easily on the person of the operator and either game can be set up quickly with the aid of a box or crate wherever or whenever the operator sees an opportunity.

Greenhorn Swindle Usually this bunco game is operated by two or more persons who pass themselves off as real estate brokers or investors. They operate from rented office space to impress their "clients." Real estate is offered at attractive prices—real estate that the operators do not own. The property is generally privately owned land, federal land, or national park property. Clients are shown this property by phony salespersons. After a period of negotiation, the victim buys the property and signs the papers. However, when the victim attempts to take possession of the newly purchased property, he or she discovers the swindle. The office through which the victim did business has meanwhile been vacated.

Money-Making Machine Despite the incredibility of this bunco scheme, it is still practiced and is often successful. In this operation, the operator, using a box of medium size planted with money, demonstrates to a victim a method of converting $1 bills or pieces of paper into $20 bills. The small denominations or pieces of paper, after being inserted through an opening on one side of the box, are cranked out the opposite side in $20 denominations. After several demonstrations of this "get rich scheme," the operator succeeds in selling the machine to the victim for a substantial amount of money.

Phony Horse Parlor This confidence game operates on the principle of "past posting." The perpetrators (usually several) set up a Western Union type office as their front, claiming to have a direct wire to the major race tracks. The fake office has several employees. A mark (victim) is taken to the "Western Union" office and introduced to a supposed "contact" there. The victim is thereafter permitted to win several small bets on tips telephonically furnished by the contact at this office. Following a big buildup of a "sure thing," the victim is induced to make a large bet on a particular race. An operator then invites the victim to a bar for a drink and to await the outcome of the particular race. When the race is over, the victim is unable to locate anyone. The victim then returns to the "Western Union" office only to find that everyone has gone.

Creepers This bunco theft is conducted by a prostitute and her accomplice, who might be female or a male. The prostitute will make contact with a victim on the street or at a bar and thereafter go to a dimly lit or dark room to perform a sex act. While the love making is taking place, the accomplice of the prostitute will creep into the room from a hidden place of concealment and remove the victim's valuables which are usually placed on a convenient chair. When the victim discovers the loss, he is generally too embarrassed to report the theft to the authorities.

Sick Engineer This bunco scheme is operated by a person who pretends to be a seriously ill mining engineer. After making contact with a potential victim, usually near a bank, the bunco artist explains the illness to the mark (victim) and speaks of the need for hospitalization. The suspect exhibits stock certificates in a newly opened mine to the victim and expresses an immediate need for cash. After some conversation regarding the illness, the suspect succeeds in selling the stock to the victim, who subsequently finds out that the certificates are valueless.

Platinum Fraud This particular fraud demonstrates the ingenuity of con artists. In a West Coast case, the misinformation was dropped "in strictest confidence" that platinum worth $285 an ounce could be purchased for $100 an ounce. The whispered story alleged that certain parties in San Diego were in touch with certain parties in Tijuana who had a lot of platinum bars smuggled in from iron curtain nations. This story was planted in various places across the United States by a well-organized band of con artists. This propaganda resulted in netting more than $500,000 from many victims, some of whom travelled thousands of miles to San Diego to "get in on the deal." One purchaser from a Midwestern city paid $120,000 for two 600-ounce bars of the supposed platinum but it turned out to be tin (selling for approximately $1.62 a pound). Suspects involved in this case were charged by the FBI with fraud by wire (long-distance telephone calls to the victims and telegraphic transfer of funds), conspiracy, and causing interstate travel in furtherance of a fraudulent scheme.

Talent Fraud This type of scheme involves such gimmicks as phony screen tests and interviews, promises of success, stardom, and pledges of jobs in the entertainment industry. Like most rackets, the scheme has many variations. The method of operation follows the same pattern. Promotors usually conduct an advertising campaign through newspaper ads or mail solicitations seeking new talent — "no experience necessary." They promise by either suggestion or outright lying that their services will lead to the victim's being employed in motion pictures, television shows, commercials, modeling, song writing, script writing, stunt work, or other areas of the entertainment industry. The promises made by the operators can't be kept. These operations have no affiliation with the industry's unions.

Interviews with applicants are conducted in a plush office with affable personnel or at a rented hotel suite. A cash outlay is requested of potential candidates for either screen tests, photographs, lessons, training, promotional expenses, security deposits, contracts, or other fees for promised services. The fees for some of the preparatory courses required vary in amounts from one hundred to several thousand dollars.

In one variation, for example, a mailing list of people with children is obtained for a selected city. Thereafter letters are sent out to families stating in effect that "your child may have the necessary qualifications for work in motion pictures or television commercials." A telephone number is provided for those parents who are interested and willing to permit their child to do this type of work. Those who respond are interviewed at a hotel suite rented by the operators. The child protégé is interviewed on a rented videotape with parents observing on a monitor in the next room. The parents are thereafter advised of the potential of their child as a star and invited back for additional tests. A contract is offered to the parents (with no guarantee of employment) for the child's services. The costs for promoting the child to producers and casting directors run from $150 to $700. The contracts invariably lead to nothing, with the operators leaving town or going out of business.

Other schemes involve a program of five or six weeks of classes for "Hollywood hopefuls" followed by a videotape screen test which allegedly will be shown to film and casting directors. The cost of this program runs around $150 for the taping and $5 a lesson. After completion of the program and waiting several weeks or months, the victim learns that the outfit has gone out of business.

Home Improvement Fraud In this bunco, an itinerant home repair worker appears at the home of a victim and offers attractive bargain home repair or improvements in such things as oiling shingles or driveway (usually using old crankcase oil), termite control or plastic siding (both phony), furnace inspection or water softeners (fake), etc. In many of these fraudulent schemes the glib salesperson assures the victim that it will cost little or nothing because the victim's house can serve as a demonstrator in the neighborhood, or the victim will receive a commission for names of prospective customers, or the victim has been selected to receive a prize or participate in an advertising plan. The "catch" is that the victim is asked to sign a contract or note against which the commission or reductions will apply. The victim's signed contract or note is thereafter sold to a financial institution and he or she is obligated to pay regardless of the fact that the commissions and bonuses never materialize.

Medical Quackery Bunco operators often prey upon people who have incurable diseases and those who dislike going to doctors. These types of victims are most prone to pay for fake remedies. The usual claim of these bunco artists is that the American Medical Association prevents their effective form of therapy from being made available to the public. Quackery claims are recognized by statements to the effect that the practitioner uses a secret formula or a machine to cure a disease; guarantees of curing; or that the method is better than surgery, x rays, or drugs.

Operators in these frauds use equipment with dials, batteries, electric cords, and meters, as well as phony case histories and testimonials. Some of the phony equipment that has come to the attention of authorities include

Plug-in vibrating cushion said to cure varicose veins and arthritis.

An electric padded rolling pin to melt fat.

A small tube containing radium. Patient's blood is treated in tube and then reinjected into body. Device supposedly cures mental retardation.

Concentrated sea water said to cure cancer, diabetes, and baldness and to "offer our bodily glands a chemical smorgasbord."

A wood and electric contrivance that bombarded a patient with static electricity (described in court as equivalent in strength to "one fly-power") said to cure all ills, provide vitamins and minerals, and improve meditation powers.

A magnetized copper bracelet supposed to cure wearer of arthritis and rheumatism.

The Badger Game This bunco game is a blackmail operation conducted by a male and female. The female (usually a prostitute), operating out of a bar, entices a patron of the bar to her room or apartment. Subsequently she gets the victim in a compromising situation at which time her real or pretended husband appears on the scene. The "indignant husband" threatens arrest at which time the woman advises the "sucker"

that her husband is only interested in money and could be induced to drop charges if the victim would pay him. The victim in most instances is willing to pay a designated sum to avoid an alleged arrest and the attendant publicity.

Auto Sales Frauds The fraudulent car dealer uses several ways of cheating customers, viz., by misrepresenting the actual purchase price of the car or by misrepresenting the interest charges and insurance coverage. The frequent result is that a person is obligated to pay for something she or he did not really want. The ultimate price is higher than he or she would pay through regularly established outlets.

Auto Repair Fraud Complaints involving fraudulent practices in auto repair are second only to mail fraud according to the Consumer Fraud Division of one state attorney general's office. In bogus practices utilized by some service stations and auto repair shops, motorists are lied to about what is really wrong with their cars. Such practices revolve around information given to the customer that the tires are leaking, defective, or in need of replacement; shock absorbers should be replaced (after squirting "leaking" oil on them); brake fluid is leaking and seals needed; radiator hose needs replacement; fan belt is defective; car has loose tie rods; etc. Lies are told about the car's condition with regard to the engine or transmission.

One fraudulent operator, in discussing bogus tire practices, stated, "You poke the tire between the tread (with a sharp pointed tool). It's easy, like cutting butter, and you can't see the hole, and the customer never sees a thing." When the tire is immersed in water, air bubbles obviously show a leak. The result—the tire is taken off to check and an alleged inside seam pointed out to the customer as defective and not repairable. The spare tire obtained from the rear trunk (away from the customers view) is likewise jabbed with the same sharp pointed tool. This often culminates in the purchase by the customer of one, two, or possibly a set of tires if the others are worn.

Other fraudulent practices involve the escalating of estimates by repair shops after taking the engine apart which results oftentimes in doubling the original quoted repair cost; misinforming the customer as to needed car repairs when in reality only minor work is required; charging for parts not replaced, or for new parts when old ones or cleaned original parts are used.

Another fraudulent practice involves overcharging on auto repairs. Repairs are often quoted from a manual of repairs. If the manual rates a certain job as nine hours and the repair actually only takes one hour, there is generally no way that most customers know this. The amount charged is consequently based on the nine hours called for in the repair manual to the detriment of the car owner.

Consumer fraud often lies on the fine line between a civil dispute and a criminal violation. The difference lies in the intent of the perpetrator. In one case, a gas station attendant advised a motorist that her car's transmission was leaking fluid and needed new seals. The cost was estimated to be under $24, to which the woman agreed. Thereafter when she returned to see if the car was ready she was told that there would be an additional $300 in repair work. When the victim demanded the station to limit the repair to the seals, she was told that they would not put the transmission back in the car—that it was unsafe. The police, on contacting the station, were told that the transmission was out of the car and being replaced. A subsequent inspection by an officer from the bunco squad disclosed a layer of road grime covering the transmission and bolts indicating that it was never disassembled. Armed with testimony from the victim and police, plus photographs of the car and transmission, the city attorney took the case to court. The matter was dismissed—the judge ruling that it was a civil matter, not criminal.

Police use various techniques in combating fraudulent auto repair practices. Undercover officers and previously inspected cars are used to ferret out bogus practices. Suspected auto repair shops or those chosen at random are checked. The cars used are of all ages and prices are taken to suspected garages to see if mechanics honestly point out the defects or suggest defects that don't exist. In one Los Angeles police case, for example, a repair bill was presented to an undercover officer for a rebuilt engine when absolutely nothing had been done. Other repair bills presented to officers working this detail listed charges for rebuilt engines when in fact used engines were installed.

Credit Card Frauds Most states have criminal code provisions making it a misdemeanor or felony to unlawfully acquire, possess, alter, forge, use, etc., a credit card for the purpose of obtaining goods or services with intent to defraud. Credit card rings involve thieves that steal, forge, and resell credit cards. Cards are stolen from mailboxes, or obtained in burglaries, robberies, and other larcenies. Stolen or forged cards and identity papers are often funneled in by small-time fences from thieves, prostitutes, dishonest cashiers, and attendants of every service trade.

Gangs operating credit card frauds are known to transfer stolen cards across the country in a matter of hours in order to increase the time lag in detection. In many cases, after obtaining a credit card, a thief will immediately purchase big-ticket items and either sell the merchandise to a "fence" or quickly return it for a cash refund, generally before the victim realizes the card is lost. Computerized credit card systems are now being widely used to signal invalid cards and unusual spending habits.

In January 1971, laws making it harder for someone to use a stolen credit card went into effect. Under an amendment to the Truth-in-Lending Act, all new credit cards issued in the United States after January 25, 1971, are required to bear some type of sure identification, usually a color picture or a signature. The same amendment also provides that no credit card holder can be held responsible for more than $50 of unauthorized purchases by someone using a lost or stolen card.

Miscellaneous Funds and Swindles In addition to the frauds and swindles mentioned above there are hundreds of other fraudulent schemes perpetrated daily on the unwary public. Frauds such as crooked gambling games, false advertising, marriage buncos, so-called business opportunities, and franchise frauds are widespread.

Federal laws applicable in bunco and confidence games

In federal law the following sections of the United States Code may be of assistance in the prosecution of these types of offenses.

Frauds and Swindles (U.S.C., title 18, sec. 1341)

Fictitious Name and Address (U.S.C., title 18, sec. 1342)

Fraud by Wire, Radio, or Television (U.S.C., title 18, sec. 1342)

Interstate Transportation of Stolen Property (Property Section, Transporting Persons Section, U.S.C., title 18, sec. 2314)

Frauds and Swindles (U.S.C., Title 18, Sec. 1341)

Whoever, having devised or intending to devise any scheme or artifice to defraud, or for obtaining money or property by means of false or fraudulent pretenses, representations, or promises, or to sell, dispose of, loan, exchange, alter, give away, distribute, supply, or furnish or procure for unlawful use any counterfeit or spurious coin, obligation, security, or other article, or anything represented to be or intimated or held out to be such counterfeit or spurious article, for the purpose of executing such scheme or artifice or attempting so to do, places in any post office or authorized depository for mail matter, any matter or thing whatever to be sent or delivered by the Post Office Department, or takes or receives therefrom, any such matter or thing, or knowingly causes to be delivered by mail according to the direction thereon, or at the place at which it is directed to be delivered by the person to whom it is addressed, any such matter or thing, shall be fined not more than $1,000 or imprisoned not more than five years, or both.

Case Illustration In this instance of mail fraud, two Los Angeles men advertised a fake travel contest in a national magazine. The pair promised free trips to Hawaii and Acapulco to persons responding to the advertisement. A postal inspector estimated that more than 57,000 persons answered the advertisement. Participants in the contest were mailed letters and "winners certificates" telling them to send a $25 deposit within ten days to confirm their prize. Over 10,000 persons mailed in their deposit.

Fictitious Name or Address (U.S.C., Title 18, Sec. 1342)

Whoever, for the purpose of conducting, promoting, or carrying on by means of the Post Office Department of the United States, any scheme or device mentioned in section 1341 of this title or any other unlawful business, uses or assumes, or requests to be addressed by, any fictitious, false, or assumed title, name, or address or name other than his own proper name, or takes or receives from any post office or authorized depository of mail matter, any letter, postal card, package, or other mail matter addressed to any such fictitious, false, or assumed title, name, or address, or name other than his own proper name, shall be fined not more than $1,000 or imprisoned not more than five years or both.

Fraud by Wire, Radio, or Television (U.S.C., title 18, Sec. 1343)

Whoever, having devised or intending to devise any scheme or artifice to defraud, or for obtaining money or property by means of false or fraudulent pretenses, representations, or promises, transmits or causes to be transmitted by means of wire, radio, or television communication in interstate or foreign commerce, any writings, signs, signals, pictures, or sounds for the purpose of executing such scheme or artifice, shall be fined not more than $1,000 or imprisoned not more than five years, or both.

Interstate Transportation of Stolen Property (U.S.C., Title 18, Sec. 2314)

1. **Property Section.** Property was stolen, converted, or taken by fraud; valued at $5,000 or more; transported in interstate or foreign commerce; transporter had knowledge property was stolen, converted, or taken by fraud.
2. **Transporting Persons.** Scheme to obtain money or property by false or fraudulent pretenses; property valued at $5,000 or more; persons are transported, caused to be transported, or induced to travel or to be transported as a result of false representations; travel is in execution or concealment of the scheme.

Investigation of Thefts

Thief catching often hinges upon the officer's thorough knowledge of the legal aspects of theft, types of thefts, methods of operation used by thieves, and the many varieties of swindles used to defraud the unsuspecting public. For example, an alert officer will know that car thieves or auto parts thieves will roam areas where vehicles are heavily parked, dark residential areas, public parking lots, rear of bars and cafes, and store parking lots. An investigator should know the activities of jewel thieves, the fact that wealthy people are "hunting grounds" for jewelry and fur thefts, that travellers, vacationers, swank resort hotels, jewelry salespersons, etc., represent victims or places to perpetrate thefts, and that many types of criminal activity can be typified by the actions of a loiterer. An investigator should be familiar with the fraudulent schemes and methods of the "bunco" or "con" artist, the shoplifter, and the pickpocket, as well as the identities of "fences" and receivers of stolen property. Officers should make it their business to know, study, and recognize the many known thieves and other types of criminals who operate in their communities.

In the investigation of theft cases it is seldom that crimes against property demand any immediate action by investigating officers. They should, unless the crime is in progress at the time of arrival, proceed slowly in the investigation. Probably the most important phase of this or any other criminal investigation is to protect the crime scene. It is a primary duty. This admonition is suggested in view of the ever present possibility of obtaining latent fingerprints or other physical evidence from a crime scene area. The fact that a criminal was present and operated in the particular area is sufficient reason for concentrated effort at a crime scene. Every bit of available information that might lead to the identification and apprehension of a suspect should be gathered.

As an initial step in the handling of a theft complaint the officer should look for clues that will aid in establishing the fact that a crime has been committed, as well as evidence that will aid in the identification of the perpetrator. In reporting the theft, loss, or recovery of any personal property, a complete list and description of all stolen or missing property, no matter how trivial, should be obtained. The minimum description of an article listed in a crime report, wherever possible should cover the quantity of the article, kind of article, physical description (color, shape, model, style), material (gold, silver, wool, etc.), condition (including age), value (present market value), trade name, identifying serial numbers, initials, or marks.

When it is an officer's responsibility to describe stolen property in the report, the officer must remember that what is recorded may later be written down in the notebooks of other officers. How accurate and complete the descriptions are will make their job either easy or difficult. It may mean the difference between recovery and nonrecovery of the stolen property.

Theft investigations should also be concerned with

Victim's occupation and residence (motel, private residence, service station, etc.).

Securing basic information from complainant and witnesses—verifying and evaluating that data prior to conducting any investigation.

Establishing ownership, actual owner, or person having property in possession at time of theft.

Signs of forced entry, method of entry and exit.

Determining date and hour of the theft or period when theft occurred or where property was last seen: for example, between 6 P.M. and 10 P.M., or between 6 P.M. 3/7/79 and 8 A.M. 3/9/79.

Corpus delicti of the offense.

Location of property immediately prior to the theft (basement of residence, dresser drawer, master bedroom, garage); if from vehicle, glove compart-ment, trunk, rear seat; if theft from person, inside coat pocket, rear pants pocket, handbag, etc.

Articles taken and those valuables left behind by the thief.

Other places in which stolen property had been previously stored.

Crime itself. Was crime possible?

Reason for placing the missing or stolen property in the location described.

Safeguards employed or the absence of safeguards where logically indicated.

Identity of the first person who discovered the loss; how it came to the person's attention; and whether this was the logical person to make the discovery.

Identity of the persons who knew the location of the property and those having access to same.

Persons acting suspiciously or persons observed carrying any suspicious objects at or near the scene.

Movements of persons having access prior and subsequent to the loss in cases where the time interval is reasonably short.

List of absentees in commercial establishment.

Proof of ownership, custody, or responsibility.

Examination of all documents and other evidence connected with the property such as bill of sale, date of purchase, identity of seller, and receipts.

Suspects named by the owner or others; descriptions and reason for suspicion (unusual behavior, financial straits, maintaining standards of living inconsistent with means, etc.).

Reconstruction of the theft from facts obtained.

Method of operation used in the particular theft.

Survey of scene for physical evidence, latent fingerprints, items left behind, discarded, etc.

Obtaining of elimination fingerprints and/or palm prints from persons known to have handled the property stolen.

Interviewing persons residing at or near the theft for any possible information of value they might be able to furnish.

Determining whether any similar offenses have occurred in the general locality of the theft occurrence.

Broadcasting of any information pertinent to case as soon as possible. This may include a tentative identification of suspect(s), car used, direction or departure taken, probable loot in possession, and any other information that might lead to the apprehension of the responsible person(s).

Photographing and sketching the crime scene where necessary.

Placing of stop notices with state identification bureaus and the FBI's National Crime Information Center (NCIC), Washington, D.C., as well as with local record bureaus.

Connecting and clearing similar unsolved crimes.

In cases of bunco and confidence games, complete details of all conversations and transactions between victim and perpetrator should be obtained. In addition, descriptions of all persons who were in any way connected with the swindle and the part taken by them. All documents, equipment, machines, etc., that were used by suspects should be secured as well as any evidence of any similar crimes by the same person or group.

Processing of property taken in thefts

Recovery Techniques Stolen property may be sold on the street, in pawnshops, to secondhand dealers, to receivers ("fences"), or at auctions where it is usually left on consignment. When property is sold on the street there is no record of the sale or trade unless the buyer, at a future time, pawns or leaves it at an auction to sell.

When reports concerning stolen property are received by a police agency, the stolen articles are indexed in the department's stolen property file which acts as a stop against the property. The various sections of the property file often include a breakdown by: serial number, description, property name, and a personalized item section. A pawnshop bulletin (listing property pawned) is also disseminated by some departments as an investigative aid. Many police departments have a separate detail that processes all reports from gun shops, pawnshops, secondhand dealers, and auction and junk dealers.

Crime by Computer

Computer fraud, also called electronic data processing (EDP) theft or computer crime, is a relatively new field in which enterprising thieves are figuring out new ways to use computers to commit their crimes. Once perpetrated, computer-related fraud is extremely difficult to detect. Today, many people have a very high level of understanding of computer capability which they sometimes use to illegal advantage. Computers are in use everywhere. They are very vulnerable to fraud and are activated by code or card. With the code or password and a typewriter-like device attached to an ordinary telephone, it is possible for a thief to call the computer and give it orders. A code or password can be stolen or a card can be duplicated. Employees can be careless with the secret password. Some sophisticated systems, however, use voiceprints or fingerprints for identification. These afford safeguards against fraudulent maneuvering.

In an East Coast case, a bank employee programmed the bank's computer to divert more than $120,000 from customers' accounts into the accounts of two co-conspirators. A programmer at another bank instructed the computer to deduct sums of money from many accounts and credit the money to him under false names.

In another case, a bank employee embezzled over a million dollars to finance his gambling by manipulating the bank's computer and by juggling deposits and withdrawals. This individual admitted to extensive gambling and betting on horse races and professional basketball. In another case, an operations manager of a large business firm tricked a computer system he had devised, and embezzled approximately $1 million. The computer accounting system was revised as a result of the investigation when this case came to light.

As with other phases of a business, the most effective way to preserve the integrity of a data processing system is through distinct separation of duties, proper internal controls, and meticulous auditing of procedures and results.

Strict accountability must be maintained for all "machine time" to prevent or detect unauthorized use of computers. Where employees operate remote equipment, special codes should be established that permit the computer to verify proper authorization before accepting or giving information. These codes must be changed frequently. The system should be tested periodically to determine any unauthorized attempts to gain access to data. An audit by a computer specialist is a most important element of any computer system in order to identify areas of weakness.

Computer fraud investigations involve such checks as vulnerable areas, security of premises, building access, computer floor access, computer room access—who has access to what, where and under what conditions? Other checks are monitoring of periods room, identification of all hazards, check of personnel and organization, and check of users against terminals. Computer fraud is now of deep concern to police agencies, business, and the banking industry. The FBI has trained experts who specialize in computer fraud. These experts conduct training seminars for police, prosecutors, and businessmen in order to combat this new area of theft.

RECEIVING STOLEN PROPERTY

Under most of the modern statutes, receiving stolen property has been made a substantive offense and is generally classified as a felony. Some state statutes make this offense a felony or a misdemeanor. In California, for example, Penal Code, section 496, provides that where the district attorney or the grand jury, in the interest of justice, and where the value of the property does not exceed $200, may specify in the accusatory pleading that the offense be a misdemeanor.

In the investigative field, the term "fence" is the popular name for the receiver of stolen property—one who purports to "buy" the goods from the thief. The elements of the *receiving statute* generally include the following:

1. The property received must have been obtained by some form of criminal act (larceny, embezzlement, false pretenses, robbery, extortion).

2. The receiver must have had knowledge of its stolen character.

3. Fraudulent intent to deprive the owner thereof.

The professional thief often steals in collaboration with receivers or "fences" in order to sell the goods. Some receivers make known their wants to the thieves they deal with. The thief will then seek out the particular items in quantity, kind, and quality desired and sell to the receiver. Many receivers obtain stolen property for $0.25 or less on the dollar depending upon the amount of "heat" generated by the theft.

In one major "fence ring" uncovered in Southern California, the group was determined to cater to burglars throughout California. The Los Angeles center served as a collection and distribution center for stolen merchandise valued at hundreds of thousands of dollars. The ring specialized in expensive jewelry, furs, clothing, appliances, and a wide variety of other property prior to their arrest by the Los Angeles Police Department. The enterprise was so prolific that the ringleader used mink stoles for rugs on the floors of the headquarters, and other expensive furs to line the dashboard of his automobile.

In another instance, officers received information of a pending burglary at a metals company. Staking out the location, the officers were able to videotape the crime in its entirety with the use of a small hand-held videotape camera; it was a type that can take pictures with a minimum of light. Three of the suspects were videotaped forcing a gate at the metals company and loading their truck with thousands of pounds of bronze ingots.

With the video camera still rolling suspects were followed to another metals company where the officers filmed a fourth "performer" purchasing the stolen ingots. At that point the officers moved in and arrested three of the suspects on charges of burglary and grand theft, and the fourth on the charge of receiving stolen property.

Through police "fence" operations financed by federal grants received from the Law Enforcement Assistance Administration (LEAA), many police agencies working with the FBI have had considerable success in recovering millions of dollars worth of stolen property. Under the Crime Control Act of 1976 the LEAA is given specific directive from Congress to bolster antifencing operations.

In these bogus fencing operations, the officers posed as big-time buyers and receivers of stolen property. Operations were set up in warehouses, hotels, or other premises. Fictitious names were given to these "fronts." Because of newspaper advertisements or the fact that the word was out on the street, thieves gravitated toward these police-operated outlets with all kinds of stolen merchandise. The operation gave an apparent assurance to the thieves that they had a safe "fence" where they could sell their stolen goods.

Property sold had been taken during muggings, armed robberies, auto thefts, purse snatchings and burglaries. Each transaction was videotaped and recorded. *Entrapment* was not a factor since those who made deals directly with the bogus fencing operation did so *after* stealing the goods. Each day the stolen merchandise bought by the police fencing operators was trucked from the ring's headquarters to police buildings. Investigators and their staff worked an average of twelve hours a day making notes on each transaction, cataloging the stolen goods, trying to find the owners, investigating leads to unsolved crimes, and drawing up arrest warrants.

During these fencing operations, a wide variety of stolen merchandise was purchased at ridiculously low prices. Items sold by the thieves included: TV sets, radios, sound recorders, cameras, credit cards, antiques, kitchen appliances, automobiles, guns, typewriters, calculators, savings bonds, and government checks. In one of the operations, a group of thieves was identified with a car theft ring capable of handling 300–400 cars per month.

Culmination of the bogus fencing operations usually came after many months with a party arranged to celebrate the success of the fencing ring. Many of the thieves dressed for the occasion arrived at the "party" in expensive cars; some wore tuxedoes. As the thieves would pass into an adjoining room, teams of uniformed officers arrested their startled "guests", informed them of their rights, handcuffed them and carted them off to jail. The thieves included men and women "customers." Often, the sellers of stolen property thought they were doing business with a Mafia operation.

Investigation of Receivers of Stolen Property

The investigation of receivers should be concerned with the following:

Having an audit made of the records if possible.

Establishing proof that the property was stolen or embezzled.

Determining when the property was received by the accused.

Reviewing records concerning the method of payment, amount, place of payment, receipts, etc.

Circumstances of the receipt of the property: From whom? When?

Location in which the property was found. Was it concealed? Had it been retransferred?

Proof that the accused knew the property was stolen.

The nature of the property, its value, the name and business of the owner.

The identity of the person from whom the property was purchased. A youth? A person with a criminal record? A person who would not likely have property of this character?

The purchase price. Was it far below its regular price or value?

Whether the resale was at an extremely low price.

Evidence of hiding, concealing, or destruction of identifying marks.

Failure to keep proper records.

Statements given to police regarding the acquisition of the stolen property.

Conduct of the accused when informed the property was stolen.

Federal law in receiving violations (U.S.C., title 18, sec. 2315)

(a) Property was stolen, unlawfully converted or taken.
(b) Property so taken in the amount of $5,000 or more was transported in interstate of foreign commerce.
(c) Person receiving, concealing, storing, bartering, selling, or disposing of the property in the amount of $5,000 or more knew it was stolen, unlawfully converted or taken.
(d) Person receiving, etc., did so while the property was moving as or was a part of or constituted interstate or foreign commerce.

Pledging Violations, Pledging of Property, U.S.C., Title 18, Sec. 2315)

(a) Property value at $500 or more was stolen, unlawfully converted, or taken.
(b) Such property was transported in interstate or foreign commerce.
(c) It was pledged or accepted as a security for a loan.
(d) The pledging or acceptance of such property as security for a loan was done while it was moving, etc., in interstate or foreign commerce.

--- SUMMARY ---

Theft is a popular name for larceny. It is a crime of opportunity and the most common of the crimes for gain. The corpus delicti of theft is the felonious taking and carrying away of the personal property (not real estate) of another, with the specific intent to permanently deprive the owner of it. The term "theft" encompasses larceny, embezzlement, obtaining of property by trick or device (bunco crimes), and the obtaining of property by false pretenses. The corpus delicti of each method of theft is similar yet distinct.

The crime of grand theft (felony) usually relates to the value of the property taken (fair market value), the area where the theft occurred (e.g., from the person), and the specific items. Other types of theft are misdemeanors. Thefts include such crimes as pickpocketing, shoplifting, confidence or bunco crimes, white-collar crimes, and computer frauds. Receivers or "fences" of stolen property are a problem to the police because they provide the thieves with an outlet to sell stolen goods. It has often been said that if "fences" could be eliminated the theft problem would be greatly curtailed.

REVIEW QUESTIONS

1. Define the term "larceny."
2. What type of crime is a white-collar worker more apt to commit?
3. In terms of confidence or bunco crimes, what is meant by a "short con"—and a "long con?"
4. How is grand theft distinguished from petty theft?
5. Name five bunco or confidence games that every investigator should know.
6. While larceny and embezzlement are both thefts, what is the difference between these two offenses?
7. A pickpocket is known by many other names. Name five.
8. Is larceny classified as a crime against the person or a crime against property?
9. Name some of the devices that a professional shoplifter might use?
10. Indicate the differences between larceny, burglary, and robbery.

WORK EXERCISE

1. Prepare a list of confidence or bunco crimes most prevalent in your area.

2. Library assignment. Research available data on computer fraud [also known as computer crime and electronic data processing (EDP) theft].

CHAPTER 14

Fraudulent Checks

Check Passers

Fraudulent check passers or "paperhangers" as they are known in criminal parlance, use their pens as weapons to "hold up" people. The typical bad check passer is nonviolent and nonaggressive. Check passing has a strong appeal for these persons, who often pride themselves as being among the "aristocracy" of the criminal underworld. The chance for making an immediate profit by passing bank checks attracts a number of check forgers. The community views them as harmless people, yet their crimes are among the most costly. According to many chiefs of police, the third most common complaint received by police is insufficient fund checks and forgeries. It is probably the easiest major crime to commit. Fraudulent check passers seek to disarm their victims by creating a most favorable impression through pleasant talk, appearance, and polite manners. Each step in the fraudulent operation has a planned purpose. Preliminary remarks or actions are frequently diversionary tactics calculated to avoid suspicion of real intent. He or she frequently has a story to tell—"car broke down," "bank closed," "unexpected guests," "just found a new apartment," etc. When a check passing takes place, it will bear all the earmarks of a legitimate transaction. Contrary to general belief, the victim in forgery cases is not wealthy. Forgers find small checks easier to pass.

Bad check passers are notorious schemers. Many of them live high and spend as fast as they can get money. The prime targets of this criminal are usually super-markets, department stores, service stations, and bars. Other victims of this offender are independent grocery stores, drugstores, liquor stores, restaurants, hotels, jewelry stores, and most any retail business. The preferred time that check passers operate is usually from the time the banks close until they open, particularly Saturdays and Sundays when they are closed. Checks are often obtained from automobile car seats, glove compartments, or over the car's sun visor.

Other documents are obtained from apartment building vestibules where mailboxes are frequently too small to hold a package of new checks, or they are "fished" out of mail slots. Careless procedures in the handling of checkbooks by office personnel have also been a source of opportunity for this criminal. During the commission of robberies, burglaries, and other thefts, thieves often take checks from the middle of a checkbook or traveler's checks as part of their loot. Thereafter, such documents are sold to a fence or fellow criminal for a price, or the thief may attempt to cash them.

Check passers are often experts at deceit. If they are "doing business" at flower shops, they pretend to be short of cash and desire to cash a check with the flower purchase. If the victim is a maternity shop, a male check passer often pretends to be buying a nicety for his "pregnant wife," and would like a check cashed. Passers may prefer rare coin or stamp shops where proprietors likewise least expect this criminal to operate. Some prefer antique shops to cash their bogus checks. After obtaining antique merchandise, the perpetrator proceeds to another antique shop and resells the newly acquired items.

A swindler often rents a car prior to a check cashing spree, obtaining the automobile under a fictitious name and using phoney identification. The perpetrator may use an extra set of license plates to prevent detection. The advent of nameplates that store employees wear for identification has been a boon to the check passer who calls employees by their first names as a method of avoiding suspicion. Frequently a check operator will visit several small stores in a selected area several times and make small cash purchases at the same hour for many days. After frequent visits of this kind, the swindler is looked upon as a store customer. Thereafter, this schemer will present a substantial check that the store will honor in the belief that the person is a regular "customer."

Check passers may don a uniform, wear working clothes, coveralls, the hard hat of a construction worker, carry a lunch box, or wear other various types of misleading apparel. Since many workers are paid weekly, check passers recognize this fact and seek to cash their "salary" checks at that time. The amounts of checks these "workers" cash are usually odd amounts, e.g., $89.25, $72.54, $61.45, etc. Sometimes their checks may bear notations to disarm people, e.g., "For Rent," "Paid in Full," "On Account," "Uncle John's Birthday," "For Services Rendered." etc.

They are often familiar with the laws of the states in which they operate. For example, in those states where it is a misdemeanor to pass checks up to $50, these offenders will try to circumvent the felony section by cashing many checks under this figure. Some states will total the amounts of the checks passed, however, and charge the perpetrator with a felony count where the total amount so justifies. Bad check passers rely on a lack of alertness by prospective victims, failure to require adequate identification, and a dismissal of prosecution when restitution is made.

In one instance a drugstore cashed a check for a check artist which was signed "U. R. Stuck." In another case a check operator passed his bogus check at a busy market bearing the signature "I. B. Smart."

Another example of check-passing deception involved two suspects who walked into a mobile homes firm on the pretext of making a purchase. One of the suspects, on a variety of ruses, lured the manager out of his office while his confederate remained behind and stole as many unsigned checks as he could find. The following day the same two suspects again returned to this mobile homes firm and again the manager was drawn away from his office leaving the second suspect alone inside the office. At a predetermined time, a third suspect walked into the local bank and attempted to cash a forged check in the amount of $6400 stolen the previous day from this firm's office. According to the plans of this group, any questions about the validity of the check were to be answered by a member of the ring left behind in the firm's office prepared to tell the bank, "Why yes, the check is good." In this case, however, the assistant manager of the bank on which the checks were drawn wasn't satisfied with the first call to the mobile homes company and instructed an assistant to make a second verification call. As the assistant dialed, the man who presented the $6400 check for cash fled. The second call to the trailer firm was answered by the company's actual owner who denied any knowledge of issuing a check for the above amount.

Frequently when check passers are apprehended, they attempt to plead ignorance of any wrongdoing. They try to sell the arresting officer a story that the check was won in a gambling game, or gained by selling someone at a bar or some other place an item of jewelry. Other seemingly plausible stories are also given by these individuals to avert arrest. A fictitious name is given as the donor of a check but a residence or business address or phone number is not known. A thorough interview into the minute details of a suspect's statements generally exposes the falsity of the "story." Often a check passer (particularly an amateur), upon apprehension, swears to make full restitution as soon as she or he obtains a job or receives funds from some alleged source.

How a check writer will take advantage of an opportunity is illustrated in one instance in which a victim lost his wallet in a supermarket parking lot. The suspect who found the wallet proceeded to fill out a blank check he found in the victim's wallet. Using the victim's identification, the suspect entered the market where he proceeded to purchase a case of beer and a box of cigars totaling $9. This check opportunist presented the forged check bearing the victim's name and exhibited identification found in the wallet, viz., a driver's license, employment badge, and a Diners Club credit card. With this identification and the carelessness on the part of the salesperson to compare the description on the license with that of the suspect, he succeeded in cashing a check for $50.

In another instance, a check passer, after observing a private ad in a local newspaper for a used automobile, visited the owner, and "tried out the car." Thereafter the suspect gave the original owner a $1250 check at which time he was given the pink slip (evidence of ownership) and keys to the car. Immediately after taking possession of the vehicle, the suspect sold it to a third party and moved from his place of residence.

Problems of Identification in Cashing Checks

There is no form of identification credential which cannot be fraudently duplicated or obtained by deceit, ruse, payment of a fee, finding, or theft. Some forgers are members of organized rings that supply them with phony or stolen identification. Operators of these rings sometimes have a printing plant that can turn out counterfeit checks complete, in some cases, with magnetically encoded account numbers that allegedly will pass through a bank's computer.

Generally speaking, there are two forms of identification that are accepted by most retail businesses: a primary identification and an accompanying one or more forms of secondary identification. There are exceptions, of course, such as a traveler's check provided it is countersigned in the presence of the person cashing the check and the signature compares favorably with the signature on the check.

An example of a primary identification generally recognized would be a motor vehicle driver's license if the signature and address on check and the driver's license agree. Other items to be checked are age, nationality, color of hair, height, and photograph where such are included on the license. Other primary identification might be an employment card with signature of firms or agencies such as the telephone company, U.S. government, city, county, and state government cards with photographs and identification data.

A primary identification would not include a temporary driver's license or learner's permit. Post office box numbers are usually not considered acceptable addresses for check cashing. Any identification that is accepted should be noted on the back of a check. A secondary, or supplemental, identification to the primary identification would be a bank passbook, current gasoline credit card or other current recognizable credit cards, bills addressed to the customer, automobile club card, library card, certain employment I.D. cards if adequate identifying information is contained, postmarked letters to the customer, and other identification material.

To counteract the bad check passer, to assist in the identification of customers, and to reduce losses by checks, many retail stores, hotels, and banks subscribe to some of the available identification systems or adopt their own rigid procedures in check cashing. The two things that a check passer objects to are being fingerprinted and photographed. However, the public continually resents such store procedure, feeling that it is put in the same class as the criminal. Some merchants require fingerprints to be placed on the back of the checks they accept and post this notice in a conspicuous place near the check-out registers. Others cash checks only for customers who have a credit card on file with their store, limit check cashing to the amount of the items purchased, or do not accept checks.

In California, for example, hundreds of supermarkets and other retail outlets subscribe to a credit system known as Telecredit, Inc., an IBM computer verification service. This particular system has over eleven million Californians cataloged by their driver's license numbers. If a record of a forgery or notice is in its file, the computer flashes a code "2" (indicating an irregularity).

A system termed *Regiscope* is another form of protective device that other merchants utilize. The system involves a Regiscope camera which simultaneously photographs both the check and check passer. The Regiscope number is placed on the check when cashed. This system identifies a questioned check with the subject who passed it, thereby practically eliminating the problem of identification.

Another system called *Regitel* is being used by department stores to detect bad checks and credit cards at the time of purchase. It is a computerized "electronic-authorization" system. Check numbers are fed into a central system that in turn warns if they have been reported stolen or come from an over-extended account.

Thumbprints are used as a means of cutting bank and business losses by check. Two of the systems using fingerprint registers are: *Identicator* (thumb signature) and *Signa-Print*. The Identicator is a device that records a check casher's thumbprint on a check without the use of ink or chemicals; thereafter, the check is processed to authenticate that the casher is the holder of the account upon which it is drawn. Signa-Print is a thumbprint-taking process which utilizes a quick drying spray on the check. Use of thumbprint register devices in banks and stores is essentially a voluntary transaction among private parties and as such has not been the subject to litigation.

Many banks now offer a service to supermarkets and other stores whereby a subscriber to the bank's program is protected against loss by fraudulent checks.

The Hotelman's Protective Association is another example of a protective system set up to protect hotel interests against the criminal element. The association operates an alert or informational system by teletype hookup. Member hotels are guarded against or can obtain information on "skips," bad check passers, and other undesirables.

The American Banker's Association (New York) *Protective Bulletin*, published by their Insurance and Protective Department, warns its association members against check artists by publishing photographs, physical descriptions, M.O.'s, handwriting specimens, whether warrant issued, and if extradition will be requested.

Recidivism of Check Passers

The check passer repeats check passing crime more than most other types of violators repeat crimes. Time and again a convicted check passer, upon prison release, reverts to swindling activity. Each arrest brings a vow of "never again," only to be broken within a short period—almost as though it were an addiction. Even during the time of institutional confinement, the check writer continually thinks only of new and better ways to swindle the public.

In one case, a convicted forger after having spent twenty-two years of his life behind bars for check passing and having been free for less than two years, was rearrested for forgery. During the time of this release, he wrote and passed fraudulent checks from coast to coast totaling $96,000. In less than a two-year period, this suspect operated under the guise of such titles and occupations as a real estate promoter, institution purchasing agent, representative of a parole board, fruit and produce owner, farmer, tire recapping business owner, seller of house trailers, newspaper publisher, government engineer, retired army colonel, apartment house owner, and auto salesperson.

In another case, a confirmed check passer spent approximately twenty-five years behind prison bars for passing worthless checks totaling less than fourteen hundred dollars. This criminal, swearing he would "never again" write another check, decided to "go the robbery route—for bigger game." Being a sixty-year-old novice robber, he mixed up a batch of mouthwash solution which a bank teller believed was nitroglycerin. The perpetrator obtained $400. In this new venture he was apprehended about a block from the bank he had victimized. After serving a few years for this robbery, this "loser" again resorted to check passing—"his first love." After passing several forged checks, the police identified and arrested this swindler who subsequently died in prison.

Types of Acts Involved in Forgery

Forgery involves the deliberate tampering of a written document for the purpose of deceit or fraud. It is an indispensable requirement that the writing be false and that if genuine, it be of legal efficacy, i.e., foundation of a legal right or liability. Handwriting examinations and expert testimony are most essential to the prosecution of check forgery cases. Forgery includes the following *two types of acts*:

Making an instrument

This includes false writing, signing the name of another without authority, making, materially altering, forging, or counterfeiting any check, bank bill, note, draft, contract, or other similar document *with the intent to defraud.*

Many people, in filling out their checks, carelessly leave space beside the numerical and word amounts. This laxness permits another word, a few letters, or numbers to be inserted. Check artists are quick to recognize this "oversight" and seize the opportunity of "doctoring" up a check for an amount much higher than the maker intended. For example, checks made out in the amounts of four, six, seven, eight, and nine are easily increased. Four can be changed to read forty or four hundred, six to read sixty or six hundred, seven to seventy or seven hundred, eight to eighty or eight hundred, and nine to read ninety or nine hundred by merely adding one or two zeros in the numerical amount and by adding the letters "ty" or the word "hundred" to the written amount. Company abbreviations may lend themselves to the fancy of a check swindler; for example, a check made payable to Martin, Inc., could easily, with pen changes, be alerted to make Inc. read Martin Ingersoll, Martin Ingraham, Martin Ingle, Martin Ingold, Martin Ingro, etc. (See Figures 14-1 and 14-2 for examples.)

Uttering a false instrument

This is to offer, put, or send an altered, forged, or counterfeit matter into circulation *with knowledge of its false character.* Proof that the check passer knew it was a forgery is essential. Questions arise as to: Did the passer commit the forgery? Did the passer forge the endorsement or write his or her own name as endorser? Did she or he pass other similar forgeries? Were other checks

Figure 14-1. A check before alteration. Note the open space to the left of the written amount and the space between the dollar sign and the first figure. *Note:* there is no code number in the lower right corner on the face of the check, because it has not been executed.

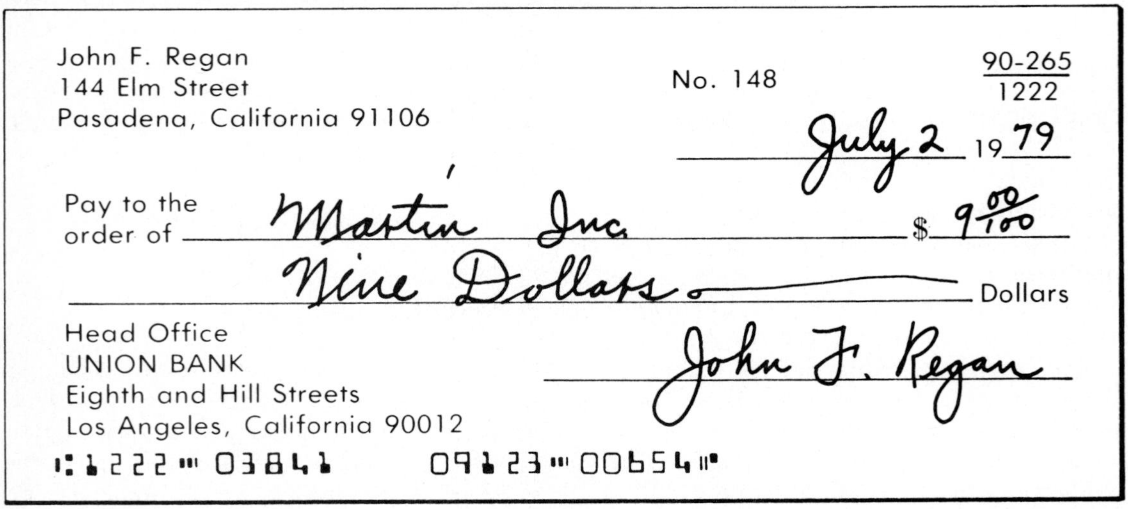

John F. Regan
144 Elm Street
Pasadena, California 91106

No. 148

$\frac{90-265}{1222}$

July 2 19 79

Pay to the order of ___ Martin Inc. ___ $ 9 00/100

Nine Dollars ___ Dollars

Head Office
UNION BANK
Eighth and Hill Streets
Los Angeles, California 90012

John F. Regan

⑆1222⑈ 03841   09123⑈00654⑈

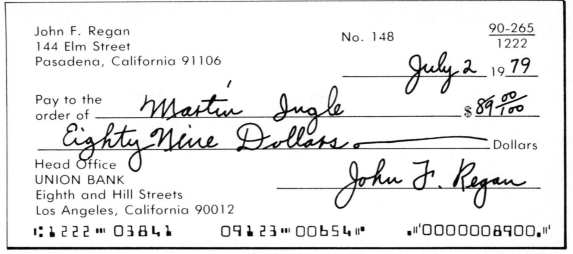

John F. Regan
144 Elm Street
Pasadena, California 91106

No. 148

$\dfrac{90\text{-}265}{1222}$

July 2, 19 79

Pay to the
order of *Martin Ingle* $ 89 00/100

Eighty Nine Dollars —————— Dollars

Head Office
UNION BANK
Eighth and Hill Streets
Los Angeles, California 90012

John F. Regan

⑈1222⑈ 03841   09123⑈00654⑈   ⑈0000008900⑈

Figure 14-2. The check in Figure 14-1 after alteration. With a few minor changes of the payee and amount of this check, the result was a profitable transaction for the forger.

found on the person when apprehended? Can goods found in passer's possession be identified with the transaction, etc.?

In both preceding instances where the check is "made or drawn" or is "uttered or delivered," the specific intent to defraud is necessary. This intent may be singular (to defraud a particular person) or the intent may be one to defraud or injure members of the public. It is a common prosecutive practice to charge both the making and the uttering of the forgery in one count although the offense does require the commission of both.

Types of Forgery and Fictitious Checks Commonly Encountered by Police

Straight forgery

This is the signing of the name of another person on business or payroll checks, as well as any document, will, note, or writing. In all cases, however, there must be an intent to defraud.

Fictitious name forgery

This type of forgery occurs where the name of a nonexistent person is signed as maker. In such a situation the officer can testify that he or she has checked the telephone directory, city directory, tax records, voting records, etc., and found no person of that name. The officer can also testify that no person of that name resides at the address given by the suspect. If a person with a similar name does reside at the address listed, that person is generally called into court to testify to the fact that she or he did not write or sign the check in question. A bank representative may testify as to the nonexistence of an account at the bank involved in the transaction.

Forgery of endorsement

In this instance, the name of the payee is forged on the check with intent to defraud. Should a person give another individual permission to sign, there is no crime. This permission need not be in writing. The fraudulent signing of a lost or stolen payroll

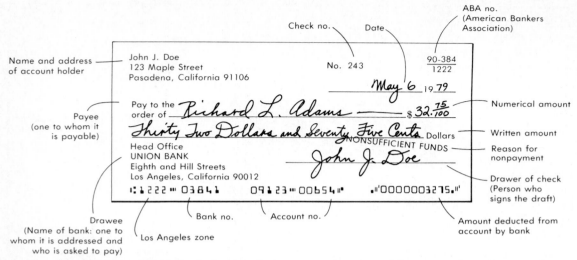

Figure 14-3. An executed check slowing the component parts and the reason for nonpayment.

check or travelers check would be classified as forgery of endorsement.

Forgery by alteration

This type of forgery includes any document, check, personal note, will, or writing on which the defendant makes some alteration in whole or in part; for example, raising the amount of a check for $8 to read $800.

Insufficient funds
or no account checks

This violation occurs when a person wilfully, *with intent to defraud,* draws or delivers a check, draft, or order upon any bank, depositary, person, or firm for the payment of money, knowing at the time that there are insufficient funds or credit on deposit; or, that there is no account in the bank on which the check is drawn. (See Figure 14-3.)

Some police departments have adopted a policy of not taking a crime report in a nonsufficient fund case where the check is less than $10, the date of the check is more than forty-five days prior to the complaint (or other time limit) or where the victim refuses to sign a form agreeing to prosecute. Other police agencies follow different procedures in processing checks of this type. The departments with such policies will take a crime report, however, in cases where the check has been stolen or forged.

Postdated check

A postdated check will also constitute a violation of the forgery statute. However, if a postdated check is given, and the defendant informs the payee at the time of delivery that sufficient funds are not yet available, there is no deception. The mere fact that the defendant fails to keep a promise to have funds available on the due date does not justify a conviction. In such an instance a civil action would be indicated.

Document Examinations

This science pertains to a minute comparison of questioned handwriting with known handwriting, the objective being to identify the writer. Handwriting is as individual in its own right as fingerprints. It is based on the fact that each person develops individual pecularities in handwriting resulting from hundreds and thousands of repeated movements of the arm and fingers. The complexity of writing is such that individual peculiarities and characteristics will appear. A document examiner can detect these characteristics and arrive at a scientific opinion. People write from habit and are not aware of the basic symbolic strokes which they put into their writing. Each individual's handwriting can be identified—provided the writing is truly representative of normal habits, written with natural speed and comfortable body posture, and if sufficient quantity exists and adequate known samples are available.

One of the first steps in the investigation of a disputed writing whether on a check, note, bills, or written instruments is to find some genuine writing with which to make a comparison. Upon locating a genuine writing and comparing handwriting, a common practice is to pick out a single letter "a," "e," "o," "t," "l," "p," etc.) and compare that particular letter wherever it appears in the questioned writing with the known writing. Thereafter, a second or different letter is noted and that too is compared (known writing against the questioned).

In conducting handwriting examinations or comparing check endorsements with signatures on driver's licenses or other documents presented, a handwriting examiner is interested in the following:

General overall form of the questioned writing (line quality, carelessness, neatness, careful preparation, misspelling, punctuation, margins, breaks in writing, added touches, and pen lifts).
Beginning, connecting, and ending strokes.
Relative height of letters.
Pressure, spacing, and letter size.
Line quality and degree of evenness.
Slant proportions.
Retracing practices.

Hesitant or halting strokes in special areas of letters.
Hooks and flourishes on letters; "t" crossings; "i" dots; formation of "o's," "p's," and capital "I's."
Formation of loops.
Use of exclamation points, underlining, and quotation marks.
Signatures. These are checked for hooks and flourishes and other peculiarities.
Attempts to "repair" or mend letter formations or numbers by overwriting or patching.
Segmentations in strokes should be noted. Hold the writing or document up to a strong light. If a stroke appears to be overlapped in a section along its length, a short stroke has been lengthened. The darker spot along the stroke is caused by ink being placed over ink.
If a check endorsement appears rather crude when compared to the signature on the identification presented, this should be a "suspicion arouser." It is extremely difficult for a skilled writer to simulate the writing of a poorly educated or unpracticed writer.
When a signature is drawn or traced, the back of the check will often bear a raised identification or a raised outline of the writing. Sometimes it is so pronounced it can be felt.

Types of document examination

The techniques used in the examination of writings involved in such criminal violations as extortion, robberies (where notes are used), kidnappings, and many other crimes are equally applicable to the examination of checks. Document examinations generally fall into certain broad classifications such as examination of paper, writing instruments, handwriting, handprinting, obliterations and alterations, forgeries, typewriting, checkwriter impressions, inks, paper, and a score of other related items. It is almost impossible to set out specifically all of the kinds of documentary examinations that can be made, or what may be disclosed through such examinations, because each piece of evidence may often present its own individual problems. Therefore, when making an examination, the document examiner considers not only the obvious aspects of the evidence but also looks for the more obscure factors that may be highly important in determining its significance.

The "no conclusion" opinion in handwriting examinations

The neutral or "no conclusion" opinion of a document examiner might result in cases where

The questioned writing was of such limited quantity that it did not reflect a substantial number of peculiarities.

The questioned writing was distorted or disguised.

The known writings were too limited in quantity or contained distortion or disguise.

The known writings consisted of letters and letter combinations that did not contain the letters and letter combinations present in the questioned material.

Caution in check investigations

A criminal investigation, as it progresses, often points to a certain person when the crime involves documents and handwritings. But, assume that the document examiner found it necessary to report "no definite conclusion was reached" with regard to a likely suspect. Investigators should at this point recognize that this type of report might serve as a "proceed with caution" signal, suggesting that careful consideration be given each incident relating to this suspect. Otherwise, the investigation might not proceed in the right direction. Could the check

passer's associate have prepared the check and tried to simulate the partner's writing? Where two or more operate as a ring, it is a common practice for one of the group to prepare a portion of the check and the second forger to prepare the balance of the document. As noted elsewhere in this chapter, a third suspect may cash the questioned check.

Check Investigations

Police departments serve as a "clearinghouse" of information relating to checks passed or issued with intent to defraud. They do *not* act as a collection agency for complainants. The police job is to gather evidence against the accused check swindler. Check cases in many departments are handled by a separate Frauds Division, Forgery Detail. The investigation usually starts after a complaint has been received arising from the return of a check accompanied by a bank rejection slip containing such notations as "lack of any account," "failure to make," "account closed," "unable to locate," "refer to maker," "uncollected funds," "payment stopped," "signature irregular," and "insufficient funds."

The police job of detecting check passers is complicated by the fact that this offense is practiced by a wide variety of types—male, female, young, and old. The offense is aggravated by the present volume of checks—$9 out of every $10 is paid by check.

The check passer constantly moves about seeking new places to exploit as well as ways to evade the law. Three victims are to be considered in these violations: (1) the person who cashed the check, (2) the person whose signature has been forged, and (3) the bank on which it is drawn. Whenever possible an investigator tries to connect a check passer with other uncleared check cases. During the course of a check investigation the investigator should

CENTER CITY POLICE DEPARTMENT

FILE NO. 79-433   DATE 2-5-79   REC'D. BY Sgt. D.A.Cole #25

SUSPECT _MASON, Howard L._ ADDRESS _1269 Main St._

RACE _W_ AGE _45_ HT. _5'11"_ WT. _175_ HAIR _Brn_ EYES _Brn_ COMPL. _Fair_

DRESS _Dk. Brn. Business Suit_ AUTO _none observed_

VICTIM (FIRM) _DIAMOND BAR RANCH MARKET_

ADDRESS _1085 Hill St. Portland, Ore._ PHONE _88-50360_

ACCEPTED BY _WILSON, George A._ DATE _2-3-79_

VICTIM CAN IDENTIFY CHECK _Yes_ SUSPECT _Yes_ WILL PROSECUTE _Yes_

MERCHANDISE REC'D. _1 Case Olympia Beer (4.80)_ CASH $ _55.20_

NAME OF BANK _Bank of America NT & SA_ BRANCH _Main Office_

CHECK NO. _115_ DATED _2-3-79_ AMOUNT $ _60.00_ POST DATED? _No_

PAYEE _BROWN, John R._ MAKER _MASON, Howard L._

ENDORSED _DIAMOND BAR RANCH MARKET_ WHY REJECTED _NSF_

OTHER WITNESSES AND/OR REMARKS _Check turned in by BROWN_
John R. (Store Owner).

CHECKS: FORM C100-14 – 1700 – 300

Figure 14-4. A type of check receipt form given to the victim when a check is taken as evidence.

Establish the corpus delicti of the check violation.

Obtain the original check for evidence. Recognize the possibility that latent fingerprints might be present on the check. Upon receipt of the questioned document place same in a clear transparent envelope before handling and furnish the victim with a receipt for the check. A sample receipt form is shown in Figure 14-4. If for some reason the questioned check cannot be obtained, arrange for a photographic or photostatic copy and advise the check holder to keep it in a secure place pending court disposition. Do not fold, bend, pin, or staple a check to a report. Identification of the check investigator should be placed on the back of the check in a corner and should contain the number, date, and officer's initials.

Record a complete description of the check in a notebook and the type of premises where the check was passed.

Interview the person(s) who actually accepted and/or approved the check. Obtain all pertinent data concerning the check transaction and the method of operation used by the check passer. Ascertain what was said by all parties present, together with complete descriptive data.

Identify and interview all witnesses who observed the check passer or talked to her or him.

Ascertain whether the check was both made out and signed by the suspect in exchange for cash or items purchased.

Inquire whether any vehicle was used. If so, obtain the year, make, model, color, and any distinctive features.

Find out if the victim was involved in any

prior dealings with the suspect. If so, gather details of all prior transactions (dates, times, purchases, identities of sales personnel, etc.) so that necessary interviews can be conducted.

Interview employees and owners of nearby stores to determine whether any similar checks have been passed in that locality by anyone answering the suspect's description.

Check names and M.O. through the police record bureau for any reference material that may be contained in the file pertaining to the suspect.

Endeavor to locate the person whose name was forged to the check in question in order to learn if the suspect was a stranger to him or her.

Secure the name of the bank witness who can testify that there is no account at the bank on which the check is drawn. Failure to find an account tends to prove that the name is forged and of a fictitious person.

Endeavor to secure evidence of other forgeries by the suspect.

Complete necessary check forms and report.

Alert surrounding law-enforcement agencies with description and M.O. of the suspect where pertinent.

Contact hotels and motels in select areas where there is indication of the suspect's possible residence.

Be alert for other possible criminal violations that the suspect can be charged with; for example, unlawful use of driver's license (where license used for identification in cashing fraudulent check), receiving stolen property, criminal conspiracy where others are involved, etc. Where a check passer prints a check in one state by use of a checkwriter and subsequently transports that checkwriter in interstate commerce, she or he could be charged with a violation of U.S.C., title

18, sec. 2314. A subdivision of this section reads:

Whoever, with unlawful or fraudulent intent, transports in interstate or foreign commerce, any tool, implement, or thing to be used or fitted to be used in falsely making, forging, altering, or counterfeiting any security or tax stamps, or any part thereof . . . shall be imprisoned for not more than ten years, or fined not more than $10,000, or both.

If a check protector or checkwriter was used, determine what kind and how it was obtained, if possible. A check through the FBI's Checkwriter Standards File may reveal the identity of the particular kind of checkwriter. A checkwriter is a machine that inscribes the amount of the check by mechanical means. The machine gives the checks an authentic appearance and makes them more readily acceptable than those that are entirely handwritten.

Submit known genuine writing of the person on whom the document is forged to the crime laboratory (in addition to any suspect's writing) so that forgery can be definitely established. Always submit as much questioned and exemplar (known handwriting) as it is possible to obtain. No amount of handwriting is excessive.

Request a search of state criminal identification and/or investigation bureau records for suspect's name and M.O.

If the suspect is not identified, request a search of the check through the FBI's National Fraudulent Check File.

Consider known narcotics addicts as possible suspects in check cases since many of them often try this means to support their addiction.

Consider burglary suspects in check investigations. Frequently a burglar obtains blank checks from a commercial firm as part of the loot. The checks are subsequently forged and passed on unsuspecting merchants often before the victimized company is aware that any of its checks are missing.

Photographs of recent prison releasees and wanted check criminals should be shown to victims and witnesses where physical descriptions are similar.

Where appropriate, prepare Ident-a-kit or artist sketch for appropriate distribution.

In the event a suspect is apprehended, ascertain who her or his close associates are; they may be accomplices in some instances. Handwriting specimens should be obtained from accomplices where deemed advisable.

On apprehended suspects, a search should be conducted (within existing legal limitations) for all articles pertinent to the pending case or that may warrant document and laboratory examinations. Such items or materials might be pens, paper, check forms, paper or pads containing indented writing, items bearing specimens of suspect's handwriting, identification cards or documents, carbon paper, checkwriter, and typewriter. Handwriting, handprinting, photographs, fingerprints, and palm prints are required as well as interrogating the suspect. Efforts should be made during this interview (if conducted) to clear up other fraudulent check matters in which the suspect may be involved. A teletype cancellation notice reflecting the suspect's apprehension should be prepared and disseminated where necessary.

Check Reports

Reporting procedures and types of forms used in fraudulent or worthless document cases are often specialized. As in all other reports, the essentials of good reporting should prevail. Check reports should include

Specific offense and code section

Case or file number

Date, time, and place of occurrence

Date and time reported

Victim's name, address, business and residence telephone numbers

Type of premises (hotel, department store, supermarket, etc.)

Names, addresses, telephone numbers, and statements of witnesses

Method used in writing the check (pen, pencil, typewriter, checkwriter)

Type of identification exhibited

What was said by all parties

Complete description of the check

Type of premises where check was cashed

Type of property obtained

Amount of loss and amount of cash suspect received

Description(s) of suspect(s) and vehicle

Reason document was not honored by the bank

Summary of the offense

For illustration purposes the following completed specimen of a type of *fraudulent document report* is set forth in order to demonstrate a report format and type of information needed (Figure 14-5).

Facilities Available in Check Investigations

Local and/or state police bulletins.

Document sections of local, county, and state crime laboratories.

Check Investigators Association.

Retail stores' protective associations.

Better Business Bureaus.

Security officers of major department stores, supermarkets, drugstore chains, oil companies, airlines, American Express Company, major credit card companies, industrial plants, railroads, gas and electric companies, and other companies or agencies with investigative staffs.

FRAUDULENT DOCUMENT REPORT

Specific Offense	CENTER CITY POLICE DEPARTMENT	Case Number
NSF Check PC 476a(b)	Reporting Department	CA 03610

NSF	RTM	Sig. Irreg.	Acc. Closed	UTL	Forged	Stolen	Fict. Print	Raised	Personal	Payroll	Money Ord.	Cred. Card
☐	☐	☐	X	☐	☐	☐	☐	☐	X	☐	☐	☐

Warrant Yes ☐ No X	APB Yes ☐ No ☐	Ident. X True Name ☐	Fict. Name ☐ True Name X	CII: Place Stop X No Action ☐	CII: Forward Record X Photo X	ACTIVE X	CLEARED ☐	ARREST ☐	UNFOUNDED ☐	INACTIVE ☐	CIVIL ☐

CAN V IDENTIFY S? YES X NO ☐	WILL V SIGN COMPL? YES X NO ☐	WAS CHECK POST DATED? YES ☐ NO X	WAS CHECK PREDATED? YES ☐ NO X	AGREEMENT TO HOLD? YES ☐ NO X	ANY PAYMENT REC'D? YES ☐ NO X

Date and time occurred 12/11/80 Mon. 1:30 PM	Location of occurrence 3456 Oak St., San Fran. Ca.	Division Detective	Date and time reported to PD or SO 12/18/80 10:00 AM

Victim's name (firm name if business) ACME LIQUORS	Residence address (business address if firm) " " " "	Residence phone -----	Business phone or address 98 24321

Person reporting offense APLIN, George (Clerk)	Residence address 621 S. Main St., San Fran.	Residence phone 98 36210	Business phone or address 98 24321

Person who accepted document REGAN, John F. (Owner)	Residence address 876 Post St., " "	Residence phone 98 42513	Business phone or address " "

Vehicle used by suspect—describe in as much detail as possible 1978 Chev. Sta. Wagon, Ca. Lic. 155KLM	Amount of loss 95.62	Amount of cash suspect received 90.00

WITNESS(ES): Name REGAN, John F.	Residence address 876 Post St., San Fran.	Residence phone 98 42513	Business phone or address 98 24321

Victim's occupation Liquor Store Owner	race	sex	age	Type of premises Liquor Store – outlying business area	Type of property obtained One-fifth I. W. Harper Whiskey

Trademarks of suspects (acts, conversation, etc.) Stated she was throwing party for eastern friends.	Identification used to pass check Driver's lic. Ca. Y123456

Was document or endorsement written in his presence? YES X NO ☐	Specify what parts, if any (face, etc.) Face	Signature of endorser John F. Regan

PEN WRITTEN ☐ BALL PEN X PENCIL ☐ TYPEWRITTEN ☐ HAND PRINTED ☐ PROTECTOGRAPHED ☐ RUBBER STAMP ☐	Sharon Lee Brown 2345 Oakhurst Ave San Francisco, Ca. (Business or personalized. Name and address) No. 105 Date: 12/11/80 Pay to the order of ACME LIQUORS (Name of Payee) $ 95.62 Ninety five and 62/100------------------------------------DOLLARS (Written amount) Bank of America, Upland Br., San Francisco, Ca., Sharon Lee Brown (Name of Bank) (City and branch) (Name of Maker)

Suspect(s)

No. 1 BROWN, Sharon Lee, 2345 Oakhurst Ave., San Francisco, Ca.

No. 2

Name	Address used	Blond Hair	Unk Eyes	5-5 Hgt.	115 Wgt.	25-28 Age	Ca. DL Y123456 Identification Number(s)	Identi-Kit Code No.

Accompanied by: Names, description, relationship, etc., of anyone with suspect(s)
WMA 30-35; 5-10; 180; brn hair; brn eyes; wearing Air Force Sgt.'s Uniform

DETAILS: Describe evidence; summarize details not given above; itemize and describe any property obtained, including serial numbers and value.
PROPERTY OBTAINED:
1. (1) Fifth of gallon I. W. Harper whiskey------------------------ $ 5.62

SUMMARY:
Female suspect accompanied by male, described above, purchased one-fifth bottle of
I.W. Harper bourbon whiskey. At time of purch. she stated she was "throwing a
party for a few friends visiting from the east;" Ca. DL No. Y123456 exhibited as
Identification. Check deposited by victim 12/12/80, ret'd 12/15/80 marked "Acc't
Closed."

How many similar checks not reported to CII?	Dates	Total amount of checks
Signature of reporting officer Charles J. Boover	Badge or Serial # #65 Det.	Signature of Supervisor approving Harry W. Wilson Lt.	Badge or Serial # 41	Date and time 12/18/80 1:00 PM

Figure 14-5. Sample of a completed fraudulent document form used in reporting check cases.

Bank special agents.

Retail credit associations.

American Bankers' Association (Washington, D.C.)

U.S. Secret Service.

Postal inspectors.

The Federal Bureau of Investigation has many facilities available to the public, such as

Monthly law-enforcement bulletin.

Typewriter Standards File.

Checkwriter Standards File.

Rubber Stamp and Printing Standards File.

Watermark file.

Ink Standards Collection.

Confidence Men File.

Prochek. This is a computer system in which the peculiarities and habits of the professional check passer are catalogued for ready retrieval. In cases where the identity of the check passer is unknown, information regarding the description, modus operandi, and check styles is quickly searched against this information "library" on known check passers.

National Fraudulent Check File. This file is a central repository for fraudulent checks passed in the United States. It is used to identify the author of bad checks. It is also used to coordinate information pertaining to fast-traveling check artists.

Identification Division. If an identification of a check passer is not made through a search of the above National Fraudulent Check File, many times an identification can be made through a comparison of the questioned signatures and endorsements on negotiable instruments with signatures on criminal fingerprint cards in the FBI's Identification Division of persons who have used similar names.

SUMMARY

Forgery includes the making, uttering, publishing, passing, or attempting to pass forged instruments as genuine—coupled with the intent to defraud. It is not necessary that any person be actually defrauded. It includes two types of acts: the making of an instrument (false writing or signing, altering), and the uttering of a false instrument (passing or giving a false instrument as a genuine one). It is a common practice to charge both the making and the uttering of the forged instrument in one count.

The identity of the person allegedly involved in check activities is the most difficult aspect to prove because the forged check is the sole basis for the investigation. Identity of the maker depends largely on handwriting examinations, although sometimes the fingerprints of the suspect are found on the document. In the investigation of check cases, modus operandi data play an extremely important role in the detection and apprehension of the check passer. Amateur check passers usually operate locally. Professional passers are recidivists who constantly keep on the move. They often have equipment or machines that duplicate and alter stolen checks as well as official identification. The strengths of a check passer are the presentation of a good image, impressive credentials, and good conversational abilities. They rely on lack of alertness by the victim, failure to require proper identification, and the dismissal of prosecution if restitution is made.

REVIEW QUESTIONS

1. In check cashing, two primary identifications are generally required. Which types are acceptable? Which are not?

2. What are the two things that a check passer most objects to?

3. What is the most important element in proving a bad check case?

4. How do amateur check passers differ from professional types?

5. Checks are usually stamped with a notation indicating the reasons for rejection when they are returned by a bank. Name five such reasons.

6. In the prosecution of check cases what type of testimony is usually most essential?

7. Forgery includes two types of acts. What are they?

8. There are six types of forgery and fictitious checks commonly encountered by the police. What are they?

9. Check passers when passing their fraudulent checks rely on three things. What are they?

10. In conducting handwriting examinations, laboratory experts are interested in many individual characteristics of a suspect's writing. Name eight.

WORK EXERCISE

From the facts of the hypothetical fraudulent check report set out below, do the following:

1. Prepare a teletype. Include all pertinent data.

2. On a report form used by your local agencies, or a facsimile of one, fill out a face sheet of the crime report. Include the necessary data that would be recorded from the facts of this case.

Facts

On Saturday, February 17, 1979, at 1800 hours, an individual representing himself as RICHARD A. MOORE approached the checkout counter of the DIAMOND BAR MARKET, 189 Baseline, Center City, and inquired of cashier JOHN R. COLE whether he could cash a payroll check in the amount of $264.60. The check was noted to have been issued by the APEX STEEL MILL, Park City, Texas, on February 14, 1979, and drawn on the Bank of America, Park City, Texas, payable to RICHARD A. MOORE. The check, No. 706, was signed by JOYCE A. HOOK, treasurer. The market checkout line at that time was quite busy.

Suspect was well-dressed, friendly, and courteous. He remarked to the cashier that he had not been able to get to the bank to cash this check and needed some money to take care of guests who arrived unexpectedly. The checkout cashier advised suspect that he would have to get an OK from

WINIFRED WILSON, the manager, and rang a buzzer. Thereafter WINIFRED WILSON came to the counter. At that time, the suspect produced a Texas drivers license B-32987, an identification card No. 640 from the APEX STEEL MILL, Park City, Texas, and a Diners Club credit card No. 885 for identification—all in the name of RICHARD A. MOORE. A local address of 1263 Chapala also was given by suspect as his temporary residence. After quickly examining the identification presented by suspect, manager WILSON approved the check, which was then cashed.

The suspect's purchases consisted of a fifth of White Horse scotch, a case of Coors beer, a carton of king size Kent cigarettes, and a box of El Toppo Corona cigars. On a hunch, cashier COLE instructed packer JIMMY SMITH to assist suspect with the purchased items to his car and quietly told the youth to obtain the license number of suspect's car. Shortly thereafter the packer returned with the license number and a description of the car, which he had recorded on a slip of paper: California 627 STG, 1979 Toyota 2-Dr. Spts. Cpe., silver grey in color, antenna on roof. The packer remarked to cashier COLE that the license plates on suspect's car "looked kind of old."

On February 26, 1979, the check presented by suspect MOORE was returned to the market by the Texas bank stamped "No Account." Thereafter WINIFRED WILSON tried to contact suspect at the local address he gave only to find that this address was a vacant lot. Neighbors in the vicinity of this address were unable to recall anyone by the name of MOORE ever living on Chapala Street, nor anyone who drove a 1979 silver grey Toyota.

Property Obtained:

One (1) case Coors Beer, 12-ounce cans	$4.50
One (1) carton Kent Cigarettes, king size	6.00
One (1) box El Toppo Corona Cigars	6.50
One (1) fifth White Horse Scotch	7.50
Currency	240.10
TOTAL LOSS	$264.60

Investigation Pending
Suspect Described: MWA, 45, 5'10–11" 175–180, Brn. Brn. Tanned complexion, high cheek bones, long nose, heavy eyebrows, small ½" circular scar left cheek bone under eye. Dress: Dk. Brn. suit, beige colored sport shirt, brn. shoes.

(Store employees' addresses)—Information for purposes of report:
   WINIFRED L. WILSON, manager, 345 E. Maple Drive Telephone 88-54221
   JOHN R. COLE, cashier, 850 Waterman Avenue Telephone 88-58621
   JIMMY SMITH, packer, 2164 Irving Place Telephone 88-69750

15———————Assaults

An assault is an unlawful attempt or threat to commit a physical injury to another, coupled with a present ability to inflict the harm contemplated. The crime of "assault" is separate and distinct from the offense of "battery." If such an attempt or threat is actually carried out, the offense would be a battery or more serious charge, as discussed below.

The above definition of assault should be understood before a further study of the more serious crimes against the person is undertaken. There are many crimes that branch out from the crime of assault and depend for their meaning on its definition. In some states, the placing of another in apprehension of a battery will support only a civil tort action. Other states have "degrees" of assault involving greater punishment,

such as aggravated assault, assault with a deadly weapon, assault with intent to rape, and assault with intent to commit murder.

Contrary to popular belief, assault is not an injury but a putting in fear. An easy way to recognize the difference between an assault and a battery is that an assault is an attempted battery. An overt act is essential in the case of an assault, e.g., striking at someone with or without a weapon. The crime of assault therefore is really an attempt. In *simple assault* there is no touching of the victim whereas in *felonious assault* it makes no difference— there may or may not be a contact. The term "simple assault" through popular usage has become a term used synonymously with the word "assault" in criminal law. An assault is complete when the assailant advances with intent to strike and comes sufficiently near the intended victim to induce a person of ordinary firmness to believe, in view of all circumstances, that she or he is about to receive a blow unless retreat or action in self-defense is undertaken. The intent may be inferred from circumstances. Specific intent need not be proved in the case of simple assault. The person attempting to commit the act must be able to carry it to a completion. For example, if "A" throws some object at "B" but has poor aim and the object misses B, the assault is complete because although the act fell short of its goal the ability to complete the act was present. In this instance, "A" could have completed the act except for poor aim. The essential elements (corpus delicti) of an assault are

1. Intent to do a corporal hurt to another.
2. Have the present ability to injure.
3. Make the attempt (overt act).

Assault versus battery

The crime of battery is most often associated with assault and is sometimes referred to as the completion of the act attempted in the assault. A battery is the willful and unlawful use of force or violence upon the person of another. With regard to the use of force or violence, the amount of force or degree of injury is immaterial. Any force applied that is unlawful is sufficient. The significant element is the unlawfulness of the act rather than its seriousness. Battery includes and implies an assault. An assault may not result in a battery but every battery necessarily includes an assault and is the greater offense. It is not necessary that the assailant directly apply the force: for example, one automobile driver forcing another off the road. Some courts require that the touching or laying hold of the person of another, or his or her clothes, be done in an angry, revengeful, rude, or hostile manner to constitute the charge of battery. A person may consent to an assault and battery, as in operations by a qualified physi-

cian, or when participating in a recognized sport according to established rules.

Justification and excuse in battery cases

In the furtherance of public justice, the law allows some persons to perform acts that would ordinarily be a battery. A battery necessarily committed by an officer performing legal duties or by any other person assisting the officer or acting under the officer's direction is not a crime and is legally justifiable. The following types of persons and instances are exempt:

Executing criminals legally convicted and sentenced to death

Peace officers using reasonable force in making an arrest

Preventing crimes or serious injury

Lawfully ejecting a trespasser if force is used in moderation by the owner or legal occupant

Guards and security officers in lawfully ejecting trespassers or preventing a disturbance of the peace on private premises such as theaters, buses, railroad stations, company property, etc.

Master of ship at sea when exercising reasonable control over employees and passengers.

A battery might be justified if it is in defense of the person or property of self, wife, husband, child, parent, other relative or member of one's family, ward, servant, master, or guests. Force resulting in death is justifiable only if there is real fear for one's life.

Investigation of Assault and Battery Cases

In an assault and/or battery case an officer must proceed with caution inasmuch as it is a misdemeanor that he or she has not witnessed. Emergency first aid and the summoning of an ambulance are first considerations at the scene. Any visible indications of injury such as bruises might assist in corroborating or disproving a suspect's story. The claim of self-defense must be anticipated.

The complainant who wishes to make the arrest in these cases should be advised as to a private person's arrest. The arrest must be made by the victim. The officer, after informing both parties that she or he is not making the arrest, accepts delivery of the arrestee and transports the person to court or to the person authorized to accept bail. The filing of the complaint may likewise be discussed with the person making the arrest. In some instances, the complainant may wish to discuss the matter with the prosecuting attorney. The officer should not, however, enter into any argument, take sides, moralize, or attempt to give legal advice. Where a disturbance of the peace occurs or the assault and battery continues in the officer's presence, then an arrest may be made by the officer. Police decisions to arrest are often based on such criteria as the nature of the assault, the seriousness of the injury, and the prior record of the assailant.

The victim, suspect, and any witnesses should be interviewed separately. Short statements should be obtained from each, including actions and words before, during, and after the assault and/or battery. Where physical force was not actually applied, as in assault cases, the nature of the threats or menacing gestures as well as the relative positions of the victim and suspect are of importance. If any weapon or instrument was used, a detailed description of it should be obtained and the object located if possible. Thereafter the weapon and other physical evidence should be collected and marked for future identification. The present ability of the suspect to commit the assault should be established. If a gun was used, ascertain whether or not it was loaded and capable of being fired.

Immediate response by police to assault and battery cases is recommended, since any delay may result in a serious injury to the victim. Where a suspect is believed to be harming a person, the officer has no choice but to intercede and arrest the aggressor should the facts so warrant. If the suspect has fled the scene, the crime report should set forth a complete description and that of the vehicle used (if any).

Assault Involving Both Spouses

The first effort of the investigating officer in these cases should be directed toward calming both parties in order to obtain their separate stories. Officers should be constantly on the alert for possible attack by either party in these situations. Determine at the outset of such cases whether the complaint is of a civil or criminal nature. In many instances the officer may be able to reason with the involved parties and effect a peaceful settlement. If this is unsuccessful, either party should be advised of his or her right to make a private person's arrest and the procedure in filing a formal complaint. It should be noted that since either side will not hesitate to use the officer, it is advisable not to take sides or enter into any argument.

In calls where there is a traumatic injury committed upon the spouse, the officer may consider such factors as the attitude of the spouse and reluctance to testify against her or his mate. Other situations calling for police action should be handled wherever a violation is indicated and the offense is of a serious nature. Calls involving custody of children are matters properly within the court's jurisdiction. When a child's health or morals are endangered, however, the officer may take any necessary action to protect the child.

In order to illustrate the extent to which complaints involving both spouses can go, the following examples are set forth. In one instance of an alleged assault by the husband against his wife, the woman contended that her husband threatened to "punch her in the nose." The victim's husband when queried by the officer as to why he had threatened his wife replied, "Because she burned my steak." Needless to say, complaints of this sort should not take up the court's time when a little calm reasoning frequently may return such a situation to normalcy. In this incident, the wife was also insistent on filing a complaint against a deputy since "he didn't arrest my husband."

In another domestic complaint, in which an officer responded to a call by a frightened homemaker, the officer was confronted at the front door by an intoxicated man armed with a rifle which he pointed at the officer's head. After some fast talking, the officer succeeded in calming the man and disarming him. In such a situation the officer has to use great discretion and treat each statement the person makes as if that person would carry it out.

In another instance, a police officer, on parking his police car in front of a complainant's home in response to a domestic disturbance call, was met by a burst of rifle fire which knocked out the police car's headlights and punctured its windshield. Fortunately, none of the shots injured the officer. The officer immediately radioed for assistance. While the officer waited for additional police assistance, the suspect kept firing his rifle in the direction of the officer and threatened to kill his children if the wife, who had slipped out of the house, did not return. While one officer talked with the suspect, two other officers entered the suspect's house through a rear door in an effort to disarm him. As the two officers approached the suspect, he turned and began firing at them. Both officers took immediate cover within the house. Thereafter, the suspect fired another shot. Silence followed. This shot turned out to be an attempt by the suspect to take his own life.

Felonious Assaults

A felonious assault is regarded as a compound assault. There are many kinds of assaults in this category. Some assaults require only a general intent—assault with a deadly weapon. Others require a specific intent—assault with intent to commit murder. The particular offense chargeable in felonious assaults depends upon the results of the act committed. For example, a single blow may result in the charge of assault, battery, mayhem, manslaughter, or murder depending upon what happens to the victim. The jury or judge (if no jury is involved) may find the defendant guilty of any offense necessarily included in that for which the suspect is charged or for an attempt to commit the offense. Where the substantive crime of robbery, for example, is not supported by the evidence, an attempt to commit robbery is a lesser included offense for which a conviction may obtain if established by the evidence.

Many of the so-called aggravated assaults are statutory felonies. Aggravated assaults are "assaults with intent" crimes and differ somewhat from state to state. A type of aggravated assault would, for example, be an unarmed robbery involving the use of strong-arm methods such as "mugging" or "yoking." This type of crime is participated in by two or more suspects. The victim is generally attacked from the rear. One of the suspects places a stranglehold on the victim's neck while one or more accomplices kick, strike, or stab the victim, removing all valuables and often leaving the victim critically injured.

Statutes in many states impose greater punishment where the assault is made with a deadly weapon. Figure 15-1 illustrates a variety of confiscated weapons, many of which could be listed in the category of deadly weapons. It has been construed by the courts that almost any instrument can be considered a deadly weapon or instrument,

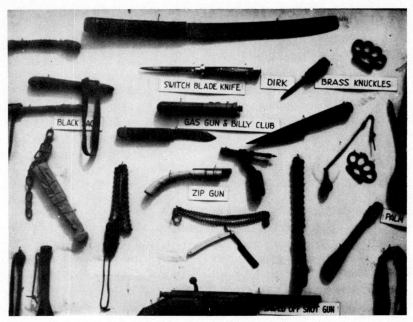

Figure 15-1. Confiscated weapons taken from various suspects. Included are several types of blackjacks, a switchblade knife, brass knuckles, a zip gun, a sawed-off shotgun, a combination gas gun and billy, razor, a dirk, and a piece of chain.

dependent upon how it is used. For example, a beer bottle or chair, although designed for lawful use, may be used as a bludgeon, club, or dagger and become a deadly weapon. In the case of a gun, however, it must be loaded unless the intent is to use the weapon as a club. Other statutes provide felony punishment for assault with caustic chemicals, drugs, or poisons. A number of states have statutes that impose felony punishment for assaults on peace officers, fire officers, or by convicts against their guards. California, for example, provides special penalties for assault with intent to commit murder, assault with intent to commit rape, sodomy, mayhem (maiming, mutilation or disfigurement), robbery, grand larceny, and assault with intent to commit any other felony.

Protection of the scene is probably one of the most important phases of an investigation of any criminal offense. Whether the pa-

trol officer later becomes the investigator of the offense or is protecting the evidence for another investigator, the officer's actions at the scene are very important to successful prosecution. The importance of this phase of an investigation is illustrated in the following assault with a deadly weapon case.

The victim and a woman friend were seated at a bar counter one night when a friend of the woman friend approached them and exchanged pleasantries. At this time, the younger woman was invited to join them for a drink. While the three of them were drinking and conversing, the suspect, who had been drinking with two other individuals, approached the trio and invited the young woman to dance with him. She declined the invitation despite the persistent pleas of suspect. As these requests and denials continued, the victim casually turned around and remarked to suspect—

"Why don't you leave her alone, she doesn't want to dance with you." After these remarks, the victim returned to his drinking and turned his back on suspect. At this time, the suspect drew a pocketknife from his pocket, stabbed the victim in the back, and walked back to his drinking partners.

The victim thereafter told his companion that he had been stabbed. He rose and fell face downward on the barroom floor, the knife still in his back. A waitress, in rendering first aid to the victim, placed a wet bar towel over the area of the wound, the towel covering the knife, which was in a half-closed position. The victim at the time was wearing a sport shirt.

The investigating officer summoned to the scene observed the victim lying face down on the floor and learned of the knifing from witnesses. He immediately called for additional assistance and an ambulance. While awaiting the arrival of this help, the officer interviewed several witnesses at the scene who identified the suspect who was placed under arrest. The officer during this preliminary investigation zealously interviewed witnesses in an effort to locate the weapon used in this offense, unaware that it was still in the victim's back. One of the serving people, on overhearing the officer's inquiries regarding the location of the weapon, proceeded to the victim and unobservedly removed the towel and knife from the victim's back. She then walked over to where the officer was standing and turned the knife over to him as a cooperative measure.

At the time the officer observed the victim lying on the floor with the bloody bar towel over the wound in the victim's back, the towel had a flat appearance. There was no pyramid or tent-shaped appearance to the towel which would suggest that a knife or other instrument was still protruding from the victim's back. In reality, however, the knife, after being thrust into the back of victim, half-closed, gave a flat semblance

to the towel. The victim fortunately survived this attack because the knife blade had missed vital areas of his body.

In this example, the action of the server in removing the knife from the victim's back broke the chain of evidence, thus affecting its admissibility. Of particular significance was the lack of protection of the victim's body and the crime scene and the failure to observe the actions of the serving person.

Investigation of felonious assault cases

While the investigation of the more serious assaults parallels that of simple assault and assault and battery cases, the felony crimes involve more in-depth investigation and are set forth below. In the handling of felonious assaults, the officer is justified in holding any person whom she or he has reasonable cause to believe may be involved. The investigator must obtain all the facts relative to the complaint. The order of investigative steps will, of necessity, be based on existing facts. The following investigation should be undertaken:

Determine if a crime has been committed. If so, what specific crime? Establish the corpus delicti of the offense.

Protect the crime scene. The court will want to know where items of evidence were found, who found them, and the condition of the evidence.

Identify and locate witnesses (the person who discovered the crime and witnesses who may have information — even hearsay information can be of assistance). Keep witnesses separated so that their statements are their own observations and accounts.

Identify and arrest the person responsible, if possible. Determine whether a "fresh pursuit" would be of value or if the suspect is still in the vicinity.

Summon any needed personnel and/or equipment.

Initiate a radio broadcast of the suspect's description (and vehicle, if one used) and where the suspect has fled. The following identifying data should be broadcast expeditiously:

Type of crime

Location of occurrence

Time of occurrence

Number and descriptions of suspects

Direction the suspect took on leaving the scene

Whether suspect was on foot or in an auto

Description of vehicle, if used

Description of weapon used.

Speed in broadcasting the above data is essential. A suspect's vehicle traveling 40 miles [65 kilometers] per hour will cover nearly 1½ miles [2½ kilometers] in two minutes. A *supplemental broadcast* should include additional information such as—a detailed description of the suspect, his or her clothing, and vehicle.

Render first aid or obtain medical help if needed. If the inflicted injury is serious, obtain a dying declaration from the victim. Prevent the body from being touched by unqualified or unauthorized persons (whether the victim is dead or alive).

Closely observe the crime scene. It may disclose obvious items such as the possible weapon used, broken articles, blood, scuff marks, overturned furniture, trampled ground, or smaller physical evidence in the nature of buttons, pieces of torn fabric, skin, hair, etc., where the victim fought with the assailant.

Begin interviewing the victim and witnesses with the suspect's first-known act and recording successive actions and words used before, during, and after the assault. What was said by whom and what were the relative positions of the victim and suspect?

Obtain professional evaluation of injuries from attending physician (if one called) and a copy of the medical report.

Photograph, sketch, make notes, and measure before moving or collecting items of evidence. Photograph injuries if possible (color photographs are preferable).

Ascertain reputation of both victim and accused for peacefulness or quarrelsomeness (useful to refute possible plea of self-defense). Determine whether there have been any previous threats, prior difficulties, and quarrels between suspect and victim. Obtain details.

Obtain victim's clothing for laboratory examination, particularly where there was physical contact between the suspect and victim. Also obtain the suspect's clothing if the suspect is apprehended.

Determine the method of operation used by the suspect. Record the unusual features of the crime that are most likely to recur from one crime to the next, e.g., the suspect asked victim for match, invited victim to room to have a drink, posed as talent scout or census taker to gain entry, etc. With regard to the force used, the report should indicate such facts as—slapped and twisted arm, slugged, choked.

Describe with particularity the weapon used. For example, if a knife was used, describe it as follows: 4-inch [10-centimeter], white-handled hunting knife; note the brand name and where it appears on the blade.

Inform suspect, if apprehended, of legal rights, prior to any interview. The fact that the suspect was advised should be placed in the officer's report. A search of suspect's person and effects for items of evidence would likewise be in order.

Where an assault is committed by means of blows from a club or blunt instrument, particular efforts should be directed toward locating the item used, as well as information that this precise instrument was used. The finding of blood, pieces of skin, or hair would tend to connect the instrument used. Hairs and fibers can be important evidence in assault cases, i.e., where a victim fought with an attacker. Fibers from suspect's clothes may be found and can be identified in much the same manner as hair. In some instances, only a few strands are needed to identify a fabric and trace it to a certain textile manufacturer. Always consider the possibility that the felonious assault might result in a charge of murder or manslaughter should the victim die within a year and a day in most jurisdictions. In California, the law provides that the death of the victim must occur within three years and a day after the stroke received or the cause of death administered for it to be considered either murder or manslaughter.

When crimes both against property and against persons are committed involving the same victim and suspect, specific reporting forms are utilized by many of the larger departments and are referred to in the initial report, e.g., see robbery, vehicle, or theft report, etc. In these situations, additional reports are made by investigating officers.

Federal Law: Assaults

The federal laws relating to assaulting or killing of federal officers and assaults on certain foreign diplomatic and other official personnel is found in U.S.C., title 18, secs. 111, 112, 1114, 1751, and 2231.

Section 111
Whoever forcibly assaults, resists, opposes, impedes, intimidates, or interferes with any person designated in section 1114 while in the performance of official duties or on account of the performance of such duties.

Section 112
[Assaults on certain foreign diplomatic and other official personnel.] Whoever assaults, strikes, wounds, imprisons, or offers violence to the person of a head of foreign state or foreign government, foreign minister, ambassador or other public minister, is in violation of the law of nations. The use of a deadly or dangerous weapon in the commission of the above acts calls for increased penalty and/or fine.

Section 1114
[Assault on or murder of any of the following federal officers (see sec. 111 above.)]

Any judge of the United States
Any United States attorney or assistant
Any U.S. marshal or deputy, or person employed to assist such marshal or deputy
Any officer or employee of the Federal Bureau of Investigation
Any postal inspector
Any officer or employee of the Secret Service
Any officer or employee of the Drug Enforcement Administration (DEA).
Any officer or enlisted person of the Coast Guard
Any officer or employee of any U.S. penal or correctional institution
Any officer, employee or agent of Customs or Internal Revenue, or any person assisting an officer in the execution of duties
Any immigration officer
Any officer or employee of the Department of Agriculture or the Department of the Interior designated by the Secretary of the Department to enforce any act of Congress for the protection, preservation, or restoration of game and other wild birds and animals
Any employee or officer of the National Park Service

Any officer or employee in the Field Service of the Bureau of Land Management

Any employee of the Agricultural Research Service, formerly Bureau of Animal Industry, of the Department of Agriculture or any employee of the Department of Agriculture designated by the Secretary of Agriculture to carry out any law or regulation, or to perform any function in connection with any federal or state program or any program of Puerto Rico, Guam, the Virgin Islands of the U.S., or the District of Columbia for the control or eradication or prevention of the introduction or dissemination of animal diseases

Any officer or employee in the Bureau of Indian Affairs

Any officer or employee of the National Aeronautics and Space Administration who is directed to guard and protect the U.S. under the administration and control of this Agency

Any security officer of the Department of State or the Foreign Service

Any officer or employee of the Department of Health, Education, and Welfare designated by the Secretary of Health, Education, and Welfare to conduct investigations or inspections under the federal Food, Drug, and Cosmetics Act while engaged in the performance of official duties, or on account of the performance of official duties

Section 1751

This section involves presidential assassination, kidnapping, and assault, and includes the President of the United States, the President-elect, the Vice President, or, if there is no Vice President, the officer next in the order of succession to the office of President, the Vice President-elect, or any individual who is acting as President under the Constitution and laws of the United States.

Section 2231

Whoever forcibly assaults, resists, opposes, prevents, impedes, intimidates or interferes with any person authorized to serve or execute search warrants or to make searches and seizures while engaged in the performance of duties as a federal officer or on account of the performance of such duties.

SUMMARY

In simple assault cases it is important to recognize that the crime of assault is separate and distinct from the offense of battery. Assault is merely an attempt or threat which, if carried out to completion, would become a battery or a more serious charge. Many crimes emanate from the crime of assault. Some examples are battery, aggravated assault, assault with a dangerous or deadly weapon, assault with intent to commit rape, and murder. Aggravated or felonious assaults are an important part of several crimes. Investigation generally focuses on the means used and the act committed. These become the determining factors of the charge brought against the accused. A single blow, for example, may result in the charge of assault and battery, mayhem, manslaughter, or murder, depending upon what happens to the victim. Many of the aggravated assaults are statutory felonies and differ somewhat from state to state. In many felonious assaults the jury or the judge (if a court trial), may find the defendant guilty of any offense necessarily included in the crime for which the subject is charged or for an attempt to commit the offense.

In a large majority of assault cases the victim generally knows the suspect and can furnish information necessary to effect her or his apprehension. Investigation of assault cases should follow good basic investigative procedures such as those set forth in this chapter.

REVIEW QUESTIONS

1. What is the corpus delicti (essential elements) of an assault?
2. In what way does the crime of assault differ from that of battery?
3. Explain what is meant by the term "felonious assault."
4. When is a battery legally justifiable?
5. What is meant by the terms "mugging" or "yoking" in aggravated assault cases?
6. In order for a felonious assault to result in a charge of murder or manslaughter, what is the period of time within which a victim must die?
7. What are the elements (corpus delicti) of an assault with a dangerous or deadly weapon?
8. Why is an immediate police response to assault and battery cases usually recommended?
9. Tire irons, beer bottles, fingernail files, pillows, and automobiles are examples of objects that have been held to be dangerous weapons. What are the criteria used when such articles are deemed to be dangerous or deadly?
10. A felonious assault may be classified as mayhem. What is the crime of mayhem?

WORK EXERCISE

There are many special types of assaults that are set out in the penal code that involve specific intent. After reviewing the penal code sections on assaults, prepare a list of types of felonious assaults which require specific intent.

CHAPTER 16 – Death Investigations

The classification of deaths into homicide, natural, suicide, and accidental is derived from ancient customs and legal procedures. The goal of this classification is to assign "responsibility" for the death in a moral and legal sense. Because of the difficulties that often arise in the determination of the cause and manner of death, it is necessary that all officers become familiar with the fundamental problems and procedures involved in various types of death cases.

Homicide

Homicide is the killing of a human being by a human being. The word "homicide" is used to describe all taking of human life by human act or agency. All murders are homicides but not all homicides are murder. For example, one may take the life of another by accident, in self-defense, by negligence, by lawful execution of a judicial sentence, or as the only possible means of arresting an escaping felon. In other words, homicide may be justified or excusable. Homicide, therefore, is not necessarily a crime. It is a necessary ingredient of the crime of murder or manslaughter. Homicide may be classified as *felonious* (murder and manslaughter) and *nonfelonious* (justifiable and excusable). Murder and manslaughter are subdivided in most states. For example, murder may be first or second degree and manslaughter, voluntary or involuntary. In most jurisdictions, to support the charge of murder or manslaughter the death must follow within a year and a day after the stroke received or the cause of death administered. By statute in California, death must occur within three years and a day after the stroke received.

Murder is generally considered the most infamous of crimes and is subject to much notoriety and publicity. Experts estimate that 20 percent of all reported deaths warrant an official investigation into the cause of death. In many cases, it is extremely difficult to determine the cause of death or to detect a murder without a complete autopsy and an investigation. But a thorough investigation will not always disclose the cause of death. Such methods as forced or induced heart attacks, feigned accidents, and traffic deaths have been used in the past to cover up the crime of murder. In most crimes, the victim is usually a major source of information. However, the investigation of a death is hampered due to the fact that the victim (deceased) is unable to furnish any information. Murder is very commonly a crime of passion, and is not committed by "criminal type" persons. A major consideration when investigating death is always whether the situation is murder, suicide, accidental, or natural death. Crime statistics bear out the fact that in most killings the victim and the killer are members of the same family, relatives, or otherwise known to each other and that the majority of murders are done with guns.

Homicide Division

Most of the 40,000 separate law-enforcement agencies in the United States do not have a specialized homicide detail functioning as such within their department's organizational structure. In smaller agencies, it is not practical or necessary to have a separate homicide detail. The chief and/or a limited number of officers quite often specialize in criminal investigation and perform most of the duties that a detective division as such would otherwise conduct. The formation of a separate homicide detail (or other specialized units) within a department generally would only be justified where there was a real need because of the volume and type of crime, where there were available personnel, and where department efficiency demanded specialized assistance.

Additional specialized units such as robbery, burglary, auto theft, worthless documents, narcotics, bunco, may be required by some departments as the need exists. Greater specialization obviously is needed in a larger force than in a small one. In the larger metropolitan departments, a homicide detail would be composed of specially qualified personnel whose assignment within a particular unit might encompass such violations as abduction, abortions, administering poison, assaults, battery, bomb threats, dead bodies, explosions, homicides, injuries, kidnapping, lynching, mayhem, missing adults, rape (except statutory), seduction, suicides and attempts, and threats of bodily harm. Regardless of the size of a particular department or the existence of a homicide detail, it is imperative that all officers have a sufficient working knowledge of homicide and related cases in order to carry out their investigative responsibility in such matters. A working knowledge of pathology and anatomy is recommended for homicide investigators.

Types of deaths investigated

The codes of various states provide for various circumstances in which a physician, funeral director, or other person shall notify the coroner's office of a particular jurisdiction when she or he has knowledge of a death that occurred under specified conditions. The code requirements generally direct the coroner's office to inquire into and determine the circumstances, manner, and cause of death occurring under the following types of conditions:

Violent, sudden or unusual deaths

Unattended deaths

Deaths wherein the deceased has not been attended by a physician in the ten days (or other specified time) before death

Deaths related to or following known or suspected self-induced or criminal abortion

Deaths related to known or suspected homicide, suicide, or accidental poisoning

Deaths known or suspected as resulting in whole or in part from or related to accident or injury either old or recent

Deaths due to drowning, fire, hanging, gunshot, stabbing, cutting, exposure, starvation, alcoholism, drug addiction, or strangulation.

Deaths in whole or in part occasioned by criminal means

Deaths associated with a known or alleged rape or with sodomy

Deaths in prison or while under sentence

Deaths known or suspected as due to contagious disease and constituting a public hazard

Deaths from occupational diseases or occupational hazards

Deaths that afford a reasonable ground to suspect that the death was caused by the criminal act of another

The coroner is generally an elected official, while the deputy coroners are selected through civil service processes. The primary duty of the coroner is to determine the cause of death. The coroner conducts a separate investigation. The coroner has an autopsy performed by a qualified pathologist (medical doctor) who is an expert in laboratory analysis. In all accidental deaths, unless the cause is obvious and well substantiated, and in all homicides or deaths from questionable causes, the coroner takes temporary custody of the property of the deceased. Most bodies, other than in obviously natural deaths, are taken by the coroner to the local morgue where an examination is conducted. If an inquest is held, witnesses are subpoenaed to testify regarding the circumstances surrounding the death. The testimony is heard by a coroner's jury (or the coroner only) who determines whether or not criminal responsibility is involved in the death. A recommendation may be made to the district attorney to file charges against the individual responsible or the coroner may present findings to a grand jury to obtain an indictment.

Role of Forensic Pathologist in Homicide Investigation

The determination of criminal responsibility in death has been developed into a specialized field of medical science called *forensic pathology*. In the last two decades a medical examiner system has developed alongside our traditional coroner's system. Many of the larger cities now have a medical examiner–coroner department. In these instances, the coroner and medical examiner operate as a team in ultimately determining the cause of death. It obviously would be ideal to have a forensic pathologist at the scene of every death that comes within a coroner's jurisdiction. However, this is not possible at this time. It is in this area (at-the-scene) of the investigation that we rely on the traditional coroner's system. There are cases wherein the burden of at-the-scene investigation rests with the police, such as homicides. Other cases present problems requiring law-enforcement officers to seek the assistance of the medical examiner or coroner.

A pathologist can assist in a homicide investigation by (1) documentation of all wounds, bruises, scratches, scars, or other marks at the time of the autopsy and (2) interpretation of the findings based on medical facts. The following questions may be answered by the pathologist:[1]

What was the cause of death?

Which wound was the fatal wound?

How long did the victim live after the injury (volitional activity after injury)?

What distance could the victim have walked or run (volitional activity after injury)?

What position was the victim in at the time of the assault?

From what direction was the force applied?

Was there evidence of a struggle or defense marks?

Was there evidence of rape?

Was there evidence of body being dragged or dumped?

What was the type of weapon involved?

What were the injuries shown: antemortem or postmortem?

Were there any characteristic signs of certain types of murders such as sex-linked crime, sadistic murder, murder by a known person or one unknown to the deceased?

Was the deceased under the influence of alcohol or any type of drug?

Were there any foreign materials recovered from the body such as bits of glass, paint in a hit-and-run case, spermatozoa (semen) in a rape case, bullet or broken knife blade?

What was the estimated time of death? How long had the victim been dead?

The role of the forensic pathologist does not stop at the autopsy table. Forensic medicine gets its name from the fact that "forensic" means to speak or argue, which thus describes medical testimony. Whether it is a criminal court or a civil court, the forensic pathologist realizes the gravity of the testimony. His or her testimony is a product of education and experience and represents an opinion. The old axiom that dead people tell no tales is false. On the autopsy table, the dead "speak" through the skill of the forensic pathologist. This is where death does delight in helping the living, and its expression is found in the courtroom testimony of the forensic pathologist.[2]

Value to the investigator in attending autopsies

During the conduct of an autopsy, an investigator can observe firsthand and ask questions pertinent to the case under investigation. The pathologist can explain the autopsy findings as they progress. As the results of the autopsy are received by the investigator firsthand from the pathologist, such information, if pertinent and requiring expeditious investigative attention, can be passed along to other investigators for immediate handling. When the investigator has a suspected weapon, comparison of the weapon with the wound can be made. The officer present at the autopsy can be the liaison with the investigation team working the case and see that all evidence is obtained during this examination. Where a coroner's inquest is conducted, the coroner's jury which is in attendance cannot hear issues of law, only issues of fact.

Ascertaining Whether a Person Is Dead

A person who is very near death will often appear quite dead to the untrained observer. Consequently, officers responding to dead

---

[1]Thomas T. Noguchi, M.D., *Homicide Investigation Syllabus,* Homicide Investigation Institute, Moorpark College, Moorpark, California, March 1970.

[2]Ibid.

body calls should, upon arrival at the scene, make a close examination of the body, being careful not to destroy any evidence. Death may be obvious because of the type of injury, condition of the body, or other facts furnished by witnesses. It is not advisable to completely rely upon the opinion of a witness or relative as to the question of death unless that person is a doctor or coroner or other trained specialist. If there is a possibility, even though remote, that the person is alive, an ambulance should be requested. First aid should be administered in such a situation pending the arrival of the ambulance. Some of the recommended methods for determining whether a person is deceased are

Pupillary reaction. The pupils of the eyes should contract when a flashlight beam is shined into the eyes.

Pulse beat. A check for a pulse may be made on the wrists or inside of the upper part of the arm.

Visible breathing. Note the movement of the chest or abdominal area.

Solar plexus. Note the action of the diaphragm.

Appearance. In death, the face becomes pale and waxy, the lower jaw drops a bit, and the mouth sags open. The eyes become soft to the touch and the eyelids are generally open or slightly open and show no motion or reflex action when touched.

Muscle resistance or muscle reflex. Muscle resistance and reflex are present in the body to some degree until death. Note if the limbs can be moved without resistance.

Identification of Homicide Victims

The importance of determining the identity of the victim provides an important basis for the investigation process since it may lead the investigator directly to other important information. The investigator's work is futile if the perpetrator of the crime is apprehended but cannot be convicted. In order to convict John Criminal of the murder of Jane Doe, it is necessary to prove that the body (if found) was, in fact, the body of Jane Doe. Since unknown bodies may deliberately be falsely identified to collect insurance proceeds, conceal criminal acts, etc., it is highly important that positive proof of the victim's identity be obtained. Many civil questions, such as the right of heirs to inherit the estate and the surviving spouse's right to remarry, depend upon proper identification of the deceased. The law requires an investigation of suspected homicides, and an inherent part of the investigation process is the proper identification of the victim.

Method of identification

Fingerprints Fingerprint identification is the most positive and quickest method of ascertaining identity. However, the prints of the deceased may not be on file, or may not be obtainable because of trauma, mutilation, incineration, or decomposition. The sole clue may be bone, a skull, or a few teeth.

Skeletal Studies Examination of the skeleton may provide a basis for identification because of individual peculiarities such as old fractures and presence of metal pins. Bones may also provide information about age, sex, and race.

Visual Inspection The victim may be recognized by someone knowing the deceased person (immediate family, relatives, friends, etc.). However, trauma, incineration, or decomposition may render the features unrecognizable. In addition, a visual inspection without further verification has the disadvantage of possible subjective error or deliberate false identification. Visual inspection combined with fingerprint evidence is a favored method for rapid, reliable identification.

Personal Effects Identification of a victim by personal effects such as jewelry may also be unreliable because of the transferability of jewelry. Jewelry can and often does provide leads for the investigator to determine positive identification.

Tattoos and Scars Identifiable scars, moles, tattoos, pockmarks, or other markings may be helpful in identification, particularly in conjunction with other findings.

Dental Evidence (Forensic Odontology) Identification based on the examination of teeth (teeth charts, fillings, inlays, crowns, bridgework, dentures, etc.) is valuable inasmuch as the teeth are probably the most durable part of the human body. When fire, decomposition, animals, and even mutilation have destroyed everything else, the teeth are often the last evidence to remain. The earliest reported use was in the identification of Nero's wife in A.D. 66.[3] There are probably no two people alive with dentitions that are completely identical in all respects. Dental evidence is legally recognized and accepted, if properly presented in court.

Clothing Articles of clothing containing cleaner's marks, labels, initials, size, color, texture, knitting, etc., have provided investigators with leads and even identification in some instances. However, identification by clothing alone has the disadvantage of depending on subjective judgment and articles of clothing can be transferred to another person. Moreover, articles of clothing are often not sufficiently unique to provide a reliable basis for identification.

---

[3]Ibid.

Photographs Identification of victims has been made by publication in bulletins, circulars, television, and other distribution media. Artist sketches, death masks, and other casts have likewise aided police in identifying "unknowns."

Estimation of Time of Death

It is important to know the time of death when there is no reliable witness to decedent's death, especially in a homicide investigation. When death is due to suicide, the time of death is important because of the exclusion clause in the insurance policy which cancels payment if such death occurs prior to the agreed time. In the case of husband and wife who apparently died from burns, explosion, traffic accident, suicide–homicide pact, or double murder, it is imperative that the pathologist determine who died first.

Estimation of the time of death based on simple examination of the body is often difficult. No pathologist is able to determine the exact time of death from examination of the body alone, contrary to the general belief. If the body is discovered a few hours after death, the estimate of time of death would be more accurate than that made when the body is discovered twenty-four hours or more after death. When the time of "last seen alive" and time of "found dead" are within one or two hours of death, the medical opinion cannot be more accurate than that supplied by a reliable witness.

Ways of determining time of death from examination of the body[4]

Conventional Method
Rigor Mortis This is the stiffening of a dead body due to accumulation of sub-

---

[4]Ibid.

stances (mainly lactic acid) in the muscles. Warm temperatures accelerate the appearance and disappearance of rigor and coldness slows down the appearance and disappearance of rigor. Other factors may likewise influence rigor. Externally, signs of rigor mortis can be determined as follows:

1. The early signs of rigor mortis are noted in the area of jaw and back of neck two to three hours after death. The signs progress downward.

2. Complete rigor will be noted in six to twelve hours after death.

3. Rigor mortis usually leaves in descending order in twenty-four to thirty-six hours.

Livor Mortis (Lividity) Often called postmortem lividity, this is a dark discoloration (usually dark blue or purplish color) found under the skin due to the settling of blood into the lowest parts of the body nearest the ground. It is important in determining whether the body may have been moved after death (particularly where the body has lain in the original position for four or five hours). These times are said to be only rough averages. Lividity should not be confused with discoloration caused by bruises on the body. The autopsy when performed will distinguish between them.

General Appearance
1. Changes in skin
2. Changes in eyes

Recent Method

Rectal Temperature and Liver Temperature The cooling of the body offers one of the more reliable methods of estimating the time that has elapsed since death, up to a period of about twenty-four hours. If the rectal temperature is 99°F [37.2°C] and the liver temperature is 100°F [37.8°C], the cooling rate of the body is about 1 to 1.5°F [0.5 to 0.9°C] per hour. However, there is a rather rapid decrease during the first three hours and this gradually tapers off, leveling close to room temperature. Influencing factors in

the cooling of the body would be the difference between the body temperature and that of the medium in which the body was found, for example, summer or winter, heavy clothing, and size, weight, and age of the victim. When a body is exposed to air, the decrease in temperature is less rapid than when submerged in cold water.

Various Physiological and Chemical Changes in Body
1. *Decomposition* is the rate at which a body breaks down due to the effects of temperature, animals, insects, and general overall conditions of the body.

2. *Cadaveric spasm* is a condition attributed to intense muscular action and exertion prior to death. It is the result of a sudden injury to the central nervous system and should not be confused with rigor mortis. It is generally most evident in suicides where a gun is used. In such situations the muscles of the hand may grip the gun tightly, making it difficult to remove from the hand.

3. *Adipocere* is a whitish gray, soapy, or waxy substance that forms on the surface of the body after about six weeks. It is a change in the fat tissues and the condition is not seen unless there is fat in the tissue beneath the skin. When a body has been buried in damp ground, or in drowning cases, this substance forms. The presence of adipocere on the body is a method of assisting the coroner in determining the approximate time of death.

Muscle Contractions by Electrical Stimuli Potassium content in spinal fluid.

Supporting autopsy findings that can be used in estimating time of death would include: stomach contents (types of meal ingested and degree of digestion) and bladder content (amount of urine contained therein).

In addition to the ways of determining the time of death from an examination of the body as set forth above, another method resulting from an investigation of the scene or location would be the amount and type of physical evidence found. Physical evidence may include a broken watch, newspapers at the door, mail in the mailbox, milk deliveries, etc. Other information obtained as a result of an investigation may be telephone calls, lights burning, habits of deceased, witnesses who last saw or talked with the deceased, etc.

Homicide Investigation

There are no hard and fast rules in homicide or any other major criminal investigation. Each case presents its own problems. The techniques and procedures used are, of necessity, based on the problems at hand. Although detectives handle the majority of dead body calls, occasions frequently arise when field officers are called upon to conduct or assist in an investigation involving a death. It is necessary therefore that all officers have a working knowledge of the problems and investigative procedures in death investigations.

It is a good initial precaution to consider all apparent homicides and even suicides as if they were actual homicides until definite proof to the contrary is established. Initially it is often difficult to distinguish homicide from accidents, suicides, or even natural deaths. Many deaths by suicide may have all the outward appearance of a murder to an untrained observer (see Figure 16-1). A person with bruises and lacerations may have fallen or been injured in some other way, or death may have resulted from a heart attack, brain hemorrhage, or other natural cause.

The body may be lying in an alley, on the seat of a vehicle, in a doorway ordinarily used by others, hanging from a stationary object, in a bathtub, or in one of numerous other locations. However, it should not be molested or moved except by a qualified doctor, coroner, or other legally authorized person and then, only after it has been

Figure 16-1. The scene of death that often confronts the first arriving officers. Is the deceased a suicide or homicide victim?

photographed from many angles, sketches made, notes taken, etc., by investigators.

The investigation at the scene is determined by the category of the death being investigated. The first officer responding to the death call must come to some general conclusion as to the cause of death inasmuch as it will dictate the type and degree of the investigation that will follow. Some of the things that will influence an officer's decision as to whether or not a homicide has occurred would be the type and amount of information furnished by the complainant and witnesses and an examination of the body (without disturbing it or anything around it). Close observation of the crime scene and body for marks of violence and other indications, such as signs of struggle, cuts, weapons, pills, poisons, lacerations, blood, bruises, or bullet holes may assist the officer in conclusions regarding homicide. Information furnished by relatives, friends, and neighbors may permit early conclusions to be drawn by the investigating officer as to the noncriminal nature of the case. For example, the person's past history of illness and absence of any signs or evidence of violent death tend to indicate death by natural causes.

Procedures in homicide investigation

Preliminary Investigation (First Arriving Officers)

Record time of notification as well as the identity of the complainant. Also record the date and location from where the call originated.

En route to the scene (depending upon the time elapsed since the alleged death), be alert for such happenings as a fleeing suspect, a person with freshly inflicted injuries, one with torn or bloody clothing, or anyone taking evasive action on foot or automobile.

Record the license numbers of vehicles parked near the scene so that they might subsequently be contacted if necessary.

Record time of arrival at the scene and exact location. Seek out and interview briefly the complainant at this time. Have that person point out the exact location of the victim's body.

Ascertain identities of those present at the scene and anyone who may have left prior to the arrival of the investigating officer. The questioning of witnesses at this stage should be brief. Complete interviews will be conducted later.

Take immediate steps to block off the area of the crime scene to prevent contamination or destruction of any evidence present. Exclude from the immediate area the public, relatives, the media, and any other persons not assigned to the investigation.

Ascertain if the victim is alive or dead. Care should be taken in approaching the body to prevent destruction of any physical evidence or leaving evidence that may confuse investigating detectives such as fingerprints, footprints, cigarette butts, empty cigarette packages, match folders.

Radio for an ambulance if there is no doctor in attendance and there is a possibility, even though remote, that the victim is alive. If the victim is taken to a hospital, one officer should accompany the injured person in the ambulance and remain at the hospital in order to obtain any pertinent information or a dying declaration.

Notify headquarters and request necessary assistance and equipment, viz., homicide detail, criminalist, photographer, and fingerprint technician. In homicide cases, request the coroner and pathologist.

Arrest the suspect if she or he is still at the location. If the suspect has fled and his or her identity is known, a radio broadcast should be made giving full description, clothing worn, method of leaving the scene, description of vehicle if one used, and other pertinent information. If the suspect was seen, but her or his identity is unknown, broadcast all available information.

Prevent anyone from entering the crime scene or approaching the body until the arrival of the detectives who will take charge of the case. The scene should be protected not only where the crime actually occurred but a wide area at and adjacent to the actual scene. This includes any portion of the surrounding area over or through which a suspect may have passed en route to or leaving the crime scene.

Footprints, tire tracks, bloodstains, soil disturbances, damaged vegetation, etc., should be protected from possible injury, especially outdoors. Such evidence may be covered with boxes or other covering, roped off, or otherwise guarded to prevent obliteration until all further reason for their preservation has ceased.

Post guards and/or use ropes, barricades, any natural barriers such as fences or ditches to keep the curious back from the critical areas; see, for example, Figure 16-2. Set out a zone into which only investigators are permitted. This zone would normally include the entire house or appropriate area if an apartment or other larger structure, a lot or other expanse, a wide zone around a vehicle, or other selected area. This zone could be enlarged or reduced in accordance with the demands of the situation.

Investigation following the arrival of homicide investigators and medical examiner

When the investigators arrive at the scene, one of them will take charge of all aspects of the case. The head investigator's job is to coordinate, direct, and make all investigative assignments. The head investigator should immediately take inventory

Figure 16-2. Scene of a homicide, showing the protection of the crime scene by use of a police vehicle and by roping off the area.

of all personnel at the scene. A recap of all information gathered during the preliminary investigation should be requested of the officer(s) who first arrived at the scene so that everyone participating in the investigation is brought up to date. The investigation under the leadership of the officer in charge will encompass the following types of duties or assignments following a preliminary survey of the crime scene:

1. Photographs of persons, places, and things should be taken as the first order of business at a homicide scene and before anything is touched or disturbed. Orientation pictures from several angles should be made to show visual proof of the type of location, approaches to, and surroundings of the death scene. Photographs should also be made of the position of the body from several angles in order to show its relation to fixed objects.

2. Photos of weapons, bloodstains, tire tracks, and other physical evidence such as bullet holes, fingerprints, or palm prints (before and after development) should be taken. It is a good practice to have an investigator accompany the photographer and point out the items of physical evidence, objects, and places of which pictures are desired.

3. Casts of footprints, heel prints, tire marks, or tool marks (if forced entry) should be made after the photographs mentioned above are taken and before crime scene investigators begin their search for evidence. Wherever possible the area containing the tool mark should be cut out and taken to the crime laboratory for examination and casting. Where such removal is not possible, a cast of the tool mark should be made at the scene. Moulage, plasticine, dental wax, modeling clay, or other suitable casting material may be used. Casts often reveal identification peculiarities not readily observable otherwise.

4. Sketch the crime scene and general location. The sketch should include all pertinent objects within the perimeter of the scene whether indoors or outdoors; the perimeter being designated by the officer in charge. The weapon and other evidentiary items must be related to the body and to fixed objects by measurements. While the sketch made need not be in proper proportion, or artistic, the measurements recorded should be accurate. Simple line drawings are preferred; include an arrow to indicate direction. From the sketches made, a scale drawing can be prepared for trial.

5. Answers should be obtained to the questions set out below as soon as possible in order to assist in reconstructing the chronology of events immediately prior to the victim's death. The answers to these queries can facilitate the progress of the investigation:

Who was the victim? (Positive identification, if possible.)

Who found the victim? What was the finder doing in the area? What is the finder's relationship to the victim? How accessible was the body?

Who was the last person to see the victim alive? When? Where? What time? With whom? What was the victim doing at the time observed?

Who was the victim planning to see, contact, or do business with prior to her or his death?

Who was the victim's closest friend?

What was the conduct of the victim prior to death? Was the victim ill or under the influence of liquor? Drugs? Was the victim obnoxious? Moody? Acting irrationally? Angry?

Why was the victim at the particular spot? Why at that time?

How much money or other valuables was the victim carrying? How much did the victim usually carry? Status of bank account? Deposits, withdrawals?

What were the spending and drinking habits of the victim?

What was the character and reputation of the victim?

6. Process the crime scene for fingerprints or palm prints. The fingerprint technician should examine all likely places and objects believed touched or handled by the killer. Doors, windows, walls, furniture, cupboards, utensils, bottles, glasses, ashtrays, telephone, and other likely possibilities should be processed.

7. The victim's fingerprints should be obtained. This will assist in subsequent identification. If fingerprints are found at the scene, the victim's prints can be quickly ruled out.

8. Obtain elimination fingerprints from all persons residing or working at the location, particularly those known to have touched or handled objects at the scene.

9. Interview witnesses separately. Taped or signed statements are preferred. Witnesses should be asked to describe in detail their exact position during the time that they gained knowledge of the crime. Any information bearing on the case should be elicited from them. Ascertain how and where they can be reached if further interviews are desired. The interviews can take place simultaneously while photographing, fingerprint processing, sketching, and casting work are being done.

10. Conduct a crime scene search. A laboratory specialist should team up with a detective if possible for this assignment. Such a team arrangement permits ready recognition of evidence, limited on-the-spot examinations, proper collection and preservation, and keeps the chain of custody as short as possible. Where such a team assignment is not possible, it is a good practice to make one detective responsible for the handling of all evidence.

The search should extend from the perimeter and proceed toward the center or begin at the center and reach to the perimeter. It may be conducted in a clockwise fashion, point-to-point, quadrant, or other method as long as it is systematic and thorough. The location of the crime scene will dictate the type of search.

11. Items of evidence should not be picked up or moved until their location and position have been photographed, sketched, measured, and recorded. This admonition is often referred to as the golden rule in homicide investigations. Following the photographing, sketching, measuring, etc., the evidence should be collected, identified, and preserved for laboratory examination.

12. Record accurately the description of the body and clothing worn. Make notes of the position of the body including position of the head, arms, hands, and legs, e.g., head to the north, face on left side. In recording a description of the body, proceed from the head to the feet. Note the color and arrangement of the hair. Observe the face for injuries, blood, dirt, extraneous matter, marks; also note eyes, mouth, and facial expression. Note victim's hands—whether clean, dirty, open, clenched, holding anything, or wearing any articles of jewelry. In observing clothing worn, note type, arrangement or disarrangement, degree of cleanliness, dry, wet, stained, torn, buttons missing, etc. Record a complete physical description of the deceased.

13. Particular attention should be given to the area immediately beneath the body after it is moved. Any items discovered there should be photographed, recorded, measured in relation to fixed objects, collected, marked for identification, and submitted to the crime laboratory. In most homicide cases the body is not moved for about two or three hours, which is about the average time needed by investigators for photographing, sketching, measuring, recording, etc.

14. Contents of wastebaskets, glasses, cups, bottles, containers, ashtrays, etc., should be carefully noted, preserved, and individually packaged for laboratory examination.

15. Search for bullets if shooting is involved. Some of the slugs will probably be found in the walls or ceiling; others may be found in furniture or other solid objects. The course and direction of the bullets should also be determined. Bullet holes in woodwork or other places should be photographed from several angles with notes, sketches, and measurements supporting the pictures taken. Bullets should be removed with great care from their location so that they are not mutilated in any way. They should be identified at the base and submitted to a ballistic expert for examination and use at the trial.

Where there is independent evidence through the statements of witnesses of the number of shots that were fired, every effort should be made to account for that many bullets. If the spent bullets are not found at the scene, request an x-ray examination of the victim's body for their possible location.

A check should be made of all rooms (if indoors) for any physical evidence that the suspect may have dropped, discarded, touched, or handled.

Consider the possibility of the crime being committed at some other place or room and the body moved to where it was discovered. The victim may have walked to another location seeking help prior to death. Thus, there is a need for a complete search and examination for evidence or clues.

Note the position or disarrangement of chairs, glasses, furniture, presence of scuff marks on floor, signs of a struggle, possible weapons, etc.

Search particularly underneath tables, chairs, desks, or other pieces of furniture for traces of blood or fingerprints. The finding of such evidence will assist in the determination that a murder had occurred and possibly furnish fingerprint, palm print, or other evidence.

Search for identifiable traces of blood in such places as the bathroom, kitchen sink, laundry tub, or other places on the premises where the assailant may have washed bloodstains off hands, body, or clothing. The search may necessitate the dismantling of plumbing fixtures (pipe traps). Washcloths, towels, rags, etc., should be obtained and transmitted to the laboratory for analysis.

Floor crevices, carpets, and contents of fireplaces should be checked for possible evidence of blood or other identifiable materials.

Endeavor to locate any written material or notes made by the victim that may disclose the identity of persons contacted, places called, or activities.

Methodically examine the terrain about the premises for damaged vegetation, footprints, items discarded or dropped, etc. Representative specimens of soil (pint carton) should be obtained from the crime scene. Specimens of botanical materials should also be gathered. These samples should be submitted to the crime laboratory for comparison with materials that may be found on a defendant's clothes or in his or her car.

The victim's body and valuables should be taken care of by the coroner.

Accompany the victim's body from the scene of the crime to the place where the autopsy is performed in order to safeguard all evidence.

Obtain the victim's clothes (including socks, shoes, and undergarments). Each item of clothing should be wrapped separately. If any of the items are wet from stain they should be air-dried over clean paper before wrapping in that paper. Thereafter the dried articles and other items should be submitted to the laboratory for analysis. Clothing may show bullet holes, particles of soil, weeds, weed seeds, grasses, grass stains, other botanical materials, bloodstains, etc.

Obtain a sample of the victim's blood, head and pubic hair, and fingernail clippings. Debris from under the fingernails may contain hair, fibers, skin, and blood from the assailant.

16. If the victim has been molested sexually, a check should be made by the examiner for such items as pubic hairs and semen stains.

17. All bruises or other marks on victim's body should be photographed (in color preferably) before and after cleansing.

18. Check the telephone calls made from victim's telephone for possible leads.

19. Interview suspect. This interview should be conducted by two detectives and only after the suspect has voluntarily waived legal rights and agrees to the interview. Prior to such interrogation, however, the interviewing detectives should make adequate preparation for the confrontation by viewing the crime scene and familiarizing themselves with all the facts. All statements made by the defendant should be recorded, typed up, and given to the suspect for reading and signature. Where a suspect is apprehended shortly after a homicide, a *gunshot residue test* of suspect's hands should be conducted to determine whether the suspect fired a gun. In this test, an adhesive-coated disc is pressed against the areas of the hands where gunshot residue is usually concentrated. A conductive coating is thereafter applied over the residue on the disc, which is then inserted directly into the scanning electron microscope (SEM). The use of the SEM and simultaneous use of x-ray analysis has been found to be very effective in gunshot residue testing.[5] Metals from gunshot residue are concentrated in particles that have specific chemical compositions and shapes.

Other investigation relating to the suspect should include:

Administering a polygraph examination if the defendant is willing and signs a waiver of legal rights.

Making a movie of the defendant's reenactment of the crime; a tape recorder may be used to record the sound.

Taking colored photographs of the suspect (both close-ups and stand-ups).

Obtaining the suspect's clothing for laboratory examination—clothes may contain hairs, fibers, particles of soil, botanical materials, bloodstains, etc., which may help to link the suspect with the crime scene or victim.

Arranging for a breathalyzer test and specimens of saliva, urine, and blood.

Obtaining fingernail clippings and hair specimens.

Examining the suspect for bites or scratches.

Taking of fingerprints and palm prints.

Determining whether suspect is right- or left-handed. Such determination may be of significance in checking the direction of stab wounds, blows, shots fired, positions, heights, and discrepancies in defendant's "story."

Obtaining of vacuumed debris, floor mats, seat cushions, and seat covers from defendant's car.

Verifying all statements furnished by defendant in order to corroborate or disprove information given.

Checking all telephone calls made by the defendant as to identities of persons called, places, times, and other evaluation.

[5]Wolten, G. M., and G. L. Loper, "Detection of Gunshot Residue Status and New Approaches," *Journal of California Law Enforcement,* January 1977, Vol. II, No. 3, p. 108.

20. Conduct a neighborhood investigation. This phase of a homicide or other major case is extremely important. Individuals residing in the immediate vicinity and surrounding pertinent areas should be personally contacted by investigators for every "bit" of information they may be able to furnish (even hearsay). Information of significance may include the barking of a dog, a scream, a loud noise, an odor, an irregularly parked auto, a casual remark, backyard gossip, etc. The names and addresses of all persons contacted should be recorded so that all residents can be accounted for.

21. Obtain a full report of all findings of the autopsy surgeon.

22. Plan on returning to the scene at the time of day the crime was committed. Additional witnesses may be located whose work takes them into that area about that time of day and day of week.

23. Investigative leads developed during the course of the investigation should be handled in the order of their importance.

24. A current log of all investigative activity should be maintained by the officer in charge of the investigation. This permits inspection, review and a ready reference checklist as to investigation conducted, assignments, work completed, investigation needing attention, and status of the case.

25. Prepare an organized, indexed, complete file (reports, statements, evidence, photographs and related data), and discuss case with prosecutor's office if trial is imminent.

26. Investigators will add additional investigative suggestions to this list according to the type of case worked and the individual requirements of each investigation.

27. Review Chapter 3, "Collection, Identification, and Preservation of Evidence."

Automobile Manslaughter Cases

Many states today have statutory classification of manslaughter. In some states, special statutory rules are applicable where death results from the negligent operation of motor vehicles; that is, "automobile homicide." California, for example, lists three kinds of manslaughter under penal code section 192: (1) voluntary manslaughter, (2) involuntary manslaughter, and (3) manslaughter with a motor vehicle. A vehicular manslaughter charge occurs where death is due to the operation of a motor vehicle with or without gross negligence. The element of gross negligence determines whether the crime is a felony or a misdemeanor. If gross negligence is not present, the crime is punishable as a misdemeanor.

Investigation of automobile manslaughter cases

The investigation of a vehicular manslaughter case may involve one or more cars, a collision with a pedestrian, or the death of one or more passengers. The following investigative suggestions are set forth to indicate some of the duties and responsibilities that may be involved in the cases:

On arrival, approach the area with caution—be careful not to destroy any evidence present.

Take steps to protect the scene from further accidents. Flares and the police unit may be used to protect the scene pending arrival of assistance. Exclude all unauthorized persons from the critical area.

Record date, time of arrival, and location.

Radio headquarters for assistance and equipment.

Determine whether the victim is alive or dead. If there is any indication of life, immediately summon an ambulance; if dead, advise coroner.

Note whether traffic control devices, if present, are functioning and can be seen.

Make notes as to weather, visibility, lighting, road conditions, obstructions, signs, signals, and markings.

Identify victim. Note all visible injuries, position of body, clothing, and physical evidence around the scene.

Identify driver of vehicle causing fatality. Make an arrest if driver is present.

Obtain vehicle identification number (VIN), license number, make, model, color, mileage, registered and legal owner of car(s) involved.

Note suspect's physical condition. Drinking? Physical impairments?

Examine suspect's car for such things as fabric marks, parts of clothing, fibers, blood, paint transfers, broken glass, missing chrome strips or headlight rims, hair, skin, tissue, and stains made by articles in the victim's possession.

If the suspect has fled the scene (as in a hit-and-run case), furnish control with all available descriptive data for local and regional broadcasts.

Interview suspect (if apprehended and waiver of rights exercised).

All alibis or excuses offered by the defendant should be checked to see if the statements are true.

Arrange for blood and urine specimens to be taken from the defendant.

Locate and interview witnesses. Obtain signed statements.

Photograph scene as it is before anything is touched or moved. Take pictures from different distances and angles in order to show intersection, streetlights, crosswalks, skid marks, or whatever other type of condition exists at the particular area.

Obtain close-up pictures of the body and its relative position to fixed objects. Do not remove the victim's body until all necessary photographs are taken and sketches, notes, and supporting measurements are made.

Include in the sketch the location of trees, poles, traffic signs and signals, building lines, hedges, etc. Outline the position of the body and evidence with chalk before removing them.

Determine the point of impact (POI) of the collision. This can be ascertained from debris at the location such as broken glass, radiator water, and dirt dislodged from the undersides of the automobiles at time of impact.

Determine the point of rest (POR) where vehicles came to rest after the accident and anything to show the positions of the vehicles in the road before the collision.

Make accurate measurements of skid marks and their relative position to fixed objects. Measure each skid mark separately. Tie any tire and skid mark to the vehicles.

Check condition of defendant's vehicle—tires (condition of tread and wear), brakes, steering, position of gear shift, emergency brake, wheels, windshield wipers, headlights and taillights, rearview mirror, position of turn indicator, mileage, etc.

Take photographs and make casts of any tire impressions if pertinent to the investigation.

Photographs of the body must be taken before and after undressing the victim at the morgue.

Obtain blood and hair specimens of victim; color photographs of injuries to victim; fingerprints, and a complete description.

The autopsy must be conducted with special attention paid to patterns. This is important in reconstructing the fatal accident.[6] Documentation of the wound pattern is vital. Bumper marks and fracture of the legs are important and should be documented as to size, exact location, and height from the heel. Any other wound pattern, such as impressions characteristic of grill work or

---

[6]Ibid.

contact with protruded ornaments must be noted. The wounds should be searched by the medical examiner for foreign materials. Any materials found in the wounds should be analyzed.

Obtain a traffic accident report and attempt to reconstruct the impact patterns in the light of the autopsy findings with special attention as to the direction of the oncoming car and the position of the victim.

Obtain victim's clothes from coroner. Wrap each item separately and submit to laboratory for processing. Clothing may contain foreign material such as glass, mud, dirt, metal, paint, tears, bloodstains, and other evidence.

Obtain a copy of the autopsy report.

Conduct any other investigation deemed necessary since it is impossible to foresee all the ramifications of any case without the knowledge of all the facts.

Complete all reports and discuss them with the district attorney for trial purposes.

The investigating officer(s) in vehicular manslaughter cases should be in a position to testify to the following:

Time call received and arrival at scene.

Location of fatal accident.

Condition of scene on arrival.

Weather, road conditions, lighting, visibility.

Whether traffic signs and signal devices (if present in the particular area) were functioning.

Street markings and general traffic conditions.

Physical hazards.

Condition of vehicles involved.

Any voluntary statements of accused.

Physical evidence such as location, identification, and disposition. Investigators must know where, when, and by whom the evidence was found and account for every item obtained during the investigation from the time the evidence was found until its introduction at the trial.

Identity of witnesses.

Photographs, measurements, diagrams, skid-mark data.

Stab Wounds

In deaths by stabbing, the investigator should pay close attention to the possibility of cuts in the palms of the hands of the victim which would indicate the probability that she or he grabbed the knife of the assailant during the struggle for life. Slashes on the outer side of a victim's forearm suggest attempts made to ward off knife thrusts. Other observations would be to check for bruised knuckles, which would indicate that the deceased struck the attacker, visible signs of a struggle at the crime scene (items such as scuff marks on floor and chairs overturned), the pattern of blood drops which may show direction of flight, the extent of the bleeding (which might indicate that the victim was dead prior to being stabbed). The appearance of a wound may suggest a knife as the possible type of instrument that was used. However, appearances are misleading inasmuch as cuts made by sharp-edged articles or objects may give the appearance of a knife wound. The medical examiner, from autopsy findings, can provide police with such information as the type of weapon, estimation as to size and shape, depth of penetration, and wound dimensions. Figure 16-3 depicts various types and shapes of wounds made by weapons and other instruments.[7]

When a knife or other weapon is located at the crime scene, it should be photographed, sketched, measured, picked up, identified, and preserved. Notes should be

_____
[7] Ibid.

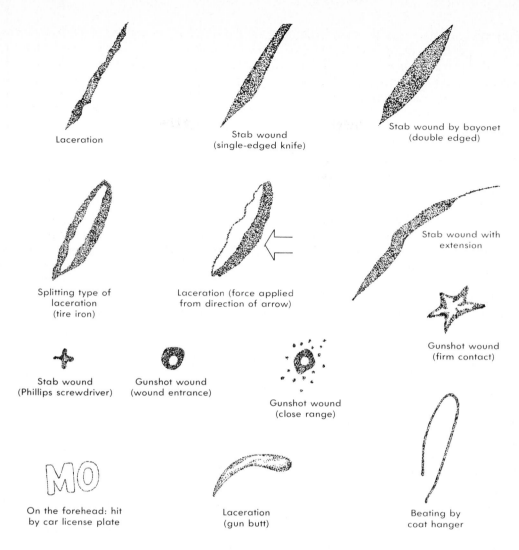

Laceration

Stab wound
(single-edged knife)

Stab wound by bayonet
(double edged)

Splitting type of
laceration
(tire iron)

Laceration (force applied
from direction of arrow)

Stab wound with
extension

Stab wound
(Phillips screwdriver)

Gunshot wound
(wound entrance)

Gunshot wound
(close range)

Gunshot wound
(firm contact)

On the forehead: hit
by car license plate

Laceration
(gun butt)

Beating by
coat hanger

Figure 16-3. Various types and shapes of wounds made by weapons and other instruments.

made to support the officer's actions and the weapon should be submitted to the laboratory for microscopic examination.

The trial of a homicide case usually requires that the position and type of wounds be shown. The use of a life-size mannequin constructed to resemble the victim has been used effectively in trials by the Los Angeles County Sheriff to illustrate knife wounds in their proper perspective.

Abortions

A death that follows from a criminal abortion is a felony in most states. It is held generally that the crime is complete whether or not miscarriage results—as long as the act is undertaken with the specific intent to procure a miscarriage. Criminal abortion offenses are committed by some unethical medical doctors, osteopaths, chiropractors, pseudo doctors (people who represent themselves as doctors), and so-called midwives with intent to procure a miscarriage. The methods employed generally involve the use of instruments (speculum, tenaculum, curette, catheter, etc.), drugs (either orally or by injection), or a douche.

Where a death occurs as the result of a criminal abortion, it is referred to police and a homicide investigation is conducted. The medical examiner's autopsy report provides investigators with valuable information as to the method of operation used (type of instruments, materials and method employed). Photographs of the victim, fingerprints, fragments of the fetus, clothing, blood and hair specimens should be obtained and preserved for analysis and evidence purposes.

The identity of the abortionist may be ascertained as a result of interviews with a victim's parents regarding their daughter's activities, friends and associates, her male friend or the father of the aborted child. Signed statements should be obtained in every instance. The victim's health record and physical condition immediately prior to the abortion should be found. Collect detailed statements made by the victim concerning her pregnancy and abortion plans, identity of persons telephonically contacted, location of places visited, and identity of persons accompanying her. In addition, collect information concerning bank account transactions or money borrowed; any written data in her possession or effects; statements from the doctor who treated the victim following the abortion; hospital records if the victim was treated at a hospital; and other pertinent information developed from the investigation.

If an abortionist suspect is identified, a full investigation of his or her activities should be undertaken. A check should be made of defendant's background, criminal record, relationship with victim, types of abortive drugs purchased, place of purchase, identity of pharmacist (as possible conspirator), corroboration of any payment received from the victim, the suspect's finances, employment, telephone calls, landlord, mail, and the identity of associates. The use of a female undercover operator (pretending to be pregnant and needing assistance) can be invaluable in revealing the suspect's activities and the possible location used in her or his "medical practices." A vigilance of the suspect's activities, and surveillance photos of women visitors may be helpful in subsequent interviews or in refuting statements, and in identifying "clients," or obtaining cooperative witnesses. Other investigation is based on developments that occur in the case.

The Battered-Child Syndrome [8]

A pathologist working in a medical examiner's or coroner's office dealing with the syndrome of the battered child is responsible for performing a complete external examination of the body with careful detailed description of all injuries, supplemented by roentgenograms of the entire skeleton, taken before the autopsy, to determine the existence of old or recent bone injury. The complete autopsy with microscopic studies must include the dissection and microscopic study of the osseous lesions (bone injuries). All findings possibly related to trauma are recorded in diagrams and photographs in color. The pathologist's findings and police reports dealing with the circumstances of the injuries and death must be evaluated with utmost care to determine whether inconsistencies exist in their statements as to the time and nature of the events associated with the injuries. When confronted with the findings, suspects frequently confess.

---

[8]Ibid.

The following two cases are illustrative of the problem of the battered-child syndrome.

Case 1

A seventeen-month-old boy was admitted to a hospital with third-degree burns of the head, torso, and extremities. Anuria (urine suppression) and septicemia (bacteria in the bloodstream) developed and the child died in one week. The father explained to the police that the child had turned on the drain valve of the hot-water heater and scalded himself. When investigating officers noted that there was no handle on the valve, the father said the child had fallen into the bathtub and when the police pointed out there was no bathtub in the house, he said the child had crawled into the shower and turned on the hot water. It was obvious that the child could not have reached the shower handle, and the father was convicted of second-degree murder.

Case 2

A ten-month-old boy was brought to a hospital by a man and a woman and was pronounced dead. They said that the child had fallen from the crib thirty minutes previously and had ceased breathing. External marks of injury were explained to the police as being the result of frequent falls while learning to walk. Autopsy revealed massive traumatic laceration of the liver and right adrenal (kidney area) with intraperitoneal hemorrhage. Police investigation elicited that the couple was operating an unlicensed foster home. As many as seventeen children of various ages were kept in a three-bedroom home. At the coroner's inquest, conflicting accounts of the fatal episode and evidence of frequent abuse of the children by the husband resulted in the couple's arrest. Examination of the remaining children in the home revealed that one had a fractured skull. The man later confessed that he had squeezed the child during a fit of anger when the child cried excessively.

Disaster and Civil Insurrection

It is a function of the medical examiner–coroner's office to investigate all deaths due to disaster and civil insurrection. Because one can never know exactly what caused a disaster until it has been thoroughly investigated, the preservation of all available evidence at the scene is vitally important. Deaths due to a disaster or civil insurrection could ultimately be classified as homicides. In view of this, the sealing off of the area where the deaths occurred is extremely important wherever possible.

Don'ts of Homicide Investigation

The following *don'ts* were compiled by the district attorney's office, Riverside County, California, for the assistance of officers in conducting homicide investigations:

Don't fail to note time you receive call, time you arrive, correct address, and manner in which you were notified.

Don't drive too close to the scene of the crime. You may obliterate or destroy footprints or tire prints, or other physical evidence.

Don't walk up to the scene until after you have made a circle checking for tire prints, footprints, and other marks or physical evidence.

Don't fail to rope off a good-sized area for a thorough investigation by identification officers and other authorized investigators.

Don't permit unauthorized persons near the scene. If there is a crowd when you arrive, clear the area at once, keep everyone back of the ropes, including peace officers.

Don't handle, change, or move anything until identified, photographed, and measured. Remember if any article is moved, it can never be put back into its original position.

Don't pick up any article that may be in evidence, unless authorized to do so. One officer will be responsible for collecting, marking, and keeping any articles to be used as evidence.

Don't forget, if the victim is dead on arrival, to keep evidence intact until the specialist arrives, or until the case is assigned to an investigator.

Don't pick up any articles of physical evidence when located. Make sure they are protected until such time as they have been photographed and picked up by persons authorized to do so.

Don't forget to examine the body at the mortuary before clothing is removed. Make note of all marks on body. Get photographs, check hands, get fingernail cuttings, hair samples, fingerprints, blood samples, and get approval of the department head before autopsy or embalming. Also note the body after clothing is removed for items such as marks and abrasions.

Don't develop a theory to the exclusion of all other thoughts. Keep an open mind to ensure thorough investigation.

Don't forget, though you may be convinced that the trial will probably be a month or two away, that evidence gathered must be beyond a reasonable doubt in order to secure conviction.

Don't be satisfied with a partial investigation. Get all the evidence and all the facts.

Don't fail, if the victim is alive and can talk, to take a statement or dying declaration at once.

Don't be in a hurry at the scene. A thorough investigation requires the time to check the entire premises for physical evidence, such as knives, guns, shells, hair, fingerprints, clothing fibers, blood spots, etc. Remember the first few minutes might

determine the success or failure of the investigation.

Don't overlook powder burns, bullet wounds, slugs, etc., in victim's clothing.

Don't forget names and addresses of witnesses and names and addresses of suspects. List all articles found on the victim. If a gun or other weapon is found, note type, make, serial number, exactly where found, or other pertinent facts.

Don't fail to put identifying marks on all evidence, in a place that will not interfere with the examination.

Don't fail to note time, place, and name of persons to whom physical evidence is released, for processing by criminalists.

Don't forget to note all wounds and marks on the body; make notes and drawings.

Don't permit witnesses to discuss the case among themselves before you take their statements.

Don't take a suicide for granted. Things are not always as they appear. Be sure! Get all the facts to prove accident, suicide, or murder.

Don't overlook the fact that the body may have been moved from one part of the house or area to another, or may have been killed in one place and moved afterwards.

Blood Analysis [9]

Laboratory examination of bloodstains

The following points must be established in identifying a stain as human blood: Is it blood? Is it human blood? If human, what blood type? Some substances at a crime scene or on objects may appear to be blood, e.g., coffee stains, iodine, fruit juices, rust, lipstick, etc. There are two commonly used

---

[9]Ibid.

tests used in identifying blood, viz., the benzidine test and the phenolphthalein test. Positive reactions in these two tests indicate a high probability that it is blood.

Benzidine Test   This test gives a blue color. A similar color reaction, however, is observed with pus, nasal secretion, plant juice, and formalin. This test gives reactions with dilutions of 1 part of blood in 300,000 parts water.

Phenolphthalein Test   This test is extremely sensitive and gives a reaction with dilutions of one part of blood in five to six million parts of water. Positive reaction is indicated by a pink color.

Other tests that are used by police crime laboratories include the *hemin crystal test* and *microscopical* examination. The hemin crystal test is also called Teichmann's crystals. A suspected stain is treated with a reagent and characteristic crystals are looked for under the microscope. A microscopical examination is made for red blood cells and determination for hemoglobin. All of the above tests indicate only that the stain is blood and does not differentiate human blood from monkey blood or blood from other species.

Precipitin Test   This test is used to determine whether the blood is human. An extract of the blood is overlaid on the antihuman serum (this is the reagent for the test) in a test tube. Positive reaction is indicated by a white ring at the contact area of the two solutions. This test is sometimes referred to as the "rabbit test" or "ring test."

Significance of the bloodstains

Inasmuch as bloodshed often plays an important role in homicide, assault, rape, burglary, robbery, and other crimes, an investigator should have a general knowledge of the significance of bloodstains and their limitations. It is very difficult to determine accurately the amount of blood at the scene, since there are many factors involved. The same amount of blood in various locations produces different sizes of bloodstains. Bloodstains may be found on the floor, wall, carpet, bedspread, or ground.

The first factor influencing the size of a bloodstain is the material's ability to absorb fluid. Materials may vary from a smooth-surfaced, nonabsorbent linoleum floor to sand, gravel, or other materials of very porous nature.

The second factor which influences the size of a bloodstain is the roughness of the surface. Blood forms a pool, and runs toward a lower position because of gravity. If the surface is rough, there is a loss of the tendency to spread. The same amount of blood on a smooth surface would produce a larger stain than on a rough surface.

A third factor is the flatness of the surface. If the surface is in a perfect horizontal plane, the blood tends to accumulate in one spot. If the surface is on a slant, the blood will tend to run in the direction of the lower level and a small amount will cover a larger area. On a vertically situated surface, such as a wall or the sides of a furniture piece, a small amount of blood will cover an even larger area because it will continue to run downward as far as it can.

Bloodstains on cloth will tend to be smaller since it absorbs more rapidly. Material such as that of a wool carpet has a rough surface and also has thickness, so the blood will be very rapidly absorbed and the expected size of the bloodstain will be approximately ⅓ or ¼ of that seen on a linoleum floor. The diameter of the stain on a nylon carpet is somewhat larger than that on a wool carpet, but the difference is not significant. The absorbency of the carpeting is mainly due to the air pockets between the fibers rather than to the material itself. Gravel or sand absorbs blood very rapidly.

Significance of the Shape of Blood-stains Depending upon the size of the bloodstain, you can approximate the height of the origin of the blood. If the blood drops from a short distance (under 20 inches [50 centimeters]), it forms a round circular spot and from higher distances the edge of the circle is likely to show radiating effects. The shape of droplets of blood on a floor or sidewalk may give indications of the direction in which the injured person was moving. Information obtained from patterns of blood drops may be of assistance to the investigator in reconstructing the crime, detecting lies, and disproving an alibi. Figure 16-4 illustrates the significance of the shape of bloodstains.

Natural Deaths

The true situation of a dead body call generally is not known until after a preliminary investigation has been conducted. The officers receiving the call have many investigative responsibilities, particularly in those instances of unattended deaths and other types coming within the purview of the coroner's office. Teamwork at the scene of death between the police and the coroner's office is essential to the determination of the cause of death. Most state laws require that the death certificate include a statement not only of the cause of death but also the mode, i.e., whether death was natural, suicidal, accidental, or a homicide. In natural deaths the coroner's office is primarily interested in establishing a diagnosis to (1) rule out unnatural causes; (2) determine whether it is an accident, suicide, or homicide; (3) eliminate dangerous conditions; and (4) determine liability.

In approaching the location of the call and on arrival at the scene, responding officers should be particularly alert for any unusual conditions or activities of a suspicious nature. Immediate steps must be taken to

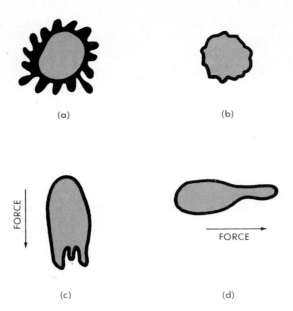

Figure 16-4. The significance of the shape of blood stains. (a) Blood dropped vertically from a height of 50 inches [1.3 meters] onto a flat surface shows a radiating, or bursting, effect; the stain is 1 inch [2.5 centimeters] in diameter. (b) The same amount of blood as in (a), but dropped vertically onto a flat surface from a height of 8 inches [20 centimeters], the stain is smaller (¾ inch—about 2 centimeters—in diameter) with a wavy edge. (c) Oval stain with spattering showing two or three spikes (splashes). Broad portions of the splashes indicate the point at which the blood first struck obliquely upon a flat surface and thus show the direction from which it came. (d) Stain shows two oval spots like an exclamation mark and indicates a left-to-right direction of blood drop.

protect the scene and property of the deceased. Nearly always present at the scene of death is a disturbance of that scene that makes it difficult at times to reach an early conclusion. Such a condition may be caused in several ways. The injured victim may be, or thought to be, alive at the time of discovery; therefore the scene will be disturbed by attempts to save a victim's life. It is possible that an assailant or some bystander may move the body for some reason. Another possibility is disturbance, in some manner, by early arrivals, sometimes inexperienced officers.

Assuming that death has been established as being due to natural causes, the following additional types of investigative duties should be conducted:

Notify desk sergeant without any unnecessary delay after verifying the validity of the complaint. Request any needed assistance and the coroner.

Determine who discovered the body.

Identify deceased: name, race, sex, age, marital status, name and relationship of next of kin, and preference of mortuary.

Determine who last saw the deceased alive: when, where, what time, with whom, activities, etc.

Obtain short statements from person(s) who witnessed death. Establish time of death.

Inquire regarding the past history of illness of the deceased. Also find out what were the actions and remarks of the victim prior to death.

Contact the victim's doctor if the victim was receiving treatment. Determine if a doctor or other legally authorized person will sign the death certificate. If no doctor or other authorized person will sign, it is a coroner's case.

Check for additional injuries or other possible causes of death, even if the cause of death is obvious.

Suicides

Suicide implies a direct connection between the deceased's "intention," the self-destructive action, and subsequent death. Suicidal actions take a great variety of forms and have different significance. Moreover, the reasons, motives, and psychological intentions of suicidal persons are quite complex. Destructive ideas or impulses that ordinarily are well controlled or mostly unconscious can be activated or released under the influence of emotional stress, physical exhaustion, or alcoholic conditions, all of which intensify suicidal behavior. Briefly summarized, some of the prominent mental trends of suicidal persons are[10]

A wish for surcease, escape, rest
Anger, rage, revenge
Guilt, shame, atonement
A wish to be rescued, reborn, start over
An "appeal" element

The most frequent methods of suicide are barbiturates and carbon monoxide poisoning in a car. Others are gunshot, hanging, and miscellaneous (cutting, stabbing, poisoning, jumping, electrocution, etc.). It is often difficult to distinguish between homicide and suicide (or accidental death) by an examination of the death scene. Many deaths by suicide have all the outward appearances of a murder to an untrained observer. This is a very important question to be answered by the officer handling the case. The instrument of death in suicide cases is, in most cases, obvious. However, many facets of a victim's personal background must be known when suicide is suspected, but is not readily apparent.

Suicide often occurs in responsible, religious, "successful" families. The fact that persons have plans for the next day or week, and tickets for vacations in resort areas, is not incompatible with simultaneous suicidal preoccupation and planning. The inescapable realization of an inability to enjoy a vacation may be the "last straw" for a depressed person.

In the investigation of suicides the investigator may encounter evasion, denial, concealment, and even direct suppression of evidence. The investigator should be alert to reconstruct the true conditions of the crime

---

[10]Ibid.

scene at the time of the discovery of the body so that erroneous conclusions are not reached. Some of the many things to be considered and resolved are:

> Temperature of the room: Was it changed from what it was at the time of discovery?
>
> Whether heaters were on or turned off.
>
> Were the windows open or closed; doors locked or unlocked.
>
> Condition of lights: They may have likely been turned on later.
>
> Identity of person who turned off automobile ignition in carbon monoxide death cases.
>
> Whether anyone touched the body, moved it, or removed any property prior to arrival of police. If rigor or livor mortis is present and the officer knows how to interpret it, this condition may indicate that the body has been moved.
>
> Identities of persons present and those who left prior to officer's arrival.

In hanging cases, the victim is often cut down and the knot untied; the plastic bag is removed from a suffocated victim; a person is pulled out of a swimming pool; and instruments and suicide notes are often removed to cover up an abortion or suicide.

Procedure in suicide investigations

Investigation of a suicide is not as complex or lengthy as in a homicide case. However, the following procedures should be taken:

> Preserve scene and evidence.
>
> Examine victim. If doubt exists as to victim being dead, call for ambulance. Administer first aid while awaiting ambulance.
>
> Where victim is obviously dead, note scene carefully for indications of a struggle, location of objects in room, position of chairs, glasses, contents of ashtrays, weapons, pills, prescription bottles, suicide note, etc.
>
> Notify headquarters of findings. Advise homicide detail. If possible, advise homicide detail of victim's identity, apparent cause of death, probable motive, and presence or absence of suicide note.
>
> Request coroner.
>
> Be alert for efforts to make victim's death appear accidental.
>
> Try to mentally reenact the death to determine whether it is logical or reasonable.
>
> Inquire about medical history, ailments, medications taken, prescriptions, type, when filled, amount remaining, etc.
>
> Note prescription labels and directions for use, e.g., directions for dissolving under the tongue probably indicates nitroglycerine, sleeping tablets are usually directed to be taken at bedtime. Drugs that are taken a certain number of times per day may be cardiovascular drugs or they may be drugs like vitamins that are not as significant. Prescription labels should have a doctor's name on them, sometimes the name of the drug, and the name of the pharmacy—all of which can furnish valuable information. Prescriptions may also indicate the date the prescription was filled and number of tablets or capsules. The amount remaining in the bottle may indicate excessive use.
>
> Note the location of the medication in relation to whether there is any indication of suicide or recent usage; or any containers (glasses, cups), loose tablets, or capsules near the body.
>
> Check with relatives, friends, and neighbors. A person with suicidal tendencies will often make such threats before committing the act.
>
> Suicide notes are very common and are generally found quite close to the body. Such a note will often be written while the person is dying. It is frequently

unfinished. If any questions of homicide arise, the handwriting on the note can be compared with the known handwriting of the deceased. The note should be preserved and turned over to the coroner. Quote the note in the complaint report.

Use discretion in titling the complaint report. Some deaths which appear suicidal are accidental. If doubtful, title the complaint report, "dead body — possible suicide."

Poisoning Cases

Although the use of poisons for the purpose of murder has greatly decreased, homicidal poisonings have to be carefully considered. In some cases an investigation may reveal that a murder has been committed. However, it may be difficult to establish that the poison was administered by the defendant. Rarely is there a witness to murder by poisoning. Careful investigation of all circumstantial evidence alone could provide a clue to a murder by poisoning. The question of suicide or homicide should be resolved.

When a death is suspected due to poisoning, a pathologist collects tissues and body fluids in separate clean jars which are labeled and stored in a cold place until they are transferred to the toxicologist for analysis. Some of the drugs and poisons can be detected easily in blood, many in the liver, yet others in urine, kidney, and brain.[11] Gaseous poisons are readily detectable in lungs and also in blood. Stomach contents are the best specimens for many poisons, especially for fast poisons. It must be remembered that all drugs used by the decedent ought to be collected and submitted with tissue specimens. A toxicologist selects the appropriate specimens from these, depending upon the class of poisons being sought. The poison is isolated and purified through long and complicated processes before it is ready for identification and quantative estimation. Once the poison is identified and quantity estimated, it is the responsibility of the toxicologist to interpret the findings, whether or not the poison isolated and the amount detected could have caused death.

Diagnosis of poisoning [12]

The diagnosis of poisoning before death by the toxin is sometimes easy but usually difficult. Many of the same symptoms seen in poisoning can also come from diseases. The one point, however, to bear in mind is that the symptoms of poisoning come suddenly upon a person who previously has been in good health, while disease is usually preceded by a number of hours, days, or even weeks of local or general indisposition. There are many diseases similar to poisoning. Those causing greatest confusion with irritant poisons are indigestion, ulceration of stomach or duodenum, gastroenteritis, appendicitis, intestinal obstruction, and hepatic or renal colic. A poison must be isolated and identified from the tissues and body fluids before it can be assumed that poison was taken, and for this purpose the most modern chemical and instrumental means available to a chemist are employed.

Classification of poisons [13]

From the standpoint of origin, the classification of poisons set out in this section could be considered appropriate. There are, however, numerous substances in each of the four classifications below that could be considered poisonous.

1. Inorganic poisons; e.g., cyanide, arsenic, mercuric chloride, antimony compounds, lead salts, phosphorus, etc.

---

[11] Ibid.

[12] Ibid.
[13] Ibid.

2. Gaseous poisons; e.g., carbon monoxide, illuminating gas, hydrogen sulfide, sulfur dioxide, etc.

3. Solvents; e.g., chloroform, ether, acetone, benzene, carbon disulfide, carbon tetrachloride, etc.

4. Organic poisons; e.g., salicylates, barbiturates, narcotics, strychnine, nicotine, etc.

In cases involving the poisoning of a human being, the evidence available may include foods or beverages as well as empty bottles, glasses, or other containers. Food and beverage samples should be placed in clean glass containers, marked, and transmitted to the laboratory for analysis.

Symptoms, which may be ascertained from interviews of the victim's friends and family or the attending physician, should include all information concerning the deceased's actions immediately prior to death. Symptoms include vomiting, abdominal pains, convulsions, coma, delirium. A chance remark by an acquaintance describing the actions of a victim prior to death may be the information needed to permit a toxicologist to make a calculated guess as the first step in determining the type of poison involved.

Deaths from Asphyxia [14]

Asphyxia is the extreme condition caused by lack of oxygen and excess of carbon dioxide in the blood, produced by sufficient interference with respiration, as in choking, suffocating, smothering, etc. Because the term is so general and actually quite vague, it must be further qualified with specific causes. Information provided by investigators, when combined with findings at autopsy and available medical history, will assist greatly in the correct interpretations essential for the further handling of a given

case. Figure 16-5 depicts some of the ways in which death can result from asphyxia or suffocation.

Strangulation

In cases involving death by strangulation, externally applied pressure occludes the airway and/or compresses the carotid arteries. Oxygen is withheld from the lungs, and the blood supply to the brain is drastically curtailed, thereby causing death. It is interesting to note that many of the oriental defense arts specialize in refinements of strangulation, with emphasis on precise control of the process.

In the investigation of suspected homicidal strangulations, look for bloody fluids at nose and mouth, tongue displacement, and assailant's marks. Also, note the scene for disturbances, signs of a struggle, the ground or floor beneath the body, fingernails for signs of possible struggle and trace evidence such as blood tissue or hair. Ligature marks will be low on the neck, transverse, and show equal pressure around the neck. Manual strangulation accomplishes the same

STRANGULATION AND HANGING COMPARED

	STRANGULATION	HANGING
Struggle	Yes	No
Notes	No	Yes, in suicidal; rarely in homicidal with attempt to simulate suicide
Other injuries	Yes	No
Angle of ligature	Transverse	High
Level of ligature	Low	High
Grooving of ligature marks	Even	Uneven; tend to be interrupted

---

[14]Ibid.

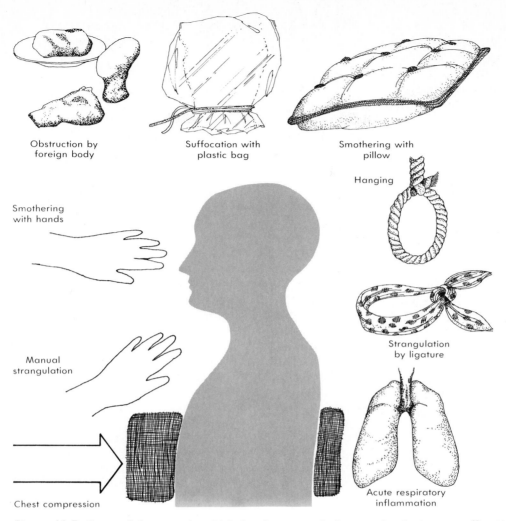

Figure 16-5. Some of the ways in which death can result from asphyxiation, or suffocation.

Labels within figure:
Obstruction by foreign body
Suffocation with plastic bag
Smothering with pillow
Smothering with hands
Hanging
Manual strangulation
Strangulation by ligature
Chest compression
Acute respiratory inflammation

final result but leaves a different pattern of soft-tissue damage. (See Figure 16-6.)

Hanging

Hanging is usually suicidal and not infrequently accidental. Victims are often found in sitting, standing, and lying positions. Belts, towels, bandages, wires, cord, strips of fabric, handkerchiefs, and other tying materials are often used. It is not necessary that the body swing free to effect a strangulation since only a little pressure is necessary to effect the result. The arteries of the neck are pressed together which prevents the flow of blood to the brain. The coroner's office considers such ligature marks as type of ligature (wire, cord, belt, etc.), pattern on skin, comparison with the weight of the body, degree of suspension (part or all off the floor), length of time

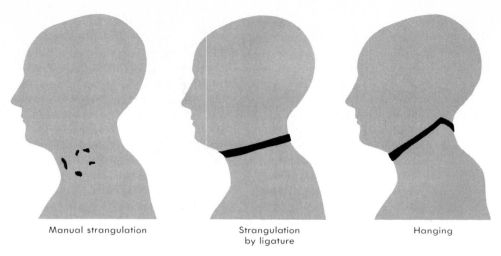

| Manual strangulation | Strangulation by ligature | Hanging |

Figure 16-6. Characteristic bruise patterns in homicidal and suicidal strangulation.

suspended (postmortem settling of marks or evidence of soft-tissue hemorrhage), and tightness of ligature.

Points to consider in the investigation of hanging are:

Was victim dead or unconscious before being placed in position of hanging?

Preservation of the knot as evidence.

Where and how ligature was tied. Type of knot. Could victim have tied these?

Inspection of the area for lack of evidence of a struggle.

Paraphernalia, including source of ligature material.

Suicide notes. Get exemplar. If no note is evident, question family members or other persons present for any notes left. The family often destroys a note.

Position of body. Did victim provide for the possibility of "stepping back" should he or she have a change of mind or hope to be discovered?

History of previous attempts.

Recent changes in behavior of deceased.

Possible organic disease (so-called rational suicide).

Financial matters.

Loss of loved one.

Was victim trying to punish someone?

Nature of telephone calls preceding death and identity of persons called.

Rigor mortis (as an aid in establishing time of death, thus the feasibility that victim was the sole active agent).

Smothering

Obstruction of the external airway (nose and mouth). Smothering is more frequently found in infants (no sign of struggle). When found in adult cases, signs of a struggle are present. When investigating these cases look for implements, such as a pillow that the assailant hopes will leave no evidence of the type of death inflicted, but could have traces of lipstick or other cosmetics, and possibly oral or nasal secretions.

Gagging

An application of an obstruction into the mouth and/or nose. Usually homicidal, but a few suicidal cases have been proved. When inserted into the mouth, a gag usually displaces the tongue in such a manner as to completely close the airway just below the larynx so that breathing by the nose would not help.

Choking

Small children often place foreign bodies, large and small into their mouths resulting in death by asphyxia. Death may be swift or lingering, dependent upon reflex factors and completeness of stoppage of the airway. Occasionally, people choke in attempting to swallow abnormally large amounts of food. Elderly persons sometimes choke to death due to their inability to swallow innocent-appearing portions of food.

Carbon monoxide (CO)

Death from this chemical source may be accidental, suicidal, or occasionally homicidal with success because the gas itself is odorless. Sources of carbon monoxide may be conflagrations, unvented gas heaters (incomplete combustion), automobile exhausts, defective automobile mufflers, and other sources. The greatest source of this poison, in general, is the exhaust of motor cars. In suicidal cases persons use this means by intentionally running their car motor in a closed garage or arranging a piece of hose from the exhaust tail pipe into the car. Cases exist where individuals forgot to turn off the ignition of their car when returning from an evening out, and the CO then entered the forced-air heating system of the house, killing all occupants during the night. Other deaths have occurred accidentally when people ran their car motors with the windows closed, to keep warm in cold weather. Carbon monoxide kills because it combines with the hemoglobin of the blood, thus making it impossible for the hemoglobin to combine with oxygen, which is a necessary life process.

Volatile intoxicant sniffing

The class of volatile intoxicants includes all substances which when sniffed or inhaled produce altered states of consciousness (ether, nitrous oxide, paint thinner, some glues, gasoline, etc.) Model airplane glue, for example (with toluene or benzene as solvents), produces a form of intoxication often accompanied by hallucinations. The glue is usually squeezed into a handkerchief or sock and placed over the nose and mouth.

Aerosol mixtures using Freon as a propellant are also used. Freon is a trademark for a group of halogenated hydrocarbons containing refrigerants and propellants. In many cases investigated, victims sprayed the contents of cans into a plastic bag or a plastic bread wrapper and then rebreathed the gases. However, this excluded oxygen and the victims suffocated.

Drug deaths

With reference to asphyxia, the respiratory center in the central nervous system becomes depressed by the drug action. Muscle paralysis, including muscles of respiration, can also occur. Narcotics and barbiturates, with and without alcohol, are the principal groups encountered. Other central nervous system depressants are implicated. There is a great variation in the tolerance of drug users to their drugs. In general, a complete autopsy must be done in cases suspected of an overdose of barbiturates or other drugs.

When someone dies in a suicide attempt because an expected rescuer failed in the allotted role, it is called a suicide by many medical examiners. For example, in one case a woman took a considerable quantity of barbiturate tablets at 4:30 P.M. and fell asleep on the kitchen floor in front of the refrigerator. She knew that every working day for the last three years her husband came home at 5 P.M. and went straight to the refrigerator for a beer. There was thus a strong possibility that she would be rescued. However, her husband was delayed and did not reach home until 7:30 P.M. Death resulted.

In the investigation of drug deaths, look for needle marks (old or recent), hypodermic kits, pills and bottles for same, and inquire into the history of the deceased. Be aware that companions may blame overdose when other possibilities exist that would implicate these individuals.

Drowning

Asphyxia, when the true sole cause of death in the water, is due to reflex closure of the glottis occurring in only 10 to 15 percent of cases. True drowning is a much more complex mechanism, varying with saltwater or freshwater. Chemical determination of right and left heart blood will differ with freshwater and saltwater. Other classifications of drowning are "wet" in which water is present in the trachea and "dry" in which water is present in the stomach. Simulation of drowning has to be ruled out by the medical examiner, i.e., whether there is a hiding of a homicide by throwing the body in the water after a killing. Death in the water from natural causes other than by drowning will be determined at the autopsy but simulation of drowning has to be ruled out.

SCUBA deaths

SCUBA (Self-Contained Underwater Breathing Apparatus) deaths usually occur because the diver becomes too confident of equipment. Mechanical failure of equipment can happen, as well as deficiencies in the compressed air supply. Expansion of air inhaled from SCUBA equipment during ascent is in accordance with Boyle's law: An ascent of 33 feet (10 meters) doubles the volume of gas. Any interference with expiration of this gas may lead to emphysema with laceration of the lungs, hemoptysis, hemothorax, or air embolism with death.

Gunshot wounds [15]

In suicides caused by a self-inflicted bullet wound, the fatal bullet must be fired from a short distance. The victim's hands should have powder burns. Clothing should have

------

[15]Ibid.

presence of powder grains. The location of the bullet wound is important. The wound is normally in the area of a vital spot such as the heart, temple, forehead, or mouth. Entrance to the wound is always larger than the diameter of the bullet. Head shots should show a powder burn pattern. The presence of several bullet wounds in a victim normally indicate a homicide. Where a weapon is found clutched in the victim's hand it is a good indication of suicide. The position of the deceased in many cases is usually one of comfort.

On occasions, it is extremely difficult to evaluate the entrance and/or exit wounds in cases of suicide. Frequently it becomes necessary to state in a positive manner whether a wound is a contact wound, a near contact wound, or one that is a result of a missile fired at a short distance or a long distance. Bullets removed from the body must be identified by the pathologist and marked on the base of the bullet.

There are certain characteristics that tend to establish an entrance wound, and these should be carefully diagrammed. Contact wounds as a rule present tearing of the margins of the skin. There may even be an increase in the size of the opening and the deposition of smudge. The deposition of smudge becomes especially useful in gunshot wounds of the head. Regardless of how much a wound bleeds, the smudge can be seen embedded on the beveled surface of the skull bone. Beveling of the internal table is found on entrance wounds. Examination should be made and all observations documented, including whether or not the discoloration in the soft tissues suggests the presence of the combustion products of the powder, usually of slate-gray color. The examination, of course, is made by the pathologist.

Entrance wounds with marginal abrasion and with the adjacent skin showing powder-fleck burns (tattoo marks) usually result from a missile fired from a distance of 3 to 9 inches [7½ to 23 centimeters]. The greater the diametric spread of the tattoo powder marks, the greater the distance of discharge from the skin surface.

Openings surrounded by marginal halo of abrasion with no other unusual markings in the skin usually represent a missile fired from a greater distance. The more concentric the halo of abrasion, the more vertical is the striking surface of the bullet to the skin. Eccentric halo patterns are frequently helpful in determining the direction from which the bullet was fired.

Need for Autopsy in Gunshot Wounds Suspected to Have Been Self-Inflicted In cases where only a wound of entry is present, or in through-and-through bullet wounds of the head, thorax, and abdomen, the medical examiner in conducting the autopsy and locating the bullet, outlines the bullet track and notes its upward or downward, medial or lateral direction through the body. The diagramming of the bullet tract becomes important where a homicide may be mistaken for a suicide and where a wound of entry must be determined from that of an exit. Thus, a determination can be made that a person was shot in the back and hence was probably a homicide victim.

Suicide by cutting

In these deaths the location of the wound is usually at a point that can be reached with ease by the arm, e.g., front or side of neck, wrists, middle of upper arm, elbow, or thighs. The appearance of several superficial wounds, usually at the neck or on the wrists, is not uncommon and is referred to as "hesitation marks." They are the result of first experiments or unsuccessful attempts.

Accidental Deaths

All accidental deaths are coroner cases. A child may swallow several aspirin tablets or drink an insecticide accidentally. Industrial poisonings due to exposure to poisonous gases may be entirely accidental. Food poisoning is not infrequent. A wrongly interpreted prescription or wrongly labeled bottle may result in death of a patient. A leaking muffler in a car or blocked chimney of a fireplace could cause accidental carbon monoxide poisoning. Accidental deaths have also resulted from such activities as "Russian roulette" to impress others rather than gambling with death, from practicing quick draws with guns, in cleaning firearms, and from hunting, home, vehicular, and railway accidents.

The procedure for handling the investigation of these cases is substantially the same as conducted in natural deaths. The main question confronting the police in cases of accidental death is whether or not the death was caused by the negligence of some other person, in which case it may amount to manslaughter.

The question as to whether death was due to an accident, suicide, or homicide is illustrated in the following case:

A young housewife was bludgeoned to death and placed in a car to make it appear she was the victim of a traffic accident. Her body was discovered in the wreckage of her small station wagon which had crashed through a concrete block wall. It was originally assumed she died from traffic injuries. However, the investigating officers discovered evidence at the victim's home that the woman had been killed in either the hallway or bathroom and that an attempt was made to clean up signs of a struggle. Inquiry disclosed that the deceased's husband was in love with another woman and the defendant killed the victim because the dead woman had what she (defendant) wanted, viz., the husband of the victim. Witnesses identified the defendant as being present at the scene of the "accident." Following a jury trial, the defendant was convicted of first degree murder.

HOMICIDE CHECK LIST

DETECTIVE ASSIGNED _____ CASE # _____

REPORTED TO _____ DATE & TIME _____

BY _____ ADDRESS & PHONE _____

WHAT SAID _____

_____

_____

_____

DATE COMMITTED _____ TIME COMMITTED _____ DATE & TIME OF DEATH _____

LOCATION OF SCENE _____

_____

HOSPITAL _____ DATE & TIME ADMITTED _____

ROOM # _____ DOCTOR(S) _____

VICTIM #1 _____ ADDRESS _____

PHYSICAL DESCRIPTION _____

_____

CLOTHING DESCRIPTION _____

X-RAYS AVAILABLE?   YES _____ NO _____ DENTAL _____ BODY _____ FROM _____

ADDRESS _____

OCCUPATION _____ BUSINESS ADDRESS _____

CRIMINAL BACKGROUND? _____

_____ CII# _____ FBI# _____

VEHICLE (IF INVOLVED) _____ LOCATION _____

VICTIM #2 _____ ADDRESS _____

PHYSICAL DESCRIPTION _____

_____

CLOTHING DESCRIPTION _____

X-RAYS AVAILABLE?   YES _____ NO _____ DENTAL _____ BODY _____ FROM _____

ADDRESS _____

OCCUPATION _____ BUSINESS ADDRESS _____

CRIMINAL BACKGROUND? _____

_____ CII# _____ FBI# _____

VEHICLE (IF INVOLVED) _____ LOCATION _____

_____

_____

1.

SUSPECT #1 _____ ADDRESS _____

PHYSICAL DESCRIPTION _____

_____

CLOTHING DESCRIPTION _____

_____

OCCUPATION _____ BUSINESS ADDRESS _____

VEHICLE _____ LOCATION _____

CRIMINAL BACKGROUND _____

_____ CII# _____ FBI# _____

ON PROBATION/PAROLE?   YES _____ NO _____ AGENCY _____ P.O. _____

P.O.'S PH: _____ MUG SHOTS AVAILABLE   YES _____ NO ___ RSD # _____ OTHER _____

RELATIONSHIP OF SUSPECT AND VICTIM _____

MISC. INFO _____

_____

_____

_____

_____

_____

(If two or more suspects, use an additional Page 2)

MODUS OPERANDI

DESCRIBE CHARACTERISTIC OF PREMISES AND AREA WHERE CRIME OCCURRED _____

_____

_____

DESCRIBE BRIEFLY HOW OFFENSE WAS COMMITTED _____

_____

_____

DESCRIBE WEAPON OR FORCE USED _____

_____

MOTIVE _____

EXTENT OF INJURIES _____

WHAT DID SUSPECT SAY?   NOTE PECULARITIES _____

_____

_____

VICTIM'S ACTIVITY JUST PRIOR TO AND/OR DURING OFFENSE _____

_____

TRADEMARK OR OTHER DISTINCTIVE ACTIONS OF SUSPECT _____

_____

VEHICLE USED _____

2.

CRIME SCENE

PERSON DISCOVERING VICTIM _____ ADDRESS _____

PH: _____ BUSINESS ADDRESS AND PHONE _____

_____

HOW DISCOVERED _____

_____

FIRST DEPUTY ON SCENE _____ DATE _____ TIME _____

DETECTIVE IN CHARGE _____ DATE _____ TIME _____

SCENE GUARDED BY _____ DATE _____ TIME _____

WEATHER _____

LIGHTING _____

ALL PERSONS – INCLUDING OFFICERS – ENTERING CRIME SCENE _____

_____

_____

DEPUTY CORONER ASSIGNED _____ 10-97 _____

I.D. TECH ASSIGNED _____ DATE _____ 10-97 _____

OTHER I.D. TECH'S AT SCENE _____ DATE _____ 10-97 _____

CRIME SCENE SKETCH BY _____

ASSISTING _____

VIDEO CAMERA OPERATOR _____

AUDIO OPERATOR _____

DATE & TIME TAKEN _____

LENGTH IN MINUTES _____

CRIME SCENE PHOTOS BY _____

B & W _____ COLOR _____

CRIME SCENE SEARCHED BY _____

_____

_____

AREA SEARCHED _____

SPECIAL ASSIGNMENTS AT SCENE (Searches, Stakeouts, Helicopter, Neighborhood Checks, etc.)

ASSIGNMENT	ASSIGNED	TIME	COMPLETED

EVIDENCE PICKED UP AT SCENE

ITEM #	ARTICLE	DATE	BY	MARKED AND TAGGED BY

(Use Continuation Report)

3.

AUTOPSY

DETECTIVE IN CHARGE _____ OTHER _____

I.D. TECHNICIAN(S) _____

DEP. CORONER _____ PATHOLOGIST _____

MORTUARY _____ ADDRESS _____

OTHERS PRESENT _____
_____

TIME I.D. START _____ FINISH _____ DATE _____

PATHOLOGIST START _____ FINISH _____ DATE _____

DESCRIBE PHOTOS TAKEN BEFORE AND AFTER CLEANUP AND DURING AUTOPSY _____
_____
_____
_____
_____
_____
_____
_____
_____

SAMPLES TAKEN

FINGERPRINTS BY _____ FINGERNAIL SCRAPINGS BY _____

HAIR SAMPLES: HEAD   ARMS   CHEST   PUBIC   LEGS   OTHER _____ BY _____

TISSUE SAMPLES _____ BY _____

BLOOD SAMPLE BY _____ TESTS REQUESTED: ALCOHOL   NARCOTICS   DRUGS

OTHER (SPECIFY) _____
_____ BY _____

BODY X-RAYS TAKEN BY _____ DESCRIBE _____
_____
_____

TESTS MADE ON BODY _____
_____ BY _____
_____

BODY IDENTIFIED BY _____ BASIS OF IDENTIFICATION _____
_____

CAUSE OF DEATH _____
_____
_____
_____
_____
_____
_____
_____

4.

EVIDENCE TAKEN AT MORTUARY (EXCLUDING SAMPLES TAKEN)

ITEM	TAKEN BY	MARKED AND TAGGED BY

ITEMS SENT FOR LABORATORY ANALYSIS

ITEM	TEST REQUIRED	BY	COMPLETED

WITNESS LIST

NAME _____

ADDRESS _____ PHONE _____

BUSINESS ADDRESS _____ PHONE _____

INTERVIEWED BY _____ DATE & TIME _____

CAN TESTIFY TO _____

_____

_____

_____

NAME _____

ADDRESS _____ PHONE _____

BUSINESS ADDRESS _____ PHONE _____

INTERVIEWED BY _____ DATE & TIME _____

CAN TESTIFY TO _____

_____

_____

NAME _____

(If additional space is required use continuation report)

5.

INVESTIGATIVE LEADS

NO.	SOURCE OF INFORMATION	DESCRIPTION OF INFORMATION	DETECTIVE & DATE ASSIGNED	DISPOSITION	REPORT DATE

6.

PRIOR REPORTS RECEIVED (MO OR PREVIOUS ARRESTS)

AGENCY	SUBJECT	REPORT #	DATE RECEIVED

PERTINENT TELETYPES OR AFB'S	DATE

DISPOSITION OF CASE

PRESENTED TO D.A./GRAND JURY ON _____ BY _____ CHARGE _____

DEPUTY D.A. ASSIGNED _____ CHARGED RETURNED _____

PRELIMINARY DATE _____ DEPUTY ASSIGNED _____ VERDICT _____

TRIAL DATE _____ D.A. DEPUTY ASSIGNED _____ VERDICT _____

FINAL DATE FOR APPEAL _____ APPEAL PENDING _____ APPELLATE DECISION _____

DISPOSITION OF PROPERTY RETAINED AS EVIDENCE _____

_____

_____

_____

_____

_____

7.

GLOSSARY OF TERMS DEALING WITH ASPHYXIA AND RELATED MATTERS*

TERM	DEFINITION
Adam's apple	Laryngeal prominence, on cartilage or larynx.
Aerosol	A system consisting of a substance dispersed in a gaseous medium.
Alveolar	Pertaining to tiny functioning spaces, as lung air sacs.
Asphyxia	Deprivation of oxygen, increase of carbon dioxide, and the consequences of same.
Aspiration	The breathing in of a substance.
Autonomic nervous system	Self-controlling, as opposed to volitional.
Barotrauma	Injuries resulting from changes in pressure.
Cadaveric spasm	So-called instantaneous rigor mortis, usually attributed to intense muscular action and exertion prior to death.
Carboxyhemoglobin	Combined form of carbon monoxide and hemoglobin such as to prevent taking up of oxygen and/or carbon dioxide and their release during circulation of the blood.
Carotid arteries	Main arteries of the neck and principal source of blood supply for the brain.
Choking	Interruption of respiration by obstruction or compression.
Congested	Excessive accumulation of blood with reddened appearance.
Conjunctiva	Delicate membrane lining the eyelid.
Cyanosis	Blue discoloration of a part due to insufficient oxygenation of the blood because of presence of oxidized heme pigment.
Diatoms	Unicellular microscopic forms of algae having a wall of silica.
Drowning	A form of suffocation occurring when the victim is submerged in water or other liquid that is inhaled into the air passages and the pulmonary alveoli.
Edema	Presence of abnormally large amounts of fluid in the intercellular spaces or specified structures of the body.
Elation	Emotional excitement marked by speeding up of mental and bodily activity.
Embolism	Sudden blocking of an artery or vein by an obstruction that has been brought to its place by the blood current.
Emphysema	Swelling or inflation of connective tissue by the presence of air (or in the pulmonary alveoli).
Endocardium	Lining membrane of the heart.
Epiglottis	Lidlike structure covering the entrance to the larynx.
Exemplar	Known specimens to which a test specimen is to be compared, as handwriting.
Gross	As perceived by the naked eye and other unassisted senses, as compared to microscopic, in the case of the autopsy.
Hanging	A form of strangulation in which the pressure upon the neck is caused by a noose, band, or other external mechanism tightened by the weight of the body.

TERM	DEFINITION
Hemoglobin	Oxygen-carrying red pigment of the red blood cells.
Hemoptysis	Expectoration of blood or bloodstained sputum.
Hemothorax	Collection of blood in the thoracic cavity.
Histotoxic	Poisonous to tissues.
Hyoid bone	Shaped like the Greek letter upsilon; U-shaped, as in the bone in the upper neck (with the ends of the U facing to the back).
Hypertonic	Having higher concentration of solutes than the physiological normal.
Identification	Recognition of an individual as determined by characteristics that distinguish that individual from all others.
Larynx	The voice box, situated between the root of the tongue and the trachea.
Lecithin	Biological compound behaving chemically somewhat as a wax; it is an emulsifying agent widely used in the food and baking industry.
Ligature	A constricting band not dependent in its action upon body weight.
Lividity	Discoloration in dependent parts, due to settling of blood in the capillaries by effect of gravity.
Membrane	A layer of tissue covering a surface or dividing a space or organ.
Narcotic	Any drug producing sleep or stupor and at the same time relieving pain; hypnotics do not relieve pain.
Natural	Not artificial or induced.
Petechial hemorrhage	Small, nonraised, round hemorrhage in skin or in submucosal membrane, usually from lack of oxygen.
Pleura	Membrane covering the lungs and lining the thoracic cavity.
Pulmonary	Pertaining to the lungs.
Putrefaction	Decomposition of proteins, accompanied by the production of foul-smelling substances.
Rigor mortis	Stiffening of a dead body, due to accumulation of substances (mainly lactic acid) in the muscles.
Sclera	The white of the eye, a tough membrane covering all but that portion covered by the cornea.
SCUBA	Self-Contained Underwater Breathing Apparatus, consisting of air tank, valve and regulator, appropriate mask and connectors, and gear to combine these into a unit to be worn by the diver.
Skin slip	Separation of the outer from underlying layers of skin due to decomposition, yielding, in the extreme, a glove effect with reference to the hand.
Smothering	Deprivation of oxygen by mechanical closing off of the external air passages by solid object or finely divided material.
Sniffing	Inhalation of toxic substances (usually liquids or gasses) for their exhilarating effect.
Sphincters	Specialized muscles closing a natural body opening.

TERM	DEFINITION
Strangulation	Occlusion of an air passage and/or arrest of circulation in a part of the body, due to compression.
Suffocation	Stoppage of respiration, or the asphyxia that results from it.
Traumatic	Pertaining to, or caused by, injury.
Vena cava Venae cavae (pl.)	Superior main vein draining the abdominal and pelvic viscera and the lower extremities.
Viscera	The large interior organs of the body.

*The terminology often referred to in deaths from asphyxia are set forth in this table for the information of investigators who are involved in asphyxia cases.

SOURCE: Thomas T. Noguchi, M.D., **Homicide Investigation Syllabus,** Homicide Investigation Institute, Moorpark College, Moorpark, California, March 1970.

SUMMARY

Deaths are classified as natural, accidental, suicidal, and homicidal. All murders are homicides but not all homicides are murder, as one may take the life of another by accident, in self-defense, as a result of negligence, or by lawful execution of a court order. These instances would be considered justifiable or excusable homicide. There is no statute of limitations for the crime of murder.

A major consideration in death investigations is the determination as to whether or not the situation is one of murder, suicide, or accidental or natural death. Before the arrival of homicide investigators, the first officers at the scene have limited duties. These are aiding the victim (if alive); apprehending the suspect if present or disseminating descriptive data if suspect is absent; protecting the scene; locating and brief questioning of witnesses; and making complete notes and preparing a report. Careful observation—seeing all that is to be seen—is a most important aspect of these investigations. Assigned investigators are responsible for a thorough and exhaustive investigation, following through on all leads, and preparing a complete, accurate, and indexed report on all phases of the case. Close liaison with the prosecutor's office during trial preparation is also extremely important.

REVIEW QUESTIONS

1. Why is the crime of murder one of the easiest to solve?
2. Name four ways in which a homicide victim might be identified.
3. Why is the time of death important to an investigator?

4. Name four ways in which the time of death is determined from an examination of the body.
5. What is the precipitin test used to determine?
6. What does the benzidine test prove?
7. What is the significance of the shape of bloodstains found at the scene of a crime?
8. What are the most frequent methods of suicide?
9. The code requirements direct the coroner to inquire into and determine the circumstances, manner, and cause of many types of death. Name six of these types.
10. What is the importance of postmortem lividity (also known as livor mortis or lividity) in estimating the time of death?
11. What is the statute of limitations in murder?
12. Homicide may be classified as felonious and non-felonious. Give an example of a non-felonious homicide.
13. Define "homicide."
14. Explain the difference between murder and manslaughter.
15. Of what value are powder patterns on a victim's body or clothing?
16. Entrance and exit wounds are important in homicide cases. Which is the larger of the two?
17. In searching the grounds surrounding the premises where a homicide has occurred, investigators check the perimeter carefully. What types of evidence and information are they seeking?
18. The first officer at the scene of a reported homicide has many duties and responsibilities. What are the principle ones?
19. How does a pathologist assist in the investigation of a violent crime?
20. In what area of the body does rigor mortis start?

WORK EXERCISE

The facts of a felonious homicide are set forth below. Information needed in the investigation of this case can be obtained by contacting the dispatcher.

Prepare a paper setting forth the investigation you would conduct in this case, beginning with your arrival at the scene. In your paper, include leads that you want covered and the information you hope to obtain as a result of such coverage. Your investigation should be logical, thorough, and systematic. All activities should be conducted in accordance with proven investigative practices.

Facts

At 1300 hours a call was received from JEANNE ADAMS, proprietor of the Sycamore Inn, a ten-unit group of rental cottages. The Inn is located on the edge of Center City at the intersection of Water Street and Highway 103. ADAMS said that she believed that someone in cottage "C" had been shot. She identified the renter of cottage as FRANK OWENS, a thirty-two year old bartender who worked a night shift at the Colonial Tavern on Highway 103. She added that "FRANK likes to play the horses." ADAMS stated that she heard what she believed to be the sound of three shots coming from cottage "C." Shortly thereafter she saw an unknown man run to a 1979 blue Chevrolet two-door sedan and drive it out of the parking lot hurriedly, heading north on Highway 103 toward Milford. ADAMS was able to furnish a partial license plate number as 13   G. She described the suspect as male, white, thirty to thirty-five years old, brown thick bushy hair, tanned complexion, full face, and wearing a brown suit coat and a pale yellow sport shirt. ADAMS believed she might be able to recognize the suspect. After the receipt of this information, the following broadcast was made:

"Unit 15A—Sycamore Inn, Water Street and Highway 103—shots fired"

Unit 15A acknowledged the broadcast.

The weather is clear and sunny. On arrival at the scene, you and your partner (an investigative team assigned to homicide), observe six cars parked in the main lot of this Inn. Ms. ADAMS meets you and your partner in the driveway and points out cottage "C." Approaching this cottage you note the door has been opened about 4 inches [10 centimeters]. You proceed to push it all the way open with your knee. Just inside the door you observe the body of a man lying on the hardwood floor face up, head to the north. His eyes and mouth are partly opened. The victim has on grey slacks, white shirt, black shoes, and black socks. ADAMS readily identifies the person as Mr. OWENS, the renter of this unit.

You further observe bloodstains on the victim's shirt near the heart, and a small pool of blood on the floor near the victim's left armpit. You also note an overturned lamp, chair, and coffee table. The glass top of the coffee table is broken into several pieces. These are all evidence of an apparent struggle. Around the body you observe several items: a chrome cigarette lighter; a black pocket comb; a square shirt button; a half-used book of matches with a lion insignia on the cover; a black, opened wallet apparently empty except for cards; and several cigarette butts (Benson & Hedges brand, filter tipped). On the north side of the lamp table, next to the sofa, you note a half-filled bottle of what appears to be Johnny Walker White Label brand scotch whiskey, and two glasses. A walnut-finished rolltop desk, located in the northwest corner of the room, appears to have been ransacked—many pieces of paper are strewn around on the floor near it.

The only bedroom is located in the northwest corner of the cottage. The dresser drawers in the bedroom appear to have been ransacked; all the drawers have been left partly opened. Other areas of the cottage seem normal. Just beyond the front door, to the left as you enter, you note a .38 cal. B/S revolver partly hidden by a large shrub. You also observe one identifiable footprint.

CHAPTER 17 ——————— Sex Crimes

Sex crimes represent a broad classification of illegal behavior. The range from the nuisance acts of voyeurism ("Peeping Tom") and exhibitionism to acts of violent behavior, viz., rape and lust murders. The investigation of sex crimes is a field for highly specialized personnel. In order to investigate a sex crime, the officer must know the type of individual involved, the crime concerned and its possible ramifications, and the corpus delicti of the particular offense. A knowledge of sociology and psychology can be of great assistance to the criminal specialist in the handling of these difficult cases.

The ramifications of sex crimes are tremendous. Sex motives project themselves into almost every type of crime that is committed, including murder, arson, theft, burglary, robbery, assault and battery, kidnapping, mayhem, etc. The infamous William Heirens, burglar, rapist, and murderer, who was eventually sentenced to life in prison, was alleged to have taken part in several hundred burglaries during which, he admitted, he received sexual satisfaction from entering strange residences. In three instances when he was interrupted in his burglarious activities he killed the females he encountered. Heirens had a fetish for women's panties which dated back to his early childhood. When arrested at the age of seventeen, Heirens had forty pairs hidden in a cardboard box under his bed. During the commission of one of his murders, Heirens wrote with lipstick on a living room wall,

"Catch me before I kill more, I cannot help myself."

The material in this chapter is not designed to teach the investigator what prompts a person to commit sex crimes, the required treatment, or how offenders should be cured or corrected. The evaluation, diagnostic process, treatment, and rehabilitative processes are within the scope of the courts and correctional fields. It is the purpose of the information set forth here, however, to help the officer gain a better understanding of sex offenses, to be conversant with their meaning and ramifications, to recognize specific violations, and to carry out the sworn duty—"to protect and serve." The sex crimes discussed herein are some of the more common offenses that constitute serious problems for most police departments.

Sex Offenders

Who are they? In terms of law enforcement, they are persons who engage in any sex practices prohibited by law. A great deal of research has been made into the intelligence, education, occupational and marital status, nationality, race, age, sex, and religion of various sex offenders without establishing any definite pattern. They appear to be of average intelligence and are often unskilled workers. Single men predominate. Their personalities have been found to be shy, timid, and nonaggresive and they are completely out of character when committing one of their vicious sex offenses. Contrary to the theory advanced by Cesare Lombroso, the noted Italian criminologist and physician, that the criminal is primarily a born type, marked by definite physical and mental stigmata, the sex offender cannot be distinguished from any other person. These criminals, as we know them, have no distinct physical characteristics and come from all walks of life.

A sex offender is classified not by the crime committed but by actions, patterns of behavior, desires, and motivations. It is not uncommon for a person to move from one of the categories below to another. However, in terms of law enforcement, the types of sex criminals are divided into three basic categories:

1. *Sex offenders* are those persons who violate the legal statutes governing the act of sexual intercourse when such violation is confined to the consummation of the act in a normal and natural manner. This generally involves such crimes as rape, seduction, abduction, prostitution, adultery, incest.

2. *Sex degenerates* are offenders who perform acts that differ from sexual intercourse. Examples are lewd and lascivious acts with a child, indecent exposure, and lewd telephone calls.

3. *Sex perverts* are individuals who, through compulsive sexual instincts, engage in "unnatural" sex acts. The term is most frequently used to describe homosexuals. In addition, it describes those who commit acts of sodomy and other sexual abnormalities. This type of person can find no gratification through conventional heterosexual —"normal"—channels.

Sex Offenses

What are sex offenses? The term "sexual offenses" represents a broad classification of illegal behavior. They can be classified into a number of types and include offenses under various names. From the viewpoint of peace officers, sex crimes may be subdivided under the topical headings in the right-hand column on the table on p. 381.

Figure 17-1 illustrates a type of rack on which a person voluntarily permits himself or herself to be strapped prior to being beaten. This is a form of masochistic perversion in which sexual satisfaction is obtained.

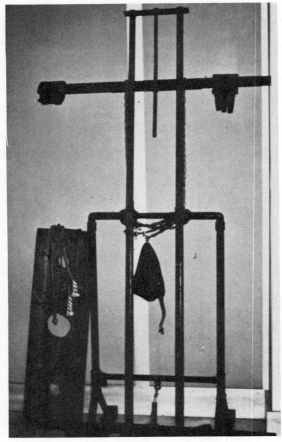

Figure 17-1. A type of rack on which a person voluntarily submits to being strapped and beaten in a masochistic form of perversion.

The victim permits herself or himself to be tied to this type of rack so that there will be no change of mind. Some baudy houses for years maintained straps, whips, and switches for individuals who came to seek their service just for this one purpose. There are cults, clubs, and groups that practice this perversion. Instances have occurred wherein women cult members were brutally flogged to death while engaged in sex orgies. Danger particularly exists where a pervert might lose control and lash the victim to death. Some holdups are staged not for the purpose of obtaining money, but so that the criminal can brutally beat the victim with a club or pistol.

Sadists are considered the most dangerous of all sex offenders. Sexual enjoyment of cruelty perpetrated upon another, or pleasure from inflicting pain, delights this person. A sadist may not only kill the victim but may also grossly mutilate the body. Lust murder is an expression of the extreme development of sadism.

Statutory laws proscribe a wide range of forbidden sex acts. However, most charges of sex crimes are made under only a few laws. Most sex offenders are dealt with under the laws forbidding rape and lewd and lascivious conduct with children. The majority of misdemeanor charges are brought under such laws as those dealing with contributing to the deliquency of a minor, lewd conduct, and exhibitionism (indecent exposure). All of these laws, vary general in nature, cover broad categories of offenses rather than specific acts. Readers are cautioned to check these offenses carefully against their own state laws.

Rape

The offense of rape is an act of heterosexual intercourse without the legal consent of the female involved. To prove innocence, the consent must be shown to have been voluntary and knowing; it is an essential element of the crime and must be proved in each case. One of the requisites of all rape is that the female must not be the wife of the perpetrator. However, a husband could be involved as a party to this crime if he assisted another in the act. The slightest sexual penetration is held sufficient to constitute sexual intercourse within the meaning of rape. An emission is unnecessary. Consent cannot legally be given by women under such conditions as unsound mind (temporary or permanent), insensibility because of drugs or anesthetic substances, or where the victim is unconscious of the nature of the act.

Voluntary	Fornication
	Adultery
	Incest
	Bigamy
	Lewd and illegal cohabitation
Involuntary	Rape
	Seduction
	Abduction
Commercial	Prostitution
	Pimping (pandering)
	Abortion
	Indecent publication
Abnormal	Sodomy
	Bestiality
	Sex perversion
	Lewd acts with a child
Nuisance offenses	Indecent exposure (exhibitionism)
	Voyeurism
	Frottage
	Transvestism
	Fetishism
	Obscenity by phone, letter, or literature
	Public obscenity by gesture or statement
	Others
Dangerous	Flagellation (sadism, masochism; see Figure 17-1)
	Anthropophagy
	Pyromania
	Piquerism
	Pedophilia
	Lust murders

See also Glossary of Terminology at the end of this chapter.

With the exception of murder, the offense of rape is considered the most serious sexual offense. It is perhaps the best known and most publicized of all the sex offenses. Convictions in forcible rape charges carry life imprisonment or long prison terms. The crime of rape has been committed under many varied circumstances and by many different classes of persons. There are many instances where females have been attacked on the street, dragged into alleys, yards or woods, and assaulted at late hours of the night. There are many instances where a criminal has been admitted to a house by the female occupant under varied pretexts advanced by the suspect, who later assaulted her. Some of these assaults have resulted in the death of the victim. There are a number of cases on record where victims have permitted themselves to be picked up by strangers to be driven home or to a shopping district only to be driven instead to a secluded spot and there assaulted by their purported benefactors. There are many cases where the victim has accepted a date with acquaintances for dinner or entertainment, and was later assaulted by her escort in an automobile or apartment. Even though some of these cases seem to reflect poor discretion on the part of the victim, they remain crimes if committed within the meaning of the statute. Rape sometimes leads to murder in order to silence the accuser. It may result in a lust murder in which the motivation itself is sexual.

Forcible Rape This classification of rape is described as an act of sexual intercourse with a female (not the wife of the perpetrator) by force or violence and against her will. The provision here is that the victim must resist and that her resistance be overcome. The force used may be actual or constructive as where submission is obtained as a result of fear or intimidation. Forcible rape as defined in the FBI National Crime Index program is "the carnal knowledge of a female through the use of force or threats of force." This offense is considered a crime of violence in the above crime index along with criminal homicide, robbery, and aggravated assault.

Statutory Rape   In this country, state statutes make it unlawful to have intercourse with females under a specified legal age. It is generally immaterial whether the accused knew of the victim's age, or whether or not she actively misled the accused as to her age. However, in a California case,[1] the court held it a reversible error to refuse to permit a defendant in a statutory rape case to present evidence showing that he had in good faith believed that the prosecutor was over eighteen years.

Some state statutes provide different punishments for sexual intercourse with a willing female over sixteen and under eighteen years if she is of previously chaste and virtuous character; other statutes recognize the previous unchaste character of the female as a defense in the consent cases if she is over fifteen years old. The statutes of the individual states must be consulted with regard to age, the admissibility of evidence, and the validity of defenses that may be offered in statutory rape cases.

Sex crimes against children

Crimes in this category include child molesting, lewd and lascivious acts with a child, indecent exposure, contributing to the deliquency of a minor, statutory rape, incest, and other statutory offenses.

Child Molesting   A child molester technically is a pedophile, a person who makes indecent advances towards children in order to obtain sexual gratification. The advances may involve all forms of sexual exploitation from fondling and exhibitionism, to rape, multilation, and murder. Many states have specific statutes covering this type of sex offender. Their acts are prosecuted under a wide range of headings dependent upon the individual acts of the molester.

Lewd and Lascivious Conduct with a Child   The elements of the crime consist of such conduct or acts upon any part of the body of a child, male or female, under a specified age, with the intention of arousing, appealing to or gratifying the lust or passions or sexual desires of the child, or of the perpetrator. If the elements of the crime are present and the suspect is positively identified, a private person arrest can be made by the victim at the scene. This applies only if the elements of the crime are present and the suspect is positively identified. If the act was observed by an officer, the officer can make the arrest.

Indecent Exposure (Exhibitionism)   This offense is regarded as the most common of the standard sex offenses. It involves the exhibition of oneself, particularly the genitals. The victim can be either a child or an adult. Such exposure may be from an auto, in a public park, or other place. The offense actively serves as a main source of sexual pleasure for the offender, who may go to extremes to accomplish that purpose. In one case a suspect cut out a portion of his trouser legs and fastened them to his shins just below the knees with rubber bands. This individual wore a shirt and tie and topcoat which gave him a semblance of being fully dressed. However, when he opened his coat, he was completely nude from the waist to just below his knees. The manner of dress was sufficient to sustain a conviction on indecent exposure.

Contributing to the Delinquency of a Minor (CDM)   Statutes of this type (CDM) impose a duty upon a parent or other adult to refrain from committing any act or omitting the performance of any duty which act or omission causes or tends to cause or encourage a minor to violate any law or otherwise lead an idle, dissolute, lewd, or immoral life. It is often a lesser included crime to other offenses, e.g., statutory rape,

---

[1] *People v. Hernandez,* 61 Cal. 2d 529 (1964).

furnishing liquor to a minor, or in felony cases wherein the minor is a principal to a crime committed by an adult.

Incest This offense is a crime of sexual intercourse or cohabitation between a man and woman who are related to each other within the degrees wherein marriage is prohibited by law. Examples are mother and son, father and daughter, brother and sister, uncle and niece. It is usually a felony. Degrees of relationship differ in the statutes of many states. One act of intercourse is enough to constitute the crime.

Suspect and Victim

In sex crimes, investigators give careful consideration to the following aspects of each case: (a) motives and condition of both parties, (b) the modus operandi of the suspect, and (c) the results of the examination of both victim and suspect.

Motives and condition of both parties
Adolescent sex experimentations
Adult males who seek sex contact with young virgins
False report to cover up acts of indiscretion
Pregnant females
Jealousy or revenge
Promiscuous females
Sex perversion
Teen-age prostitutes

Examination of both victim and suspect
Take blood tests if necessary
Find evidence that may prove that there was bodily contact between parties
Find stains, hairs, dirt
Find traces of victim's powder and lipstick on suspect

Modus operandi
Administration of liquor or drugs
Arouse passion of victim
Assault on street
Forcible entry into dwelling
Kidnapping for purpose of rape
Offering ride to victim
Pick up at bar or other public place
Presentation of gift or money to victim
Taking advantage of feeble-minded victims
Use of weapon

Investigation of Sex Offenses

There is certain essential information needed in sex offenses to establish the significant facts of the crime being investigated. Items of particular attention include the following:

Date and time of occurrence; date and time reported.
Classification of offense.
Age of victim (including date of birth).
Location or scene of occurrence; exact address including room or apartment number, street, alley, park, etc. If outside, nearest address or distance and direction from a known point.
Weather, lighting, visibility.
Condition of victim: mental condition—presence of drugs, intoxicants; physical condition—bruises, scratches; medical examination findings; indication of pregnancy—how long?
Condition of victim's clothing—tears, stains, disarray.
Statement of victim in detail (with female police officer present).
Modus operandi—way in which suspect attracted victim's attention—honking horn, rapping on window, offering ride, speaking to victim, approach in bar, theater, or other public place.
If car involved, all available descriptive

data including upholstery, seat covers, color of dash, accessories, objects or articles in car, major dents, scratches, etc.

Corroboration of victim's statements.

Character and reputation of victim.

Detailed description of the route traveled (if travel is involved).

Description of suspect and clothing.

Statements of witnesses.

Neighborhood investigation to determine whether anyone observed suspect and/or victim or heard anything relevant.

Establishment of all elements of the particular offense.

Physical evidence—clothing, personal belongings, articles discarded or left by victim or suspect, blood, hairs, fibers fingerprints, semen stains, foot and tire impressions, soil, and botanical materials.

If suspect apprehended—advise of rights.

Establishment of suspect's employment and hours of work.

List of items found in suspect's car (road maps, newspapers, rags).

Statement in detail from suspect as to actions and activities during pertinent times.

Complete description of suspect, and colored photographs.

Photographs of crime scene including general view and close-ups of pertinent points of interest.

Investigation of rape cases

The investigation of rape offenses should answer the questions who, what, when, where, how, and why. The procedures undertaken should include

Accompaniment of the victim by a female police officer to the hospital or place of examination.

Examination of victim by a physician as soon as practicable. Vaginal smears should be obtained for laboratory examination. The identity of the examining physician should be obtained as she or he is an important witness in all rape cases.

Recording of all visible indications of injury, e.g., bruises and lacerations. Colored photographs should be taken wherever possible, for court purposes.

Obtaining of all garments worn by victim. Identify, wrap separately, and transport to the crime laboratory for examination.

Taking of a detailed statement (written or recorded) from victim as soon as she is able to give a coherent account of the events. This statement is usually taken by a female police officer who should be present at the questioning. In many cases, however, another investigator may assist in the interview, preferably another female officer. The interview with the victim should be monitored by an experienced detective. Victims, especially younger victims are reluctant to discuss intimacies in the presence of a male. The statement should include the age and marital status of the victim. It should be detailed as to events preceding the crime—for example, where a victim accepted a ride with her eventual attacker. The statement should include the location, and why the victim accepted the ride. It should cover conversations with the suspect, routes, locations, and persons having any knowledge of prior or subsequent events. Other data of significance include the fears the victim may express, and, if the suspect is known to her, when and where they first met, frequency of meetings, times, dates, places, description of force used, and resistance offered.

Ascertaining the character and reputation of victim.

Possible motives (pregnancy, jealousy, revenge, false report to cover up indiscreet acts, etc.).

Transporting victim to the location of the alleged assault in order that she might point out the exact location. This procedure provides the opportunity for a careful search for evidence—shoe impressions, tire tracks, bloodstains, articles of jewelry, buttons, hairs, items of clothing, handkerchiefs, discarded protectives, signs of a struggle, and other evidence to prove the crime of rape or to disprove the allegations. If offense was committed indoors, bedclothing (if pertinent) should be obtained and forwarded to the crime laboratory for examination. Complaints of rape are sometimes unfounded and are prompted by the complainant's fear of pregnancy as the result of an illicit intercourse or by a malicious desire to bring punishment to the suspect.

The value of recognizing evidence at a crime scene, no matter how insignificant it may seem at the time, was demonstrated in a successful solution of a rape case by an Eastern police department. Detectives in that case traced a distributor's stamp on the cellophane wrapper of a cigarette package to a nearby town where the distributor informed them that he had made deliveries to only two stores in their city. Upon contacting both stores, one of them was able to identify the rapist from a description that the police had obtained from the victim.

Additional procedures should include:

Photographing and sketching the crime scene. Adequate notes should be made prior to collecting, identifying, preserving, and transporting evidence to the laboratory. Photographs can assist in corroborating victim's statements and help to expose false assertions.

Obtaining suspect's clothing, if possible. The clothing (including shoes) should be submitted to the crime laboratory with the request that all articles be examined for soil specimens, weed seeds, grasses, and other botanical materials that might be identified with the crime scene (if out of doors).

Impounding of suspect's vehicle. It should be processed for identifiable materials such as stains (blood and semen), hairs, fibers, and other transfer materials. In sex offenses it is often possible to show contact between two individuals or between one individual and some other object by comparing transferred fibers.[2] Such examinations are only of value when it is known that no contact occurred between the individuals or objects prior to or subsequent to the offense. Extreme care must be exercised to keep all articles of clothing and other objects separated. Each garment should be separately packaged in plastic or paper bags. Large garments may be laid on clean sheets of paper on a table and separately rolled up in the paper. Mark each exhibit. If the clothing of either subject is permitted to touch the clothing of the other or is even laid down on a table or placed on a car seat previously contacted by the clothing of the other subject, the comparisons may have no value. Should the garments involved be wet with stains, they should be air-dried before packing.

The following sexual assault case illustrates the transfer of fibers, hair, blood, seminal stains, and other evidence between

[2]*Physical Evidence Manual,* Division of Law Enforcement, Investigative Services Branch, Department of Justice, State of California, March 1976.

a victim and a suspect, which caused the suspect to enter a guilty plea in view of the overwhelming scientific findings against him. In this instance, a young couple, while parked on a country road were approached by an unknown suspect who threatened to kill the young people if they interfered. This suspect then proceeded to sexually assault the young woman. The victim's clothing was carefully identified, each item separately packaged, and transmitted to the laboratory for examination.

Thereafter, the investigation developed a suspect residing in the general vicinity of the crime area. His clothing was obtained and forwarded to the laboratory. Seven different types of fibers similar to those composing the trousers of the suspect were found on the clothing of the girl. Fibers matching the fibers of which the girl's dress was composed were found on the T-shirt and trousers of the suspect. A fragment of hair was found on the dress of the victim which, in all observable characteristics, matched the known hair samples of the suspect. A button, with a sewing thread still attached, was found on the rear floor of the car and matched the thread with which the remaining buttons were sewn to the suspect's trousers.

In addition, human head hairs which matched known head hairs of the victim were found on the trousers of the suspect, as was pubic hair. Human blood on the fly of the suspect's trousers belonged to the same international blood group as the blood of the victim and could not have come from the suspect as his blood was of another group. Seminal stains were found on the clothing of both the victim and the suspect.

Sample of a Completed Kidnap-Rape Offense Report with Supporting Data

As an aid in visualizing the reporting structure of reports prepared by an officer im-

mediately following the investigation of a kidnap-rape offense, for example, Figure 17-2 demonstrates the type of "paper work" involved.

White Slave Traffic Act (The Mann Act: U.S.C., title 18)

Sec. 2421. Transportation generally

Whoever knowingly transports in interstate or foreign commerce, or in the District of Columbia or in any Territory or Possession of the United States, any woman or girl for the purpose of prostitution or debauchery or for any other immoral purpose, or with the intent and purpose to induce, entice, or compel such woman or girl to become a prostitute or to give herself up to debauchery, or to engage in any other immoral practice; or

Whoever knowingly procures or obtains any ticket or tickets, or any form of transportation or evidence of the right thereto, to be used by any woman or girl in interstate or foreign commerce, or in the District of Columbia or any Territory or Possession of the United States, in going to any place for the purpose of prostitution or debauchery, or any other immoral purpose, or with the intent or purpose on the part of such person to induct, entice, or compel her to give herself up to the practice of prostitution, or to give herself up to debauchery, or any other immoral practice, whereby any such woman or girl shall be transported in interstate or foreign commerce, or in the District of Columbia or any Territory or Possession or the United States, shall be fined not more than $5,000 or imprisoned not more than five years, or both.

Sec. 2422. Coercion or enticement of female

Whoever knowingly persuades, induces, entices, or coerces any woman or girl to go from one place to another in interstate or foreign commerce, or in the District of Columbia or in any Territory or Possession of the

81-316

CENTER CITY POLICE DEPARTMENT 3402

2. CODE SECTION 207, 261.3 PC	3. CRIME KIDNAP-RAPE	4. CLASSIFICATION PARKING LOT - KNIFE	5 REPORT AREA Div. 4

| 6. DATE AND TIME OCCURRED - DAY 3/14/79 2300 hrs | 7. DATE AND TIME REPORTED 3/15/79 0030 | 8. LOCATION OF OCCURRENCE City Park, Oak & 38th Sts,Center City |

| 9. VICTIM'S NAME LAST, FIRST, MIDDLE (FIRM IF BUSINESS) WILSON, MARY A. | 10. RESIDENCE ADDRESS 1178 Main St., Apt. "C" | 11. RES PHONE 88-50326 |

| 12. OCCUPATION Nurse | 13. RACE - SEX WFA | 14. AGE 28 | 15. DOB 2/25/51 | 16. BUSINESS ADDRESS (SCHOOL IF JUVENILE) 805 N.Maple St. Center City | 17. BUS PHONE 88-62145 |

CODES FOR BOXES 20 AND 30 — V=VICTIM W=WITNESS P=PARENT RP=REPORTING PARTY DC=DISCOVERED CRIME — 18. CHECK IF MORE NAMES IN CONTINUATION BOX

19. NAME - LAST, FIRST, MIDDLE	20. CODE	21. RESIDENCE ADDRESS	22. RESIDENCE PHONE
23.OCCUPATION	24. RACE - SEX	25. AGE	26. DOB	27. BUSINESS ADDRESS (SCHOOL IF JUVENILE)	28. BUSINESS PHONE
29. NAME - LAST, FIRST, MIDDLE		30. CODE	31. RESIDENCE ADDRESS	32. RESIDENCE PHONE
33. OCCUPATION	34.RACE - SEX	35 AGE	36.DOB	37. BUSINESS ADDRESS (SCHOOL IF JUVENILE)	38. BUSINESS PHONE

MODUS OPERANDI (SEE INSTRUCTIONS)

39. DESCRIBE CHARACTERISTICS OF PREMISES AND AREA WHERE OFFENSE OCCURRED
Carport, rear of Apt.Complex, Resid./Apt.neighborhood and City Park

40. DESCRIBE BRIEFLY HOW OFFENSE WAS COMMITTED
Grabbed victim from rear. Knife held at throat. Taken to City Park where
both suspects took turns raping V. Dish towel used as gag.

41. DESCRIBE WEAPON, INSTRUMENT, EQUIPMENT, TRICK, DEVICE OR FORCE USED
Hands & hunting knife and threats

42. MOTIVE - TYPE OF PROPERTY TAKEN OR OTHER REASON FOR OFFENSE
Sexual gratification

43. ESTIMATED LOSS VALUE AND/OR EXTENT OF INJURIES — MINOR, MAJOR
Contusions and abrasions of the knees, elbows and forehead

44. WHAT DID SUSPECT/S SAY — NOTE PECULIARITIES
"If you make one sound I'll slit your throat. Come with us and you won't
get hurt"

45. VICTIM'S ACTIVITY JUST PRIOR TO AND/OR DURING OFFENSE
Walking from carport to apartment

46. TRADEMARK — OTHER DISTINCTIVE ACTION OF SUSPECT/S
Suspect #1 spoke with a lisp

47. VEHICLE USED — LICENSE NO. - ID NO. - YEAR - MAKE - MODEL - COLORS (OTHER IDENTIFYING CHARACTERISTICS)
Chevrolet, Lic. unk. 4-dr.sedn. 1979, grey, auto-shift, blk. uph. w/sidewalls

| 48. SUSPECT NO. 1 (LAST, FIRST, MIDDLE) HALL, RALPH S. | 49.RACE - SEX WMA | 50 AGE 32 | 51 HT 6 | 52 WT 175 | 53.HAIR Brn | 54 EYES Brn | 55 ID NO. OR DOB 2/4/47 | 56 ARRESTED YES ☒NO |

57. ADDRESS, CLOTHING AND OTHER IDENTIFYING MARKS OR CHARACTERISTICS brn trousers
984 Mission Rd, Center City; Brn shirt, Blk jacket, blk half-boots

| 58. SUSPECT NO.2 (LAST, FIRST, MIDDLE) SMITH, JOHN W. | 59.RACE - SEX MWA | 60 AGE 26 | 61.HT. 5'8 | 62 WT 150 | 63.HAIR Brn | 64 EYES Brn | 65 ID NO. OR DOB 3/2/53 | 66 ARRESTED YES ☒NO |

67 ADDRESS, CLOTHING AND OTHER IDENTIFYING MARKS OR CHARACTERISTICS blk shoes
397 N. Wall St., Center City; Wh. "T" shirt, Blue Denim jkt/pnts

68. CHECK IF MORE NAMES IN CONTINUATION

| REPORTING OFFICERS J.F.JENSEN #22; F.R.King #18 | RECORDING OFFICER JENSEN | TYPED BY wrj | DATE AND TIME 3/15/79 0315 | ROUTED BY |

FURTHER ACTION ☒ YES ☐ NO
COPIES TO: ☒ DETECTIVE ☒ CII DOJ
☐ JUVENILE ☐ PATROL
☒ DIST. ATTNY ☐ OTHER
☐ SO./P.D. ☐ OTHER

REVIEWED BY Lt. J. L. ROBERTS #14   3/15/79
DATE

Figure 17-2. A completed, hypothetical ten-page felony rape-kidnap report.

		69 CASE NO.
		81-316

CENTER CITY POLICE DEPARTMENT   CA 0354

70 CODE SECTION	71 CRIME	72. CLASSIFICATION		
207, 261.3 PC	KIDNAP-RAPE	PARKING LOT - KNIFE		
73 VICTIM'S NAME - LAST, FIRST, MIDDLE (FIRM IF BUS.)		74. ADDRESS	RESIDENCE BUSINESS	75 PHONE
WILSON, MARY A.		1055 Main St. Apt. "C"		88-50326

ASSIGNMENT:

On 3/15/79 at 0305 hrs. reporting officers were assigned to contact Miss MARY A. WILSON at the N. E. corner of Oak and 38th Sts. Radio control advised that she allegedly had just been forcibly raped by two unknown white males at City Park.

SUMMARY:

On 3/14/79, 11 PM. victim, a white, female, age 28 was walking from her carport toward her apartment when she was grabbed from the rear by suspect #1. Suspect #2 placed a 4" hunting knife at her throat threatening to cut it unless she did as she was told. Victim forced into front seat of a 1979 Chev. 4-dr. sdn, grey, between suspects and then driven (Susp. #2 driver) to an isolated area of City Park where she was forced to have sexual intercourse with both suspects. Each suspect held victim while the other sexually assaulted her. Suspect #1 gagged victim with dishtowel during occurrence. Victim was left at the scene and was warned by suspect #1 to remain there for ten minutes and not to call the police or they would return and kill her. After suspects drove away, victim immediately called police.

INTERVIEW WITH VICTIM MARY A. WILSON

Miss Mary A. WILSON, age 28, was contacted at 0310 hrs. at the above location at which time she furnished the following information. She related that at about 11:00 PM 3/14/79 she parked her car in the carport section at the rear of the apartment house where she resides - 1055 Main Street, Center City. She stated that while proceeding from the carport to her apartment building she noticed two unknown men standing near the sidewalk entrance to this building. She related that as she proceeded past them the taller of the two (Susp. #1) grabbed her from behind pinning her arms. At that time, according to Miss WILSON, the shorter of the two (Susp. #2) placed an approximate 4" hunting-type knife close to her throat stating "If you make one sound, I'll slit your throat. Come with us and you won't get hurt."

Victim advised that she was then forced to walk to the rear of the apartment where their car was parked and forced into the front seat - seated between the two suspects. She stated that they then drove her to City Park - suspect #2 driving. Miss WILSON stated that suspects took her to the south side of this park at which time they made her walk about 300 ft. from the road to a grassy area surrounded by a lot of shrubs and trees. There, she stated, suspect #1

REPORTING OFFICERS		RECORDING OFFICER	TYPED BY	DATE AND TIME	ROUTED BY
FURTHER ACTION ☐ YES COPIES TO: ☐ DETECTIVE ☐ CII					
☐ NO ☐ JUVENILE ☐ PATROL					
☐ DIST. ATTNY. ☐ OTHER					
☐ SO/PD ☐ OTHER		REVIEWED BY		DATE	

		GS CASE NO
CENTER CITY POLICE DEPARTMENT CA 0354		81-316

70 CODE SECTION	71 CRIME	72 CLASSIFICATION		
207, 261.3	KIDNAP - RAPE	PARKING LOT - KNIFE		
73 VICTIM'S NAME - LAST, FIRST, MIDDLE (FIRM IF BUS)		74 ADDRESS [X] RESIDENCE [ ] BUSINESS		75 PHONE
WILSON, MARY A.		1055 Main St. Apt. "C"		88-50326

pushed her to the ground tore her panties off and while suspect #2 held her, suspect #1 had intercourse with her against her will. She indicated that during the time she was physically assaulted, suspect #1 placed a dishtowel type cloth in her mouth as a gag. Victim related that she struggled with suspect #1 and scratched him on the left side of his face at which time he slapped her face. Miss WILSON advised that she did not resist further fearing for her safety. She stated that after suspect #1 raped her, he then held her while suspect #2 also had intercourse with her. Both suspects had emissions while raping her, according to victim.

Victim stated that when suspect #2 had sexually assaulted her suspect #1 warned her "don't get up for ten minutes after we leave or we will return and kill you." Also, that "if you know what is good for you you don't say anything about this to anyone." She advised that suspects then walked to their car and drove away. Victim said that as soon as she heard their car drive away she went to a phone and contacted the police.

CRIME SCENE:

Inasmuch as the location where victim was sexually assaulted was near the place where officers interviewed victim, Miss WILSON voluntarily accompanied officers to the spot in City Park where the alleged sex assault had occurred. The location was noted to be an isolated grassy, bushy area with a lot of shrubs and trees. This section of the park was approximately 100 yards southwest of the intersection of Oak and 38th Sts. On searching the designated area, officer KING found a pair of white panties which victim identified as hers; also, a pale yellow dishtowel which she stated appeared to be the one with which suspect #1 gagged her. Both these items were collected by officer KING, placed in separate cellophane envelopes and identified with the initials F.R.K. Officer KING also found a cigarette butt at this location - Kent Brand, filter tip, which he likewise identified and placed in a small cellophane envelope evidence envelope. Several footprints were noted in the grassy turf. However, due to the grassy condition of the turf it was not possible to obtain any identifiable prints. Six small specimens of grass and earth plugs were obtained from this area by officer JENSEN. These specimens were placed in separate evidence containers, sealed and identified by officer JENSEN with his initials J.F.J. and notes made as to the location where obtained. Five flash photographs of the crime scene were taken by officer KING.

After completing this search, victim was transported to the Benson Emergency Hospital where an examination of the victim was made by Dr. CHARLES THOMAS and a Rape Kit completed. This kit was initialed and sealed by Dr. THOMAS and turned over to officer JENSEN.

FURTHER ACTION	[ ] YES [ ] NO	COPIES TO	[ ] DETECTIVE [ ] JUVENILE [ ] DIST. ATTNY [ ] SO/PD	[ ] CII [ ] PATROL [ ] OTHER [ ] OTHER		
					REVIEWED BY	DATE

CENTER CITY POLICE DEPARTMENT   CA 0354

CASE NO
81-316

CODE SECTION	71 CRIME	72 CLASSIFICATION
207, 261.3 PC	KIDNAP-RAPE	PARKING LOT, KNIFE

VICTIM'S NAME - LAST, FIRST, MIDDLE (FIRM IF BUS.)	74 ADDRESS X RESIDENCE	BUSINESS	75 PHONE
WILSON, MARY A.	1055 Main St. Apt. "C"		88-50326

EVIDENCE REPORT

ITEM   DESCRIPTION

1........... One (1) Cigarette butt (Kent Brand,filter tip)..Tag #82761

2........... One (1) Pale yellow dishtowel...................Tag #82762

3........... One (1) Pair woman's white panties.............Tag #82763

4........... Six (6) Small plugs of grass and earth.........Tag #s 82764-69
               incl.

5........... One (1) Carton containing a skirt, blouse,
            sweater, stockings, and shoes of victim
            MARY A. WILSON................................Tag #s 82770-74
               incl.

6........... One (1) Rape Kit #7341 delivered to laboratory
            technician J. P. ARDEN by officer KING.........Tag #82775

7........... Five (5) Photographs of crime scene taken by
            officer KING..................................Tag #82776

8........... One (1) Four-inch hunting knife, brown plastic
            handle taken from suspect SMITH by officer KING.Tag #82777

9........... One (1) Carton containing shoes and clothing
            of suspect RALPH S. HALL (blk half-boots,
            brn shirt, brn trousers, blk jacket and tan
            undershorts)..................................Tag #s 82778-82
               incl.

10........... One (1) Carton containing shoes and clothing
            of suspect JOHN W. SMITH (white "T" shirt,
            white undershorts, blue denim trousers, blue
            denim jacket,and blk shoes)...................Tag #s 82783-87
               incl.

(Items 1,2,3,7,9 and 10 were collected, marked for
identification by officer F.R.KING and turned over
to the crime lab. by KING on 3/15/79).

(Items 4, 5, 6 and 8 were collected, marked for
identification by officer JENSEN and turned over
to the crime lab. by JENSEN on 3/15/79).

(5)

ARREST REPORT

DEFENDANT

LAST	FIRST	MIDDLE
SMITH,	JOHN	W.

Date of Report___3/15/79_____

Crime___KIDNAP-RAPE_____

Booking #___2134_____

File #___81-316____

	SEX	RACE	AGE	DOB		HEIGHT	WEIGHT	HAIR	EYES
Description	Male	W	26	3-2-53	/	5'8 /	150 /	brn /	brn

Address___397 N. Wall St., Center City___   Phone #___88-16632

Place of Arrest___2500 blk W. Highland Ave___   Date___3/15/79___ Time___0400 hrs.

Arresting Officers___J. F. JENSEN #22; F. R. KING #18___ Divn-Sta___#4____

Arrested on Warrant #___No___   Without Warrant___XXX

FULL DETAILS OF ARREST AND COURT ACTION BELOW

At 0400 hrs while patrolling in the vicinity of Highland St. and Sterling Ave, a 1979 Chevrolet 4-dr. sedan, grey, containing two occupants were observed travelling west on Highland St. with only parking lights showing. This car was noted to match the description of a car wanted in connection with a rape attack on this date. A pull-over of the suspect's car was ordered. Upon approaching the vehicle the driver appeared to be perspiring freely and **shaking** noticeably. A record check of this car disclosed that it was registered to JOHN W. SMITH and that SMITH had one burglary arrest and conviction in 1976. The passenger in this car was identified as RALPH S. HALL whose record reflected 3 prior arrests for sex offenses. Both SMITH and HALL had several stains on their trousers which appeared to be grass stains.

Both suspects were placed under arrest and searched for possible weapons. A four-inch hunting knife with brown plastic handle was found in suspect SMITH's right rear trouser pocket by officer JENSEN. Suspect HALL had no weapons on his person. It was observed that suspect SMITH was smoking a Kent filter tip cigarette. Following the search suspects were taken to the Center City jail where they were booked on the above charge by officer JENSEN.

SEE: EVIDENCE REPORT

Signature of Arresting Officers_____   _____/_____

DISPOSITION

	DATE	TIME	BY		DATE	TIME	BY
Rel. on Bail	____/	____/	_____	Rel. No Comp.	____/	____/	_____
Comp. Filed	____/	____/	_____	Arraigned	____/	____/	_____

Original

ARREST REPORT

Date of Report___3/15/79_____

Crime__KIDNAP-RAPE_____

DEFENDANT

LAST	FIRST	MIDDLE
HALL,	RALPH	S.

Booking #___2134_____

File #___**81-316**_____

	SEX	RACE	AGE	DOB	HEIGHT	WEIGHT	HAIR	EYES
Description	Male	W	32	2-4-47	/ 6	/ 175	/ brn	brn

Address__984 Mission Rd. Center City_____   Phone #___88-14682

Place of Arrest____2500 blk W. Highland Ave____   _Date_3/15/79_____Time___0400 hrs

Arresting Officers__J. F. JENSEN #22; F. R. KING #18__ Divn-Sta_#4

Arrested on Warrant #___No_____   Without Warrant__XXX

FULL DETAILS OF ARREST AND COURT ACTION BELOW

At 0400 hrs while patrolling in the vicinity of Highland St. and Sterling Ave, a 1979 Chevrolet 4-dr. sedan, grey, containing two occupants were observed travelling west on Highland with only parking lights showing. This car was noted to match the description of a car wanted in connection with a rape attack which occurred a few hours previous. A pull-over of the suspect's car was ordered. Upon approaching the vehicle the driver appeared to be perspiring freely and shaking noticeably. A record check of this vehicle disclosed that the car was registered to JOHN S. SMITH and that SMITH had one burglary arrest and conviction in 1976. The passenger in this car was identified as RALPH S. HALL whose record reflected 3 prior arrests for sex offenses. Both SMITH and HALL had several stains on their trousers which appeared to be grass stains.

Both suspects were placed under arrest and searched for possible weapons. A four-inch hunting knife with brown plastic handle was found in suspect SMITH's right rear trousers pocket by officer JENSEN. Suspect HALL had no weapons on his person. It was noted that suspect SMITH was smoking a Kent filter tip cigarette (a brand of cigarette found at the crime scene). Following the search suspects were taken to the Center City jail where they were booked on the above charge.

SEE: EVIDENCE REPORT

Signature of Arresting Officers_____   _____/_____

DISPOSITION

	DATE	TIME	BY		DATE	TIME	BY
Rel. on Bail	_____/	_____/	_____	Rel. No Comp.	_____/	_____/	_____
Comp. Filed	_____/	_____/	_____	Arraigned	_____/	_____/	_____

		69. CASE NO.
CENTER CITY POLICE DEPARTMENT CA 0354		81-316

70 CODE SECTION 207, 261.3 PC	71 CRIME KIDNAP-RAPE	72. CLASSIFICATION PARKING LOT - KNIFE			
73 VICTIM'S NAME - LAST, FIRST, MIDDLE (FIRM IF BUS.) WILSON, Mary A.		74. ADDRESS 1055 Main St. Apt. "C"	RESIDENCE	BUSINESS	75 PHONE 88-50236

INTERVIEW WITH SUSPECT RALPH S. HALL

On 3/15/79, at 0430 hrs. suspect HALL was advised of his rights by officer
J. F. JENSEN per Miranda at the Center City jail. Mr. HALL stated that he
understood his rights and that he did not wish to say anything without the
advice of counsel. Interview discontinued.

INTERVIEW WITH SUSPECT JOHN W. SMITH

On 3/15/79 at 0445 hrs. suspect SMITH was advised of his rights by officer
F. R. KING per Miranda at the Center City jail. Mr. SMITH stated that he
understood his rights but did not wish to make any statements without the
advice of counsel. Interview discontinued.

REPORTING OFFICERS	RECORDING OFFICER	TYPED BY	DATE AND TIME	ROUTED BY

FURTHER ACTION	YES	COPIES TO:	DETECTIVE	CII		
	NO		JUVENILE	PATROL		
			DIST. ATTNY.	OTHER		
			SO./PD.	OTHER	REVIEWED BY	DATE

(SEX SHEET) (8)

CENTER CITY
POLICE DEPARTMENT

| SEX FILE NUMBER (1-4) | | Date 3/15/79 | Time 0445 hrs. |

DATE OF ARREST 3/15/79 | PLACE OF ARREST 2500 Blk. W. Highland

SUSPECT'S NAME (5-28) HALL, Ralph S. | Alias Harry Adams

SUSPECT'S ADDRESS (5-28) 984 Mission Rd. | CITY Center City | OCCUPATION Welder

SUSPECT'S AGE (29-30) 32 | DATE OF BIRTH 2/4/47 | PLACE OF BIRTH Chicago, Illinois

OFFENSE (31-32) Kidnap-Rape | DATE OF OFFENSE 3/14/79 | TIME OF OFFENSE 2300 hours

LOCATION OF CRIME City Park, Oak and 38th Sts. Center City

SUSPECT'S AUTO: MAKE (33-34) - | COLOR (35) - | YEAR (36-37) -

AUTO TYPE (38) - | LICENSE NO. - | MISC.

REMARKS MADE BY SUSPECT "If you know whats good for you don't say anything about this

TRADEMARK (How crime committed) MO (39-46) Grab V near Apt.-threaten with knife -(to anyone.

VICTIM'S NAME WILSON, Mary A. (take to City Pk -rape | AGE 28 | SEX F

REGISTRATION STATUS (47) Reg.X-Con | ARRESTING OFFICERS JENSEN,J.F.;KING,F.R. | DISTRICT (48) Div.4

DEPARTMENT Center City PD | CASE FILE NO. 81-316 | GRID KEY (49-52)

---

(53) COLOR & SEX
1 (X) White Male
2 ( ) White Female
3 ( ) Mexican Male
4 ( ) Mexican Female
5 ( ) Negro Male
6 ( ) Negro Female
7 ( ) Indian Male
8 ( ) Indian Female
9 ( ) Others Male
10 ( ) Others Female

(54) Height
1 ( ) Short (Up to 5'6)
2 ( ) Med. (5'6 to 5'10)
3 (X) Tall (Over 5'10)
4 Exact Height 6'

(55) WEIGHT
1 ( ) Light (Up to 140 lbs.)
2 (X) Med. (141 to 179 lbs.)
3 ( ) Heavy (180 lbs & over)
4 Exact Weight 175

(56) BUILD
1 ( ) Slender
2 (X) Medium
3 ( ) Heavy

(57) COMPLEXION
1 (X) Sallow
2 ( ) Light-Fair
3 ( ) Ruddy
4 ( ) Dark-Swarthy
5 ( ) Freckled
6 ( ) Ginger or Lt Brown
7 ( ) Drk Brown or Negro
8 ( ) Chocolate or Black
9 (X) Pockmarked

(58) TATOO MARKS
1 ( ) Right Arm
2 ( ) Right Hand
3 ( ) Right Fingers
4 (X) Left Arm (Anchor)
5 ( ) Left Hand
6 ( ) Left Fingers
7 ( ) Visible Neck or Chest

(59) HAIR COLOR
1 ( ) Blonde
2 ( ) Red
3 (X) Brown
4 ( ) Black
5 ( ) Gray
6 ( ) Partially Gray

(60) HAIR TYPE
1 ( ) Bald
2 ( ) Partially Bald
3 ( ) Bobbed
4 ( ) Curly
5 (X) Straight
6 ( ) Unkempt
7 ( ) Bushy

(61) EYE COLOR
1 ( ) Blue
2 ( ) Gray
3 ( ) Hazel
4 (X) Maroon or Brown
5 ( ) Black
6 ( ) Separate Colors

(62) EYE DEFECTS (None)
1 ( ) Cast, Right eye
2 ( ) Cast, Left eye
3 ( ) Right eye missing or artificial
4 ( ) Left eye missing or artificial
5 ( ) Near Sighted
6 ( ) Wears Glasses
7 ( ) Glasses occasionally

(63) VISIBLE SCARS or MOLES (None)
1 ( ) Face & Head, R. Side
2 ( ) Face & Head, L. Side
3 ( ) Face & Head, both sides
4 ( ) Neck
5 ( ) Nose, include broken
6 ( ) R. Hand, wrist or arm
7 ( ) L. Hand, wrist or arm
8 ( ) Both Hands, wrists or arms
9 ( ) Chin, including cleft

(64) MUSTACHE
1 ( ) Yes
2 (X) No

(65-66) AMPUTATIONS & (None) DEFORMITIES
1 ( ) Right Ear
2 ( ) Left Ear
3 ( ) Right Arm
4 ( ) Right Leg
5 ( ) Left Arm
6 ( ) Left Leg
7 ( ) Right Hand
8 ( ) Left Hand
9 ( ) Right Foot
10 ( ) Left Foot
11 ( ) Finger Right Hand
12 ( ) Finger Left Hand
13 ( ) Hunch Back
14 ( ) Lame
15 ( ) Crippled Right Arm
16 ( ) Crippled Left Arm
17 ( ) Crippled Right Leg
18 ( ) Crippled Left Leg
19 ( ) Left Handed

(67) TEETH
1 ( ) Protruding Uppers
2 ( ) Protruding Lowers
3 (X) Irregular
4 ( ) Gold, visible
5 ( ) Stained
6 ( ) Decay, visible
7 ( ) False
8 ( ) Missing, visible
9 ( ) Good

(68) SPEECH
1 ( ) Soft or Low
2 ( ) Southern Accent
3 ( ) Loud
4 ( ) Refined
5 ( ) Vulgar
6 ( ) Foreign or broken
7 (X) Impediment (lisp)
8 ( ) Stuttering
9 ( ) Rapid
10 ( ) Dumb

(69) DRESS
1 ( ) Neat
2 ( ) Well Dressed
3 (X) Rough
4 ( ) Uniform

CENTER CITY
POLICE DEPARTMENT

SEX FILE NUMBER (1-4) | Date 3/15/79 | Time 0445 hrs.
DATE OF ARREST 3/15/79 | PLACE OF ARREST 2500 Blk. W. Highland

SUSPECT'S NAME (5-28) SMITH, John W. | Alias Robert Mason
SUSPECT'S ADDRESS (5-28) 397 N. Wall St. | CITY Center City | OCCUPATION Carpenter
SUSPECT'S AGE (29-30) 26 | DATE OF BIRTH 3/2/53 | PLACE OF BIRTH Bradford, Ma.
OFFENSE (31-32) Kidnap - Rape | DATE OF OFFENSE 3/14/79 | TIME OF OFFENSE 2300 hours
LOCATION OF CRIME City Park, Oak and 38th Sts. Center City
SUSPECT'S AUTO: MAKE (33-34) Chevrolet | COLOR (35) Grey | YEAR (36-37) 1979
AUTO TYPE (38) Sedan - 4-Dr. | LICENSE NO. 165 SAM | MISC.
REMARKS MADE BY SUSPECT "If you make one sound I'll slit your throat."
TRADEMARK (How crime committed) MO (39-46) Grab V near Apt.-threaten with knife - take to City Park - rape V
VICTIM'S NAME WILSON, Mary A. | AGE 28 | SEX F
REGISTRATION STATUS (47) Reg.X-con ARRESTING OFFICERS JENSEN, J.F. KING, F.R. DISTRICT (48) Div. 4
DEPARTMENT Center City PD | CASE FILE NO. 81-316 | GRID KEY (49-52)

(53) COLOR & SEX
1 (X) White Male
2 ( ) White Female
3 ( ) Mexican Male
4 ( ) Mexican Female
5 ( ) Negro Male
6 ( ) Negro Female
7 ( ) Indian Male
8 ( ) Indian Female
9 ( ) Others Male
10 ( ) Others Female

(54) Height
1 ( ) Short (Up to 5'6)
2 (X) Med. (5'6 to 5'10)
3 ( ) Tall (Over 5'10)
4 Exact Height 5'8

(55) WEIGHT
1 ( ) Light (Up to 140 lbs.)
2 (X) Med. (141 to 179 lbs.)
3 ( ) Heavy (180 lbs. & over)
4 Exact Weight 150

(56) BUILD
1 ( ) Slender
2 (X) Medium
3 ( ) Heavy

(57) COMPLEXION
1 (X) Sallow
2 ( ) Light-Fair
3 ( ) Ruddy
4 ( ) Dark-Swarthy
5 ( ) Freckled
6 ( ) Ginger or Lt. Brown
7 ( ) Drk. Brown or Negro
8 ( ) Chocolate or Black
9 ( ) Pockmarked

(58) TATOO MARKS
1 (X) Right Arm (ROSE)
2 ( ) Right Hand
3 ( ) Right Fingers
4 ( ) Left Arm
5 ( ) Left Hand
6 ( ) Left Fingers
7 ( ) Visible Neck or Chest

(59) HAIR COLOR
1 ( ) Blonde
2 ( ) Red
3 (X) Brown
4 ( ) Black
5 ( ) Gray
6 ( ) Partially Gray

(60) HAIR TYPE
1 ( ) Bald
2 ( ) Partially Bald
3 ( ) Bobbed
4 ( ) Curly
5 (X) Straight
6 ( ) Unkempt
7 ( ) Bushy

(61) EYE COLOR
1 ( ) Blue
2 ( ) Gray
3 ( ) Hazel
4 (X) Maroon or Brown
5 ( ) Black
6 ( ) Separate Colors

(62) EYE DEFECTS (None)
1 ( ) Cast, Right eye
2 ( ) Cast, Left eye
3 ( ) Right eye missing or artificial
4 ( ) Left eye missing or artificial
5 ( ) Near Sighted
6 ( ) Wears Glasses
7 ( ) Glasses occasionally

(63) VISIBLE SCARS or MOLES (None)
1 ( ) Face & Head, R. Side
2 ( ) Face & Head, L. Side
3 ( ) Face & Head, both sides
4 ( ) Neck
5 ( ) Nose, include broken
6 ( ) R. Hand, wrist or arm
7 ( ) L. Hand, wrist or arm
8 ( ) Both Hands, wrists or arms
9 ( ) Chin, including cleft

(64) MUSTACHE
1 ( ) Yes
2 (X) No

(65-66) AMPUTATIONS & (None) DEFORMITIES
1 ( ) Right Ear
2 ( ) Left Ear
3 ( ) Right Arm
4 ( ) Right Leg
5 ( ) Left Arm
6 ( ) Left Leg
7 ( ) Right Hand
8 ( ) Left Hand
9 ( ) Right Foot
10 ( ) Left Foot
11 ( ) Finger Right Hand
12 ( ) Finger Left Hand
13 ( ) Hunch Back
14 ( ) Lame
15 ( ) Crippled Right Arm
16 ( ) Crippled Left Arm
17 ( ) Crippled Right Leg
18 ( ) Crippled Left Leg
19 ( ) Left Handed

(67) TEETH
1 ( ) Protruding Uppers
2 ( ) Protruding Lowers
3 (X) Irregular
4 ( ) Gold, visible
5 ( ) Stained
6 ( ) Decay, visible
7 ( ) False
8 ( ) Missing, visible
9 ( ) Good

(68) SPEECH
1 ( ) Soft or Low
2 ( ) Southern Accent
3 ( ) Loud
4 ( ) Refined
5 ( ) Vulgar
6 ( ) Foreign or broken
7 ( ) Impediment
8 ( ) Stuttering
9 (X) Rapid
10 ( ) Dumb

(69) DRESS
1 ( ) Neat
2 ( ) Well Dressed
3 (X) Rough
4 ( ) Uniform

DEPARTMENT OF CALIFORNIA HIGHWAY PATROL

VEHICLE REPORT	TYPE (CHECK ONE)	USE REVERSE SIDE FOR STOLEN OR EMBEZZLED VEHICLES
	[X] IMPOUNDED [ ] RECOVERED [ ] STORED [ ] RELEASED	

REPORTING DEPARTMENT	AREA OR DIVISION	DATE	FILE NUMBER
CENTER CITY POLICE DEPARTMENT	Div. 4	3/15/79	81-316

DESCRIPTION OF VEHICLE

YEAR	MAKE	MODEL	BODY TYPE	LICENSE NUMBER(S)	YEAR	STATE	COLOR (COMBINATION)
1979	Chev		Sed. 4-Dr	FRONT 165 SAM / REAR 165 SAM	1979	Ca.	

VEHICLE IDENTIFICATION NUMBER (VIN)	DOES VIN COMPARE WITH REG CARD?	DOES VIN APPEAR ALTERED?	IS VIN CLEAR IN AUTO STATIS?	IS LICENSE NUMBER CLEAR IN AUTO STAT?	SPEEDOMETER READING
1D35H3K401527	[X] YES [ ] NO	[ ] YES [X] NO	[X] YES [ ] NO	[X] YES [ ] NO	12521

ENGINE NUMBER (EN)	IF A RECOVERED STOLEN VEHICLE, HAS NEIGHBORHOOD OR AREA BEEN CHECKED FOR LEADS OR CLUES?
Same	[ ] YES [ ] NO (LIST LEADS OR CLUES IN REMARKS)

REGISTERED OWNER	ADDRESS	HOME PHONE 88-16632 BUSINESS PHONE
JOHN W. SMITH	397 N. Wall St. Center City	

LEGAL OWNER	ADDRESS	PHONE
Bank of America, Center City	650 S. Broadway	88-57381

CIRCUMSTANCES

NAME OF GARAGE	ADDRESS	PHONE
Bell's Garage	45 Oak St., Center City	88-44326

LOCATION TOWED FROM	TIME AND DATE TOWED
Highland & Sterling	5:00 AM 3/15/79

PERSON REPORTING OCCURRENCE	ADDRESS	PHONE	TIME AND DATE REPORTED
J. F. Jensen #22	Center City Police Dept.	88-44102	

CONDITION OF VEHICLE	DRIVEABLE?	WRECKED?	STRIPPED?	IF STRIPPED, INDICATE MAJOR COMPONENT PARTS MISSING
	[X] YES [ ] NO	[ ] YES [X] NO	[ ] YES [X] NO	[ ] ENGINE [ ] TRANS [ ] BUCKET SEATS [ ] TIRES & WHEELS

WAS VEH RETURNED TO OWNER?	IF STOLEN, NAME, DATE AND CASE NO. OF REPORTING AGENCY	STOLEN TELETYPE NO.
[ ] YES [X] NO		

REMARKS (IF ARREST MADE, INDICATE FULL NAMES, CHARGES, AND WHERE DETAINED)   STORAGE AUTHORITY

SMITH, John W. — Defendant   Center City Jail

207, 261.3   — Charge
Kidnap-Rape

V.I.N. 1D35H3K401527

VEHICLE INVENTORY

ITEMS	YES	NO	ITEMS	YES	NO	ITEMS	YES	NO	ITEMS	CONDITION	LIST PROPERTY, TOOLS, AND OTHER ITEMS
SEAT (FRONT)	✓		ENGINE	✓		TRANSMISSION			L. F. TIRE	New	Sun glasses
SEAT (REAR)	✓		BATTERY	✓		AUTOMATIC ( )	✓		R. F. TIRE	New	bumper jack
RADIO	✓		CARBURETOR	✓		3 SPEED ( )			L. R. TIRE	New	8" Crescent wrench
TAPE STEREO		✓	AIR COND	✓		4 SPEED ( )	✓		R. R. TIRE	New	3/8" Screw driver
TAPES (#)		✓	GENERATOR	✓		FOG LIGHT(S)			SPARE TIRE	New	1 book Green stamps
CLOCK	✓		ALTERNATOR	✓		SIDE VIEW MIRROR(#)	✓		FENDERS	Good	1 Flashlight 2-cell
IGNITION KEY	✓		HUB CAPS(#)	✓		WINDSHIELD WIPER(#)	✓		BODY HOOD	Good	1 pr. Work gloves-grey
REGISTRATION	✓		JACK	✓		GRILL	✓		TOP	Good	1 Sm. Kodak Camera

OFFICER ORDERING VEH STORED (SIGNATURE)	I.D. NO.	GARAGE PRINCIPAL OR AGENT STORING VEH (SIGNATURE)	TIME AND DATE
X /s/ J. F. JENSEN	22	X /s/ R. R. Bell	5:15 AM 3/15/79

APPRAISING OFFICER'S SIGNATURE (SEC 22704 VC)	I.D. NO.	APPRAISED VALUE	TIME AND DATE OF APPRAISAL

FOR OFFICE USE ONLY

REQUIRED NOTICES SENT TO REGISTERED AND LEGAL OWNERS AND GARAGE (SEC. 22852 VC)	IF NO IS CHECKED, INDICATE REASON	RECOVERY TELETYPE (DATE AND NUMBER)
[ ] YES [ ] NO	[ ] VEHICLE NOT STORED [ ] VEHICLE RECLAIMED BY OWNER [ ] OTHER	

IMPOUND RELEASE NOTIFICATION

TO	ADDRESS	DATE

RELEASE VEHICLE TO	ADDRESS

SIGNATURE OF CLERK OR OFFICER RELEASING	CERTIFICATION: *I, THE UNDERSIGNED, DO HEREBY CERTIFY THAT I AM LEGALLY AUTHORIZED AND ENTITLED TO TAKE POSSESSION OF ABOVE DESCRIBED VEHICLE.*
	SIGNATURE OF OWNER OR LEGAL OWNER OR AGENT OF OWNER

NOTE: THIS FORM IS FURNISHED BY THE HIGHWAY PATROL TO ALL CALIFORNIA PEACE OFFICERS.

U.S., for the purpose of prostitution or de-bauchery, or for any other immoral purpose, or with the intent and purpose on the part of such person that such woman or girl shall engage in the practice of prostitution or debauchery, or for any other immoral prac-tice, whether with or without her consent, and thereby knowingly causes such woman or girl to go and to be carried or transported as a passenger upon the line or route of any common carrier or carriers in interstate or foreign commerce, or in the District of Co-lumbia or in any Territory or Possession of the United States, shall be fined not more than $5,000 or imprisoned not more than five years, or both.

Sec. 2423. Coercion or enticement of minor female

Whoever knowingly persuades, induces, en-tices, or coerces any woman or girl who has not attained her eighteenth birthday, to go from one place to another by common carrier, in interstate commerce or within the District of Columbia or any Territory or Pos-session of the United States, with intent that she be induced or coerced to engage in prostitution, debauchery or other immoral practice, shall be fined not more than $10,000 or imprisoned not more than ten years, or both.

GLOSSARY OF TERMINOLOGY USED TO IDENTIFY FORMS OF SEXUAL BEHAVIOR

Adamism	A form of exhibitionism in which the subject shows himself in the nude.
Adultery	Voluntary intercourse by a married man or married woman with person other than his or her spouse.
Analingus	Sexual pleasure obtained through the use of the mouth on the rectum.
Anthropophagy	Cannabalism: the eating of human flesh.
Bestiality	Sexual act with a beast.
Bisexual	One who is sexually attracted to both sexes.
Buggery	Unnatural sexual intercourse.
Cabareting	The underworld name for indulging in abnormal fantasies or daydreams to resolve the sex drive.
Cain complex	Aggressive rivalry between brothers and/or sisters for the affection of one or both parents.
Compulsive neurosis	A neurosis of obsessive ideas and urges to perform complicated and senseless acts.
Confabulation	A psychopathic symptom in which imaginary experiences are related as true.
Coprolagnia	Sexual excitement brought on by sight or thought of feces.
Coprolalia	Irresistible impulse to use obscene language.
Coprophagy	The eating of fecal excrement.
Coprophilia	A condition in which a person becomes sexually excited by excretory organs; inordinate interest in feces.
Coprophobia	Neurotic fear of feces.
Coprophrasia	A mental disorder characterized by use of obscene language or collec-tion of pornographic literature.
Cunnilingus	The application of the mouth to the external genitalia of the female; also called cunnilinctus.

Ectasy intoxication	The moment when the sadist has reached the top of his affectivity.
Electra complex	The sex desire, unconscious and unrecognized, of the very young daughter for the father with definite antagonism and rivalry toward the mother.
Exhibitionism	Intentional exposure of sex organs or the nude body under inappropriate conditions (usually compulsive).
Fellatio	Stimulation of the penis by friction in the mouth of another person.
Fetish	An object (or some part of the body not normally directly associated with sex) that begins having special sexual significance to a person, and the presence of which is often necessary for sexual satisfaction.
Fetishism	A sex abnormality in which certain objects or certain parts of the body become symbols that often are necessary to the deviate in order to derive sexual satisfaction.
Fire-water complex	This condition is found as a part of the symptoms occurring in sex pyromaniacs. After lighting a fire there is a period of exhibitionism followed by a desire to urinate.
Flagellation	A psychosexual perversion characterized by an intense passion either to whip (sadist) or to be whipped (masochist); whipping becomes a means of arousing sexual emotions.
Flagellomania	Sexual excitement from whipping or being whipped.
Fornication	Voluntary sexual intercourse involving an unmarried woman; literally used, any sexual intercourse outside marriage.
Frottage	Sexual gratification obtained by rubbing against another person.
Frotteur	One who seeks sexual gratification by rubbing against another person; also called hugger or rubber.
Gerontophilia	The choice of older people of the opposite sex as sexual objects or partners.
Heterosexual	A person who is attracted to one of the opposite sex only, and is considered to be "normal."
Homosexual	A person who has a tendency to find sexual gratification with a person of the same sex. Other names for males: "gay" persons, inverts, "faggots," "queers," "nances," "pansies," "queens," "fruits," "swishes." Other names for females: "gay" persons, lesbians, sapphists ("lady lovers"), or tribads ("bull dykes"), according to activities.
Impairing morals	Sexual acts performed by adults upon juveniles or in their presence which would weaken or damage the moral standard of the juveniles.
Incest	Sexual intercourse between closely related persons of the opposite sex, the marriage of whom would be prohibited by law.
Invert	Another term for homosexual.
Kleptomania	Obsessive impulse to steal, especially in the absence of any economic motive or personal desire, often with sexual overtones.
Lesbians	Commonly applied to all female homosexuals.

Libido	Basic human desires.
Lust murder	Murder committed in sadistic, brutal manner; the victim's body usually shows evidence of mutilation, particularly of the privates.
Masochism	Erotic or sexual excitement and/or satisfaction from being subjected to pain, whether by oneself or another.
Masturbation	The induction of erection and the obtaining of sexual satisfaction, in either sex, from manual or other artificial mechanical stimulation of the genitals.
Narcissism	A high valuation of one's own bodily qualities, and, by extension, of one's deeds and personal qualities — self-love.
Narcissist	An individual who is love with her or his own body and has an excessive desire to exhibit it.
Necrophilia	Sexual attraction to corpses.
Nymphomania	A morbid and excessive sexual desire in the female.
Oedipus complex	The sexual desire of the son for the mother with definite antagonism and rivalry towards the father.
Paraphilia	A distortion or anomaly of sexuality.
Pederasty	Anal coitus with a boy or young man.
Pederosis	The use of children by adults as sexual objects.
Pedophilia	An adult's sexual attraction to children.
Pervert	One who indulges in unnatural sexual acts or fantasies.
Piquerism	Sexual inclinations to stab, pierce, slash, or cut. Sexual gratification is obtained from the shedding of blood, the tearing of flesh, and/or the pain and suffering of the victim.
Prostitution	Act or practice of engaging in sexual intercourse for money.
Psychopathic personalities	Abnormal persons who suffer from their abnormality, and, through the same abnormality, make society suffer.
Pygmalionism	Perversion characterized by the desire to have sex acts with inanimate objects, such as a statue or mannikin.
Pyromania	Uncontrollable impulse to set things afire. Sex pyromaniacs are individuals who secure sexual satisfaction through setting fires.
Rape, forcible	Sexual intercourse with a woman against her will and consent and despite her resistance.
Rape, statutory	Carnal knowledge by a male over the statutory age of a female under the statutory age, without force and with consent and penetration.
Sadism	The tendency to associate sexual satisfaction with the infliction of pain upon another.
Sadomasochism	This is a dual deviation in which the individual can secure sexual satisfaction either from the inflicting of pain or from suffering.
Sapphists	Women homosexuals who engage in cunnilingus as well as other lesbian practices.

Satyriasis	A morbid sex desire in the male.
Scoptophilia	Sexual pleasure derived from peeping to observe disrobed human figures or sexual acts; also called scopophilia, scotophilia, voyeurism, Peeping Tomism.
Seduction	The offense of a man inducing a woman to have unlawful sexual intercourse with him.
Sex maniacs	Persons who are definitely irresponsible in sexual matters by virtue of insanity.
Sex offenders	Adult individuals who engage in any sexual practice that falls outside the socially accepted and legally defined scope of normal sexuality.
Sexual anomaly	Behavior in the sexual sphere that deviates rather sharply from the normal but is not considered to be necessarily pathological.
Sexual psychopaths	Persons who are not insane or mentally defective, but who cannot control their impulses toward the commission of sex crimes and offenses.
Sodomy	Any "unnatural" sexual relation, especially anal.
Symbolic sadism	The condition in which the sadistic impulses are expressed by acts of mutilation on some symbol that has specific meaning.
Symbolism	The process in which one thing stands for something else.
Transvestism	Persistent association of sexual excitement with dressing in the clothes of the opposite sex.
Tribad	Most aggressive of female homosexuals. The aggressor assumes the role of the man either through artificial means or the unusual formation of her own body. Also called "bull dykes," "bull doggers," "dykes."
Triolism	A form of exhibitionism wherein the subject desires to perform sexual acts with several partners or in the presence of numerous people.
Urolagnia	Association of sexual excitement with urine or urination.
Vampirism	Act or practice of bloodsucking.
Voyeur	One who seeks sexual gratification by peeping, a Peeping Tom.
Voyeurism	Sexual gratification by peeping. Also called scotophilia, scoptophilia, scopophilia.
Zooerasty	Sexual intercourse with an animal.
Zoophilia	A peculiarity involving an unnatural fondness for animals.

SUMMARY

Sex crimes vary widely from nuisance acts, such as voyeurism, to lust murders. A sex offender may be young, middle-aged, or old; educated or uneducated; married or single; and of any race, religious persuasion, or occupation. Of the various types of sex offenders, sadists are considered the most dangerous. They often delight in killing and mutilating their victims.

The crime of rape is the best known and most publicized among sex offenses. State statutes make it unlawful to have intercourse with females under a specified legal age. Forcible rape is a crime of violence; conviction carries penalties ranging from long-term imprisonment to death in some states. Sex crime investigations are usually handled by specialized law-enforcement personnel. The White Slave Traffic Act (also known as the Mann Act) has specific U.S. Code sections prohibiting the transportation of women in interstate or foreign commerce for the purposes of prostitution or debauchery. A specific section of the Act covers coercion, inducement, or enticement of females; another section applies to female minors.

REVIEW QUESTIONS

1. What type of sex offender is considered to be the most dangerous?
2. Name five sex crimes against children.
3. What type of offender is a voyeur?
4. What is the difference between a sadist and a masochist?
5. Are there any ways that an investigator can use to pick out a sex offender from other types of criminal offenders?
6. In terms of law enforcement, types of sex criminals are divided into three basic categories. What are they?
7. What is the difference between statutory rape and forcible rape?
8. What kinds of crime are included in the category of sex crimes against children?
9. What is the Mann Act?
10. "Transfer evidence" is always sought in rape cases. What is the meaning of this term?

WORK EXERCISE

1. The facts set forth below represent a grave problem which you, as the investigator are confronted with. After carefully reviewing the facts below, write a short paper on the decision you would make under these circumstances. Include an explanation for your conduct.

Facts

A fourteen-year-old girl was kidnapped while walking to church on a Sunday morning. She is the daughter of good, responsible parents of ordinary circumstances. Investigation discloses that she had been picked up by a man by the name of HARRIS and thereafter taken to the madam of a house of prostitution located some distance from Center City. The girl remained there three days. During this time, the madam of this house said the girl appeared to be heavily drugged and exceedingly ill. Finally the madam became nervous, contacted HARRIS, and ordered him to take the girl out of the house. She was afraid of both the girl's age and physical condition.

Several days later, HARRIS was apprehended at a bar in Center City and transported to the Center City jail. Two vice officers were assigned to interrogate HARRIS and try to determine the facts of the case and the location of the girl. Although HARRIS waived his Miranda rights, he would not admit any knowledge of the girl or her whereabouts. He was obviously lying, although this did not seem to bother him. The officers have now arrived at a point where all approaches of legal interrogation have been used. But these methods failed to obtain any information about this missing girl. You and your partner are convinced he knows where the girl is. You are further convinced that the element of time is of the greatest importance and that the girl's life is endangered. You are certain that if this man will tell you what he knows you can save the innocent child's life. You must get this information from the suspect or release him. What is your decision?

2. The following problem is for class discussion and/or research.

Facts

You have a suspect accused of rape under arrest at headquarters. In order to expedite the interview with this suspect you tell him that if he does not tell you the truth about his involvement, it will be necessary for you to involve his whole family—including his wife and children—and his employer. Assume this approach works, and that the suspect confesses to you to avoid a lot of unnecessary embarrassment. Would such a confession be admissible? Explain your answer.

Narcotics and Dangerous Drugs

Narcotics

The term "narcotic," which originally referred to a variety of substances inducing altered states of consciousness, in current usage means opium, its derivatives, or synthetic substitutes for it. These produce tolerance and dependence, both psychological and physical.[1] Opium is the coagulated juice of a species of poppy plant scientifically known as *Papaver somniferum*. Its original home was probably the Mediterranean region and the Middle East. The plant has a

smooth branching stem 2 to 3 feet [0.6 to 0.9 meter] tall; and large, dull, green, smooth leaves and solitary, single flowers varying from white to purple in color. Juice obtained from pods (unripe capsules) is the source from which raw opium is obtained. (See Figure 18-1.)

Opium contains a series of closely related alkaloids, but only three of these are of medical importance: (1) morphine and its related compounds, marketed as Dilaudid, Percodan, dionine, heroin, pantapon; (2) codeine; and (3) papaverine. Morphine is the chief alkaloid of opium and is used primarily to relieve pain. It is a central nervous system depressant. Codeine, used mainly in the treatment of coughs, is also a central ner-

---

[1] *Drug Enforcement,* Drug Enforcement Administration, U.S. Department of Justice, Washington, D.C., Spring 1975.

Figure 18-1. Poppies. (a) Turkish peasants harvesting crude opium; (b) crude opium oozing from slit poppypods. (Photographs courtesy of the Drug Enforcement Administration, U.S. Department of Justice)

vous system depressant. Papaverine is a drug that relaxes smooth muscles, particularly those of blood vessels. The alkaloids constitute the base from which the various opiate drugs are manufactured. These opium derivatives are classified as narcotics. They differ widely in their uses, effects, and addiction potential. Several synthetic drugs such as Demerol and methadone are classed as narcotics. Any substance that is derived directly or indirectly from opium is classified as an opiate. Opium derivatives, such as morphine, heroin, codeine, and Percodan, constitute the chief danger as far as opiate addiction is concerned. Addiction to opiates consists of actual physical dependence. This is augmented by the development of a tolerance requiring larger and larger amounts to avoid the beginning of withdrawal symptoms. Manufacturers and distributors of medicinal opiates are stringently controlled by the federal government through laws designated to keep these products available only for legitimate medical use. Those who distribute these drugs are registered with federal authorities and must comply with specific record-keeping and drug security requirements.

Narcotic drug abuse

The abuse of narcotic drugs dates back to ancient times. Their use today is still a serious problem. The appeal of morphine-like drugs (heroin, codeine, Percodan, Hycodan, Dilaudid, etc.) lies in their ability to reduce sensitivity to both psychological and physical stimuli and to produce a state of euphoria. These drugs dull fear, tension, and anxiety. Under the influence of morphine-like narcotics, the drug-dependent person is usually lethargic and indifferent to her or his environment and personal situation. Chronic use leads to both physical and psychological dependence. Tolerance develops and ever-increasing doses are required in order to achieve the desired effect. As the need for the drug increases, the addict's activities become increasingly drug centered.

With the deprivation of morphine or heroin, the first withdrawal signs are usually experienced shortly before the time of the next scheduled dose. Complaints, pleas, and demands by the addict are prominent, increasing in intensity and peaking from thirty-six to seventy-two hours after the last dose, then gradually subsiding. Symptoms such as watery eyes, runny nose, yawning, and perspiration appear about eight to twelve hours after the last dose. Thereafter the addict may fall into a restless sleep.

As the abstinence syndrome progresses, restlessness, irritability, loss of appetite, insomnia, gooseflesh, tremors, and, finally, violent yawning and severe sneezing occur. These physical symptoms reach their peak at forty-eight to seventy-two hours after the last dose. The patient is weak and depressed with nausea and vomiting. Stomach cramps and diarrhea are common. Heart rate and blood pressure are elevated. Chills alternating with flushing and excessive sweating are also characteristic symptoms. Pains in the bones and muscles of the back and extremities occur, as do muscle spasms and kicking movements—which may be the source of the expression "kicking the habit." At this time an individual may become suicidal. Without treatment, the syndrome eventually runs its course and most of the symptoms will disappear in from seven to ten days. How long it takes to restore physiological and psychological equilibrium, however, is unpredictable.[2]

In addition, addicts exhibit the following characteristics: pupillary constriction (pupils of the eyes contract to the size of pinpoints); frequent burning of clothes or fingers with lighted cigarettes during drowsy stage (sometimes referred to as "nodding"); slovenly, unwashed appearance and poor hygiene; sickness and malnutrition; craving for sugar or foods with high sugar content; and preference for long-sleeve garments to hide needle marks on arms.

Addicts may not confine injections to their arms. They have been known to inject heroin into their legs, between their toes, and even under their tongues in order to hide needle marks. They will scratch themselves often, due to the effect of heroin on nerve endings.

There is also a mental preoccupation with where and when to get the next "fix," as well as with ways of financing the "habit." Addict's hands are often cold and clammy; they invariably feel cold. The clothing worn is generally not in accord with the weather, as addicts have a tendency to overdress.

[2]Ibid.

Withdrawal symptoms drive addicts to lie, cheat, steal, and turn to prostitution in order to obtain money to purchase additional drugs. Because addicts are preoccupied with drug taking, they usually neglect themselves. They often contract infections because their nutritional status is poor, they may be injecting contaminated drugs intravenously, and they are likely to be using poor or unsterilized injection techniques. These factors may result in serious or fatal septicemia (blood poisoning), hepatitis, and abscesses of the liver, brain, and lungs. (See Figure 18-2.)

Figure 18-2. Body of a young female narcotic addict showing multiple, generalized, infected ulcers of the skin, secondary to the effects of diminished physical resistance (pyoderma gangrenosum).

Opium

Opium is obtained from a poppy plant called *Papaver somniferum* by making incisions into the unripened seedpod of the poppy. The incisions are made in the late afternoon. (See Figure 18-1.) Then a milky substance oozes out and turns to reddish brown upon contact with the air. The exuded substance is collected the following morning. If it is destined for legitimate medical use, it is graded on its morphine content, which must be at least 9.5 percent. Thereafter the substance is further refined and the various alkaloids extracted. If, however, it is intended for illegal use, it is mixed with glycerin and water and boiled down to the consistency of heavy molasses. The substance is processed further by cooking to evaporate the water, with the remaining glycerin keeping the opium pliable. It is then placed in various containers and sold to the underworld to be further processed for smoking or ultimately to become illegal morphine or heroin.

In discussing opium, there is sometimes a confusion between the terms "alkaloid" and "narcotic." It should be stressed that not all alkaloids are narcotics, and that not all narcotics are alkaloids. A narcotic is generally defined as a drug which produces sleep or stupor and relieves pain. Many alkaloids do not meet these specifications.[3] American addicts seldom use opium but rather its derivatives, morphine and heroin. Opium is known in the argot by such names as "o," "mud," "tar," and many others.

Procedure Used in Smoking Opium
The opium pipe is the usual tool of the addict. A small rolled ball of opium, known as *yen pok*, is placed upon a long needle-

---

[3] *Van Nostrand's Scientific Encyclopedia*, 5th ed., Van Nostrand Reinhold, New York, 1976, p. 830.

type instrument known as a *yen hok*, and held over the flame of an opium lamp until the ball commences to burn. At this point the opium gives off a fume having a sickly, sweet odor. The opium ball is then placed on the bowl of a long-stemmed hollow pipe where the fumes (not the smoke) are drawn deeply into the lungs of the user. The pipe may be beautifully ornamented and very expensive, or it may well be an improvised device consisting of a bottle and a long tube attached thereto. A residue, or ash, known as *yen shee,* which collects in the bowl and stem of the pipe is scraped out with an instrument known as a *gow* and saved. This ash contains varying amounts of the active alkaloid depending upon the grade of opium smoked, and it is retained for use when a supply of opium is not available, or is sold to less fortunate users. Sometimes the *yen shee* is mixed with an alcoholic beverage to ensure preservation, and in this condition is known as *yen shee suey.* Generally, this fluid is taken orally, but it may be injected when opium is not available and withdrawal symptoms are otherwise inevitable.

Effects Initially, the effects produced by smoking opium are hallucinations and pleasant dreams; however, the addict ultimately finds that it is necessary not only to use more opium but to smoke it more frequently in order to forestall the excruciating agony of the withdrawal symptoms, and he or she no longer experiences pleasant dreams.[4]

Morphine

Morphine is the principal alkaloid of opium. It was first isolated by F. W. A. Sertürner in 1806. Since morphine is a condensed extract, it is approximately three times stronger than opium. There is a wide variety of legitimate uses for morphine as a medicinal or pain-relieving agent. Users

addicted to morphine from an illegal source seek methods of gaining the legitimate medication when their own source is temporarily cut off. These methods are usually robbery, burglary, forgery, and confidence schemes.

In its natural state, morphine is not readily soluble in water. Therefore, it is treated with sulfuric acid. The resultant, morphine sulfate, is quite soluble and is the most common form used. Morphine is white and comes in three principal forms: powder, cubes, and ⅛ to ½ grain tablets. The texture is light, very similar to that of chalk dust. Peddlers adulterate the powder with milk sugar, cutting the potency considerably. The drug is taken orally and intravenously. Most addicts prefer intravenous injection because the effects are more immediate and pronounced. The improvised hypodermic "outfit" is the same as that used to inject heroin. Morphine is known in the argot by such names as "morph," "white stuff," "Miss Emma," "Mary Ann," and others. The effects of morphine upon the user are like those of heroin.

Heroin

Heroin is another of the opiates. Public concern as to the opiates is focused primarily on heroin, regarded as the chief drug of addiction in the United States. Heroin is known to the addicts as "H," "horse," "joy powder," "Harry," "scag," "white stuff," "sugar," "smack," and by many other names. It is sold as a diluted powder mostly in flat packets called "decks" or in capsules called "caps." (See Figure 18-3.) Heroin is synthesized from morphine and, grain for grain, is up to ten times more potent in its pharmacological effects. Heroin acts as a depressant to the spinal cord. The tolerance for this drug builds up faster than any other opiate. Consequently, the danger of drug dependency is considerably greater. It has come to be known as the most dangerous and enslaving drug. As a result, the United

---

[4]From the Los Angeles Police Department.

Figure 18-3. Forms of heroin.

States government has legislated against the importation or manufacture of heroin.

Appearance   In its pure state, heroin is a crystalline substance that is virtually colorless. After exposure to air, it may assume a light tan coloration. In the United States it appears in a wide variety of off-white colors, including tan, grey, and brown. This coloration is caused by the diluent used in the adulteration process.

Method of Illegal Packaging, Distribution, and Use   After processing, heroin is sold by the kilo [2.2 pounds] with prices ranging generally from $30,000 to $45,000, and as high as $58,000. The high cost of heroin is attributed to the scarcity brought about by the Mexican government's poppy eradication program and increased pressure on drug traffickers. The purity of Mexican heroin ("Mexican Brown") is said to range generally from 30 to 35 percent. The purchaser of pure heroin expects to cut it at least three times, thus making 3 kilos [6.6 pounds] out of each kilo.

Diluents used to cut heroin include many substances: sugar, lactose, starch, mannitol, quinine, and other materials. The trafficker will then sell it by the pound with the going rate ranging between $10,000 and $18,000.

The subsequent buyer also expects to adulterate the purchase and will sell heroin by the ounce with prices ranging from $500 to $1000.

Thereafter the heroin is cut into "quarters" and then put into smaller bags for street sale. Papers, caps [capsules, balloons (a gram or less)], or prophylactics are prevalent methods of packaging for street sales. The average addict uses from 2 to 5 grams per day at a cost of approximately $50 per gram, making the daily cost around $100. Street heroin runs from 2 to 5 percent pure. Since addicts cannot legitimately earn this amount, they resort to crime—thefts, burglaries, and sometimes robberies of small businesses. In their thievery, addicts usually get less than one-third of the value of the stolen property, since the underworld knows that addicts are in no position to bargain.

During the sequence of buying and selling, dope peddlers take advantage of one another whenever possible. Hijacking and confidence schemes taking place between the parties usually lead to additional crimes, particularly burglary and homicide.

A "mule" in narcotic slang is a drug user who sells or transports drugs for a regular peddler, usually in order to obtain drugs for her or his own use. The enforcement officer finds that most "mules" are excellent "pushers" (sellers). The ironic justice is that many peddlers become users either out of curiosity or because the "hypes" themselves are continually suggesting it to them. More often it is an occupational hazard. The nonuser peddler cannot identify or test the quality of the merchandise he or she is about to buy; the judgment of the "hype" (addict) who is testing for her or him must be trusted. The "hype" sometimes enters into a secret agreement with the drug seller, agreeing to indicate to the drug buyer (the peddler) that the quality of the drug is excellent when, in reality, the material is plain milk sugar. The buyer will not know the difference until he or she begins to sell it.

Figure 18-4. Paraphernalia (often referred to as "outfit," "fit," "artillery") used by addicts to administer narcotics intravenously.

Meanwhile, the "hype" tester has received one-half of the money paid and promptly proceeds to increase her or his habit with the new windfall. The peddlers therefore soon decide to try an injection or two merely to be their own testers; then one morning they awaken to find themselves going through the symptoms of withdrawal.

The "outfit" is a term representing the paraphernalia used to inject narcotics. The makeup of an "outfit" varies, but usually will include a teaspoon, hypodermic needle, eyedropper, small piece of cotton, matches, and a tie rag (see Figure 18-4). Most addicts have more than one "outfit," and conceal them in every place imaginable.

Injecting Process[5] Following is a description of the injecting process: a small amount of heroin is placed in the vessel of the spoon and enough water to cover the heroin is added. (See Figure 18-5.) The handle of the spoon is bent in order that the liquid will not spill when the spoon is set on a flat surface. The mixture is then heated with two or three matches or a candle. It actually boils in the spoon and becomes a solution. A small piece of cotton is then placed in the vessel of the spoon. At this

[5]Ibid.

point, either the eyedropper or hypodermic needle is placed in the cotton and the solution is then drawn into the eyedropper or syringe. The cotton is used in this fashion to remove the impurities from the poison about to be injected.

Next, the tie rag (anything from a necktie to a piece of string) is used as a tourniquet. This makes the vein more prominent and the injection easier. The needle is then placed on top of the upraised vein and the puncture made. The "hype" is careful not to miss the vein and sometimes several punctures are necessary. When the point of the needle has entered the vein, blood will force its way up through the needle and be visible in the eyedropper. This is an indication to the user that the point of the needle is actually inside the vein and has not passed through it or completely missed it. The bulb of the dropper is then squeezed; and blood and solution enter the vein.

The cotton is saved to be reused and finally boiled to obtain whatever drug residue it may contain. The reverse side of the spoon is blackened from the matches, and the tie rag is spotted with small bloodstains. These are all collected by the "hype" and put into a hiding place until the next injection. There is no attempt to sterilize. Frequently, the users congregate, and the same outfit is

Figure 18-5. A makeshift "hype" outfit.

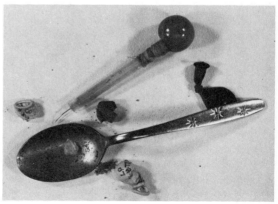

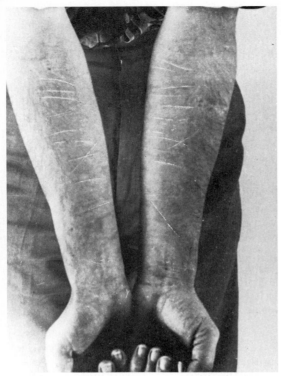

After several injections, the wall of the vein collapses, following which the addict looks elsewhere on his body for a suitable vein. A close examination of a suspected addict's arms may reveal evidence of "tracks" (old injection marks along vein), as in Figure 18-8. Observation of a suspect's arms may also show fresh puncture marks.

Marks Left by Injection   The needle marks generally appear in a pattern over the veins in the elbow folds, along the inner forearm, top sides of the hands and on the legs. These areas are the most accessible large veins in the body. Injections in these areas can be easily self-administered. If right-handed, an addict often starts by using the left arm. Continued self-injection in a vein causes the vein to collapse, thereby causing a long scar or "track" as in Figure 18-8. Tracks are indications of previous use only. In the case of recent use, a series of small scabs will be seen. These scabs last from approximately ten days to two weeks. The scabs are due to small infections

Figure 18-6. Scars resulting from narcotics injections. The forearms were cut with a razor blade and narcotics were inserted.

Figure 18-7. An arm showing the ulcerated condition (encircled) that resulted from the use of unsterile injection equipment.

passed from one to the other without it so much as being wiped off.

The method described above is the common practice of all narcotic users. There are, of course, improvisations. If a spoon is not available, a bottle cap or some other device is used. If there is no hypodermic needle, the user punctures the vein with a safety pin or a razor blade, then literally pours the solution into the vein with the eyedropper. Figure 18-6 depicts the two forearms of an addict and the resulting scars from injections where a razor blade was used.

When an addict uses an improvised needle, abscesses and ulcers invariably result because of the unsterile condition of such equipment. Figure 18-7 illustrates an ulcerated condition brought about by such means.

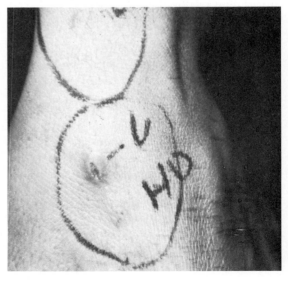

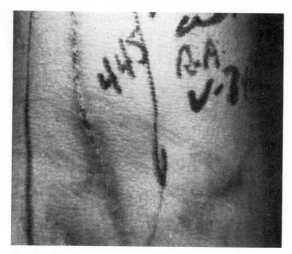

Figure 18-8. A portion of an arm showing old tracks. This condition is a result of numerous narcotic injections that brought about vein collapse.

brought about by the unsterilized injection outfit that the addict uses to administer the drug and because of the drug's impurities. Users occasionally burn the needle-mark area with a lighted cigarette, cut the skin with a knife, or scratch the area in an attempt to obliterate the marks. Sometimes needle marks are hidden in a tattoo that the addict has placed over the main vein.

The amount of narcotics injected varies in accordance with the habit of the user. Because of tolerance, either the dose must be increased or the same dose taken more frequently. Those persons just starting a life of addiction probably use one or two capsules a day. In a relatively short period of time they will be injecting five and ten capsules at one time and "fixing" (injecting) three or four times a day. This is not true only of the isolated circumstance, but also applies to the average case. If the heroin is not available, the user can only foresee the inevitable onslaught of withdrawal symptoms. The more severe the habit, the more severe the suffering.

In addition to the above effects, addiction causes a complete moral breakdown. Such a breakdown is well described in the "Psalm of Heroin Addiction" written by a twenty-year-old narcotics addict:

Psalm of Heroin Addiction

King heroin is my shepherd, I shall always want.
He maketh me to lie down in the gutters.
He leadeth me beside the troubled waters.
He destroyeth my soul.
He leadeth me in the paths of wickedness for the effort's sake.
Yea, I shall walk through the valley of poverty and will fear all evil
For thou, heroin, art with me.
The needle and capsule try to comfort me.
Thy strippest the table of groceries in the presence of my family.
Thou robbest my head of reason.
My cup of sorrow runneth over.
Surely heroin addiction shall stalk me all the days of my life.
And I dwell in the house of the damned forever.

The above typewritten "psalm" was found in a telephone booth by an officer of the Long Beach, California, police department. On the back of the card on which it was typed appeared the following—written in longhand:

Truly this is my psalm. I am a young woman, 20 years of age and for the past year and one-half I have been wandering down the nightmare alley of the junkies. I want to quit taking dope and I try but I can't.
Jail didn't cure me. Nor did hospitalization help me for long.
The doctor told my family it would have been better and indeed kinder if the person who first got me hooked on dope to have taken a gun and blown my brains out, and I wish to God she had. My God how I do wish it.

Most of the heroin now in the United States originates in Mexico. From 60 to 80 percent or more of the illicit heroin coming into the United States is Mexican. The Mexican heroin enters the United States through a variety of ways: by smugglers at crossing points; by illegal crossings at various points along the border; by illegal aircraft; by private boats and cargo vessels; and by cars and trucks. The 1248-mile- [2080-kilometer-] long common border with Texas and the 150-mile [250-kilometer] common border with California make it a real challenge for the federal, state, and local law enforcement to curb the flow of Mexican heroin ("Mexican Brown") into the United States.

Once the heroin is safely across the Mexican border into California, Arizona, or Texas, the heroin pipeline moves rapidly within a short period of time into many of the larger cities across the country, where further distribution takes place. Mexican heroin ranges in color from off-white to a deep brown. When this heroin is cut, it may be almost white as a result of the use of diluents such as lactose, quinine, mannitol, powdered milk, starch, sugar. Color does not assure potency since traffickers add dyes to produce a darker cast and thereby enhance consumer acceptance.

It is the concern of drug officials that should Mexico's efforts to defoliate poppy fields, as well as other law-enforcement procedures being used, succeed, the traffickers in Mexican heroin will probably turn once again to Southeast Asia's "Golden Triangle" (Thailand, Burma, Laos), which now provides between 10 and 15 percent of the street heroin circulating in the United States.

Codeine

This drug is one of the most common addictive drugs derived from opium. It is the least addictive of the opium derivatives and very similar in appearance to morphine (a white crystalline powder). The narcotic is used illicitly in the same manner as morphine and heroin. Codeine is a common ingredient of pills, powders, and cough syrups—serving as a pain reliever or as a repressant. It is occasionally used by addicts deprived of their sources of heroin. The potency of codeine is only about one-sixth that of morphine, and is the weakest derivative of opium. Its primary effects include dulled perception, straying attention, and lack of awareness of surroundings. Users may be dazed or act mildly intoxicated. When withdrawal symptoms occur, they are less severe than with more potent drugs (heroin, morphine).

Percodan (oxycodone, dihydrohydroxycodeinone)

Percodan is an extremely important analgesic (painkiller), according to authorities. The drug-addictive liability of dihydrohydroxycodeinone, the narcotic ingredient of Percodan, is between morphine and codeine; but it is much closer to morphine in its effect. Percodan and codeine are taken orally by some addicts when heroin supplies are not available. Addicts dissolve Percodan tablets in water, filter out the insoluble binders and inject the active drug intravenously.

Methadone

In response to a shortage of morphine during World War II, German chemists synthesized methadone. Although chemically unlike morphine or heroin, it produces many of the same effects. It is administered orally or by injection. Tolerance and physical dependence can develop. Withdrawal symptoms develop more slowly and are less severe than in withdrawal from morphine or heroin. But methadone withdrawal symptoms may be more prolonged. Methadone was introduced in the United States in 1947 as an analgesic and distributed under such names as Amidone, Dolophine, and Methadon.

Since the 1960s, methadone has become widely used in detoxification of heroin addicts and in methadone maintenance pro-

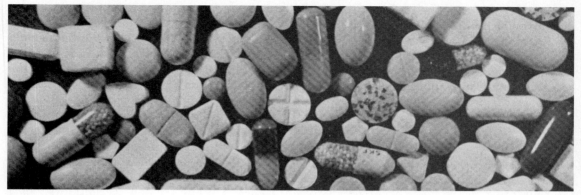

Figure 18-9. Dangerous drugs, such as stimulants, depressants, and hallucinogens, are made in various shapes and colors of capsules and tablets. These drugs affect the mind and produce changes in mood and behavior. Illicit traffic and use constitute a major enforcement problem.

grams. There are special restrictions imposed by the Federal Food, Drug, and Cosmetic Act as well as the Controlled Substances Act (CSA) for both the manufacture and use of methadone. With the passage of the Narcotic Treatment Act of 1974, DEA was given significantly greater authority to monitor methadone maintenance programs.[6]

A longer lasting heroin substitute called LAAM is being considered as a substitute for methadone in treating opiate-dependent persons. Switching from methadone to LAAM as soon as its safety and efficacy have been determined will permit patients to visit drug clinics only three times a week. LAAM should reduce diversion, cost, and interference with patient's work schedules.[7]

Dangerous Drugs

The term "dangerous drugs" is commonly used to refer to the non-medical use of prescription or over-the-counter tranquilizers, barbiturates, and amphetamines and other stimulants.[8] (See Figure 18-9.) Barbiturates are primarily a diversion problem; methamphetamines are primarily a problem of illicit production; and amphetamines are obtained from both sources. The various "dangerous drugs" present a special problem, for, unlike heroin, cocaine, and marijuana — which are illegal — these categories of drugs are frequently prescribed by doctors for valid medical purposes. But because of their popularity among abusers, the Drug Enforcement Administration estimates over 200 million doses are diverted from legal channels annually.[9] Some of the drugs are lost through theft and forged prescriptions or are stolen from truck shipments. Some are illegally handled by a handful of corrupt doctors, pharmacists, osteopaths, veterinarians, dentists, nurses, and other medical professionals.

There are three important sources of "dangerous drugs": (1) diversion from legitimate domestic production and distribution; (2) illicit domestic production; and (3)

---

[6]*Drug Enforcement,* Spring 1975, loc. cit.

[7]*White Paper on Drug Abuse, A Report to the President from the Domestic Council Drug Abuse Task Force,* Sept. 1975.

[8]*White paper on Drug Abuse,* loc. cit.

[9]*Drug Enforcement,* Drug Enforcement Administration, U.S. Department of Justice, Washington, D.C., Feb. 1977.

illicit foreign production and smuggling. It is possible to estimate the share of the illicit market from each source by looking for tell-tale "signatures" on seizures and undercover purchases made by law-enforcement officers. The identification of "signatures" is possible due to faulty processing and/or other identifiable characteristics of tablets seized.

Stimulants

Stimulants are a group of drugs, most of which are amphetamines. They directly stimulate the central nervous system (brain and spinal cord). They induce a transient sense of well-being, self-confidence, alertness, and wakefulness. The degree of these effects depends on the dosage. Their medical uses include the suppression of appetite and the reduction of fatigue or mild depression. Stimulants include cocaine, amphetamines, methamphetamines, phenmetrazine (Preludin), and methylphenidate (Ritalin). Methamphetamine is commonly referred to as "speed" or "crystal." Stimulants are also known as "pep pills" or "uppers." Criminals have been known to use amphetamines to bolster their courage before committing a crime. Athletes have been known to take them to excel. Students use them in "cramming" for an examination.

Amphetamines are usually taken orally in the form of tablets or capsules. Crystal methamphetamine and cocaine can be inhaled or "snorted" through the nose. They can also be injected into the veins, in which case the effects are immediate and more intense. The drugs are produced in a wide variety of physical forms. Most of the amphetamines found will be of legal manufacture.

Because amphetamines are available only through prescription, any such drugs collected should be left in the container. The container should be identified and processed for possible fingerprints. A record should be made of the quantity, color, shape, and markings of all tablets and capsules. Do not open a capsule. Place drugs in container, seal, identify, and transmit to the laboratory for analysis. Prior to analysis by the laboratory, drugs should not be identified solely on the basis of appearance. The officer's notes should refer only to the physical description and quantity of the substances.

Identification of Stimulants Illicit amphetamines are most often found in tablet and capsule form, although they have been found in powder and liquid form. Although brand name stimulants have trademarks or other identifying symbols, the tablets may vary widely in size, shape, and color. Tablets may be unscored, or single scored or double scored. The shape of the tablets may be round, oval, heart, triangular, square, etc. Tablets may be flat or curved, vary in thickness, and have beveled or unbeveled edges. Some may be candy coated. Amphetamine capsules are most often clear and filled with powder or multi-colored time-disintegration beads.

Examples of Amphetamines

Amphetamine sulfate in rose-colored, heart-shaped tablets is known as "peaches," "roses," "hearts," or "bennies."

Amphetamine sulfate in round, white, double-scored tablets is called "cartwheels," "whites," or "bennies."

Long-acting amphetamine sulfate capsules found in many colors are known as "coast-to-coast," "L.A. turnabouts," "copilots," or "browns."

Amphetamine sulfate in oval-shaped tablets of various colors is called "footballs" or "greenies."

Injectable amphetamine is called "bombido," "jugs," or "bottles."

Dextroamphetamine sulfate in orange-colored, heart-shaped tablets is known as "hearts," "oranges," or "dexies" (after a trade name).

Side Effects Tolerance develops rapidly with the use of amphetamines, requiring increased dosage to obtain the original effect. Too large a dose or too sudden an increase in dose, however, may produce bizarre mental effects such as delusions or hallucinations. These effects are more likely if the drug is injected intravenously in diluted, powdered form than if it is taken orally in tablet form. The early signs include repetitive grinding of the teeth; touching and picking the face and extremities; performing the same task over and over; a preoccupation with one's own thought processes; suspiciousness; and a feeling of being watched. Paranoia with auditory and visual hallucinations characterize the toxic syndrome resulting from continued high doses. Dizziness, tremors, agitation, hostility, panic, headaches, flushed skin, chest pains with palpitations, excessive sweating, vomiting, and abdominal cramps are among the symptoms of a sublethal dose. In the absence of medical intervention, high fever, convulsions, and cardiovascular collapse may precede the onset of death. Since death is due in part to the consequences of a marked increase in body temperature, it should be added that physical exertion and environmental temperature may greatly increase the hazards of stimulant use. Fatalities under conditions of extreme exertion have been reported among athletes who have taken stimulants in moderate amounts.

Whether or not these drugs produce physical dependence is still open to question. However, the chronic high-dose users do not easily or quickly return to normal if withdrawn from stimulants. Profound apathy and depression, fatigue, and disturbed sleep of up to twenty hours a day characterize the immediate withdrawal syndrome, which may last for several days.[10]

Methamphetamine Marketed under the trade name Methedrine, this drug is chemically related to amphetamine, but it has more central nervous system activity and correspondingly less effect on blood pressure and heart rate than amphetamines. The slang name for this drug is "speed." "Meth," "flash," or "crystals" are other names. The drug is available as tablets, powder, or capsules. When used under the careful supervision of a physician, methamphetamine has several benefits. However, it can be extremely dangerous when improperly taken. The most prevalent method of use of this drug is by intravenous injection using paraphernalia similar to that used by heroin addicts. When used intravenously the puncture wounds are more pronounced than those caused by the injection of heroin and the same areas of the body are used. On occasions, heroin addicts will inject methamphetamine to alleviate the distress of withdrawal. This drug is soluble in water—the user does not have to "cook" the mixture as a heroin user would have to do. It is injected in the same manner as narcotics.

Psychological Effects.[11] Following the injection of methamphetamine, effects may be felt immediately or any time within twenty minutes. Usually there is a period of elation and euphoria that lasts for approximately one-half hour. This period is called the "rush." During this period, the user experiences the sensation of objects and time passing at a rapid pace, hence the street or slang name "speed." There are hallucinations and, in some cases, periods of blurred vision coupled with double vision (diplopia). In addition, the user is unable to coordinate thoughts. After the "rush" the user starts down from the "high" and maintains a level of intoxication for an average of seven to eight hours, depending upon the amount taken. This period is called "wiring" or "maintaining." At the end of the "wiring" period, the user comes all the way down from the "high." This period is called "crashing."

---

[10]*Drug Enforcement,* Spring 1975, loc. cit.

[11]From the Los Angeles Police Department.

"Crashing" is also known as "going to sleep." The "crash" produces mental depression along with nausea, vomiting, diarrhea, nervousness, sleepiness, increased appetite, and indolence. To some users this depression is so great the user will obtain more methamphetamine and "shoot up" (inject) again to escape the feeling. Generally the methamphetamine user will not feel hungry while high. But users who stay high for a long period of time sometimes smoke marijuana to get hungry. Usually when the user stays high, she or he will experience a loss of weight.

Taken orally or sniffed, the drug produces the same symptoms. A longer period of time elapses before the "rush" is felt when the drug is sniffed. The method of sniffing is to place the "meth" on a "sniffing board" and spread the granules out. Then a drinking straw or rolled-up piece of paper is inserted into to one nostril while the other nostril is closed off. The user then sniffs the methamphetamine through the straw into the nasal passage. The membranes of the nose are injured when the drug is sniffed.

How Obtained   Amphetamines and the related methamphetamine are easily obtained. Having consulted medical books for the symptoms of maladies that are treated with these drugs, the user can easily simulate these symptoms and obtain prescriptions for the drugs, or forge prescriptions and pass them at local pharmacies. The user can also steal the drugs from pharmacies, doctor's offices, or the manufacturers' warehouses. Finally, the user can obtain the drugs from sources not regulated by the Food and Drug Administration.

Medical authorities estimate that the life expectancy of a person who "mainlines," i.e., injects methamphetamine is approximately five years.[12]

Phenmetrazine   (Preludin)   and Methylphenidate (Ritalin)   The effects,

medical indications, patterns of abuse, and adverse effects of phenmetrazine and methylphenidate compare closely with those of other stimulants. The primary use of phenmetrazine is as an appetite suppressant. Methylphenidate is used mainly for treatment of hyperkinetic behavioral disorders in children. These drugs have been subject to abuse in countries where they are freely available. In a few localities in the U.S., there are doctors who write prescriptions on demand. While the abuse of phenmetrazine involves both oral and intravenous use, most of that associated with methylphenidate results from injection after the drug in tablet form is dissolved in water. Complications arising from such use are common, since the tablets contain insoluble materials, which, upon injection, cause the occurrence of blood clots and abscesses, especially in the lungs.[13]

Prices   The price range of amphetamines, like other drugs, varies in accordance with the going "street price" and their availability. Amphetamines can be purchased by the *barrel* (100,000) for $4000 to $5000; *keg* (50,000), $1800 to $2800; *pillow* (25,000), $900 to $1400; *jar* (1000), $55 to $100; *bottle* (100), $15 to $30; or *roll* (3 to 10), $1.

Cocaine

This drug, the principal active ingredient of the South American plant called *Erythroxylon coca*, is one of the family of psychotropic drugs whose primary effect is to alter mood and behavior by acting on the central nervous system. (See Figure 18-9.) It is the most powerful natural stimulant.[14] The coca plant grows plentifully in Bolivia, Chile, Colombia, Ecuador, and Peru. Coca plants are harvested from two to six times

---

[12]*Van Nostrand's Scientific Encyclopedia,* loc. cit.

[13]*Drug Enforcement,* Spring 1975, loc. cit.

[14]*Drug Enforcement,* Drug Enforcement Administration, U.S. Department of Justice, Washington, D.C., Spring 1974.

each year. The leaves, after they have been stripped from the plants by hand, are dried in the sun before shipment. After the harvest and drying process, the coca leaf is converted to coca paste in a large number of mobile laboratories which are widely dispersed geographically. Most of these laboratories have small production capacity, making batches of coca paste of about 2–3 kilograms at a time. Thereafter, the coca paste is converted to cocaine hydrochloride in illicit laboratories in Chile, Bolivia, Peru, Ecuador, Colombia, Argentina, Mexico, and the United States.

Cocaine is a white, odorless, crystalline powder resembling snow, Epsom salt, or camphor. As an analgesic it has been largely supplanted by synthetic drugs. Its medical applications are now mainly restricted to operations of the ear, eye, nose, and throat. While the demand for licit cocaine has been going down, however, the clandestine supply to the United States market has been rising. Virtually all the cocaine available in this country is of illicit origin. It is sold on the street in the form of a white crystalline powder containing usually from 5–10 percent pure cocaine, cut with other white powders such as procaine, lidocaine and lactose.[15]

The effects of cocaine include a stimulation of the central nervous system and increases in the heart rate, blood pressure, and body temperature. Because of its central nervous system effects, the drug is habit-forming. The pleasurable effects of cocaine are mixed with hallucinations. A commonly reported hallucination is that of insects crawling on the skin. Cocaine is extremely dangerous because it can produce psychosis, and an overdose can result in death. Synthetic local anesthetics such as procaine (Novocaine), Butyn, Nupercaine, and Metycaine are now generally preferred by the medical profession over cocaine.[16]

[15]*Drug Enforcement,* Spring 1975, loc. cit.
[16]*Van Nostrand's Scientific Encyclopedia,* loc. cit.

Cocaine has a fairly fast effect. When inhaled through the nose, it goes to the back of the nasal cavity, combines with mucus, and drips down the back of the throat. The nose and upper gum become numb and then the "high" begins. If the drug is "mainlined" (taken intravenously), all the infections associated with heroin use can occur, including abscesses and hepatitis. Some heroin addicts will combine heroin and cocaine in one injection. This is called a "speedball" or a "coke-jab." The effects of the two drugs are directly opposite to one another and the body is severely abused by their combined use.

Concealment of cocaine

Drugs have been found on the young and old, on the affluent and poor, and on people of many professions. Smugglers and "mules" (transporters of narcotics) have tried every conceivable method to conceal cocaine and other drugs. Some of the ways that have been used to conceal cocaine, for example, include: sewing it in the lining of a coat; swallowing balloons or prophylactics filled with the drug (which has resulted in death in some instances when the balloons or prophylactics burst in the persons' stomachs); placing it in the padding of a wheelchair; hiding it in surgical body girdles or taping it to the body; and hiding it inside hollow water skis and fishing rods. Other methods are inserting the drug in body cavities; concealment in diving tanks; placing cocaine (liquefied) in seemingly unopened liquor bottles; and placement in portable hairdryers after removing electric motor. Other hiding places include airplane engines scheduled for repairs, photographic frames, shoes, hollow heels, false-bottom suitcases, fountain pens, book covers, flashlights after batteries are removed, false bottoms of furniture, hollow crutches, handbags, food cans, briefcases, loaves of bread, plastic statues, wooden artificial legs, gas tanks, radiators, auto parts, door panels, tires, behind headlights, in wall plaques, tennis rackets, and children's toys.

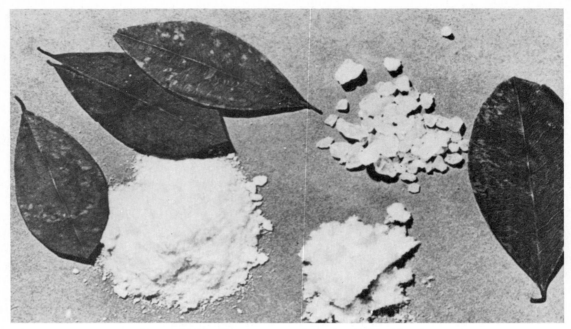

Figure 18-10. Coca leaves and cocaine hydrochloride.

Cost of cocaine

The price of illicit cocaine is governed by the availability of the drug and the going street price. However, a sampling of existing price ranges for this drug could be given approximately as follows: kilo—$35,000 to $45,000; pound—$18,000 to $25,000; ounce—$1000 to $1800; gram—$80 to $100.

Cocaine use in this country seemed insignificant as late as the early 1960s. Since then, however, use has increased rapidly. From 1970 on, there has been a steady upward trend in the amount of cocaine seized en route to the United States from South America and within this country. This drug does not produce true addiction nor does it seem that the user develops a tolerance. However, it can produce psychological dependence. In the illicit trade, it is known by such names as "C," "Cecil," "chalk," "Charlie," "happy dust," "coconuts," "Bernice,"

"big C," "blow," "gold dust," "white girl," "flake," "snow," and others. It has also been referred to as the new "in" drug. In addition, it is known as the "Cadillac of drugs" and the "champagne of drugs" because of its high market price.

Traffic in cocaine

Cocaine is smuggled into the United States either directly or circuitously via Panama, Jamaica, Mexico, Bermuda, the United Kingdom, and Tahiti. Colombia is said to be the most significant center for the illicit manufacture and traffic of cocaine in South America.[17] Colombia's 500-mile-[830-kilometer-] long Caribbean coast with

---

[17]*Drug Enforcement,* Drug Enforcement Administration, U.S. Department of Justice, Washington, D.C., Spring 1976.

its sparsely populated ports, coves, deserted beaches, and natural airstrips lends itself ideally to cocaine smuggling.

One of the many cocaine smuggling rings uncovered in a Drug Enforcement Administration operation involved 66 pounds [30 kilograms] of cocaine worth $14 million. It was successfully concluded with the arrest and conviction of the ring's leader and members of the group after many months of investigation. Such areas were involved as Los Angeles; New York; Miami; Bogota, Colombia; and Brasilia, Brazil. In this case cocaine was smuggled into the United States in aerosol cans disguised as toiletry items. The cans were brought into this country two or three at a time by couriers. The aerosol cans were altered so that the top of the cans could be removed. Small plastic inserts, which could spray for about two minutes, were placed under the nozzle in an attempt to duplicate the real thing, should the cans be tested. Investigation established that the cocaine was prepared in an illicit laboratory in Bogota, Colombia.

Injecting process, use and effects

Cocaine can be administered by mouth but the preferred routes are through the nose, called sniffing or "snorting," or by intravenous injection. If the drug is sniffed, the small crystals are abrasive to the blood vessels in mucous membranes lining the nose. These membranes become reddened and irritated and often bleed. After continued use of cocaine, the blood vessels of the nose become constricted, preventing nutrients from reaching the area. Necrosis and perforation of the nasal septum may occur.[18]

Some cocaine users like what they call "frosties"—having a friend put cocaine on a piece of paper and blow it into the backs of their mouths. Most often it is sniffed or

---

[18]*Drug Enforcement*, Spring 1974, loc. cit.

"snorted." In this "snorting" procedure, cocaine powder is put on a clean flat surface such as a mirror. A razor blade is then used to divide the powder into lines. Thereafter, with plastic straws (cocaine granules would stick to a paper straw), the drug is inhaled into the nose. Sometimes rolled-up currency or match covers are used as straws.

Depressants (sedatives and hypnotics)

The barbiturates made from barbituric acid constitute the largest group of sedatives. Their effects are opposite to those of the amphetamines. They are the most frequently prescribed drug to induce sleep and to reduce daytime tension and anxiety. They are known as hypnotics and are commonly referred to as "sleeping pills." Because of their sedative effect they are also called "downers" by drug users. People can legally buy and use these drugs only with a doctor's prescription. Prescriptions are extensively abused. This group of drugs depresses the central nervous system and relieves anxiety. Barbiturates are valuable when used properly but extremely dangerous when abused.

Barbiturates are addicting. Signs of physical dependence appear with doses well above therapeutic level. Withdrawal from barbiturates is especially dangerous and is characterized by accompanying convulsions and delirium.

About 2500 derivatives of barbituric acid have been synthesized, but of these only about 15 remain in widespread use. Small therapeutic doses tend to calm nervous conditions, and larger amounts cause sleep from twenty to sixty minutes after oral administration. As in the case of alcohol, some individuals may experience a sense of excitement before sedation takes effect. If dosage is increased, however, the effects of the barbiturates may progress through successive stages of sedation, sleep, and coma, to death from respiratory arrest and cardiovascular complications.[19]

Barbiturates have often been diverted from legitimate channels. Popular brand name depressants bear trademarks or other identifying symbols. Their trade names are usually recognizable by the ending "al" (Secon*al*, Nembut*al*, Amyt*al*, Lumin*al*). Individual barbiturates are distinguished from one another by the colors of the gelatin capsules in which they are packed. Some of the better known barbiturates commonly found among drug offenders are

> *Seconal* (secobarbital)—A white powder, in a red, pink, or reddish-orange capsule, referred to as "reds," "red birds," or "red devils." A variation of secobarbital sodium is manufactured in a pink capsule and is called "pinks," "pinkies," or "pink ladies."
>
> *Nembutal* (pentobarbital)—A white powder in a yellow capsule, referred to as "yellows," "yellow jackets," or "nimbies."
>
> *Amytal Sodium* (amobarbital sodium)—A white powder in a blue capsule, referred to as "blues," "blue heavens," or "blue velvets." It is available as either a small white tablet or light blue capsule. The capsules are the most common and are called "blue velvets."
>
> *Tuinal* (equal parts secobarbital sodium and amobarbital sodium)—A white powder in a blue and red capsule, referred to as "rainbows" or "double trouble."

Methaqualone This drug is a synthetic sedative chemically unrelated to the barbiturates, glutethimide, or chloral hydrate. It has been widely abused because it was once mistakenly thought to be safe and nonaddictive and to have aphrodisiac qualities. Actually, methaqualone has caused many cases of serious poisoning. It is administered orally. Large doses cause coma and may be accompanied by thrashing movements or convulsions. Continued heavy use of large doses leads to tolerance and dependence. Methaqualone has been marketed in the United States under various brand names such as Quaalude, Parest, Optimil, Somnafac, and Sopor.[20] Quaalude is becoming very popular on some school campuses, a pill selling for up to $4.00.

Symptoms of Barbiturate Intoxication[21] Barbituric intoxication produces symptoms similar to alcoholic intoxication but without the odor of alcohol. Some of the symptoms that the user exhibits are disorientation, depression, thick and lethargic speech; a lack of muscular coordination; involuntary oscillation of the eyes and inability of the eyes to hold a fixed position; and defective judgment. The degree of intoxication can produce symptoms which may vary from a euphoric "high" to sloppy drunkenness or unconsciousness. Persons even mildly under the influence of barbiturates create a serious hazard when they drive a car.

Habituation and Withdrawal Anyone who ceases to take or abruptly curtails the amount of a depressant on which he or she has become dependent will encounter symptoms of withdrawal more severe than in an otherwise comparable case of narcotics addiction (such as heroin). Some of the withdrawal symptoms from barbiturates include nervousness, headaches, anxiety, nose twitching, tremors, weakness, insomnia, nausea, change in blood pressure, mental confusion, delirium, hallucinations, convulsions, and exhaustion. Sudden complete withdrawal from barbiturates by an addicted person results in convulsions. Often temporary psychosis results.

---

[19]*Drug Enforcement,* Spring 1975, loc. cit.

[20]*Drug Enforcement,* Spring 1975, loc. cit.

[21]From the Los Angeles Police Department.

Sometimes abrupt withdrawal may cause death. Withdrawals from depressants should be supervised under the controlled conditions of a hospital.[22]

Dangers The addict frequently becomes semiconscious and unknowingly takes additional pills; the result is often accidental death mistaken as suicide. The user often takes a hypnotic and a stimulant in combination. This is called a "speedball." The effects of the drugs are opposite, and the body fights them both to remain normal.

The depressants vary with respect to their lethal overdose potential. Moderate depressant overdose closely resembles alcoholic inebriation. The symptoms of severe depressant poisoning are coma, cold and clammy skin, weak and rapid pulse, and slow or rapid, shallow respiration. Death will follow if the reduced respiration and low blood pressure are not counteracted by proper medical treatment.[23]

Cost of Barbiturates The price range of barbiturates, like other drugs obtained illicitly, varies in accordance with the going "street price" and their availability. Barbiturates can be purchased on the drug market for the following approximate prices: *keg* (50,000), $3200 to $7250; *jar* (1000), $120 to $160; *bottle* (100), $25; individually, $1.

Hallucinogens

Hallucinogens (also called psychedelics or consciousness-expanding drugs) and psychotomimetics (mimicking insanity) are drugs capable of provoking changes of sensation, thinking, self-awareness, and emotion. Alterations of time and space perception, illusions, hallucinations, and delusions may be either minimal or overwhelming depending on the dose. The results are very variable: a "high" or a "bad trip" ("freakout" or "bummer") may occur in the same person on different occasions. LSD is the most potent and best-studied hallucinogen.

LSD (Lysergic Acid Diethylamide) In 1938 Dr. Albert Hofmann, a biochemist at Sandoz Laboratories in Basel, Switzerland, first synthesized LSD. At that time, his firm was particularly interested in the ingredients of a dark purple fungus named ergot—which had spoiled rye fields during a wet European summer. Dr. Hofmann took up the study of one of ergot's constitutents, lysergic acid, and made a series of new compounds from it, including diethylamide of lysergic acid. On an April afternoon in 1943, Dr. Hofmann was attempting to separate LSD from its isomer when he accidentally inhaled an infinitesimal amount of the new compound. He recognized its perception-altering properties and repeated his intake a few days later to confirm his findings.[24]

LSD has since become known as one of the most powerful drugs. The National Institute of Mental Health (NIMH) is the primary federal agency responsible for supporting and overseeing research on LSD.

Physical Effects[25] An average dose of LSD amounting to a tiny speck (1 ounce is enough to provide 300,000 average doses) has an effect lasting eight to twelve hours. Users typically take it in a pill, sugar cube, or capsule form, although the amount of active material is so small it can be placed on almost anything. The physical effects consist of enlarged pupils, a flushed face, chilliness, perhaps a rise in temperature and heart beat, and a slight increase in blood pressure. LSD is not an addictive drug; that

---

[22]Ibid.
[23]Ibid.

[24]Sidney Cohen, M.D., *The Beyond Within.* Atheneum, New York, 1964.
[25]*LSD: Some Questions and Answers.* Public Health Service Publication No. 1828, U.S. Department of Health, Education, and Welfare, Washington, D.C., June 1971.

is, even though the user may use it regularly and become tolerant to its effects, no withdrawal symptoms result if it is suddenly discontinued.

Psychological Effects The psychological effects of LSD vary considerably according to the amount taken, the personality of the user, and the circumstances under which the drug is taken. Effects can be notably different at different times, even in the same person. Marked changes in sensation are typical. Vision is significantly altered. Users are likely to see unusual patterns, and the meaning of what is seen is often transformed. One sensory experience may be translated or merged into another: for example, smells may be felt, sounds may be seen. These are called synesthesias. Illusions and hallucinations can occur, and delusional thoughts are sometimes expressed. The sense of time and of self are strangely altered. Emotional variations are marked, ranging from bliss to horror, sometimes within a single experience. One of the most confusing, yet common, reactions among users is the feeling of two strong and opposite feelings at the same time—they can feel both happy and sad at the same time, or depressed and elated, or relaxed and tense. Arms and legs may feel both heavy and light. Users also report a sensation of losing the normal feelings of boundaries between one's body and space.

Users of LSD often refer to "good" and "bad trips." By a good trip is meant a drug experience in which pleasant sensations and imagery are predominant, while a bad trip or "bummer" is the opposite. During the bad trip the images are terrifying and the emotional state is one of dread and horror. Because of the impaired time sense, a few minutes may seem like hours. Such an experience can assume the proportions of a terrible nightmare from which one cannot easily awaken. Unfortunately, there is no way to predict definitely who will have a good or bad trip, and a history of having had good trips is no guarantee that the next trip experience will not be horrifying.[26]

Case A twenty-three-year-old college student, on being questioned by police, stated, "Yes, officer, I'm under the influence of LSD, but I haven't taken any for eight weeks. I see worms crawling out of my fingers. They are little black worms and I pick them out of my fingers and throw them on the floor. I see the same worms crawling right back in the same holes. I have worms crawling out of my ears, eyes, head, and neck. My teeth are on fire. My eyeballs feel like buckets of blood."

Dangers of LSD Clinical reports on the illicit use of LSD have warned of definite dangers.[27] These include

1. *Panic.* The user may grow frightened because she or he cannot "turn off" the drug's action. The user may forget that a drug can change thinking and feeling, and fear that he or she is going insane.

2. *"Flashbacks."* A flashback is a recurrence of some of the features of the LSD state days or months after the last dose. A flashback occurring without apparent cause can be very frightening and cause the user to believe that she or he is becoming psychotic. In some individuals this concern has caused fear and depression leading to suicide.

3. *Accidental death.* Because the LSD user may sometimes have paranoid feelings of being invulnerable or even of being able to fly, there have been cases of accidental death resulting from these beliefs. Users have been known to walk in front of moving cars or to attempt to fly, i.e., jump from a high window or from other heights, and fall to their deaths.

Case In one instance a young man under the influence of LSD was restrained from diving off a cliff into the rocks and ocean below. Later he explained that he felt

---

[26]Ibid.
[27]Ibid.

the breaking waves were a silk scarf and he wanted to dive into it.

Identification of LSD[28] LSD, in its pure form, is odorless, tasteless, and colorless. It is therefore possible for unsuspecting persons to take or be given the drug without their knowledge. Due to the microscopic amount needed, the drug is diluted or mixed with other ingredients to prepare it for packaging. If the drug has an odor, taste, or color, it can generally be attributed to the diluent, mixing agent, or impurities in its manufacture.

LSD obtained on the street often contains a number of impurities. Sometimes other compounds (among them atropine) are sold as LSD. Black-market doses, usually diluted as they are passed on, contain an unknown amount of LSD. LSD has been obtained in liquid form in small ampules and then has been transferred to large bottles labeled as mouthwash. It may also be found in crystalline form, capsules, bulk powder, and tablets. LSD is most commonly administered orally. A sugar cube is saturated with LSD and eaten. When in powder form, LSD is usually dissolved in a sweet liquid or water and ingested. The drug has been placed on animal crackers, candy wafers, gum drops, licorice, sugar cubes, chewing gum, gummed flaps of envelopes, cigarette tobacco, and marijuana. The drug may also be "skin popped" (injected under the skin) or taken intravenously.

Experienced narcotics investigators are able to identify many drugs by their texture, smell, and, sometimes, taste. Since the introduction of LSD, however, officers *do not* attempt to identify any drug in this manner for fear of the dangerous consequences. Narcotics officers have found that sellers or distributors of LSD find it more profitable than marijuana, easier to handle, and easier to dispose of if necessary.

Marijuana is consumed in this country by smoking it in the form of a cigarette. The characteristics of marijuana are easily distinguished from ordinary cigarettes. LSD, on the other hand, is very difficult to detect due to the many forms of camouflage. The amount of LSD reaching the consumer may be so minute that it would barely be visible to the naked eye (thus making analysis a difficult task for the lab technician). The amount of LSD placed on the item to be consumed varies from 100 micrograms to 500 micrograms or more. The micrograms of LSD on the item will determine its value.[29]

Hallucinogens other than LSD In addition to LSD, a large number of synthetic and natural hallucinogens are known. These include DMT (dimethyltryptamine), found in the seeds of certain plants; DOM, popularly known as "STP," derived in a chemical laboratory; mescaline, obtained from the peyote cactus; psilocybin and psilocyn, obtained from certain mushrooms grown in Mexico; MDA and MMDA, PCP, PHP, and many other substances that produce altered states of consciousness.

DMT (Dimethyltryptamine) DMT is a short-acting hallucinogen found in the seeds of certain plants native to the West Indies and parts of South America. The powdered seeds have been used for centuries as a snuff, called "cohoba," in religious ceremonies to produce a state of mind that the Haitian natives claimed enabled them to communicate with their gods. It is also produced synthetically by clandestine chemists. DMT is not taken orally, but its vapor is inhaled from the smoke given off by burning the ground seeds or powder mixed with tobacco, parsley leaves, or marijuana. It can also be injected. The effects of a single dose—60 to 150 milligrams—last only from forty-five to sixty minutes and mainly produce halluci-

---

[28]Ibid.

[29]From the Los Angeles Police Department.

nations. It may cause psychological but not physical dependence.[30]

DOM   Known popularly as "STP," this drug appeared on the psychedelic scene in the early spring of 1967. Articles in the underground newspapers promoted its use, claiming STP (serenity, tranquility, peace) to be stronger than LSD. The compound was identified by Food and Drug Administration chemists to be 4-methyl-2,5-dimethoxy-amphetamine or DOM. Little is known about the therapeutic, pharmacological, or psychological effects. However, doses of one to three milligrams produce euphoria and doses of more than three milligrams can cause pronounced hallucinogenic effects lasting eight to ten hours. "STP" is not found in nature, but is synthesized in the laboratory and has appeared in illegal channels in tablet form.[31]

Mescaline (Peyote)   Mescaline, which is derived from the buttons of the peyote cactus plant, has been used for centuries by various Indian tribes of Central America and the southeastern United States. The Native American Church, which uses peyote in religious ceremonies, has been exempted from certain provisions of the federal law. Generally ground into a powder, peyote is taken orally. Because of its bitter taste, the drug is often ingested with tea, coffee, milk, orange juice, or some other beverage. Mescaline is available on the illicit market, however, as a crystalline powder, in capsules, or as a liquid in ampules or vials. A dose of 350 to 500 milligrams of mescaline produces illusions and hallucinations for five to twelve hours. Like LSD, mescaline is not likely to produce physical dependence but may cause psychological dependence.[32]

Psilocybin and Psilocyn   Also derived from plants, psilocybin and psilocyn are ob-

tained from certain mushrooms generally grown in Mexico. Like mescaline, they have been used in Indian rites for centuries. Their effects are similar to those of mescaline, except that a smaller dose of 4–8 milligrams is ample. Psilocybin and psilocyn are available in crystalline, powdered, or liquid form. They are said to cost about the same as LSD on the illicit market. The experience lasts for approximately six hours. The extracts from these plants do not produce physical dependence, although users have been known to develop a tolerance to them.[33]

PHP   (Phenylcylclohexyl   Pyrollidine)   In a recent case involving the arrest and shooting of a suspect by a police officer in Southern California, an autopsy disclosed that the suspect had taken the drug PHP. At the coroner's inquest, a Los Angeles County deputy coroner who was a medical doctor performed the autopsy and testified that the suspect had .01 milligrams of PHP in his blood and .02 milligrams of this drug in his liver. It was indicated at the inquest that PHP is an analogue of the hallucinogen PCP, known as "angel dust." Dr. Sydney Cohen, a noted physician and psychiatrist at the University of California at Los Angeles who specializes in the study of drugs, testified at the inquest. He said that not too much work had been done on PHP, but that one could conclude "it would show similar effect" to "angel dust," which often causes bizarre behavior.

MDA and MMDA   Chemically, MDA and MMDA are related to the amphetamines, mescaline, and DOM (STP). They are controlled as hallucinogens; they also produce some stimulation and a sense of well-being. The MDA sold on the street is synthesized illicitly and sold in powder, tablet, or liquid form. It is usually taken orally but may be "snorted" through the nose or injected intravenously. The MDA experience is re-

---

[30]*Facts Sheet No. 10: Hallucinogens.* Bureau of Narcotics and Dangerous Drugs, U.S. Department of Justice, Washington, D.C., 1970.
[31]Ibid.
[32]*Drug Enforcement,* Spring 1975, loc. cit.

[33]Ibid.

ported to be devoid of the visual and auditory distortions which mark that of LSD.[34]

Phencyclidine (PCP) This drug is referred to in the drug culture as "angel dust," "peace pill," "DOA" ("dead on arrival"), "hog," or "killer weed" (when combined with marijuana or other plant material). PCP, developed in the 1950s, is now licitly manufactured as a veterinary anesthetic under the trade name Sernylan. Since 1967 it has also been produced in clandestine laboratories, frequently in dangerously contaminated forms. The prevailing patterns of street-level abuse are by oral ingestion of tablets or capsules containing the drug in powder form, both alone and in combination with other drugs, and by smoking the drug after it has been sprinkled on parsley, marijuana, or tobacco. It is sometimes sold to unsuspecting consumers as LSD, THC, or mescaline.

Reported experiences under the influence of phencyclidine are mainly nondescript or unpleasant. In low doses the experience usually proceeds in three successive stages: changes in body image, sometimes accompanied by feelings of depersonalization; perceptual distortions, infrequently evidenced as visual or auditory hullucinations; and feelings of apathy or estrangement. The experience often includes drowsiness, inability to verbalize, and feelings of emptiness or "nothingness." Reports of difficulty in thinking, poor concentration, and preoccupation with death are common. Common signs of phencyclidine use include flushing and profuse sweating. Analgesia, involuntary eye movements, muscular incoordination, double vision, dizziness, nausea, and vomiting may also be present.[35] Users of PCP feel the effects within two to five minutes after smoking a small amount and the feelings peak in about fifteen to thirty minutes. The "high" continues for four to six hours, but the user does not feel normal for twenty-four to forty-eight hours.

In one case involving a sophisticated illicit manufacturer and distributor of illegal amphetamines and PCP, a clandestine laboratory was located on a remote hill top. The laboratory was surrounded by an electric fence and television cameras for external surveillance in the event of a raid. Despite these precautions, after a successful raid on the premises by sheriff's deputies and DEA agents, the "mastermind" of this operation confessed that he got involved in the enterprise because of his interest in drugs and the challenge in avoiding capure. Invoices were found ordering chemicals that would have made over 1000 pounds [46 kilograms] of PCP. The "mastermind" (a recent law school graduate), was described by one of his associates in the drug operation as a young "James Bond" on the wrong side of the law.

Case Involving PCP (Phencyclidine) and MDA (3,4 Methylenedioxyamphetamine) At approximately 1720 hours, JOHN R. COOK, nineteen years old, was traveling on Lake Road near Centerville. The vehicle became disabled and COOK, along with two companions, began walking west. COOK apparently went berserk and threatened his companions. COOK attempted to strike the men with a tree limb; the two men became frightened and ran.

Approximately ten minutes later a Highway Patrol officer, ROBERT D. HALL, passed the disabled vehicle and shortly thereafter came upon COOK walking in the center of the roadway. Officer HALL stopped his police car 20 to 25 feet [6 to 8 meters] behind COOK to determine if he was in need of assistance.

Before the officer could exit, COOK saw the patrol vehicle, ran to the right side of it, opened the front door, entered and attempted to tear the shotgun from the Lektro-lok mounting. HALL saw that the subject was grunting and groaning. The officer pushed COOK out the door. HALL

---

[34]*Drug Enforcement*, Spring 1975, loc. cit.

[35]*Drug Enforcement*, Spring 1975, loc. cit.

radioed, "11-99, I have a subject on a bad trip." COOK ran around to the left side of the patrol car as officer HALL was completing the radio broadcast. COOK was ordered to the left of the road. COOK then attempted to forcibly enter the patrol vehicle through the driver's door.

Officer HALL pushed the subject away several times. COOK started to walk away, enabling HALL to obtain his baton. Due to the remote location the nearest assistance was 15 miles [25 kilometers] away.

Again the subject attempted to enter the patrol car, forcing his way past the officer and trying to start the car. HALL had previously removed the keys. Again COOK was pushed from the patrol car. The officer was unable to restrain or control the subject. HALL radioed, "11-99, hurry up." COOK circled around the vehicle and assaulted the officer.

Three fishermen happened by the scene. They stopped to see if they could possibly render assistance. HALL advised the fishermen of his problem and asked them to help him. COOK had been calling out the name "RAY." The officer, attempting to keep COOK away, told him, "Go find RAY." COOK would not leave. COOK continued his assault, causing the officer to use his baton. Officer HALL struck the subject across the hands and wrists several times. This did not affect COOK. The officer struck COOK solidly in the chest area with the end of the baton, again with no effect. COOK continued the assault. He was struck in the sides by HALL, who swung his baton in a full arc, using both hands—to no effect. The officer then struck the subject on the head across the temple area with no deterring effect.

COOK reached out and grabbed the baton with both hands. While the two men stood face to face, grappling with the baton, COOK lifted the officer off the ground and swung him in an arc. Both individuals fell into a grassy ditch alongside the highway. The subject landed on top of the officer. HALL called to the fishermen for help and as they moved forward the subject stood up. The officer was then able to regain his footing; and he radioed an "11-99."

Subject COOK again attacked, and was successful in wrestling the baton away from the officer. Now swinging the baton, COOK advanced. HALL was struck numerous times as he backed away. COOK began swinging at the officer's head. HALL realized that if he was struck in the head and dazed or rendered unconscious that COOK would have access to his service revolver. The officer feared for the lives of the three fishermen as well as his own.

HALL drew his service revolver, pointed it at the ground and ordered the subject to throw down the baton. The officer repeated the order while backing away as COOK continued the assault. HALL fired two rounds at the subject's legs, hoping to disable him. One round struck COOK in the leg. COOK continued swinging at officer HALL's head. A third shot was fired into the chest of COOK with no visible effect. COOK continued to aggressively swing the baton at the officer's head. A fourth shot was fired which also struck COOK in the chest. COOK then went down to a sitting position. Officer HALL was carrying issue .38 caliber ammunition in a .357 magnum revolver.

An ambulance was requested. As the officer attempted to control the bleeding, COOK attempted to continue his attack. COOK attempted to grab any person that walked within arm's reach. HALL had placed a gauze bandage on the subject's wounds; COOK tore the bloody compress from his body and threw it at the officer, striking him in the chest.

At 1820 hours, an ambulance arrived and transported subject COOK to Centerville Hospital. At 1906 hours, the subject was pronounced dead upon arrival at the hospital.

An autopsy revealed that COOK was

under the influence of two powerful hallucinogens, PCP (phencyclidine) and MDA
(3,4 Methylenedioxyamphetamine). One
bullet was found to have broken the femur
bone near the hip of one leg. The two bullets
that struck COOK in the chest passed completely through his body without striking
any major organs.

When interviewed by the Central County
Sheriff's Department, the three witnesses
indicated that they believed their lives were
in danger. In addition, they said that the
officer had no choice in taking the action he
did.

HALL had attempted to control the irra-
tional subject by reasoning with him, physically restraining him, and by using his
baton with no effect while awaiting assistance. He did not receive any actual physical
assistance from the three witnesses. As a
last resort, and then only when he was in
fear for the lives of the witnesses and his
own, did he fire his revolver in self-defense.

(*Note*: The above are true facts. The
names and places, however, are fictitious.)

The National Institute on Drug Abuse
(NIDA) has issued a special bulletin on the
dangers of PCP. It is an animal tranquilizer
that has become popular, particularly among
teen-agers. High doses of this synthetic
drug, which is easily—and illegally—manufactured, can turn the user to violence
and bring on coma and death. NIDA has
alerted all emergency rooms, medical examiners, drug clinics, and coroners to the dangers of this drug.[36]

Marijuana Marijuana is a dried plant
material obtained from the Indian hemp
plant (*Cannabis sativa*). It has very limited
medical use in the United States. The plant
grows in mild climates throughout the
world, especially in Mexico, Africa, India,
the Middle East, and the United States.

---

[36]*U.S. News & World Report*, Jan. 23, 1978.

Figure 18-11. (a) Leaf formation of a marijuana
plant. (b) Clusters of seeds on a marijuana plant
(fruit of the plant).

Marijuana is frequently cultivated for its commercial value in the production of such items as twine, rope, bags, and clothing. The sterilized seeds are occasionally used in various feed mixtures, particularly bird seed. The marijuana plant (Figure 18-11) grows in the form of a shrublike plant from 4 to 20 feet [1 to 6 meters] high. The leaves have from five to eleven (always an uneven number) leaflets or fingers. These leaflets are from 2 to 6 inches [5 to 15 centimeters] long, are slender, pointed almost equally at both ends, and have sawlike edges and pronounced ridges running from the center diagonally to the edges. The leaf is of a deep green color on the upper side and lighter green on the lower. The green plant has a peculiar odor, is sticky to the touch, and is covered with fine hairs that are barely visible to the naked eye. An almost positive identification of marijuana can be made by identifying the "cystolith hairs" on particles by a microscope.

The female of the species contains an abundant amount of cannabinol, which is the actual narcotic resin. Marijuana varies greatly in strength, depending upon where it is grown, whether it is wild or specifically cultivated for smoking or eating, and which portions of the plant actually go into the drug mixture. Marijuana is sometimes adulterated with other materials such as its own seeds and stems, tea, catnip, or oregano. These reduce the strength of the resulting mixture. Hashish ("hash") is the potent dark-brown resin which is collected from the tops of high-quality cannabis. Because of the high concentration of resin, hashish is often five to six times stronger than the usual marijuana, although the active drug ingredients are the same. The marijuana used in the United States is perhaps one-fifth the strength of hashish.[37]

---

[37]*Drug Enforcement*, Spring 1975, loc. cit.

Colombian marijuana is regarded as a high-grade, expensive type which sells from $50 to $70 an ounce. Another cannabis strain is a seedless variety called Sinsemilla. It is very strong and sells for up to $120 a lid.

Hashish Oil This substance is a concentrate of cannabis. Hashish is produced by a process of repeated extractions to yield a dark viscous liquid, samples of which have been found to contain from 20 to 60 percent THC. A drop or two of this oil on a cigarette is equal in psychoactive effect to an entire marijuana cigarette. The concentrate serves to reduce the smuggler's risks, while compounding those of the consumer.

In one case, officers confiscated 6 gallons of this oil plus several pounds of marijuana and hashish. Arrests and seizures resulted after an undercover officer succeeded in purchasing 2.5 liters of hashish oil from a member of the drug ring for $26,000. In addition, 19 liters of hashish oil were located in a trunk at the site.

In another case, a plush three-story hillside home in a beach city was uncovered by officers as the location of a major narcotics and dangerous drugs "factory." Among the contraband materials seized by police and narcotics agents were a gallon of hashish oil, thousands of LSD tablets, a quantity of cocaine and marijuana (some canned and sealed for shipment). Order forms and notes found at this "factory" disclosed that the group had been doing hundreds of thousands of dollars worth of business. Blank birth certificates, driver's licenses, and marriage forms were also found at this residence— "everything to make a guy a new person," according to the arresting officers. In addition, thousands of dollars in $20, $50, and $100 bills were unearthed in the cellar at this location.

THC (Tetrahydrocannabinol) This is considered to be the basic active ingredient in marijuana and hashish. The THC content of the plant, varying from none to more than 2 percent THC, determines its mind-altering activity. Because THC is somewhat unstable, its content in marijuana decreases as time passes. The plant that grows wild in the United States is low in THC content compared to cultivated marijuana, or the Mexican, Lebanese, or Indian varieties. Plant strain, climate, soil conditions, the time of harvesting, and other factors determine the potency.

For use as a drug, the leaves and flowering tops of the plant are dried in indirect heat, then manicured, or processed, to remove seeds and stems. When processed, it resembles catnip or tea, which is the origin of one of the nicknames of marijuana. Although there are several methods of using marijuana throughout the world, the most prevalent method employed in the United States is by smoking, usually in the form of a cigarette. In the vernacular of the street, they are called "reefers," "joints," or "sticks." It may also be smoked in ordinary pipes or water pipes or occasionally incorporated into food and eaten. When the drug is smoked, the smoke smells like burning rope or alfalfa. Because of the distinctive odor, users sometimes burn incense to mask the smell.

Marijuana Cigarette The marijuana cigarette is composed of two cigarette papers and a small quantity of marijuana. Two papers are used in order to prevent the marijuana fragments from piercing the single paper while passing through the custody of many persons before finally reaching the user. The papers used in preparing the cigarette may be brown or white in color. When the cigarette is "rolled," it looks like a roll-your-own cigarette with the ends tucked in or twisted. The cigarettes will vary in size and shape. The finished cigarette is easily distinguished from a regular tobacco cigarette. Marijuana cigarettes are difficult to light and must be kept ignited by continuous puffing. They burn with a brighter glow

than tobacco and are more easily seen in the dark. Knowledge of the characteristics of the small egg-shaped seeds should be helpful in identification when the drug is found in suspected material, clothing, or on the floor of a suspected automobile. The seeds have encircling ridges with motley lacy markings on the surface. (See Figure 18-12.)

Smoking The ends are opened and a match held to one end. The smoke is inhaled deeply, retained as long as possible, and then exhaled slowly. If more than one person is present, only one cigarette is usually lighted and passed around. Marijuana smokers are gregarious and prefer to smoke in the company of others. The "roach" (butt end) is wholly consumed by using a "crutch" or a "bridge." The "crutch" is used to hold the remnants of the cigarette. The "crutch" may be an alligator clip, paper clip, hair clip, or the back of a match cover rolled into a funnel. When smoking, the users make a noise that resembles the sound of air being sucked between puckered lips. If the smoking is done in an automobile, the windows are usually rolled up to prevent the

Figure 18-12. Manicured marijuana cigarettes.

smoke from escaping. Occasionally seeds are found in the cigarette and will make a popping noise as they burn. The intoxicating effects of marijuana smoke can last from two to four hours.

How Does Marijuana Work? After inhalation, effects begin within minutes, peak within one hour, and are dissipated within three hours. After ingestion, effects begin in thirty minutes to two hours, peak at three hours, and persist for four to six hours. The acute physiologic effects of cannabis are dose-related. Psychoactive effects are highly variable and depend on the dose, the route of administration, the personality of the user, prior experience with the drug, personal expectations, and the environmental and social setting in which the drug is used.

Enhanced perception of colors, sounds, patterns, textures, and taste is common. Moods are complex and a sense of increased well-being is frequently experienced, although anxiety and depression may be increased by the drug as well. Drowsiness or hyperactivity and hilarity may occur. Ideas expressed may seem disconnected, rambling, and assume altered importance. Time seems to pass slowly, and short-term memory may be impaired. Motor performance is variably impaired, as is reaction time. Although attention can be maintained in certain situations, it is probable that alterations in attention are responsible for some of the reported gradual reduction in performance and learning.[38]

Packaging and Sale of Marijuana Marijuana is usually compressed into "bricks" similar to a miniature bale of hay. Some are square and others are oblong. (See Figure 18-13.) The "bricks" weigh 1 kilo (2.2 pounds). The price of a kilo may range from $200–$500 (bulk price), depending on the supply and demand and other factors such as the quality and distance from the source. Kilos are subdivided into 1-pound units (each sells for approximately $100–$225). Other units sell in ½-pound, 1-ounce, and sometimes smaller quantities. The 1-ounce quantities are referred to as "cans," "lids," or "baggies." A 1-ounce lid price is about $15–$25 and contains enough marijuana for fifty or more cigarettes. Cigarettes are priced from $.50–$2.00. (See Figure 18-14.)

Investigation of Illicit Drug Cases

The investigation of illicit drug cases involves generally the same basic investigative practices as applied to other criminal violations. However, the nature of this type of case requires specialized investigative approaches. With all types of crimes except one, the victims, their relatives, and associates are anxious to report them as soon as possible—the exception is illicit narcotics. The victim of a narcotics peddler is part of the crime itself. The victim is an accessory who must cooperate with the criminal who sells the drugs in order to preserve her or his source of supply. Relatives and friends of illicit drug users are protective and ashamed and often do not want to become involved.

Illicit drug cases require special skills, familiarization with narcotics and dangerous drugs, and a knowledge of applicable laws. A narcotics investigation requires native craftiness and adaptability along with glibness enough to enter into the confidence of violators. Nearly all field work in these cases is undercover investigation in which an officer assumes another identity for the purposes of gathering evidence or making a "buy" of evidence. Reports of undercover operators should be prepared as soon as possible after any observable violation of the law. The reports should contain as much of

---

[38]Robert B. Millman, M.D., "Cannabis (Marijuana and Hashish)," in Paul B. Beeson and Walsh McDermott, M.D., *Textbook of Medicine*, 14th ed., W. B. Saunders Company, Vol. 1, No. 344, p. 594, 1975.

Figure 18-13. Kilo bricks of marijuana.

the actual transaction as the operator can remember. Undercover operators should be observed in any "buy" operation, for corroboration purposes, and to protect them from physical harm. The use of informants to obtain leads and arrange introductions is also a standard and essential practice. The use of informants, however, should be considered only where the information sought cannot be otherwise obtained. Other investigative approaches, aids, methods, and considerations include

Recognition of characteristic behavior of illicit drug users and physical symptoms resulting from the use of narcotics and dangerous drugs.

Case buildup approach in order to identify as many participants as possible, and the extent of their involvement.

Figure 18-14. Retail forms of marijuana.

Recognition of identifying "telltale" marks and punctures on the arms and bodies of drug users; types of conditions or appearances indicative of illicit drug use.

Familiarization with the type of paraphernalia used in preparation and injection of illicit drugs: spoon or bottle cap ("cooker"), medicine dropper or eyedropper, hypodermic syringes and needles ("spikes"), tie rags (straps, heavy rubber bands, handkerchiefs, string, belts, etc.) to make veins stand out, and drug containers.

Knowledge of places and areas frequented by narcotics users and methods of operation.

Knowledge of the street jargon of narcotics and dangerous drugs.

Recognition of narcotics violators residing or frequenting specific areas of a community.

Identification of cars and license numbers of suspects, and knowledge of criminal records.

Use of surveillance procedures.

Application of scientific aids wherever necessary—electronic equipment, tape recorders, binoculars, motion pictures, camera equipment with telephoto lens, miniature cameras, disguised vehicles, use of identifiable currency, tracing powders, etc.

Collection, identification, preservation, and disposition of evidence. This includes supportive notes.

Preparation of accurate and detailed reports setting forth results of medical and clinical examinations, photographs, facts that constitute probable cause for arrest, testimony that participating officers or witnesses can provide as to the sale, finding of evidence, location where found, identification, time, place, preservation, chain of custody, statement of suspect, and other pertinent data.

Searches

There is no magic formula for searching persons, property, premises, or vehicles. Illicit drugs may be found in a variety of places or containers. The predominant rule in all searches is to be extremely methodical and thorough. In all instances, however, the search must be a legal one: (1) with valid consent, oral or written. (The courts will examine the circumstances of each case to determine if the consent was freely, clearly, and intelligently given, with the individual aware of constitutional rights.); (2) by search warrant; or (3) a search incidental to the arrest (search limited to the area within suspect's reach for weapons or evidence he or she may destroy as stated in the case of *Chimel v. California*.[39] If the officer desires to search beyond this area, a search warrant is required).

Search of Persons Suspects have been known to conceal illicit drugs on various parts of their body and clothing. Searches of the body include hair, ears, mouth (under tongue), body cavities, groin area, tape on body, soles of feet, and between toes. Other areas that should be searched are hat, hat bands, hat linings, coats or jackets (lapels, linings, seams), ties, belts, socks, shoes (soles, heels). In one instance a narcotic suspect concealed narcotics by drilling a hole into the back of one of the heels of Western-style boots and inserting the contraband. A small leather plug was used to close the opening of the drilled compartment.

Search of Vehicle The *Chimel* opinion, above, preserves a limited exception applicable to the search of vehicles, holding that, "assuming the existence of probable cause, automobiles and other vehicles may be searched without warrants 'where it is not practicable to secure a warrant because the vehicle can be quickly moved out of the

---

[39]*Chimel v. California,* 395 U.S. 752 (1969).

locality or jurisdiction in which the warrant must be sought'. ...." The Court's decision does not alter the rule, however, that a search of a vehicle as an incident of arrest must bear a reasonable relation to the particular arrest. For example, in arresting for traffic violations, the officer cannot conduct an incidental search since there are no fruits, instrumentalities, or contraband usually connected with traffic violations. Even in traffic stops, however, an officer should always keep an eye open for any contraband, weapons, burglary tools, etc., that may be visible within any vehicle—possession of which is in violation of a law. Such items, if observed, may lawfully be seized.

Vehicles have often been used to transport and conceal narcotics and dangerous drugs. A variety of places within, outside, and under a car have been used to conceal contraband. Illicit narcotics and drugs may be found in ashtrays, glove compartments and contents, taped to windows that have been rolled down, under horn buttons, beneath seats, in air vents, under dashboards, in car upholstery, in door panels, in engine compartments, behind headlights, under hubcaps, in trunk compartment, in spare tires, in specially constructed or double gas tanks, welded or tied to undercarriage, in back of bumpers, under fenders, and in many other places limited only by the imagination and patience of the searching officer.

Search of Premises In conducting a lawful search of a premises, search sections or rooms in a systematic, thorough manner. Tools and equipment that may be useful in searching include camera, measuring tape, screwdriver, wrench (for plumbing traps), light (flashlight and/or portable floodlight), extension cord, shovel, and metal rod for probing flower beds or places indicating soil disturbances. The searchers should look into, around, under, and through all objects, containers, materials, and places. A recorder should be appointed to take notes of any evidence found during a search. If narcotics or drugs are found, ask the suspect (if present) what they are, get admission about ownership; and keep notes on exact conversations. Both the searcher and recorder should mark any found evidence. The officer finding the evidence should retain it before turning it over to the crime laboratory for technical examination and identification. The name of the manager or landlord of the concerned residence should be obtained for report purposes.

Narcotics have been secreted in a number of places in rooms and other areas of premises. Some of the suggested places to search for illicit drugs include: the bathroom medicine cabinet (pill bottles, e.g., aspirin bottles may not contain aspirin, other bottles may be mislabled or tablets and pills misstamped), hampers of dirty clothes (unfold all clothing), underside of washbowl, under toilet tank lid, inside tank float ball, in bottom of water tank bowl, within tube of toilet paper roll, in lipstick tubes, face powder, tissue boxes, submerged in face cream, cosmetic containers, hollowed-out bars of soap, behind wall and light fixtures and other ducts, in door jambs and top of doors, behind venetian blinds, and under floor coverings. Other places include the kitchen area—illegal drugs may be submerged in coffee, tea, flour, soap chips, or in jars, wine bottles, pans, and utensils. Searches of bedroom, living room, and other parts of the house should include closets, clothing, chairs, sofas, radios and TVs, beneath rugs, linoleum, loose floorboards, moldings, beds, bedposts, mattresses, pillows, stuffed toys, playpens, baby carriages, dressers, in containers hung by string outside windows, in books, objects, articles and other innumerable places. Basements, areas beneath houses, porches, stairs, attics, and garages are also used to conceal contraband. When searching the grounds about a premises, it is well to look for indications of recently disturbed earth, well-travelled paths or other locations leading to air vents or other places as evidenced by obvious foot traffic impressions.

Jail Smuggling Drug users have attempted to conceal narcotics by saturating and reironing handkerchiefs, pockets of clothing, shirttails, ties, sheets of paper, etc., with a concentration of narcotics substance. These impregnated articles are carried by a suspect in case of arrest so that the narcotic will be available by soaking it out while incarcerated. In the jail-booking area, visitors may drop or discard empty cigarette packages, gum wrappers, or impregnated cigarette butts containing narcotics for trustees to retrieve. In an effort to conceal narcotics, persons about to be arrested or those permitted weekend passes have swallowed balloons containing narcotics with a string tied to the balloon in order that they might regurgitate their cache when needed. Others have swallowed toy balloons filled with narcotics and retrieved them after a bowel movement. Narcotics have been placed in rubber balls and tossed or thrown onto acreage of prison farms adjoining highways, or on the grounds of penal institutions, thus permitting trustees to obtain their narcotic "supplies." Female jail visitors have orally passed narcotics to inmates when kissing their loved ones. Other secretive ways of "delivering" narcotic substances to inmates are continually being devised.

Arrest situations
Whenever an arrest is made:

Use sufficient personnel to handle the arrest.

In addition to arrest warrant, have search warrant if possible; be mindful of legal limits in searching.

Brief all participating officers on the part each is to play.

Move fast on all locations (if more than one) and simultaneously. If circumstances justify it, use force to enter, since it takes only seconds to flush evidence down the toilet. In these instances, entry should be made only within legal limitations.

As soon as suspect is in custody, handcuff hands behind back; advise of legal rights; search; if necessary call in a doctor for an internal body search.

If a suspect has needle marks, photograph them.

Names, addresses, and telephone numbers found in suspect's effects should be checked; many of these names will furnish valuable investigative leads as to associates and possible meeting places.

Request crime laboratory analysis of all materials and substances believed to contain narcotics.

Consider blood test, urine test, Nalline test, medical examination, and polygraph examination of suspect where advisable. A small dose of Nalline (a narcotic antagonist) will cause a mild withdrawal reaction such as a dilation of the pupils in the eyes of subjects who have taken narcotics recently.

A check of the jail register of visitors and mail may provide investigative leads.

Drug Enforcement Administration (DEA) The DEA was established in the U.S. Department of Justice on July 1, 1973, by Reorganization Plan 2 of 1973. The DEA enforces the controlled substances laws and regulations. This agency provides the evidence necessary for the prosecution of those persons involved in the growing, manufacture, or distribution of controlled substances appearing in or destined for the illicit traffic in the United States. DEA provides the leadership in narcotics and dangerous drug suppression at the national and international levels by reducing the supply of illicit drugs entering this country or being pro-

WEIGHTS AND MEASURES USED IN ILLEGAL NARCOTIC TRAFFIC	
Paper or bindle (glassine packet)	1 or more grains (one ounce to one spoon which is about 20 caps)
Cap or capsule	1-1/2 grains, clear no. 5 gelatin capsule
15 grains	1 gram
1/2 spoon	1 gram (level half-teaspoon)
1 spoon	2 grams (level teaspoon)
16 spoons	1 ounce
32 grams	1 ounce
1 ounce	480 grains (refers to ounces of narcotics — usually of heroin)
16 ounces	1 pound
Kilo	2.2 pounds
Can/lid	1 ounce of marijuana
Stick	0.5 to 1 gram, varies (marijuana cigarette)
Matchbox	1/5 (approx.) of a lid
Balloon(s)	1 gram or less (heroin); also larger quantities
Roll	3 to 10 amphetamines (Benzedrine, Dexedrine, Methedrine) wrapped in aluminum foil
Bottle	100 tablets or capsules (amphetamines or barbiturates)
Jar	1000 tablets or capsules (amphetamines or barbiturates)
Pillow	25,000 amphetamine tablets
Keg	50,000 tablets/capsules (amphetamines or barbiturates)
Barrel	100,000 units (amphetamines)

duced domestically. In addition, it aids in reducing the diversion of legally controlled substances to the illicit market. DEA conducts domestic and internal investigations of major drug traffickers and continually strives to immobilize international and domestic trafficking conspiracies, clandestine manufacturers, and sources of diversion from legitimate channels.

DEA exchanges intelligence data with local, state, and other federal agencies as well as appropriate foreign governments. In its overseas operations, DEA performs under the policy guidance of the Cabinet Committee on International Narcotic Controls. DEA regulates the legal trade in narcotics and dangerous drugs. This entails the establishment of import-export and manu-

facturing quotas for various controlled drugs; registering all authorized handlers of drugs; inspecting the premises and records of manufacturers and major distributors; and investigating instances of criminal diversion.[40]

Spanish-Language Miranda Warnings In view of the interrogation problems that confront law enforcement as a result of the flow of heroin, marijuana, and other drugs across U.S. borders, and the increased use of Spanish language interpreters by law-enforcement agencies, the need for a standardized Spanish translation of the Miranda warnings has become in-

---

[40]U.S. Government Manual, 1977–78.

creasingly evident. The following Spanish translation was prepared for the California Department of Justice by two special consultants: Professors George L. Voyt of the University of California at Los Angeles and Joseph M. Puig of Los Angeles Valley College.

Advertencia y Renuncia de Derechos

1. Usted tiene el derecho de guardar silencio—de no hablar.

2. Lo que usted diga se puede usar y se usará en contra de usted en la corte.

3. Usted tiene el derecho de consultar a un abogado antes que nosotros hablemos con usted, y tiene el derecho de pedir la presencia del abogado durante todo el tiempo que nosotros lo estemos interrogando a usted.

4. Si usted no tiene dinero para emplear un abogado, se le nombrará uno para que lo represente a usted, antes de hacérsele a usted cualquier clase de preguntas. Este abogado no le costará nada a usted. Los servicios de él son gratuitos.

5. ¿Comprende usted cada uno de estos derechos que yo le acabo de explicar?

6. Entonces, sabiendo usted cuáles son sus derechos, ¿quiere usted hablar con nosotros o no, en este momento?

Concerning the above Miranda warnings, two words of caution are necessary: first, the Spanish warnings should be used only by Spanish interpreters. Officers should not attempt to "Mirandize" suspects in Spanish and converse with them in English. Secondly, records of the giving of the Miranda warnings in Spanish should note the *Spanish* version of what was said rather than the English translation. Likewise, the suspect's waiver of rights should be recorded exactly as given, rather than in its English translation.

GLOSSARY OF NARCOTICS AND DANGEROUS DRUG EXPRESSIONS

EXPRESSION	DEFINITION
Acapulco gold	Marijuana
Ace	Marijuana cigarette
Acid	LSD
Angel dust	PCP (Phencyclidine)
Artillery	Equipment for injecting drugs
Bag	Container of drugs
Bagman	Drug supplier
Balloon	Rubber toy balloon used for storing or packaging drugs
Bang	To inject narcotics
Barbs	Barbiturates
Beans	Benzedrine tablets
Beast	LSD
Bennies	Benzedrine and amphetamine tablets
Bernice	Cocaine
Bhang	Marijuana
Big bloke	Cocaine
Big "C"	Cocaine
Big "H"	Heroin
Big "O"	Opium
Bindle	Small quantity or packet of narcotics; **see** PAPER
Bird's eye	A very small amount of narcotics

EXPRESSION	DEFINITION
Biz	Equipment for injecting drugs
Black beauties	Amphetamines
Blackbirds	Amphetamines
Black Russians	Amphetamines
Black Stuff	Opium
Blast	To smoke a marijuana cigarette
Block	Barbiturate
Blow	To smoke a marijuana cigarette
Blown mind	Extreme hallucination
Blue angels	Amytal (amobarbital sodium), a barbiturate
Bluebirds	Amytal (amobarbital sodium), a barbiturate
Blue devils	Amytal (amobarbital sodium), a barbiturate
Blue heaven	LSD
Blue mist	LSD
Blues	Amytal (amobarbital sodium), a barbiturate
Bomb	A large marijuana cigarette
Bombed	Intoxicated on drugs
Bombido	Injectable amphetamine
Booster	Consumption or injection of additional dosage
Boy	Heroin
Bread	Money
Brick	Kilo of marijuana in compressed form
Bridge	Alligator clamp or other device used to hold marijuana cigarette while smoking same; **see** CRUTCH, ROACH HOLDER
Broccoli	Marijuana
Brown	Heroin
Brown dots	LSD
Brown sugar	Heroin
Bumblebees	Amphetamines
Bummer	Bad LSD experience
Bush	Marijuana
Businessmen's high	MDA, a hallucinogen
Busted	Arrested
Busters	Barbiturates
Butter flowers	Marijuana
Buttons	Peyote buttons (sections of the peyote cactus)
Buy	To buy drugs
Buzzing	Trying to make a purchase of drugs
C	Cocaine
Caballo	Heroin
Cactus	Money
California sunshine	LSD
Can	1 ounce of marijuana; if opium, usually 3-1/2 or 6-2/3 ounces
Candy	Barbiturates

GLOSSARY OF NARCOTICS AND DANGEROUS DRUG EXPRESSIONS (Continued)

EXPRESSION	DEFINITION
Cap	Capsule containing 1 grain of narcotics
Cartwheel	Amphetamine tablet (round, white, double scored)
Cecil	Cocaine
Chalk	Methamphetamine
Charlie	Cocaine
Chicken powder	Amphetamine
Chinese red	Heroin
Chippy	Drug abuser taking small, irregular amounts; also, a prostitute
Chiva	Heroin
Chocolate chips	LSD
Christmas trees	Barbiturates
Coasting	Feeling drowsy after shooting heroin; under the influence of drugs
Cocktail	A regular cigarette into one end of which a partially smoked marijuana cigarette is inserted so as to waste none of the drug
Coffee	LSD
Coke	Cocaine
Coke kit	Mirror, razor blade, spoon, and cocaine container
Cold turkey	Sudden drug withdrawal
Come down	To come off drugs
Contact lens	LSD
Connect	To buy drugs
Cook a pill	Prepare opium for smoking; heat opium for smoking
Cooker	Bottle cap for heating drug powder with water
Copilot	Amphetamine tablet
Cop	Purchase drug
Cop-out	Confession
Corinne	Cocaine
Cottons	Bits of cotton saturated with narcotic solution
Crank	Amphetamine
Crap	Heroin
Crash	The effects of stopping the use of amphetamines
Crutch	Device used to hold marijuana cigarette when it has burned down to the fingers; **see** BRIDGE, ROACH HOLDER
Crystal	Amphetamine
Cube	LSD (sugar cube impregnated with)
Cupcakes	LSD
Cut	Adulterate narcotics by adding a diluent (lactose, sugar, mannitol, quinine etc.)
Dabble	Take small amounts of drugs on an irregular basis
Dealer	Drug supplier
Deck	A bindle or paper containing narcotics
Dexies	Dexedrine, Dexamyl
Dime bag	Ten-dollar purchase of narcotics
Dirty	Possessing narcotics; found with injection marks

GLOSSARY OF NARCOTICS AND DANGEROUS DRUG EXPRESSIONS (Continued)

EXPRESSION	DEFINITION
DMT	Hallucinogen, a short-acting psychedelic that is injected or smoked
DOA	"Dead on arrival," PCP
Dollies	Dolophine, a synthetic narcotic; methadone
Domino	To purchase drugs
Doojee	Heroin
Dope	Any narcotic
Double cross	Amphetamine tablets (double scored)
Double trouble	Tuinal, a barbiturate
Downer	A barbiturate (depressant)
Dream	Cocaine
Dummy	Purchase that did not contain narcotics
Dust	Cocaine
Dynamite	High-grade heroin
Emma (Miss)	Morphine
Eye-openers	Amphetamines
Factory	Equipment for injecting drugs
Fall out	Lose consciousness from drugs
Fat	Describing someone who has a good supply of drugs
Fiend	Morphine addict
First line	Morphine
Fit	Equipment for injecting drugs
Fix	To inject drugs or one dose of a particular drug
Flake	Cocaine
Flash	Initial high feeling when injecting amphetamines and other drugs
Flea powder	Poor quality narcotics
Flip	Take psychedelic drugs
Floating	Under influence of drugs
Foolish powder	Heroin
Footballs	Oval-shaped amphetamine sulfate tablets
Freak	A person who injects amphetamines
Freak out	Bad experience with psychedelics
Frosties	Having a friend put cocaine on a piece of paper and blow it into the back of the user's mouth
Fuzz	Police
Gage	Marijuana
Ganga	Marijuana
Garbage	Poor-quality drugs
Gassing	Sniffing gasoline fumes
Geeze	Injection of narcotic
Girl	Cocaine
Gold dust	Cocaine
Good trip	Happy experience with psychedelics
Goofballs	Any barbiturate tablet or capsule

GLOSSARY OF NARCOTICS AND DANGEROUS DRUG EXPRESSIONS (Continued)

EXPRESSION	DEFINITION
Goofed up	Under the influence of barbiturates
Gow head	Opium addict
Gram	Gram of heroin (approximately ten capsules)
Grass	Marijuana
Grasshopper	Marijuana user
Greens, Greenies	Heart-shaped tablets, dextroamphetamine sulfate and amobarbital
Green Dragon	Barbiturate (sodium amytal)
Greta	Marijuana
Griffo	Marijuana
Guide	Babysitter for psychedelic user during experience
Gun	Needle used to inject narcotics; **see** OUTFIT
"H"	Heroin
Habit	Physical or psychological dependency on drugs
Half-can	1/2 ounce of marijuana
Hand-to-hand	Delivery of narcotics person to person
Hard stuff	Morphine, heroin
Harry	Heroin
Hash/Hashish	A concentrated resinous derivative of marijuana
Hashbury	Haight-Ashbury district of San Francisco
Hay	Marijuana
Haze	LSD
Hearts	Benzedrine or Dexedrine that comes in heart-shaped tablets
Heat	Police
Heaven dust	Cocaine
Heavy	Heroin
Helen	Heroin
Hemp	Marijuana
High	Under the influence of narcotics
Hit	One dose of a particular drug
Hocus	Morphine
Hog	Addict who uses all the drugs he or she can get; **see** PIG; also, a user of PCP
Holding	Possessing narcotics
Hooked	Addicted; confirmed addiction
Hop	Opium
Hophead	Narcotics addict
Horning	Sniffing or "snorting" narcotics through nasal passage
Horse	Heroin
Hot shot	Fatal dosage; **see** OVERDOSE
Hype	Narcotics addict
Hype outfit	**See** "outfit"
Ice cream habit	Small, irregular drug habit
"I'm flush"	I have money
"I'm holding"	I have narcotics

GLOSSARY OF NARCOTICS AND DANGEROUS DRUG EXPRESSIONS (Continued)

EXPRESSION	DEFINITION
"I'm looking"	I wish to buy
"I'm way down"	I need marijuana
In power	Selling narcotics; **see also** PUSHER
"J"	Marijuana cigarette
Jail plant	Narcotics concealed on person to be used in jail
Jamming	Losing one's "cool"; being at a loss for words
Jane	Marijuana
Jay	Marijuana
Jive	Marijuana or in-group talk
Jive sticks	Marijuana cigarettes
Joint	Marijuana cigarette
Jolt	An injection of narcotics
Joy pop	An occasional injection of narcotics
Joy powder	Heroin
Junk	Heroin
Junker, Junkie	Narcotics addict
Kee	**See** KILO
Kick	To abandon a drug habit
Kicking the habit	Trying to break the habit of drug use
Kif	Hashish
Kilo	Approximately 2.2 pounds of marijuana, heroin, or cocaine; also called **kee**
Killer weed	PCP
Kit	Paraphernalia for injecting heroin into the bloodstream
"L"	LSD (lysergic acid diethylamide)
Lab	Equipment used to manufacture drugs illegally
Layout	Equipment for injecting drugs (needle, dropper, spoon, cotton, tie rag, etc.); **see also** OUTFIT
Lemonade	Poor heroin
Lid	Approximately 1 ounce of marijuana
Lid poppers	Amphetamines
Loaded	Under the influence of narcotics or drugs
Locoweed	Marijuana
Looking	Wishing to buy
LSD	Lysergic acid diethylamide
Lusher	One preferring alcohol to narcotics
"M"	Morphine
Machinery	Equipment for injecting drugs
Mainline	Vein of body, usually in the arm; to inject drugs directly into the veins (intravenously)
Mainliner	An addict who injects narcotics directly into the veins (intravenously)
Make a buy	Purchase drugs

EXPRESSION	DEFINITION
Man (The)	A drug supplier; police officer
Manicure	Preparation of marijuana for use in cigarettes, removal of dirt, seeds, and stems from the drug
Marks	Scars caused by hypodermic injection
Marshmallow reds	Barbiturates
Mary Jane	Marijuana
Matchbox	1/5 (approx.) of a lid
Meth	Methamphetamine
Mexican mud	Heroin
Mexican reds	Barbiturates
Mickey (Finn)	Chloral hydrate
Mikes	Micrograms
Mindblower	Pure unadulterated drugs
Miss Emma	Morphine
Mohasky	Marijuana
Mojo	Narcotics
Monkey	Drug habit where physical dependency is present
Moragrita	Marijuana
Morf	Morphine
Mota	Marijuana (Spanish slang)
Mud	Opium
Muggles	Marijuana
Mule	One who sells or transports for a regular peddler
Mutha	Marijuana
Nailed	Caught, arrested
Nebbies	Barbiturates
Needle	Hypodermic needle
Nimbies	Barbiturates (Nembutal capsules)
Nose candy	Cocaine
Nuggets	Amphetamines
"O"	Opium
O.D.	Overdose of narcotics; **see** HOT SHOT
On a trip	Under the influence of LSD or other hallucinogen
On the beam	Feeling fine
On the needle	Addicted to heroin
On the nod	Under the influence of drugs
On the street	Out of jail
Oranges	Dexedrine tablets (amphetamines)
Outfit	Paraphernalia used to inject narcotics (needle, dropper, spoon, cotton, handkerchief, etc.); **also called** HYPE OUTFIT; **see** GUN, WORKS
Pad	User's residence
Panama red	Marijuana
Paper	Small quantity of heroin; **see** BINDLE

GLOSSARY OF NARCOTICS AND DANGEROUS DRUG EXPRESSIONS (Continued)

EXPRESSION	DEFINITION
Paper acid	LSD
Paradise	Cocaine
PCP	Hallucinogen (Phencyclidine)
Peace pill	PCP
Peaches	Dexedrine (a light orange tablet)
Peanuts	Barbiturates
Pep pills	Amphetamines
Per	Prescription
Piece	One ounce of heroin
Pig	**See** HOG
Pill Head	Amphetamine or barbiturate user
Pin shot	To make a hole in skin with pin and use an eyedropper to inject drugs
Pinkies, Pinks	Barbiturates
Pink ladies	Barbiturates
Plant	Place where narcotics are concealed
Pleasure smoker	One who smokes narcotics occasionally
Pop	Inject drugs; a subcutaneous injection; take a pill (amphetamine)
Pot	Marijuana
Psychedelics	Mind-altering drugs
Pure	Pure heroin, prior to adulteration
Purple hearts	Barbiturates
Pusher	One who sells narcotics; **see also** IN POWER
Quarter moon	Hashish
Quill	Folded matchbook cover from which narcotics are sniffed or "snorted"
Rainbows	Barbiturate (Tuinal)
Rainy day woman	Marijuana
Reds	Barbiturates (Seconal capsules)
Red birds	Barbiturates (Seconal capsules)
Red devils	Barbiturates (Seconal capsules)
Red and blues	Barbiturates
Reefers	Marijuana cigarettes
Roach	Marijuana cigarette butt
Roach holder	Device for holding butt of a marijuana cigarette; **see** BRIDGE, CRUTCH
Roll	Aluminum foil containing pills, either barbiturates or amphetamines
Rope	Marijuana
Roses	Benzedrine tablets
Rough stuff	Marijuana as it comes from the plant
Royal blue	LSD
Sam	Federal narcotics agent
Sativa	Marijuana
Scar a joint	Swallow a marijuana cigarette
Scag	Heroin
Scat	Heroin

GLOSSARY OF NARCOTICS AND DANGEROUS DRUG EXPRESSIONS (Continued)

EXPRESSION	DEFINITION
Score	To make a purchase
Script	Prescription
Seggy	Seconal capsule (barbiturate)
Shine	Reject
Shit	Heroin
Shot	An injection
Shooting gallery	Place where narcotic addicts inject drugs
Sick	Withdrawal from narcotics
Skin popping	Injecting drugs under skin
Smack	Heroin
Sniff	Sniff narcotics, usually cocaine, through nose
Snorting	Inhalation of cocaine through nose
Snow	Cocaine
Snowbird	Cocaine user
Soles	Hashish
Speed	Methamphetamine
Speedball	Injection of a stimulant and a depressant
Speed freak	Habitual user of methamphetamine
Spike	A hypodermic needle
Splash	Methamphetamine
Spoon	About 2 grams of heroin
Spot you	To pay first, take delivery later
Square	A nonuser
Square joint	Commercial tobacco cigarette
Stack	A quantity of marijuana cigarettes
Stardust	Cocaine
Stash	A cache of narcotics
Stick	Marijuana cigarette
Stoned	Overindulgence in drugs; high
Stoolie	Informer
Squirrels	LSD
STP	Hallucinogen
Straight person	Person who does not take drugs; sometimes used to describe a person under the influence of drugs
Straw	Marijuana
Strawberry fields	LSD
Strung out	Heavily addicted
Stuff	Narcotics
Stumblers	Barbiturates
Suey	A liquid solution of opium pipe residue
Sugar	LSD; powdered narcotics (heroin)
Sunshine	LSD
Super grass	PCP in parsley (California expression)
Sweet Lucy	Marijuana
Swing man	Drug supplier

GLOSSARY OF NARCOTICS AND DANGEROUS DRUG EXPRESSIONS (Continued)

EXPRESSION	DEFINITION
Tall	Good
Tar	Opium
Tea	Marijuana
Tea blower	Marijuana smoker
Tea head	Marijuana addict
Teenie-boppers	Upper- or middle-class youths seeking experiences with drugs
Texas tea	Marijuana
Things	Balloons of heroin
Thirteen ("13")	Marijuana
Thrusters	Amphetamines
Toke	Puff of marijuana cigarette
To the mouth	Swallow evidence
Tootsie	Barbiturate (Tuinal capsule)
Torch up	To light up a marijuana cigarette
TNT	Heroin
Tracks	Scars along veins after many injections
Travel agent	Person who acts as a guide through psychedelic experience
Trip, Tripping	Being high on hallucinating drugs
Truck drivers	Amphetamines
Turkey	Capsule reported to be narcotics but actually filled with nonnarcotic substance
Turnabouts	Amphetamines
Turned off	Withdrawn from drugs
Turned on	Under the influence of drugs
Turning tricks	Prostituting
Underground railway	System which supplies food and lodging to runaways
Uppers	Amphetamines
Uptight	Tense and frightened
User	Addict
Vacuum cleaners	Cocaine users who sniff or "snort"
Vodka acid	Vodka that contains LSD
Wake-ups	Amphetamines
Weed	Marijuana
Weed head	Marijuana user
Weekend habit	Small irregular habit
Whiskers	Federal narcotics agent
Whites, Whities	Benzedrine (amphetamine sulfate tablets)
White girl	Cocaine
White junk	Heroin
White lightning	LSD
White stuff	Morphine
Wigging	High on drugs
Window pane	LSD

EXPRESSION	DEFINITION
Wiped out	To have lost consciousness from use of dangerous drugs
Works	Equipment used for injecting drugs; **see** OUTFIT
Yellow jackets	Barbiturates (Nembutal)
Yellows	Barbiturates
Yen	Craving for drugs
Yen hock	Instrument for cooking opium pill
Yen shee	Residue from inside opium 'pipe
Yen shee suey	Residue from inside opium pipe mixed with water or other liquid and taken as a drink
Zap	To destroy
Zig Zag	Brand of cigarette paper that has been used to roll marijuana cigarettes

SUMMARY

The term "narcotic" refers to opium, its derivatives and synthetic substitutes for it. These produce tolerance and dependence, both psychological and physical. While narcotics afford relief of physical or psychic suffering in a short-lived euphoric state, they also result in drug dependence. Methods of administration include oral ingestion and subcutaneous or intravenous injection. When the narcotic supply is cut off, withdrawal symptoms develop with the intensity of sickness varying with the degree of physical dependence and the amount of drug customarily used. Since there is no simple way to ascertain the purity of a drug that is sold on the street, the effects of illicit narcotics are unpredictable, compounding the dangers of overdose and death. Heroin is regarded as the chief addictive drug. A considerable amount of the drug comes from Mexico. The drug dependent person usually has little access to legitimate sources of money or drugs and must devote all her or his time and energy to the acquisition of heroin to supply the "habit." A drug dependent person may lie, cheat, and steal in order to obtain money to purchase additional drugs.

"Dangerous drugs" are divided into three general categories: depressants (barbiturates), stimulants (usually amphetamines), and hallucinogens (psychedelics). Some have medical value when used under medical supervision; others serve no legitimate purpose. Barbiturates constitute the largest group of depressants; the more common ones used by drug offenders are Seconal, Nembutal, Amytal, and Tuinal. Barbiturates cause dependence.

Stimulants most commonly used are amphetamine sulfate (Benzedrine), dextroamphetamine sulfate (Dexedrine), and methamphetamine (Methedrine). They are produced in a wide variety of physical forms. These drugs stimulate the central nervous system. They are taken orally as pills but can be injected intravenously in liquid form. Cocaine, a powerful stimulant, is often inhaled or "snorted" through the nose. Continued use of stimulants leads to psychological dependence.

Hallucinogens, often referred to as psychedelics, are drugs capable of provoking many changes. Minimal or overwhelming alterations of time, space, and perception, as well as illusions, hallucinations, and delusions, may occur. LSD is the most potent of the hallucinogens. Others include DMT, DET, DOM ("STP"), PCP, MDA, psilocybin, and mescaline. They are taken in capsule or tablet form. LSD has been taken in other forms such as on candy, in chewing gum, on crackers, toothpicks, and handkerchiefs.

Marijuana and hashish are derived from the hemp plant. All parts of both the male and female plants contain varying amounts of the major psychoactive substance, THC. Hashish, the varnish-like resin obtained from the flowering tops of the hemp plant, is collected and compressed into a mass. Hashish is said to be much more potent than marijuana. The acute physiologic effects of cannabis are dose related. The drug has many psychoactive effects. Hashish oil, a concentrate of cannabis, contains from 20 to 60 percent THC. One drop or two on a cigarette is equal in psychoactive effect to an entire marijuana cigarette. Scientific evidence has recently indicated that the effects of marijuana may be considerably more hazardous than once suspected. Scientific research on the effects of marijuana is being conducted both in the United States and other countries to resolve the issue of marijuana's possible hazardous effects.

REVIEW QUESTIONS

1. What is the chief alkaloid of opium?
2. To what does "opiate" refer?
3. Which is considered the stronger of the two narcotics, morphine or heroin?
4. What is the chief drug of addiction in the United States?
5. What is a "mule"?
6. What type of pupillary reaction is caused by heroin?
7. What is the difference between barbiturates and amphetamines?
8. Is cocaine considered a stimulant or a depressant?
9. Under what department of the United States government is the Drug Enforcement Agency (DEA)?
10. What is the most widely used illicit drug?
11. In a discussion of drugs involving opiates, depressants and hallucinogens, under which of these categories would STP, DMT, DOM, and PCP fall?
12. For what drug is "snow" the slang expression?

13. A stimulant generally excites the central nervous system. Which of the following are stimulants—heroin, opium, morphine, cocaine, barbiturates?
14. How are the various types of barbiturates distinguished?
15. Name three addictive drugs.
16. What is the botanical name for marijuana?
17. In what plant is the drug mescaline found?
18. What do the following slang expressions mean?
    Yen shee
    Smack
    Outfit
    Kilo
    Bird's eye
    Dynamite
    Deck
    Double trouble
    Yellow jacket
    Blue devil
    Peace pill
19. From what plant is cocaine derived?
20. What are the most commonly used barbiturates?

────────── WORK EXERCISE ──────────

Classify each of the twenty-five terms listed below as either: (A) opiate; (B) stimulant; (C) barbiturate; (D) hallucinogen; (E) marijuana, cannabis, hashish; or (F) none of these.

1. Beans	2. Reds	3. Buttons
4. Purple hearts	5. Angel dust	6. Charlie
7. Mota	8. Green dragon	9. Wake-ups
10. Blackbirds	11. Killer weed	12. Bernice
13. Hocus	14. Pinks, pinkies	15. Kif
16. Flat tire	17. Chiva	18. Brown sugar
19. Peace pill	20. Mud	21. Broccoli
22. Stumbler	23. Scag	24. Thirteen
25. Nose candy		

Arson
and
Bomb
CHAPTER
19—Investigation

Arson

In a broad sense, arson may be defined as the malicious or intentional act of setting fire to buildings or property. In most jurisdictions, the crime of arson covers all kinds of buildings and structures, crops and forests, the personal property of another, and even one's own property if burned with the intent of defrauding an insurer of that property. Intent implies that the act was done knowingly, purposely, and intentionally. Intent may also be inferred from the act itself if the inevitable consequences of the act are the burning of a building or property. The crime of arson cannot be consummated without burning. The offense is complete, however,

if any part of the wood is charred (not mere discoloration), if the fiber of the wood is destroyed or its identity is changed.

Arson is usually a felony under modern statutes. Where death occurs as a result of arson, it is statutory first-degree murder in many states. In the prosecution for arson, as in all criminal cases, it is incumbent upon the state to prove the *corpus delicti,* viz.,

> That there was a fire (must be scorching of the property)
> That the fire was of human origin and by incendiary means
> That the fire was caused willfully and maliciously (not by accidental or natural causes)

In proving the corpus delicti, the fire department's records will show that a fire occurred at a specific location on a certain date and time; that something was burned; the type of structure or property; occupants; name of owner; identity of person turning in the alarm or reporting the fire; the damage; and value and insurance data. Other information the fire department can provide is the result of their examination and inspection—whether there was evidence of multiple fires or trailers to lead a fire from one part of a building to another; of an accelerant, mechanical device, or chemical compound; whether the electrical system was short-circuited; or of other unlawful or irregular activities. Conviction of an arsonist in nearly every instance is based on circumstantial or indirect evidence. Courts of all states have held that all the elements of an arson case can be established by circumstantial evidence (indirect evidence), i.e., a chain of circumstances and physical evidence that may prove the commission of the crime.

The *detection of arson* is primarily the responsibility of the fire department. Most of the arson cases are brought to the attention of the police arson detail by the fire department. A case can be won or lost by what the fire fighter may see, hear, or do at the scene of a fire. A knowledge of fire chemistry, patterns of fire, building construction features, and burning characteristcs of building contents permits arson detection specialists to arrive at a conclusion regarding fire origins. In all fires of suspicious origin the cooperation and teamwork of both fire and police specialists are needed for successful solutions and convictions. However, once the probability of arson is arrived at by the fire department, the necessary investigation in order to provide the proof that the district attorney needs to prosecute the person(s) responsible is conducted by a police agency.

The crime of arson is generally committed under cover of darkness, at times and in a manner calculated to divert suspicion. Only the criminal or those acting in concert with him or her are usually present at the scene of their covert activities. The perpetrator hopes to destroy any incriminating evidence by means of the fire itself. Arson offenses are peculiar in that the perpetrator(s) may be hours, days, and miles away from the scene at the time of the fire. An alibi offered by the accused of being "miles away from the scene at the time of the fire and consequently could not have set fire without being present" is a common defense. However, this alibi is weakened when the state's evidence shows that the fire was set by means of a contrivance that would cause a lapse of time before the fire was discovered. Relevant facts and circumstances tending to show the accused present at the crime scene are the means of rebuttal by the prosecution. If a defendant is prosecuted as a conspirator or as an accessory, physical presence at the scene of the fire is unnecessary, and alibi evidence may have no importance. In those instances where the facts so warrant, the prosecution may charge a suspected arsonist with attempted arson.

Importance of Motive in Arson Cases

Motive is *not* an element of the crime of arson, or any other crime. Conviction can be obtained although the prosecution is unable to show any motive that may have influenced the act(s) of the accused. However, whenever a motive can be shown, it is helpful to a prosecution in showing why the accused acted that way, what there was to gain, or for other purposes.

Types of motives

Destroy evidence
Monetary: defrauding insurance companies

Revenge, spite, grudge, jealousy
Intimidation
Settle an estate
Destroy records
To aid commission of crime: diversionary tactic
Crime cover-up: burglary, homicide, embezzlement, etc.
Get rid of distressed or outmoded merchandise
Secure employment as a guard
Eliminate competition: business rival
Landlord-tenant feuds
Hero complex
Tax frauds
Secure a building wrecking contract
Contents overinsured
Suicidal
Sabotage: cripple machinery, slow down work, destroy finished products, disable a plant
Pyromania: compulsion to set things on fire
Vandalism

Fire Triangle

The fire triangle below illustrates the requirements which must be met if any fire is to occur. Fire can take place only where *oxygen* or other oxidizing agent, *fuel*, and a sufficient temperature (*heat*) to maintain combustion are present. Removal of any one of the factors will result in the extinguishment of the fire.

Fuel
Liquid, solid or gas; mostly compounds of carbon and hydrogen. The fuel must be in proper form and be mixed with oxygen in proper proportions.

Oxygen
Supports combustion. The earth's atmosphere is 21 percent oxygen of which *air* is the primary source. Oxygen is found in abundance in compounds that include nitrates, chlorates, peroxides, etc.

Heat
Sparks, flames, chemical reactions, friction, compression. The heat must be in sufficient quantity in relation to the fuel and of sufficient temperature.

Classification of Fires

Class "A" fires
Fires in this category may occur in ordinary combustibles (wood, paper, rags, straw, rubbish) and are probably the most common type of fire encountered.

Class "B" fires
These are fires involving flammable liquids (petroleum products, paints, cooking oils, ether, etc.). Flammable liquids are said to be the most frequent problems confronting the fire prevention, protection, and suppression fields. The flammable liquid itself does not burn; the vapors from the liquid burn.

Class "C" fires
These are fires involving live electrical equipment that may be encountered in transformers, switch rooms, conduits and raceways, or electrical appliances and motors.

Class "D" fires
These are fires involving combustible metals, magnesium, potassium, zinc, titanium, sodium, etc. Such fires may be encountered in some industrial and missile industries.

Class "E" fires

These are fires involving radioactive materials.

Point of Origin

Point of origin (point of ignition) and cause of fire must be determined as soon as possible in arson investigation. Any theory concerning the possibility of arson in a given case should not be advanced until a thorough investigation has been conducted, possible causes eliminated, and all data reviewed and evaluated. Once the point of origin is determined, however, emphasis should be placed on a search of that particular area for evidence of arson intent—materials, equipment, traces of accelerants, contrivances, or parts thereof. The search should be conducted as soon as feasible since many highly volatile fluids will eventually be lost through evaporation. Fortunately, the use of water in fire extinguishment assists in slowing the loss of volatile fluids by cooling, covering, and insulating materials into which flammable substances have soaked. The search for traces of flammable fluids may be facilitated by use of a highly sensitive combustible vapor detector.

In small fires or fires that have been brought under control in the early stages, the starting place of the fire is generally obvious. In more severe fires, the physical appearance (charring or "alligatoring") may furnish the answer to the point of origin. Usually the origin is the area where there is the greatest depth of char. (See Figure 19-1.)

In instances where there is complete destruction, interviews with witnesses may disclose the starting place, assuming the witnesses observed the fire in its early stages. The first fire fighter or police officer at the scene may also furnish the necessary clues to substantiate the point of origin.

Figure 19-1. Point of origin of a fire. Note the pattern of deep charring ("alligatoring") that indicates the location where the fire originated.

Causes of Fire

Natural or accidental causes

All fires are presumed to be of accidental origin. Any evidence of incendiarism, however, will rebut this presumption. In proof of the corpus delicti of arson cases, all possible accidental causes must be eliminated. All wiring, appliances, and sources of heat should be checked during the course of the fire investigation. The elimination process should consider those that occur through *sources of ignition*—rays of sun, lightning, static electricity, electrical energy, chemical sources, gas leaks, painting equipment, paint, linseed oil, turpentine, solvents, paint rags, cigarettes and matches, gas pilot lights, frictional heat (mechanical heat energy), slipping belts, nonlubricated metal moving parts, defective switches, deteriorated wire insulation, faulty wiring, spontaneous ignition, etc. (See Figure 19-2.)

COMMON ARSON DEVICES

Plants	Accelerants or "boosters" used to spread the progress of the fire (kerosene, gasoline, paint thinner, lighter fluid, lacquers, stove oil, solvents, etc.)
Trailers	Paper, black powder, wicks, strips of film, and other materials that may be used to convey the fire from one place to another
Chemicals	Phosphorus dissolved in disulfide of carbon, sulphuric acid dropped in mixtures of potassium chlorate and powdered sugar, illuminating gas, etc.
Flammable liquids	In various containers — gasoline, kerosene, paint thinner, lighter fluid, etc.
Electric timers	To trigger another device or combination of electrical-mechanical equipment hooked up to combustible materials or volatile liquid
Timing devices	Attached to accelerants to provide alibi of not being present at time of fire
Candles	As direct or indirect ignitor
Cigarette	As ignitor
Flares	As ignitor
Electric appliances	Arranged to simulate an accidental fire (hot plate, electric iron, electric blanket, soldering iron, all left on intentionally)
Fuses	Bridged with pennies, foil, or wire
Electrical overloading of circuit	Short-circuiting
Pilot light	Gas leakage

In addition *accidental sources* (combustibles near heat) where fire may occur should be checked: clothing hung near fireplace to dry, light bulbs and fixtures, careless smoking and disposal of cigarettes, cigars, or hot pipe ashes, fireplace and chimney leaks, heating and cooking appliances, washers, dryers, radios, TVs, misuse of flammable liquids (gasoline, kerosene, paint thinner, lacquers, alcohol, etc.), mishandling and storage of such liquids, and many others.

Incendiary

In arson cases or other fires of a suspicious nature the search for evidence of incendiarism should be conducted in a systematic, thorough manner. The ignition (fire setting) by an arsonist may be *direct* or *delayed*.

Direct ignition is simply setting fire to the property by applying matches or other flame. Gasoline, kerosene, paint thinner, lighter fluid, or other combustible material may be thrown or spread over the part to be damaged and there will follow a more rapid spread of the flame as well as a more complete combustion of the affected area. (See Figure 19-3.)

In *delayed ignition,* the fire setter seeks to accomplish the purpose through a mechanical or other timing device (candle, cigarette-matchbook combination), which is designed to either permit escape or to delay the ignition until a time when the property is not well guarded and susceptible to greater damage.

Fire devices that did not ignite or that failed to continue burning may be discovered during the examination of burned or unburned areas. The arson investigator should carefully scrutinize and inspect all suspect areas for incendiary materials, equipment, contrivances, or other means that may have been employed by the fire setter.

Figure 19-2. Photo taken after debris was carefully removed, showing the cause of the fire to be deteriorated wire insulation. This permitted the wire to come in contact with a gas pipe, thus causing a short-circuit, resulting in fire.

Odors

The odors emitted by fires (gasoline, kerosene, sulphur, ammonia, turpentine, paint thinner, lacquer, linseed oil) are of value in determining what flammable substances are present. All such items have peculiarly distinct odors and are recognizable.

Size of fire and rapid spread of flames

The size of the fire and the rapidity in which it spread from the time of discovery until the alarm was received and arrival of equipment at the scene are important considerations that may indicate the fire to be of an incendiary origin.

Holes in plaster walls and floors

Holes in plaster walls are frequently made to expose raw wood and to increase draft once the fire is started. Holes bored in ceilings are sometimes made to accelerate the fire to upper floors.

Evidence of tampering with alarm and protection equipment

This may involve "trailers" between fires (paper, rags, rope soaked in kerosene, film,

Indications of Arson

In addition to the incendiary materials, devices, or contrivances set forth above, a search should be made for indications of arson intent. Frequently such incendiary intent is manifested by some obvious indicators.

Multiple fires

These are separate fires burning in different places at the same time. Many arsonists start fires in buildings in widely separated places.

Figure 19-3. Fragments of a Molotov cocktail: glass jar, parts of fuse, and accellerant residue used in an arson attempt.

etc.), flammable liquids, candles, timing devices, electrical equipment, and appliances.

Indications of tampering with doors or windows

Particular observation should be made of doors and windows for evidence of pry marks on the window sills or door jambs, or other forcible entry. Were the doors left open or blocked open? Or propped up purposefully? Consideration should also be given to the possibility that the burning was committed to cover up the commission of another crime (burglary, homicide, theft, embezzlement, etc.). (See Figure 19-4.) Tools used to gain entrance or cut objects may contain microscopic bits of evidence.

Color of smoke

The color and quantity of the smoke often gives fire officers an indication of the type of fire that they have to encounter. In addition, they indicate the probable types of substances involved.

White Smoke This is generally emitted by the burning of vegetable compounds, burning hay, or phosphorous.

Yellow or Brownish-Yellow Smoke This may represent burning material

Figure 19-4. A broken window, gallon can (which contained gasoline residue), and a hammer used to break the window. The arsonist set fire to the premises to conceal the crime of burglary.

such as films, nitric acid, sulphur, burning smokeless gun powder, hydrochloric acid. Yellow smoke would be particularly significant where the premises involved did not have these types of materials.

Black Smoke Generally represents the burning of petroleum or petroleum-base products (tar, coal, turpentine, rubber, etc.). Of importance to the investigation would be the fact that such products were not part of the burning building or contents.

Evidence of application of petroleum products to wood

Petroleum often penetrates cracks and crevices, causing burns underneath the floor upon which it was poured. The char marks of petroleum products poured on the floor burn in the pattern of the liquid, which often runs in the cracks and burns downward, beneath the floor upon which it was applied. Since fire burns upwards (and sometimes sidewards), such charring under the floor level is suspect. Even though gasoline, paint thinner, solvents and similar liquids are highly volatile and flammable, they frequently do not burn completely. Identifiable residues of such fluids can therefore be recovered in many cases when large fires have occurred.

Intensity of heat and difficulty of extinguishment

The fact that the heat generated by the fire was particularly intense suggests to the fire investigator the strong possibility that flammable liquids or compounds were added to the normal contents of the building. The process of quenching the fire with water in such instances will cause flashbacks and increased intensity and color. The difficulties encountered in extinguishing the fire may be indicative of the presence of unusual conditions. These observations, coupled with odors emitted, are indications of the probability of arson.

Other observations

Suspicious persons and circumstances that should be taken into account include

The presence of familiar faces (those observed at other fires).

Mentally deranged persons.

Persons showing an undue interest in the fire.

Overly helpful or solicitous people.

Person who discovered fire and seeks credit as the "hero."

Suspects—evidence of accelerant materials on hands, fingernails, clothing, shoes.

Type and amount of merchandise in store (distressed, outdated).

Unusual circumstances such as removal of furniture, paintings, typewriter, clothing, or other items of sentimental value (diplomas, birth and marriage certificates, canaries, fish, photographs, etc.).

Tracks, footprints, fingerprints, or other physical evidence that is foreign to the scene.

Receptacles (cans, jars, etc.) containing residue of accelerants.

Timing devices or parts thereof.

Residues of wax or paraffin. Wax from the burned candles often soaks into the pores of wood and can be identified by the investigator. The spot on which the candle rested is usually not burned as much as the wood surrounding this spot.

Fire Investigation and Flammable Fluids [1]

The types of evidence that may be encountered in a fire investigation are potentially

---

[1] *Physical Evidence Manual,* Investigative Services Branch, Department of Justice, State of California, Mar. 1976.

as broad as in any other type of criminal case. The recovery and interpretation of physical evidence in this type of case, however, are frequently complicated due to partial or complete destruction produced by the fire. In the case of large structural fires, exhibits of importance may be covered by debris and therefore be difficult to locate. Fire fighting operations, including forcible entry, hose stream evolutions, ventilation and mop-up, also may cause evidence destruction, affect burn patterns or otherwise alter the scene.

During the processing of a fire scene for evidence of arson, the following tools and equipment have been found to be useful: shovel, rake, wire cutters, saw, steel tape, broom, portable lighting equipment, glass containers, clean cans with lids, plastic bags, cellophane envelopes, evidence stickers, protective clothing, etc. In addition, specialized equipment (such as a hydrocarbon detector) is of use at places that indicate the probability of use of accelerants.

Special procedures applicable to fire investigations

Limit mop-up after the fire is suppressed until a search for all possible physical evidence can be conducted. This is important since normal fire department procedures employed after fire suppression may cause loss of evidence when positions of furniture and other items are altered or material is removed from the scene. If overhaul has started, it should be stopped immediately until an investigator has sanctioned the removal of materials.

Fire fighters observing evidentiary material should be instructed to leave it alone until it can be examined and processed by an experienced fire investigator.

The search should extend throughout the whole area of the building involved.

Fire sets that did not ignite or that failed to continue burning may be present in unburned areas.

Attempts should always be made to reexamine scenes of large fires during daylight hours and after heat and burn odors have been allowed to dissipate. Far more can be observed under natural illumination than at night, even when excellent floodlights are available. Further, smoke and fumes may make the human nose incapable of detecting odors from small quantities of volatile fluids.

As part of any fire investigation, all early arriving fire fighters, as well as other persons at the fire scene, should be questioned as to any unusual observations that they might have made. This may assist in locating the point of origin of the fire, establish window and door conditions, indicate unusual flame or smoke colors and quantity, or supply other useful information.

Type of information that a witness may furnish

Time of the fire and general weather conditions.

What attracted her or his attention to the fire?

Exact place fire was burning when first observed (point of ignition).

Color and volume of the smoke.

Intensity of the flame and rapidity of spread.

Any unusual odors detected.

Possibility of observing more than one fire burning at the location.

Whether any explosions were heard before or during the fire.

Possible identities of persons at fire scene, in vicinity, or any suspicious circumstances.

Vehicles observed at or leaving the scene.

Figure 19-5. Business structure in which five distinct explosions were reported by witnesses. Search of the fire debris and materials uncovered 5 cubic centimeters of unburned gasoline. Investigation disclosed that the gasoline had been used to spread the fire throughout the building.

Detection of flammable fluids

Petroleum products and other flammable fluids are among the most common types of materials employed in arson cases involving structures. Even though alcohol, gasoline, stove oil, paint thinners, solvents, and other similar fluids are highly volatile and flammable, they frequently do not burn completely. Identifiable residues of such fluids can therefore be recovered in many cases even when large fires have occurred. (See Figure 19-5.)

The detection of the most concentrated deposits of many volatile fluids, such as gasoline, by odor may become difficult if much of such fluid is present. This is due to the fact that the human nose loses its sensitivity to many odors if exposed to large quantities over a period of time. Trace amounts of volatile fluid odors may also be masked by other odors at the fire scene. This is particularly true in the case of those produced by burned plastic and rubber.

It is important to realize that many flammable fluids have little or no odor. Included are such substances as some alcohols, deodorized kerosene, charcoal lighters.

The search for traces of flammable fluid may be facilitated by use of a highly sensitive combustible vapor detector.

Flammable fluid evidence recovery[2]

Samples of volatile fluids found in open jars or cans should be poured into clean metal or glass containers and sealed to prevent any loss of the fluid. In those instances where glass or plastic containers or cans are found that contain just an odor or trace of fluid, the container should be sealed immediately. Traces of flammable fluid may remain even though wet from fire fighting operations.

New clean paint cans are the best storage containers for recovered material suspected of containing flammable fluids. They have lids which may be readily sealed, and are not liable to breakage and loss of volatile fluids and vapors. Such paint cans are readily available from paint stores and hardware stores. Glass jars may be used for flammable liquids if they contain lids that can be tightly sealed. Mason jars that have rubber seals on the lids should be avoided since many fluids will soften or dissolve such seals and permit leakage and loss of contents. Plastic or wax containers should not be used for storage of flammable materials.

When specimens believed to contain small amounts of flammable fluid are obviously not damp with water, it is preferable to add a small amount of water to the container on top of the specimen. This tends to retard evaporation.

Identification of trace amounts of fluid in samples recovered frequently requires distillation. This means that specimens must be cut up into relatively small size pieces that will fit into glass distillation flasks. For this reason it is normally desirable that the investigator saw or chop large exhibits at the time of evidence recovery and place small pieces in containers. This usually is a superior method and easier than attempting to deliver large sections of wood, carpets, and similar exhibits to the laboratory even when the latter can be done rapidly and little loss of fluids is likely to occur.

All containers should be marked properly. Include name of person recovering the exhibit, date, time, and location of recovery. Postal or other carrier regulations should also be followed closely when shipping evidence.

Flammable fluid analyses[3]

Even when present in minute amounts or as residues from which the more volatile fractions have been lost, it is frequently possible to identify the original fluid employed. Comparisons are sometimes possible between residues recovered at the scene and samples of volatile fluids obtained from suspects. At times it is also possible to indicate the common origin of different flammable fluid specimens recovered in gasoline theft and other investigations as well as in arson cases. This type of study may be very complex and will usually require special sample recovery procedures. For this reason the crime laboratory should always be contacted by telephone for special instructions when this type of study is necessary. This will ensure that all necessary standard and control samples are properly secured.

Other arson evidence

Mechanical, electrical, or other fire ignition devices may be identified as to their nature and operation even if burned in a fire. All parts of such devices should be searched for and recovered. It may also be possible to compare the recovered evidence with similar material found in the possession of a suspect.

Residues from fuses and other chemical igniters or fuels are usually identifiable. Candle wax can be identified as to type and compared with candles or wax deposits on

[2] Ibid.

[3] Ibid.

clothing or other objects found in the possession of suspects.

Finding charred paper will be largely dependent on the extent of burning, intensity of the heat, and duration of the exposure of the paper to such heat. The possibility of finding the physical and chemical characteristics of the paper and ink is also dependent on these factors. Infrared photography has been used to reproduce the writing or printing on charred paper. Photographic filters, lighting, and chemical treatment with solutions of different reagents may assist in reproducing the original contents.

Deaths from burns

In any case where death from burns occurs in an individual living alone or where the manner of death has not been witnessed, it is usually mandatory that an autopsy be performed, including examination of the brain. The purpose of this procedure is to rule out the possibility of lack of recognition of such things as bullet wounds or stab wounds on the charred skin surface. This procedure does not apply to those cases of burns where the visual inspection of skin surfaces is sufficient to rule out the wound mentioned. Look for soot in the tracheobronchial tree to establish whether the deceased was alive at the time of the fire.[4]

Vehicle Fires

In a vehicle fire it is incumbent upon the investigator to establish, beyond all reasonable doubt, that a crime has been committed. It must be proven that no malfunction or other accidental happening could have contributed to, or in fact caused, the fire. Fires do not just happen; they are the result of

_____

[4]Thomas T. Noguchi, M.D., _Homicide Investigation Syllabus_, Homicide Investigation Institute, Moorpark College, Moorpark, California, March 1970.

chemical actions which produce certain and definite causes. The mobility of the automobile plus its collateral value lends itself readily to the overt act of arson. Whether the motive is financial, mechanical, or domestic trouble, the operator of the vehicle usually perpetrates the criminal act at a late hour. The ability to determine the cause and/or correctly evaluate physical evidence after a vehicle fire is of utmost importance to the completion of a successful arson investigation. So-called "breaks" in a case do not just happen; they are created by the diligence and hard work of the investigator.

Characteristics consistent with vehicle fires of incendiary origin

Odor of flammable liquids
Car burned up too rapidly
Top of car badly buckled or sagged
Glass flowed and taffied
Seat springs devoid of material
Floor covering showed effects of more intense fire and reduced to ash in some areas
Paint burned off of a far greater portion of the exterior of the body
Burns underneath floor mat or door panel
Obscured location of vehicle

Extinguishing car fires

In these fires, it is very advisable that the fire be put out with fog or similar sprays, and mopped up with a dribble of water in persistent areas. If a solid stream of water hits the auto, it breaks up brittle and charred remains of evidence, changes their location, or even knocks valuable evidence out of the vehicle. A solid stream of water will tear the remnants of upholstery to shreds, eliminating burn patterns, and voiding the possibility of the investigator determining whether the fire originated at the floor level or at the seat level. If the floor covering is not torn, it is often possible to determine by the visible burn patterns whether a flammable liquid has been used. This is true even when the floor covering is charred and brittle.

Case:

1. Ash from a mechanic's rag resting on the top of seat springs was the determining factor in securing a statement of guilt.

2. Finding an unusual quantity of wadded-up paper ash under the front edge of the front seat brought about a statement of guilt.

In both of the above cases, had a solid stream of water been used, important bits of evidence would have been readily washed away thereby preventing the conclusion of possible incendiarism.

Whenever vehicles are found burned in an isolated area, the immediate vicinity of the burned vehicle should be checked for footprints and/or tire tracks that may furnish valuable leads as to the identity of the perpetrator. The car itself should be carefully processed for possible fingerprints, missing items from the car, etc. The search of the crime scene may disclose bits of valuable evidence in the form of discarded items, cans, bottles or other containers, matches, cigarette or cigar butts, etc. A neighborhood investigation in the vicinity may also furnish additional information of value. Any containers that may possibly have been used to hold flammable liquids should be sealed and taken to the laboratory for analysis and fingerprint examination.

Note-Taking in Fire Investigations

The first step in any case is to gather all the information which is available concerning the incident. Thereafter, and as soon as possible, all data should be segregated in accordance with the plan or outline the investigator wishes to follow in dictating, typ-ing, or recording the report. The true test of adequacy is whether or not it clearly portrays all the facts in a clear, concise, accurate, and complete manner. Many inexperienced officers state that one of their biggest problems in compiling information during an investigation is in not knowing what questions to ask. Unfortunately there is no slide rule that can be used to obtain required information. However, answers to the questions Who, What, Where, When, Why, and How can provide a wealth of data for a report.

Who?

Who was the victim
Who made the report
Who discovered the fire
Who was the first person to observe the fire
Who was the last person to pass by before the fire
Who had a motive for setting the fire
Who set the fire
Who helped that person
Who will sign the complaint
Who has been interviewed
Who else should be interviewed
Who marked the evidence
Who was it turned over to
With whom did the suspect associate
With whom are the witnesses connected
With whom did the incendiarist set the fire
With whom did you talk at the scene and at other times
With whom did you work on the investigation

What?

What happened
What was the type of fire
What actions were taken by the suspect
What do the witnesses know about it
What evidence was obtained

What was done with the evidence
What was used to set the fire
What accelerants were used
What "plants" were used
What action did the fire fighters take
What further investigative action is needed
What knowledge or skill was needed in setting the fire
What was the condition of the doors, windows, and furnishings
What was removed
What other agencies were notified
What was reported but did not occur
What witnesses were not contacted
What time was the fire set
What time was it reported
What was the time of your arrival
What means of transportation did the suspect use to reach the location
With what devices was the fire set
With what trade or profession are any tools used associated
With what other crime is this fire associated

Where?

Where was the fire
Where was the fire discovered
Where did the fire occur
Where were the "plants" or accelerants obtained
Where was the witness
Where did the suspect live
Where did the suspect spend time
Where would the suspect most likely go
Where was the suspect apprehended
Where was the evidence marked
Where was the evidence stored

When?

When was the fire started
When was it discovered

When were the authorities notified
When did they arrive at the scene
When was the guilty party arrested
When was the suspect last seen
When was the arrest made
When will the complaint be signed

How?

How was the fire set
How did the incendiarist get to the scene
How did the guilty party get away
How did the incendiarist obtain information in order to commit the crime
How was the fire concealed
How was the fire first discovered
How were "plants" or accelerants used
How did you get your information regarding the fire
How was the arrest effected

Why?

Why was the fire set
Why were "plants" and accelerants used
Why were the witnesses reluctant to tell anything
Why was the witness anxious to point out the guilty party
Why did so much time elapse before the fire was reported
Why was this particular method of entry used

How much?

How much damage was done
How much property was removed prior to the fire
How much knowledge was necessary to set the fire
How much money was taken
How much did the victim claim was lost in the fire

How much trouble was it to carry property away

How much information are witnesses not giving out

How much is property owner or tenant withholding

How much additional information do you need to help solve the fire case

———— BOMB INVESTIGATION ————

A bomb is defined by the Interstate Commerce Commission (ICC) as any chemical compound, mixture, or device, the primary or common purpose of which is to function by explosion, with substantially instantaneous release of gas and heat. The bomb is regarded by many as the ultimate weapon of terrorism. The mentally ill, racists, anarchists, militants, syndicated criminals, and others have all employed the bomb with varying degrees of success.

Bomb complaints, generally, are received by law-enforcement agencies or private persons by telephone or letter. The caller or writer usually advises that there is a bomb planted in a particular building or other place, and that it is set to explode at a certain time. The caller is invariably anonymous and the source of the call or location from which it emanates is unknown. Such communications, oral or written, demand immediate attention. They should never be considered the work of a crank or prankster without other available facts to warrant such conclusion. The function of the police in bomb matters concerns itself with the protection of human life and property, removal of the bomb menace, and the investigation and apprehension of the bomb perpetrators or threateners. The object of this portion of the chapter is to give investigators a few facts and suggestions on explosives and procedures. Persons other than those trained in explosive matters should never attempt to disarm a suspected bomb.

Explosives

Generally speaking all explosive materials may be classified into one of two general groups: "high order" or "low order." The classification by "high" or "low" is based on the rate of velocity of explosion or detonation. Each group requires a particular ignition system.

High order
Here the rate of change to gaseous state is very rapid: detonation results. Explosives in this category include dynamite (various grades), TNT, RDX, and composition C-4 plastic explosive. High-order explosives will detonate only by the shock of a blasting cap to which a fuse is attached or by an electric detonator. A detonating cord (with its primary high-order-explosive core) is also used to detonate charges of high-order explosives. Explosives that are used as initiators or detonators for high-order explosives are generally referred to as primary explosives. High-order explosives have a *shattering effect*. The explosive waves produce a high degree of fragmentation near the focus of the charge and less intensive fragmentation of objects at greater distance from the detonation point. The location of the explosive can be determined by a critical study of the fragmentation and the direction of the explosives as noted from a study of various parts of the original structure. The velocity of high-order explosives ranges from about 3200 to over 27,000 feet per second (975 to over 8200 meters per second).

Low order
The rate of change to gaseous state is quite slow: deflagration results. Low-order explosives are principally propellant powders such as used in loading ammunition

Figure 19-6. A pipe bomb.

(black powder, smokeless powder), dust or grain explosions, gas explosions, and volatile vapors. Low-order explosives must be ignited by heat, friction, or spark, and they do not require the shock of a blasting cap. They should not be regarded as low in hazard. Some of these substances are among the most dangerous, as the history of major explosions involving black powder demonstrates. In low-order explosions with black or smokeless powder, explosion depends upon the burning of one particle setting off the next.

Low-order explosions are used in blasting operations; they have a "pushing" (rather than a shattering) effect, and a twisting and tearing type of deformation. Velocities of low-order explosives range from 1200 to about 3200 feet per second. Black powder, or smokeless powder has been frequently used to load pipe bombs (see Figure 19-6), which are generally lighted by a safety fuse. The safety fuse transmits the flame to the low-order explosive inside the pipe. When ignited, the low-order explosive inside the pipe explodes. The gases produced result in a blast and fragmentation of the pipe by the pressure.

Factors influencing violence of explosion

Nature of material, chemical structure
Concentration of air
Turbulence of the mixture
Particle size, in case of dust
Oxygen concentration
Pressure of flammable material
Temperature of flammable material
Condition and shape of container
Point of origin of explosion with respect to position of vents
Size and nature of vent closure

Explosive Accessories

Electric squibs

These are also known as electric matches. They are similar in appearance to an electric blasting cap and are sometimes used to ignite black powder. The squibs provide a spurt of flame similar to that produced by a safety fuse.

Blasting caps

These are used for initiating high-order explosives. They contain small amounts of a sensitive, powerful explosive. It is the function of the blasting cap to impart to the explosive an initial impulse of sufficient strength to set up a detonating wave that will be propagated throughout the charge. Two types of blasting caps generally are used:

1. *Electric blasting caps* are used where there is a source of electricity available. Under certain circumstances radio frequency waves emitted by a transmitter can detonate an electric blasting cap. Some caps are connected with lighting circuits. When lights are turned on, the bomb explodes.

2. *Nonelectric blasting caps* are designed to detonate from the spurt of flame provided by a safety fuse or other flame-producing device.

All types and sizes of blasting caps are sensitive to shock, friction, and heat. Many serious injuries and deaths have been caused by the careless handling of blasting caps. The handling and transportation of blasting caps should be left to experienced explosives personnel. Figure 19-7 illustrates a safety program poster that is distributed nation-wide warning of the dangers of blasting caps and depicting various types.

Safety fuse

The flame is conveyed through this medium at a continuous and uniform rate to a nonelectric blasting cap for ignition purposes; or, in the case of blasting powder, for the direct firing of the charge. Safety fuses consist of a fine core of special black powder enclosed in and protected by various kinds of coverings and waterproofing materials, according to grade. The speed at which most domestic fuses burn is thirty or forty seconds per foot. Pressure, degree of confinement, temperature, and moisture are all factors tending to influence the rate of burning. Most safety fuses cannot be extinguished by water or by foot. If necessary to save a life and as a last resort, pull the fuse out; or cut ahead of the burning. Cutting ahead of the fuse, however, involves a calculated risk. In many fuses it is not possible to determine the progress of the fire through the powder core by observation of the exterior. Therefore, it is extremely hazardous to estimate the length of time before an explosion of a burning fuse.

Detonating cords

These cords are frequently known by a brand name, such as Primacord, Primex, Detacord, and others. A detonating cord is a round, flexible cord, similar in appearance to

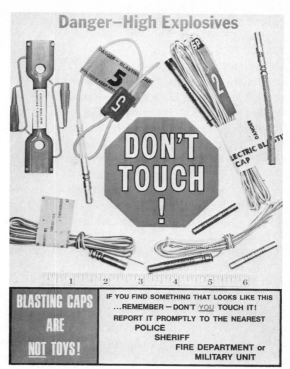

Figure 19-7. Educational poster depicting different types of blasting caps and warning against touching.

a safety fuse. The explosive core of the detonating cord is protected by a sheath of various textiles, waterproofing materials, or plastics. Various coloring and textile patterns differentiate the particular strengths and types of detonating cords. They are used in various ways to detonate charges of high-order explosives in the same manner as blasting caps.

Bombs

Bombs generally can be placed in the category of (1) *open-type* or (2) *concealed* or *disguised bomb*. The problem of bomb handling varies, of course, for both types. No attempt should be made by a nonexpert explosives handler to touch, move, handle, or remove any device in these two classifications.

Open-type bomb

This type bomb makes no effort to conceal its identity; it is easily recognizable. Examples of some of the more common homemade bombs include pipe bombs, or several sticks of dynamite taped or tied together and to which a blasting cap or "primacord" is fastened. Other open-type bombs are often of the hand-thrown or firebomb varieties such as Molotov cocktails, firecrackers of the M80 type, and others. Homemade bombs are the kinds of devices with which police are often confronted. The list of materials and chemical compounds that can be used to make homemade bombs is virtually unlimited. Contrary to popular opinion, neither commercial explosives nor blasting caps are necessary for the construction of effective bombs. Underground literature often provides information on bomb construction with materials that can be purchased in any hardware store or pharmacy.

Pipe Bombs This open-type bomb is popular inasmuch as the component parts are readily obtainable and easy to construct. A short piece of pipe is capped at both ends with a hole drilled through one of the capped ends, or through the side of the pipe itself. (See Figure 19-6.) Black or smokeless powder is used to fill the interior of the pipe. This type of bomb may be loaded with a stick of dynamite, in which case a shattering of the metal would be caused. A pipe bomb can also be activated by attaching electric blasting cap leg wires to a house current, flashlight batteries, telephone, or doorbell. In some instances, the safety fuse is replaced by an electric detonator.

Dynamite Sticks This open-type bomb is usually made of several sticks of dynamite taped or tied together and a blasting cap, or safety fuse attached. (See Figure 19-8.) The

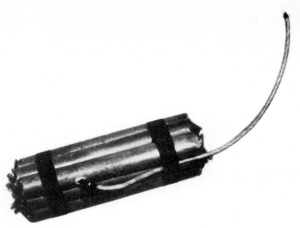

Figure 19-8. Open-type bomb consisting of several sticks of dynamite taped together along with a detonating fuse.

dynamite (chemicals and materials) is encased in a waterproof, cardboard cylinder, usually 1¼ by 8 inches [3 by 20 centimeters] in size, although there are other sizes, shapes, and strengths. The explosion of dynamite is brought about by strong shock, initiated by electric or nonelectric caps or detonating cord. Dynamite residue can be microscopically identified as such by various chemical tests. The basic types of dynamites in use are straight dynamites, ammonia dynamites, gelatin dynamites, ammonia–gelatin dynamites, and military dynamites.

Molotov Cocktail This open-type, crude incendiary grenade was popularized during World War II by the Russians. It was named after Vyacheslav Mikhailovich Molotov, a Russian statesman. The device consists of a bottle filled with a flammable liquid (principally gasoline) and a saturated wick that is ignited before throwing. Contrary to popular belief, the container does not have to have a small neck or opening. The main concern in selecting a container is that it break on impact and have proper ignition. Molotov cocktails are generally soda bottles, half-gallon wine bottles, mason jars, 5-gallon water jugs, milk bottles, liquor bot-

Figure 19-9. Open-type unexploded Molotov cocktail (incendiary grenade) with cloth wick; usually filled with a petroleum product.

tles, etc. The wicks used may be cloth, paper, tape and matches, etc. The size of the container is determined by how the bomb is to be used. If thrown, a small container is required. If dropped from overhead, a large container has a greater effect. Figure 19-9 depicts a typical Molotov cocktail made with a soda-type bottle.

Gasoline is often used in Molotov cocktails because of its ready availability. During some riots, rioters have taken automobiles into a disturbance area, siphoned gas from the gas tank, and made numerous bombs at or near the scene. Gasoline bombs cover a greater area on street pavement. The hard surface invariably breaks the container. Large containers of gasoline, with a piece of cloth inserted under the lid (extending one or two inches outside the lid) have been used. The container is carried right side up. When needed the container is merely inverted, the cloth saturated, ignited, and thrown.

M80 Firecracker This is a low-velocity explosive. If exploded in a confined area such

Figure 19-10. A powerful firecracker that has been doctored with wire staples to cause injury when exploded.

as a room or office, it can cause serious injury to the eyes and ears. Firecrackers of this sort are readily obtainable in Mexico. Figure 19-10 shows an M80 to which shrapnel in the form of wire staples has been attached by a putty substance.

Flashbulb A homemade bomb (Figure 19-11) can be made by drilling a small hole into the neck of a large photo flashbulb into which a quantity of black or smokeless powder is poured. Thereafter the bulb replaces the conventional light bulb in the room or office of an intended victim. Should the room light wallswitch be turned on, an explosion occurs causing severe injury to the victim's eyes or ears. In another variation of the use of this explosive device, ball bearings or

Figure 19-11. Homemade bomb using a large photo flashbulb filled with black or smokeless powder.

other shrapnel are added. The resultant explosion would disperse the shrapnel over a wide area causing possible serious injury to the intended victim.

Concealed or disguised bombs

Explosives in this classification generally are: (1) a *time bomb* (chemical or mechanical) that explodes automatically at a predetermined time or (2) a *trigger bomb* that can be set off by such natural acts as opening or raising the lid of a box, untying a string, removing a wrapper, inverting the container, or other acts normally involved in the handling or movement of such a container or part of it. Disguised bombs may be rigged in containers such as: lunch box, first aid kit, flower box, flashlight, cigar box, briefcase, handbag, suitcase, food containers, or other surprise devices or "booby traps."

Letter and Package Bombs　In March of 1977, a letter bomb contained in a 9- by 6-inch envelope was addressed to President Jimmy Carter in Washington, D.C. The Secret Service discovered the bomb when the envelope was passed through an x-ray machine. It was subsequently destroyed by the District of Columbia police. Terrorists' letter bombs sent from one country to another country's diplomats and officials have been intercepted and deactivated. Quite often these letters have been addressed to a specific individual, position, or unit in an organization, e.g., to a "Chairman of the Board" or a "First Vice President." The letters are often marked for special handling. Envelopes are the usual sizes, in various colors, and have the name and address written, printed, or typed on an affixed label; delivery methods may also vary. Thicknesses may vary from 1/8 inch to 5/16 inch. Weight is approximately 1.7 ounces. These dimensions and weights vary with different clandestine devices used.

The letter bomb also often comes in a manila envelope. It is stiffer than the usual letter, particularly in the center. The device is initiated by a pressure-release mechanism. Opening the letter releases a floating cocked firing pin—a rod through the center of the envelope. (See Figure 19-12.)

Package bombs likewise may vary widely in size, shape, and color. They appear to be objects such as gifts or books placed inside manila envelopes. They may be mailed from a foreign country and indicate some form of special handling: registered mail, certified mail, special delivery, etc. Some packages contain a spring device. Frequently, the spring is held open by a cord which is cut or untied when the package is examined. For this reason, no suspected package should be opened by cutting or untying strings. Turning of a hinge or lifting of the cover may release a spring trigger mechanism. In other arrangements the circuits are closed by tilting the package or shaking it. Sometimes mercury is caused to flow to make electrical contact when the package is disturbed. Whenever a letter or package is suspected of

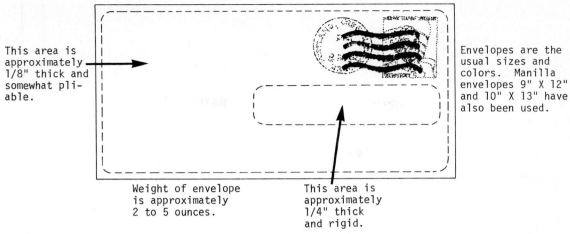

This area is approximately 1/8" thick and somewhat pliable.

Envelopes are the usual sizes and colors. Manilla envelopes 9" X 12" and 10" X 13" have also been used.

Weight of envelope is approximately 2 to 5 ounces.

This area is approximately 1/4" thick and rigid.

Figure 19-12. Schematic of a type of mechanical letter bomb.

containing a possible explosive device, the police should be notified immediately.

All such devices have the explosive power to kill or maim. Some letter and package bombs have electrical wiring systems concealed within paperback books. The book is hollowed out to enclose a device with an electrical firing pin. Terrorists may construct any number of explosive letter or package gimmicks. *Never* try to deactivate such a device. As previously stated, notify the police bomb squad.

In one instance concerning a homemade package bomb, two uniformed officers each lost a hand when the suspect package blew up as they tried to move it. This bomb incident was an outgrowth of a business dispute between two individuals who were old acquaintances. The subject of this case agreed to sell his laundry business to his friend, but the latter changed his mind when he discovered that the business' indebtedness was greater than the subject had represented to him. The subject then became infuriated with his friend, and rigged a package bomb. The subject left the concealed device at his friend's office. When the intended victim found the package, he went home before opening it. But later that day he had second thoughts about the package, and he asked the police to investigate. He arranged to meet them at his office about midnight. At that time two uniformed officers met the intended victim at his office and admonished him to stand back as they proceeded to move the package outside of the building. The package blew up as it was being moved, resulting in the maiming of the two officers and minor injuries to the intended victim. The subject later pleaded guilty to two counts of mayhem as a result of the incident. He was sentenced to from one to fourteen years imprisonment. Both officers have since successfully brought civil suits against subject.

Police Officer Averts a Tragedy—a Positive Lesson In this instance, an alert officer spotted a homemade bomb and ordered radio silence to avoid setting it off. As a result of an anonymous telephone call, a Los Angeles police officer was dispatched to a parking lot behind a large church in Hollywood. On arriving at the location, the officer found a package about the size of a cigar box leaning against a retaining wall near the rear of the church. The package was bound by a coil of wire. The officer spotted three electrical blasting caps just behind the package. The officer alertly recognized the device as one that was designed to spark coil by a radio signal, so he backed out of the parking lot and drove about a block away where he radioed for additional personnel, including the bomb squad. He then radioed all patrol cars in the area to maintain a radio silence until the bomb could be disarmed. Bomb squad specialists soon confirmed his suspicion. They indicated that the coil was set to attract a spark from police radio frequency transmission. The spark would have set off the blasting caps, which in turn would have initiated the explosion. The officer's astute action ended the threat of a very serious explosion—police training had paid off.

As a security precaution in London, England, underground railway cars, platforms, stations, buses, terminals, and other places have signs posted warning the public to be on the alert for any suspicious packages. The posters set forth specific instructions for people to follow if an unattended package is observed. (See Figure 19-13.)

Chemical and Mechanical Delay Devices A *chemical* delay explosive time device generally involves the time required for acid or liquid to decompose metal or other material, or time required for a solvent to dissolve a soluble material. Chemicals offer almost limitless possibilities in constructing explosives and may even consume themselves in the process.

A *mechanical* delay explosive device is likewise homemade and is constructed with the aid of an alarm clock, watch, or other time contrivance. It should be kept in mind that time bombs do not necessarily tick as they may be set off by a chemical fuse. Should a suspected package tick, there is a real likelihood that it is a time bomb and timed to explode at some particular hour. There is generally no way of telling what that hour is. Time bombs may sometimes be

If you see an unattended package or bag on the Underground

1. DON'T touch it.
2. DON'T pull the red emergency handle between stations.
3. PULL the emergency handle once the train has stopped at the next station.
4. TELL the Guard or any London Transport staff immediately.
5. TELL other passengers to leave the car.

Figure 19-13. Poster used in London in underground cars and stations, busses, and other places to alert the public to the danger of unattended packages.

detected by placing a contact microphone against the suspected package and listening at a distance with the aid of an amplifier.

The use of x-ray and fluoroscopic equipment has been a valuable aid to police in determining first, whether the concealed or disguised package, box, suitcase, lunch box, etc., actually is a bomb; and second, its construction and possible method of detonation. Either fluoroscopic examinations or x-ray photographs should be made from all possible angles without disturbing the ques-

Figure 19-14. Portable x-ray mini-equipment for bomb investigation.

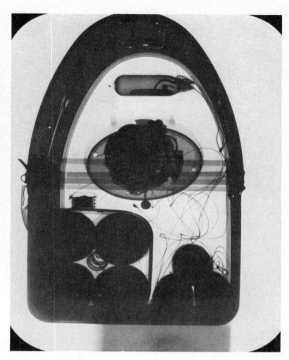

Figure 19-15. X-ray photo of a metal lunch box showing concealed bomb mechanism and construction. This photo was made with a portable, flashlight-sized x-ray tubehead.

tioned article. Figure 19-14 illustrates a type of portable x-ray equipment that can be used indoors with a power supply and cable lengths up to 100 feet; or anywhere with a battery pack. X-ray photos can be made at the scene with film that develops dry in seconds, thus permitting examination and disarming capabilities for the bomb technician.

The following illustrations demonstrate the use of x-ray and fluoroscopic equipment. X-ray photographs of suspected packages, articles, objects, etc., permit trained bomb-disposal personnel to make the necessary evaluation and decisions for the appropriate handling and/or dismantling operations of explosive devices. See Figures 19-15 to 19-18 for illustrations of the use of x-rays in bomb detection and handling.

Operations and Procedures in Bomb Incidents

Actions taken in bomb incidents are controlled by the characteristics of the sus-pected bomb. Operating procedures generally should take into account the latitude required by the various skill levels of personnel involved in a bomb incident response. Analysis of the typical bomb incident suggests that three basic skill requirements are involved:[5]

Protective. Skills involved in responding to the need to protect life and property. Includes ability to deal with and control excited or frightened persons, make or influence decisions under

[5]*Development of Bomb Incident: Policy and Procedure,* Arson and Bomb Investigation Institute, Moorpark College, Moorpark, California, February 1971.

Figure 19-16. Photo made with portable x-ray equipment that permitted penetration and good visualization through a 2-inch pipe bomb.

stress, conduct search operations, and employ damage control measures. Relative personal risk: *minimal* to *moderate.*

Technical. Skills involved in neutralizing incendiary and explosive devices through disarming or detonation. Includes ability to recognize and defeat a wide range of fusing systems, work under stress, and safely dispose of all commonly encountered explosives. Relative personal risk: *high.*

Investigative. Skills involved in working with physical and human evidence to identify persons responsible for bombing incidents. Includes knowledge of legal requirements and ability to make maximum use of investigative resources. Relative personal risk: *normal.*

In some agencies a single officer may be expected to process an entire incident provided she or he is well trained and fully qualified in all aspects of the assignment. In another agency, three or more different skill requirements may be required in order to perform in the three areas of skill requirements demanded. Twenty-four-hour coverage by a public safety agency will, of necessity, require assignment of sufficient trained personnel to meet anticipated needs in terms of time of day and volume of work. Because of the high level of skill and risk involved, the following four functional assignments and their relationship to each other and the bomb incident are suggested:[6]

Public safety officer (patrol officer, fire fighter, guard)
Incident response
Recognition of explosive and incendiary devices
Basic evacuation procedures
Basic search procedures
Basic damage control measures
Reporting and recording

Bomb scene officer
Incident response
Recognition of explosive and incendiary devices
Evacuation procedures
Search procedures
Damage control measures
Movement of devices to safe area under certain prescribed conditions in the absence of a bomb technician
Reporting and recording

---

[6]Ibid.

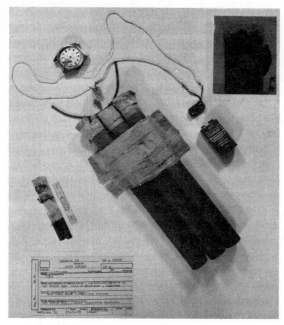

Figure 19-17. A homemade incendiary bomb discovered under a vending machine in a bar and diagnosed with the aid of x-ray photographs, permitting dismantling by a bomb technician. The insert shows the opaque covering on the bomb as it was found.

Some insight into the various skill levels can be gained by comparing the estimated *minimum* bomb-incident-training period required for each assignment.

Public safety officer	4 hours
Bomb scene officer	24 hours
Investigator	24 hours
Bomb disposal technician	120 hours

All public safety officers should be trained in basic evacuation, damage control, and bomb identification techniques. Their responsibilities must be stated in such a manner to leave no doubt as to the limitations of their skills and the hazards of exceeding these limits. Bomb scene officers, on the other hand, should not only be trained in the basic public safety officer skills but also in more advanced procedures. In the area of damage control, for example, bomb scene officers may be expected to do more than open windows and doors. They may be given instruction in the construction of protective works and the use of shielding devices. Their skills in identification might include the use of a stethoscope or portable x-ray. In some

Bomb disposal technician
Damage control measures
Evaluation of devices
Disarming
Detonation/ignition, transportation
Disposal of explosive materials
Processing of evidence at scene (detonation/ignition)
Reporting and recording

Investigator
Processing of evidence at scene (detonation/ignition)
Follow-up of investigative leads
Searches and arrests
Case preparation
Reporting and recording

Figure 19-18. A type of x-ray surveillance system used for examining luggage, packages, and other questionable articles.

instances it may be desirable to train, equip, and authorize them to remotely remove a bomb from a facility. Their responsibilities should be based on their levels of training and skill. In no case should their titles or stated responsibilities authorize or imply authority to attempt a disarming or any other high-risk procedure.

It is highly recommended that every public safety agency should include at least one individual trained in basic bomb recognition, evacuation, and damage control procedures. This basic training is available to all departments through the Department of the Army Explosive Ordnance Disposal Detachments, which are located throughout the United States. A list of these units can be obtained from any local military installation.

Investigative Procedures and Suggestions

Many police agencies have procedural plans for the handling of bomb incidents. Trained personnel, equipment, and resources are usually part of such plans. (See Figure 19-19.) It is the purpose of this section to acquaint the police science student with some basic facts in the form of suggestions and procedures that are frequently used or considered in hazardous situations involving bomb threats, unexploded bombs, and exploded bombs.

Bomb threats

The decision to evacuate or not to evacuate business premises is one of the perplexing problems of bomb threat cases. Any decision to evacuate or not to evacuate bears with it resulting economic loss, confusion, and numerous other problems. Management may make it an overall policy that, in the event of a bomb threat, evacuation will be automatic. This decision obviously circumvents the calculated risk and gives prime consideration to the safety of personnel in the building. The alternative is for management to make the decision at the time of the receipt of the threat. In some places, such as New York City, for example, evacuation of threatened buildings is mandatory under law. Thus the police have a

Figure 19-19. Types of equipment used in bomb investigations.

legal responsibility to evacuate a building. Los Angeles, on the other hand, prefers to leave the decision regarding evacuation up to the management of the company or building.

Management decisions regarding evacuation are influenced by such factors as nature of the call; whether caller's voice is that of a child; caller known to company as chronic complainant; past experience; relationship call may have to a known situation; employee unhappiness; recent dismissal; and unrest in the community. If the caller has stated that a device is to be placed in the building, there obviously is no need to make a decision to evacuate; added security precautionary measures, however, would be in order. If it has been stated that a device is in the building, then the evacuation and judgment must be made more quickly with the prime consideration being that of saving human life. The amount of time available may dictate management's action.

If evacuation is requested by the building official, the danger area should be cleared of all occupants. No arbitrary distance is a safe one because of possible flying shrapnel should an explosion occur. It may be necessary to clear an entire floor as well as portions of the floor above and below the critical area.

Bomb Threats by Letter or Note If the bomb threat is received by letter or note, the document should be carefully preserved, identified, and processed by the laboratory for fingerprints, handwriting, ink examination, and other paper examinations. If typewritten, an examination for make, model, key defects, and other identifying imperfections should be made. The Anonymous Letter File of the FBI should be checked as a method of connecting two or more cases involving threats of a similar nature.

Telephone Bomb Threats In such instances the caller should be kept on the line as long as possible. Record the conversation. Endeavor to trace the call while it is being received. The following type of information can be most helpful in the initial evaluation of a bomb threat and for evidence and investigation follow-up:[7]

Time call received.
Time caller hung up.
Exact words of person placing call.

Questions to ask caller
When is bomb going to explode?
Where is the bomb right now?
What kind of a bomb is it?
What does it look like?
Why did you place the bomb?

Description of caller's voice
Male, female?
Young, middle-aged, old?
Tone of voice: muffled, calm, hysterical?
Accent?
Background noise?
Is voice familiar?
If so, who did it sound like?
Was message accompanied by any threats as to race, religion, nationality?

Person receiving or monitoring call
Department
Telephone number
Home address and telephone number
Date

Procedural Steps

Necessity of immediate police attention in these cases is paramount. Most departments, upon receipt of such complaints, require a supervisor to take charge and proceed to the victim location.

The decision to call out the bomb detail or explosives specialist is made at the

---

[7]Ibid.

scene by the supervisor following initial evaluation of all the facts and circumstances: nature of threat, kinds of troubles intended victim has been having, solid possibility of explosion, location of alleged bomb, presence of people, and other hazards.

Arrangements for adequate communication, equipment, and personnel, as well as material resources are early considerations on the part of the supervisor following on-the-spot appraisal.

If a building search is ordered, assignments of specific areas should be made. Record the identity and assignments of all searchers. Prior to the search, however, the searchers should be instructed as to the objectives of the search, their duties on finding a suspected package or device, and whatever other procedures they are expected to follow. In addition, *precautionary instructions* as to the dangers involved in touching, jarring, tilting, or otherwise handling any part of a suspect package or items attached in any way to the article should be given.

Searchers should possess flashlights and light-bending adapters for directing light into small openings. Other tools found useful include a multibladed knife, screwdriver, wrench, probing rod, etc., for assistance in exploration. However, it is to be reemphasized that should a suspect package or device be discovered, an explosives technician should be immediately summoned.

The search must be conducted in a thorough, methodical manner. A recommended procedure, in a building search, is to start from the outside and work toward the inside; or when inside, start from the bottom and work upward. In many instances, certain employees of a building can render valuable assistance in identifying or eliminating foreign articles, "strange" boxes, packages, etc., since they are more familiar with the building and contents than the searcher is. Every conceivable place within a building should be carefully examined in order to locate the alleged bomb. The search should include lockers, storage closets, behind pipes, in air-conditioning ducts, rest rooms, elevator wells and shafts, tunnels, cabinets, wastepaper receptacles, lighting fixtures, hanging decorations, filing drawers, briefcases, handbags, and all other places and containers since concealment is limited only by the imagination and ingenuity of the bomb threatener.

Upon completing a search assignment, the particular area searched should be marked or otherwise identified as having been searched.

In halls, auditoriums, and theaters, a search of the facilities should include the outside areas: vents, ducts, window ledges, fire escape area, behind equipment affixed to the building, and other places that the structure of the particular building may suggest. The search should proceed within the building: the basement area, lockers, cabinets, miscellaneous containers, fixtures, tunnels, storage areas, beneath stages, speaker's platforms, etc. Search areas in and around all seats. Decorations, light fixtures, air-conditioning units, banquet rooms, rest rooms, etc., should be examined closely.

In out-of-doors area searches, explosive devices may be located in drainage systems, trash or garbage receptacles, incinerators, mailboxes, street and sidewalk sewer holes, parked cars and trucks, and any other place suggested by the particular locality.

In view of the many ways in which an automobile can be wired or triggered to explosive materials, any search of a vehicle should be conducted by a trained explosives technician. The search of a vehicle generally is directed around the outside (front, sides, and rear) and the entire undercarriage. Examination includes area beneath tires, hubcaps, wheel rims, fenders, wheel well, exhaust system and muffler, and gas tank. Where there is evidence of forced entry, the car's battery cable should be disconnected before any interior search. The search includes such places as panels, arm rests, under floor mats, accelerator, brake pedal, area of dashboard, glove compartment, radio and speaker, heater and ducts, engine compartment, trunk, spare tire and other places where devices could be secreted. Other critical areas requiring examination include light switches, dome light, ignition switch, cigarette lighter front and rear, clock, windshield wiper, and other wiring.

The search of an aircraft should begin at the outside and work inward and from the bottom up. Aircrew can be of valuable assistance in these searches because of their familiarity with plane construction, equipment, supplies, etc. Whenever airline personnel conduct searches, however, they should be instructed as to their duties whenever suspicious items or materials are discovered. In making thorough searches, searchers must look in, around, and through all accessible areas, crevices, containers, equipment, shelves, lockers, cabinets, seats, etc. In checking luggage, passengers can be helpful in identifying and opening their belongings for the searchers. This procedure can assist in pinpointing bombs in unclaimed luggage. Freight can likewise be checked to account for all cargo.

Unexploded Bombs

Whenever a bomb or explosive device is located, the first consideration should be the protection of human life and property. In view of the almost infinite possible varieties of bombs, and the ever present danger of the bomb exploding, many investigative steps must be taken. Under no circumstances should a nonqualified person touch or handle a suspected package, device, or anything attached thereto (unless as a last resort for the saving of human life). The immediate considerations on finding an explosive device are

Immediate movement to scene with qualified bomb personnel should be made in order to evaluate the suspected bomb and take whatever action is necessary to disarm or remove the device.

In the event the police agency has no technical personnel trained to handle a bomb disposal assignment, a list of explosives specialists, and how they can be reached, should be readily available at each department. In addition, special equipment that can be used in bomb emergencies should be available. These include bomb blankets or other baffling materials to direct an explosion upwards or downwards, protective shields and armor, x-ray and fluoroscope equipment, blast tube or other explosive carriers, etc. Outside of larger metropolitan areas, the only qualified bomb disposal technicians available are military explosive ordnance disposal units. These units are located throughout the United States.

The danger area should be cleared of all occupants to ensure as much safety as possible. An acceptable ruse or excuse might be used for evacuation in order to prevent panic and possible injury to people when exiting.

A guard should be established outside the danger area to prevent the possibility of injury or damage should an explosion occur. Only authorized personnel should be permitted to enter the danger zone.

The scene should be protected and preserved so that all possible physical evidence might be obtained.

Headquarters should be kept advised of all developments and/or needs.

It should be noted whether or not the package is ticking. Is it attached to anything? Fastened down? Close observation should be made without touching or disturbing. The authority to decide how or if a bomb is to be rendered safe should rest solely with the bomb disposal technician at the scene.

The person who discovered the bomb should be interviewed for all pertinent information. Any other persons at scene should be interviewed concerning the identity of persons or automobiles observed in the area prior to the finding of the bomb. Why a particular building was selected for a bomb attempt should be ascertained.

A neighborhood inquiry should obtain any possible information concerning suspicious persons or cars in the pertinent area, or fleeing from the scene around the time in question.

Surveillance of the crowd of spectators should be undertaken to identify possible suspects.

Photographs should be taken of the crowd to determine whether the pictures will reveal any familiar faces that appeared at previous bombing incidents. Suspect may be among the "curious spectators."

If deemed advisable, any flammable materials should be removed from the immediate area of the suspected bomb in order to eliminate any additional injury or damage should an explosion occur.

Fire department, rescue, and medical units, should be alerted.

Shutting off power, gas, and fuel lines leading into danger area should be considered if type of bomb warrants this action. It could prevent any additional explosions that might add to the impending disaster.

Bomb should be preserved after dismantling for fingerprint examination and determination of source of parts for possible tracing.

Sources or suppliers of explosive materials in the area should be contacted to identify purchasers who might be considered possible suspects.

Any standby alerts should be called off after danger is over.

Caution: In no instance should any dangerous chemicals, powders, explosives, or other suspected bomb devices be shipped or delivered to a crime laboratory for examination. Evidence should be shipped or delivered *only* if it is *known* to be safe. If any doubt exists, the laboratory should be telephoned prior to shipping or delivering exhibits. Federal and state laws restrict the transportation of such dangerous materials.

Exploded Bombs

The primary object of an investigation following the explosion of a bomb is to (1) establish the nature of the bomb, (2) find out the method of ignition, and (3) obtain any other evidence that may assist in the identification and apprehension of the person(s) responsible. Investigative procedures and considerations include

Figure 19-20. Uniformed police officers in New York City using wooden barriers to keep unlookers away from the site of an early morning explosion.

Necessity of immediate response to the scene by explosive specialists (bomb detail). Supervision, organization, communication, coordination, and control at scene are of vital importance.

Action upon arrival, based upon initial evaluation, existing facts, conditions, and the order of urgency; e.g., whether ambulance, medical assistance, or the fire department is needed; necessity of shutting off power, gas, and fuel lines; or other expediency.

Clearing danger area of all occupants. Establish a perimeter in order to protect and preserve the critical area from all unauthorized persons. Limit access to as few persons as possible. Guards, barricades, ropes, may assist in defining forbidden areas. (See Figure 19-20.)

Removal of flammable materials from the surrounding area to prevent any further damage.

Taking exterior and interior photographs (if a building) once the structure has been examined and declared safe from any possibility of collapsing. Many times a reevaluation of the overall appearance of the scene is required. Without proper photographs, this study is practically impossible. Photographs of the structure before the bombing should be obtained, if available, for additional study and comparison.

Taking of close-up or special photos of physical evidence, evidence of forced entry, appliances (if involved as source of power for detonation), or any other pictures that may be pertinent.

Taking of photographs of spectators at different intervals. Persons appearing in picture may be identifed as "spectators" at previous bombing incidents.

Making sketch of pertinent areas to show the damage and relation of the affected objects to each other.

Designation of one or more persons to evaluate each item of evidence recovered, see that it is photographed, charted, and recorded as to exact location, time found, by whom, and properly preserve items for laboratory examination. This procedure helps to keep the chain of evidence short.

Interviewing of witnesses and victim(s) at scene. Ascertain who was there and has since left; determine everything that happened before officers arrived. Ascertain what type of sound the explosion made, what was the force of the explosion and its direction, color of smoke, flame, odor of any gas, etc. Arrange to show any available photographs or albums of known bomb suspects to witnesses for possible identification.

Recording of license numbers of automobiles at or near scene, or entering or leaving the area of the explosion. The identity of the owners of the vehicles and check of available identification records may assist in identifying a bombing suspect.

Search and screening of debris. Look for the location or placement of the explosive charge, evidence of type of container, ignition device, fragments of detonators, blasting caps, pieces of fuse, parts of battery, wire, clock mechanism or parts, packaging materials, string, etc. Items of this type should be photographed, recorded in notebook as to location, carefully collected, identified, preserved, and transmitted to the laboratory for examination. Surgeon-type gloves should be worn in handling any materials that may possibly contain fingerprints.

Special attention to the recovery of residue deposits to establish the source of the explosive used.

If a plant or business is a victim of a bombing, consideration of recent dismissals, employee grievances, and labor troubles.

Looking for evidence of forced entry such as jimmied doors or windows.

Obtaining samples of soil areas. If gasoline or other petroleum products are part of the bomb, liquid will often collect in soil near the structure. Use clean 1-gallon paint cans with lids to collect samples.

Tracing any physical evidence found. Contact suppliers of materials that have been used in the construction of the bomb, for identification of possible suspects.

Conducting an extensive neighborhood investigation for any suspects and/or vehicles observed in the area before, during, or after the bombing that may indicate possible implication.

If suspects develop during the investigation, consideration of such traditional relevant factors as evidence of motive, plan, design or scheme, ability and opportunity, possessing the means, fabrication, destruction and suppression of evidence, faking an alibi, making of false statements, and other indications of a consciousness of guilt.

Checking local mental institutions for any releasees who might have potentialities as bombers.

Studying other bomb cases to determine whether they might contribute to the solution of the case under investigation.

If persons are killed or injured, determining their identities as soon as possible. Identification of the victims may provide a reason for the bombing and lead to possible suspects or other valuable investigative information.

Identification of Bomb Threatener

The identification and apprehension of a bomb threatener is brought about by the use of maximum investigative resources. Techniques of interviews, surveillances, voice identification, employee checks, use of informants, analysis of similar incidents, handwriting examinations, if applicable, and many other investigative channels, as applicable, should be used.

Reference Files and Scientific Aids Available in Bomb Cases

Although it is not possible to list herein the many reference files and scientific aids available in investigations of this type, the following sources should be noted:

FBI

This organization has information on the construction of various types of bombs, collection of dynamite wrappers, explosive materials, blasting caps, fuses, detonators, photograph albums, anonymous letter file, typewriter standards file, fingerprints of bomb suspects.

LEAA National Bomb Data Center, Picatinny Arsenal

Located in New Jersey, this Center is operated for the Law Enforcement Assistance Administration, U.S. Department of Justice, by the Federal Bureau of Investigation, and the U.S. Army Materiel Command. The Center collects and distributes statistical data on bombings and provides technical advice on bomb disposal to public safety agencies.

Bomb center services include:

Collection and analysis of data relating to bombing incidents, materials, techniques, and targets. That data is published in summary reports that are distributed to authorized municipal, county, state, and federal public safety agencies.

Publication and distribution of procedural bulletins that cover methods for improving the security of potential targets; techniques to use at bombing sites; technical information about explosives, fire bombs, and home-made devices; and bomb disposal services. These bulletins are made available to authorized public safety personnel.

Development of standarized instructional lessons and materials concerning bombings. These are used in basic, in-service, and specialized law-enforcement training programs.

Maintenance of an annotated bibliography concerning bombings and incendiary devices. The Center provides copies on request.

National Crime Information Center (NCIC)

This is the FBI's computerized system linked to over 100 control terminals tied to their computer in Washington, D.C., and provides service to all of the fifty states and to Canada.

Federal Aviation Administration Behavioral Profile

This Profile alerts authorities to potential troublemakers.

X-ray and fluoroscopic surveillance equipment

This can be used to inspect bomb devices in boxes, luggage, briefcases, and other miscellaneous containers.

Magnetometers

These can be used to register presence of metallic objects.

Trained dogs

They can "sniff out" explosives.

Laboratory techniques

Aids available in scientifically processing crime scene evidence include ultraviolet and other special lamps, chromotography (to separate mixtures by chromotrography), neutron activation (radiometric methods of analysis), atomic absorption (atomic absorption spectrometry), emission and mass spectrography, radiography (photography by x-ray radiation or by the gamma rays of radium or radioactive substances), and practically all other accessory equipment required for criminalistic operations.

Bomb Threats, Explosives, and Incendiary Devices

U.S.C., title 18, sec. 844 (d) through 844 (i)

844(d) Whoever transports or receives, or attempts to transport or receive, in interstate or foreign commerce any explosive with the knowledge or intent that it will be used to kill, injure, or intimidate any individual or unlawfully to damage or destroy any building, vehicle, or other real or personal property, shall be imprisoned for not more than 10 years, or fined not more than $10,000, or both; and if personal injury results shall be imprisoned for not more than 20 years or fined not more than $20,000, or both; and if death results, shall be subject to imprisonment for any term of years, or to the death penalty or to life imprisonment as provided in section 34 of title 18.

844(e) Whoever, through the use of the mail, telephone, telegraph, or other instrument of commerce, willfully makes any threat, or maliciously conveys false information knowing the same to be false, concerning an attempt or alleged attempt being made, to kill, injure, or intimidate any individual or unlawfully to damage or destroy any building, vehicle, or other real or personal property by means of an explosive shall be imprisoned for not more than five years or fined not more than $5,000, or both.

844(f) Whoever maliciously damages or destroys, or attempts to damage or destroy, by means of an explosive, any building, vehicle, or other personal or real property in whole or in part owned, possessed, or used by, or leased to, the United States, or any department or agency thereof, or any institution or organization receiving federal financial assistance shall be imprisoned for not more than ten years, or fined not more than $10,000, or both; and if death results shall be subject to imprisonment for any term of years, or to the death penalty or to life imprisonment as provided in section 34 of Title 18.

844(g) Whoever possesses an explosive in any building in whole or in part owned, possessed, or used by, or leased to, the United States or any department or agency thereof, except with the written consent of the agency, department, or other person responsible for the management of such building, shall be imprisoned for not more than one year, or fined not more than $1,000, or both.

844(h) Whoever (1) uses an explosive to commit any felony which may be prosecuted in a court of the United States or (2) carries an explosive unlawfully during the commission of any felony which may be prosecuted in a court of the United States, shall be sentenced to a term of imprisonment for not less than 1 year nor more than 10 years. In the case of his second or subsequent conviction under this subsection, such person shall be sentenced to a term of imprisonment for not less than 5 years nor more than 25 years, and, not withstanding any other provision of law, the court shall not suspend the sentence of such person or give him a probationary sentence.

844(i) Whoever maliciously damages or destroys, or attempts to damage or destroy, by means of an explosive, any building, vehicle, or other real or personal property used in interstate or foreign commerce or in any activity affecting interstate or foreign commerce shall be imprisoned for not more than 10 years, or fined not more than $10,000, or both; and if personal injury results shall be imprisoned for not more than 20 years or fined not more than $20,000, or both; and if death results shall also be subject to imprisonment for any term of years, or to the death penalty or to life imprisonment as provided in section 34 of this title.

For the purposes of the above subsections, "explosive" means gunpowders, powders used for blasting, all high-order explosives, blasting materials, fuses (other than electric circuit breakers), detonators and other detonating agents, smokeless powders, and other explosive or incendiary devices within the meaning of paragraph (5) of section 232 of this title. This also includes any chemical compound, mechanical mixture, or device that containes oxidizing and combustible units or other ingredients, in such proportions, quantities, or packing that ignition by fire, friction, concussion, percussion, or detonation may cause an explosion.

Statutory jurisdiction of the above violations of federal law lies concurrently with the Attorney General, FBI, and the Secretary of the Treasury Department. The Alcohol, Tobacco, and Firearms Division (ATFD) of the Treasury Department handles incidents involving property or functions of the Treasury Department and any investigation the Department may request in accord with section 844(i).

SUMMARY

The crime of arson involves the willful and malicious burning of all kinds of buildings and structures, as well as crops, forests, and personal property of another. Even one's own property can be involved if burned with the intent to defraud. It is usually a felony under modern statutes. The detection of arson is primarily the responsibility of the fire department. However, arson investigations are conducted jointly by police and fire department arson investigators. The conviction of an arsonist is nearly always based on circumstantial evidence.

A knowledge of fire chemistry, patterns of fire, building construction features, and burning characteristics of buildings and contents permit investigative specialists to arrive at conclusions regarding fire origins. Teamwork of police and fire arson squad specialists are a necessity in arson solving.

Bomb investigations require trained explosive specialists to combat the wide variety of commercial and homemade explosives that confront the police. The police function in bomb matters includes the protecting of life and property, removal of bomb menace by explosive specialists, and the investigation and apprehension of bomb perpetrators or threateners. Tactical plans for handling bomb emergencies are needed by every police agency.

1. What is the corpus delicti of arson?
2. List eight motives in arson cases.
3. What three things—often referred to as the "fire triangle"—are necessary to produce a fire?
4. Is a confession of setting an incendiary fire sufficient to establish the criminal origin of the fire?
5. Which of the following areas of physical evidence are most likely to reveal criminal design: the outer shell; the inner shell; the point of origin; or the point of greatest damage?
6. Can the offense of arson be committed without the occurrence of a burning?
7. When death occurs as a result of arson, what penalty is prescribed in your state?
8. When a defendant is prosecuted as a conspirator in an arson case, does the prosecutor have to show that the person was actually at the scene of the fire when it occurred, or at any other time?
9. What types of fires are included in the class "B" fire category?
10. Name ten common arson devices.
11. What are six indications of arson?
12. What types of information should you try to obtain from a witness to a fire?
13. Indicate briefly the general difference between high-order and low-order explosives.
14. Is black powder considered a high-order or a low-order explosive?
15. Bombs can generally be classifed in one of two broad categories. What are these two?
16. If you were to take a bomb-threat telephone call, list all the possible information you would attempt to obtain from the caller.
17. What is meant by a "Molotov cocktail"?
18. Where is the National Bomb Data Center located?
19. Of all the questions you might ask an anonymous bomb-threat caller, which of the following would you consider the most important ones: Why did you place the bomb? What does the bomb look like? When is the bomb set to go off? Where is the bomb right now? What is your name?
20. What is the function of the police in bomb matters?

WORK EXERCISE

Write a paper on the actual procedures you would take following the receipt of information set forth in the two problems below. Obviously, you would notify control. What else must be done in order to save lives and property? For example, in problem number 1, how, precisely, would you get the people to leave the theatre without causing panic? What else must be done? In problem number 2, what advice would you give the manager? Keep in mind the content of the letter. What would your plan of action be? Explain. *Note:* As an alternative, these two problems may be the subject of class discussion.

Problem Number 1

At 1900 hours, while proceeding south on Main Street in downtown Center City, your unit (car 18A) is flagged down by a well-dressed man in front of the Majestic Theatre, 605 South Main Street. The individual is quite excited. He identifies himself as manager of the Majestic Theatre, and proceeds to tell you that he just received a telephone call from an unknown person advising him that there was a bomb planted in his theatre. He states that the caller cursed him and hung up before he could obtain any additional information. The manager says that his theatre is just about full and wants to know what he should do as "this is the first time this has ever happened to me."

Problem Number 2

At 1330 hours, an unknown man enters the Acme Supermarket carrying a package wrapped in green paper with a white envelope attached to the top with cellophane tape. The envelope is addressed to J. B. LONG, manager of the market. LONG opens the envelope and notes that the letter was apparently printed on a toy printing press. The note reads as follows:

Acme Supermarket, Mr. J.B. Long

This is a holdup. Do not alarm this man. I repeat: do not alarm this man. He does not know he is robbing your market.

There are 2 bombs in your market and unless you fill this box with bills, I will set them off. I want all bills, no change. Rewrap the package and give it to the man quietly. One little noise and I'll blow you all to hell.

As a safety precaution, I also wired your home residence. So don't try to be a hero.

Don't try to follow this man or walk out of the market to get his license number. I'll be watching.

You have 15 minutes to send this man out your front door with the money or else. Be foolish and I'll blow you all apart.

Pick up the box, go to the safe and fill it up as instructed. Then return, tell the man the product is unsatisfactory. Do not move or call for sixty minutes, or you will kill innocent people. Get busy, Mr. Long.

Suggested for additional study:

Brodie, Thomas G., *Bombs and Bombings,* Charles C. Thomas Co., Springfield, Ill., 1973.

Lenz, Robert R., *Explosives and Bomb Disposal Guide,* Charles C. Thomas Co., Springfield, Ill., 1973.

Meidl, James H., *Explosives and Toxic Hazardous Materials,* Glencoe Press, Beverly Hills, Ca., 1970.

Kidnapping and Extortion

Kidnapping

Crimes against persons, including kidnapping, taking of hostages, extortion, and the threat of violence associated with these crimes, have been increasing in recent years. Kidnappers are demanding millions of dollars in ransom from wealthy persons and business leaders. Terrorists have for years used kidnapping and bombings to force governmental changes or release of their associates from prison. Businesses as well as goverments are becoming targets. Kidnapping and other hostage-type criminal acts are among the most heinous encountered by any law-enforcement agency and are among the most difficult cases to investigate. In these cases, the safety and welfare of the victim(s) are the primary concern of law enforcement.

People have a keen interest in every type of kidnap case. In no other type of crime does public sympathy extend so thoroughly to the victim; people readily cooperate with law enforcement. In kidnap for ransom crimes, particularly during the period in which the victim's fate hangs in the balance, considerable interest in all aspects of these cases is shown by the mass media. Considerable restraint must be exercised by the media in order to ensure the safety of the victim. Kidnap for ransom violations, as well as other types of kidnapping involves two phases in the investigation. The first occurs during the time the victim's fate remains in question. The second happens after the victim has been released and is safe.

The Lindbergh case

This case marks the beginning of federal kidnapping legislation. The early 1930s saw a wave of kidnappings committed by organized gangs. The Lindbergh case of 1932 resulted in many changes in kidnapping laws both by Congress and state legislatures. Today every jurisdiction has kidnap laws similar to the federal statute, which is often referred to as the "Lindbergh Law." Under modern statutes kidnapping is a felony. The special form of kidnapping for ransom is regarded as one of the gravest of crimes; perpetrators frequently receive the death penalty where physical injury or death is involved. Some states have provided for aggravated kidnapping beyond the holding for ransom, such as kidnap for robbery, kidnap for rape, and other forms.

Facts of the Lindbergh Case On March 1, 1932, between 8 P.M. and 10 P.M., Charles Augustus Lindbergh, Jr., twenty-month-old son of Charles Augustus Lindbergh, the famous aviator, and Ann Morrow Lindbergh, the author, was kidnapped. He was taken from his nursery room located on the second floor of his home near Hopewell, New Jersey. The child's absence was discovered at approximately 10 P.M. by his nurse. A search of the premises was immediately made, during which the following ransom note was found on the nursery window sill:

> Dear Sir
>   Have 50000$ ready 25000$ in 20$ bills 15000$ in 10$bills and 10000 in 5$ bills After 2-4 days we will inform you were to deliver the mony. We warn you for making anyding public or for notify the police The child is in gut care
>   Indication for all letters are singnature and three holes

The "signature" was a symbol of two overlapping blue circles. The overlap was colored red. A square hole pierced each of the three parts:

After the Hopewell officers were notified, the report was telephoned to the New Jersey Sate Police, who assumed charge of the investigation. At that time there was no federal kidnapping law. In the search at the scene of the kidnapping, traces of mud were found on the floor of the nursery. Footprints which were impossible to measure were found under the nursery window. A three-section ladder was found about 50 feet [15 meters] from the house. Impressions in the mud under the nursery window revealed where the ladder had been placed to effect access to the nursery window. The two sections of the ladder had been used in reaching the window. One of the two sections was split where it joined the other, indicating that the ladder had been broken during the ascent or descent. There were no bloodstains in or about the nursery. Search and examination failed to reveal any fingerprints. Household and estate employees were questioned and investigated. Colonel Lindbergh designated certain acquaintances to communicate with the kidnapper. Widespread appeals to the kidnapper to start negotiations were made.

A *second* ransom note was received by Colonel Lindbergh on March 6, 1932. It was postmarked Brooklyn, New York, March 4. The note increased the ransom demand to $70,000.

The *third* ransom note was received by Colonel Lindbergh's attorney on March 8, 1932. The third note said that an intermediary appointed by the Lindberghs would not be accepted. It also requested a note in the press; this request was complied with.

On the same date, Dr. John F. Condon ("Jafsie"), a retired school principal from Bronx, New York, published in the *Bronx Home News* an offer to act as go-between and to pay an additional $1000 ransom. The following day, the *fourth* ransom note was received by Condon, which indicated he would be acceptable as a go-between. This was approved by Colonel Lindbergh. About March 10, 1932, $70,000 in currency was received by Condon. He also received the authority to pay out the money as ransom. He immediately started negotiations through newspaper columns for payment of the ransom money.

About 8:30 P.M., March 12, 1932, after receiving an anonymous telephone call, Condon received the *fifth* ransom note. It was delivered by Joseph Perrone, a taxicab driver, who received it from an unidentified stranger. The message said that another note would be found beneath a stone at a vacant stand, 100 feet [30 meters] from an outlying subway station. This note, the *sixth,* was found by Condon, in the place indicated. Following the instructions given in the sixth note, he met an unidentified man, who called himself "John," at Woodlawn Cemetery in New York City. They discussed payment of the ransom money. The stranger agreed to furnish a token of the child's identity. Condon was accompanied by a bodyguard, except when he talked to "John." During the next few days, Condon repeated his advertisements, urging further contact and stating his willingness to pay the ransom.

A baby's sleeping suit, furnished as a token of identity, and a *seventh* ransom note, was received by Condon on March 16, 1932. The suit was delivered to Colonel Lindbergh and later identified. Condon continued his advertisements. The *eighth* ransom note was received by Condon on March 21, 1932. It insisted on complete compliance and told that the kidnapping had been planned for a year. On March 29, 1932, Betty Gow, the Lindbergh nurse, found the infant's thumb guard, worn at the time of the kidnapping, near the entrance to the estate.

The following day, the *ninth* ransom note was received by Condon, threatening to increase the demand to $100,000 and refusing a code for use in newspaper columns. The *tenth* ransom note, received by Condon on April 1, 1932, instructed him to have the money ready the following night, to which Condon replied by an ad in the press. The *eleventh* ransom note was delivered to Condon on April 2, 1932, by an unidentified taxi driver who said he received it from an unknown man. Condon found the *twelfth* ransom note under a stone in front of a greenhouse in The Bronx, as instructed in the eleventh note.

That same evening, by following the instructions contained in the twelfth note, Condon again met a man whom he believed to be "John" in Saint Raymond's cemetery in The Bronx. He persuaded John to reduce the demand to $50,000. This amount was handed to the stranger in exchange for a receipt and the *thirteenth* note, containing instructions to the effect that the kidnapped child could be found on a boat named "Nellie" near Martha's Vineyard, Massachusetts. The stranger then walked north into the park woods. The following day an unsuccessful search for the infant was made near Martha's Vineyard. The search was later repeated. Condon was positive that he would recognize "John" if he ever saw him again.

On May 12, 1932, the body of the kidnapped baby was accidentally found, partly buried and badly decomposed, about 4½ miles [7½ kilometers] southeast of the Lindbergh home. It was 45 feet [14 meters] from the highway, near Mount Rose, New Jersey. The head was crushed; there was a hole in the skull. The body was partially dismembered. The body was positively identified and later cremated at Trenton, New Jersey on May 13, 1932. The coroner's examination showed that the child had been dead for about two months and that death was caused by a blow on the head. The discovery of the Lindbergh child was made by a truck driver's helper.

Three months after the kidnapping, on June 22, 1932, Congress passed an act known as the Lindbergh Kidnap Law which, as later amended, provided the death penalty for transporting a kidnapped person across a state line. The FBI was given jurisdiction and designated by President Franklin D. Roosevelt to coordinate all federal investigative activities. The case developed into a cooperative effort between the New Jersey State Police, the New York City Police, and the FBI.

One of the most significant turns of events in this case came when, in April, 1933, President Roosevelt issued a proclamation requiring the return to the U.S. Treasury of all gold and gold certificates. This was particularly helpful, in view of the fact that $40,000 of the ransom money had been paid in gold certificates. From August 20, 1934, to September of 1934, sixteen gold certificates turned up. Each one was pinpointed on a large map as having come from the metropolitan New York area. The description of the passer of these notes in each instance fitted that of the person described by Condon as "John." On September 18, 1934, the big break in the case came when an official at the Corn Exchange Bank and Trust Company, located in New York City, called the FBI's New York office and said that the bank had received a $10 gold certificate that date. An immediate check of this particular bill disclosed that it had been presented to the bank by a gasoline service station located in New York City. At the service station, an attendant was interviewed. The attendant told a team of New York City Police, New Jersey State Police, and FBI agents that he had received the certificate from a person whom he believed to be of Scandinavian extraction. The attendant's description of the person was noted to fit that of the passer

of other bills in previous weeks. The attendant, suspicious of the certificate (inasmuch as these bills had been recalled), recorded on the bill the license number of suspect's automobile. The license number was traced to Bruno Richard Hauptmann, who lived in The Bronx.

A surveillance was conducted at Hauptmann's residence throughout the night of September 18, 1934. At 9 A.M. the next day, Hauptmann was taken into custody as he was about to enter his automobile. A $20 bill, one of those paid as ransom, was found on Hauptmann. In his house a pair of shoes was found which had been purchased with a $20 bill—also part of the ransom—recovered on September 8. He admitted to several other purchases which had been made with ransom certificates. On the night of September 19, Hauptmann was positively identified by Joseph Perrone, the taxi driver who had received the fifth ransom note.

The following day, ransom certificates in excess of $13,000 were found secreted in the garage of Hauptmann. Shortly thereafter he was identified by Condon as the "John" to whom the ransom had been paid. It was also ascertained that Hauptmann was in possession of a 1931 Dodge sedan automobile which answered the description of a car seen in the vicinity of the Lindbergh home the day prior to the kidnapping. Hauptmann's handwriting was identified by FBI handwriting experts as being identical with that of the ransom notes.

The trial of Hauptmann began on January 3, 1935, at Flemington, New Jersey and continued for five weeks. On February 13, a verdict of guilty was returned against Hauptmann. He was sentenced by the court to be executed during the week of March 18. His attorneys appealed the verdict and the sentence. The New Jersey Supreme Court on October 9 upheld the verdict of the lower court. Hauptmann's appeal to the United States Supreme Court was denied on December 9, 1935. He was to be electrocuted on

January 17, 1936. He was granted a thirty-day reprieve by the governor of New Jersey. On February 17, he was resentenced to be electrocuted during the week of March 30. On March 30, the pardon court of New Jersey denied Hauptmann's petition for clemency. He was electrocuted on April 3.

One of the by-products of the Lindbergh case was a mass of misinformation received from well-meaning but uninformed, highly imaginative individuals. Another was a deluge of letters written by demented persons, publicity seekers, and frauds. It was essential, however, that all possible clues, regardless of their prospects of success, be carefully reviewed and checked for relevancy.

In one of the frauds perpetrated in this case, a man named Gaston B. Means succeeded in obtaining $100,000 from Evalyn Walsh McLean, a wealthy woman from Washington, D.C. McLean endeavored through Means, an acquaintance, to assist Colonel Lindbergh in gaining the return of his child by paying the ransom money. Means, who obtained $100,000 in ransom money from McLean, had succeeded in convincing her that he was in contact with the kidnappers. He fabricated a fabulous tale of having been approached to participate in a "big kidnapping." When McLean demanded the return of her $100,000 and the additional money she had advanced Means for "expenses," he said that he had turned the money over to an unknown man called "The Fox"—the alleged leader of the kidnappers. "The Fox" was subsequently identified by the FBI as Norman T. Whitaker, a disbarred Washington attorney. The FBI's investigation of Means resulted in his conviction of embezzlement and larceny after trust, for which he was sentenced to fifteen years in a federal penitentiary. In addition, both Means and Whitaker were convicted of conspiracy to defraud; Both received prison sentences for this crime.

The Federal Kidnapping Statute[1] com-monly known as the "Lindbergh Law," was passed on June 22, 1932, making it a federal violation to transport in interstate or foreign commerce a kidnapped person for purpose of ransom, reward, or otherwise. Included in the "or otherwise" clause of the kidnapping statute were such offenses as sex cases, bank cases, hitchhikers, and parents taking a child without their having legal custody. After twenty-four hours, there is a presumption that a victim may have been taken out of the state. This presumption permits the FBI to enter the case and work cooperatively with the local police on such kidnappings. In the event that evidence developed as a result of the investigation indicates that there was no interstate transportation involved, the FBI will terminate its investigation and cooperate with local authorities in every way possible. The kidnap statute was amended October 24, 1972, to establish a federal kidnap offense which requires no interstate transportation when the victim is a specified foreign official or official guest of the United States. In addition, a kidnapping within the special maritime, territorial, or aircraft jurisdictions of the United States is now a federal offense regardless of the occurrence of interstate transportation.

Kidnap Investigations

Kidnap where no ransom is involved

When a complaint alleging a kidnapping is received, one of the major problems is to get as much information as possible from the complainant. Advise the person calling to remain calm and to please stay on the line. Tell the person certain information is needed. At this time, police are interested in answers to questions involving who, how, what, when, and where. There is a tendency on the part of many complainants to label every disappearance as a kidnapping. Police must distinguish between legitimate cases

---

[1] United States Code, title 18, secs. 1201 and 1202.

Figure 20-1. Photo showing value of an artist's sketch of a kidnap robbery suspect.

and hoax cases involving runaways, one spouse leaving another, "mother complex" kidnappings (baby-sitter taking child), child stealing by one of the parents not legally entitled to custody, etc. At this time the specific type of kidnapping should be determined: kidnap in connection with another crime (robbery), kidnap for sex (rape), kidnap for transportation (hitchhiking), etc. The following types of information should be the first considerations in a kidnap investigation:

1. Name and address of the caller, telephone number, present location.
2. Date and time of abduction.
3. Place of kidnap.
4. Brief rundown of what happened. Was any force used?
5. Activities of victim previous to abduction.
6. Description of victim, including clothing worn, if victim is still missing.
7. Description of suspect, including clothing worn.
8. Whether or not a vehicle was involved.

Get description, license number, and distinguishing features.
9. Direction of travel when last seen.
10. Whether there are any witnesses or suspects.

When the above information is received, a broadcast should be made, the watch commander notified, and an immediate investigation undertaken by detective specialists. This investigation should include such investigative procedures as a thorough interview with the victim as soon as possible; search of the crime scene; interview with witnesses; initiation of follow-up broadcasts and teletypes; exhibiting specialized criminal mug books to victim and witnesses; checking similar M.O.'s; preparing an Ident-a-kit picture or having an artist's sketch made (see Figure 20-1); maintaining liaison with other law-enforcement agencies for possible suspects; eliminating suspects by checking out their activities and whereabouts on the day in question; and pursuing other investigation based on case developments.

Kidnap where ransom is involved

During phase 1, while the victim's life still is in jeopardy, there are two objectives:

1. Safe return of the victim
2. Identifying and apprehending the person responsible

When a call is received from a complainant indicating a kidnap and ransom demand, the caller should be requested to remain on the line in order that the officer might obtain certain needed information. Generally complaint or desk officers immediately channel a call of this type to the particular division that handles kidnap cases. Initially, the same data as that sought in cases where no ransom is involved should be obtained. In addition, the following types of information, questions, requests, procedures or instructions are in order:

Ask if there has been a demand for payment of money.

If a ransom letter, note or telephone call has been received, obtain the exact wording.

Advise caller not to handle the note or letter and to see that no one else handles it.

Ask if anyone else knows of the contents of the letter or note or call; if so, ascertain that person's identity.

Advise the complainant to refrain from divulging the contents of the letter, note, or telephone call to anyone except police officials.

Emphasize the importance of silence as being essential to the victim's safety; say that this matter must be treated with utmost secrecy.

Caution the caller not to disturb anything at the scene and to keep others from walking around or disturbing anything in the areas involved.

Start a log in which the watch commander or other high-ranking officer chronologically records facts, things done, assignments, etc.

Arrange for a personal interview.

This interview should be conducted by a high-ranking officer at victim's residence. Every action should be guarded. All activity around the victim's home should be kept at a low profile to avoid arousing suspicion of the kidnapper or the public. The interview with the victim's family should include the telling of police procedures in kidnap cases; the obtaining of the family confidence by citing experiences in these cases; and soliciting the family's full cooperation. Questions asked of the victim's family should be penetrating and exhaustive. As much information as possible should be obtained.

Should members of the press have information that a kidnapping has occurred, the officer in charge should solicit their cooperation in order to bring about the mutual objective—the safe return of the vicitm. All press inquiries should be handled by the ranking officer. Members of the press can unwittingly destroy evidence, frighten or alarm the kidnapper, and block efforts to return the victim or complete the ransom negotiations. Withholding of information from the press is temporary and is no infringement upon the "people's right to know" because the information ultimately will be published when the immediate danger to the victim has passed. If kidnappers are kept in the dark, they can only guess at whether the family has contacted the authorities, what investigative measures have been taken, what evidence has been found, and other such information.

Other types of procedures, questions, requests, or instructions that are often very helpful to the investigation involve the following:

Determine the method of entry used so

that the area can be processed for possible evidence.

Obtain and preserve the ransom note for laboratory processing.

Furnish the family with an exact copy of the note in the event it is needed by them for negotiations.

Review the ransom note, letter, or telephone instructions with the family to make sure that they understand the contents.

Make sure that the person answering the suspect's telephone call follows instructions of the officer in charge.

Determine the financial status of the family.

Determine if the family intends to pay the ransom; officers should avoid giving any opinion as to ransom payments.

Ascertain how the members of the family can raise the ransom money and have it available should they decide to meet the demand.

Help parents in their decision as to who will make the payoff.

Obtain information concerning all cars that might be used in payoff negotiations—complete description, license plate, accessories.

Discuss with family ways in which they can verify if victim is alive.

Obtain permission for officers to stay in home of family during crisis. Knowledge of the presence of investigators in the victim's home should be carefully guarded.

Arrange for private telephone line and tracing of all incoming calls.

Arrange to obtain serial numbers of all ransom bills.

Obtain permission from family to intercept mail/telegrams should they be received.

Discuss with family placing of a newspaper ad should such an action be necessary.

Obtain a complete description of the victim (including clothing worn) and the best available photograph of her or him.

Determine if there is anything unusual in the family background.

Obtain family history—particularly concerning the victim.

Request permission of family to examine personal possesions of the victim, such as a diary or letters, for possible leads.

Ascertain whether fingerprints of victim are available anywhere.

Identify all associates of victim.

Obtain the names of the family doctor, dentist, priest or minister, and hospital should such information be needed.

Arrange with family to make recordings of all calls.

Obtain specimens of victim's handwriting.

Ascertain the identity of servants employed in the household. Investigate their backgrounds, how their positions were obtained, who gave recommendations for them, etc.

Ascertain the identity of tradespeople, delivery persons, and other past employees with whom members of family have had disagreements.

Obtain the location of victim's place of employment or business.

Determine the action of the family for an appropriate time prior to and including the day of the kidnapping—get specific times and places.

Assign unmarked mobile units to strategic areas for surveillance and ready availability should circumstances warrant. In all instances, however, the assigned officers must refrain from conducting any investigative activity that would jeopardize the safety of the victim.

Based on the facts and circumstances, conduct any other appropriate investigation that can be accomplished without endangering the life of the victim.

A kidnap/ransom attempt that could have involved $2 million to $8 million was cleared in short order. Two masked, armed suspects were killed as they were about to kidnap an automobile tire magnate from his home in a wealthy suburb of a large metropolitan city. In this case, the two suspects, after parking their vehicle in the driveway of the victim's home, donned rubber Halloween ghoul masks and surgical gloves. They then walked up to the front door of the victim's estate. When a female police officer, posing as a maid, inquired as to who was at the door, one of the suspects replied, "Parcel post delivery, ma'am." Four detectives were stationed inside the house at the time. Peering out the windows, detectives saw both suspects with pistols in their hands at the front door. One of the detectives opened the front door quickly and jumped to the side. Both suspects dashed inside the house with drawn guns. Officers opened fire with shotguns and pistols, dropping both of the outlaws. One of them died immediately, and the other died shortly after being taken to the hospital.

Notes found on one of the suspects indicated that they had hoped to hold the victim for $2 million to $8 million in ransom. In the suspects' car, police found another pair of surgical gloves, a rope, a blanket, ammunition, a rifle, and another ghoul mask. In a wallet of one of the suspects was a scrap of paper which showed these calculations: 10 × $200,000 = $2 million; 20 × $400,000 = $8 million. The victim's telephone number was also listed on the paper.

The police had talked the victim into getting out of the house during the time they occupied it, following a tip they had received about the possible kidnapping. Both suspects had long police records.

The Chowchilla kidnapping

One of the most extraordinary kidnappings in recent years occurred on July 15, 1976, sometime after 2:30 P.M., near the town of Chowchilla, California. Chowchilla is 120 miles [200 kilometers] southeast of San Francisco. Three stocking-masked, armed suspects forced the driver of a school bus containing twenty-six children to stop the vehicle by blocking the roadway with a white Dodge van. The van was the size of a delivery truck. As the driver halted the bus to avoid the van, a stocking-masked man, dressed in white coveralls and armed with two guns, stepped out of the van. The suspect ordered the bus driver to open the bus door. At that time, the first suspect was joined by two other stocking-masked suspects (also wearing white coveralls), who had driven up in a second van of approximately the same size. The school bus was then driven by one of the suspects about a mile to a dry creek bed, where it was concealed behind a cluster of tall bamboo canes. The bus was located later that day by a sheriff's air search.

After hiding the bus, the suspects transferred the school children (ages five to fifteen) and the bus driver to the two small vans mentioned above. After driving around for about eleven hours, the suspects drove both vans into a rock quarry near Livermore, California, about 95 miles [160 kilometers] northwest of Chowchilla. At the quarry, all the captives were ordered into a large moving van. This van had been buried in one section of the rock quarry. The two small vans were parked close to the moving van's shaft entrance. A tarpaulin was placed over the shaft entrance and the panel truck door to keep the children and their bus driver from knowing their whereabouts. The moving van was approximately 25 feet long, 8 feet wide, and 7 feet high [7½ × 2½ × 2 meters]. It had an opening cut into the roof with a ladder leading down into the interior. As the children were ordered one by one into the van, each child's name, age, and a personal item or piece of clothing was obtained from them to prove that the twenty-seven had indeed been kidnapped and could be identified. A list of the names was written on a brown paper bag. The trousers, boots, and identification of the bus driver were also taken from him. He was ordered into the buried van and a flashlight was given to him.

When all the captives had entered the van, the opening was sealed off with sheets of scrap metal, plywood, dirt, debris, and heavy truck batteries. The moving van itself had obviously been prepared in advance for the abduction. It contained water, bread, potato chips, and breakfast cereal. In addition, it had a makeshift portable toilet, several mattresses, and a ventilation system consisting of two pieces of 4-inch flexible rubber tubing connected to two 5-inch openings at the front and side of the van. Air was pumped in and out of the van with two battery-driven fans.

On the following day, after approximately twenty-seven hours of captivity (sixteen in the buried moving van), the bus driver, with the help of some of the older children, succeeded in digging out of the underground prison. They used an 18-inch piece of 3- by 4-inch wood used for bracing inside the bus. After freeing all captives, the bus driver and the children walked to the lights in the rock quarry, where they contacted an employee of the company who in turn notified the police. Thereafter the children were given the necessary medical treatment and then returned to their parents.

Aspects of the Chowchilla Kidnapping Investigation The moving van used to imprison the children and bus driver was determined to have been purchased on November 20, 1975, from the Palo Alto Transfer and Storage Company. The van was bought by a person using the name Mark Hall who was later identified as defendant Fred N. Woods.

A security guard at the rock quarry told the police of an incident at the quarry in November, 1975, in which three men were questioned about their digging of a trench. They used a bulldozer. Only one name was recorded: Fred N. Woods, the owner's son. The owner, when questioned by the security officer, confirmed the fact that his son had the run of the rock quarry. This incident was a significant lead in pinpointing defendant Woods as a logical suspect.

The California license number 1C91414 of one of the two small vans was jotted down by a Chowchilla woman. She was suspicious of the occupants, whom she had observed in Chowchilla the day before the kidnapping. The license number was subsequently traced to defendant Woods through an Oakland, California, surplus dealer, who recognized Woods' photo. The dealer identified him as the person to whom he sold two vans on November 24 or 25, 1975.

Under voluntary hypnosis, the school bus driver was able to furnish the license number (1C91414) of one of the two vans used by suspects, as well as all but one digit of the license number of the second van.

Some of the school children recalled hearing the names Fred and James used during the kidnap ordeal—which were the first names of two of the defendants.

The police checked the personnel (past and present) employed in the rock quarry. One of the employees remembered that the owner's son, Frederick Newhall Woods IV, had been arrested "back somewhere up in the mountains for some kind of petty thing or other." A check of Downieville, California, police records showed that on October 6, 1974, three young men were arrested on a charge of joyriding. They pleaded guilty and paid a fine of $125 each plus completing one years' probation. A photograph of Woods was obtained from the Downieville Police Department and shown to kidnap victims. James Schoenfeld and his younger brother Richard Allen Schoenfeld were determined to be close associates of Woods. These three were then considered the principal suspects of this case.

A handwritten ransom note containing the names of twenty-six Chowchilla school-children and their bus driver was found in one of the housing units in the Portola Valley 78-acre estate belonging to the Woods family. The note had never been sent. The defendants planned to demand $5 million as a ransom for the children's return. The plan called for the ransom money to be air-dropped to the defendants in a remote, desolate area of the Santa Cruz mountains. The money was to be placed in a shatterproof container.

It was determined that defendant James Schoenfeld rented a 40-foot mobile home on the outskirts of Reno, Nevada on April 23, 1976. The mobile home was rented under the name of Ralph Lester Snider. The owner of the trailer park recalled seeing both Schoenfeld and a person whom he believed to be defendant Woods together at the mobile park on July 17, 1976, two days after the kidnapping. They were cleaning out the mobile unit. The trailer park address was given by James Schoenfeld when he obtained a Nevada driver's license under the name of Ralph Snider earlier in 1976. It was also found that the name Ralph Lester Snider, which defendants James Schoenfeld and Fred Woods both used, belonged to a six-year-old boy who had died in an auto accident in San Jose, California, in 1960. (It is not uncommon for "street wise" suspects to use identification documents based on birth certificates of deceased persons.)

James Schoenfeld, three days after the kidnapping, tried unsuccessfully to enter Canada. On two occasions he was denied entry. Canadian border officers recalled that he had some guns in his car and two identifications other than his own: those of Fred Woods and Ralph Lester Snider. He also had some back-packing and camping equipment.

The FBI's investigation disclosed that James Schoenfeld sold guns and ammunition to a sporting goods store in Spokane, Washington on July 19, 1976, and other guns to a pawn shop in Coeur D'Alene, Idaho, on July 20. Agents combed Idaho newspaper classified advertising of vehicles for sale. Seeking an ad that asked for about the same amount of cash that Schoenfeld had raised through the sale of the guns, agents located a Coeur D'Alene man who sold Schoenfeld a 1955 Chevrolet van for $250. The defendant was arrested in this van on July 29 by officers of the Menlo Park, Redwood City, and Atherton, California, police departments. James Schoenfeld's younger brother, Richard Allen Schoenfeld, surrendered to the Alameda County District Attorney at Oakland, California, on July 23.

Based on information furnished by the FBI, the Royal Canadian Mounted Police arrested defendant Fred N. Woods on July 29 at Vancouver, British Columbia, after he had called for mail at the general delivery section of the downtown post office. At the time, Woods was using the name Ralph Snider, but he later admitted his true name. He was released to the FBI in Blaine, Washington, and was later returned to Madera County, California, by sheriff's deputies.

The evidence in this kidnapping case consisted of 4800 items, according to the disclosure made by the prosecution at a pretrial hearing. Some of the evidence released after guilty pleas were entered by the three defendants indicated that the kidnapping had been planned for about a year. The defense chose a court trial rather than a jury trial for all defendants, in the belief that a jury would be antagonistic because children were involved in the case. All three defendants were convicted of twenty-four counts of kidnapping for ransom and three counts of kidnapping with bodily harm. James L. Schoenfeld and Frederick Newhall Woods IV were sentenced to life imprisonment without parole, and Richard Allen Schoenfeld to life imprisonment.

Investigation during the second phase (after the victim has been returned or the body has been located)

When victim has been returned, the first thing to be done if a child is involved, is to let the parents know that their loved one is alive and safe. Then the investigation changes. An all-out investigation is conducted in accordance with the second objective—to identify and apprehend the persons responsible for the kidnapping. Since the life of the victim no longer hangs in the balance, the media can be of great help. Assistance of the media might consist of the publication or showing of such things as description of the wanted suspect; an artist's sketch or Ident-a-kit photo; identity of suspect; the type of vehicle being sought; ransom lists; and partial details of the crime. Such publicity can cause persons to come forward with information. This may result in new leads and evidence.

There are, however, some facts of a case that *should not be given publicity*. These include confidential investigative techniques; the plan of the investigation; the investigative steps being taken; the identities of witnesses; details of the ransom note; information concerning the payoff spot; and other information of a confidential nature. There also may be information, which, if disclosed, could jeopardize the defendant's right to a fair trial. Facts of a confidential nature are kept secret so that law-enforcement authorities can be sure that a suspect has direct knowledge of the crime, rather than information published in news releases.

During the investigation, the officer in charge should conduct regular briefings in order that all investigative personnel working on the kidnap case are kept informed. Investigation should be conducted in every aspect of the case suggested by the information received. Investigative activities and procedures include

Thorough interview with the victim. All minute details should be obtained.

Obtaining of victim's clothing for laboratory examination. Clothing may contain some transfer evidence (hair or fibers, for example).

Coverage of all leads in the order of priority. As leads are covered they are checked off, and new leads given to the investigator as the case expands.

Thorough crime-scene searches of the areas where victim disappeared, where victim is hidden (if known), and where ransom is paid. In addition, photographs of all pertinent areas should be taken.

Collecting of soil samples from the immediate area of the crime scene and from various other locations near the scene, at distances of 10, 50, and 100 feet [3, 15, and 30 meters] in all compass directions. Each sample should be numbered and identified.

Reinterviews of all witnesses where necessary.

Placing stops against suspects and/or vehicles.

Preparing an artist's sketch or Ident-a-kit photo.

Contacting informants for possible leads.

Conducting surveillances as needed.

Processing for fingerprints of all areas where suspect might have been.

Finding out why a particular victim was picked for abduction. Answers could furnish possible leads.

Determining whether kidnapper (writer of ransom note) is familiar with victim's residential area, habits, financial status, etc.

Obtaining handwriting, fingerprints, palm prints of all members of family and household.

Maintaining liaison with other law-enforcement agencies for possible suspects and coverage of leads.

Covering neighborhoods of pertinent areas involved for possible suspects. Interviews with neighbors in such areas should be exhaustive and cover a period of time prior to the kidnapping.

Dictating or preparing inserts for report on all case developments and coverage of leads. These inserts should be prepared so that they can be included in the finished report prepared in the case.

Conducting all pertinent investigation based upon developments in the case, as well as upon other areas, as experience dictates.

Hostage Kidnappings

Many of the larger police departments, the FBI, and other federal agencies now have *hostage negotiators* ready to deal with cases involving hostages. The idea behind negotiating is to resolve hostage incidents without bloodshed—to diffuse potentially explosive situations by talking the suspect into reacting rationally. Hostage negotiation was pioneered by a volunteer team of three New York City detectives. The FBI now has trained hostage negotiators in each of its fifty-nine field offices. The Los Angeles Police Department uses highly trained and disciplined SWAT (special weapons and tactics) units to handle barricaded suspects and other hostage situations.

When people are taken as hostages, the last thing captors are interested in is having to kill the hostages; hostages are the leverage of terrorists. Once they kill the hostages, they lose all their bargaining power. In these situations, the specific moves made by police toward terrorists must often be improvised to meet the specific circumstances of the case and to take advantage of the personality quirks of the kidnapper. No rigid rules can be laid down since every hostage situation involves many different factors.

Hostage/kidnap cases involve three important rules. The first is: *Give the terrorist a chance to save face.* Orders for unconditional surrender place the hostage in needless danger. Strategy takes place in the area of ego, it has been said. The kidnapper has an ego, the police chief has an ego, and agents have egos. Law-enforcement personnel working on these situations must remain flexible. Efforts must be made to get suspects to feel that they can walk out and still be human beings. Law-enforcement officers should use toughness only as a last resort. In rare cases where a person is bent on wanton killing or self-destruction, negotiation techniques can be ineffective, and armed assault may be proper. Negotiating is not the solution to every situation. There are times when words have to be replaced with weapons. However, hostage negotiations give the police another way to do their job.

The second rule is: *Always tell the truth.* Police authorities cannot get themselves into a position of lying, since it weakens the position of the negotiator, who must establish credibility. It is better to tell the captor that something is impossible than to make promises which cannot be kept.

The third rule is: *Be patient.* No effort should be made to force the situation. Time is always on the side of the people on the outside. A basic concept to follow in critical situations is that good decisions are based on complete and accurate facts. The fundamental goal should be to proceed in such a way that no one is hurt. Terrorists can be caught and property can be replaced, but human life can never be restored.

On March 9, 1977, twelve Hanafi Muslim terrorists led by Hamaas Abdul Khaalis and armed with long knives, pistols, and sawed-off shotguns, broke into three Washington, D.C. buildings. They seized 134 hostages. The raiders stated they wanted revenge for the 1973 murders of fellow Hanafi Muslims. Negotiating teams which included the metropolitan police of Washington, D.C., the FBI, and government representatives and ambassadors from Egypt, Iran, and Pakistan were employed. The teams were successful in causing the release of the 134 hostages after thirty hours of captivity.

It is interesting to note that just six hours prior to the release Khaalis vowed to begin cutting off heads of hostages and proceed to hang the headless bodies out of the window. At that time, Khaalis was reminded by negotiators that he had promised to feed his captives and urged him to permit lunch to be sent in. By the time the lunch orders were filled, Khaalis had cooled off. Diverting his attention from killing to a minor item like food proved to be a good tactic. The *wait and talk strategy* employed by the negotiators ultimately persuaded the terrorist leader to release the hostages. Khaalis, during a conversation with the negotiators, indicated that he considered it humiliating to be arrested and taken to jail. The negotiators acted in accordance with the first rule (giving the suspect a chance to save face): an agreement was made for Khaalis to be freed without bond. However, no stipulation was made that he would be immune from prosecution.

Hostage takers are said to fall into one of three categories: (1) the ordinary or professional criminal, (2) the political terrorist, and (3) the mentally unbalanced or psychotic hostage. Kidnappers in category 1 are regarded as the most predictable. They usually do not intend to take hostages. But when they are trapped, they use their victims or customers to bargain for escape. Sometimes a criminal will use the manager of a bank or supermarket as a hostage in demanding money. Hostage takers in cate-

gory 2 are the most dangerous. They seldom agree to negotiate and are usually acting in accordance with their ideals, or a cause. In this instance the negotiator tries to redirect the hostage taker's thinking. Terrorists usually claim to be revolutionaries fighting for a cause. They often vow to die as martyrs in support of that cause. They usually avoid costly assaults where there is little chance of success. Mass kidnappings generally offer terrorists too many problems; the larger the number of victims, the more improbable the success is. This is why the majority of kidnappings involve only one victim. The major exception occurs in the hijacking of planes, because they cannot be immobilized without a catastrophe to all within. Hijacking ultimately depends on the expectation that a friendly state will give the kidnappers sanctuary.

Mentally unbalanced or psychotic hostage takers usually are looking for forums to get their messages across. They regard themselves as being trapped by society or unknown forces. They often have a wish for someone to take control and talk them out of dying. This is one of the areas where negotiators can best function. It is not uncommon for those who harbor strong feelings of frustration to commit suicide.

In any hostage situation, one of the initial steps is to establish a line of communication with the captor. The telephone is a good way and gives the negotiator an opportunity to develop a one-to-one relationship with the hostage taker. Negotiators can also be valuable in hijackings where hostages are being held aboard a grounded airplane or in instances where a band of political terrorists is holding hostages. Negotiators try to formulate a psychological profile of the suspect after he makes his first move. Friends, neighbors, associates, relatives are interviewed regarding all aspects of the captor's personality. Knowing how the hostage taker will react enables police to plan tactics that are specifically designed for the situation.

Considerable interest in terrorism has been shown by many United States firms with overseas operations. Corporate executives are likewise showing considerable interest in this criminal problem and are taking various types of training to cope with it. Security consultants and bodyguards are now in great demand. The Society for Industrial Security has held many conferences on defense strategy and tactics against bombing, bombing threats, extortion, kidnapping, and assassination. As a result of terrorist activity, many new anti-terrorist and anti-kidnapping devices in the electronic, tear gas, protective body armor, and automobile safety equipment and other protective areas are now being sold by various companies. The Central Intelligence Agency (CIA) has expressed fears that terrorism will increase in the years ahead.

Throughout all negotiations, the hostage taker and the victims should be contained within a confined area. In addition, an outer perimeter should be established to keep out traffic and curious people to prevent interference with the police operation.

Child Stealing

This offense is legally against the parent or other legal guardian and not against the child. It is only necessary that the abduction be against the will or without the consent of the parent, guardian, or person having legal custody. In the absence of any judicial decree granting the custody of the child to one spouse, the other spouse would not be guilty of child stealing if she or he takes the child away against the other parent's will. In the statute on child stealing, the consent of the child under the age specified is no defense to a charge of that crime, because the child is considered to be incapable of giving legal consent.

In one case, a woman stole her four-year-old son during a visit with him arranged through a county welfare department adoption agency at an agency office. The boy was a ward of the court at the time. He was in the custody and care of foster parents, who were in the process of adopting the boy. About the time of the child's disappearance, the foster parents were waiting for the boy in a car parked outside the adoption agency. In this case, prosecutive action was instituted against the mother for child stealing.

Extortion

Extortion is the obtaining of property from another with that person's consent, but where such consent is induced by wrongful use of force or fear; it is also the act of forcing a public officer to do some official act by means of threats. To constitute extortion, the wrongful use of force or fear must produce consent.[2] Typical are ordinary cases of *blackmail*. Extortion in some jurisdictions is called blackmail. It differs from robbery in that choice is given to the victim. In robbery, the intimidation is so extreme as to overcome the will of the victims and cause them to part with money or property without consent.

Victims of extortion cases can be railroads, airlines, ships, banks, amusement centers, water supplies, power plants, municipal stadiums, famous people, movie stars, politicians, corporation executives, ordinary people or even presidents. Extortionists have been known to pick names at random from newspaper articles, directories, or telephone books.

Threats to kill, kidnap, or injure a person; ransom demands for release of a kidnapped person; and threats to destroy property are investigated by the FBI under the Federal

---

[2] *People v. Biggs*, 172 P. 152, 153.

Extortion Statute.[3] The FBI can work on these threats if they are transmitted in interstate commerce or sent through the United States Postal Service. Where letters accuse a person of a crime or injure his or her reputation, they are investigated by postal inspectors if the letters are sent through the mails. Federal prosecution under the Hobbs Act is often used against extortioners who attempt to obtain money from federally insured banks or loan companies by threats against employees and their families. This act prohibits interfering with commerce by robbery, extortion, or attempting or conspiring to do so.

Extortionists deliver their threats by telephone or by letters. Threats can include personal injury, mutilation, or killing. Others involve damaging, burning, or blowing up property (houses, hotels, business establishments, etc.). In some cases, threats are used merely to antagonize or frighten a victim or to cause mental anguish. An extortionist often sends letters to families of kidnap victims demanding money for the return of the victim, thereby taking advantage of the family's predicament. Invariably the threats will indicate harm or injury should the police be notified. The extortioner usually works alone, despite the sending of messages which may carry the pronoun "we." Threats made are seldom actually carried out. However, threats against life or property cannot be ignored—appropriate police action must be taken.

Payoff locations chosen by an extortionist may be any place that suits the suspect's purpose. The location may be a church, a trash barrel, an alley, a telephone booth, a cemetery, near a certain monument, in a ravine, etc. Suspects have been known to send victims on several false runs to prospective payoff spots in an effort to see whether the police are covering a particular

area. Sometimes a suspect will ride a bus or drive a car by the location, hoping to spot police surveillance activity. The extortioner may even call the victim and accuse him or her of contacting the police, hoping to further intimidate the victim into full compliance.

Investigation of extortion

The solution of extortion cases often depends upon the complete cooperation of the victim. In these cases, the first concern of police is the safety of the victim; recovery of extortion money and apprehension of suspects is secondary. If a letter is involved, both the letter and envelope may furnish valuable evidence as to the educational background of the writer; spelling, choice of words, punctuation, etc, should be studied. A thorough interview with the victim often results in the description of a logical suspect. The suspect may be a discharged or disgruntled employee, a business competitior, or a jealous suitor. She or he could be someone seeking revenge for some past incident, someone with a long-standing hatred or jealousy of victim, or a vindictive neighbor. Seemingly irrelevant information may not mean much to the complainant during an interview, but such "trivia" may provide valuable answers to the investigator in identifying a suspect.

In the coverage of extortion payoffs, many things must be taken into account. These include coordination, the number of surveillants needed, means of communication, photographic equipment, vehicles, types of communication equipment or other methods of contact, observation posts, aircraft support, dress, meals, and relief. Considerations vary, depending upon the facts, circumstances, location, and terrain to be traversed. In many respects extortion investigation procedures are similar to those of kidnap investigations. Investigations are governed by the identity and lifestyle of the victim, location of occurrence, and other ac-

---

[3]United States Code, title 18, secs. 873, 875, 876, and 877.

tivities of the victim—employment, recreation, social, etc.

Extortion threats where a telephone is used.

The following procedures are in order in telephone extortion threats:

Ascertain date and exact time call was received.

Determine what was said and by whom it was said.

Find out what threats were made and what instructions were given.

Inquire whether any background noises were heard: music, traffic, churchbells, etc.

Ask if the suspect stated that she or he would call again. Ask if suspect stated when that would happen.

Ascertain whether any regional or foreign accent was detected in the suspect's voice.

The victim should be advised that if any additional calls are received, he or she should cooperate with the caller, take detailed notes of the message, and record the exact time, date, and directions of payoff. If possible, arrange to record the call: have the victim ask the caller to repeat instructions, even if they are understood by the victim. In addition, have instructions repeated to make sure they are accurate. Endeavor to have the call traced by keeping the caller on the line as long as possible. The victim should ask questions such as "With whom am I talking?" "How do I know this isn't a joke?" "Why did you pick me?" "What denominations of money do you want?" "Where is the money to be delivered?" "When will I get further instructions?" "How will I know when I reach the location?" "What guarantees do I have that you will keep your word?" Have the intended victim ask as many of these questions as possible.

In one attempted extortion case, the manager of a supermarket received a telephone call from an unknown person, stating he was holding the manager's wife and child hostage in his car. He advised the manager to meet him at a designated spot with all the money in the store to secure their safe release. The manager immediately telephoned his home, knowing that his wife had not planned to leave the house that afternoon. The manager received no answer. He then called the police, who sent a unit to the manager's residence. It was then determined that the wife and child were at home and unharmed.

When asked why she had not answered the phone when her husband called, the wife replied that she had received a call a short time prior to her husband's attempt to reach her. The call was from a person identifying himself as a telephone company lineman. He informed her that the line was being worked on, and told her not to answer the phone for at least an hour. The payoff spot was covered by the police but the extortioner failed to show up.

Later the same day, the manager of a supermarket in a city 70 miles [115 kilometers] distant received a similar extortion telephone call. This manager also called his residence, received no answer, and then notified the police. The same M.O. had been used in this instance, but this time the extortioner made his appearance at the payoff spot. He was apprehended by police. The suspect had a loaded automatic pistol and a loaded revolver in his possession at the time of his arrest.

Extortion threats where a letter is received

The following procedures are in order in extortion cases involving letters:

Ask when the letter was received.

Find out how it was delivered.

Get the postmark and date on the letter.

Learn if the letter was handwritten, hand printed, or typed.

Note the signature on the letter.

Request the recipient to maintain absolute secrecy and not to handle the letter or envelope or permit anyone else to touch it; instruct the complainant not to reveal the contents to anyone except law-enforcement authorities.

Instruct complainant to maintain a normal routine around house and office.

Ask complainant whether she or he suspects anyone of sending letter.

Find out if any prior communication has been received.

Obtain and preserve the extortion letter for laboratory examination.

Interview victim in depth for possible suspects.

Tape record all calls—with victim's permission.

Consult with telephone company officials regarding the tracing of calls to victim's home or office.

Brief all personnel involved in the case; keep everyone fully informed.

Find out the identity, license numbers, and description of all cars which victim owns or has access to, should they be used in a payoff transaction.

Make certain that victim's movements are coordinated with police instructions at all times during the crisis.

Organize personnel, vehicles and equipment for any necessary surveillance procedures.

Get fingerprints and palm prints of victim and others who are known to have handled the letter or envelope.

Investigate the area of the victim's residence if it is relevant to the facts, circumstances, location, etc., of the case. Extortionists have been known to observe their intended victims before and during the period of the extortion demands in order to check on victims' reaction to their threats.

Oversee the preparation of the extortion package.

Alert all personnel and the victim to the danger of the suspect stopping or intercepting the victim at any point along the payoff route and relieving him or her of the package.

Check anonymous letter file of local and state police, and FBI for similar letters.

Trace the paper and envelope used by the extortioner.

Record license numbers of all cars passing a payoff location; a motion picture camera or a camera with a telephoto lens, as well as binoculars, can assist in this surveillance. Should a payoff fail to materialize, a review of car license numbers may suggest possible suspects. Suspects have been known to drive or ride a bus by the payoff location in an effort to spot police coverage.

If a suspect is taken into custody, fingerprints and palm prints should be taken for comparison with the unknown prints obtained in the investigation. Handwriting or hand printing specimens should also be obtained from the suspect, depending upon whether the letter was written or printed. Voiceprint samples should also be obtained for comparison with tape recordings made during the extortion calls. It should also be determined whether the suspect has access to a particular make of typewriter similar to that used to prepare the extortion letter (if the extortion letter was typed). In one case, a fingerprint of a suspect was found on a typewriter ribbon spool. Typewriter ribbons may also disclose identifying data. Other investigation can be conducted as the case progresses.

In an unusual recent Florida extortion plot, the suspect—an attorney—was apprehended as he attempted to recover an extorted package of money. The victim, the widow of the chairman of the board of a large Southern liquor distillery, received a 400-

word message punched out in plastic tape and attached to several sheets of paper. The extortion note stated, "Whether you live or die depends on the decision you are about to make. You will deliver $200,000 according to directions or die." The victim was directed to check a package that had been left on the balcony of her apartment. The message also said, "It is harmless, but the meaning is clear"—a dead fish was found in the package.

To further emphasize the extortioner's demand, the note told the victim to "have one of your servants stand on the balcony between 9 and 9:05 A.M. tomorrow. A steel-jacketed bullet fired from a high-powered rifle will tear off a portion of his skull." The extortionist directed one of victim's employees, who was named in the note, to take the money to a bank of telephones at Miami International Airport that evening. The victim's representative was then directed to proceed to a Miami Beach restaurant. Successive telephone calls directed him to go to a motel, then another restaurant, and then to walk along a causeway bridge until he saw a piece of string tied to the bridge railing. Here the messenger was to drop the money into the water.

During the time in which the messenger was trying to locate the string, surveillance detectives noticed a movement on the surface of the water under the bridge in the area where the money was to be dropped. At that time, the officers arrested a suspect swimming under the bridge wearing a black wetsuit, diving mask, snorkel, and fins. The investigation disclosed that the suspect had an accomplice who made the extortion calls while he waited in the water for the extortion money.

SUMMARY

In kidnap cases, the primary concern of law-enforcement officers is the safe return of the victim. Secondary considerations are the identification and apprehension of the persons responsible. The famous Lindbergh case brought about the enactment of the Federal Kidnap Statute, better known as the "Lindbergh Law," which makes it a federal crime to take a victim across a state line or a foreign border. The FBI enters these cases after twenty-four hours under a presumption that the victim may have been taken out of the state. Abduction cases involve such offenses as kidnapping, kidnapping for ransom, kidnapping for robbery, and kidnapping for sex. Where a victim's life is in jeopardy, all investigation is kept at a low profile. However, once the victim has been released, an all-out effort is made to bring the perpetrators to justice.

The use of hostage negotiators is now being used by law-enforcement agencies in hostage/kidnap cases to deal with terrorists, ordinary criminals, and mentally unbalanced suspects. The aim of the negotiator is to resolve hostage incidents by talking the suspect into reacting rationally. Armed assault against the suspect is used only as a last resort when the suspect is bent on wanton killing. Three important rules in these situations include giving the suspect a chance to save face; being patient, since time is on the side of people on the outside; and always telling the truth—don't make promises that cannot be kept.

The crime of extortion, or blackmail, as it is typically referred to, is the obtaining of property from another by wrongful use of force or fear to produce consent. It is also an act of extortion to force a public official to do an official act under threat of force or fear.

Extortion differs from robbery in that choice is given to the victim. In robbery, the intimidation is so extreme as to cause the victim to part with money or property without consent. The solution of extortion cases often depends upon the complete cooperation of the victim. The investigation in extortion cases is similar to that conducted in kidnap cases.

REVIEW QUESTIONS

1. By what name is the Federal Kidnapping Statute popularly known?

2. In a kidnap for ransom case where the victim's life is in jeopardy, what are the two objectives of the investigation?

3. If a kidnapping involves a foreign official or an official guest of the United States, and no interstate transportation of the victim is involved, can it be called a federal violation?

4. Which of the following crimes are necessarily included in the crime of kidnapping? (a) Mayhem, (b) kidnapping for robbery, (c) kidnapping for extortion, (d) false imprisonment, (e) none of these.

5. After a kidnap victim has been released and the kidnapper is still at large, should the press be given the full story? If not, what types of information should be withheld.

6. In order to determine whether a caller in a kidnap case is the actual kidnapper, what type of questions should be asked by the family so that they know they are dealing with the right person?

7. If a kidnapping occurs within the special maritime, territorial or aircraft jurisdiction of the United States, and no interstate transportation is involved, would this come under the Federal Kidnapping Statute?

8. Upon the receipt of a kidnapping complaint which involves a letter demanding ransom, what information would you obtain and what instructions would you give to the complainant?

9. In cases involving hostages, many departments now have hostage negotiators. What is the principle involved in this type of approach?

10. Hostage takers fall into three categories. The first is the ordinary criminal. What are the other two?

11. "Obtaining property from another when that person's consent is induced by wrongful use of force or fear" is the best definition of a) robbery b) larceny c) extortion d) kidnapping e) none of these.

12. By what other name is extortion often referred to?

13. When an extortion threat is received by telephone, what types of information would you request of the complainant?

14. Robbery and extortion are quite similar. What is the difference between these two crimes?

15. Name twelve things that must be taken into account in preparation for coverage of the payoff in an extortion case.

WORK EXERCISE

1. Below are the contents of an unsigned, typed, ransom note received at noon by CLAIRE HARRIS, president of Acme Industries, Inc., from an unknown individual. The note, in a sealed envelope, was delivered by a twelve-year-old BOB ADAMS, who stated that he was given $10 by an unknown woman at 11 A.M. in front of the YWCA to deliver to MRS. HARRIS at Acme Industries, Inc., Center City. MRS. HARRIS immediately telephoned her home in an attempt to talk with her husband, but was told by a servant that he had gone to a gym about 10 A.M. and had not returned. MR. HARRIS is known to be driving his personal car—a 1979, blue, Cadillac, two-door sports coupé, license number 605 AVE.

After reviewing the contents of the note, write a paper on the actions and procedures that you think should be undertaken in this investigation.

Text of typed ranson demand:

MRS. HARRIS. FOR THE SAFE RETURN OF YOUR HUSBAND WE ARE DEMANDING $100,000 IN CASH, ALL UNMARKED BILLS. YOU WILL TAKE ALL PRECAUTION AGAINST SUSPICION IN DRAWING THE MONEY FROM THE BANK. THE MONEY IS TO BE DELIVERED IN A SUITCASE LARGE ENOUGH TO HOLD THIS AMOUNT.

YOU WILL HAVE THE MONEY READY AND BE AT THE INTERSECTION OF HIGHWAY 5 AND 64 AT EXACTLY 3 P.M. AT EXACTLY 3:05 P.M. YOU WILL CALL YOUR HOME FOR FURTHER INSTRUCTIONS.

YOU WILL USE YOUR CAR, LICENSE 154 LAM. YOU WILL BE PINPOINTED ALL ALONG THE WAY.

WE KNOW THE PENALTY FOR KIDNAPPING AND WE KNOW WE ARE GAMBLING OUR LIVES. IF YOU WANT TO GAMBLE THE LIFE OF YOUR HUSBAND CALL IN THE POLICE OR MARK THE MONEY.

DON'T ENTERTAIN ANY NOTION OF CALLING THE POLICE OR FBI IF YOU EVER WANT TO SEE YOUR HUSBAND AGAIN. SAVE THIS NOTE AND PLACE IT IN THE SUITCASE WITH THE MONEY.

2. The two questions below concern the victim's importance in kidnapping and extortion cases. What is your answer to each of these questions? State your opinions and give reasons for your position.

A. Should legislation be passed to prevent a payment of ransom in kidnap cases?

B. Should legislation be passed to prevent the payment of money in extortion (blackmail) cases?

Index